7

Stata Reference Manual

Release 7

Volume 1 A-G

Stata Press
College Station, Texas

Stata Press, 4905 Lakeway Drive, College Station, Texas 77845

Copyright © 1985–2001 by Stata Corporation
All rights reserved
Version 7.0
Typeset in TeX
Printed in the United States of America

10 9 8 7 6 5 4 3 2

ISBN 1-881228-47-9 (volumes 1–4)
ISBN 1-881228-48-7 (volume 1)
ISBN 1-881228-49-5 (volume 2)
ISBN 1-881228-50-9 (volume 3)
ISBN 1-881228-51-7 (volume 4)

The suggested citation for this software is

StataCorp. 2001. *Stata Statistical Software: Release 7.0*. College Station, TX: Stata Corporation.

Full Contents of Reference Volumes 1–4

Contents of Reference Volume 1

intro . . . . Introduction to reference manual

about . . . . Display information about my version of Stata
adjust . . . . Tables of adjusted means and proportions
alpha . . . . Cronbach's alpha
anova . . . . Analysis of variance and covariance
append . . . . Append datasets
arch . . . . Autoregressive conditional heteroskedasticity (ARCH) family of estimators
areg . . . . Linear regression with a large dummy-variable set
arima . . . . Autoregressive integrated moving average models

binreg . . . . Generalized linear models: extensions to the binomial family
biprobit . . . . Bivariate probit models
bitest . . . . Binomial probability test
boxcox . . . . Box–Cox regression models
brier . . . . Brier score decomposition
bstrap . . . . Bootstrap sampling and estimation
by . . . . Repeat Stata command on subsets of the data

canon . . . . Canonical correlations
cd . . . . Change directory
centile . . . . Report centile and confidence interval
cf . . . . Compare two datasets
checksum . . . . Calculate checksum of file
ci . . . . Confidence intervals for means, proportions, and counts
clogit . . . . Conditional (fixed-effects) logistic regression
cloglog . . . . Maximum-likelihood complementary log-log estimation
cluster . . . . Introduction to cluster analysis commands
cluster averagelinkage . . . . Average linkage cluster analysis
cluster completelinkage . . . . Complete linkage cluster analysis
cluster dendrogram . . . . Dendrograms for hierarchical cluster analysis
cluster generate . . . . Generate summary and grouping variables from a cluster analysis
cluster kmeans . . . . Kmeans cluster analysis
cluster kmedians . . . . Kmedians cluster analysis
cluster notes . . . . Place notes in cluster analysis
cluster singlelinkage . . . . Single linkage cluster analysis
cluster utility . . . . List, rename, use, and drop cluster analysis
cnsreg . . . . Constrained linear regression
codebook . . . . Produce a codebook describing the contents of data
collapse . . . . Make dataset of means, medians, etc.
compare . . . . Compare two variables
compress . . . . Compress data in memory
constraint . . . . Define and list constraints
contract . . . . Make dataset of frequencies
copy . . . . Copy file from disk or URL
copyright . . . . Display copyright information
corr2data . . . . Create a dataset with a specified correlation structure

correlate .... Correlations (covariances) of variables or estimators
corrgram .... Correlogram
count .... Count observations satisfying specified condition
cox .... Estimate Cox proportional hazards model
cross .... Form every pairwise combination of two datasets
ct .... Count-time data
ct ctset .... Declare data to be count-time data
ct cttost .... Convert count-time data to survival-time data
cumsp .... Cumulative spectral distribution
cumul .... Cumulative distribution
cusum .... Cusum plots and tests for binary variables

data types .... Quick reference for data types
describe .... Describe contents of data in memory or on disk
destring .... Change string variables to numeric
dfuller .... Augmented Dickey–Fuller test for unit roots
diagplots .... Distributional diagnostic plots
dir .... Display filenames
display .... Substitute for a hand calculator
do .... Execute commands from a file
doedit .... Edit do-files and other text files
dotplot .... Comparative scatterplots
drawnorm .... Draw a sample from a normal distribution
drop .... Eliminate variables or observations
dstdize .... Direct and indirect standardization

edit .... Edit and list data using Data Editor
egen .... Extensions to generate
eivreg .... Errors-in-variables regression
encode .... Encode string into numeric and vice versa
epitab .... Tables for epidemiologists
erase .... Erase a disk file
error messages .... Error messages and return codes
estimation commands .... Quick reference for estimation commands
exit .... Exit Stata
expand .... Duplicate observations

factor .... Principal components and factor analysis
fillin .... Rectangularize dataset
for .... Repeat Stata command
format .... Specify variable display format
fracpoly .... Fractional polynomial regression
functions .... Quick reference for functions

generate .... Create or change contents of variable
glm .... Generalized linear models
glogit .... Logit and probit on grouped data
grmeanby .... Graph means and medians by categorical variables
gsort .... Ascending and descending sort

Contents of Reference Volume 2

hadimvo . . . . Identify multivariate outliers
hausman . . . . Hausman specification test
heckman . . . . Heckman selection model
heckprob . . . . Maximum-likelihood probit estimation with selection
help . . . . Obtain on-line help
hetprob . . . . Maximum-likelihood heteroskedastic probit estimation
hilite . . . . Highlight a subset of points in a two-way scatterplot
hist . . . . Categorical variable histogram
hotel . . . . Hotelling's T-squared generalized means test

icd9 . . . . ICD-9-CM diagnostic and procedure codes
impute . . . . Predict missing values
infile . . . . Quick reference for reading data into Stata
infile (fixed format) . . . . Read ASCII (text) data in fixed format with a dictionary
infile (free format) . . . . Read unformatted ASCII (text) data
infix (fixed format) . . . . Read ASCII (text) data in fixed format
input . . . . Enter data from keyboard
insheet . . . . Read ASCII (text) data created by a spreadsheet
inspect . . . . Display simple summary of data's characteristics
ipolate . . . . Linearly interpolate (extrapolate) values
ivreg . . . . Instrumental variables and two-stage least squares regression

jknife . . . . Jackknife estimation
joinby . . . . Form all pairwise combinations within groups

kappa . . . . Interrater agreement
kdensity . . . . Univariate kernel density estimation
ksm . . . . Smoothing including lowess
ksmirnov . . . . Kolmogorov–Smirnov equality of distributions test
kwallis . . . . Kruskal–Wallis equality of populations rank test

label . . . . Label manipulation
ladder . . . . Ladder of powers
level . . . . Set default confidence level
limits . . . . Quick reference for limits
lincom . . . . Linear combinations of estimators
linktest . . . . Specification link test for single-equation models
list . . . . List values of variables
lnskew0 . . . . Find zero-skewness log or Box–Cox transform
log . . . . Echo copy of session to file or device
logistic . . . . Logistic regression
logit . . . . Maximum-likelihood logit estimation
loneway . . . . Large one-way ANOVA, random effects, and reliability
lorenz . . . . Inequality measures
lrtest . . . . Likelihood-ratio test after model estimation
ltable . . . . Life tables for survival data
lv . . . . Letter-value displays

matsize .... Set the maximum number of variables in a model
maximize .... Details of iterative maximization
means .... Arithmetic, geometric, and harmonic means
memory .... Memory size considerations
merge .... Merge datasets
meta .... Meta analysis
mfx .... Obtain marginal effects or elasticities after estimation
mkdir .... Create directory
mkspline .... Linear spline construction
ml .... Maximum likelihood estimation
mlogit .... Maximum-likelihood multinomial (polytomous) logistic regression
more .... The —more— message
mvencode .... Change missing to coded missing value and vice versa
mvreg .... Multivariate regression

nbreg .... Negative binomial regression
net .... Install and manage user-written additions from the net
net search .... Search Internet for installable packages
newey .... Regression with Newey–West standard errors
news .... Report Stata news
nl .... Nonlinear least squares
nlogit .... Maximum-likelihood nested logit estimation
notes .... Place notes in data
nptrend .... Test for trend across ordered groups

obs .... Increase the number of observations in dataset
ologit .... Maximum-likelihood ordered logit estimation
oneway .... One-way analysis of variance
oprobit .... Maximum-likelihood ordered probit estimation
order .... Reorder variables in dataset
orthog .... Orthogonal variables and orthogonal polynomials
outfile .... Write ASCII-format dataset
outsheet .... Write spreadsheet-style dataset

pcorr .... Partial correlation coefficients
pctile .... Create variable containing percentiles
pergram .... Periodogram
pk .... Pharmacokinetic (biopharmaceutical) data
pkcollapse .... Generate pharmacokinetic measurement dataset
pkcross .... Analyze crossover experiments
pkequiv .... Perform bioequivalence tests
pkexamine .... Calculate pharmacokinetic measures
pkshape .... Reshape (pharmacokinetic) Latin square data
pksumm .... Summarize pharmacokinetic data
plot .... Draw scatterplot using typewriter characters
poisson .... Poisson regression
pperron .... Phillips–Perron test for unit roots
prais .... Prais–Winsten regression and Cochrane–Orcutt regression
predict .... Obtain predictions, residuals, etc., after estimation
probit .... Maximum-likelihood probit estimation
prtest .... One- and two-sample tests of proportions

Contents of Reference Volume 3

qc .... Quality control charts
qreg .... Quantile (including median) regression
quadchk .... Check sensitivity of quadrature approximation
query .... Display system parameters

range .... Numerical ranges, derivatives, and integrals
recast .... Change storage type of variable
recode .... Recode categorical variable
reg3 .... Three-stage estimation for systems of simultaneous equations
regress .... Linear regression
regression diagnostics .... Regression diagnostics
rename .... Rename variable
reshape .... Convert data from wide to long and vice versa
#review .... Review previous commands
roc .... Receiver Operating Characteristic (ROC) analysis
rreg .... Robust regression
runtest .... Test for random order

sample .... Draw random sample
sampsi .... Sample size and power determination
save .... Save and use datasets
saved results .... Saved results
scobit .... Maximum-likelihood skewed logit estimation
sdtest .... Variance comparison tests
search .... Search Stata documentation
separate .... Create separate variables
serrbar .... Graph standard error bar chart
set .... Quick reference for system parameters
shell .... Temporarily invoke operating system
signrank .... Sign, rank, and median tests
simul .... Monte Carlo simulations
sktest .... Skewness and kurtosis test for normality
smooth .... Robust nonlinear smoother
snapspan .... Convert snapshot data to time-span data
sort .... Sort data
spearman .... Spearman's and Kendall's correlations
spikeplot .... Spike plots and rootograms
st .... Survival-time data
st stbase .... Form baseline dataset
st stci .... Confidence intervals for means and percentiles of survival time
st stcox .... Estimate Cox proportional hazards model
st stdes .... Describe survival-time data
st stfill .... Fill in by carrying forward values of covariates
st stgen .... Generate variables reflecting entire histories
st stir .... Report incidence-rate comparison
st stphplot .... Graphical assessment of the Cox proportional hazards assumption
st stptime .... Calculate person-time, incidence rates, and SMR
st strate .... Tabulate failure rates and rate ratios
st streg .... Estimate parametric survival models

st sts . . . . Generate, graph, list, and test the survivor and cumulative hazard functions
st sts generate . . . . Create survivor, hazard, and other variables
st sts graph . . . . Graph the survivor and the cumulative hazard functions
st sts list . . . . List the survivor and the cumulative hazard functions
st sts test . . . . Test equality of survivor functions
st stset . . . . Declare data to be survival-time data
st stsplit . . . . Split and join time-span records
st stsum . . . . Summarize survival-time data
st sttocc . . . . Convert survival-time data to case–control data
st sttoct . . . . Convert survival-time data to count-time data
st stvary . . . . Report which variables vary over time
stack . . . . Stack data
statsby . . . . Collect statistics for a command across a by list
stb . . . . STB installation instructions
stem . . . . Stem-and-leaf displays

Contents of Reference Volume 4

summarize . . . . Summary statistics
sureg . . . . Zellner's seemingly unrelated regression
svy . . . . Introduction to survey commands
svy estimators . . . . Estimation commands for complex survey data
svydes . . . . Describe survey data
svylc . . . . Estimate linear combinations after survey estimation
svymean . . . . Estimate means, totals, ratios, and proportions for survey data
svyset . . . . Set variables for survey data
svytab . . . . Tables for survey data
svytest . . . . Test linear hypotheses after survey estimation
sw . . . . Stepwise maximum-likelihood estimation
swilk . . . . Shapiro–Wilk and Shapiro–Francia tests for normality
symmetry . . . . Symmetry and marginal homogeneity tests

table . . . . Tables of summary statistics
tabstat . . . . Display table of summary statistics
tabsum . . . . One- and two-way tables of summary statistics
tabulate . . . . One- and two-way tables of frequencies
test . . . . Test linear hypotheses after model estimation
testnl . . . . Test nonlinear hypotheses after model estimation
tobit . . . . Tobit, censored-normal, and interval regression
translate . . . . Print and translate logs and graphs
treatreg . . . . Treatment effects model
truncreg . . . . Truncated regression
tsreport . . . . Report time-series aspects of dataset or estimation sample
tsset . . . . Declare data to be time-series data
ttest . . . . Mean comparison tests
tutorials . . . . Quick reference for Stata tutorials
type . . . . Display contents of files

update . . . . Update Stata

vce . . . . Display covariance matrix of the estimators
view . . . . View files and logs
vwls . . . . Variance-weighted least squares

weibull . . . . Estimate Weibull and other parametric survival-time models
which . . . . Display location and version for an ado-file
wntestb . . . . Bartlett's periodogram-based test for white noise
wntestq . . . . Portmanteau (Q) test for white noise

xcorr . . . . Cross-correlogram for bivariate time series
xi . . . . Interaction expansion
xpose . . . . Interchange observations and variables
xt . . . . Cross-sectional time-series analysis
xtabond . . . . Arellano–Bond linear, dynamic panel-data estimator
xtclog . . . . Random-effects and population-averaged cloglog models
xtdata . . . . Faster specification searches with xt data
xtdes . . . . Describe pattern of xt data
xtgee . . . . Estimate population-averaged panel-data models using GEE
xtgls . . . . Estimate panel-data models using GLS
xtintreg . . . . Random-effects interval data regression models
xtivreg . . . . Instrumental variables and two-stage least squares for panel-data models
xtlogit . . . . Fixed-effects, random-effects, and population-averaged logit models
xtnbreg . . . . . . Fixed-effects, random-effects, and population-averaged negative binomial models
xtpcse . . . . OLS or Prais–Winsten models with panel-corrected standard errors
xtpois . . . . Fixed-effects, random-effects, and population-averaged Poisson models
xtprobit . . . . Random-effects and population-averaged probit models
xtrchh . . . . Hildreth–Houck random coefficients models
xtreg . . . . Fixed-, between-, and random-effects, and population-averaged linear models
xtregar . . . . Fixed- and random-effects linear models with an AR(1) disturbance
xtsum . . . . Summarize xt data
xttab . . . . Tabulate xt data
xttobit . . . . Random-effects tobit models

zip . . . . Zero-inflated Poisson and negative binomial models

Contents of Programming Manual

intro . . . . Introduction to programming manual

assert . . . . Verify truth of claim

break . . . . Suppress Break key
byable . . . . Make programs byable

capture . . . . Capture return code
char . . . . Characteristics
cluster subroutines . . . . Add cluster analysis routines
cluster utilities . . . . Cluster analysis programming utilities
confirm . . . . Argument verification
continue . . . . Break out of loops

#delimit . . . . Change delimiter
discard . . . . Drop automatically loaded programs
display . . . . Display strings and values of scalar expressions

error . . . . Display generic error message and exit
estimates . . . . Post and redisplay estimation results
exit . . . . Exit from a program or do-file

file formats .dta . . . . Description of .dta file format
foreach . . . . Loop over items
forvalues . . . . Loop over consecutive values
functions . . . . Functions for programmers

gettoken . . . . Low-level parsing

hexdump . . . . Display hexadecimal report on file

if . . . . if programming command

macro . . . . Macro definition and manipulation
macro system . . . . Quick reference for system macros
mark . . . . Mark observations for inclusion
matrix . . . . Introduction to matrix commands
matrix accum . . . . Form cross-product matrices
matrix constraint . . . . Constrained estimation
matrix define . . . . Matrix definition, operators, and functions
matrix get . . . . Access system matrices
matrix mkmat . . . . Convert variables to matrix and vice versa
matrix rowname . . . . Name rows and columns
matrix score . . . . Score data from coefficient vectors
matrix svd . . . . Singular value decomposition
matrix symeigen . . . . Eigenvalues and vectors of symmetric matrices
matrix utility . . . . List, rename, and drop matrices
more . . . . Pause until key is pressed

numlist . . . . Parse numeric lists

pause . . . . Program debugging command
postfile . . . . Save results in Stata dataset
_predict . . . . Obtain predictions, residuals, etc., after estimation programming command
preserve . . . . Preserve and restore data
program . . . . Define and manipulate programs

quietly . . . . Quietly and noisily perform Stata command

return . . . . Return saved results
_rmcoll . . . . Remove collinear variables
rmsg . . . . Return messages
_robust . . . . Robust variance estimates

scalar . . . . Scalar variables
sleep . . . . Pause for a specified time
smcl . . . . Stata Markup and Control Language
sortpreserve . . . . Sorting within programs
st st_is . . . . Survival analysis subroutines for programmers
syntax . . . . Parse Stata syntax
sysdir . . . . Set system directories

tabdisp . . . . Display tables
tokenize . . . . Divide strings into tokens
tsrevar . . . . Time-series operator programming command

unab . . . . Unabbreviate variable list

version . . . . Version control

while . . . . Looping
window . . . . Programming menus, dialogs, and windows
window control . . . . Create dialog-box controls
window dialog . . . . Create dialog box
window fopen . . . . Display open/save dialog box
window manage . . . . Manage window characteristics
window menu . . . . Create menus
window push . . . . Copy command into Review window
window stopbox . . . . Display message box

Subject Table of Contents

Getting Started

[GS] Getting Started manual . . . . Getting Started with Stata for Macintosh
[GS] Getting Started manual . . . . Getting Started with Stata for Unix
[GS] Getting Started manual . . . . Getting Started with Stata for Windows
[U]   User's Guide, Chapter 2 . . . . Resources for learning and using Stata
[R]   help . . . . Obtain on-line help
[R]   tutorials . . . . Quick reference for Stata tutorials

Data manipulation and management

Basic data commands

[R]   describe . . . . Describe contents of data in memory or on disk
[R]   display . . . . Substitute for a hand calculator
[R]   drop . . . . Eliminate variables or observations
[R]   edit . . . . Edit and list data using Data Editor
[R]   egen . . . . Extensions to generate
[R]   generate . . . . Create or change contents of variable
[R]   list . . . . List values of variables
[R]   memory . . . . Memory size considerations
[R]   obs . . . . Increase the number of observations in dataset
[R]   sort . . . . Sort data

Functions and expressions

[U]   User's Guide, Chapter 16 . . . . Functions and expressions
[R]   egen . . . . Extensions to generate
[R]   functions . . . . Quick reference for functions
[P]   functions . . . . Functions for programmers

Dates

[U]   User's Guide, Section 15.5.3 . . . . Date formats
[U]   User's Guide, Section 16.3.3 . . . . Date functions
[U]   User's Guide, Chapter 27 . . . . Commands for dealing with dates
[R]   functions . . . . Quick reference for functions

Inputting and saving data

[U]   User's Guide, Chapter 24 . . . . Commands to input data
[R]   edit . . . . Edit and list data using Data Editor
[R]   infile . . . . Quick reference for reading data into Stata
[R]   insheet . . . . Read ASCII (text) data created by a spreadsheet
[R]   infile (free format) . . . . Read unformatted ASCII (text) data
[R]   infix (fixed format) . . . . Read ASCII (text) data in fixed format
[R]   infile (fixed format) . . . . Read ASCII (text) data in fixed format with a dictionary
[R]   input . . . . Enter data from keyboard
[R]   outfile . . . . Write ASCII-format dataset
[R]   outsheet . . . . Write spreadsheet-style dataset
[R]   save . . . . Save and use datasets

Combining data

[U] User's Guide, Chapter 25 .... Commands for combining data
[R] append .... Append datasets
[R] merge .... Merge datasets
[R] joinby .... Form all pairwise combinations within groups

Reshaping datasets

[R] collapse .... Make dataset of means, medians, etc.
[R] contract .... Make dataset of frequencies
[R] compress .... Compress data in memory
[R] cross .... Form every pairwise combination of two datasets
[R] expand .... Duplicate observations
[R] fillin .... Rectangularize dataset
[R] obs .... Increase the number of observations in dataset
[R] reshape .... Convert data from wide to long and vice versa
[R] separate .... Create separate variables
[R] stack .... Stack data
[R] statsby .... Collect statistics for a command across a by list
[R] xpose .... Interchange observations and variables

Labeling, display formats, and notes

[U] User's Guide, Section 15.5 .... Formats: controlling how data are displayed
[U] User's Guide, Section 15.6 .... Dataset, variable, and value labels
[R] format .... Specify variable display format
[R] label .... Label manipulation
[R] notes .... Place notes in data

Changing and renaming variables

[U] User's Guide, Chapter 28 .... Commands for dealing with categorical variables
[R] destring .... Change string variables to numeric
[R] encode .... Encode string into numeric and vice versa
[R] generate .... Create or change contents of variable
[R] mvencode .... Change missing to coded missing value and vice versa
[R] order .... Reorder variables in dataset
[R] recode .... Recode categorical variable
[R] rename .... Rename variable

Examining data

[R] cf .... Compare two datasets
[R] codebook .... Produce a codebook describing the contents of data
[R] compare .... Compare two variables
[R] count .... Count observations satisfying specified condition
[R] gsort .... Ascending and descending sort
[R] inspect .... Display simple summary of data's characteristics
[R] pctile .... Create variable containing percentiles
[R] st stdes .... Describe survival-time data
[R] summarize .... Summary statistics
[R] svytab .... Tables for survey data
[R] table .... Tables of summary statistics
[P] tabdisp .... Display tables

[R] tabstat .... Display table of summary statistics
[R] tabsum .... One- and two-way tables of summary statistics
[R] tabulate .... One- and two-way tables of frequencies
[R] xtdes .... Describe pattern of xt data

Miscellaneous data commands

[R] corr2data .... Create a dataset with a specified correlation structure
[R] drawnorm .... Draw a sample from a normal distribution
[R] icd9 .... ICD-9-CM diagnostic and procedures codes
[R] ipolate .... Linearly interpolate (extrapolate) values
[R] range .... Numerical ranges, derivatives, and integrals
[R] sample .... Draw random sample

Utilities

Basic utilities

[U] User's Guide, Chapter 8 .... Stata's on-line help and search facilities
[U] User's Guide, Chapter 18 .... Printing and preserving output
[U] User's Guide, Chapter 19 .... Do-files
[R] about .... Display information about my version of Stata
[R] by .... Repeat Stata command on subsets of the data
[R] copyright .... Display copyright information
[R] do .... Execute commands from a file
[R] doedit .... Edit do-files and other text files
[R] exit .... Exit Stata
[R] help .... Obtain on-line help
[R] level .... Set default confidence level
[R] log .... Echo copy of session to file or device
[R] obs .... Increase the number of observations in dataset
[R] #review .... Review previous commands
[R] search .... Search Stata documentation
[R] translate .... Print and translate logs and graphs
[R] tutorials .... Quick reference for Stata tutorials
[R] view .... View files and logs

Error messages

[U] User's Guide, Chapter 11 .... Error messages and return codes
[R] error messages .... Error messages and return codes
[P] error .... Display generic error message and exit
[P] rmsg .... Return messages

Saved results

[U] User's Guide, Section 16.6 .... Accessing results from Stata commands
[U] User's Guide, Section 21.8 .... Accessing results calculated by other programs
[U] User's Guide, Section 21.9 ..... Accessing results calculated by estimation commands
[U] User's Guide, Section 21.10 .... Saving results
[P] return .... Return saved results
[R] saved results .... Saved results

Internet

[U]	User's Guide, Chapter 32 .... Using the Internet to keep up to date
[R]	checksum .... Calculate checksum of file
[R]	net .... Install and manage user-written additions from the net
[R]	net search .... Search Internet for installable packages
[R]	news .... Report Stata news
[R]	stb .... STB installation instructions
[R]	update .... Update Stata

Data types and memory

[U]	User's Guide, Chapter 7 .... Setting the size of memory
[U]	User's Guide, Section 15.2.2 .... Numeric storage types
[U]	User's Guide, Section 15.4.4 .... String storage types
[U]	User's Guide, Section 16.10 .... Precision and problems therein
[U]	User's Guide, Chapter 26 .... Commands for dealing with strings
[R]	compress .... Compress data in memory
[R]	data types .... Quick reference for data types
[R]	limits .... Quick reference for limits
[R]	matsize .... Set the maximum number of variables in a model
[R]	memory .... Memory size considerations
[R]	recast .... Change storage type of variable

Advanced utilities

[P]	assert .... Verify truth of claim
[R]	cd .... Change directory
[R]	checksum .... Calculate checksum of file
[R]	copy .... Copy file from disk or URL
[R]	dir .... Display filenames
[P]	discard .... Drop automatically loaded programs
[R]	erase .... Erase a disk file
[R]	for .... Repeat Stata command
[P]	hexdump .... Display hexadecimal report on file
[R]	mkdir .... Create directory
[R]	more .... The —more— message
[R]	query .... Display system parameters
[P]	quietly .... Quietly and noisily perform Stata command
[R]	set .... Quick reference for system parameters
[R]	shell .... Temporarily invoke operating system
[P]	smcl .... Stata markup and control language
[P]	sysdir .... Set system directories
[R]	type .... Display contents of files
[R]	which .... Display location and version for an ado-file

Graphics

[G]	Graphics Manual .... Stata Graphics Manual
[R]	boxcox .... Box–Cox regression models
[R]	corrgram .... Correlogram
[R]	cumsp .... Cumulative spectral distribution
[R]	cumul .... Cumulative distribution

[R] cusum .... Cusum plots and tests for binary variables
[R] diagplots .... Distributional diagnostic plots
[R] dotplot .... Comparative scatterplots
[R] factor .... Principal components and factor analysis
[R] grmeanby .... Graph means and medians by categorical variables
[R] hadimvo .... Identify multivariate outliers
[R] hilite .... Highlight a subset of points in a two-way scatterplot
[R] hist .... Categorical variable histogram
[R] kdensity .... Univariate kernel density estimation
[R] ksm .... Smoothing including lowess
[R] lv .... Letter-value displays
[R] mkspline .... Linear spline construction
[R] pergram .... Periodogram
[R] plot .... Draw scatterplot using typewriter characters
[R] qc .... Quality control charts
[R] regression diagnostics .... Regression diagnostics
[R] roc .... Receiver Operating Characteristic (ROC) analysis
[R] serrbar .... Graph standard error bar chart
[R] smooth .... Robust nonlinear smoother
[R] spikeplot .... Spike plots and rootograms
[R] st stphplot .... Graphical assessment of the Cox proportional hazards assumption
[R] st streg .... Graph estimated survival, hazard, and cumulative hazard functions
[R] st sts graph .... Graph the survivor and the cumulative hazard functions
[R] stem .... Stem-and-leaf displays
[R] wntestb .... Bartlett's periodogram-based test for white noise
[R] xcorr .... Cross-correlogram for bivariate time series

Statistics

Basic statistics

[R] egen .... Extensions to generate
[R] anova .... Analysis of variance and covariance
    [R] oneway .... One-way analysis of variance
[R] bitest .... Binomial probability test
[R] ci .... Confidence intervals for means, proportions, and counts
[R] correlate .... Correlations (covariances) of variables or estimators
[R] logistic .... Logistic regression
[R] prtest .... One- and two-sample tests of proportions
[R] regress .... Linear regression
    [R] predict .... Obtain predictions, residuals, etc., after estimation
    [R] regression diagnostics .... Regression diagnostics
    [R] test .... Test linear hypotheses after model estimation
[R] sampsi .... Sample size and power determination
[R] sdtest .... Variance comparison tests
[R] signrank .... Sign, rank, and median tests
[R] statsby .... Collect statistics for a command across a by list
[R] summarize .... Summary statistics
[R] table .... Tables of summary statistics

[R]   tabstat .... Display table of summary statistics
[R]   tabsum .... One- and two-way tables of summary statistics
[R]   tabulate .... One- and two-way tables of frequencies
[R]   ttest .... Mean comparison tests

ANOVA and ANCOVA

[R]   anova .... Analysis of variance and covariance
[R]   loneway .... Large one-way ANOVA, random effects, and reliability
[R]   oneway .... One-way analysis of variance

Linear regression and related maximum-likelihood regressions

[U]   User's Guide, Chapter 29 .... Overview of model estimation in Stata
[U]   User's Guide, Section 23.11 .... Obtaining robust variance estimates
[R]   estimation commands .... Quick reference for estimation commands
[R]   areg .... Linear regression with a large dummy-variable set
[R]   cnsreg .... Constrained linear regression
[R]   cox .... Estimate Cox proportional hazards model
[R]   eivreg .... Errors-in-variables regression
[R]   fracpoly .... Fractional polynomial regression
[R]   glm .... Generalized linear models
[R]   heckman .... Heckman selection model
[R]   impute .... Predict missing values
[R]   ivreg .... Instrumental variables and two-stage least squares regression
[R]   mvreg .... Multivariate regression
[R]   nbreg .... Negative binomial regression
[R]   newey .... Regression with Newey–West standard errors
[R]   nl .... Nonlinear least squares
[R]   orthog .... Orthogonal variables and orthogonal polynomials
[R]   poisson .... Poisson regression
[R]   prais .... Prais–Winsten regression and Cochrane–Orcutt regression
[R]   qreg .... Quantile (including median) regression
[R]   reg3 .... Three-stage estimation for systems of simultaneous equations
[R]   regress .... Linear regression
[R]   regression diagnostics .... Regression diagnostics
[R]   roc .... Receiver Operating Characteristic (ROC) analysis
[R]   rreg .... Robust regression
[R]   st stcox .... Estimate Cox proportional hazards model
[R]   st streg .... Estimate parametric survival models
[R]   sureg .... Zellner's seemingly unrelated regression
[R]   svy estimators .... Estimation commands for complex survey data
[R]   sw .... Stepwise maximum-likelihood estimation
[R]   tobit .... Tobit, censored-normal, and interval regression
[R]   treatreg .... Treatment effects model
[R]   truncreg .... Truncated regression
[R]   vwls .... Variance-weighted least squares
[R]   weibull .... Estimate Weibull and other parametric survival-time models
[R]   xtabond .... Arellano–Bond linear, dynamic panel-data estimator
[R]   xtgee .... Estimate population-averaged panel-data models using GEE
[R]   xtgls .... Estimate panel-data models using GLS
[R]   xtintreg .... Random-effects interval data regression models
[R]   xtivreg ...... Instrumental variables and two-stage least squares for panel-data models

[R] xtnbreg Fixed-effects, random-effects, and population-averaged negative binomial models
[R] xtpcse . . . . OLS or Prais–Winsten models with panel-corrected standard errors
[R] xtpois . . . . Fixed-effects, random-effects, and population-averaged Poisson models
[R] xtrchh . . . . Hildreth–Houck random coefficients models
[R] xtreg . . . . Fixed-, between-, and random-effects and population-averaged linear models
[R] xtregar . . . . Fixed- and random-effects linear models with an AR(1) disturbance
[R] zip . . . . Zero-inflated Poisson and negative binomial models

Logistic and probit regression

[U] User's Guide, Chapter 29 . . . . Overview of model estimation in Stata
[U] User's Guide, Section 23.11 . . . . Obtaining robust variance estimates
[R] biprobit . . . . Bivariate probit models
[R] clogit . . . . Conditional (fixed-effects) logistic regression
[R] cloglog . . . . Maximum-likelihood complementary log-log estimation
[R] constraint . . . . Define and list constraints
[R] glogit . . . . Logit and probit on grouped data
[R] heckprob . . . . Maximum-likelihood probit estimation with selection
[R] hetprob . . . . Maximum-likelihood heteroskedastic probit estimation
[R] logistic . . . . Logistic regression
[R] logit . . . . Maximum-likelihood logit estimation
[R] mlogit . . . . Maximum-likelihood multinomial (polytomous) logistic regression
[R] nlogit . . . . Maximum-likelihood nested logit estimation
[R] ologit . . . . Maximum-likelihood ordered logit estimation
[R] oprobit . . . . Maximum-likelihood ordered probit estimation
[R] probit . . . . Maximum-likelihood probit estimation
[R] scobit . . . . Maximum-likelihood skewed logit estimation
[R] svy estimators . . . . Estimation commands for complex survey data
[R] sw . . . . Stepwise maximum-likelihood estimation
[R] xtclog . . . . Random-effects and population-averaged cloglog models
[R] xtgee . . . . Estimate population-averaged panel-data models using GEE
[R] xtlogit . . . . Fixed-effects, random-effects, and population-averaged logit models
[R] xtprobit . . . . Random-effects and population-averaged probit models

Pharmacokinetic statistics

[R] pk . . . . Pharmacokinetic (biopharmaceutical) data
[R] pkcollapse . . . . Generate pharmacokinetic measurement dataset
[R] pkcross . . . . Analyze crossover experiments
[R] pkexamine . . . . Calculate pharmacokinetic measures
[R] pkequiv . . . . Perform bioequivalence tests
[R] pkshape . . . . Reshape (pharmacokinetic) Latin square data
[R] pksumm . . . . Summarize pharmacokinetic data

Survival analysis

[U] User's Guide, Chapter 29 . . . . Overview of model estimation in Stata
[U] User's Guide, Section 23.11 . . . . Obtaining robust variance estimates
[R] cox . . . . Estimate Cox proportional hazards model
[R] ct . . . . Count-time data
[R] ct ctset . . . . Declare data to be count-time data
[R] ct cttost . . . . Convert count-time data to survival-time data
[R] ltable . . . . Life tables for survival data
[R] snapspan . . . . Convert snapshot data to time-span data

[R]   st .... Survival-time data
                                  (multiple entries related to st commands)

   [P]   st st_is .... Survival analysis subroutines for programmers
   [R]   st stbase .... Form baseline dataset
   [R]   st stci .... Confidence intervals for means and percentiles of survival time
   [R]   st stcox .... Estimate Cox proportional hazards model
   [R]   st stdes .... Describe survival-time data
   [R]   st stfill .... Fill in by carrying forward values of covariates
   [R]   st stgen .... Generate variables reflecting entire histories
   [R]   st stir .... Report incidence-rate comparison
   [R]   st stphplot .... Graphical assessment of the Cox proportional hazards assumption
   [R]   st stptime .... Calculate person-time, incidence rates, and SMR
   [R]   st strate .... Tabulate failure rates and rate ratios
   [R]   st streg .... Estimate parametric survival models
   [R]   st sts   Generate, graph, list, and test the survivor and cumulative hazard functions
   [R]   st sts generate .... Create survivor, hazard, and other variables
   [R]   st sts graph .... Graph the survivor and the cumulative hazard functions
   [R]   st sts list .... List the survivor and the cumulative hazard functions
   [R]   st sts test .... Test equality of survivor functions
   [R]   st stset .... Declare data to be survival-time data
   [R]   st stsplit .... Split and join time-span records
   [R]   st stsum .... Summarize survival-time data
   [R]   st sttocc .... Convert survival-time data to case–control data
   [R]   st sttoct .... Convert survival-time data to count-time data
   [R]   st stvary .... Report which variables vary over time
 [R]   sw .... Stepwise maximum-likelihood estimation
 [R]   weibull .... Estimate Weibull and other parametric survival-time models

Time series

   [U]   User's Guide, Section 14.4.3 .... Time-series varlists
   [U]   User's Guide, Section 15.5.4 .... Time-series formats
   [U]   User's Guide, Section 16.3.4 .... Time-series functions
   [U]   User's Guide, Section 16.8 .... Time-series operators
   [U]   User's Guide, Section 27.3 .... Time-series dates
   [U]   User's Guide, Section 29.12 .... Models with time-series data
   [R]   arch .... Autoregressive conditional heteroskedasticity (ARCH) family of estimators
   [R]   arima .... Autoregressive integrated moving average models
   [R]   corrgram .... Correlogram
   [R]   cumsp .... Cumulative spectral distribution
   [R]   dfuller .... Augmented Dickey–Fuller test for unit roots
   [R]   pergram .... Periodogram
   [R]   pperron .... Phillips–Perron test for unit roots
   [R]   spikeplot .... Spike plots and rootograms
   [R]   tsreport .... Report time-series aspects of dataset or estimation sample
   [P]   tsrevar .... Time-series operator programming command
   [R]   tsset .... Declare data to be time-series data
   [R]   wntestb .... Bartlett's periodogram-based test for white noise
   [R]   wntestq .... Portmanteau (Q) test for white noise
   [R]   xcorr .... Cross-correlogram for bivariate time series

Cross-sectional time series (panel data)

[U] User's Guide, Chapter 29 .... Overview of model estimation in Stata
[R] quadchk .... Check sensitivity of quadrature approximation
[R] xt .... Cross-sectional time-series analysis
[R] xtabond .... Arellano–Bond linear, dynamic panel-data estimator
[R] xtclog .... Random-effects and population-averaged cloglog models
[R] xtdata .... Faster specification searches with xt data
[R] xtdes .... Describe pattern of xt data
[R] xtgee .... Estimate population-averaged panel-data models using GEE
[R] xtgls .... Estimate panel-data models using GLS
[R] xtintreg .... Random-effects interval data regression models
[R] xtivreg ...... Instrumental variables and two-stage least squares for panel-data models
[R] xtlogit .... Fixed-effects, random-effects, and population-averaged logit models
[R] xtnbreg Fixed-effects, random-effects, and population-averaged negative binomial models
[R] xtpcse .... OLS or Prais–Winsten models with panel-corrected standard errors
[R] xtpois .... Fixed-effects, random-effects, and population-averaged Poisson models
[R] xtprobit .... Random-effects and population-averaged probit models
[R] xtrchh .... Hildreth–Houck random coefficients models
[R] xtreg .... Fixed-, between-, and random-effects and population-averaged linear models
[R] xtregar .... Fixed- and random-effects linear models with an AR(1) disturbance
[R] xtsum .... Summarize xt data
[R] xttab .... Tabulate xt data
[R] xttobit .... Random-effects tobit models

Auxiliary regression commands

[U] User's Guide, Section 16.5 .... Accessing coefficients and standard errors
[U] User's Guide, Chapter 23 .... Estimation and post-estimation commands
[R] estimation commands .... Quick reference for estimation commands
[R] adjust .... Tables of adjusted means and proportions
[R] constraint .... Define and list constraints
[R] correlate .... Correlations (covariances) of variables or estimators
[R] hausman .... Hausman specification test
[R] lincom .... Linear combinations of estimators
[R] linktest .... Specification link test for single-equation models
[R] lrtest .... Likelihood-ratio test after model estimation
[R] maximize .... Details of iterative maximization
[R] mfx .... Obtain marginal effects or elasticities after estimation
[R] mkspline .... Linear spline construction
[R] predict .... Obtain predictions, residuals, etc., after estimation
[R] regression diagnostics .... Regression diagnostics
[P] _robust .... Robust variance estimates
[R] test .... Test linear hypotheses after model estimation
[R] testnl .... Test nonlinear hypotheses after model estimation
[R] vce .... Display covariance matrix of the estimators
[R] xi .... Interaction expansion

Commands for epidemiologists

[R] binreg .... Generalized linear models: extensions to the binomial family
[R] dstdize .... Direct and indirect standardization
[R] epitab .... Tables for epidemiologists
[R] icd9 .... ICD-9-CM diagnostic and procedures codes

[R]   roc .... Receiver Operating Characteristic (ROC) analysis
[R]   st .... Survival-time data
[R]   symmetry .... Symmetry and marginal homogeneity tests
[R]   tabulate .... One- and two-way tables of frequencies

Analysis of survey data

[U]   User's Guide, Chapter 30 .... Overview of survey estimation
[U]   User's Guide, Chapter 29 .... Overview of model estimation in Stata
[R]   svy .... Introduction to survey commands
[R]   svy estimators .... Estimation commands for complex survey data
[R]   svydes .... Describe survey data
[R]   svylc .... Estimate linear combinations after survey estimation
[R]   svymean .... Estimate means, totals, ratios, and proportions for survey data
[R]   svyset .... Set variables for survey data
[R]   svytab .... Tables for survey data
[R]   svytest .... Test linear hypotheses after survey estimation
[P]   _robust .... Robust variance estimates

Transforms and normality tests

[R]   boxcox .... Box–Cox regression models
[R]   fracpoly .... Fractional polynomial regression
[R]   ladder .... Ladder of powers
[R]   lnskew0 .... Find zero-skewness log or Box–Cox transform
[R]   sktest .... Skewness and kurtosis test for normality
[R]   swilk .... Shapiro–Wilk and Shapiro–Francia tests for normality

Nonparametrics

[R]   kdensity .... Univariate kernel density estimation
[R]   ksm .... Smoothing including lowess
[R]   ksmirnov .... Kolmogorov–Smirnov equality of distributions test
[R]   kwallis .... Kruskal–Wallis equality of populations rank test
[R]   nptrend .... Test for trend across ordered groups
[R]   qreg .... Quantile (including median) regression
[R]   roc .... Receiver Operating Characteristic (ROC) analysis
[R]   runtest .... Test for random order
[R]   signrank .... Sign, rank, and median tests
[R]   smooth .... Robust nonlinear smoother
[R]   spearman .... Spearman's and Kendall's correlations
[R]   symmetry .... Symmetry and marginal homogeneity tests

Cluster analysis

[R]   cluster .... Introduction to cluster analysis commands
[R]   cluster averagelinkage .... Average linkage cluster analysis
[R]   cluster completelinkage .... Complete linkage cluster analysis
[R]   cluster dendrogram .... Dendrograms for hierarchical cluster analysis
[R]   cluster generate .... Generate summary and grouping variables from a cluster analysis
[R]   cluster kmeans .... Kmeans cluster analysis
[R]   cluster kmedians .... Kmedians cluster analysis
[R]   cluster notes .... Place notes in cluster analysis
[P]   cluster subroutines .... Add cluster analysis routines
[P]   cluster utilities .... Cluster analysis programming utilities

[R]   cluster singlelinkage .... Single linkage cluster analysis
[R]   cluster utility .... List, rename, use, and drop cluster analysis

Factor analysis

[R]   alpha .... Cronbach's alpha
[R]   canon .... Canonical correlations
[R]   factor .... Principal components and factor analysis
[R]   impute .... Predict missing values

Do-it-yourself maximum likelihood estimation

[P]   matrix .... Introduction to matrix commands
[R]   ml .... Maximum likelihood estimation

Quality control

[R]   qc .... Quality control charts
[R]   serrbar .... Graph standard error bar chart

Other statistics

[R]   alpha .... Cronbach's alpha
[R]   brier .... Brier score decomposition
[R]   bstrap .... Bootstrap sampling and estimation
[R]   canon .... Canonical correlations
[R]   centile .... Report centile and confidence interval
[R]   hotel .... Hotelling's T-squared generalized means test
[R]   impute .... Predict missing values
[R]   jknife .... Jackknife estimation
[R]   kappa .... Interrater agreement
[R]   means .... Arithmetic, geometric, and harmonic means
[R]   pcorr .... Partial correlation coefficients
[R]   pctile .... Create variable containing percentiles
[R]   range .... Numerical ranges, derivatives, and integrals
[R]   simul .... Monte Carlo simulations

Matrix commands

Basics

[U]   User's Guide, Chapter 17 .... Matrix expressions
[P]   matrix .... Introduction to matrix commands
[P]   matrix define .... Matrix definition, operators, and functions
[P]   matrix utility .... List, rename, and drop matrices

Programming

[P]   matrix accum ....,..... Form cross-product matrices
[R]   ml .... Maximum likelihood estimation
[P]   estimates .... Post and redisplay estimation results
[P]   matrix rowname .... Name rows and columns
[P]   matrix score .... Score data from coefficient vectors

Other

[P]   matrix constraint .... Constrained estimation
[P]   matrix get .... Access system matrices
[P]   matrix mkmat .... Convert variables to matrix and vice versa
[P]   matrix svd .... Singular value decomposition
[P]   matrix symeigen .... Eigenvalues and vectors of symmetric matrices

Programming

Basics

[U]   User's Guide, Chapter 21 .... Programming Stata
[U]   User's Guide, Section 21.3 .... Macros
[U]   User's Guide, Section 21.11 .... Ado-files
[P]   program .... Define and manipulate programs
[P]   macro .... Macro definition and manipulation
[P]   return .... Return saved results

Program control

[U]   User's Guide, Section 21.11.1 .... Version
[P]   version .... Version control
[P]   continue .... Break out of loops
[P]   foreach .... Loop over items
[P]   forvalues .... Loop over consecutive values
[P]   if .... if programming command
[P]   while .... Looping
[P]   error .... Display generic error message and exit
[P]   capture .... Capture return code

Parsing and program arguments

[U]   User's Guide, Section 21.4 .... Program arguments
[P]   syntax .... Parse Stata syntax
[P]   confirm .... Argument verification
[P]   gettoken .... Low-level parsing
[P]   numlist .... Parse numeric lists
[P]   tokenize .... Divide strings into tokens

Console output

[P]   display .... Display strings and values of scalar expressions
[P]   tabdisp .... Display tables

Commonly used programming commands

[P]   by .... Program byable ado-files
[P]   #delimit .... Change delimiter
[P]   exit .... Exit from a program or do-file
[P]   quietly .... Quietly and noisily perform Stata command
[P]   mark .... Mark observations for inclusion
[P]   more .... Pause until key is depressed
[P]   preserve .... Preserve and restore data
[P]   matrix .... Introduction to matrix commands

[P]   scalar .... Scalar variables
[P]   smcl .... Stata markup and control language
[P]   tsrevar .... Time-series operator programming command

Debugging

[P]   pause .... Program debugging command
[P]   program .... Set trace debugging command

Advanced programming commands

[P]   break .... Suppress Break key
[P]   char .... Characteristics
[P]   estimates .... Post and redisplay estimation results
[P]   macro .... Macro definition and manipulation
[P]   macro system .... Quick reference for system macros
[R]   ml .... Maximum likelihood estimation
[P]   postfile .... Save results in Stata dataset
[P]   _predict   ... Obtain predictions, residuals, etc., after estimation programming command
[P]   _rmcoll .... Remove collinear variables
[P]   unab .... Unabbreviate variable list
[P]   window .... Programming menus, dialogs, and windows
[P]   window control .... Create dialog-box controls
[P]   window dialog .... Create dialog box
[P]   window fopen .... Display open/save dialog box
[P]   window menu .... Create menus
[P]   window stopbox .... Display message box

Special interest programming commands

[P]   cluster subroutines .... Add cluster analysis routines
[P]   cluster utilities .... Cluster analysis programming utilities
[P]   st st_is .... Survival analysis subroutines for programmers
[P]   tsrevar .... Time-series operator programming command

File formats

[P]   file formats .dta .... Description of .dta file format
[G]   file formats .gph .... Description of .gph file format

Interface features

[R]   doedit .... Edit do-files and other text files
[R]   edit .... Edit and list data using Data Editor
[P]   sleep .... Pause for a specified time
[P]   smcl .... Stata markup and control language
[P]   window .... Programming menus, dialogs, and windows
[P]   window control .... Create dialog-box controls
[P]   window dialog .... Create dialog box
[P]   window fopen .... Display open/save dialog box
[P]   window manage .... Manage window characteristics
[P]   window menu .... Create menus
[P]   window push .... Copy command into Review window
[P]   window stopbox .... Display message box

Title

> **intro** — Introduction to reference manual

Description

This entry describes the layout of the *Stata Reference Manual*.

Remarks

Arrangement of the manual

The *Stata Reference Manual* is arranged like an encyclopedia—alphabetically. At the beginning of Volume 1 is a full table of contents for all four volumes, followed by a table of contents for the *Programming Manual*. After this is a subject table of contents for the *Reference Manual* and the *User's Guide*. At the end of Volume 4 is an index for the *Reference Manual* and the *User's Guide*.

Most entries in the *Reference Manual* are Stata commands. Be sure to see the subject table of contents, located immediately before this entry.

The `search` command can also be used to find the Stata commands that relate to a particular statistical topic; see [R] **search**. For an introduction to Stata's basic commands, see the *Getting Started* manual. For an overview of Stata, see the *User's Guide*. For information about Stata's graphics, see the *Stata Graphics Manual*. For information about Stata's matrix or programming commands, see the *Stata Programming Manual*.

The Stata user community has written many additions to Stata. Use the `net search` command to search for user-written additions across the Internet; see [R] **net search**.

Arrangement of each entry

Each entry in this manual is generally arranged in the following format:

Syntax

Entries begin with a syntax diagram. A command's syntax diagram shows how to type the command, indicates all possible options, and gives the minimal allowed abbreviations for all the items in the command. For instance, the syntax diagram for the `list` command is

$\underline{\texttt{l}}\texttt{ist}$ $\big[\textit{varlist}\big]$ $\big[\texttt{if } \textit{exp}\big]$ $\big[\texttt{in } \textit{range}\big]$ $\big[\texttt{, } \big[\underline{\texttt{no}}\big]\texttt{display}\big]$ $\big[\underline{\texttt{nol}}\texttt{abel}\big]$ $\big[\underline{\texttt{noobs}}\big]$ $\big[\underline{\texttt{do}}\texttt{ublespace}\big]$ $\big]$

by ... : may be used with `list`; see [R] **by**.

Items in the `typewriter-style font` should be typed exactly as they appear in the diagram, although they may be abbreviated. <u>Underlining</u> is used to indicate the shortest abbreviations where abbreviations are allowed. For instance, `list` may be abbreviated `l`, `li`, or `lis`, or it may be spelled out completely. Items in the typewriter font that are not underlined may not be abbreviated; thus, `if` and `in` may not be abbreviated.

1

The square brackets denote optional items. In the first line of the syntax diagram, *varlist*, if *exp*, and in *range* are optional. Nested square brackets are used to denote optional items within optional items. Thus, the last half of the syntax diagram (from the comma through doublespace) is optional, as is any part of it. The strange item [no]display means that you may specify the option display, which may be abbreviated d, or the option nodisplay, which may be abbreviated nod.

To make the diagrams easier to read, we will often omit the plethora of brackets around the options since you are supposed to know that each of the options is itself optional. Thus, a cleaner but less precise form of the above syntax diagram is

list [*varlist*] [in *range*] [if *exp*] [, [no]display nolabel noobs doublespace]

by ... : may be used with list; see [R] **by**.

Items typed in *italics* represent arguments for which you are to substitute variable names, observation numbers, and the like.

The diagrams employ the following symbols:

#	Indicates a literal number, e.g., 5; see [U] **15.2 Numbers**.
[ ]	Anything enclosed in brackets is optional.
{ }	At least one of the items enclosed in braces must appear.
|	The vertical bar separates alternatives.
%fmt	Any Stata format, e.g., %8.2f; see [U] **15.5 Formats: controlling how data are displayed**.
exp	Any algebraic expression, e.g., (5+myvar)/2; see [U] **16 Functions and expressions**.
filename	Any filename; see [U] **14.6 File-naming conventions**.
newvar	A variable that will be created by the current command; see [U] **14.4.2 Lists of new variables**.
numlist	A list of numbers; see [U] **14.1.8 numlist**.
oldvar	A previously created variable; see [U] **14.4.1 Lists of existing variables**.
options	A list of options; see [U] **14.1.7 options**.
range	An observation range, e.g., 5/20; see [U] **14.1.4 in range**.
"*string*"	Any string of characters enclosed in double quotes; see [U] **15.4 Strings**.
varlist	A list of variable names; see [U] **14.4 varlists**. If *varlist* allows time-series operators, a note to that effect will be shown below the syntax diagram; see [U] **14.4.3 Time-series varlists**.
varname	A variable name; see [U] **14.3 Naming conventions**.
weight	A [*wgttype*=*exp*] modifier; see [U] **14.1.6 weight** and [U] **23.13 Weighted estimation**.
xvar	The variable to be displayed on the horizontal axis.
yvar	The variable to be displayed on the vertical axis.

If a command allows the by prefix—and most commands do—this will be indicated immediately following the syntax diagram. The list command allows by.

Description

Following the syntax diagram is a brief description of the purpose of the command.

Options

If the command allows any options, they are explained here.

Remarks

The explanations under *Description* and *Options* are exceedingly brief and technical; they are designed to provide a quick summary of the command. The remarks explain in English what the preceding technical jargon means.

Saved Results

Commands are classified as e class, r class, s class, or n class, according to whether they save calculated results in e(), r(), s(), or not at all. These results can then be used in subroutines by other programs (ado-files). Such saved results are documented here; see [U] **21.8 Accessing results calculated by other programs** and [U] **21.9 Accessing results calculated by estimation commands**.

Methods and Formulas

The techniques and/or formulas used in obtaining the results are described here, as tersely and technically as possible. If a command is implemented as an ado-file, that is indicated here.

References

Published sources are listed that either were directly referenced in the preceding text or might be of interest.

Also See

Other manual entries are listed that, if this entry interested you, might also interest you. These entries are labeled as "Complementary", "Related", or "Background". Complementary entries are for commands that you might use with the command at which you are looking. Related entries are for commands that you might use instead of the command at which you are looking. Background entries provide background information that you may need in order to use the command at which you are looking.

Also See

Complementary:	[R] **net search**, [R] **search**
Background:	[U] **1.1 Getting Started with Stata**

Title

> **about** — Display information about my version of Stata

Syntax

```
about
```

Description

about displays information about the Stata that you are running.

Remarks

about displays information about the release number, flavor, serial number, and license for your Stata. If you are running Stata for Windows, information on memory is also displayed:

```
. about
Intercooled Stata 7.0 for Windows
Born 01 Dec 2000
Copyright (C) 1985-2001
Total physical memory:      64948 KB
Available physical memory:  11292 KB
10-user Stata for Windows (network) perpetual license:
        Serial number:  197040000
          Licensed to:  Alan R. Riley
                        StataCorp
```

or

```
. about
Intercooled Stata 7.0 for Macintosh
Born 01 Dec 2000
Copyright (C) 1985-2001
Single-user Stata for Macintosh perpetual license:
        Serial number:  47040001
          Licensed to:  Chinh Nguyen
                        Stata Corporation
```

Also See

Related:	[R] **which**
Background:	[U] **4 Flavors of Stata**

4

Title

adjust — Tables of adjusted means and proportions

Syntax

adjust [*var* [= #] ...] [if *exp*] [in *range*] , by(*varlist*) [{ xb | pr | exp }

     { se | stdf } generate(*newvar1* [*newvar2*]) ci level(#) vertical

     equation(*eqno*) nooffset replace label(*text*) selabel(*text*) cilabel(*text*)

     nokey noheader format(%*fmt*) *tabdisp_options*]

Description

After an estimation command (see [R] **estimation commands**), adjust provides adjusted predictions of $x\beta$ (the means in a linear-regression setting), probabilities (available after some estimation commands), or exponentiated linear predictions. The estimate is computed for each level of the by() variable(s), setting the variable(s) specified in [*var* [= #] ...] to their mean or to the specified number if the = # part is specified. Variables used in the estimation command but not included in either the by() variable list or the adjust variable list are left at their current values, observation by observation. In this case, adjust displays the average estimated prediction (or the corresponding probability or exponentiated prediction) for each level of the by variables.

Options

by(*varlist*) is required and specifies the variable(s) whose levels determine the subsets of the data for which adjusted predictions are to be computed. The variables in by() are not required to be involved in the original estimation command. A maximum of seven variables may be specified in the by() option.

xb indicates that the linear prediction from the estimation command is to be displayed. This produces predicted values (means in the linear-regression setting) and is equivalent to the xb option of predict. Realize that, depending on the estimation command, the xb values may not be in the original units of the dependent variable. The default is xb if pr or exp are not specified.

pr is an alternative to xb and indicates that predicted probabilities are to be displayed. The pr option is not available after all commands.

exp is an alternative to xb and indicates that exponentiated linear predictions, $\exp(x\beta)$, are to be displayed. Depending on the estimation command, the resulting quantities might be called "incidence rates", "hazard ratios", etc.

se indicates that the standard error of the linear prediction is to be displayed. This is equivalent to the stdp option of predict.

stdf indicates that the standard error of the forecast of the linear prediction is to be displayed. This is equivalent to the stdf option of predict and is only available after estimation commands that support the stdf predict option.

5

generate(*newvar1* [*newvar2*]) generates one or two new variables. If one variable is specified, then the adjusted linear predictions for each observation are generated in *newvar1* (holding the appropriate variables to their means or other specified values). If `pr` is specified, then the adjusted linear predictions are transformed to probabilities. If `exp` is specified, then the exponentiated predictions are returned. If *newvar2* is specified, then the standard errors from either the `se` option or the `stdf` option are placed in the second variable.

ci specifies that confidence intervals are to be displayed. The confidence intervals are for the displayed estimates as determined by the choice of the `xb`, `pr`, or `exp` options—producing intervals for the adjusted linear prediction, probability, or exponentiated linear predictions. When `stdf` is specified, prediction intervals are produced. These are, by definition, wider than the corresponding confidence intervals.

level(*#*) specifies the confidence level, in percent, for confidence or prediction intervals. The default is `level(95)` or as set by `set level`; see [R] **level**.

vertical requests that the endpoints of confidence or prediction intervals be stacked vertically on display.

equation(*eqno*) specifies which equation in a multiple-equation system is to be used in the `adjust` command. This option is allowed only following multiple-equation estimation commands.

nooffset is relevant only if you specified `offset(`*varname*`)` or `exposure(`*varname*`)` when you estimated your model. It modifies the calculations made by `adjust` so that they ignore the offset or exposure variable.

replace specifies that the data in memory are to be replaced with data containing one observation per cell corresponding to the table produced by the `adjust` command.

label(*text*), selabel(*text*), and cilabel(*text*) allow you to change the labels for the displayed predictions (from the `xb`, `pr`, or `exp` options); error terms (from the `se` or `stdf` options); and confidence intervals (from the `ci` option). `label()` and `selabel()` also change the variable labels for the variables created by the `generate()` option.

nokey and noheader suppress the display of the table key and header information.

format(*%fmt*) specifies the display format for presenting the numbers in the table; see [U] **15.5 Formats: controlling how data are displayed**. `format(%8.0g)` is the default. Standard errors and confidence intervals are further formatted for output by automatic enclosure within parentheses or square brackets.

The allowed *tabdisp_options* are `center`, `left`, `cellwidth(`*#*`)`, `csepwidth(`*#*`)`, `scsepwidth(`*#*`)`, and `stubwidth(`*#*`)`; see [P] **tabdisp**.

Remarks

adjust is a post-estimation command; see [U] **23 Estimation and post-estimation commands**. adjust is really a front-end process for `predict`; see [R] **predict**. It sets up the values at which predictions are desired and then displays the predictions in tabular form; the data remain unchanged. adjust's options control the labeling of the predictions, errors, and confidence intervals. tabdisp is used to produce the final table. Several options from tabdisp are available for control over the final appearance of the table.

If you restricted your estimation command to a portion of the data using `if` or `in`, then you will generally want to use the same conditions with `adjust`. This is easily done by including `if e(sample)` with the `adjust` command. However, there may be legitimate reasons for using different data to perform the estimation and to obtain adjusted predictions (i.e., out-of-sample adjusted predictions).

Note: If you performed an estimation command using weights and follow that with the `adjust` command letting some of the variables vary observation by observation, the weights will not be used in constructing the adjusted table. This is not a concern when all variables of the estimation command are specified in `adjust`'s variable list and `by()` option variable list.

An interesting way to use `adjust` is after using `xi` with the estimation command. Another interesting use of `adjust` is to specify a categorical variable both in the variable list being set to a specific value and as a `by` variable. This is helpful in examining the predictions for several groups as if they were set at a particular group's value (possibly also holding some other variables to certain values also).

▷ Example

Using the automobile dataset, let's understand automobile price as a function of whether the car was manufactured domestically. We first look at the average price for domestic and foreign cars.

```
. table foreign, c(mean price sd price) format(%8.3f)
```

Car type	mean(price)	sd(price)
Domestic	6072.423	3097.104
Foreign	6384.682	2621.915

These average prices do not seem very far apart. However, we do not think that these averages are telling us the full story since there are other variables that have an impact on the price of automobiles. As an (admittedly fake) first attempt at modeling automobile price, we decide to perform a regression.

```
. regress price mpg weight turn foreign
```

Source	SS	df	MS		Number of obs =	74
					F(4, 69) =	19.23
Model	334771309	4	83692827.3		Prob > F =	0.0000
Residual	300294087	69	4352088.22		R-squared =	0.5271
					Adj R-squared =	0.4997
Total	635065396	73	8699525.97		Root MSE =	2086.2

price	Coef.	Std. Err.	t	P>|t|	[95% Conf. Interval]	
mpg	-.4660076	73.51407	-0.01	0.995	-147.1226	146.1905
weight	4.284532	.7404967	5.79	0.000	2.807282	5.761782
turn	-229.2059	114.2423	-2.01	0.049	-457.1131	-1.298679
foreign	3221.415	706.4847	4.56	0.000	1812.017	4630.813
_cons	1368.197	4887.597	0.28	0.780	-8382.292	11118.69

We now ask ourselves what the price of domestic and foreign cars would be if they were compared at identical values of the explanatory variables: `turn`, `weight`, and `mpg` under this regression model. We compare the prices predicted from the model with these three variables set at their respective mean values. The `adjust` command provides the answer.

```
. adjust mpg weight turn, by(foreign) se ci center
```

```
   Dependent variable: price     Command: regress
Covariates set to mean: mpg = 21.297297, weight = 3019.4595, turn = 39.648647
```

Car type	xb	stdp	lb	ub
Domestic	5207.54	(320.823)	[4567.52	5847.56]
Foreign	8428.95	(552.515)	[7326.72	9531.19]

Key:	xb	=	Linear Prediction
	stdp	=	Standard Error
	[lb , ub]	=	[95% Confidence Interval]

We see that under this regression model foreign cars are predicted to be more expensive than domestic cars when compared at the average value of mpg, weight, and turn. The standard errors and confidence intervals are also presented. What if instead of prediction standard errors and confidence intervals we wanted to know the forecast standard errors and prediction intervals?

. adjust mpg weight turn, by(foreign) stdf ci center

Dependent variable: price   Command: regress
Covariates set to mean: mpg = 21.297297, weight = 3019.4595, turn = 39.648647

Car type	xb	stdf	lb	ub
Domestic	5207.54	(2110.69)	[996.826	9418.25]
Foreign	8428.95	(2158.09)	[4123.68	12734.2]

Key:	xb	=	Linear Prediction
	stdf	=	Standard Error (forecast)
	[lb , ub]	=	[95% Prediction Interval]

Understand the difference between these two tables. The reported means are the same but their reported standard errors differ. The first table uses the se option (stdp option of predict), the standard error of the linear prediction. This standard error measures uncertainty of the mean originating from the uncertainty of the estimated model coefficients. Were our model estimated on an infinite population, we would be certain as to the model's coefficients and hence the mean of each population. These standard errors would then be zero.

Even if we knew the mean with certainty—even if the stdp standard errors were zero—we would be uncertain as to the price of each individual car. This is because individual cars have individual prices drawn from a distribution whose mean we would know; $price_j = \mu_j + \epsilon_j$.

In the second table, the reported standard errors are noticeably larger than those in the first. These standard errors reflect our total uncertainty as to the price of individual cars, $\sqrt{\sigma_\mu^2 + \sigma_\epsilon^2}$. This uncertainty is based on our uncertainty of the mean itself, σ_μ—the prediction's standard error—and the inherent uncertainty because of the unmeasured characteristics of the individual cars themselves, σ_ϵ, the residual standard error. These two components, appropriately combined, are called the forecast standard error and are obtained with the stdf option.

Also note that the first table presents confidence intervals based on the stdp standard error and that the second table presents what are commonly called prediction intervals based on the larger stdf forecast standard errors. Confidence intervals are intervals on our prediction for the mean. Prediction intervals are intervals on our prediction for individual observations.

◁

▷ Example

We also want to know the predicted cost for domestic and foreign cars when some of the variables are set at particular values. For instance, if we want to compare the predicted price when mpg is 25, turn is 35.2, and weight is at its mean value, we do the following:

```
. adjust mpg=25 weight turn=35.2, by(foreign)
```

```
          Dependent variable: price     Command: regress
       Covariate set to mean: weight = 3019.4595
     Covariates set to value: mpg = 25, turn = 35.2
```

Car type	xb
Domestic	6225.47
Foreign	9446.88

```
     Key:  xb  =  Linear Prediction
```

Imagine that we now want to find the predicted average price of foreign and domestic cars under this regression model when mpg and weight are set to their overall means but the turn variable is left alone, meaning it takes on the values observed car by car.

```
. adjust mpg weight, by(foreign) se gen(pred err)
```

```
          Dependent variable: price     Command: regress
           Created variables: pred, err
         Variable left as is: turn
       Covariates set to mean: mpg = 21.297297, weight = 3019.4595
```

Car type	xb	stdp
Domestic	4796.42	(342.766)
Foreign	9400.69	(621.791)

```
     Key:  xb    =  Linear Prediction
           stdp  =  Standard Error
```

Specifying gen(pred err) generates prediction and error variables that we can use. Let's take a look at a few observations and compare them to the actual price and the predicted price using predict without any constraints.

```
. predict pred2 , xb
. list foreign turn price pred2 pred err in 47/58
```

	foreign	turn	price	pred2	pred	err
47.	Domestic	42	5,798	7585.93	4668.595	373.002
48.	Domestic	42	4,934	6600.487	4668.595	373.002
49.	Domestic	45	5,222	4798.425	3980.978	628.3688
50.	Domestic	40	4,723	5901.609	5127.007	314.9057
51.	Domestic	43	4,424	6156.588	4439.389	445.2716
52.	Domestic	41	4,172	3484.962	4897.801	325.7249
53.	Foreign	37	9,690	8226.297	9036.04	548.7275
54.	Foreign	36	6,295	5196.463	9265.246	589.1915
55.	Foreign	34	9,735	8138.971	9723.657	719.4052
56.	Foreign	35	6,229	6711.028	9494.451	647.5291
57.	Foreign	32	4,589	5893.468	10182.07	890.1414
58.	Foreign	34	5,079	6554.16	9723.657	719.4052

Note the differences in the predictions from the `predict` command and those from `adjust`. `predict` uses each observation's individual values for the variables in the regression model. `adjust` substitutes certain values for some or all of the variables in the regression model depending on what was specified in the `adjust` command. The first produces predicted values for the cars. The second produces predicted values for the cars with certain characteristics changed.

◁

▷ Example

Say we wish to look at the predicted cost of domestic and foreign cars by repair record (`rep78`) under the current regression model holding `mpg` and `weight` to their mean and allowing `turn` to vary. `adjust` allows us to do this even though we did not include `rep78` in the regression model.

```
. adjust mpg weight, by(rep78 foreign) se ci center format(%9.2f)
```

```
         Dependent variable: price     Command: regress
         Variable left as is: turn
    Covariates set to mean: mpg = 21.289856, weight = 3032.0291
```

Repair Record 1978	Car type Domestic	Foreign
1	4951.66 (322.08) [4309.13,5594.19]	
2	4407.30 (471.15) [3467.38,5347.21]	
3	4790.37 (351.31) [4089.51,5491.22]	9471.91 (632.09) [8210.93,10732.89]
4	4722.45 (368.21) [3987.90,5457.01]	9548.31 (653.36) [8244.89,10851.73]
5	6097.69 (579.71) [4941.19,7254.19]	9420.97 (618.80) [8186.50,10655.45]

```
    Key:  Linear Prediction
          (Standard Error)
          [95% Confidence Interval]
```

This is an example of a two-way table produced by `adjust`. Up to seven-way tables are possible.

You may have noticed that the means of `mpg` and `weight` in this run of `adjust` are not the same as in the previous runs. This is due to the fact that the `rep78` variable (which was not a part of the regression) has five missing values and `adjust` does casewise deletion when confronted with missing values.

◁

▷ Example

What if we wanted to find the predicted cost of foreign and domestic cars under this regression model while setting `weight` to its mean, letting `mpg` and `turn` vary, and pretending for the moment that all the cars are domestic? `adjust` handles this since it allows variables to be set to a specific value for the prediction and yet these variables may still differentiate subsets of the data in the `by()` option.

```
. adjust weight foreign=0, by(foreign) se ci center
```

```
      Dependent variable: price     Command: regress
    Variables left as is: mpg, turn
   Covariate set to mean: weight = 3019.4595
  Covariate set to value: foreign = 0
```

Car type	xb	stdp	lb	ub
Domestic	4797.11	(363.698)	[4071.55	5522.66]
Foreign	6177.65	(637.952)	[4904.97	7450.33]

```
     Key:  xb         =  Linear Prediction
           stdp       =  Standard Error
           [lb , ub]  =  [95% Confidence Interval]
```

In this table, we obtain the predicted prices of all cars as if they were domestic. The $6,178 prediction, for instance, is the average predicted price of our sample of foreign cars were they instead domestic and if they had average weight. The foreign-car sample has a different prediction than the domestic-car sample because the cars in the two samples have different `mpg` and `turn` and we left these differences just as we observed them.

We now do the same thing except we treat all cars as if they were foreign by typing

```
. adjust weight foreign=1, by(foreign) se ci center
```

```
      Dependent variable: price     Command: regress
    Variables left as is: mpg, turn
   Covariate set to mean: weight = 3019.4595
  Covariate set to value: foreign = 1
```

Car type	xb	stdp	lb	ub
Domestic	8018.52	(627.607)	[6766.48	9270.56]
Foreign	9399.07	(685.01)	[8032.51	10765.6]

```
     Key:  xb         =  Linear Prediction
           stdp       =  Standard Error
           [lb , ub]  =  [95% Confidence Interval]
```

Put either way, the tables report the same difference in prices due to `mpg` and `turn` between the domestic and foreign car samples: 9399.07 − 8018.52 or 6177.65 − 4797.11.

◁

▷ Example

What if we decide to include the `rep78` variable in the regression model of our earlier examples? An easy way to do that is with `xi`; see [R] **xi**.

```
. xi : regress price mpg weight turn I.rep78
I.rep78          _Irep78_1-5          (naturally coded; _Irep78_1 omitted)
```

Source	SS	df	MS			
Model	242819042	7	34688434.6			
Residual	333977917	61	5475047.82			
Total	576796959	68	8482308.22			

```
Number of obs =      69
F(  7,    61) =    6.34
Prob > F      =  0.0000
R-squared     =  0.4210
Adj R-squared =  0.3545
Root MSE      =  2339.9
```

price	Coef.	Std. Err.	t	P>|t|	[95% Conf. Interval]	
mpg	-86.24749	84.98694	-1.01	0.314	-256.1894	83.69441
weight	3.39851	.8279604	4.10	0.000	1.742901	5.05412
turn	-321.7209	136.6736	-2.35	0.022	-595.0167	-48.42515
_Irep78_2	1143.126	1860.47	0.61	0.541	-2577.113	4863.365
_Irep78_3	1074.757	1715.121	0.63	0.533	-2354.84	4504.354
_Irep78_4	1541.853	1759.521	0.88	0.384	-1976.527	5060.234
_Irep78_5	2813.323	1849.747	1.52	0.133	-885.4749	6512.121
_cons	9030.873	5599.464	1.61	0.112	-2165.946	20227.69

Now we wish to return to our two-way adjusted table presented in an earlier example and examine the adjusted predictions under this new regression model. We will set `mpg` and `weight` to their mean values and allow `turn` to vary and obtain the predictions for domestic and foreign cars by repair record.

```
. adjust mpg weight, by(foreign rep78) se
```

```
Dependent variable: price     Command: regress
Variables left as is: turn, _Irep78_2, _Irep78_3, _Irep78_4, _Irep78_5
Covariates set to mean: mpg = 21.289856, weight = 3032.0291
```

Car type	Repair Record 1978				
	1	2	3	4	5
Domestic	4308.5	4687.54	5156.86	5528.63	8730.43
	(1655.28)	(861.486)	(509.245)	(677.039)	(880.691)
Foreign			7206.34	7780.68	8873.42
			(759.055)	(798.379)	(910.117)

```
Key:  Linear Prediction
      (Standard Error)
```

`adjust` can take advantage of the original `rep78` variable in the `by` option. You will notice that the output says that the `xi` created variables are left as is along with the `turn` variable. This is true, but with the `rep78` variable in the `by` option, `adjust` still produces the results desired.

If you have used `xi` in your estimation command, you can freely use in the `by()` option the original variables on which `xi` operated. The same is not true for setting these variables to specific values. In that case, you must use the names produced by `xi`. For example, let's say that we wish to create the same adjusted prediction table as before but we now want to treat all the data as if it had a repair record of 3. Here is how we would do it:

```
. adjust mpg weight _Irep78_2=0 _Irep78_3=1 _Irep78_4=0 _Irep78_5=0, by(for rep78) se
```

```
     Dependent variable: price      Command: regress
     Variable left as is: turn
  Covariates set to mean: mpg = 21.289856, weight = 3032.0291
 Covariates set to value: _Irep78_2 = 0, _Irep78_3 = 1, _Irep78_4 = 0,
                          _Irep78_5 = 0
```

Car type	1	Repair Record 1978 2	3	4	5
Domestic	5383.26 (468.873)	4619.17 (653.654)	5156.86 (509.245)	5061.54 (530.558)	6991.86 (687.006)
Foreign			7206.34 (759.055)	7313.58 (796.544)	7134.85 (734.568)

```
Key:  Linear Prediction
      (Standard Error)
```

If you wanted to do the same thing except set the repair record to 1 (the level dropped by xi), then in the adjust command, set all the xi created variables to zero.

```
. adjust mpg weight _Irep78_2=0 _Irep78_3=0 _Irep78_4=0 _Irep78_5=0, by(for rep78) se
  (output omitted )
```
◁

▷ Example

The adjust command also works after multiple-equation estimation models. Let us take our first example regression and replace it with a corresponding multivariate regression using mvreg:

```
. mvreg gear_ratio price displ = mpg weight turn foreign
```

Equation	Obs	Parms	RMSE	"R-sq"	F	P
gear_ratio	74	5	.2632419	0.6854	37.58139	0.0000
price	74	5	2086.166	0.5271	19.2305	0.0000
displacement	74	5	40.98463	0.8118	74.38435	0.0000

	Coef.	Std. Err.	t	P>|t|	[95% Conf. Interval]	
gear_ratio						
mpg	.0098519	.0092763	1.06	0.292	-.0086538	.0283577
weight	-.0002951	.0000934	-3.16	0.002	-.0004815	-.0001087
turn	.012322	.0144156	0.85	0.396	-.0164364	.0410804
foreign	.4308748	.0891474	4.83	0.000	.2530305	.6087191
_cons	3.079496	.6167391	4.99	0.000	1.849135	4.309857
price						
mpg	-.4660076	73.51407	-0.01	0.995	-147.1226	146.1905
weight	4.284532	.7404967	5.79	0.000	2.807282	5.761782
turn	-229.2059	114.2423	-2.01	0.049	-457.1131	-1.298679
foreign	3221.415	706.4847	4.56	0.000	1812.017	4630.813
_cons	1368.197	4887.597	0.28	0.780	-8382.292	11118.69
displacement						
mpg	.2235286	1.444251	0.15	0.877	-2.657673	3.10473
weight	.1003079	.0145477	6.90	0.000	.071286	.1293298
turn	-.4931961	2.244395	-0.22	0.827	-4.970641	3.984249
foreign	-26.13646	13.87953	-1.88	0.064	-53.82537	1.552458
_cons	-83.01403	96.02129	-0.86	0.390	-274.5713	108.5432

We simply indicate which equation from the multiple-equation model is to be used by `adjust`. The equation may be specified by number or by name. We use `equation(price)` below but could have specified `equation(#2)` instead.

```
. adjust mpg weight turn, by(foreign) se ci center equation(price)
```

```
                Equation: price      Command: mvreg
    Covariates set to mean: mpg = 21.297297, weight = 3019.4595, turn = 39.648647
```

Car type	xb	stdp	lb	ub
Domestic	5207.54	(320.823)	[4567.52	5847.56]
Foreign	8428.95	(552.515)	[7326.72	9531.19]

```
      Key:  xb          =  Linear Prediction
            stdp        =  Standard Error
            [lb , ub]   =  [95% Confidence Interval]
```

As expected, this table is the same as produced in the first example.

◁

▷ Example

`adjust` following `anova` helps explore the underlying cause for significant terms in the ANOVA or ANOCOVA table. The `sysage.dta` dataset illustrating ANOCOVA in [R] **anova** provides an example.

```
. anova systolic drug disease drug*disease age, continuous(age)
```

```
                    Number of obs =      58     R-squared     =  0.6826
                    Root MSE      =  8.1164     Adj R-squared =  0.5980
```

Source	Partial SS	df	MS	F	Prob > F
Model	6375.73983	12	531.311652	8.07	0.0000
drug	2762.01519	3	920.671731	13.98	0.0000
disease	605.323109	2	302.661555	4.59	0.0153
drug*disease	608.728232	6	101.454705	1.54	0.1871
age	2116.40132	1	2116.40132	32.13	0.0000
Residual	2964.41534	45	65.8758965		
Total	9340.15517	57	163.862371		

We see that `age` is a significant covariate and that `drug` and `disease` are significant factors while the interaction is not. However, the interaction does not look as if it can be completely ignored. To further explore this interaction we use `adjust`:

```
. adjust age, by(disease drug) se f(%6.3f) replace label(Predicted Systolic)
```

```
      Dependent variable: systolic     Command: anova
    Covariate set to mean: age = 45.155174
```

Patient's Disease	Drug Used			
	1	2	3	4
1	28.641 (3.316)	26.972 (3.634)	15.184 (4.690)	19.164 (3.760)
2	29.809 (4.068)	32.427 (4.063)	4.288 (3.630)	12.294 (3.315)
3	17.999 (3.654)	19.153 (3.318)	7.427 (4.063)	13.630 (3.631)

Key: Predicted Systolic
      (Standard Error)

From this table, it appears that drug 3 gives the lowest predicted systolic measure. Also notice that the systolic measure for disease 2 appears to vary more widely across the different drugs (a low of 4.288 for drug 3 and a high of 32.427 for drug 2).

We specified the `replace` option so that at this point the data from the adjusted table are now in memory. Remember to specify `replace` only if you have previously saved your original data.

```
. list drug disease xb stdp

          drug   disease         xb        stdp
   1.        1         1   28.64146    3.315753
   2.        2         1   26.97245    3.634287
   3.        3         1   15.18372    4.690391
   4.        4         1   19.16392    3.760155
   5.        1         2   29.80869    4.067505
   6.        2         2   32.42668    4.062614
   7.        3         2   4.287933    3.629817
   8.        4         2   12.29404    3.314871
   9.        1         3   17.99923    3.654392
  10.        2         3   19.15318    3.318073
  11.        3         3   7.426678    4.062614
  12.        4         3   13.63019    3.631155
```

A graph of the interaction can be produced from this data.

```
. graph xb drug, c(L) s([disease]) xlab(1/4)
```

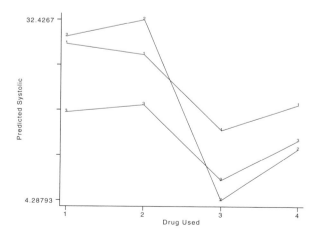

This simple example shows one of the many uses of the data after using the `replace` option.

◁

▷ Example

To illustrate the `pr` option of `adjust`, we turn to the low birth weight dataset illustrated in [R] **logistic** that was obtained from Hosmer and Lemeshow (1989, Appendix 1). Below we show a `logistic` model (`probit`, `logit`, and several other commands are also allowed with the `pr` option of `adjust`).

```
. xi : logistic low age lwt i.race smoke , nolog
i.race          _Irace_1-3          (naturally coded; _Irace_1 omitted)
```

```
Logit estimates                              Number of obs   =       189
                                             LR chi2(5)      =     20.08
                                             Prob > chi2     =    0.0012
Log likelihood = -107.29639                  Pseudo R2       =    0.0856
```

low	Odds Ratio	Std. Err.	z	P>|z|	[95% Conf. Interval]	
age	.9777443	.0334083	-0.66	0.510	.9144097	1.045466
lwt	.9875761	.006305	-1.96	0.050	.9752956	1.000011
_Irace_2	3.425372	1.771281	2.38	0.017	1.243215	9.437768
_Irace_3	2.5692	1.069301	2.27	0.023	1.136391	5.808555
smoke	2.870346	1.09067	2.77	0.006	1.363	6.044672

In this case, we will ask for adjusted probability estimates under this model, setting `lwt` to its mean and `age` to 30. We will ask for these adjusted probability estimates by `race` and `smoke`.

```
. adjust age = 30 lwt , by(race smoke) pr ci format(%7.4f)
```

```
Dependent variable: low      Command: logistic
  Variables left as is: _Irace_2, _Irace_3
Covariate set to mean: lwt = 129.8201
Covariate set to value: age = 30
```

race	smoked during pregnancy	
	0	1
white	0.1226	0.2863
	[0.0572,0.2434]	[0.1670,0.4452]
black	0.3237	0.5787
	[0.1412,0.5822]	[0.3110,0.8070]
other	0.2642	0.5075
	[0.1464,0.4291]	[0.2838,0.7283]

```
Key:  Probability
      [95% Confidence Interval]
```

The confidence interval is for the adjusted estimated probabilities. Both the probabilities and confidence intervals are obtained by first computing the linear predictions and associated confidence intervals and then transforming them to probabilities. If the `pr` option were not specified, we would have obtained the adjusted linear predictions.

```
. adjust age = 30 lwt , by(race smoke) ci format(%7.4f) noheader
```

race	smoked during pregnancy 0	1
white	-1.9681 [-2.8020,-1.1341]	-0.9136 [-1.6070,-0.2202]
black	-0.7368 [-1.8053,0.3317]	0.3176 [-0.7954,1.4305]
other	-1.0245 [-1.7633,-0.2856]	0.0300 [-0.9259,0.9859]

```
Key:  Linear Prediction
      [95% Confidence Interval]
```

It is easy to confirm that the entries in this table can be transformed to the probabilities in the previous table. For instance, $.1226 = \exp(-1.9681)/\{1 + \exp(-1.9681)\}$.

◁

▷ Example

In this example, we specify the `exp` option for `adjust` following a `cox` regression on the `drugtr.dta` data introduced in the section *Cox regression with censored data* in [R] **st stcox**. To make the `adjust` table more meaningful, we generate a new age variable that has the minimum age in the data (47 in this case) subtracted from the age. This will produce hazard ratios in the `adjust` table relative to someone age 47 instead of to a newborn.

```
. gen age0 = age-47
. stcox drug age0 , nolog
         failure _d: died
   analysis time _t: studytime

Cox regression -- Breslow method for ties

No. of subjects =          48                  Number of obs   =          48
No. of failures =          31
Time at risk    =         744
                                               LR chi2(2)      =       33.18
Log likelihood  =    -83.323546                Prob > chi2     =      0.0000
```

_t _d	Haz. Ratio	Std. Err.	z	P>|z|	[95% Conf. Interval]	
drug	.1048772	.0477017	-4.96	0.000	.0430057	.2557622
age0	1.120325	.0417711	3.05	0.002	1.041375	1.20526

Using either `age0` or `age` with `stcox` produces identical results—the reported hazard ratios are relative to a one unit change in the variable. If we wanted to see the hazard ratios for the placebo and treatment drug when `age` is 50 (`age0` is 3) with `age` 47 (`age0` is 0) as the base, we could use `adjust`:

```
. adjust age0=3, by(drug) exp stubwidth(11) label(Hazard Ratio)
```

```
      Dependent variable: _t      Command: cox
   Covariate set to value: age0 = 3
```

Drug type (0=placebo)	exp(xb)
0	1.40615
1	.147473

```
     Key: exp(xb)  =  Hazard Ratio
```

These hazard ratios are for 50 year olds with respect to 47 year olds on placebo. Without the `exp` option, we would have obtained a table of the linear predictions instead of the hazard ratios.

◁

Methods and Formulas

`adjust` is implemented as an ado-file.

Acknowledgment

The `adjust` command is based in part on the `adjmean` and `adjprop` commands (Garrett 1995, 1998) written by Joanne Garrett of the University of North Carolina at Chapel Hill.

References

Garrett, J. M. 1995. sg33: Calculation of adjusted means and adjusted proportions. *Stata Technical Bulletin* 24: 22–25. Reprinted in *Stata Technical Bulletin Reprints*, vol. 4, pp. 161–165.

——. 1998. sg33.1: Enhancements for calculation of adjusted means and adjusted proportions. *Stata Technical Bulletin* 43: 16–24. Reprinted in *Stata Technical Bulletin Reprints*, vol. 8, pp. 111–123.

Higbee, K. T. 1998. sg89: Adjusted predictions and probabilities after estimation. *Stata Technical Bulletin* 44: 30–37. Reprinted in *Stata Technical Bulletin Reprints*, vol. 8, pp. 165–173.

Hosmer, D. W., Jr., and S. Lemeshow. 1989. *Applied Logistic Regression*. New York: John Wiley & Sons. (*Second edition forthcoming in 2001.*)

Also See

Related:	[R] **epitab**, [R] **svytab**, [R] **table**
Background:	[U] **23 Estimation and post-estimation commands**,
	[R] **predict**,
	[P] **tabdisp**

Title

alpha — Cronbach's alpha

Syntax

> alpha *varlist* [if *exp*] [in *range*] [, <u>a</u>sis <u>c</u>asewise <u>d</u>etail <u>g</u>enerate(*newvar*)
>
> <u>item</u> <u>label</u> <u>min</u>(#) <u>reverse</u>(*varlist*) <u>std</u>]

by ... : may be used with alpha; see [R] **by**.

Description

alpha computes the interitem correlations or covariances for all pairs of variables in *varlist* and Cronbach's α statistic for the scale formed from them. At least two variables must be specified with alpha.

Options

asis indicates that the sense (sign) of each item should be taken as presented in the data. The default is to empirically determine the sense and reverse the scorings for any that enter negatively.

casewise specifies that cases with missing values should be deleted listwise. The default is pairwise computation of covariances/correlations.

detail lists the individual interitem correlations and covariances.

generate(*newvar*) specifies that the scale constructed from *varlist* is to be stored in *newvar*. Unless asis is specified, the sense of items entering negatively is automatically reversed. If std is also specified, the scale is constructed using standardized (mean 0, variance 1) values of the individual items. Unlike most Stata commands, generate() does not employ casewise deletion. A score is created for every observation for which there is a response to at least one item (one variable in *varlist* is not missing). The summative score is divided by the number of items over which the sum is calculated.

item specifies that item-test and item-rest correlations and the effects of removing an item from the scale are displayed. item is valid only when more than two variables are specified in *varlist*.

label requests that the detailed output table be displayed in a compact format that enables the inclusion of variable labels.

min(#) specifies that only cases with at least # observations be included in the computations. casewise is a shorthand for min(k) where k is the number of variables in *varlist*.

reverse(*varlist*) specifies that the signs (directions) of the variables (items) in *varlist* should be reversed. Any variables specified in reverse() that are not also included in alpha's *varlist* are ignored.

std specifies that the items in the scale are to be standardized (mean 0, variance 1) before summing.

Remarks

Cronbach's alpha (Cronbach 1951) assesses the reliability of a summative rating (Likert 1932) scale composed of the variables (called items) specified. The set of items is often called a test or battery. A scale is simply the sum of the individual item scores, reversing the scoring for statements that have negative correlations with the factor (e.g., attitude) being measured. Scales can be formed using the raw item scores or standardized item scores.

The reliability α is defined as the square of the correlation between the measured scale and the underlying factor. If one thinks of a test as being composed of a random sample of items from a hypothetical domain of items designed to measure the same thing, α represents the expected correlation of one test with an alternative form containing the same number of items. The square root of α is the estimated correlation of a test with errorless true scores (Nunnally and Bernstein 1994, 235). The value of α in the case of dichotomous items is often referred to as "Kuder–Richardson Formula 20" (KR-20); see Kuder and Richardson (1937), Allen and Yen (1979, 83–85), and Nunnally and Bernstein (1994, 235).

In addition to reporting α, `alpha` will generate the summative scale from the items (variables) specified and automatically reverse the sense of any when necessary. Stata's decision can be overridden by specifying the `reverse(`*varlist*`)` option.

Since α concerns reliability in measuring an unobserved factor, it is related to factor analysis. The test should be designed to measure a single factor and, since the scale will be composed of an unweighted sum, the factor loadings should all contribute roughly equal information to the score. Both of these assumptions can be verified with `factor`; see [R] **factor**. Equality of factor loadings can also be assessed using the `item` option.

▷ Example

To illustrate `alpha` we apply it, first without and then with the `item` option, to the automobile dataset after randomly introducing missing values:

```
. alpha price headroom rep78 trunk weight length turn displ, std
Test scale = mean(standardized items)
Reversed item: rep78

Average interitem correlation:      0.5251
Number of items in the scale:            8
Scale reliability coefficient:      0.8984
```

The scale derived from our somewhat arbitrarily chosen automobile items (variables) appears rather good since the estimated correlation between it and the underlying factor it measures is $\sqrt{.8984} \approx .9478$ and the estimated correlation between this battery of eight items and all other eight-item batteries from the same domain is .8984. Since the "items" are not on the same scale, it is important that `std` was specified so that the scale and its reliability were based on the sum of standardized variables. Note that we could obtain the scale in a new variable called `sc` with the option `gen(sc)`.

Though the scale appears good, to determine if all the items fit the scale, we include the `item` option:

```
. alpha price headroom rep78 trunk weight length turn displ, std item
Test scale = mean(standardized items)
```

Item	Obs	Sign	item-test correlation	item-rest correlation	interitem correlation	alpha
price	70	+	0.5260	0.3719	0.5993	0.9128
headroom	66	+	0.6716	0.5497	0.5542	0.8969
rep78	61	−	0.4874	0.3398	0.6040	0.9143
trunk	69	+	0.7979	0.7144	0.5159	0.8818
weight	64	+	0.9404	0.9096	0.4747	0.8635
length	69	+	0.9382	0.9076	0.4725	0.8625
turn	66	+	0.8678	0.8071	0.4948	0.8727
displa~t	63	+	0.8992	0.8496	0.4852	0.8684
Test					0.5251	0.8984

"Test" denotes the additive scale; in this case, .5251 is the average interitem correlation and .8984 is the alpha coefficient for a test scale based on all items.

"Obs" shows the number of nonmissing values of the items; "Sign" indicates the direction in which an item variable entered the scale; a "−" denotes that the item was reversed. The remaining four columns in the table provide information on the effect of a single item on the scale.

Column four gives the item-test correlations. Apart from the sign of the correlation for items that entered the scale in reversed order, these correlations are the same numbers as those computed by the commands

```
. alpha price headroom rep78 trunk weight length turn displ, std
. correlate price headroom rep78 trunk weight length turn displ
```

Typically, the item-test correlations should be roughly the same for all items. Item-test correlations may actually not be very adequate to detect items that fit poorly, because the poorly fitting items may distort the scale. Accordingly, it may be more useful to consider item-rest correlations (Nunnally and Bernstein 1994), i.e., the correlation between an item and the scale that is formed by all other items. The average interitem correlations (covariances if **std** is omitted) of all items, excluding one, are shown in column six. Finally, column seven gives Cronbach's α for the test scale that consist of all but the one item.

In this example, neither the **price** item nor the **rep78** item seem to fit well in the scale in all respects. The item-test and item-rest correlations of **price** and **rep78** are much lower than for the other items. The average interitem correlation increases substantially by removing either **price** or **rep78**; apparently they do not correlate strongly with the other items. Finally, we see that Cronbach's α coefficient will increase from .8984 to .9128 if the item **price** is dropped, and it will increase from .8984 to .9143 if **rep78** is dropped. For well-fitting items, we would of course expect that α decreases by shortening the test.

The variable names for the automobile data are reasonably informative. This may not always be true; items in batteries commonly used to measure personality traits, attitudes or values, etc., are usually named with indexed names such as **item12a**, **item12b**, etc. The **label** option forces **alpha** to produce the same statistical information in a more compact format that leaves room to include variable (item) labels. In this compact format, **alpha** excludes the number of nonmissing values of the items, displays the statistics using fewer digits, and uses somewhat cryptic headers:

```
. alpha price headroom rep78 trunk weight length turn displ, std item label det
Test scale = mean(standardized items)

Items      | S  it-cor  ir-cor  ii-cor   alpha   label
-----------+-----------------------------------------------------------------
price      | +   0.526   0.372   0.599   0.913   Price
headroom   | +   0.672   0.550   0.554   0.897   Headroom (in.)
rep78      | -   0.487   0.340   0.604   0.914   Repair Record 1978
trunk      | +   0.798   0.714   0.516   0.882   Trunk space (cu. ft.)
weight     | +   0.940   0.910   0.475   0.863   Weight (lbs.)
length     | +   0.938   0.908   0.473   0.862   Length (in.)
turn       | +   0.868   0.807   0.495   0.873   Turn Circle (ft.)
displa~t   | +   0.899   0.850   0.485   0.868   Displacement (cu. in.)
-----------+-----------------------------------------------------------------
Test       |                     0.525   0.898   mean(standardized items)

Interitem correlations (reverse applied) (obs=pairwise, see below)
        c1       c2       c3       c4       c5       c6       c7       c8
r1   1.0000
r2   0.1174   1.0000
r3  -0.0479   0.1955   1.0000
r4   0.2748   0.6841   0.2777   1.0000
r5   0.5093   0.5464   0.3624   0.6486   1.0000
r6   0.4511   0.5823   0.3162   0.7404   0.9425   1.0000
r7   0.3528   0.4067   0.4715   0.5900   0.8712   0.8569   1.0000
r8   0.5537   0.5166   0.3391   0.6471   0.8753   0.8422   0.7723   1.0000

Pairwise number of observations
                     price     headroom      rep78        trunk
        price          70
     headroom          62          66
        rep78          59          54          61
        trunk          65          61          59          69
       weight          60          56          52          60
       length          66          61          58          64
         turn          62          58          56          62
 displacement          59          58          51          58

                    weight      length        turn   displacement
       weight          64
       length          60          69
         turn          57          61          66
 displacement          54          58          56          63
```

Since the **detail** option was also specified, the interitem correlation matrix was printed, together with the number of observations used for each entry (since these varied across the matrix). Note the negative sign attached to **rep78** in the output indicating the sense in which it entered the scale.

◁

Users of **alpha** require some standard for judging values of α. We paraphrase Nunnally and Bernstein (1994, 265): In the early stages of research, modest reliability of 0.70 or higher will suffice; values in excess of 0.80 are often wasteful of time and funds. In contrast, where measurements on individuals are of interest, a reliability of 0.80 may not be nearly high enough. Even with a reliability of 0.90, the standard error of measurement is almost one-third as large as the standard deviation of test scores; a reliability of 0.90 is the minimum that should be tolerated and a reliability of 0.95 should be considered the desirable standard.

Saved Results

alpha saves in r():

Scalars

r(alpha)	scale reliability coefficient
r(k)	number of items in the scale
r(rho)	average interitem covariance (correlation if std is specified)

Methods and Formulas

alpha is implemented as an ado-file.

Let x_i, $i = 1, \ldots, k$, be the variables over which α is to be calculated. Let s_i be the sign with which x_i enters the scale. If asis is specified, $s_i = 1$ for all i. Otherwise, principal factor analysis is performed on x_i and the first factor's score predicted; see [R] **factor**. s_i is -1 if correlation of the x_i and the predicted score is negative and $+1$ otherwise.

Let r_{ij} be the correlation between x_i and x_j, c_{ij} the covariance, and n_{ij} the number of observations used in calculating the correlation or covariance. The average correlation is

$$\bar{r} = \frac{\sum_{i=2}^{k} \sum_{j=1}^{i-1} s_i s_j n_{ij} r_{ij}}{\sum_{i=2}^{k} \sum_{j=1}^{i-1} n_{ij}}$$

and the average covariance similarly is

$$\bar{c} = \frac{\sum_{i=2}^{k} \sum_{j=1}^{i-1} s_i s_j n_{ij} c_{ij}}{\sum_{i=2}^{k} \sum_{j=1}^{i-1} n_{ij}}$$

Let c_{ii} denote the variance of x_i, and define the average variance as

$$\bar{v} = \frac{\sum_{i=1}^{k} n_{ii} c_{ii}}{\sum_{i=1}^{k} n_{ii}}$$

If std is specified, the scale reliability α is calculated as defined by the general form of the Spearman–Brown Prophecy Formula (Nunnally and Bernstein 1994, 232; Allen and Yen 1979, 85–88):

$$\alpha = \frac{k\bar{r}}{1 + (k-1)\bar{r}}$$

This corresponds to α under the assumption that the summative rating is the sum of the standardized variables (Nunnally and Bernstein 1994, 234). If std is not specified, α is defined (Nunnally and Bernstein 1994, 232, 234) as

$$\alpha = \frac{k\bar{c}}{\bar{v} + (k-1)\bar{c}}$$

Let x_{ij} reflect the value of item i in the jth observation. If `std` is specified, the jth value of the scale computed from the k x_{ij} items is

$$S_j = \frac{1}{k_j} \sum_{i=1}^{k} s_i S(x_{ij})$$

where $S()$ is the function that returns the standardized (mean 0, variance 1) value if x_{ij} is not missing and zero if x_{ij} is missing. k_j is the number of nonmissing values in x_{ij}, $i = 1, \ldots, k$. If `std` is not specified, $S()$ is the function that returns x_{ij}, or missing if x_{ij} is missing.

Acknowledgment

This improved version of `alpha` was written by Jeroen Weesie of Utrecht University, the Netherlands.

References

Allen, M. J. and W. M. Yen. 1979. *Introduction to Measurement Theory*. Monterey, CA: Brooks/Cole Publishing Company.

Bleda, M. J. and A. Tobias. 2000. sg143: Cronbach's alpha one-sided confidence interval. *Stata Technical Bulletin* 56: 26–27.

Cronbach, L. J. 1951. Coefficient alpha and the internal structure of tests. *Psychometrika* 16: 297–334.

Kuder, G. F. and M. W. Richardson. 1937. The theory of the estimation of test reliability. *Psychometrika* 2: 151–160.

Likert, R. A. 1932. A technique for the measurement of attitudes. *Archives of Psychology* 140: 5–55.

Nunnally, J. C. and I. H. Bernstein. 1994. *Psychometric Theory*. 3d ed. New York: McGraw–Hill.

Tarlov, A. R., J. E. Ware, Jr., S. Greenfield, E. C. Nelson, E. Perrin, and M. Zubkoff. 1989. The medical outcomes study. *Journal of the American Medical Association* 262: 925–930.

Weesie, J. 1997. sg66: Enhancements to the alpha command. *Stata Technical Bulletin* 35: 32–34. Reprinted in *Stata Technical Bulletin Reprints*, vol. 6, pp. 176–179.

Also See

Related: [R] **factor**

Title

| **anova** — Analysis of variance and covariance |

Syntax

<u>an</u>ova *varname* $\left[term \left[/\right] \left[term \left[/\right] \ldots \right] \right]$ $\left[weight \right]$ $\left[\text{if } exp \right]$ $\left[\text{in } range \right]$ $\left[, \left[\underline{no} \right] \underline{an}ova \right.$

> <u>categ</u>ory(*varlist*) <u>cl</u>ass(*varlist*) <u>nocons</u>tant <u>cont</u>inuous(*varlist*)

> <u>repeat</u>ed(*varlist*) bse(*term*) bseunit(*varname*) <u>group</u>ing(*varname*) <u>detail</u>

> <u>p</u>artial <u>s</u>equential <u>regr</u>ess $\left. \right]$

where *term* is of the form   *varname*$\left[\left\{ \, * \mid \mid \, \right\} varname \left[\ldots \right] \right]$

by ... : may be used with anova; see [R] **by**.

aweights and fweights are allowed; see [U] **14.1.6 weight**.

anova shares the features of all estimation commands; see [U] **23 Estimation and post-estimation commands**.

Syntax for predict

predict after anova follows the same syntax as predict after regress and can provide predictions, residuals, standardized residuals, studentized residuals, the standard error of the residuals, the standard error of the prediction, the diagonal elements of the projection (hat) matrix, and Cook's D. See [R] **regress** for details.

Description

The **anova** command estimates analysis-of-variance (ANOVA) and analysis-of-covariance (ANOCOVA) models for balanced and unbalanced designs, including designs with missing cells; for repeated measures ANOVA; and for factorial, nested, or mixed designs. **anova** can also be used to produce regression estimates by those who have no interest in ANOVA and ANOCOVA output.

Users wanting to estimate one-way ANOVA models may find the **oneway** or **loneway** commands more convenient; see [R] **oneway** and [R] **loneway**.

Options

$\left[no \right]$**anova** indicates that the ANOVA table is or is not to be displayed. The **anova** command typically displays the ANOVA table and in those cases the **noanova** option suppresses the display. For instance, typing **anova, detail noanova** would show the **detail**-output for the last ANOVA model while suppressing the ANOVA table itself.

If you specify the **regress** option, the ANOVA table is automatically suppressed. In that case, also specifying the **anova** option would show both the regression output and the ANOVA table.

category(*varlist*) indicates the names of the variables in the *terms* that are categorical or class variables. Stata ordinarily assumes that all variables are categorical variables so, in most cases, this option need not be specified. If you specify this option, however, the variables referenced in the *terms* that are not listed in the **category()** option are assumed to be continuous. Also see the **class()** and **continuous()** options.

class(*varlist*) is a synonym for category(*varlist*).

noconstant suppresses the constant term (intercept) from the ANOVA or regression model.

continuous(*varlist*) indicates the names of the variables in the *terms* that are continuous. Stata ordinarily assumes that all variables are categorical variables. Also see the category() and class() options.

repeated(*varlist*) indicates the names of the categorical variables in the *terms* that are to be treated as repeated measures variables in a repeated measures ANOVA or ANCOVA.

bse(*term*) indicates the between-subjects error term in a repeated measures ANOVA. This option is needed only in the rare case when the anova command cannot automatically determine the between-subjects error term.

bseunit(*varname*) indicates the variable representing the lowest unit in the between-subjects error term in a repeated measures ANOVA. This option is rarely needed since the anova command automatically selects the first variable listed in the between-subjects error term as the default for this option.

grouping(*varname*) indicates a variable that determines which observations are grouped together in computing the covariance matrices that will be pooled together and used in a repeated measures ANOVA. This option is rarely needed since the anova command automatically selects the combination of all variables except the first (or as specified in the bseunit option) in the between-subjects error term as the default for grouping observations.

detail presents a table showing the actual values of the categorical variables along with their mapping into level numbers. You do not have to specify this option at the time of estimation. You can obtain the output at any time by typing anova, detail.

partial presents the ANOVA table using partial (or marginal) sums of squares. This is the default. Also see the sequential option.

sequential presents the ANOVA table using sequential sums of squares.

regress presents the regression output corresponding to the specified model. Specifying regress implies the noanova option, so if you want both the regression output and the ANOVA table, you must also specify the anova option. You need not specify the regress option at the time of estimation. You can obtain the underlying regression estimates at any time by typing anova, regress.

Remarks

Remarks are presented under the headings

> *One-way analysis of variance*
> *Two-way analysis of variance*
> *N-way analysis of variance*
> *Analysis of covariance*
> *Nested designs*
> *Mixed designs*
> *Latin square designs*
> *Repeated measures analysis of variance*
> *Weighted data*
> *Obtaining the covariance matrix*
> *Testing effects*
> *Obtaining symbolic forms*
> *Testing coefficients*
> *How Stata numbers levels*
> *anova as an alternative to regress*

anova uses least squares to fit linear models and can report both regression and ANOVA output. The command is designed to be most useful to persons wishing to estimate analysis-of-variance or analysis-of-covariance models (henceforth referred to simply as ANOVA models), but is also useful for persons wishing to estimate regression models with numerous categorical variables.

If your interest is in formal ANOVA, you should read this entire entry. If your interest is solely in regression, you may want to skip to *anova as an alternative to regress*.

Persons interested in regression should also see [R] **regress**.

If your interest is in one-way ANOVA, you may find the oneway command more convenient; see [R] **oneway**.

Analysis of variance was pioneered by Fisher in 1925. Fisher (1935) considered the design of factorial experiments. Many books discuss analysis of variance; see, for instance, Altman (1991), Cobb (1998), Snedecor and Cochran (1989), Steel and Torrie (1980), or Winer, Brown, and Michels (1991). For a classic source, see Scheffé (1959). Kennedy and Gentle (1980) discuss the computing problems of analysis of variance. Edwards (1985) is primarily concerned with the relationship between multiple regression and analysis of variance. Rabe-Hesketh and Everitt (2000, Chapters 4 and 5) illustrate their discussion with Stata output. Repeated measures analysis of variance is discussed in Winer, Brown, and Michels (1991), Kuehl (1994), and Milliken and Johnson (1984). Pioneering work in repeated measures analysis of variance can be found in Box (1954), Geisser and Greenhouse (1958), Huynh and Feldt (1976), and Huynh (1978).

One-way analysis of variance

anova, entered without options, performs and reports standard ANOVA. For instance, to perform a one-way layout of a variable called endog on exog, type anova endog exog.

▷ Example

You run an experiment varying the amount of fertilizer used in growing apple trees. You test four concentrations, using each concentration in three groves of twelve trees each. Later in the year, you measure the average weight of the fruit.

If all had gone well, you would have had three observations on the average weight for each of the four concentrations. Instead, two of the groves were mistakenly leveled by a confused man on a large bulldozer. You are left with the following data:

```
. use apple
(Apple trees)

. list

      treatm~t     weight
  1.         1      117.5
  2.         1      113.8
  3.         1      104.4
  4.         2       48.9
  5.         2       50.4
  6.         2       58.9
  7.         3       70.4
  8.         3       86.9
  9.         4       87.7
 10.         4       67.3
```

To obtain one-way analysis-of-variance results, you type

```
. anova weight treatment

                          Number of obs =     10     R-squared      =  0.9147
                          Root MSE      = 9.07002    Adj R-squared  =  0.8721

                Source |  Partial SS     df       MS             F     Prob > F

                 Model |  5295.54433      3   1765.18144        21.46    0.0013

             treatment |  5295.54433      3   1765.18144        21.46    0.0013

              Residual |  493.591667      6   82.2652778

                 Total |   5789.136       9   643.237333
```

You find significant (at better than the 1% level) differences among the four concentrations.

Although the output is a usual analysis-of-variance table, let's run through it anyway. Above the table is a summary of the underlying regression. The model was estimated on 10 observations, and the root mean square error (Root MSE) is 9.07. The R^2 for the model is 0.9147 and the adjusted R^2 (R_a^2) is 0.8721.

The first line of the table summarizes the model. The sum of squares (Partial SS) for the model is 5295.5 with 3 degrees of freedom (df). This results in a mean square (MS) of $5295.5/3 \approx 1765.2$. The corresponding F statistic is 21.46 and has a significance level of 0.0013. Thus, the model appears to be significant at the 0.13% level.

The next line summarizes the first (and only) term in the model, treatment. Since there is only one term, the line is identical to that for the overall model.

The third line summarizes the residual. The residual sum of squares is 493.59 with 6 degrees of freedom, resulting in a mean square error of 82.27. It is the square root of this latter number that is reported as the Root MSE.

The model plus the residual sum of squares equal the total sum of squares, which is reported as 5789.1 in the last line of the table. This is the total sum of squares of weight after removal of the mean. Similarly, the model plus the residual degrees of freedom sum to the total degrees of freedom, 9. Remember that there are 10 observations. Subtracting 1 for the mean, we are left with 9 total degrees of freedom.

◁

❏ Technical Note

Rather than using the anova command, we could have performed this analysis using the oneway command. The first example in [R] **oneway** repeats this same analysis. You may wish to compare the output.

❏

It is possible and even probable that you will want to see the underlying regression corresponding to a model after seeing the ANOVA table. After estimating an ANOVA model using the anova command, you can obtain the regression output by typing anova, regress.

▷ Example

Returning to the apple tree experiment, we found that the fertilizer concentration appears to affect the average weight of the fruit significantly. Although that is interesting, we next want to know which concentration appears to grow the heaviest fruit. To find out, we examine the underlying regression coefficients.

```
. anova, regress
      Source |      SS        df      MS              Number of obs =      10
-------------+-------------------------------        F( 3,    6) =    21.46
       Model | 5295.54433      3  1765.18144         Prob > F     =  0.0013
    Residual | 493.591667      6  82.2652778         R-squared    =  0.9147
-------------+-------------------------------        Adj R-squared =  0.8721
       Total | 5789.136        9  643.237333         Root MSE     =    9.07

      weight |     Coef.    Std. Err.      t     P>|t|     [95% Conf. Interval]
-------------+----------------------------------------------------------------
       _cons |      77.5    6.413473    12.08   0.000      61.8068     93.1932
   treatment |
          1  |      34.4    8.279758     4.15   0.006     14.14016    54.65984
          2  | -24.76667    8.279758    -2.99   0.024    -45.02651   -4.506828
          3  |      1.15    9.070021     0.13   0.903    -21.04354    23.34354
          4  | (dropped)
```

See [R] **regress** for an explanation of how to read this table. In summary, we find that concentration 1 produces significantly heavier fruits when compared with concentration 4, the omitted (`dropped`) group; concentration 2 produces significantly lighter fruits; concentrations 3 and 4 appear to be roughly equivalent.

◁

❏ Technical Note

After estimating the model using `anova`, we could have simply typed `regress` rather than `anova, regress` to obtain the same output. `regress` typed without arguments reshows the last regression. Since `anova` defines a regression, typing `regress` after `anova` is another way of displaying the regression.

❏

If you type `anova` without any arguments, the ANOVA table will be redisplayed.

▷ Example

We previously typed `anova wgt treat` to produce and display the ANOVA table for our apple tree experiment. We typed `anova, regress` to obtain the regression coefficients. If we want to redisplay the ANOVA table, we can type `anova` without arguments:

```
. anova
                       Number of obs =       10    R-squared     =  0.9147
                       Root MSE      = 9.07002    Adj R-squared =  0.8721

       Source |  Partial SS    df       MS            F      Prob > F
--------------+----------------------------------------------------------
        Model | 5295.54433      3  1765.18144       21.46      0.0013

    treatment | 5295.54433      3  1765.18144       21.46      0.0013

     Residual | 493.591667      6  82.2652778
--------------+----------------------------------------------------------
        Total |   5789.136      9  643.237333
```

◁

Two-way analysis of variance

You can include multiple explanatory variables with the anova command, and you can specify interactions by placing '*' between the variable names. For instance, typing anova y a b performs a two-way layout of y on a and b. Typing anova y a b a*b performs a full two-way factorial layout.

Note: With the default partial sums of squares, when you specify interacted terms, the order of the terms does not matter. Typing anova y a b a*b is the same as typing anova y b a b*a.

▷ Example

The classic two-way factorial ANOVA problem, at least as far as computer manuals are concerned, is a two-way analysis-of-variance design from Afifi and Azen (1979).

Fifty-eight patients, each suffering from one of three different diseases, were randomly assigned to one of four different drug treatments, and the change in their systolic blood pressure was recorded. Here are the data:

	Disease 1	Disease 2	Disease 3
Drug 1	42, 44, 36 13, 19, 22	33, 26, 33 21	31, –3, 25 25, 24
Drug 2	28, 23, 34 42, 13	34, 33, 31 36	3, 26, 28 32, 4, 16
Drug 3	1, 29, 19	11, 9, 7 1, –6	21, 1, 9 3
Drug 4	24, 9, 22 –2, 15	27, 12, 12 –5, 16, 15	22, 7, 25 5, 12

Let's assume that we have entered these data into Stata and stored the data as systolic.dta. Below we use the data, list the first 10 observations, summarize the variables, and tabulate the control variables:

```
. use systolic
(Systolic Blood Pressure Data)

. list in 1/10

        drug   disease   systolic
 1.       1        1         42
 2.       1        1         44
 3.       1        1         36
 4.       1        1         13
 5.       1        1         19
 6.       1        1         22
 7.       1        2         33
 8.       1        2         26
 9.       1        2         33
10.       1        2         21

. summarize

    Variable |      Obs        Mean    Std. Dev.       Min        Max
    ---------+-------------------------------------------------------
        drug |       58         2.5    1.158493         1          4
     disease |       58    2.017241    .8269873         1          3
    systolic |       58    18.87931    12.80087        -6         44
```

```
. tabulate drug disease
```

| | Patient's Disease | | | |
Drug Used	1	2	3	Total
1	6	4	5	15
2	5	4	6	15
3	3	5	4	12
4	5	6	5	16
Total	19	19	20	58

Each observation in our data corresponds to one patient, and for each patient we record `drug`, `disease`, and the increase in the systolic blood pressure, `systolic`. The tabulation reveals that the data are not balanced—there are not equal numbers of patients in each `drug`–`disease` cell. Stata does not require that the data be balanced. We can perform a two-way factorial analysis of variance by typing

```
. anova systolic drug disease drug*disease
```

| | | Number of obs = | | 58 | R-squared | = 0.4560 |
| | | Root MSE | = 10.5096 | | Adj R-squared = | 0.3259 |

Source	Partial SS	df	MS	F	Prob > F
Model	4259.33851	11	387.212591	3.51	0.0013
drug	2997.47186	3	999.157287	9.05	0.0001
disease	415.873046	2	207.936523	1.88	0.1637
drug*disease	707.266259	6	117.87771	1.07	0.3958
Residual	5080.81667	46	110.452536		
Total	9340.15517	57	163.862371		

You should also be familiar with Stata's `table` command; see [R] **table**. Although it will not perform analysis of variance, it can produce useful summary tables of your data:

```
. table drug disease, c(mean systolic) row col f(%8.2f)
```

| | Patient's Disease | | | |
Drug Used	1	2	3	Total
1	29.33	28.25	20.40	26.07
2	28.00	33.50	18.17	25.53
3	16.33	4.40	8.50	8.75
4	13.60	12.83	14.20	13.50
Total	22.79	18.21	15.80	18.88

◁

❏ Technical Note

A few words should be said about how to interpret the significance of terms like `drug` and `disease` in unbalanced data. If you are familiar with SAS, the sums of squares and the F statistic reported by Stata correspond to SAS type III sums of squares. (Stata can also calculate sequential sums of squares, but we will postpone that topic for now.)

Let's think in terms of the following tableau:

	Disease 1	Disease 2	Disease 3	
Drug 1	μ_{11}	μ_{12}	μ_{13}	$\mu_{1\cdot}$
Drug 2	μ_{21}	μ_{22}	μ_{23}	$\mu_{2\cdot}$
Drug 3	μ_{31}	μ_{32}	μ_{33}	$\mu_{3\cdot}$
Drug 4	μ_{41}	μ_{42}	μ_{43}	$\mu_{4\cdot}$
	$\mu_{\cdot 1}$	$\mu_{\cdot 2}$	$\mu_{\cdot 3}$	$\mu_{\cdot\cdot}$

In this diagram, μ_{ij} is the mean increase in systolic blood pressure associated with drug i and disease j, $\mu_{i\cdot}$ is the mean for drug i, $\mu_{\cdot j}$ is the mean for disease j, and $\mu_{\cdot\cdot}$ is the overall mean.

If the data are balanced, meaning that there are an equal number of observations going into the calculation of each mean μ_{ij}, then the row means $\mu_{i\cdot}$ are given by

$$\mu_{i\cdot} = \frac{\mu_{i1} + \mu_{i2} + \mu_{i3}}{3}$$

In our case the data are not balanced, but we define the $\mu_{i\cdot}$ according to that formula anyway. The test for the main effect of drug amounts to the test that

$$\mu_{1\cdot} = \mu_{2\cdot} = \mu_{3\cdot} = \mu_{4\cdot}$$

To be absolutely clear, the F test of the term **drug**, called the *main effect* of drug, is formally equivalent to the test of the three constraints:

$$\frac{\mu_{11} + \mu_{12} + \mu_{13}}{3} = \frac{\mu_{21} + \mu_{22} + \mu_{23}}{3}$$

$$\frac{\mu_{11} + \mu_{12} + \mu_{13}}{3} = \frac{\mu_{31} + \mu_{32} + \mu_{33}}{3}$$

$$\frac{\mu_{11} + \mu_{12} + \mu_{13}}{3} = \frac{\mu_{41} + \mu_{42} + \mu_{43}}{3}$$

In our data we obtain a significant F statistic of 9.05, and thus reject those constraints.

❑

❑ Technical Note

Stata can display the symbolic form underlying the test statistics it presents as well as display other test statistics and their symbolic forms; see *Obtaining symbolic forms* below. Without explanation, here is the result of requesting the symbolic form for the main effect of **drug** in our data:

```
. test drug, symbolic
_cons          0
drug
        1       r1
        2       r2
        3       r3
        4       -(r1+r2+r3)
disease
        1       0
        2       0
        3       0
```

```
drug*disease
    1   1        1/3 r1
    1   2        1/3 r1
    1   3        1/3 r1
    2   1        1/3 r2
    2   2        1/3 r2
    2   3        1/3 r2
    3   1        1/3 r3
    3   2        1/3 r3
    3   3        1/3 r3
    4   1       -1/3 (r1+r2+r3)
    4   2       -1/3 (r1+r2+r3)
    4   3       -1/3 (r1+r2+r3)
```

This says exactly what we said in the previous technical note.

❑

❑ Technical Note

As anyone familiar with ANOVA knows, the statement that there is no main effect of a variable is not the same as the statement that it has no effect at all, but it is still worth repeating. Stata's ability to perform ANOVA on unbalanced data can easily be put to ill use.

For example, consider the following table of the probability of surviving a bout with one of two diseases according to the drug administered to you:

	Disease 1	Disease 2
Drug 1	1	0
Drug 2	0	1

If you have disease 1 and are administered drug 1, you live. If you have disease 2 and are administered drug 2, you live. In all other cases, you die.

This table has no main effects of either drug or disease, although there is a large interaction effect. You might now be tempted to reason that since there is only an interaction effect, you would be indifferent between the two drugs in the absence of knowledge about which disease infects you. Given an equal chance of having either disease, you reason that it does not matter which drug is administered to you—either way, your chances of surviving are 0.5.

You may not, however, have an equal chance of having either disease. If you knew that disease 1 were 100 times more likely to occur in the population, and if you knew that you had one of the two diseases, you would express a strong preference for receiving drug 1.

When you calculate the significance of main effects on unbalanced data, you must ask yourself why the data are unbalanced. If the data are unbalanced for random reasons and you are making predictions for a balanced population, then the test of the main effect makes perfect sense. If, however, the data are unbalanced because the underlying populations are unbalanced, and you are making predictions for such unbalanced populations, the test of the main effect may be practically—if not statistically—meaningless.

❑

▷ Example

Stata not only has the ability to perform ANOVA on unbalanced populations, it can perform ANOVA on populations that are so unbalanced that entire cells are missing. For instance, using our systolic blood pressure data, let's re-estimate the model eliminating the drug 1 disease 1 cell. Since **anova** follows the same syntax as all other Stata commands, we can explicitly specify the data to be used by typing the **if** qualifier at the end of the **anova** command. In this case, we want to use the data that are not drug 1 and disease 1:

```
. anova systolic drug disease drug*disease if ~(drug==1 & disease==1)
```

| | Number of obs = | | 52 | R-squared | = | 0.4545 |
| | Root MSE | = | 10.1615 | Adj R-squared = | | 0.3215 |

Source	Partial SS	df	MS	F	Prob > F
Model	3527.95897	10	352.795897	3.42	0.0025
drug	2686.57832	3	895.526107	8.67	0.0001
disease	327.792598	2	163.896299	1.59	0.2168
drug*disease	703.007602	5	140.60152	1.36	0.2586
Residual	4233.48333	41	103.255691		
Total	7761.44231	51	152.185143		

◁

❑ Technical Note

The test of the main effect of drug in the presence of missing cells is more complicated than that for unbalanced data. Our underlying tableau is now of the form:

	Disease 1	Disease 2	Disease 3	
Drug 1		μ_{12}	μ_{13}	
Drug 2	μ_{21}	μ_{22}	μ_{23}	$\mu_{2\cdot}$
Drug 3	μ_{31}	μ_{32}	μ_{33}	$\mu_{3\cdot}$
Drug 4	μ_{41}	μ_{42}	μ_{43}	$\mu_{4\cdot}$
		$\mu_{\cdot 2}$	$\mu_{\cdot 3}$	

The hole in the drug 1 disease 1 cell indicates that the mean is unobserved. Considering the main effect of drug, the test is unchanged for the rows in which all the cells are defined:

$$\mu_{2\cdot} = \mu_{3\cdot} = \mu_{4\cdot}$$

The first row, however, requires special attention. In this case, we want the average outcome for drug 1, which is averaged over just diseases 2 and 3, to be equal to the average values of all other drugs averaged over those same two diseases:

$$\frac{\mu_{12} + \mu_{13}}{2} = \frac{(\mu_{22} + \mu_{23})/2 + (\mu_{32} + \mu_{33})/2 + (\mu_{42} + \mu_{43})/2}{3}$$

Thus, the test contains three constraints:

$$\frac{\mu_{21} + \mu_{22} + \mu_{23}}{3} = \frac{\mu_{31} + \mu_{32} + \mu_{33}}{3}$$

$$\frac{\mu_{21} + \mu_{22} + \mu_{23}}{3} = \frac{\mu_{41} + \mu_{42} + \mu_{43}}{3}$$

$$\frac{\mu_{12} + \mu_{13}}{2} = \frac{\mu_{22} + \mu_{23} + \mu_{32} + \mu_{33} + \mu_{42} + \mu_{43}}{6}$$

❑

Stata can calculate two types of sums of squares, *partial* and *sequential*. If you do not specify which sums of squares to calculate, Stata calculates partial sums of squares. The technical notes above have gone into great detail about the definition and use of partial sums of squares. Use the `sequential` option to obtain sequential sums of squares.

❏ Technical Note

Before illustrating sequential sums of squares, consider one more feature of the partial sums. If you know how such things are calculated, you may worry that the terms must be specified in some particular order, that Stata would balk or, even worse, produce different results if you typed, say, `anova drug*disease drug disease` rather than `anova drug disease drug*disease`. We assure you that is not the case.

When you type a model, Stata internally reorganizes the terms, forms the cross-product matrix, inverts it, converts the result to an upper-Hermite form, and then performs the hypothesis tests. As a final touch, Stata reports the results in the same order that you typed the terms.

❏

▷ Example

You wish to estimate the effects on systolic blood pressure of drug and disease using sequential sums of squares. You want to introduce disease first, then drug, and finally, the interaction of drug and disease:

```
. anova systolic disease drug disease*drug, sequential
```

	Number of obs =	58	R-squared	= 0.4560
	Root MSE	= 10.5096	Adj R-squared =	0.3259

Source	Seq. SS	df	MS	F	Prob > F
Model	4259.33851	11	387.212591	3.51	0.0013
disease	488.639383	2	244.319691	2.21	0.1210
drug	3063.43286	3	1021.14429	9.25	0.0001
disease*drug	707.266259	6	117.87771	1.07	0.3958
Residual	5080.81667	46	110.452536		
Total	9340.15517	57	163.862371		

The F statistic on disease is now 2.21. When we estimated this same model using partial sums of squares, the statistic was 1.88.

◁

N-way analysis of variance

You may include high-order interaction terms, such as a third-order interaction between the variables A, B, and C, by typing A*B*C.

▷ Example

You wish to determine the operating conditions that maximize yield for a manufacturing process. There are three temperature settings, two chemical supply companies, and two mixing methods under investigation. Three observations are obtained for each combination of these three factors.

```
. use manuf
(manufacturing process data)

. describe

Contains data from manuf.dta
  obs:            36                          manufacturing process data
  vars:            4                          5 Jul 2000 16:24
  size:          288 (93.5% of memory free)

              storage  display    value
variable name   type   format     label      variable label

temperature     byte   %9.0g      temp       machine temperature setting
chemical        byte   %9.0g      supplier   chemical supplier
method          byte   %9.0g      meth       mixing method
yield           byte   %9.0g                 product yield

Sorted by:
```

You wish to perform a three-way factorial analysis of variance.

```
. anova yield temp chem temp*chem meth temp*meth chem*meth temp*chem*meth
                       Number of obs =      36     R-squared     =  0.5474
                       Root MSE      = 2.62996     Adj R-squared =  0.3399

            Source │  Partial SS    df       MS           F     Prob > F

             Model │    200.75      11      18.25         2.64    0.0227

       temperature │     30.50       2      15.25         2.20    0.1321
          chemical │     12.25       1      12.25         1.77    0.1958
 temperature*chemical │   24.50       2      12.25         1.77    0.1917
            method │     42.25       1      42.25         6.11    0.0209
 temperature*method │    87.50       2      43.75         6.33    0.0062
   chemical*method │       .25       1        .25         0.04    0.8508
 temperature*chemical*
            method │      3.50       2       1.75         0.25    0.7785

          Residual │    166.00      24   6.91666667

             Total │    366.75      35   10.4785714
```

The interaction between temperature and method appears to be the important story in this data. A table of means for this interaction is given below.

```
. table method temp, c(mean yield) row col f(%8.2f)

mixing │  machine temperature setting
method │    low    medium    high    Total

  stir │   7.50     6.00      6.00    6.50
  fold │   5.50     9.00     11.50    8.67

 Total │   6.50     7.50      8.75    7.58
```

You decide to use the folding method of mixing and a high temperature in your manufacturing process.

◁

Analysis of covariance

You can include multiple explanatory variables with the anova command, but unless you explicitly state otherwise, all the variables are interpreted as *categorical variables*. Using the continuous(*varlist*) option, you can designate variables as *continuous* and thus perform analysis of covariance.

▷ Example

Let's now return to the systolic blood pressure example. Remember that the data contained three variables: systolic, the increase in systolic blood pressure; disease, which of four diseases the patient endured; and drug, which of three drugs were administered. We have another variant of this data that includes one more variable, the age of the patient, age. (This example, which was based on real data, now enters the fictional world. We concocted the age data based on nothing more than our own fanciful imagination.)

```
. use sysage
(Systolic Blood Pressure Data)

. summarize age
```

Variable	Obs	Mean	Std. Dev.	Min	Max
age	58	45.15517	13.9985	20	73

Let's now estimate systolic as a function of drug, disease, age, and disease interacted with age:

```
. anova systolic drug disease age disease*age, continuous(age)
```

Number of obs =   58   R-squared   = 0.6221
Root MSE   = 8.48737   Adj R-squared = 0.5604

Source	Partial SS	df	MS	F	Prob > F
Model	5810.41855	8	726.302318	10.08	0.0000
drug	2791.94475	3	930.648251	12.92	0.0000
disease	129.092158	2	64.5460789	0.90	0.4148
age	1817.80067	1	1817.80067	25.23	0.0000
disease*age	43.4069507	2	21.7034754	0.30	0.7412
Residual	3529.73663	49	72.0354414		
Total	9340.15517	57	163.862371		

◁

We typed anova systolic drug disease age disease*age, continuous(age) to obtain the above estimates. Rather than typing continuous(age), we could have typed category(drug disease).

In general, we can specify either the continuous variables or the categorical variables. If we do not specify either option, Stata assumes that all the variables are categorical. If we specify the continuous(*varlist*) option, Stata assumes the remaining variables are categorical. If we specify the category(*varlist*) option, Stata assumes that the remaining variables are continuous. We suggest typing whichever list is shorter.

You can type class(*varlist*) rather than category(*varlist*) if the word class is more appealing. They are synonyms.

Remember that you can specify interactions by typing *varname*∗*varname*. You have seen examples of interacting categorical variables with categorical variables and, directly above, a categorical variable (disease) with a continuous variable (age).

You can also interact continuous variables with continuous variables. To include an age^2 term in our model, we could type age*age. If we also wanted to interact the categorical variable disease with the age^2 term, we could type disease*age*age (or even age*disease*age).

Nested designs

In addition to specifying interaction terms, nested terms can also be specified in an analysis of variance. A vertical bar is used to indicate nesting: A|B is read as A nested within B. A|B|C is read as A nested within B which is nested within C. A|B*C is read as A is nested within the interaction of B and C. A*B|C is read as the interaction of A and B, which is nested within C.

Different error terms can be specified for different parts of the model. The forward slash is used to indicate that the next term in the model is the error term for what precedes it. For instance, anova y A / B|A indicates that the F test for A is to be tested using the mean square from B|A in the denominator. Error terms (terms following the slash) are generally not tested unless they are themselves followed by a slash. Residual error is the default error term.

For example, consider A / B / C, where A, B, and C may be arbitrarily complex terms. Then anova will report A tested by B and B tested by C. If we add one more slash on the end to form A / B / C /, then anova would also report C tested by the residual error.

▷ Example

You have collected data from a manufacturer that is evaluating which of five different brands of machinery to buy to perform a particular function in an assembly line. Twenty assembly line employees were selected at random for training on these machines with four employees assigned to learn a particular machine. The output from each employee (operator) on the brand of machine for which they were trained was measured during four trial periods. In this example, the operator is nested within machine. Due to sickness and employee resignations the final data are not balanced. The following table gives the mean output and sample size for each machine and operator combination.

```
. use machine
(machine data)

. table machine operator, c(mean output n output) col f(%8.2f)
```

five brands of machine	operator nested in machine				
	1	2	3	4	Total
1	9.15	9.48	8.27	8.20	8.75
	2	4	3	4	13
2	15.03	11.55	11.45	11.52	12.47
	3	2	2	4	11
3	11.27	10.13	11.13		10.84
	3	3	3		9
4	16.10	18.97	15.35	16.60	16.65
	3	3	4	3	13
5	15.30	14.35	10.43		13.63
	4	4	3		11

Assuming that `operator` is random (i.e., you wish to infer to the larger population of possible operators) and `machine` is fixed (i.e., only these five machines are of interest), the typical test for `machine` uses `operator` nested within `machine` as the error term. `operator` nested within `machine` can be tested by residual error. Our earlier warning concerning designs with unplanned missing cells and/or unbalanced cell sizes also applies to interpreting the ANOVA results from this unbalanced nested example.

```
. anova output machine / operator|machine /
                    Number of obs =      57     R-squared      =  0.8661
                    Root MSE      = 1.47089     Adj R-squared =  0.8077

          Source |  Partial SS    df      MS              F    Prob > F
    -------------+----------------------------------------------------
           Model |  545.822288    17   32.1071934        14.84   0.0000

         machine |  430.980792     4  107.745198         13.82   0.0001
 operator|machine|  101.353804    13    7.79644648
    -------------+----------------------------------------------------
 operator|machine|  101.353804    13    7.79644648         3.60   0.0009

        Residual |  84.3766582    39    2.16350406
    -------------+----------------------------------------------------
           Total |  630.198947    56   11.2535526
```

First notice that `operator|machine` is preceded by a slash, indicating that it is the error term for the term(s) before it (in this case `machine`). `operator|machine` is also followed by a slash that indicates it should be tested with residual error. Notice that the output lists the `operator|machine` term twice, once as the error term for machine, and again as a term tested by residual error. A line is placed in the ANOVA table to separate the two. In general, a dividing line is placed in the output to separate the terms into groups that are tested with the same error term. The overall model is tested by residual error and is separated from the remainder of the table by a blank line at the top of the table.

The results indicate that the machines are not all equal and that there are significant differences between operators.

◁

▷ Example

A medical researcher comes to you for help in analyzing some data he has collected. Two skin rash treatment protocols were tested at eight clinics (four clinics for each protocol). Three doctors were selected at random from each of the clinics to administer the particular protocol to four of their patients. Each patient was treated for four separate rash patches and the response was measured. The data are described below.

(Continued on next page)

```
. use rash
(skin rash data)

. describe

Contains data from rash.dta
  obs:          384                           skin rash data
  vars:           5                           21 Jun 2000 13:29
  size:       3,456 (93.0% of memory free)    (_dta has notes)

              storage  display   value
variable name   type   format    label       variable label

response        byte    %9.0g
treatment       byte    %9.0g                 2 treatment protocols
clinic          byte    %9.0g                 4 clinics per treatment
doctor          byte    %9.0g                 3 doctors per clinic
patient         byte    %9.0g                 4 patients per doctor

Sorted by:
```

The researcher wants to determine if the treatment protocols are significantly different. He would also like to know if the clinic, doctor, or patient are significant effects. In this analysis, treatment is a fixed factor whereas clinic, doctor, and patient are random factors. Your first thought when presented with this data is that there are more powerful experimental designs that could have been used. For instance, a better design would be to test both treatments on each patient. However, the data have already been collected, so you proceed with the analysis of this fully nested ANOVA design.

Notice that in the following **anova** command, we use abbreviations for the variable names. This can sometimes make long ANOVA model statements easier to type and read. Also, with larger ANOVA models, the **matsize** will need to be increased; see [R] **matsize**.

```
. set matsize 140

. anova response t / c|t / d|c|t / p|d|c|t /

                            Number of obs =       384    R-squared     =  0.5040
                            Root MSE      = 11.6192    Adj R-squared =  0.3404

            Source |    Partial SS     df        MS              F      Prob > F

             Model |    39505.9896     95    415.852522         3.08     0.0000

         treatment |    4240.04167      1    4240.04167         9.79     0.0204
    clinic|treatment |  2599.48958      6    433.248264

    clinic|treatment |  2599.48958      6    433.248264         0.93     0.4982
doctor|clinic|treatment |  7429.58333   16    464.348958

doctor|clinic|treatment |  7429.58333   16    464.348958        1.32     0.2065
    patient|doctor|clinic|
            treatment |  25236.875     72    350.512153

    patient|doctor|clinic|
            treatment |  25236.875     72    350.512153         2.60     0.0000

          Residual |    38882.00      288    135.006944

             Total |    78387.9896    383    204.66838
```

You conclude that the two treatment protocols are significantly different. You also see that clinic and doctor are not significant while patient is significant. The mean response for the two treatment protocols is shown below.

```
. table treatment , c(mean response) f(%8.2f) stubwidth(11)
```

2 treatment protocols	mean(response)
1	39.18
2	45.83

Treatment protocol two gives the largest response. We will return to this example when we explore the use of `test` after `anova`.

◁

Mixed designs

An analysis of variance can consist of both nested and crossed terms. A split-plot ANOVA design provides an example.

▷ Example

Two reading programs and three skill enhancement techniques are under investigation. Ten classes of first grade students were randomly assigned so that five classes were taught with one reading program and another five classes were taught with the other. The 30 students in each class were divided into six groups with five students each. Within each class, the six groups were divided randomly so that each of the three skill enhancement techniques was taught to two of the groups within each class. At the end of the school year a reading assessment test was administered to all the students. In this split-plot ANOVA, the whole-plot treatment is the two reading programs and the split-plot treatment is the three skill enhancement techniques.

```
. use reading
(Reading experiment data)

. describe

Contains data from reading.dta
  obs:            300                         Reading experiment data
  vars:             5                         5 Jul 2000 16:32
  size:         2,700 (86.2% of memory free)  (_dta has notes)
```

variable name	storage type	display format	value label	variable label
score	byte	%9.0g		reading score
program	byte	%9.0g		reading program
class	byte	%9.0g		class nested in program
skill	byte	%9.0g		skill enhancement technique
group	byte	%9.0g		group nested in class and skill

```
Sorted by:
```

In this split-plot ANOVA, the error term for `program` is `class` nested within `program`. The error term for `skill` and the `program` by `skill` interaction is the `class` by `skill` interaction nested within `program`. Other terms are also involved in the model and can be seen below.

Our `anova` command is longer than will fit on a single line of this manual. Where we have chosen to break the command into multiple lines is arbitrary. If you were typing this command into Stata, you would just type along and let Stata automatically wrap across lines as necessary.

```
. anova score prog / class|prog skill prog*skill / class*skill|prog /
         group|class*skill|prog /
```

| | Number of obs = | 300 | R-squared | = | 0.3738 |
| | Root MSE | = 14.6268 | Adj R-squared = | | 0.2199 |

Source	Partial SS	df	MS	F	Prob > F
Model	30656.5167	59	519.601977	2.43	0.0000
program	4493.07	1	4493.07	8.73	0.0183
class|program	4116.61333	8	514.576667		
skill	1122.64667	2	561.323333	1.54	0.2450
program*skill	5694.62	2	2847.31	7.80	0.0043
class*skill|program	5841.46667	16	365.091667		
class*skill|program	5841.46667	16	365.091667	1.17	0.3463
group|class*skill| program	9388.10	30	312.936667		
group|class*skill| program	9388.10	30	312.936667	1.46	0.0636
Residual	51346.40	240	213.943333		
Total	82002.9167	299	274.257246		

The `program*skill` term is significant as is the `program` term for this particular data. Let us look at a table of mean scores by `program` and `skill`.

```
. table prog skill, c(mean score) row col f(%8.2f)
```

reading program	skill enhancement technique 1 2 3 Total
1	68.16 52.86 61.54 60.85
2	50.70 56.54 52.10 53.11
Total	59.43 54.70 56.82 56.98

It appears that the first reading program and the first skill enhancement technique perform best when combined. It is also clear that there is an interaction between the reading program and the skill enhancement technique.

◁

❑ Technical Note

There are several valid ways to write complicated anova terms. In the reading experiment example, we had a term `group|class*skill|program`. This can be read as: group is nested within both class and skill and further nested within program. You can also write this term as `group|class*skill*program` or `group|program*class*skill` or `group|skill*class|program` etc. All variations will produce the same result. Some people prefer having only one '|' in a term and would use `group|class*skill*program` which is read as: group nested within class, skill, and program.

❑

Latin square designs

It is possible to use `anova` to analyze a Latin square design. Consider the following example published in Snedecor and Cochran (1989).

▷ Example

Data from a Latin square design is as follows:

Row	Column 1	Column 2	Column 3	Column 4	Column 5
1	257(B)	230(E)	279(A)	287(C)	202(D)
2	245(D)	283(A)	245(E)	280(B)	260(C)
3	182(E)	252(B)	280(C)	246(D)	250(A)
4	203(A)	204(C)	227(D)	193(E)	259(B)
5	231(C)	271(D)	266(B)	334(A)	338(E)

In Stata, it might appear as follows:

```
        row       c1       c2       c3       c4       c5
 1.       1      257      230      279      287      202
 2.       2      245      283      245      280      260
 3.       3      182      252      280      246      250
 4.       4      203      204      227      193      259
 5.       5      231      271      266      334      338
```

Before `anova` can be used on this data, it must be organized so that the outcome measurement is in one column. `reshape` is not sufficient for this task because there is information about the treatments in the sequence of these observations. `pkshape` is designed to reshape this type of data; see [R] **pkshape**.

```
. pkshape row row c1-c5, order(beacd daebc ebcda acdeb cdbae)
. list

         sequence    outcome    treat    carry    period
  1.          1         257       1        0        1
  2.          2         245       5        0        1
  3.          3         182       2        0        1
  4.          4         203       3        0        1
  5.          5         231       4        0        1
  6.          1         230       2        1        2
  7.          2         283       3        5        2
  8.          3         252       1        2        2
  9.          4         204       4        3        2
 10.          5         271       5        4        2
 11.          1         279       3        2        3
 12.          2         245       2        3        3
 13.          3         280       4        1        3
 14.          4         227       5        4        3
 15.          5         266       1        5        3
 16.          1         287       4        3        4
 17.          2         280       1        2        4
 18.          3         246       5        4        4
 19.          4         193       2        5        4
 20.          5         334       3        1        4
 21.          1         202       5        4        5
 22.          2         260       4        1        5
 23.          3         250       3        5        5
 24.          4         259       1        2        5
 25.          5         338       2        3        5
```

```
. anova outcome sequence period treat

                        Number of obs =        25    R-squared     =  0.6536
                        Root MSE      = 32.4901    Adj R-squared =  0.3073

           Source | Partial SS    df       MS               F     Prob > F

            Model |  23904.08     12   1992.00667          1.89     0.1426

         sequence |  13601.36      4      3400.34          3.22     0.0516
           period |   6146.16      4      1536.54          1.46     0.2758
            treat |   4156.56      4      1039.14          0.98     0.4523

         Residual |  12667.28     12   1055.60667

            Total |  36571.36     24   1523.80667
```

These methods will work with any type of Latin square design, including those with replicated measurements. For more information, see [R] **pk**, [R] **pkcross**, and [R] **pkshape**.

Repeated measures analysis of variance

One of the underlying assumptions for the F tests in ANOVA is independence of the observations. In a repeated measures design, this assumption is almost certainly violated or at least suspect. In a repeated measures ANOVA, the subjects (or whatever the experimental units are called) are observed for each level of one or more of the other categorical variables in the model. These variables are called the repeated measure variables. Observations from the same subject are likely to be correlated.

The approach used in repeated measures ANOVA to correct for this lack of independence is to apply a correction to the degrees of freedom of the F test for terms in the model that involve repeated measures. This correction factor, ϵ, lies between the reciprocal of the degrees of freedom for the repeated term and 1. Box (1954) provided the pioneering work in this area. Milliken and Johnson (1984) refer to the lower bound of this correction factor as Box's conservative correction factor. Winer, Brown, and Michels (1991) simply call it the conservative correction factor.

Geisser and Greenhouse (1958) provide an estimate for the correction factor that is called the Greenhouse–Geisser ϵ. This value is estimated from the data. Huynh and Feldt (1976) show that the Greenhouse–Geisser ϵ tends to be conservatively biased. They provide a revised correction factor called the Huynh–Feldt ϵ. The Huynh–Feldt ϵ can exceed 1. When this happens it is set to 1. Thus there is a natural ordering for these correction factors: Box's conservative $\epsilon \leq$ Greenhouse–Geisser $\epsilon \leq$ Huynh–Feldt $\epsilon \leq 1$. A correction factor of 1 is the same as no correction.

The **anova** command with the **repeated()** option computes these correction factors and displays the revised test results in a table that follows the standard ANOVA table. In the resulting table, H-F stands for Huynh–Feldt, G-G stands for Greenhouse–Geisser, and Box stands for Box's conservative ϵ.

▷ Example

This example is taken from Table 4.3 of Winer, Brown, and Michels (1991). The reaction time for five subjects each tested with four drugs was recorded in the variable **score**. Here is a table of the data (see [P] **tabdisp** if unfamiliar with **tabdisp**):

```
. use t43
(T4.3 -- Winer, Brown, Michels)

. tabdisp person drug, cellvar(score)
```

	drug			
person	1	2	3	4
1	30	28	16	34
2	14	18	10	22
3	24	20	18	30
4	38	34	20	44
5	26	28	14	30

drug is the repeated variable in this simple repeated measures ANOVA example. The ANOVA is specified as follows:

```
. anova score person drug, repeated(drug)
```

```
                          Number of obs =      20    R-squared     = 0.9244
                          Root MSE      = 3.06594    Adj R-squared = 0.8803
```

Source	Partial SS	df	MS	F	Prob > F
Model	1379.00	7	197.00	20.96	0.0000
person	680.80	4	170.20	18.11	0.0001
drug	698.20	3	232.733333	24.76	0.0000
Residual	112.80	12	9.40		
Total	1491.80	19	78.5157895		

```
Between-subjects error term:  person
                    Levels:  5           (4 df)
      Lowest b.s.e. variable:  person

Repeated variable: drug
                              Huynh-Feldt epsilon           = 1.0789
                              *Huynh-Feldt epsilon reset to 1.0000
                              Greenhouse-Geisser epsilon =    0.6049
                              Box's conservative epsilon =    0.3333
```

			——— Prob > F ———			
Source	df	F	Regular	H-F	G-G	Box
drug	3	24.76	0.0000	0.0000	0.0006	0.0076
Residual	12					

Notice that in this case, the Huynh–Feldt ϵ is 1.0789, which is larger than 1. It is reset to 1, which is the same as making no adjustment to the standard test computed in the main ANOVA table. The Greenhouse–Geisser ϵ is 0.6049 and its associated p-value is computed from an F ratio of 24.76 using 1.8147 ($= 3\epsilon$) and 7.2588 ($= 12\epsilon$) degrees of freedom. Box's conservative ϵ is set equal to the reciprocal of the degrees of freedom for the repeated term. In this case it is 1/3, so that Box's conservative test is computed using 1 and 4 degrees of freedom for the observed F ratio of 24.76.

Even using Box's conservative ϵ, drug is significant with a p-value of 0.0076. The following table gives the mean score (i.e., response time) for each of the four drugs:

```
. table drug, c(mean score) f(%8.2f)
```

drug	mean(score)
1	26.40
2	25.60
3	15.60
4	32.00

The ANOVA table for this example provides an F test for **person**. This F test should be ignored. An appropriate test for **person** would require replication (i.e., multiple measurements for **person** and **drug** combinations). Also without replication there is no test available for investigating the interaction between **person** and **drug**.

◁

▷ Example

The glucose metabolism rate in three brain regions is under investigation. Ten subjects were involved in the experiment and four measurements were taken in each brain region for each subject. Unlike our previous example, this example has replication within subjects. The following table gives the mean of the four glucose measurements for each subject and brain region.

```
. use glucose
(Brain Glucose Data)
. table region subject, c(mean glucose) f(%6.2f) row col center
```

Brain region	subject 1	2	3	4	5	6	7	8	9	10	Total
1	76.25	68.00	58.00	64.50	67.00	78.50	61.25	78.00	74.75	67.25	69.35
2	72.25	70.00	85.50	77.50	83.50	80.75	82.25	82.00	65.50	51.00	75.03
3	89.75	89.25	85.75	79.00	81.75	79.75	79.00	81.50	76.50	70.75	81.30
Total	79.42	75.75	76.42	73.67	77.42	79.67	74.17	80.50	72.25	63.00	75.22

In this experiment, **region** is a fixed factor (i.e., we are only interested in these three brain regions) and is the repeated variable since subjects are measured at each brain region. **subject** and **rep** (replication) are random factors (i.e., we are interested in drawing conclusions to a larger population). The appropriate test for **subject** uses **rep|subject** as the error term. **region** is tested with **region*subject**, while this interaction is tested by residual error.

(Continued on next page)

```
. anova glucose subject / rep|subject region / region*subject / , repeated(region)
```

	Number of obs =	120	R-squared	= 0.9290
	Root MSE = 3.64501		Adj R-squared =	0.8591

Source	Partial SS	df	MS	F	Prob > F
Model	10425.7583	59	176.707768	13.30	0.0000
subject	2801.675	9	311.297222	22.75	0.0000
rep|subject	410.583333	30	13.6861111		
region	2858.45	2	1429.225	5.91	0.0107
region*subject	4355.05	18	241.947222		
region*subject	4355.05	18	241.947222	18.21	0.0000
Residual	797.166667	60	13.2861111		
Total	11222.925	119	94.3102941		

```
Between-subjects error term: rep|subject
                     Levels: 40        (30 df)
      Lowest b.s.e. variable: rep
      Covariance pooled over: subject   (for repeated variable)
Repeated variable: region
```

	Huynh-Feldt epsilon	= 1.3869
	*Huynh-Feldt epsilon reset to	1.0000
	Greenhouse-Geisser epsilon =	0.9961
	Box's conservative epsilon =	0.5000

| | | | —— Prob > F —— | | |
Source	df	F	Regular	H-F	G-G	Box
region	2	5.91	0.0107	0.0107	0.0108	0.0380
region*subject	18					
region*subject	18	18.21	0.0000	0.0000	0.0000	0.0000
Residual	60					

The repeated measure ϵ corrections are applied to any terms that are tested in the main ANOVA table and have the repeated variable in the term. These ϵ corrections are given in a table below the main ANOVA table. In this case, the repeated measures tests for region and region*subject are presented.

From this ANOVA we determine that there are significant differences in glucose metabolism for the brain regions. Both the subject and the subject by brain region interaction are also significant and should not be ignored when making conclusions concerning glucose metabolism in these three brain regions.

◁

❏ Technical Note

The computation of the Greenhouse–Geisser and Huynh–Feldt epsilons in a repeated measures ANOVA requires the number of levels and degrees of freedom for the between-subjects error term. It also requires a value computed from a pooled covariance matrix. The observations are grouped based on all but the lowest level variable in the between-subjects error term. The covariance over the repeated variables is computed for each resulting group and then these covariance matrices are pooled. The dimension of the pooled covariance matrix is the number of levels of the repeated variable (or combination of levels for multiple repeated variables). In the glucose metabolism example, there are three levels of the repeated variable (region), so the resulting covariance matrix is 3×3.

The `anova` command attempts automatically to determine the between-subjects error term and the lowest level variable in the between-subjects error term in order to group the observations for computation of the pooled covariance matrix. `anova` will issue an error message indicating that the `bse()` or `bseunit()` option is required when it is unable to determine them. The user may also override the default selections of `anova` by specifying the `bse()`, `bseunit()`, or `grouping()` options. The term specified in the `bse()` option must be a term in the ANOVA model.

The default selection for the between-subjects error term (the `bse()` option) is the interaction of the nonrepeated categorical variables in the ANOVA model. The first variable listed in the between-subjects error term is automatically selected as the lowest level variable in the between-subjects error term but can be overridden with the `bseunit()` option. This is often a term such as subject or replication within subject and is most often listed first in the term due to the nesting notation of ANOVA. This makes sense in most repeated measures ANOVA designs when the terms of the model are written in standard form. For instance, in the glucose metabolism example there are three categorical variables (`subject`, `rep`, and `region`), with `region` the repeated variable. In this case, `anova` looked for a term involving only `subject` and `rep` to determine the between-subjects error term. It found `rep|subject` as the term with 40 levels and 30 degrees of freedom. `anova` then picked `rep` as the default for the `bseunit()` option (the lowest variable in the between-subjects error term) since it was listed first in the term.

The grouping of observations proceeds based on the different combinations of values of the variables in the between-subjects error term excluding the lowest level variable (as found by default or as specified with the `bseunit()` option). The user may specify the `grouping()` option to change the default grouping used in computing the pooled covariance matrix.

The between-subjects error term, number of levels, degrees of freedom, lowest variable in the term, and grouping information are presented after the main ANOVA table and before the rest of the repeated measures output.

❑

▷ Example

Table 7.7 of Winer, Brown, and Michels (1991) provides another repeated measures ANOVA example. There are four dial shapes and two methods for calibrating dials. Subjects are nested within calibration method and an accuracy score is obtained. The data are shown below.

```
. use t77
(T7.7 -- Winer, Brown, Michels)
. tabdisp shape subject calib, cell(score)
```

4 dial shapes	2 methods for calibrating dials and subject nested in calib					
	── 1 ──			── 2 ──		
	1	2	3	1	2	3
1	0	3	4	4	5	7
2	0	1	3	2	4	5
3	5	5	6	7	6	8
4	3	4	2	8	6	9

The calibration method and dial shapes are fixed factors whereas subjects are random. The appropriate test for calibration method uses the nested subject term as the error term. Both the dial shape and the interaction between dial shape and calibration method are tested with the dial shape by subject interaction nested within calibration method. In this case, we drop this term from the `anova` command and it becomes residual error. The dial shape is the repeated variable since each subject is tested with all four dial shapes. Here is the anova command that produces the desired results:

```
. anova score calib / subject|calib shape calib*shape , repeated(shape)
```

| | Number of obs = | 24 | R-squared | = 0.8925 |
| | Root MSE | = 1.11181 | Adj R-squared = | 0.7939 |

Source	Partial SS	df	MS	F	Prob > F
Model	123.125	11	11.1931818	9.06	0.0003
calib	51.0416667	1	51.0416667	11.89	0.0261
subject|calib	17.1666667	4	4.29166667		
shape	47.4583333	3	15.8194444	12.80	0.0005
calib*shape	7.45833333	3	2.48611111	2.01	0.1662
Residual	14.8333333	12	1.23611111		
Total	137.958333	23	5.99818841		

```
Between-subjects error term:  subject|calib
                     Levels:  6         (4 df)
        Lowest b.s.e. variable:  subject
        Covariance pooled over:  calib     (for repeated variable)
Repeated variable: shape
```

	Huynh-Feldt epsilon	= 0.8483
	Greenhouse-Geisser epsilon =	0.4751
	Box's conservative epsilon =	0.3333

Source	df	F	Regular	H-F	G-G	Box
shape	3	12.80	0.0005	0.0011	0.0099	0.0232
calib*shape	3	2.01	0.1662	0.1791	0.2152	0.2291
Residual	12					

Calibration method is significant as is dial shape. The interaction between calibration method and dial shape is not significant. The repeated measure ϵ corrections do not change these conclusions, but they do change the significance level for the tests on shape and calib*shape. Also notice that in this example, unlike the previous two examples, the Huynh–Feldt ϵ is less than 1.

The following table gives the mean score for dial shapes and calibration method. Since the interaction was not significant we focus our attention on the row and column labeled "Total".

```
. table shape calib , c(mean score) row col f(%8.2f)
```

4 dial shapes	2 methods for calibrating dials		
	1	2	Total
1	2.33	5.33	3.83
2	1.33	3.67	2.50
3	5.33	7.00	6.17
4	3.00	7.67	5.33
Total	3.00	5.92	4.46

▷ Example

Data with two repeated variables are given in Table 7.13 of Winer, Brown, and Michels (1991). The accuracy scores of subjects making adjustments to three dials during three different periods of time are recorded. Three subjects are exposed to a certain noise background level while a different set of three subjects is exposed to a different noise background level. Here is a table of accuracy scores for the noise, subject, period, and dial variables:

```
. use t713
(T7.13 -- Winer, Brown, Michels)
. tabdisp subject dial period, by(noise) cell(score) stubwidth(11)
```

noise background and subject nested in noise		10 minute time periods and dial								
		─── 1 ───			─── 2 ───			─── 3 ───		
		1	2	3	1	2	3	1	2	3
1										
	1	45	53	60	40	52	57	28	37	46
	2	35	41	50	30	37	47	25	32	41
	3	60	65	75	58	54	70	40	47	50
2										
	1	50	48	61	25	34	51	16	23	35
	2	42	45	55	30	37	43	22	27	37
	3	56	60	77	40	39	57	31	29	46

noise, period, and dial are fixed whereas subject is random. Both period and dial are repeated variables. The ANOVA for this example is specified below.

```
. anova score noise / subject|noise period noise*period / period*subject|noise dial
         noise*dial / dial*subject|noise period*dial noise*period*dial ,
         repeated(period dial)
```

```
                         Number of obs =      54    R-squared     = 0.9872
                         Root MSE      = 2.81859    Adj R-squared = 0.9576
```

Source	Partial SS	df	MS	F	Prob > F
Model	9797.72222	37	264.803303	33.33	0.0000
noise	468.166667	1	468.166667	0.75	0.4348
subject|noise	2491.11111	4	622.777778		
period	3722.33333	2	1861.16667	63.39	0.0000
noise*period	333.00	2	166.50	5.67	0.0293
period*subject|noise	234.888889	8	29.3611111		
dial	2370.33333	2	1185.16667	89.82	0.0000
noise*dial	50.3333333	2	25.1666667	1.91	0.2102
dial*subject|noise	105.555556	8	13.1944444		
period*dial	10.6666667	4	2.66666667	0.34	0.8499
noise*period*dial	11.3333333	4	2.83333333	0.36	0.8357
Residual	127.111111	16	7.94444444		
Total	9924.83333	53	187.261006		

```
   Between-subjects error term:  subject|noise
                        Levels:  6         (4 df)
        Lowest b.s.e. variable:  subject
        Covariance pooled over:  noise     (for repeated variables)
```

Repeated variable: period

```
                                     Huynh-Feldt epsilon      =  1.0668
                                     *Huynh-Feldt epsilon reset to 1.0000
                                     Greenhouse-Geisser epsilon =  0.6476
                                     Box's conservative epsilon =  0.5000
```

| | | | | ————— Prob > F ————— | | | |
Source		df	F	Regular	H-F	G-G	Box
period		2	63.39	0.0000	0.0000	0.0003	0.0013
noise*period		2	5.67	0.0293	0.0293	0.0569	0.0759
period*subject|noise		8					

Repeated variable: dial

```
                                     Huynh-Feldt epsilon      =  2.0788
                                     *Huynh-Feldt epsilon reset to 1.0000
                                     Greenhouse-Geisser epsilon =  0.9171
                                     Box's conservative epsilon =  0.5000
```

		df	F	Regular	H-F	G-G	Box
Source				————— Prob > F —————			
dial		2	89.82	0.0000	0.0000	0.0000	0.0007
noise*dial		2	1.91	0.2102	0.2102	0.2152	0.2394
dial*subject|noise		8					

Repeated variables: period*dial

```
                                     Huynh-Feldt epsilon      =  1.3258
                                     *Huynh-Feldt epsilon reset to 1.0000
                                     Greenhouse-Geisser epsilon =  0.5134
                                     Box's conservative epsilon =  0.2500
```

		df	F	Regular	H-F	G-G	Box
Source				————— Prob > F —————			
period*dial		4	0.34	0.8499	0.8499	0.7295	0.5934
noise*period*dial		4	0.36	0.8357	0.8357	0.7156	0.5825
Residual		16					

For each repeated variable and for each combination of interactions of repeated variables there are different ϵ correction values. The anova command produces tables for each applicable combination.

The two most significant factors in this model appear to be dial and period. The noise by period interaction also may be significant depending on which correction factor you use. Below are tables of the mean accuracy score for dial and period by noise.

```
. table dial , c(mean score) f(%8.2f)
```

dial	mean(score)
1	37.39
2	42.22
3	53.22

```
. table noise period, c(mean score) f(%8.2f) row col stubwidth(10)
```

noise background	10 minute time periods 1	2	3	Total
1	53.78	49.44	38.44	47.22
2	54.89	39.56	29.56	41.33
Total	54.33	44.50	34.00	44.28

We see that dial shape 3 produces the highest score and that the scores tend to decrease over the time periods.

◁

The previous example had two repeated measurement variables. Up to four repeated measurement variables may be specified in the **anova** command.

Weighted data

Like all estimation commands, **anova** can produce estimates on weighted data. See [U] **14.1.6 weight** for details on specifying the weight.

▷ Example

You wish to investigate the prevalence of byssinosis, a form of pneumoconiosis to which workers exposed to cotton dust are subject. You have data on 5,419 workers in a large cotton mill. You know whether each worker smokes, his or her race, and the dustiness of the work area. The variables are

> **smokes**   Smoker or nonsmoker in the last five years.
> **race**   White or other.
> **workplace** 1 (most dusty), 2 (less dusty), 3 (least dusty).

You wish to estimate an ANOVA model explaining the prevalence of byssinosis according to a full factorial model of **smokes**, **race**, and **workplace**.

The data are unbalanced. Moreover, although you have data on 5,419 workers, the data are grouped according to the explanatory variables along with some other variables, resulting in 72 observations. For each observation, you know the number of workers in the group (**pop**), the prevalence of byssinosis (**prob**), and the values of the three explanatory variables. Thus, you wish to estimate a three-way factorial model on grouped data.

We begin by showing you a bit of the data. The data are from Higgins and Koch (1977).

```
. use byssin
(Byssinosis incidence)

. describe

Contains data from byssin.dta
  obs:           72                          Byssinosis incidence
  vars:           5                          21 Jun 2000 13:25
  size:       1,152 (89.7% of memory free)
```

variable name	storage type	display format	value label	variable label
smokes	int	%8.0g	smokes	Smokes
race	int	%8.0g	race	Race
workplace	int	%8.0g	workplace	
				Dustiness of workplace
pop	int	%8.0g		Population size
prob	float	%9.0g		Prevalence of byssinosis

```
Sorted by:

. list in 1/5
      smokes     race  workpl~e      pop      prob
  1.     yes    white      most       40      .075
  2.     yes    white      less       74         0
  3.     yes    white     least      260  .0076923
  4.     yes    other      most      164   .152439
  5.     yes    other      less       88         0
```

The first observation in the data represents a group of 40 white workers who smoke and work in a "most" dusty work area. Of those 40 workers, 7.5% have byssinosis. The second observation represents a group of 74 white workers who also smoke, but who work in a "less" dusty environment. None of those workers has byssinosis.

Almost every Stata command allows weights. In this case, we want to weight the data by pop. We can, for instance, make a table of the number of workers by their smoking status and race:

```
. tabulate smokes race [freq=pop]
```

Smokes	Race other	white	Total
no	799	1431	2230
yes	1104	2085	3189
Total	1903	3516	5419

The [freq=pop] at the end of the tabulate command tells Stata to count each observation as representing pop persons. When making the tally, tabulate treats the first observation as representing 40 workers, the second as representing 74 workers, and so on.

Similarly, we can make a table of the dustiness of the workplace:

```
. tabulate workplace [freq=pop]
```

Dustiness of workplace	Freq.	Percent	Cum.
least	3450	63.66	63.66
less	1300	23.99	87.65
most	669	12.35	100.00
Total	5419	100.00	

We can discover the average incidence of byssinosis among these workers by typing

```
. summarize prob [freq=pop]
    Variable |       Obs        Mean    Std. Dev.        Min         Max

        prob |      5419    .0304484    .0567373          0     .287037
```

We discover that 3.04% of these workers have byssinosis. Across all cells, the byssinosis rates vary from 0 to 28.7%. Just to prove to you that there might be something here, let's obtain the average incidence rates according to the dustiness of the workplace:

```
. table workplace smokes race [freq=pop], c(mean prob)
```

Dustiness of workplace	Race and Smokes			
	— other —		— white —	
	no	yes	no	yes
least	.0107527	.0101523	.0081549	.0162774
less	.02	.0081633	.0136612	.0143149
most	.0820896	.1679105	.0833333	.2295082

Enough preliminary. Let's now estimate the ANOVA model.

```
. anova prob workplace smokes race workplace*smokes workplace*race smokes*race
         workplace*smokes*race  [aweight=pop]
(sum of wgt is   5.4190e+03)
```

		Number of obs =	65	R-squared	=	0.8300
		Root MSE	= .025902	Adj R-squared =		0.7948

Source	Partial SS	df	MS	F	Prob > F
Model	.173646538	11	.015786049	23.53	0.0000
workplace	.097625175	2	.048812588	72.76	0.0000
smokes	.013030812	1	.013030812	19.42	0.0001
race	.001094723	1	.001094723	1.63	0.2070
workplace*smokes	.019690342	2	.009845171	14.67	0.0000
workplace*race	.001352516	2	.000676258	1.01	0.3718
smokes*race	.001662874	1	.001662874	2.48	0.1214
workplace*smokes*race	.000950841	2	.00047542	0.71	0.4969
Residual	.035557766	53	.000670901		
Total	.209204304	64	.003268817		

Of course, if we want to see the underlying regression, we could type **anova, regress** or simply **regress**.

◁

Obtaining the covariance matrix

After estimating with **anova**, you can obtain the covariance matrix of the estimators in the same way as after **regress**. You can refer to **e(V)** as in **matrix list e(V)**. (Alternatively, you can use the vce command; see [R] **vce**.)

Testing effects

After estimating an ANOVA model using the **anova** command, you can test for the significance of effects in the ANOVA table as well as effects that are not reported in the ANOVA table by using the **test** command. You follow **test** by the list of effects you wish to test. By default, **test** uses the residual mean square error in the denominator of the F ratio. You can specify other error terms using the slash notation just as you would with **anova**.

▷ Example

Returning to our byssinosis data, we can easily obtain a test on a particular term from the ANOVA table. Here are two examples:

```
. test smokes
```

Source	Partial SS	df	MS	F	Prob > F
smokes	.013030812	1	.013030812	19.42	0.0001
Residual	.035557766	53	.000670901		

```
. test smokes*race
```

Source	Partial SS	df	MS	F	Prob > F
smokes*race	.001662874	1	.001662874	2.48	0.1214
Residual	.035557766	53	.000670901		

Both of these tests use residual error by default and agree with the ANOVA table produced earlier.

◁

❑ Technical Note

After **anova** you can use the '/' syntax in **test** to perform tests with a variety of non-$\sigma^2 \mathbf{I}$ error structures. However, be warned that in most unbalanced models the mean squares are not independent and do not have equal expectations under the null hypothesis. Also be warned that you assume responsibility for the validity of the test statistic.

❑

▷ Example

We return to the nested ANOVA example where five brands of machinery were compared in an assembly line. We can obtain appropriate tests for the nested terms using **test** even if we had run the **anova** command without initially indicating the proper error terms.

```
. use machine
(machine data)
. anova output machine operator|machine
```

	Number of obs =	57	R-squared	=	0.8661
	Root MSE	= 1.47089	Adj R-squared =		0.8077

Source	Partial SS	df	MS	F	Prob > F
Model	545.822288	17	32.1071934	14.84	0.0000
machine	430.980792	4	107.745198	49.80	0.0000
operator|machine	101.353804	13	7.79644648	3.60	0.0009
Residual	84.3766582	39	2.16350406		
Total	630.198947	56	11.2535526		

In this ANOVA table, `machine` is tested with residual error. With this particular nested design, the appropriate error term for testing `machine` is `operator` nested within `machine`. This is easily obtained from `test`.

```
. test machine / operator|machine
```

Source	Partial SS	df	MS	F	Prob > F
machine	430.980792	4	107.745198	13.82	0.0001
operator|machine	101.353804	13	7.79644648		

This result from `test` matches what we obtained from our original `anova` command as presented in our discussion of nested designs.

◁

▷ Example

The other nested ANOVA example was based on the skin rash data. The ANOVA table is presented here again. As before we will use abbreviations of variable names in typing in the commands.

```
. use rash
(skin rash data)
. anova response t / c|t / d|c|t / p|d|c|t /
```

	Number of obs =	384	R-squared	=	0.5040
	Root MSE	= 11.6192	Adj R-squared =		0.3404

Source	Partial SS	df	MS	F	Prob > F
Model	39505.9896	95	415.852522	3.08	0.0000
treatment	4240.04167	1	4240.04167	9.79	0.0204
clinic|treatment	2599.48958	6	433.248264		
clinic|treatment	2599.48958	6	433.248264	0.93	0.4982
doctor|clinic|treatment	7429.58333	16	464.348958		
doctor|clinic|treatment	7429.58333	16	464.348958	1.32	0.2065
patient|doctor|clinic| treatment	25236.875	72	350.512153		
patient|doctor|clinic| treatment	25236.875	72	350.512153	2.60	0.0000
Residual	38882.00	288	135.006944		
Total	78387.9896	383	204.66838		

In practice it is often beneficial to pool nonsignificant nested terms to increase the power of tests on remaining terms. One rule of thumb is to allow the pooling of a term whose p-value is larger than 0.25. In this skin rash example, the p-value for the test of `clinic` is 0.4982. This indicates that the clinic effect is negligible and might be ignored. Currently `treatment` is tested by `clinic|treatment` which has only 6 degrees of freedom. If we pool the `clinic` and `doctor` terms and use this pooled estimate as the error term for `treatment` we would have a term with 22 degrees of freedom.

Below are two tests. The first is a test of `treatment` with the pooled `clinic` and `doctor` terms. The second is a test of this pooled term by `patient`.

```
. test t / c|t d|c|t
```

Source	Partial SS	df	MS	F	Prob > F
treatment	4240.04167	1	4240.04167	9.30	0.0059
clinic|treatment doctor| clinic|treatment	10029.0729	22	455.866951		

```
. test c|t d|c|t / p|d|c|t
```

Source	Partial SS	df	MS	F	Prob > F
clinic|treatment doctor| clinic|treatment	10029.0729	22	455.866951	1.30	0.2014
patient|doctor|clinic| treatment	25236.875	72	350.512153		

Notice that in the first example, we include two terms after the forward slash (c|t and d|c|t). test after anova allows multiple terms both before and after the slash. The terms before the slash are combined and are then tested by the combined terms that follow the slash (or residual error if no slash is present).

The p-value for treatment using the pooled term is 0.0059. Originally it was 0.0204. The increase in the power of the test is due to the increase in degrees of freedom for the pooled error term.

We can get identical results if we drop clinic from the anova model. (Realize that this dataset has unique numbers for each doctor so that there is no confusion of doctors when clinic is dropped.)

```
. anova response t / d|t / p|d|t /
```

```
Number of obs =      384     R-squared     =  0.5040
Root MSE      = 11.6192     Adj R-squared =  0.3404
```

Source	Partial SS	df	MS	F	Prob > F
Model	39505.9896	95	415.852522	3.08	0.0000
treatment	4240.04167	1	4240.04167	9.30	0.0059
doctor|treatment	10029.0729	22	455.866951		
doctor|treatment	10029.0729	22	455.866951	1.30	0.2014
patient|doctor| treatment	25236.875	72	350.512153		
patient|doctor| treatment	25236.875	72	350.512153	2.60	0.0000
Residual	38882.00	288	135.006944		
Total	78387.9896	383	204.66838		

This agrees with our earlier test results.

◁

Another example of test after anova is given as the last example in the section *anova as an alternative to regress*. In that example two terms from the anova are jointly tested (pooled).

Obtaining symbolic forms

test can also produce the symbolic form of the estimable functions and symbolic forms for particular tests.

▷ Example

After estimating an ANOVA model, you type test, symbolic to obtain the symbolic form of the estimable functions. For instance, returning to our blood pressure data, let's begin by re-estimating systolic on drug, disease, and drug*disease:

```
. anova systolic drug disease drug*disease
```

		Number of obs =		58	R-squared	= 0.4560
		Root MSE	= 10.5096		Adj R-squared =	0.3259

Source	Partial SS	df	MS	F	Prob > F
Model	4259.33851	11	387.212591	3.51	0.0013
drug	2997.47186	3	999.157287	9.05	0.0001
disease	415.873046	2	207.936523	1.88	0.1637
drug*disease	707.266259	6	117.87771	1.07	0.3958
Residual	5080.81667	46	110.452536		
Total	9340.15517	57	163.862371		

To obtain the symbolic form of the estimable functions, type

```
. test, symbolic
_cons         r0
drug
        1     r1
        2     r2
        3     r3
        4     r0 - (r1+r2+r3)
disease
        1     r5
        2     r6
        3     r0 - (r5+r6)
drug*disease
    1   1     r8
    1   2     r9
    1   3     r1 - (r8+r9)
    2   1     r11
    2   2     r12
    2   3     r2 - (r11+r12)
    3   1     r14
    3   2     r15
    3   3     r3 - (r14+r15)
    4   1     r5 - (r8+r11+r14)
    4   2     r6 - (r9+r12+r15)
    4   3     r0 - (r1+r2+r3+r5+r6-r8-r9-r11-r12-r14-r15)
```

◁

▷ Example

To obtain the symbolic form for a particular test, you type test *term* [*term* ...], symbolic. For instance, the symbolic form for the test of the main effect of drug is

```
. test drug, symbolic
_cons         0
drug
        1     r1
        2     r2
        3     r3
        4     -(r1+r2+r3)
disease
        1     0
        2     0
        3     0
drug*disease
    1   1     1/3 r1
    1   2     1/3 r1
    1   3     1/3 r1
    2   1     1/3 r2
    2   2     1/3 r2
    2   3     1/3 r2
    3   1     1/3 r3
    3   2     1/3 r3
    3   3     1/3 r3
    4   1     -1/3 (r1+r2+r3)
    4   2     -1/3 (r1+r2+r3)
    4   3     -1/3 (r1+r2+r3)
```

If we omit the symbolic option, we instead see the result of the test:

```
. test drug
```

Source	Partial SS	df	MS	F	Prob > F
drug	2997.47186	3	999.157287	9.05	0.0001
Residual	5080.81667	46	110.452536		

◁

Testing coefficients

The test command will allow you to perform tests directly on the coefficients of the underlying regression model. This case is very much like using test after regress; you specify the test as 'test *exp* = *exp*'. See [R] **test** and remember two additional facts:

1. Syntax 2 of test (test *coefficientlist* as defined in [R] **test**) is not available to you after estimating an ANOVA model. Stata assumes the *coefficientlist* is really a list of terms and so interprets what you type as a list of effects (syntax 3). You would be testing effects rather than coefficients. (We understand that in certain instances these are the same thing. If you understand that, too, then feel free. Remember, however, they are not always the same thing.)

2. When you specify the expressions, you must enclose references to coefficients in _coef[]; see [U] **16.5 Accessing coefficients and standard errors**. For instance, the coefficient on the first level of drug and the second level of disease is referred to as _coef[drug[1]*disease[2]]. If you were to omit the _coef[], Stata would think you are trying to multiply two things together rather than referring to the coefficient on the interaction of two terms.

▷ Example

Let's begin by testing whether the coefficient on the first drug is equal to the coefficient on the second in our blood pressure data. We have already estimated the model anova systolic drug disease drug*disease and you can see the results of that estimation in the opening example of *Obtaining symbolic forms*. Even though we have done quite a bit since we estimated the model, Stata still remembers and we can perform tests at any time.

```
. test _coef[drug[1]]=_coef[drug[2]]
 ( 1)   drug[1] - drug[2] = 0.0
        F(  1,     46) =     0.12
              Prob > F =     0.7272
```

We find that the two coefficients are not significantly different, at least at any significance level smaller than 73%. Let's now add the constraint that the coefficient on the first drug interacted with the first disease is equal to the coefficient on the second drug again interacted with the first disease. We do that by typing the new constraint and adding the accumulate option (see [R] **test**):

```
. test _coef[drug[1]*disease[1]]=_coef[drug[2]*disease[1]], accumulate
 ( 1)   drug[1] - drug[2] = 0.0
 ( 2)   drug[1]*disease[1] - drug[2]*disease[1] = 0.0
        F(  2,     46) =     0.08
              Prob > F =     0.9200
```

Let's continue. Our goal is to determine whether the first drug is significantly different from the second drug. So far our test includes the equality of the two drug coefficients along with the equality of the two drug coefficients when interacted with the first disease. We must add two more equations, one for each of the remaining two diseases.

```
. test _coef[drug[1]*disease[2]]=_coef[drug[2]*disease[2]], accumulate
 ( 1)   drug[1] - drug[2] = 0.0
 ( 2)   drug[1]*disease[1] - drug[2]*disease[1] = 0.0
 ( 3)   drug[1]*disease[2] - drug[2]*disease[2] = 0.0
        F(  3,     46) =     0.22
              Prob > F =     0.8806
. test _coef[drug[1]*disease[3]]=_coef[drug[2]*disease[3]], accumulate
 ( 1)   drug[1] - drug[2] = 0.0
 ( 2)   drug[1]*disease[1] - drug[2]*disease[1] = 0.0
 ( 3)   drug[1]*disease[2] - drug[2]*disease[2] = 0.0
 ( 4)   drug[1]*disease[3] - drug[2]*disease[3] = 0.0
        Constraint 4 dropped
        F(  3,     46) =     0.22
              Prob > F =     0.8806
```

The overall F statistic is 0.22, which is hardly significant. We cannot reject the hypothesis that the first drug has the same effect as the second drug.

You may notice that we also got the message "Constraint 4 dropped". For the technically inclined, the last constraint was unnecessary given the normalization of the model. You need not worry about such problems because Stata handles them automatically.

◁

❏ Technical Note

You can use `test` to perform other, more complicated tests. In such cases, you will probably want to review the symbolic forms of particular tests and you will certainly want to review the symbolic form of the estimable functions. We explained how to do that above.

Let's check that Stata gives the right answers by laboriously typing the gory details of the test for the main effect of drug. Stata already told us the symbolic form in the previous subsection. The obsessed among you have no doubt already worked through the algebra and established that Stata was correct. Our chances of typing all the constraints correctly, however, are so small that we typed them into a do-file:

```
. do mainef
. #delimit ;
delimiter now ;
. test _coef[drug[1]] +
        (_coef[drug[1]*disease[1]] + _coef[drug[1]*disease[2]] +
        _coef[drug[1]*disease[3]] - _coef[drug[4]*disease[1]] -
        _coef[drug[4]*disease[2]] - _coef[drug[4]*disease[3]])/3 = 0 ,
        notest ;
. test _coef[drug[2]] +
        (_coef[drug[2]*disease[1]] + _coef[drug[2]*disease[2]] +
        _coef[drug[2]*disease[3]] - _coef[drug[4]*disease[1]] -
        _coef[drug[4]*disease[2]] - _coef[drug[4]*disease[3]])/3 = 0 ,
        accumulate notest ;
. test _coef[drug[3]]+
        (_coef[drug[3]*disease[1]] + _coef[drug[3]*disease[2]] +
        _coef[drug[3]*disease[3]] - _coef[drug[4]*disease[1]] -
        _coef[drug[4]*disease[2]] - _coef[drug[4]*disease[3]])/3 = 0 ,
        accumulate ;
 (1)   drug[1] + .3333333 drug[1]*disease[1] + .3333333 drug[1]*disease[2] +
       .3333333 drug[1]*disease[3] - .3333333 drug[4]*disease[1] -
       .3333333 drug[4]*disease[2] - .3333333 drug[4]*disease[3] = 0.0
 (2)   drug[2] + .3333333 drug[2]*disease[1] + .3333333 drug[2]*disease[2] +
       .3333333 drug[2]*disease[3] - .3333333 drug[4]*disease[1] -
       .3333333 drug[4]*disease[2] - .3333333 drug[4]*disease[3] = 0.0
 (3)   drug[3] + .3333333 drug[3]*disease[1] + .3333333 drug[3]*disease[2] +
       .3333333 drug[3]*disease[3] - .3333333 drug[4]*disease[1] -
       .3333333 drug[4]*disease[2] - .3333333 drug[4]*disease[3] = 0.0
       F(  3,    46) =    9.05
             Prob > F =    0.0001
end of do-file
```

We have our result. The F statistic has 3 degrees of freedom and is 9.05. This is the same result we obtained when we typed `test drug`. Typing `test drug` was easier, however.

❏

How Stata numbers levels

We have covered all aspects of the `anova` command except one mechanical detail: the definition of a categorical variable. Throughout the above text, we have made statements like "Stata assumes all the variables are categorical unless you explicitly state otherwise". Although the statement makes perfect sense, anyone familiar with statistical programs knows that it left something unsaid. Most programs place additional requirements on the definition of categorical variables, namely, that they be sequential integers.

Stata does not care whether your variables are integers, whether they are positive, or whether the numbering scheme is sequential or jumps around helter-skelter. Stata will figure it out.

▷ Example

Let's prove our claim. Below we have a small dataset containing three variables: outcome, scheme1, and scheme2.

```
. list
        outcome    scheme1    scheme2
   1.        28          2       -1.1
   2.        23          2       -1.1
   3.        34          2       -1.1
   4.        42          2       -1.1
   5.        13          2       -1.1
   6.        29          3          2
   7.        19          3          2
   8.         9          5        2.1
   9.        -2          5        2.1
  10.        15          5        2.1
```

Let's think of an ANOVA model of outcome on scheme1 and outcome on scheme2. If you look closely, you will see that scheme1 and scheme2 are two different ways of labeling the same thing. In scheme1, the levels are labeled 2, 3, and 5; in scheme2, those same levels are labeled -1.1, 2, and 2.1.

anova produces the same output no matter which labeling scheme we use:

```
. anova outcome scheme1
                        Number of obs =       10    R-squared     =  0.5474
                        Root MSE      =  9.86094    Adj R-squared =  0.4181

          Source |   Partial SS     df        MS             F      Prob > F

           Model |   823.333333      2   411.666667          4.23     0.0624

         scheme1 |   823.333333      2   411.666667          4.23     0.0624

        Residual |   680.666667      7  97.2380952

           Total |      1504.00      9  167.111111
```

```
. anova outcome scheme2
                        Number of obs =       10    R-squared     =  0.5474
                        Root MSE      =  9.86094    Adj R-squared =  0.4181

          Source |   Partial SS     df        MS             F      Prob > F

           Model |   823.333333      2   411.666667          4.23     0.0624

         scheme2 |   823.333333      2   411.666667          4.23     0.0624

        Residual |   680.666667      7  97.2380952

           Total |      1504.00      9  167.111111
```

◁

❑ Technical Note

Although statistical results are unaffected by the numbering scheme you use, there is a minor difference in how Stata presents regression results (as well as the results of test with the symbolic option). Below we use anova with the regress option to re-estimate our model based on scheme1. The regress option tells Stata to present the regression table rather than the ANOVA output.

```
. anova outcome scheme1, regress
      Source |     SS      df      MS                Number of obs =      10
-------------+------------------------------         F(  2,     7) =    4.23
       Model | 823.333333    2  411.666667           Prob > F      =  0.0624
    Residual | 680.666667    7  97.2380952           R-squared     =  0.5474
-------------+------------------------------         Adj R-squared =  0.4181
       Total |    1504.00    9  167.111111           Root MSE      =  9.8609

     outcome |     Coef.   Std. Err.     t    P>|t|    [95% Conf. Interval]
-------------+----------------------------------------------------------------
       _cons |  7.333333   5.693215    1.29   0.239   -6.128981    20.79565
     scheme1 |
          2  |  20.66667   7.201411    2.87   0.024    3.638036      37.6953
          3  |  16.66667   9.001763    1.85   0.107   -4.619122    37.95245
          5  | (dropped)
```

Notice that in labeling the regression coefficients, Stata used our numbering scheme. The first level of scheme1 is labeled 2, the second level 3, and the third level 5, just as we numbered them.

Let's now repeat the experiment using the scheme2 numbering scheme:

```
. anova outcome scheme2, regress
      Source |     SS      df      MS                Number of obs =      10
-------------+------------------------------         F(  2,     7) =    4.23
       Model | 823.333333    2  411.666667           Prob > F      =  0.0624
    Residual | 680.666667    7  97.2380952           R-squared     =  0.5474
-------------+------------------------------         Adj R-squared =  0.4181
       Total |    1504.00    9  167.111111           Root MSE      =  9.8609

     outcome |     Coef.   Std. Err.     t    P>|t|    [95% Conf. Interval]
-------------+----------------------------------------------------------------
       _cons |  7.333333   5.693215    1.29   0.239   -6.128981    20.79565
     scheme2 |
          1  |  20.66667   7.201411    2.87   0.024    3.638036      37.6953
          2  |  16.66667   9.001763    1.85   0.107   -4.619122    37.95245
          3  | (dropped)
```

Remember that scheme2 labeled the first level -1.1, the second level 2, and the third level 2.1. This time, however, our regression results are labeled 1, 2, and 3.

Stata uses our numbering scheme to label results whenever all our numbers are positive integers less than 99. The first numbering scheme meets that criterion; the second numbering scheme does not. In the second case, Stata created a mapping of our values onto the set of sequential integers. Thus, level -1.1 is labeled 1, level 2 is labeled 2, and level 2.1 is labeled 3.

Stata will show us the mapping if we specify the detail option. We request that Stata show us only the mapping and not present the ANOVA table:

```
. anova, detail noanova
   Factor     Value        Value        Value        Value
 ----------------------------------------------------------------
   scheme2    1 -1.1        2 2          3 2.1
```

Stata makes a small table. In each entry, the number to the left is how Stata labels the level in its regression output. The number to the right is the true value of the underlying variable.

❏

❏ Technical Note

Since the labeling affects only the output of regression and test with the symbolic option, it may not seem important. There is, however, a case when you need to know how Stata labels the levels. If you use the test command to construct your own tests that explicitly refer to individual coefficients of the underlying regression model, you need to refer to those levels as Stata refers to them. Before you panic, realize that you are unlikely to be performing tests of that type. Most tests can be performed without explicitly referring to the coefficients and so the labeling is irrelevant.

Nevertheless, the coefficient on the "third" level of scheme2, which you crazily labeled 2.1, is referred to as _coef[scheme2[3]]; see [U] **16.5 Accessing coefficients and standard errors**. On the other hand, the "third" level of scheme1, which you more reasonably labeled 5, is referred to as _coef[scheme1[5]]. You can find out how Stata labeled the levels from the regression output or from the detail output.

If this seems confusing and you are planning on performing tests directly on the coefficients of the underlying regression, label your levels sequentially with integers starting at 1 as most other programs require. Or, if you decide to opt for the freedom of having arbitrary labeling schemes, adopt a labeling scheme that uses only positive integers less than 99. This way, your labeling scheme will be Stata's labeling scheme. If you use a truly arbitrary labeling scheme that contains floating-point numbers, however, Stata will create a mapping and you will have to know that mapping to refer to the coefficients.

❏

Even with nested designs the scheme you use in numbering the nested levels does not matter except as noted in the above technical note. If you have B|A (meaning B nested within A) you may choose to number the levels of B within each level of A

$$
\begin{array}{ccccccc}
\text{A} & 1 & 1 & 1 & 2 & 2 & 2 \\
\text{B} & 1 & 2 & 3 & 1 & 2 & 3
\end{array}
$$

or you may number the levels of B disregarding A:

$$
\begin{array}{ccccccc}
\text{A} & 1 & 1 & 1 & 2 & 2 & 2 \\
\text{B} & 1 & 2 & 3 & 4 & 5 & 6
\end{array}
$$

The numbering of the levels does not have to be sequential or composed of integer values.

▷ Example

The machine example used to describe the anova nesting notation provides an illustration. In this example, each operator was numbered sequentially starting with 1 within each machine. We create op2 that numbers the operators in a strange way and show the result of running anova substituting op2 for operator.

```
. use machine
(machine data)

. gen op2 = 100.4*machine + 10.3*operator
```

```
. anova output machine / op2|machine / , detail
```

Factor	Value	Value	Value	Value
machine	1 1	2 2	3 3	4 4
	5 5			
op2	1 110.7	2 121	3 131.3	4 141.6
	5 211.1	6 221.4	7 231.7	8 242
	9 311.5	10 321.8	11 332.1	12 411.9
	13 422.2	14 432.5	15 442.8	16 512.3
	17 522.6	18 532.9		

```
                          Number of obs =      57    R-squared     =  0.8661
                          Root MSE      = 1.47089    Adj R-squared =  0.8077
```

Source	Partial SS	df	MS	F	Prob > F
Model	545.822288	17	32.1071934	14.84	0.0000
machine	430.980792	4	107.745198	13.82	0.0001
op2|machine	101.353804	13	7.79644648		
op2|machine	101.353804	13	7.79644648	3.60	0.0009
Residual	84.3766582	39	2.16350406		
Total	630.198947	56	11.2535526		

which agrees with our previous result.

◁

anova as an alternative to regress

Even if you have no interest in formal ANOVA, you may still find the **anova** command useful. It has the ability to construct dummy variables on the fly, and when you are estimating regressions containing many dummy variables, **anova** is quicker than **regress** in producing the estimates.

Read the first part of this entry (the part you probably skipped) just to become familiar with the **anova** syntax. Then remember the following rules-of-thumb:

1. Specify the **regress** option on the end of the **anova** command. This way, you will see only the regression table and not be bothered with the ANOVA table.

2. Specify the **continuous**(*varlist*) option so that Stata will know which variables in your model are continuous or, if it is more convenient, specify the **category**(*varlist*) option so that Stata will know which variables are categorical.

3. Use the ANOVA table to obtain the overall significance of categorical variables (dummy sets) in certain circumstances, namely, when the categorical variable is not interacted with any other categorical variable in the model. For instance, if you type

```
anova drate region age, continuous(age)
```

the F statistic reported in the ANOVA table for **region** is the overall significance of the dummy set for region. The same is true if you type

```
anova drate region age region*age, continuous(age)
```

The same is *not* true if you type

```
anova drate region age region*sex, continuous(age)
```

In this case, the F statistic on `region` is the effect of `region` after orthogonalization with the `region*sex` dummies. If you do not understand this rule, shy away from the ANOVA table.

▷ Example

You have Census data recording the death rate (`drate`) and median age (`age`) for each state. The dataset also includes the region of the country in which each state is located (`region`):

```
. summarize drate age region
    Variable |      Obs        Mean    Std. Dev.        Min        Max

       drate |       50        84.3     13.07318         40        107
         age |       50        29.5     1.752549         24         35
      region |       50        2.66     1.061574          1          4
```

`age` is coded in integral years from 24 to 35 and `region` is coded from 1 to 4, with 1 standing for the Northeast, 2 for the North Central, 3 for the South, and 4 for the West.

When you examine the data more closely, you discover large differences in the death rate across regions of the country:

```
. tabulate region, summarize(drate)
     Census |       Summary of Death Rate
     region |     Mean     Std. Dev.       Freq.

         NE |  93.4444        7.0553           9
    N Cntrl |  88.9167        5.5834          12
      South |  88.3125        8.5457          16
       West |  68.7692       13.3426          13

      Total |  84.3000       13.0732          50
```

Naturally, you wonder if these differences might not be explained by differences in the median ages of the populations. To find out, you estimate a regression model of `drate` on `region` and `age`. In this case, you decide to start by looking at the ANOVA table because there are no interacted variables. The table will report exactly what you expect it to report—the significance of dummy sets.

```
. anova drate region age
                             Number of obs =      50    R-squared     = 0.7927
                             Root MSE      = 6.7583     Adj R-squared = 0.7328

      Source |  Partial SS     df        MS              F      Prob > F

       Model |  6638.86529     11    603.533208          13.21    0.0000

      region |  1320.00973      3    440.003244           9.63    0.0001
         age |  2237.24937      8    279.656171           6.12    0.0000

    Residual |  1735.63471     38    45.6745977

       Total |     8374.50     49    170.908163
```

You have the answer to your question: Differences in median ages do not eliminate the differences in death rates across the four regions. The ANOVA table summarizes the two terms in the model, `region` and `age`. The `region` term contains 3 degrees of freedom and the `age` term contains 8 degrees of freedom. Both are significant at better than the 1% level.

It is worth noting that the **age** term contains 8 degrees of freedom. Since you did not explicitly indicate that **age** was to be treated as a continuous variable, it was treated as *categorical*, meaning unique coefficients were estimated for each level of age. The only clue of this is that the number of degrees of freedom associated with the **age** term exceeds 1. This becomes more obvious if you review the regression coefficients:

```
. anova, reg

      Source |       SS       df       MS                Number of obs =      50
 ------------+------------------------------            F( 11,    38) =   13.21
       Model | 6638.86529     11  603.533208            Prob > F      =  0.0000
    Residual | 1735.63471     38  45.6745977            R-squared     =  0.7927
 ------------+------------------------------            Adj R-squared =  0.7328
       Total |    8374.50     49  170.908163            Root MSE      =  6.7583
```

drate	Coef.	Std. Err.	t	P>|t|	[95% Conf. Interval]	
_cons	93.925	7.295544	12.87	0.000	79.15594	108.6941
region						
1	13.37147	4.195344	3.19	0.003	4.878439	21.8645
2	13.81431	2.974005	4.65	0.000	7.793748	19.83486
3	13.075	2.747792	4.76	0.000	7.512391	18.63762
4	(dropped)					
age						
24	-38.925	9.944825	-3.91	0.000	-59.05724	-18.79275
26	-53.925	9.944825	-5.42	0.000	-74.05724	-33.79275
27	-24.61666	8.015933	-3.07	0.004	-40.84407	-8.389257
28	-26.26488	7.393098	-3.55	0.001	-41.23143	-11.29834
29	-20.064	7.23115	-2.77	0.009	-34.7027	-5.425299
30	-18.05497	7.074489	-2.55	0.015	-32.37652	-3.733414
31	-9.011922	8.011676	-1.12	0.268	-25.23071	7.206869
32	-11.89646	8.384027	-1.42	0.164	-28.86904	5.07611
35	(dropped)					

If you want to treat **age** as a continuous variable, you must include the **continuous**(*varlist*) option. In the following case, only one variable, **age**, is continuous.

```
. anova drate region age, continuous(age)

                      Number of obs =      50    R-squared     =  0.7203
                      Root MSE      = 7.21483    Adj R-squared =  0.6954
```

Source	Partial SS	df	MS	F	Prob > F
Model	6032.08254	4	1508.02064	28.97	0.0000
region	1645.66228	3	548.554092	10.54	0.0000
age	1630.46662	1	1630.46662	31.32	0.0000
Residual	2342.41746	45	52.0537213		
Total	8374.50	49	170.908163		

The **age** term now has 1 degree of freedom. The regression coefficients are

```
. anova, reg
```

Source	SS	df	MS
Model	6032.08254	4	1508.02064
Residual	2342.41746	45	52.0537213
Total	8374.50	49	170.908163

Number of obs	=	50
F(4, 45)	=	28.97
Prob > F	=	0.0000
R-squared	=	0.7203
Adj R-squared	=	0.6954
Root MSE	=	7.2148

drate	Coef.	Std. Err.	t	P>|t|	[95% Conf. Interval]	
_cons	-41.97859	19.88906	-2.11	0.040	-82.03722	-1.919959
region						
1	13.37578	3.723447	3.59	0.001	5.876378	20.87519
2	15.16831	3.022157	5.02	0.000	9.081374	21.25525
3	14.07378	2.865756	4.91	0.000	8.301846	19.8457
4	(dropped)					
age	3.922947	.7009425	5.60	0.000	2.511177	5.334718

Although we started analyzing this data in an attempt to explain the regional differences in death rate, let's focus on the effect of age for a moment. In our first model, each level of **age** had a unique death rate associated with it. For instance, the predicted death rate in a northeastern state with a median age of 24 was

$$93.93 + 13.37 - 38.93 \approx 68.37$$

whereas the predicted death rate from our current model is

$$-41.98 + 13.38 + 3.92 \cdot 24 \approx 65.48$$

Our previous model had an R^2 of 0.7927 whereas our current model has an R^2 of 0.7203. This "small" loss of predictive power accompanies a gain of 7 degrees of freedom, so we suspect that the continuous age model is as good as the discrete age model.

◁

❑ Technical Note

There is enough information in the two ANOVA tables to attach a statistical significance to our suspicion that the loss of predictive power is offset by the savings in degrees of freedom. To wit: Since the continuous-age model is nested within the discrete-age model, we can perform a standard Chow test. For those of us who know such formulas off the top of our heads, the F statistic is

$$\frac{(2342.41746 - 1735.63471)/7}{45.6745977} = 1.90$$

There is, however, a better way.

We can find out whether our continuous model is as good as our discrete model by putting **age** in the model twice, once as a continuous variable and once as a categorical variable. The categorical variable will then measure deviations around the straight line implied by the continuous variable, and the F test for the significance of the categorical variable will test whether those deviations are jointly zero.

There is no way to tell Stata that the variable **age** in a model is in one instance continuous and in another categorical. As far as Stata is concerned, every variable in the model is either continuous or categorical, so we must fool Stata by creating the same variable with two different names:

```
. generate cage=age
. anova drate region cage age, continuous(cage)
```

	Number of obs =		50	R-squared	= 0.7927
	Root MSE	= 6.7583		Adj R-squared =	0.7328

Source	Partial SS	df	MS	F	Prob > F
Model	6638.86529	11	603.533208	13.21	0.0000
region	1320.00973	3	440.003244	9.63	0.0001
cage	91.9613243	1	91.9613243	2.01	0.1641
age	606.782747	7	86.6832496	1.90	0.0970
Residual	1735.63471	38	45.6745977		
Total	8374.50	49	170.908163		

We first created a new variable called **cage** that is identical to the **age** variable. We then told Stata to estimate an ANOVA model of **drate** on the variables **region**, **cage**, and **age**, where the variable **cage** is continuous. Since we did not specify otherwise, Stata assumes that the other two variables, **region** and **age**, and most importantly, **age**, are categorical.

We find that the F test for the significance of the (categorical) **age** variable is 1.90, just as we calculated above. It is significant at the 9.7% level. If we hold to a 5% significance level, we cannot reject the hypothesis that the effect of **age** is linear.

❑

▷ Example

In our Census data, we still find significant differences across the regions after controlling for the median age of the population. We might now wonder whether the regional differences are differences in level—independent of age—or are instead differences in the regional effects of age. Just as you can interact categorical variables with other categorical variables, you can interact categorical variables with continuous variables.

```
. anova drate region age region*age, continuous(age)
```

	Number of obs =		50	R-squared	= 0.7365
	Root MSE	= 7.24852		Adj R-squared =	0.6926

Source	Partial SS	df	MS	F	Prob > F
Model	6167.7737	7	881.110529	16.77	0.0000
region	188.713602	3	62.9045339	1.20	0.3225
age	873.425599	1	873.425599	16.62	0.0002
region*age	135.691162	3	45.2303874	0.86	0.4689
Residual	2206.7263	42	52.5411023		
Total	8374.50	49	170.908163		

The **region*age** term in our model measures the differences in slopes across the regions. We cannot reject the hypothesis that there are no such differences. We also note that the **region** effect is now "insignificant". This does not mean that there are no regional differences in death rates since each test is a *marginal* or *partial* test. In this example, with **region*age** included in the model, **region** is being tested at the point where **age** is zero. Apart from this value not existing in the dataset, it is also a long way from the mean value of **age**, so the test of **region** at this point is pretty meaningless (although quite valid if you acknowledge what is being tested).

To obtain a more sensible test of `region` we can subtract the mean from the `age` variable and use this in the model.

```
. quietly summarize age

. generate mage = age - r(mean)

. anova drate region mage region*mage, continuous(mage)
```

| | | Number of obs = | 50 | R-squared | = | 0.7365 |
| | | Root MSE | = 7.24852 | Adj R-squared = | | 0.6926 |

Source	Partial SS	df	MS	F	Prob > F
Model	6167.7737	7	881.110529	16.77	0.0000
region	1166.14735	3	388.715783	7.40	0.0004
mage	873.425599	1	873.425599	16.62	0.0002
region*mage	135.691162	3	45.2303874	0.86	0.4689
Residual	2206.7263	42	52.5411023		
Total	8374.50	49	170.908163		

`region` is significant when tested at the mean of the `age` variable.

◁

▷ Example

We can `test` for the overall significance of `region` in the last model. See *Testing effects* earlier in this entry for an explanation of the use of the `test` command after `anova`. The simple form of the `test` syntax is

> test [*term* [*term* [...]]]

After running the model `anova drate region mage region*mage, continuous(mage)`, type

```
. test region region*mage
```

Source	Partial SS	df	MS	F	Prob > F
region region*mage	1781.35344	6	296.89224	5.65	0.0002
Residual	2206.7263	42	52.5411023		

The overall F statistic associated with the `region` and `region*mage` terms is 5.65 and it is significant at the 0.02% level.

If `test` works, typing `test` followed by a single term in our model should produce output that exactly matches that provided by the `anova` command. If you look back at the ANOVA output, you will see that the `region` term, by itself, had a sum of squares of 1166.15, which, based on 3 degrees of freedom, yielded an F statistic of 7.40 and a significance level of 0.0004.

```
. test region
```

Source	Partial SS	df	MS	F	Prob > F
region	1166.14735	3	388.715783	7.40	0.0004
Residual	2206.7263	42	52.5411023		

`test` yields the same result.

◁

Saved Results

anova saves in e():

Scalars

e(N)	number of observations
e(mss)	model sum of squares
e(df_m)	model degrees of freedom
e(rss)	residual sum of squares
e(df_r)	residual degrees of freedom
e(r2)	R-squared
e(r2_a)	adjusted R-squared
e(F)	F statistic
e(rmse)	root mean square error
e(ll)	log likelihood
e(ll_0)	log likelihood, constant-only model
e(N_bse)	number of levels of the between-subjects error term
e(df_bse)	degrees of freedom for the between-subjects error term
e(box#)	Box's conservative epsilon for a particular combination of repeated variable(s) (repeated() only)
e(gg#)	Greenhouse–Geisser epsilon for a particular combination of repeated variable(s) (repeated() only)
e(hf#)	Huynh–Feldt epsilon for a particular combination of repeated variable(s) (repeated() only)

Macros

e(cmd)	anova
e(depvar)	name of dependent variable
e(varnames)	name(s) of the right-hand-side variables
e(repvars)	name(s) of repeated variable(s) (repeated() only)
e(repvar#)	name(s) of repeated variable(s) for a particular combination (repeated() only)
e(model)	ols
e(wtype)	weight type
e(wexp)	weight expression
e(predict)	program used to implement predict

Matrices

e(b)	coefficient vector
e(V)	variance–covariance matrix of the estimators
e(Srep)	covariance matrix based on repeated measures (repeated() only)

Functions

e(sample)	marks estimation sample

References

Afifi, A. A. and S. P. Azen. 1979. *Statistical Analysis: A Computer-Oriented Approach.* 2d ed. New York: Academic Press.

Altman, D. G. 1991. *Practical Statistics for Medical Research.* London: Chapman & Hall.

Box, G. E. P. 1954. Some theorems on quadratic forms applied in the study of analysis of variance problems, I. Effect of inequality of variance in the one-way classification. *Annals of Mathematical Statistics* 25: 290–302.

Cobb, G. W. 1998. *Introduction to Design and Analysis of Experiments.* New York: Springer-Verlag.

Edwards, A. L. 1985. *Multiple Regression and the Analysis of Variance and Covariance.* 2d ed. New York: W. H. Freeman and Company.

Fisher, R. A. 1925. *Statistical Methods for Research Workers.* Edinburgh: Oliver & Boyd.

——. 1935. *The Design of Experiments.* Edinburgh: Oliver & Boyd.

——. 1990. *Statistical Methods, Experimental Design, and Scientific Inference.* Oxford: Oxford University Press. Facsimile reprint of *Statistical Methods for Research Workers* (1925, 14/e 1970), *The Design of Experiments* (1935, 8/e 1966), and *Statistical Methods and Scientific Inference* (1956, 3/e 1973).

Geisser, S. and S. Greenhouse. 1958. An extension of Box's results on the use of the F distribution in multivariate analysis. *Annals of Mathematical Statistics* 29: 885–891.

Gleason, J. R. 1999. sg103: Within subjects (repeated measures) ANOVA, including between subjects factors. *Stata Technical Bulletin* 47: 40–45. Reprinted in *Stata Technical Bulletin Reprints*, vol. 8, pp. 236–243.

——. 2000. sg132: Analysis of variance from summary statistics. *Stata Technical Bulletin* 54: 42–46. Reprinted in *Stata Technical Bulletin Reprints*, vol. 9, pp. 328–332.

Higgins, J. E. and G. G. Koch. 1977. Variable selection and generalized chi-square analysis of categorical data applied to a large cross-sectional occupational health survey. *International Statistical Review* 45: 51–62. (Data reprinted in *Data*, ed. D. F. Andrews and A. M. Herzberg. New York: Springer-Verlag, 1985.)

Huynh, H. 1978. Some approximate tests for repeated measurement designs. *Psychometrika* 43: 161–175.

Huynh, H. and L. S. Feldt. 1976. Estimation of the Box correction for degrees of freedom from sample data in randomized block and split-plot designs. *Journal of Educational Statistics* 1: 69–82.

Kennedy, W. J., Jr., and J. E. Gentle. 1980. *Statistical Computing.* New York: Macmillan.

Kuehl, R. O. 1994. *Statistical Principles of Research Design and Analysis.* Belmont, CA: Duxbury Press.

Milliken, G. A. and D. E. Johnson. 1984. *Analysis of Messy Data, Volume 1: Designed Experiments.* New York: Van Nostrand Reinhold.

Rabe-Hesketh, S. and B. Everitt. 2000. *A Handbook of Statistical Analysis using Stata.* 2d ed. Boca Raton, FL: Chapman & Hall/CRC.

Scheffé, H. 1959. *The Analysis of Variance.* New York: John Wiley & Sons.

Snedecor, G. W. and W. G. Cochran. 1989. *Statistical Methods.* 8th ed. Ames, IA: Iowa State University Press.

Steel, R. G. D. and J. H. Torrie. 1980. *Principles and Procedures of Statistics.* 2d ed. New York: McGraw–Hill.

Winer, B. J., D. R. Brown, and K. M. Michels. 1991. *Statistical Principles in Experimental Design.* 3d ed. New York: McGraw–Hill.

Also See

Complementary:	[R] **adjust**, [R] **encode**, [R] **linktest**, [R] **predict**, [R] **test**, [R] **vce**, [R] **xi**
Related:	[R] **loneway**, [R] **oneway**, [R] **regress**
Background:	[U] **16.5 Accessing coefficients and standard errors**,
	[U] **23 Estimation and post-estimation commands**

Title

append — Append datasets

Syntax

append using *filename* [, nolabel]

Description

append appends a Stata-format dataset stored on disk to the end of the dataset in memory. If *filename* is specified without an extension, .dta is assumed.

Note that Stata also has the capability to join observations from two datasets into a single observation; see [R] **merge**. Also see [U] **25 Commands for combining data** for a comparison of append, merge, and joinby.

Options

nolabel prevents Stata from copying the value label definitions from the disk dataset into the dataset in memory. Even if you do not specify this option, label definitions from the disk dataset never replace definitions already in memory.

Remarks

The disk dataset must be a Stata-format dataset; that is, it must have been created by save; see [R] **save**.

▷ Example

You have two datasets stored on disk that you want to combine into a single dataset. The first dataset, called even.dta, contains the sixth through eighth positive even numbers. The second dataset, called odd.dta, contains the first five positive odd numbers. The datasets are

```
. use even
(6th through 8th even numbers)
. list
        number        even
1.          6          12
2.          7          14
3.          8          16
. use odd
(First five odd numbers)
. list
        number        odd
1.          1           1
2.          2           3
3.          3           5
4.          4           7
5.          5           9
```

We will append the even data onto the end of the odd. Since the odd is already in memory (we just used it above), we type `append using even`. The result is

```
. append using even

. list
        number        odd        even
  1.         1          1           .
  2.         2          3           .
  3.         3          5           .
  4.         4          7           .
  5.         5          9           .
  6.         6          .          12
  7.         7          .          14
  8.         8          .          16
```

Since the variable `number` is in both datasets, the variable was extended with the new data from the file `even.dta`. Since there is no variable called `odd` in the new data, the additional observations on `odd` were forward-filled with *missing*. Since there is no variable called `even` in the original data, the first observations on `even` were back-filled with *missing*.

◁

▷ Example

The order of variables in the two datasets is irrelevant. Stata always appends variables by name:

```
. use odd1
(First five odd numbers)

. describe

Contains data from odd1.dta
  obs:             5                          First five odd numbers
  vars:            2                          5 Jul 2000 17:00
  size:           60 (99.9% of memory free)   (_dta has notes)

              storage  display   value
variable name   type   format    label      variable label

odd            float   %9.0g                Odd numbers
number         float   %9.0g

Sorted by:  number

. describe using even

Contains data                               6th through 8th even numbers
  obs:             3                          5 Jul 2000 17:00
  vars:            2
  size:           30

              storage  display   value
variable name   type   format    label      variable label

number          int    %8.0g
even           float   %9.0g                Even numbers

Sorted by:
```

```
. append using even
. list
          odd      number       even
  1.       1          1           .
  2.       3          2           .
  3.       5          3           .
  4.       7          4           .
  5.       9          5           .
  6.       .          6          12
  7.       .          7          14
  8.       .          8          16
```

The results are the same as in the first example.

◁

When Stata appends two datasets, the definitions of the dataset in memory, called the *master* dataset, override the definitions of the dataset on disk, called the *using* dataset. This extends to value labels, variable labels, characteristics, and date–time stamps. If there are conflicts in numeric storage types, the more precise storage type will be used regardless of whether this storage type was in the *master* dataset or the *using* dataset. If a variable is stored as a `str#` in one dataset and a numeric storage type in the other, the definition in the *master* dataset will prevail. If a variable is stored as a longer string in one dataset than in the other, the longer `str#` storage type will prevail.

❏ Technical Note

If a variable is a string in one dataset and numeric in the other, Stata issues a warning message and then appends the data. If the using dataset contains the string variable, the combined dataset will have numeric missing values for the appended data on this variable; the contents of the string variable in the using data are ignored. If the using dataset contains the numeric variable, the combined dataset will have null strings for the appended data on this variable; the contents of the numeric variable in the using data are ignored.

❏

▷ Example

Since Stata has five numeric variable types—`byte`, `int`, `long`, `float`, and `double`—it is possible that you may attempt to append datasets containing variables with the same name but of different numeric types; see [U] **15.2.2 Numeric storage types**.

Let's `describe` the datasets in the example above:

```
. describe using odd
Contains data                          First five odd numbers
  obs:          5                      5 Jul 2000 17:03
  vars:         2
  size:        60
```

variable name	storage type	display format	value label	variable label
number	float	%9.0g		
odd	float	%9.0g		Odd numbers

```
Sorted by:
```

```
. describe using even
Contains data                                      6th through 8th even numbers
  obs:            3                                5 Jul 2000 17:00
  vars:           2
  size:          30
```

variable name	storage type	display format	value label	variable label
number	int	%8.0g		
even	float	%9.0g		Even numbers

```
Sorted by:
. describe using oddeven
Contains data                                      First five odd numbers
  obs:            8                                5 Jul 2000 17:04
  vars:           3
  size:         128
```

variable name	storage type	display format	value label	variable label
number	float	%9.0g		
odd	float	%9.0g		Odd numbers
even	float	%9.0g		Even numbers

```
Sorted by:
```

The variable `number` was stored as a `float` in `odd.dta` but as an `int` in `even.dta`. Since `float` is the more precise storage type, the resulting dataset, `oddeven.dta` had `number` stored as a `float`. Had we, instead, appended `odd.dta` to `even.dta`, `number` would still have been stored as a `float`:

```
. use even
(6th through 8th even numbers)
. append using odd
number was int now float
. describe
Contains data from even.dta
  obs:            8                                6th through 8th even numbers
  vars:           3                                5 Jul 2000 17:00
  size:         128 (99.8% of memory free)         (_dta has notes)
```

variable name	storage type	display format	value label	variable label
number	float	%8.0g		
even	float	%9.0g		Even numbers
odd	float	%9.0g		Odd numbers

```
Sorted by:
      Note:  dataset has changed since last saved
```

◁

▷ Example

Suppose you have a dataset in memory containing the variable `educ` and you have previously given a `label variable educ "Education Level"` command so that the variable label associated with `educ` is "Education Level". You now `append` a dataset called `newdata.dta` that also contains a variable named `educ`, except that its variable label is "Ed. Lev". After appending the two datasets, the variable `educ` is still labeled "Education Level". See [U] **15.6.2 Variable labels**.

◁

▷ Example

Assume that the values of the variable `educ` are labeled with a value label named `educlbl`. Further assume that in `newdata.dta`, the values of `educ` are also labeled by a value label named `educlbl`. Thus, there is one definition of `educlbl` in memory and another (although perhaps equivalent) definition in `newdata.dta`. When you `append` the new data, you will see the following:

```
. append using newdata
label educlbl already defined
```

When `append` comes upon a situation where one label in memory and another on disk have the same name, it warns you of the problem and sticks with the definition currently in memory, ignoring the definition in the disk file.

◁

❑ Technical Note

When you `append` two datasets that both contain definitions of the same value label, there is a danger that the codings are not equivalent. That is why Stata warns you with a message like "label educlbl already defined". If you do not know that the two value labels are equivalent, you should convert the value labeled variables into string variables, append the data, and then construct a new coding. `decode` and `encode` make this easy:

```
. use newdata, clear
. decode educ, gen(edstr)
. drop educ
. save newdata, replace
. use basedata
. decode educ, gen(edstr)
. drop educ
. append using newdata
. encode edstr, gen(educ)
. drop edstr
```

See [R] **encode**.

You can specify the `nolabel` option to force `append` to ignore all the value label definitions in the incoming file, whether or not there is a conflict. In practice, you will probably never want to do this.

❑

Also See

Complementary:	[R] **save**
Related:	[R] **cross**, [R] **joinby**, [R] **merge**
Background:	[U] **25 Commands for combining data**

Title

> **arch** — Autoregressive conditional heteroskedasticity (ARCH) family of estimators

Syntax

> arch *depvar* $[$*varlist*$]$ $[$*weight*$]$ $[$if *exp*$]$ $[$in *range*$]$ $[$, arch(*numlist*) garch(*numlist*)
>
> saarch(*numlist*) tarch(*numlist*) aarch(*numlist*) narch(*numlist*) narchk(*numlist*)
>
> abarch(*numlist*) atarch(*numlist*) sdgarch(*numlist*) earch(*numlist*) egarch(*numlist*)
>
> parch(*numlist*) tparch(*numlist*) aparch(*numlist*) nparch(*numlist*) nparchk(*numlist*)
>
> pgarch(*numlist*) het(*varlist*) archm archmlags(*numlist*) archmexp(*exp*)
>
> ar(*numlist*) ma(*numlist*) arima($#_p$,$#_d$,$#_q$) noconstant constraints(*numlist*)
>
> hessian opg robust score(*newvarlist* | *stub**) arch0(*cond_method*)
>
> arma0(*cond_method*) condobs(#) savespace detail level(#)
>
> *maximize_options* from(*initial_values*) gtolerance(#)
>
> bhhh dfp bfgs nr bhhhbfgs(#,#) bhhhdfp(#,#) $]$

To estimate an ARCH($#_m$) model, type

> . arch *depvar* ... , arch(1/$#_m$)

To estimate a GARCH($#_m$, $#_k$) model, type

> . arch *depvar* ... , arch(1/$#_m$) garch(1/$#_k$)

Estimation of other models is possible.

You must tsset your data before using arch; see [R] **tsset**.

depvar and *varlist* may contain time-series operators; see [U] **14.4.3 Time-series varlists**.

iweights are allowed; see [U] **14.1.6 weight**.

arch shares the features of all estimation commands; see [U] **23 Estimation and post-estimation commands**.

Details of syntax

The basic model arch estimates is

$$y_t = \mathbf{x}_t\boldsymbol{\beta} + \epsilon_t$$
$$\mathrm{Var}(\epsilon_t) = \sigma_t^2 = \gamma_0 + A(\boldsymbol{\sigma}, \boldsymbol{\epsilon}) + B(\boldsymbol{\sigma}, \boldsymbol{\epsilon})^2 \tag{1}$$

The y_t equation may optionally include ARCH-in-mean and/or ARMA terms:

$$y_t = \mathbf{x}_t\boldsymbol{\beta} + \sum_i \psi_i g(\sigma_{t-i}^2) + \mathrm{ARMA}(p, q) + \epsilon_t$$

If no options are specified, $A() = B() = 0$ and the model collapses to linear regression. The following options add to $A()$ (α, γ, and κ represent parameters to be estimated):

Option	Terms added to $A()$
`arch()`	$A() = A() + \alpha_{1,1}\epsilon_{t-1}^2 + \alpha_{1,2}\epsilon_{t-2}^2 + \cdots$
`garch()`	$A() = A() + \alpha_{2,1}\sigma_{t-1}^2 + \alpha_{2,2}\sigma_{t-2}^2 + \cdots$
`saarch()`	$A() = A() + \alpha_{3,1}\epsilon_{t-1} + \alpha_{3,2}\epsilon_{t-2} + \cdots$
`tarch()`	$A() = A() + \alpha_{4,1}\epsilon_{t-1}^2(\epsilon_{t-1} > 0) + \alpha_{4,2}\epsilon_{t-2}^2(\epsilon_{t-2} > 0) + \cdots$
`aarch()`	$A() = A() + \alpha_{5,1}(|\epsilon_{t-1}| + \gamma_{5,1}\epsilon_{t-1})^2 + \alpha_{5,2}(|\epsilon_{t-2}| + \gamma_{5,2}\epsilon_{t-2})^2 + \cdots$
`narch()`	$A() = A() + \alpha_{6,1}(\epsilon_{t-1} - \kappa_{6,1})^2 + \alpha_{6,2}(\epsilon_{t-2} - \kappa_{6,2})^2 + \cdots$
`narchk()`	$A() = A() + \alpha_{7,1}(\epsilon_{t-1} - \kappa_7)^2 + \alpha_{7,2}(\epsilon_{t-2} - \kappa_7)^2 + \cdots$

The following options add to $B()$:

Option	Terms added to $B()$
`abarch()`	$B() = B() + \alpha_{8,1}|\epsilon_{t-1}| + \alpha_{8,2}|\epsilon_{t-2}| + \cdots$
`atarch()`	$B() = B() + \alpha_{9,1}|\epsilon_{t-1}|(\epsilon_{t-1} > 0) + \alpha_{9,2}|\epsilon_{t-2}|(\epsilon_{t-2} > 0) + \cdots$
`sdgarch()`	$B() = B() + \alpha_{10,1}\sigma_{t-1} + \alpha_{10,2}\sigma_{t-2} + \cdots$

Each of the options requires a *numlist* argument (see [U] **14.1.8 numlist**). The *numlist* determines the lagged terms included. For instance, `arch(1)` specifies $\alpha_{1,1}\epsilon_{t-1}^2$, `arch(2)` specifies $\alpha_{1,2}\epsilon_{t-2}^2$, `arch(1,2)` specifies $\alpha_{1,1}\epsilon_{t-1}^2 + \alpha_{1,2}\epsilon_{t-2}^2$, `arch(1/3)` specifies $\alpha_{1,1}\epsilon_{t-1}^2 + \alpha_{1,2}\epsilon_{t-2}^2 + \alpha_{1,3}\epsilon_{t-3}^2$, etc.

If options `earch()` and/or `egarch()` are specified, the basic model estimated is

$$y_t = \mathbf{x}_t\boldsymbol{\beta} + \sum_i \psi_i g(\sigma_{t-i}^2) + \text{ARMA}(p, q) + \epsilon_t$$

$$\ln \text{Var}(\epsilon_t) = \ln\sigma_t^2 = \gamma_0 + C(\ln\boldsymbol{\sigma}, \mathbf{z}) + A(\boldsymbol{\sigma}, \boldsymbol{\epsilon}) + B(\boldsymbol{\sigma}, \boldsymbol{\epsilon})^2 \tag{2}$$

where $z_t = \epsilon_t/\sigma_t$. $A()$ and $B()$ are given as above, but note that $A()$ and $B()$ now add to $\ln\sigma_t^2$ rather than σ_t^2. (The options corresponding to $A()$ and $B()$ are rarely specified in this case.) $C()$ is given by

Option	Terms added to $C()$
`earch()`	$C() = C() + \alpha_{11,1}z_{t-1} + \gamma_{11,1}(|z_{t-1}| - \sqrt{2/\pi})$ $+ \alpha_{11,2}z_{t-2} + \gamma_{11,2}(|z_{t-2}| - \sqrt{2/\pi}) + \cdots$
`egarch()`	$C() = C() + \alpha_{12,1}\ln\sigma_{t-1}^2 + \alpha_{12,2}\ln\sigma_{t-2}^2 + \cdots$

Alternatively, if options `parch()`, `tparch()`, `aparch()`, `nparch()`, `nparchk()`, and/or `pgarch()` are specified, the basic model estimated is

$$y_t = \mathbf{x}_t\boldsymbol{\beta} + \sum_i \psi_i g(\sigma_{t-i}^2) + \text{ARMA}(p, q) + \epsilon_t$$

$$\{\text{Var}(\epsilon_t)\}^{\varphi/2} = \sigma_t^\varphi = \gamma_0 + D(\boldsymbol{\sigma}, \boldsymbol{\epsilon}) + A(\boldsymbol{\sigma}, \boldsymbol{\epsilon}) + B(\boldsymbol{\sigma}, \boldsymbol{\epsilon})^2 \tag{3}$$

where φ is a parameter to be estimated. $A()$ and $B()$ are given as above, but note that $A()$ and $B()$ now add to σ_t^φ. (The options corresponding to $A()$ and $B()$ are rarely specified in this case.) $D()$ is given by

Option	Terms added to $D()$
parch()	$D() = D() + \alpha_{13,1}\epsilon_{t-1}^\varphi + \alpha_{13,2}\epsilon_{t-2}^\varphi + \cdots$
tparch()	$D() = D() + \alpha_{14,1}\epsilon_{t-1}^\varphi(\epsilon_{t-1} > 0) + \alpha_{14,2}\epsilon_{t-2}^\varphi(\epsilon_{t-2} > 0) + \cdots$
aparch()	$D() = D() + \alpha_{15,1}(|\epsilon_{t-1}| + \gamma_{15,1}\epsilon_{t-1})^\varphi + \alpha_{15,2}(|\epsilon_{t-2}| + \gamma_{15,2}\epsilon_{t-2})^\varphi + \cdots$
nparch()	$D() = D() + \alpha_{16,1}|\epsilon_{t-1} - \kappa_{16,1}|^\varphi + \alpha_{16,2}|\epsilon_{t-2} - \kappa_{16,2}|^\varphi + \cdots$
nparchk()	$D() = D() + \alpha_{17,1}|\epsilon_{t-1} - \kappa_{17}|^\varphi + \alpha_{17,2}|\epsilon_{t-2} - \kappa_{17}|^\varphi + \cdots$
pgarch()	$D() = D() + \alpha_{18,1}\sigma_{t-1}^\varphi + \alpha_{18,2}\sigma_{t-2}^\varphi + \cdots$

Commonly estimated models

Common term	Options to specify
ARCH (Engle 1982)	arch()
GARCH (Bollerslev 1986)	arch() garch()
ARCH-in-mean (Engle et al. 1987)	archm arch() [garch()]
GARCH with ARMA terms	arch() garch() ar() ma()
EGARCH (Nelson 1991)	earch() egarch()
TARCH, threshold ARCH (Zakoian 1990)	abarch() atarch() sdgarch()
GJR, form of threshold ARCH (Glosten et al. 1993)	arch() tarch() [garch()]
SAARCH, simple asymmetric ARCH (Engle 1990)	arch() saarch() [garch()]
PARCH, power ARCH (Higgins and Bera 1992)	parch() [pgarch()]
NARCH, nonlinear ARCH	narch() [garch()]
NARCHK, nonlinear ARCH with a single shift	narchk() [garch()]
A-PARCH, asymmetric power ARCH (Ding et al. 1993)	aparch() [pgarch()]
NPARCH, nonlinear power ARCH	nparch() [pgarch()]

In all cases, you type

$$\text{arch } depvar \; [indepvars], \; options$$

where you obtain the options from the table above. Each option requires that you specify a *numlist* as its argument; the *numlist* specifies the lags to be included. For the vast majority of ARCH models, that value will be 1. For instance, to estimate the classic first-order GARCH model on cpi, you would type

```
. arch cpi, arch(1) garch(1)
```

If you wanted to estimate a first-order GARCH model of cpi on wage, you would type

```
. arch cpi wage, arch(1) garch(1)
```

If, for any of the options, you want first- and second-order terms, specify *optionname*(1/2). Specifying garch(1) arch(1/2) would estimate a GARCH model with first- and second-order ARCH terms. If you specified simply arch(2), only the lag 2 term would be included.

Reading arch output

The regression table reported by `arch` will appear as

op.depvar		Coef.	Std. Err.	z	P>|z|	[95% Conf. Interval]
depvar						
x1		# ...				
x2						
	L1	# ...				
	L2	# ...				
_cons		# ...				
ARCHM						
sigma2		# ...				
ARMA						
ar						
	L1	# ...				
ma						
	L1	# ...				
HET						
z1		# ...				
z2						
	L1	# ...				
	L2	# ...				
ARCH						
arch						
	L1	# ...				
garch						
	L1	# ...				
aparch						
	L1	# ...				
etc.						
_cons		# ...				
POWER						
power		# ...				

Dividing lines separate "equations".

The first one, two, or three equations report the mean model

$$y_t = \mathbf{x}_t\boldsymbol{\beta} + \sum_i \psi_i g(\sigma^2_{t-i}) + \mathrm{ARMA}(p, q) + \epsilon_t$$

The first equation reports $\boldsymbol{\beta}$ and the equation will be named [*depvar*]. (Say you estimated a model on d.cpi; then the first equation would be named [cpi].) In Stataese, the coefficient on x1 in the above example could be referred to as [*depvar*]_b[x1]. The coefficient on the lag 2 value of x2 would be referred to as [*depvar*]_b[L2.x2]. Such notation would be used, for instance, in a subsequent `test` command; see [R] **test**.

The [ARCHM] equation reports the ψ coefficient(s) if your model includes ARCH-in-mean terms; see *Options for specifying ARCH-in-mean terms*. Most ARCH-in-mean models include only a contemporaneous variance term, so the term $\sum_i \psi_i g(\sigma^2_{t-i})$ becomes $\psi\sigma^2_t$. The coefficient ψ will be, in Stataese, [ARCHM]_b[sigma2]. If your model includes lags of σ^2_t, the additional coefficients will be [ARCHM]_b[L1.sigma2], and so on. If you specify a transformation $g()$ (option archmexp()), the coefficients will be [ARCHM]_b[sigma2ex], [ARCHM]_b[L1.sigma2ex], and so on. sigma2ex refers to $g(\sigma_t^2)$, the transformed value of the conditional variance.

The [ARMA] equation reports the ARMA coefficients if your model includes them; see *Options for specifying ARIMA terms*. This equation includes one or two "variables" named ar and ma. In subsequent test statements, one could refer to the coefficient on the first lag of the autoregressive term by typing [ARMA]_b[L1.ar] or simply [ARMA]_b[L.ar] because the L operator is assumed to be lag 1 if you do not specify otherwise. The second lag on the moving-average term, if there were one, could be referred to by typing [ARMA]_b[L2.ma].

The last one, two, or three equations report the variance model.

The [HET] equation reports the multiplicative heteroskedasticity if the model includes such; see *Other options affecting specification of variance*. When you estimate such a model, you specify the variables (and their lags) determining the multiplicative heteroskedasticity and, after estimation, their coefficients are simply [HET]_b[*op*.*varname*].

The [ARCH] equation reports the ARCH, GARCH, etc., terms by referring to "variables" arch, garch, and so on. For instance, if you specified arch(1) garch(1) when you estimated the model, the conditional variance is given by $\sigma_t^2 = \gamma_0 + \alpha_{1,1}\epsilon_{t-1}^2 + \alpha_{2,1}\sigma_{t-1}^2$. The coefficients would be named [ARCH]_b[_cons] (γ_0), [ARCH]_b[L.arch] ($\alpha_{1,1}$), and [ARCH]_b[L.garch] ($\alpha_{2,1}$).

The [POWER] equation appears only if you are estimating a variance model the form of equation (3) above; the estimated φ is the coefficient [POWER]_b[power].

The naming convention for estimated ARCH, GARCH, etc., parameters is (definitions for parameters α_i, γ_i, and κ_i can be found in the tables for $A()$, $B()$, $C()$, and $D()$ above)

Option	1st parameter	2nd parameter	common parameter
arch()	$\alpha_1 =$ [ARCH]_b[arch]		
garch()	$\alpha_2 =$ [ARCH]_b[garch]		
saarch()	$\alpha_3 =$ [ARCH]_b[saarch]		
tarch()	$\alpha_4 =$ [ARCH]_b[tarch]		
aarch()	$\alpha_5 =$ [ARCH]_b[aarch]	$\gamma_5 =$ [ARCH]_b[aarch_e]	
narch()	$\alpha_6 =$ [ARCH]_b[narch]	$\kappa_6 =$ [ARCH]_b[narch_k]	
narchk()	$\alpha_7 =$ [ARCH]_b[narch]	$\kappa_7 =$ [ARCH]_b[narch_k]	
abarch()	$\alpha_8 =$ [ARCH]_b[abarch]		
atarch()	$\alpha_9 =$ [ARCH]_b[atarch]		
sdgarch()	$\alpha_{10} =$ [ARCH]_b[sdgarch]		
earch()	$\alpha_{11} =$ [ARCH]_b[earch]	$\gamma_{11} =$ [ARCH]_b[earch_a]	
egarch()	$\alpha_{12} =$ [ARCH]_b[egarch]		
parch()	$\alpha_{13} =$ [ARCH]_b[parch]		$\varphi =$ [POWER]_b[power]
tparch()	$\alpha_{14} =$ [ARCH]_b[tparch]		$\varphi =$ [POWER]_b[power]
aparch()	$\alpha_{15} =$ [ARCH]_b[aparch]	$\gamma_{15} =$ [ARCH]_b[aparch_e]	$\varphi =$ [POWER]_b[power]
nparch()	$\alpha_{16} =$ [ARCH]_b[nparch]	$\kappa_{16} =$ [ARCH]_b[nparch_k]	$\varphi =$ [POWER]_b[power]
nparchk()	$\alpha_{17} =$ [ARCH]_b[nparch]	$\kappa_{17} =$ [ARCH]_b[nparch_k]	$\varphi =$ [POWER]_b[power]
pgarch()	$\alpha_{18} =$ [ARCH]_b[pgarch]		$\varphi =$ [POWER]_b[power]

Syntax for predict

predict [*type*] *newvarname* [if *exp*] [in *range*] [, *statistic*]

    t0(*time_constant*) <u>structural</u>

    <u>dynamic</u>(*time_constant*) at({*varname*$_\epsilon$ | #$_\epsilon$} {*varname*$_{\sigma^2}$ | #$_{\sigma^2}$})]

where *statistic* is

xb	predicted values for mean equation—the differenced series; the default
y	predicted values for the mean equation in y—the undifferenced series
<u>var</u>iance	predicted values for the conditional variance
<u>h</u>et	predicted values of the variance considering only the multiplicative heteroskedasticity
<u>res</u>iduals	residuals or predicted innovations
<u>yr</u>esiduals	residuals or predicted innovations in y—the undifferenced series

and *time_constant* is a # or a time literal such as d(1jan1995) or q(1995q1), etc.; see [U] **27.3 Time-series dates**.

These statistics are available both in and out of sample; type predict ... if e(sample) ... if wanted only for the estimation sample.

Description

arch estimates models of autoregressive conditional heteroskedasticity (ARCH) using conditional maximum likelihood. In addition to ARCH terms, models may include multiplicative heteroskedasticity.

Concerning the regression equation itself, models may also contain ARCH-in-mean and/or ARMA terms.

Options

Options for specifying terms appearing in A()

arch(*numlist*) specifies the ARCH terms (lags of ϵ_t^2).

Specify arch(1) to include first-order terms, arch(1/2) to specify first- and second-order terms, arch(1/3) to specify first-, second-, and third-order terms, etc. Terms may be omitted. Specify arch(1/3 5) to specify terms with lags 1, 2, 3, and 5. All the options work like this.

arch() may not be specified with aarch(), narch(), narchk(), nparchk(), or nparch() as this would result in collinear terms.

garch(*numlist*) specifies the GARCH terms (lags of σ_t^2).

saarch(*numlist*) specifies the simple asymmetric ARCH terms. Adding these terms is one way to make the standard ARCH and GARCH models respond asymmetrically to positive and negative innovations. Specifying saarch() with arch() and garch() corresponds to the SAARCH model of Engle (1990).

saarch() may not be specified with narch(), narchk(), nparchk(), or nparch() as this would result in collinear terms.

tarch(*numlist*) specifies the threshold ARCH terms. Adding these is another way to make the standard ARCH and GARCH models respond asymmetrically to positive and negative innovations. Specifying tarch() with arch() and garch() corresponds to one form of the GJR model (Glosten, Jagannathan, and Runkle 1993).

Note that tarch() may not be specified with tparch() or aarch() as this would result in collinear terms.

aarch(*numlist*) specifies the lags of the two-parameter term $\alpha_i(|\epsilon_t| + \gamma_i\epsilon_t)^2$. This term provides the same underlying form of asymmetry as including arch() and tarch(); it is just expressed in a different way.

aarch() may not be specified with arch() or tarch() as this would result in collinear terms.

narch(*numlist*) specifies the lags of the two-parameter term $\alpha_i(\epsilon_t - \kappa_i)^2$. This term allows the minimum conditional variance to occur at a value of lagged innovations other than zero. For any given term specified at lag L, the minimum contribution to conditional variance of that lag occurs when $\epsilon_{t-L}^2 = \kappa_L$—the squared innovations at that lag are equal to the estimated constant κ_L.

narch() may not be specified with arch(), saarch(), narchk(), nparchk(), or nparch() as this would result in collinear terms.

narchk(*numlist*) specifies the lags of the two-parameter term $\alpha_i(\epsilon_t - \kappa)^2$; note that this is a variation on narch() with κ held constant for all lags.

narchk() may not be specified with arch(), saarch(), narch(), nparchk(), or nparch() as this would result in collinear terms.

Options specifying terms appearing in B()

abarch(*numlist*) specifies lags of the term $|\epsilon_t|$.

atarch(*numlist*) specifies lags of $|\epsilon_t|(\epsilon_t > 0)$, where $(\epsilon_t > 0)$ represents the indicator function returning 1 when true and 0 when false. Like the TARCH terms, these ATARCH terms allow the effect of unanticipated innovations to be asymmetric about zero.

sdgarch(*numlist*) specifies lags of σ_t. Combining atarch(), abarch(), and sdgarch() produces the model by Zakoian (1990) that the author called the TARCH model. The acronym TARCH, however, is often used to refer to any model using thresholding to obtain asymmetry.

Options for terms appearing in C()

earch(*numlist*) specifies lags of the two-parameter term $\alpha z_t + \gamma(|z_t| - \sqrt{2/\pi})$. These terms represent the influence of news—lagged innovations—in Nelson's (1991) EGARCH model. For these terms, $z_t = \epsilon_t/\sigma_t$ and arch assumes $z_t \sim N(0,1)$. Nelson (1991) derived the general form of an EGARCH model for any assumed distribution and performed estimation assuming a Generalized Error Distribution (GED). See Hamilton (1994) for a derivation where z_t is assumed normal. The z_t terms can be parameterized in at least two equivalent ways; arch uses Nelson's (1991) original parameterization; see Hamilton (1994) for an equivalent alternative.

egarch(*numlist*) specifies lags of $\ln(\sigma_t^2)$.

Options for terms appearing in D()

Note: The model is parameterized in terms of $h(\epsilon_t)^\varphi$ and σ_t^φ. A single φ is estimated even when more than one option is specified.

parch(*numlist*) specifies lags of $|\epsilon_t|^\varphi$. parch() combined with pgarch() corresponds to the class of nonlinear models of conditional variance suggested by Higgins and Bera (1992).

tparch(*numlist*) specifies lags of $(\epsilon_t > 0)|\epsilon_t|^\varphi$, where $(\epsilon_t > 0)$ represents the indicator function returning 1 when true and 0 when false. As with tarch(), tparch() specifies terms that allow for a differential impact of "good" (positive innovations) and "bad" (negative innovations) news for lags specified by *numlist*.

Note that tparch() may not be specified with tarch() as this would result in collinear terms.

aparch(*numlist*) specifies lags of the two-parameter term $\alpha(|\epsilon_t| + \gamma\epsilon_t)^\varphi$. This asymmetric power ARCH model, A-PARCH, was proposed by Ding et al. (1993) and corresponds to a Box–Cox function in the lagged innovations. The authors estimated the original A-PARCH model on over 16,000 daily observations of the Standard and Poor's 500, and not without good reason. As the number of parameters and the flexibility of the specification increase, larger amounts of data are required to estimate the parameters of the conditional heteroskedasticity. See Ding et al. (1993) for a discussion of how 7 popular ARCH models nest within the A-PARCH model.

Note that when γ goes to 1, the full term goes to zero for many observations and this point can be numerically unstable.

nparch(*numlist*) specifies lags of the two-parameter term $\alpha|\epsilon_t - \kappa_i|^\varphi$.

nparch() may not be specified with arch(), saarch(), narch(), narchk(), or nparchk() as this would result in collinear terms.

nparchk(*numlist*) specifies lags of the two-parameter term $\alpha|\epsilon_t - \kappa|^\varphi$; note that this is a variation on nparch() with κ held constant for all lags. This is the direct analog of narchk() except for the power of φ. nparchk() corresponds to an extended form of the model of Higgins and Bera (1992) as presented by Bollerslev et al. (1994). nparchk() would typically be combined with the option pgarch().

nparchk() may not be specified with arch(), saarch(), narch(), narchk(), or nparch() as this would result in collinear terms.

pgarch(*numlist*) specifies lags of σ_t^φ.

Other options affecting specification of variance

het(*varlist*) specifies that *varlist* be included in the specification of the conditional variance. *varlist* may contain time-series operators. This varlist enters the variance specification collectively as multiplicative heteroskedasticity; see Judge et al. (1985). If het() is not specified, the model will not contain multiplicative heteroskedasticity.

Assume the conditional variance is thought to depend on variables x and w while also having an ARCH(1) component. We request this specification by using the options het(x w) arch(1), and this corresponds to the conditional-variance model

$$\sigma_t^2 = \exp(\lambda_0 + \lambda_1 x_t + \lambda_2 w_t) + \alpha\epsilon_{t-1}^2$$

Multiplicative heteroskedasticity enters differently with an EGARCH model because the variance is already specified in logs. For the options het(x w) earch(1) egarch(1), the variance model is

$$\ln(\sigma_t^2) = \lambda_0 + \lambda_1 x_t + \lambda_2 w_t + \alpha z_{t-1} + \gamma(|z_{t-1}| - \sqrt{2/\pi}) + \delta\ln(\sigma_{t-1}^2)$$

Options for specifying ARCH-in-mean terms

archm specifies that an ARCH-in-mean term be included in the specification of the mean equation. This term allows the expected value of *depvar* to depend on the conditional variance. ARCH-in-mean is most commonly used in evaluating financial time series when a theory supports a trade-off between asset riskiness and asset return. By default, no ARCH-in-mean terms are included in the model.

archm specifies that the contemporaneous expected conditional variance be included in the mean equation. For example, typing

    . arch y x, archm arch(1)

specifies the model

$$y_t = \beta_0 + \beta_1 \mathbf{x}_t + \psi \sigma_t^2 + \epsilon_t$$
$$\sigma_t^2 = \gamma_0 + \gamma \epsilon_{t-1}^2$$

archmlags(*numlist*) is an expansion of archm and specifies that lags of the conditional variance σ_t^2 be included in the mean equation. To specify a contemporaneous and once-lagged variance, either specify archm archmlags(1) or specify archmlags(0/1).

archmexp(*exp*) specifies the transformation in *exp* be applied to any ARCH-in-mean terms in the model. The expression should contain an X wherever a value of the conditional variance is to enter the expression. This option can be used to produce the commonly used ARCH-in-mean of the conditional standard deviation. Using the example from archm, typing

    . arch y x, archm arch(1) archmexp(sqrt(X))

specifies the mean equation $y_t = \beta_0 + \beta_1 \mathbf{x}_t + \psi \sigma_t + \epsilon_t$. Alternatively, typing

    . arch y x, archm arch(1) archmexp(1/sqrt(X))

specifies $y_t = \beta_0 + \beta_1 \mathbf{x}_t + \psi / \sigma_t + \epsilon_t$.

Options for specifying ARIMA terms

ar(*numlist*) specifies the autoregressive terms to be included in the model. These are the autoregressive terms of the structural model disturbance. For example, ar(1/3) specifies that lags of 1, 2, and 3 of the structural disturbance are to be included in the model. ar(1,4) specifies that lags 1 and 4 are to be included, possibly to account for quarterly effects.

If the model does not contain any regressors, these terms can also be considered autoregressive terms for the dependent variable; see [R] **arima**.

ma(*numlist*) specifies the moving average terms to be included in the model. These are the terms for the lagged innovations—white noise disturbances.

arima($\#_p$,$\#_d$,$\#_q$) is an alternate, shorthand notation for specifying models that are autoregressive in the dependent variable. The dependent variable and any independent variables are differenced $\#_d$ times, 1 through $\#_p$ lags of autocorrelations are included, and 1 through $\#_q$ lags of moving averages are included. For example, the specification

    . arch y, arima(2,1,3)

is equivalent to

    . arch D.y, ar(1/2) ma(1/3)

The former is easier to write for "classic" ARIMA models of the mean equation but is not nearly as expressive as the latter. If gaps in the AR or MA lags are to be modeled, or if different operators are to be applied to independent variables, the latter syntax will generally be required.

Other options affecting the mean and/or variance specifications

noconstant suppresses the constant term (intercept) in the equation for the conditional mean.

constraints(*numlist*) specifies the constraint numbers of the linear constraints to be applied during estimation. The default is to perform unconstrained estimation. Constraints are specified using the constraint command; see [R] **constraint** (also see [R] **reg3** for the use of constraint in multiple-equation contexts).

Options affecting the estimated standard errors

hessian and opg specify how standard errors are to be calculated. The default is opg unless one of the options bfgs, dfp, or nr is specified, in which case the default is hessian.

hessian specifies that the standard errors and coefficient covariance matrix be estimated from the full Hessian—the matrix of negative second derivatives of the log likelihood function. These are the estimates produced by most of Stata's maximum likelihood estimators.

opg specifies that the standard errors and coefficient covariance matrix be estimated using the outer product of the coefficient gradients with respect to the observation likelihoods.

hessian and opg provide asymptotically equivalent estimates of the standard errors and covariance matrix and there is no theoretical justification for preferring either estimate.

If you obtain your standard errors from the Hessian, because you either specify hessian or use an optimization method that implies hessian, be aware that the part of the calculation that occurs after convergence can take a while. Evaluating the second derivatives numerically to estimate the covariance matrix is an $O(k^2/2)$ process, where k is the number of parameters. If the model contains 5 parameters, producing the covariance matrix at the final step will take about 12.5 times longer than a single iteration in finding the maximum. If you have 10 parameters, it will take about 50 times longer. (This is assuming you did not use method nr. Method nr requires the longer time at every iteration.)

robust specifies that the Huber/White/sandwich estimator of variance is to be used in place of the traditional calculation; see [U] **23.11 Obtaining robust variance estimates**.

For ARCH models the robust or quasi-maximum likelihood estimates (QMLE) of variance are robust to symmetric nonnormality in the disturbances. The robust variance estimates are not generally robust to functional misspecification of the mean equation; see Bollerslev and Wooldridge (1992).

Note that the robust variance estimates computed by arch are based on the full Huber/White formulation as discussed in [P] **_robust**. Many software packages report robust estimates that in fact set some terms to their expectations of zero (Bollerslev and Wooldridge 1992), which saves them from having to calculate second derivatives of the log-likelihood function.

score(*newvarlist* | *stub**) creates a new variable for each parameter in the model. Each new variable contains the derivative of the model log-likelihood with respect to the parameter for each observation in the estimation sample: $\partial L_t / \partial \beta_k$, where L_t is the log likelihood for observation t and β_k is the kth parameter in the model.

If score(*newvarlist*) is specified, the *newvarlist* must contain a new variable for each parameter in the model. If score(*stub**) is specified, variables named *stub#* are created for each parameter in the model. The *newvarlist* is filled, or the #'s in *stub#* are created, in the order in which the estimated parameters are reported in the estimation results table.

Unlike scores for most other models, the scores from `arch` are individual gradients of the log likelihood with respect to the variables, not with respect to $\mathbf{x}_t\boldsymbol{\beta}$. Since the ARCH model is inherently nonlinear, the scores with respect to $\mathbf{x}_t\boldsymbol{\beta}$ could not be used to reconstruct the gradients for the individual parameters.

Options affecting conditioning (priming) values

`arch0`(*cond_method*) is a rarely used option to specify how the conditioning (presample or priming) values for σ_t^2 and ϵ_t^2 are to be computed. In the presample period, it is assumed that $\sigma_t^2 = \epsilon_t^2$ and that this value is constant. If `arch0()` is not specified, the priming values are computed as the expected unconditional variance given the current estimates of the β coefficients and any ARMA parameters.

`arch0(xb)` is the default. It specifies that the priming values are the expected unconditional variance of the model, which is $\sum_1^T \widehat{\epsilon}_t^2 / T$, where $\widehat{\epsilon}_t$ is computed from the mean equation and any ARMA terms.

`arch0(xb0)` specifies that the priming values are the estimated variance of the residuals from an OLS estimate of the mean equation.

`arch0(xbwt)` specifies that the priming values are the weighted sum of the $\widehat{\epsilon}_t^2$ from the current conditional mean equation (and ARMA terms) that places more weight on estimates of ϵ_t^2 at the beginning of the sample.

`arch0(xb0wt)` specifies that the priming values are the weighted sum of the $\widehat{\epsilon}_t^2$ from an OLS estimate of the mean equation (and ARMA terms) that places more weight on estimates of ϵ_t^2 at the beginning of the sample.

`arch0(zero)` specifies that the priming values are 0. Unlike the priming values for ARIMA models, 0 is generally not a consistent estimate of the presample conditional variance or squared innovations.

`arch0(#)` specifies that $\sigma_t^2 = \epsilon_t^2 = \#$ for any specified nonnegative #. Thus, `arch0(0)` is equivalent of `arch0(zero)`.

`arma0`(*cond_method*) is a rarely used option to specify how the ϵ_t values are initialized at the beginning of the sample for the ARMA component of the model, if it has such a component. This option has an effect only when AR or MA terms are included in the model (options `ar()`, `ma()`, or `arima()` specified).

`arma0(zero)` is the default. This specifies that all priming values of ϵ_t are to be taken to be 0. This estimates the model over the entire requested sample and takes ϵ_t to be its expected value of 0 for all lags required by the ARMA terms; see Judge et al. (1985).

`arma0(p)`, `arma0(q)`, and `arma0(pq)` specify that the estimation begin after priming the recursions for a certain number of observations. p specifies that estimation begin after the pth observation in the sample, where p is the maximum AR lag in the model; q specifies that estimation begin after the qth observation in the sample, where q is the maximum MA lag in the model; and pq specifies that estimation begin after the $(p + q)$th observation in the sample.

During the priming period the recursions necessary to generate predicted disturbances are performed, but results are used only for the purpose of initializing pre-estimation values of ϵ_t. Understand the definition of pre-estimation: say you estimate a model in 10/100. If the model is specified with `ar(1,2)`, then pre-estimation refers to observations 10 and 11.

The ARCH terms σ_t^2 and ϵ_t^2 are also updated over these observations. Any required lags of ϵ_t prior to the priming period are taken to be their expected value of 0 while ϵ_t^2 and σ_t^2 take the values specified in `arch0()`.

arma0($\#$) specifies that the presample values of ϵ_t are to be taken as $\#$ for all lags required by the ARMA terms. Thus, arma0(0) is equivalent to arma0(zero).

condobs($\#$) is a rarely used option to specify a fixed number of conditioning observations at the start of the sample. Over these priming observations, the recursions necessary to generate predicted disturbances are performed but only for the purpose of initializing pre-estimation values of ϵ_t, ϵ_t^2, and σ_t^2. Any required lags of ϵ_t prior to the initialization period are taken to be their expected value of 0 (or the value specified in arma0()) and required values of ϵ_t^2 and σ_t^2 assume the values specified by arch0(). condobs() can be used if conditioning observations are desired for the lags in the ARCH terms of the model. If arma() is also specified, the maximum of the number of conditioning observations required by arma() and condobs($\#$) is used.

Other options exclusive of optimization options

savespace specifies that memory use be conserved by retaining only those variables required for estimation. The original dataset is restored after estimation. This option is rarely used and should be specified only if there is insufficient space to estimate a model without the option. Note that arch requires considerably more temporary storage during estimation than most estimation commands in Stata.

detail specifies that a detailed list of any gaps in the series be reported. These include gaps due to missing observations or missing data for the dependent variable or independent variables.

level($\#$) specifies the confidence level, in percent, for confidence intervals of the coefficients.

Options for controlling maximization

maximize_options control the maximization process; see [R] **maximize**. These options are often more important for ARCH models than other maximum likelihood models because of convergence problems associated with ARCH models—ARCH model likelihoods are notoriously difficult to maximize.

Several alternate optimization methods such as Berndt–Hall–Hall–Hausman (BHHH) and Boyd–Fletcher–Goldfarb–Shanno (BFGS) are provided for arch models. Since each method attacks the optimization differently, some problems can be successfully optimized by an alternate method when one method fails.

The default optimization method for arch is a hybrid method combining BHHH and BFGS iterations. This combination has been found operationally to provide good convergence properties on difficult likelihoods. However, sometimes a likelihood is particularly deceptive to one, or both of these methods.

from(*initial_values*) allows specifying the initial values of the coefficients. ARCH models may be sensitive to initial values and may have coefficient values that correspond to local maxima. The default starting values are obtained via a series of regressions producing results which, based on asymptotic theory, are consistent for the β and ARMA parameters and are, we believe, reasonable for the rest. Nevertheless, these values will sometimes prove to be infeasible in that the likelihood function cannot be evaluated at the initial values arch first chooses. In such cases, the estimation is restarted with ARCH and ARMA parameters initialized to zero. It is possible, but unlikely, that even these values will be infeasible and you will have to supply initial values yourself.

The standard syntax for from() accepts a matrix, a list of values, or coefficient name value pairs; see [R] **maximize**. In addition, arch allows the following:

from(archb0) specifies that the starting value for all the ARCH/GARCH/... parameters in the conditional-variance equation be set to 0.

from(armab0) specifies that the starting value for all ARMA parameters in the model be set to 0.

from(archb0 armab0) specifies that the starting value for all ARCH/GARCH/... and ARMA parameters be set to 0.

gtolerance(#) specifies the threshold for the relative size of the gradient; see [R] **maximize**. The default for arch is gtolerance(.05).

gtolerance(999) may be specified to disable the gradient criterion. If the optimizer becomes stuck with repeated "(backed up)" messages, it is likely that the gradient still contains substantial values, but an uphill direction cannot be found for the likelihood. With this option, results can often be obtained, but it is unclear whether the global maximum likelihood has been found.

When the maximization is not going well, it is also possible to set the maximum number of iterations, see [R] **maximize**, to the point where the optimizer appears to be stuck and to inspect the estimation results at that point.

bhhh, dfp, bfgs, nr, bhhhbfgs(), bhhhdfp() specify how the likelihood function is to be maximized. bhhhbfgs(5,10) is the default.

bhhh specifies that the Berndt–Hall–Hall–Hausman (BHHH, Berndt et al. 1974) method be used. While it is difficult to make general statements about convergence properties of nonlinear optimization methods, BHHH tends to do well in areas far from the maximum, but does not have quadratic convergence in areas near the maximum.

dfp specifies that the Davidon–Fletcher–Powell (DFP) method be used; see Press et al. (1992). As currently implemented, dfp requires substantially less temporary storage space than the other methods (with the exception of bfgs) and this may be an advantage for models with many parameters.

bfgs specifies that the Boyd–Fletcher–Goldfarb–Shanno (BFGS) method be used; see Press et al. (1992). BFGS optimization is similar to DFP with second-order terms included when updating the Hessian. bfgs, like dfp, requires little memory.

nr specifies that Stata's modified Newton–Raphson method be used. Since all derivatives for arch are taken numerically, this method can be slow for models with many parameters. However, its choice of direction is computed quite differently from DFP, BFGS, and BHHH, and so nr is sometimes successful when the other methods have difficulty. (When you specify nr, arch automatically specifies the maximizer's difficult option for you; see [R] **maximize**.)

bhhhbfgs($\#_1$,$\#_2$) specifies BHHH and BFGS be combined. $\#_1$ designates the number of BHHH steps; $\#_2$, the number of BFGS steps. Optimization alternates between these sets of BHHH and BFGS steps until convergence is achieved. The default optimization method is bhhhbfgs(5, 10).

bhhhdfp($\#_1$,$\#_2$) specifies that BHHH and DFP be combined. $\#_1$ designates the number of BHHH steps; $\#_2$, the number of DFP steps. The optimization alternates between these sets of BHHH and DFP steps until convergence is achieved.

Options for predict

Six statistics can be computed by using predict after arch: the predictions of the mean equation (option xb, the default), the undifferenced predictions of the mean equation (option y), the predictions of the conditional variance (option variance), the predictions of the multiplicative heteroskedasticity component of variance (option het), the predictions of residuals or innovations (option residuals), and the predictions of residuals or innovations in terms of y (option yresiduals). Given the dynamic nature of ARCH models and that the dependent variable might be differenced, there are alternate ways of computing each statistic. We can use all the data on the dependent variable available right up to the time of each prediction (the default, which is often called a one-step prediction), or we can use the data up to a particular time, after which the predicted value of the dependent variable is used recursively to make subsequent predictions (option `dynamic()`). Either way, we can consider or ignore the ARMA disturbance component (the component is considered by default and ignored if you specify option `structural`). We might also be interested in predictions at certain fixed points where we specify the prior values of ϵ_t and σ_t^2 (option `at()`).

xb (the default) calculates the predictions from the mean equation. If D.*depvar* is the dependent variable, these predictions are of D.*depvar* and not *depvar* itself.

y specifies that predictions of *depvar* are to be made even if the model was specified in terms of, say, D.*depvar*.

variance calculates predictions of the conditional variance $\widehat{\sigma}_t^2$.

het calculates predictions of the multiplicative heteroskedasticity component of variance.

residuals calculates the residuals. If no other options are specified, these are the predicted innovations ϵ_t, i.e., they include any ARMA component. If option `structural` is specified, these are the residuals from the mean equation ignoring any ARMA terms; see `structural` below. The residuals are always from the estimated equation, which may have a differenced dependent variable; if *depvar* is differenced, they are not the residuals of the undifferenced *depvar*.

yresiduals calculates the residuals in terms of *depvar*, even if the model was specified in terms of, say, D.*depvar*. As with `residuals`, the `yresiduals` are computed from the model including any ARMA component. If option `structural` is specified, any ARMA component is ignored and `yresiduals` are the residuals from the structural equation; see `structural` below.

t0(*time_constant*) specifies the starting point for the recursions to compute the predicted statistics; disturbances are assumed to be 0 for $t <$ `t0()`. The default is to set `t0()` to the minimum t observed in the estimation sample, meaning that observations prior to that are assumed to have disturbances of 0.

> t0() is irrelevant if `structural` is specified because in that case all observations are assumed to have disturbances of 0.

> t0(5) would begin recursions at $t = 5$. If your data were quarterly, you might instead type t0(q(1961q2)) to obtain the same result.

> Note that any ARMA component in the mean equation or GARCH term in the conditional-variance equation makes `arch` recursive and dependent on the starting point of the predictions. This includes one-step ahead predictions.

structural specifies that the calculation is to be made considering the structural component only, ignoring any ARMA terms, thus producing the steady-state equilibrium predictions.

dynamic(*time_constant*) specifies how lags of y_t in the model are to be handled. If `dynamic()` is not specified, actual values are used everywhere lagged values of y_t appear in the model to produce one-step ahead forecasts.

> dynamic(*time_constant*) produces dynamic (also known as recursive) forecasts. *time_constant* specifies when the forecast is to switch from one-step ahead to dynamic. In dynamic forecasts, references to y evaluate to the prediction of y for all periods at or after *time_constant*; they evaluate to the actual value of y for all prior periods.

> dynamic(10) would calculate predictions where any reference to y_t with $t < 10$ evaluates to the actual value of y_t and any reference to y_t with $t \geq 10$ evaluates to the prediction of y_t. This means that one-step ahead predictions are calculated for $t < 10$ and dynamic predictions thereafter.

Depending on the lag structure of the model, the dynamic predictions might still reference some actual values of y_t.

In addition, you may specify `dynamic(.)` to have `predict` automatically switch from one-step to dynamic predictions at $p + q$, where p is the maximum AR lag and q is the maximum MA lag.

`at(varname_\epsilon | #_\epsilon  varname_{\sigma^2} | #_{\sigma^2})` specifies that very static predictions are to be made. `at()` and `dynamic()` may not be specified together.

`at()` specifies two sets of values to be used for ϵ_t and σ_t^2, the dynamic components in the model. These specified values are treated as given. In addition, lagged values of *depvar*, if they occur in the model, are obtained from the real values of the dependent variable. All computations are based on actual data and the given values. The purpose of `at()` is to allow static evaluation of results for a given set of disturbances. This is useful, for instance, in generating the news response function.

`at()` requires that you specify two arguments. Each argument can be either a variable name or a number. The first argument supplies the values to be used for ϵ_t; the second supplies the values to be used for σ_t^2. If σ_t^2 plays no role in your model, the second argument may be specified as '.' to indicate missing.

Remarks

The basic premise of ARCH models is that the volatility of a series is not constant through time. Instead, periods of relatively low volatility and periods of relatively high volatility tend to be grouped together. This is a commonly observed characteristic of economic time-series and is even more pronounced in many frequently-sampled financial series. ARCH models seek to estimate this time-dependent volatility as a function of observed prior volatility. In some cases, the model of volatility is of more interest than the model of the conditional mean. As implemented in `arch`, the volatility model may also include regressors to account for a structural component in the volatility—usually referred to as multiplicative heteroskedasticity.

ARCH models were introduced by Engle (1982) in a study of inflation rates and there has since been a barrage of proposed parametric and nonparametric specifications of autoregressive conditional heteroskedasticity. Overviews of the literature can found in Bollerslev, Engle, and Nelson (1994) and Bollerslev, Chou, and Kroner (1992). Introductions to basic ARCH models appear in many general econometrics texts, including Davidson and MacKinnon (1993), Greene (2000), Kmenta (1997), Johnston and DiNardo (1997), and Wooldridge (2000). Harvey (1989) and Enders (1995) provide introductions to ARCH in the larger context of econometric time-series modeling and Hamilton (1994) provides considerably more detail in the same context.

`arch` estimates models of autoregressive conditional heteroskedasticity (ARCH, GARCH, etc.) using conditional maximum likelihood. By "conditional" is meant that the likelihood is computed based on an assumed or estimated set of priming values for the squared innovations ϵ_t^2 and variances σ_t^2 prior to the estimation sample; see, for example, Hamilton (1994) or Bollerslev (1986). Sometimes additional conditioning is done on the first a, g, or $a + g$ observations in the sample; where a is the maximum ARCH term lag and g is the maximum GARCH term lag (or the maximum lag(s) from the other ARCH family terms).

The original ARCH model proposed by Engle (1982) modeled the variance of a regression model's disturbances as a linear function of lagged values of the squared regression disturbances. We can write an ARCH(m) model as

$$y_t = \mathbf{x}_t\boldsymbol{\beta} + \epsilon_t \qquad \text{(conditional mean)}$$
$$\sigma_t^2 = \gamma_0 + \gamma_1\epsilon_{t-1}^2 + \gamma_2\epsilon_{t-2}^2 + \cdots + \gamma_m\epsilon_{t-m}^2 \qquad \text{(conditional variance)}$$

where

$$\epsilon_t \sim N(0, \sigma_t^2)$$

ϵ_t^2 is the squared residuals (or innovations)

γ_i are the ARCH parameters

The ARCH model has a specification for both the conditional mean and the conditional variance, and the variance is a function of the size of prior unanticipated innovations—ϵ_t^2. This model was generalized by Bollerslev (1986) to include lagged values of the conditional variance—a GARCH model. The GARCH(m, k) model is written as

$$y_t = \mathbf{x}_t \boldsymbol{\beta} + \epsilon_t$$
$$\sigma_t^2 = \gamma_0 + \gamma_1 \epsilon_{t-1}^2 + \gamma_2 \epsilon_{t-2}^2 + \cdots + \gamma_m \epsilon_{t-m}^2 + \delta_1 \sigma_{t-1}^2 + \delta_2 \sigma_{t-2}^2 + \cdots + \delta_k \sigma_{t-k}^2$$

where

γ_i are the ARCH parameters

δ_i are the GARCH parameters

Without proof, we note that the GARCH model of conditional variance can be considered an ARMA process in the squared innovations, although not in the variances as the equations might seem to suggest; see, for example, Hamilton (1994). Specifically, the standard GARCH model implies that the squared innovations result from the process

$$\epsilon_t^2 = \gamma_0 + (\gamma_1 + \delta_1)\epsilon_{t-1}^2 + (\gamma_2 + \delta_2)\epsilon_{t-2}^2 + \cdots + (\gamma_k + \delta_k)\epsilon_{t-k}^2 + w_t - \delta_1 w_{t-1} - \delta_2 w_{t-2} - \delta_3 w_{t-3}$$

where

$$w_t = \epsilon_t^2 - \sigma_t^2$$

w_t is a white-noise process that is fundamental for ϵ_t^2

One of the primary benefits of the GARCH specification is parsimony in identifying the conditional variance. As with ARIMA models, the ARMA specification in GARCH allows the structure of the conditional variance to be modeled with fewer parameters than with an ARCH specification alone. Empirically, many series with a conditionally heteroskedastic disturbance have been found to be adequately modeled with a GARCH(1,1) specification.

An ARMA process in the disturbances can be easily added to the mean equation. For example, the mean equation can be written with an ARMA$(1, 1)$ disturbance as

$$y_t = \mathbf{x}_t \boldsymbol{\beta} + \rho(y_{t-1} - \mathbf{x}_{t-1}\boldsymbol{\beta}) + \theta \epsilon_{t-1} + \epsilon_t$$

with an obvious generalization to ARMA(p, q) by adding additional terms; see [R] **arima** for more discussion of this specification. This change affects only the conditional-variance specification in that ϵ_t^2 now results from a different specification of the conditional mean.

Much of the literature on ARCH models has focused on alternate specifications of the variance equation. `arch` allows many of these alternate specifications to be requested using the options `saarch()` through `pgarch()`. In all cases, these options imply that one or more terms be changed or added to the specification of the variance equation.

One of the areas addressed by many of the alternate specifications is asymmetry. Both the ARCH and GARCH specifications imply a symmetric impact of innovations. Whether an innovation ϵ_t^2 is positive or negative makes no difference to the expected variance σ_t^2 in the ensuing periods: only the size of the innovation matters—good news and bad news have the same effect. Many theories, however, suggest that positive and negative innovations should vary in their impact. For risk-averse investors, a large unanticipated drop in the market is more likely to lead to higher volatility than a large unanticipated increase (see Black 1976, Nelson 1991). The options saarch(), tarch(), aarch(), abarch(), earch(), aparch(), tparch() allow various specifications of asymmetric effects.

The options narch(), narchk(), nparch(), nparchk() also imply an asymmetric impact, but of a very specific form. All of the models considered so far have a minimum conditional variance when the lagged innovations are all zero. "No news is good news" when it comes to keeping the conditional variance small. The narch(), narchk(), nparch(), nparchk() options also have a symmetric response to innovations, but they are not centered at zero. The entire news response function (response to innovations) is shifted horizontally such that minimum variance lies at some specific positive or negative value for prior innovations.

ARCH-in-mean models allow the conditional variance of the series to influence the conditional mean. This is particularly convenient for modeling the risk/return relationship in financial series; the riskier an investment, all else equal, the lower its expected return. ARCH-in-mean models modify the specification of the conditional mean equation to be

$$y_t = \mathbf{x_t}\boldsymbol{\beta} + \psi\sigma_t^2 + \epsilon_t \qquad \text{(ARCH-in-mean)}$$

While this linear form in the current conditional variance has dominated the literature, arch allows the conditional variance to enter the mean equation through a nonlinear transformation $g()$, and for this transformed term to be included contemporaneously or lagged.

$$y_t = \mathbf{x_t}\boldsymbol{\beta} + \psi_0 g(\sigma_t^2) + \psi_1 g(\sigma_{t-1}^2) + \psi_2 g(\sigma_{t-2}^2) + \cdots + \epsilon_t$$

Square root is the most commonly used $g()$ transformation because researchers want to include a linear term for the conditional standard deviation, but any transform $g()$ is allowed.

▷ Example

We will consider a simple model of the US Wholesale Price Index (WPI) (Enders 1995, 106–110) which we also consider in [R] **arima**. The data are quarterly over the period 1960q1 through 1990q4.

In [R] **arima** we estimate a model of the continuously compounded rate of change in the WPI, $\ln(\text{WPI}_t) - \ln(\text{WPI}_{t-1})$. The graph of the differenced series—see [R] **arima**—clearly shows periods of high volatility and other periods of relative tranquility. This makes the series a good candidate for ARCH modeling. Indeed, price indices have been a common target of ARCH models. Engle (1982) presented the original ARCH formulation in an analysis of UK inflation rates.

The first-order generalized ARCH model (GARCH, Bollerslev 1986) is the most commonly used specification for the conditional variance in empirical work and is typically written GARCH$(1, 1)$. We can estimate a GARCH$(1, 1)$ process for the log-differenced series by typing

(Continued on next page)

```
. arch D.ln_wpi, arch(1) garch(1)

(setting optimization to BHHH)
Iteration 0:   log likelihood =   355.2346
Iteration 1:   log likelihood =  365.64589
 (output omitted )
Iteration 10:  log likelihood =  373.23397

ARCH family regression

Sample:  1960q2 to 1990q4                      Number of obs     =        123
                                               Wald chi2(.)      =          .
Log likelihood =    373.234                    Prob > chi2       =          .
```

D.ln_wpi	Coef.	OPG Std. Err.	z	P>|z|	[95% Conf. Interval]	
ln_wpi						
_cons	.0061167	.0010616	5.76	0.000	.0040361	.0081974
ARCH						
arch						
L1	.4364123	.2437428	1.79	0.073	−.0413147	.9141394
garch						
L1	.4544606	.1866605	2.43	0.015	.0886126	.8203085
_cons	.0000269	.0000122	2.20	0.028	2.97e-06	.0000508

We have estimated the ARCH(1) parameter to be .436 and the GARCH(1) parameter to be .454, so our estimated GARCH(1, 1) model is

$$y_t = .0061 + \epsilon_t$$
$$\sigma_t^2 = .436\,\epsilon_{t-1}^2 + .454\,\sigma_{t-1}^2$$

where $y_t = \ln(\mathtt{wpi}_t) - \ln(\mathtt{wpi}_{t-1})$.

Note that the model Wald test and probability are both reported as missing (.). By convention Stata reports the model test for the mean equation. In this case, and fairly often for ARCH models, the mean equation consists only of a constant and there is nothing to test.   ◁

▷ Example

We can retain the GARCH(1, 1) specification for the conditional variance and model the means as an AR(1) and MA(1) process with an additional seasonal MA term at lag 4 by typing

```
. arch D.ln_wpi, ar(1) ma(1 4) arch(1) garch(1)

(setting optimization to BHHH)
Iteration 0:   log likelihood =  380.99952
Iteration 1:   log likelihood =  388.57801
Iteration 2:   log likelihood =  391.34179
Iteration 3:   log likelihood =  396.37029
Iteration 4:   log likelihood =  398.01112
(switching optimization to BFGS)
Iteration 5:   log likelihood =  398.23657
BFGS stepping has contracted, resetting BFGS Hessian (0)
Iteration 6:   log likelihood =  399.21491
Iteration 7:   log likelihood =  399.21531  (backed up)
 (output omitted )
Iteration 12:  log likelihood =   399.4934  (backed up)
Iteration 13:  log likelihood =  399.49607
Iteration 14:  log likelihood =  399.51241
(switching optimization to BHHH)
```

```
Iteration 15:  log likelihood =  399.51441
Iteration 16:  log likelihood =  399.51443

ARCH family regression -- ARMA disturbances

Sample:  1960q2 to 1990q4                    Number of obs    =      123
                                             Wald chi2(3)     =   153.60
Log likelihood =  399.5144                   Prob > chi2      =   0.0000
```

D.ln_wpi		Coef.	OPG Std. Err.	z	P>|z|	[95% Conf. Interval]	
ln_wpi							
_cons		.0069556	.0039511	1.76	0.078	-.0007884	.0146996
ARMA							
ar							
	L1	.7922546	.1072028	7.39	0.000	.5821409	1.002368
ma							
	L1	-.3417593	.1499399	-2.28	0.023	-.6356361	-.0478824
	L4	.2452439	.1251166	1.96	0.050	.00002	.4904679
ARCH							
arch							
	L1	.2037791	.1243096	1.64	0.101	-.0398632	.4474214
garch							
	L1	.6953231	.1890604	3.68	0.000	.3247715	1.065875
_cons		.0000119	.0000104	1.14	0.253	-8.51e-06	.0000324

To clarify exactly what we have estimated, we could write our model

$$y_t = .007 + .792\,(y_{t-1} - .007) - .342\,\epsilon_{t-1} + .245\,\epsilon_{t-4} + \epsilon_t$$
$$\sigma_t^2 = .204\,\epsilon_{t-1}^2 + .695\,\sigma_{t-1}^2$$

where $y_t = \ln(\mathtt{wpi}_t) - \ln(\mathtt{wpi}_{t-1})$.

The ARCH(1) coefficient, .204, is not significantly different from zero, but it is clear that collectively the ARCH(1) and GARCH(1) coefficients are significant. If there is any doubt, you can check the conjecture with **test**.

```
. test [ARCH]L1.arch [ARCH]L1.garch

 ( 1)  [ARCH]L.arch = 0.0
 ( 2)  [ARCH]L.garch = 0.0

        chi2(  2) =     85.10
      Prob > chi2 =     0.0000
```

(Note that for comparison we estimated the model over the same sample used in the example in [R] **arima**; Enders estimates this GARCH model, but over a slightly different sample.)

◁

❏ Technical Note

The rather ugly iteration log on the prior result is not atypical. Difficulty in converging is common in ARCH models. This is actually a fairly well behaved likelihood for an ARCH model. The "switching optimization to ..." messages are standard messages from the default optimization method for **arch**. The "backed up" messages are typical of BFGS stepping as the BFGS Hessian is often over-optimistic, particularly during early iterations. These are nothing to be concerned about.

Nevertheless, watch out for the messages "BFGS stepping has contracted, resetting BFGS Hessian" and "backed up". Both can flag problems. Problems, if they arise, will result in an iteration log that goes on and on; Stata will never report convergence and so will never report final results. The question is: when do you give up and press *Break* and, if you do, what do you do then?

The "BFGS stepping has contracted" message, if it occurs repeatedly (more than, say, five times), often indicates that convergence will never be achieved. Literally it means that the BFGS algorithm was stuck and needed to reset its Hessian and take a steepest descent step.

The "backed up" message, if it occurs repeatedly, also indicates problems, but only if the likelihood value is simultaneously not changing. If the message occurs repeatedly but the likelihood value is changing, as it did above, all is going well: it is just going slowly.

If you have convergence problems, you can specify options attempting to assist the current maximization method or try a different method. Or, it simply might be that your model specification and your data lead to a likelihood that is nonconvex in the allowable region and thus cannot be maximized.

Concerning the "backed up" message with no change in the likelihood: You can try resetting the gradient tolerance to a larger value. Specifying option `gtolerance(999)` will disable gradient checking, allowing convergence to be declared more easily. This does not guarantee that convergence will be declared and, even if convergence is declared, it is unclear whether the global maximum likelihood has been found.

You can also try to specify initial values.

Finally, see *Options for controlling maximization*. You can try a different maximization method.

Realize that the ARCH family of models are notorious for convergence difficulties. Unlike most estimators in Stata, it is not uncommon for convergence to require many, many steps or even to fail. This is particularly true of the explicitly nonlinear terms such as `aarch()`, `narch()`, `aparch()`, or `archm` (ARCH-in-mean) and any model with several lags in the ARCH terms. There is not always a solution. Alternate maximization methods or possibly different starting values can be tried, but if your data do not support your assumed ARCH structure, convergence simply may not be possible.

ARCH models can be susceptible to irrelevant regressors or unnecessary lags, whether in the specification of the conditional mean or in the conditional variance. In these situations, `arch` will often continue to iterate, making little to no improvement in the likelihood. We view this conservative approach as better than declaring convergence prematurely when the likelihood has not been fully maximized. `arch` is estimating the conditional form of second sample moments, often with flexible functions, and that is asking much of the data.

❑

❑ Technical Note

if *exp* and *in* *range* have a somewhat different interpretation with commands accepting time-series operators. The time-series operators are resolved *before* the conditions are tested. We believe this is what one would expect when typing a command, but it may lead to some confusion. Note the results of the following `list` commands:

```
. list t y l.y in 5/10

              t          y        L.y
   5.      1961q1      30.8       30.7
   6.      1961q2      30.5       30.8
   7.      1961q3      30.5       30.5
   8.      1961q4      30.6       30.5
   9.      1962q1      30.7       30.6
  10.      1962q2      30.6       30.7
```

```
. keep in 5/10
(124 observations deleted)

. list t y l.y
             t          y        L.y
   1.     1961q1      30.8         .
   2.     1961q2      30.5       30.8
   3.     1961q3      30.5       30.5
   4.     1961q4      30.6       30.5
   5.     1962q1      30.7       30.6
   6.     1962q2      30.6       30.7
```

We have one additional lagged observation for y in the first case. l.y was resolved before the in restriction was applied. In the second case, the dataset no longer contains the value of y to compute the first lag. This means that

```
. arch y l.x, arch(1), if twithin(1930, 1990)
```

is not the same as

```
. keep if twithin(1930, 1990)

. arch y l.x, arch(1)
```

❑

▷ Example

Continuing with the WPI data, we might be concerned that the economy as a whole responds differently to unanticipated increases in wholesale prices than it does to unanticipated decreases. Perhaps unanticipated increases lead to cash flow issues that affect inventories and lead to more volatility. We can see if the data supports this supposition by specifying an ARCH model that allows an asymmetric effect of "news"—innovations or unanticipated changes. One of the most popular such models is EGARCH (Nelson 1991). The full first-order EGARCH model for the WPI can be specified as

```
. arch D.ln_wpi, ar(1) ma(1 4) earch(1) egarch(1)
(setting optimization to BHHH)
Iteration 0:   log likelihood =    227.5251
Iteration 1:   log likelihood =   381.69189
 (output omitted )
Iteration 21:  log likelihood =   405.31453

ARCH family regression -- ARMA disturbances
Sample:  1960q2 to 1990q4              Number of obs    =        123
                                      Wald chi2(3)     =     156.04
Log likelihood =  405.3145            Prob > chi2      =     0.0000
```

D.ln_wpi		Coef.	OPG Std. Err.	z	P>|z|	[95% Conf. Interval]	
ln_wpi _cons		.0087343	.0034006	2.57	0.010	.0020692	.0153994
ARMA ar							
	L1	.7692304	.0968317	7.94	0.000	.5794438	.9590169
ma							
	L1	-.3554775	.1265674	-2.81	0.005	-.603545	-.10741
	L4	.241473	.086382	2.80	0.005	.0721674	.4107787
ARCH earch							
	L1	.4064035	.1163528	3.49	0.000	.1783561	.6344509
earch_a							
	L1	.2467611	.1233453	2.00	0.045	.0050088	.4885134
egarch							
	L1	.8417318	.0704089	11.95	0.000	.7037329	.9797307
_cons		-1.488376	.6604486	-2.25	0.024	-2.782831	-.1939203

Our result for the variance is

$$\ln(\sigma_t^2) = -1.49 + .406\, z_{t-1} + .247 \left| z_{t-1} - \sqrt{2/\pi} \right| + .842 \ln(\sigma_{t-1}^2)$$

where $z_t = \epsilon_t/\sigma_t$, which is distributed as $N(0,1)$.

We have a strong indication for a leverage effect. The positive L1.earch coefficient implies that positive innovations (unanticipated price increases) are more destabilizing than negative innovations. The effect appears quite strong (.406) and is substantially larger than the symmetric effect (.247). In fact, the relative scales of the two coefficients imply that the positive leverage completely dominates the symmetric effect.

This can readily be seen if we plot what is often referred to as the news response or news impact function. This curve just shows the resulting conditional variance as a function of unanticipated news, in the form of innovations. That is, it is the conditional variance σ_t^2 as a function of ϵ_t. Thus, we need to evaluate σ_t^2 for various values of ϵ_t—say -4 to 4—and then graph the result.

predict, at() will calculate σ_t^2 given a set of specified innovations $(\epsilon_t, \epsilon_{t-1}, \ldots)$ and prior conditional variances $(\sigma_{t-1}^2, \sigma_{t-2}^2, \ldots)$. The syntax is

. predict *newvar*, variance at(*epsilon sigma2*)

epsilon and *sigma2* are either variables or numbers. The use of *sigma2* is a little tricky because you specify values of σ_t^2, and σ_t^2 is what predict is supposed to predict. *predict* does not simply copy variable *sigma2* into *newvar*. Rather, it uses the lagged values contained in *sigma2* to produce the currently predicted value of σ_t^2, it does this for all t, and those results are stored in *newvar*. (If you are interested in dynamic predictions of σ_t^2, see *Options for predict*.)

We will generate predictions for σ_t^2 assuming the lagged values of σ_t^2 are 1, and we will vary ϵ_t from -4 to 4. First we will create variable et containing ϵ_t, and then we will create and graph the predictions:

. gen et = (_n-64)/15

. predict sigma2, variance at(et 1)

. graph sigma2 et in 2/1, s(.) c(1) title(News response function) xlab ylab

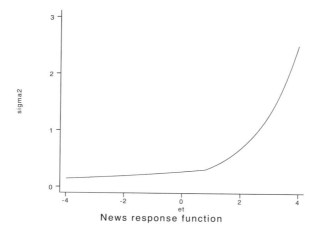

News response function

The positive asymmetry does indeed dominate the shape of the news response function. In fact, the response is a monotonically increasing function of news. The form of the response function shows that, for our simple model, only positive unanticipated price increases have the destabilizing effect which we observe as larger conditional variances.

◁

▷ Example

As an example of a frequently sampled, long-run series, consider the daily closing indices of the Dow Jones Industrial Average, variable `dowclose`. Only data after 1jan1953 is used to avoid the first half of the century when the New York Stock Exchange was open for Saturday trading. The compound return of the series is used as the dependent variable and is graphed below.

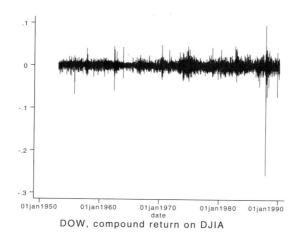

DOW, compound return on DJIA

We should probably examine how we formed this difference, because it is somewhat different from most time series.

We formed this difference by referring to `D.ln_dow`, but only after playing a trick. The series is daily and each observation represents the Dow closing index for the day. Our data included a time variable recorded as a daily date. We wanted, however, to model the log differences in the series and we wanted the span from Friday to Monday to appear as a single-period difference. That is, the day before Monday is Friday. As our dataset was `tsset` with `date`, the span from Friday to Monday was 3 days. The solution was to create a second variable that sequentially numbered the observations. By `tsset`ing the data with this new variable, we obtained the desired differences.

```
. gen t = _n
. tsset t
```

Now, our data look like

```
. gen dayofwk = dow(date)
. list date dayofwk t ln_dow D.ln_dow in 1/8
             date    dayofwk          t      ln_dow    D.ln_dow
    1.  02jan1953          5          1    5.677096           .
    2.  05jan1953          1          2    5.682899    .0058026
    3.  06jan1953          2          3    5.677439   -.0054603
    4.  07jan1953          3          4    5.672636   -.0048032
    5.  08jan1953          4          5    5.671259   -.0013762
    6.  09jan1953          5          6    5.661223   -.0100365
    7.  12jan1953          1          7    5.653191   -.0080323
    8.  13jan1953          2          8    5.659134    .0059433
. list date dayofwk t ln_dow D.ln_dow in -8/1
             date    dayofwk          t      ln_dow    D.ln_dow
 9334.  08feb1990          4       9334    7.880188    .0016198
 9335.  09feb1990          5       9335    7.881635    .0014472
 9336.  12feb1990          1       9336    7.870601    -.011034
 9337.  13feb1990          2       9337    7.872665    .0020638
 9338.  14feb1990          3       9338    7.872577   -.0000877
 9339.  15feb1990          4       9339     7.88213     .009553
 9340.  16feb1990          5       9340    7.876863   -.0052676
 9341.  20feb1990          2       9341    7.862054   -.0148082
```

We can see that the difference operator D spans weekends because the currently specified time variable t is not a true date and has a difference of 1 for all observations. We must leave this contrived time variable in place during estimation, or `arch` will be convinced that our dataset has gaps. If we were using calendar dates, we would indeed have gaps.

Ding, Granger, and Engle (1993) estimated an A-PARCH model of daily returns of the Standard and Poor's 500 (S&P 500) 3jan1928 through 30aug1991. We will estimate the same model for the Dow data shown above. The model includes an AR(1) term as well as the A-PARCH specification of conditional variance.

```
. arch D.ln_dow, ar(1) aparch(1) pgarch(1)
(setting optimization to BHHH)
Iteration 0:   log likelihood =  31138.767
Iteration 1:   log likelihood =  31350.761
Iteration 2:   log likelihood =  31351.092   (backed up)
Iteration 3:   log likelihood =  31351.414   (backed up)
Iteration 4:   log likelihood =  31351.729   (backed up)
(switching optimization to BFGS)
Iteration 5:   log likelihood =  31352.038   (backed up)
Iteration 6:   log likelihood =  31368.841
  (output omitted )
Iteration 56:  log likelihood =  32273.555   (backed up)
Iteration 57:  log likelihood =  32273.555   (backed up)
BFGS stepping has contracted, resetting BFGS Hessian (5)
Iteration 58:  log likelihood =  32273.555
```

```
ARCH family regression -- AR disturbances
Sample:  2 to 9341                          Number of obs    =      9340
                                            Wald chi2(1)     =    175.46
Log likelihood =  32273.56                  Prob > chi2      =    0.0000
```

D.ln_dow		Coef.	OPG Std. Err.	z	P>|z|	[95% Conf. Interval]	
ln_dow _cons		.0001786	.0000875	2.04	0.041	7.15e-06	.00035
ARMA ar	L1	.1410944	.0106519	13.25	0.000	.1202171	.1619717
ARCH aparch	L1	.0626331	.0034308	18.26	0.000	.0559089	.0693572
aparch_e	L1	-.3645082	.0378483	-9.63	0.000	-.4386896	-.2903268
pgarch	L1	.9299009	.0030998	299.98	0.000	.9238254	.9359765
_cons		7.19e-06	2.53e-06	2.84	0.004	2.23e-06	.0000121
POWER power		1.585176	.0629186	25.19	0.000	1.461858	1.708494

Turning first to the iteration log, we note that the final iteration reports the message "backed up". Ending on a "backed up" message for most estimators would be a cause for great concern, but not with `arch` or, for that matter, `arima`, as long as you do not specify option `gtolerance()`. That is because `arch` and `arima`, by default, monitor the gradient and declare convergence only if, in addition to everything else, the gradient is sufficiently small.

The estimated model demonstrates substantial asymmetry with the large negative `L1.aparch_e` coefficient indicating that the market responds with much more volatility to unexpected drops in returns, "bad news", than it does to increases in returns, "good news".

◁

▷ Example

Engle's (1982) original model that sparked the interest in ARCH provides an example requiring constraints. Most current ARCH specifications make use of GARCH terms to provide flexible dynamic properties without estimating an excessive number of parameters. The original model was limited to ARCH terms and to help cope with the collinearity of the terms, a declining lag structure was imposed in the parameters. The conditional variance equation was specified as

$$\sigma_t^2 = \alpha_0 + \alpha(.4\,\epsilon_{t-1} + .3\,\epsilon_{t-2} + .2\,\epsilon_{t-3} + .1\,\epsilon_{t-4})$$
$$= \alpha_0 + .4\,\alpha\epsilon_{t-1} + .3\,\alpha\epsilon_{t-2} + .2\,\alpha\epsilon_{t-3} + .1\,\alpha\epsilon_{t-4}$$

From the earlier `arch` output we know how the coefficients will be named. In Stataese, the formula is

$$\sigma_t^2 = [\text{ARCH}]\_\text{cons} + .4\,[\text{ARCH}]\text{L1.arch}\,\epsilon_{t-1} + .3\,[\text{ARCH}]\text{L2.arch}\,\epsilon_{t-2}$$
$$+ .2\,[\text{ARCH}]\text{L3.arch}\,\epsilon_{t-3} + .1\,[\text{ARCH}]\text{L4.arch}\,\epsilon_{t-3}$$

We could specify these linear constraints any number of ways, but the following seems fairly intuitive; see [R] **constraint** for syntax.

```
. constraint define 1 (3/4)*[ARCH]l1.arch = [ARCH]l2.arch
. constraint define 2 (2/4)*[ARCH]l1.arch = [ARCH]l3.arch
. constraint define 3 (1/4)*[ARCH]l1.arch = [ARCH]l4.arch
```

The original model was estimated on UK inflation; we will again use the WPI data and retain our earlier specification of the mean equation, which differs from Engle's UK inflation model. With our constraints, we type

```
. arch D.ln_wpi, ar(1) ma(1 4) arch(1/4) constraint(1/3)

(setting optimization to BHHH)
Iteration 0:   log likelihood =  396.80192
Iteration 1:   log likelihood =  399.07808
  (output omitted )
Iteration 9:   log likelihood =  399.46243

ARCH family regression -- ARMA disturbances

Sample: 1960q2 to 1990q4                      Number of obs    =       123
                                              Wald chi2(3)     =    123.32
Log likelihood =  399.4624                    Prob > chi2      =    0.0000

Constraints:
 ( 1)   .75 [ARCH]L.arch - [ARCH]L2.arch = 0.0
 ( 2)   .5 [ARCH]L.arch - [ARCH]L3.arch = 0.0
 ( 3)   .25 [ARCH]L.arch - [ARCH]L4.arch = 0.0
```

		OPG					
		Coef.	Std. Err.	z	P>|z|	[95% Conf. Interval]	
ln_wpi							
_cons		.0077204	.0034531	2.24	0.025	.0009525	.0144883
ARMA							
ar							
	L1	.7388168	.1126811	6.56	0.000	.517966	.9596676
ma							
	L1	-.2559691	.1442861	-1.77	0.076	-.5387646	.0268264
	L4	.2528922	.1140185	2.22	0.027	.02942	.4763644
ARCH							
arch							
	L1	.2180138	.0737787	2.95	0.003	.0734101	.3626174
	L2	.1635103	.055334	2.95	0.003	.0550576	.2719631
	L3	.1090069	.0368894	2.95	0.003	.0367051	.1813087
	L4	.0545034	.0184447	2.95	0.003	.0183525	.0906544
_cons		.0000483	7.66e-06	6.30	0.000	.0000333	.0000633

L1.arch, L2.arch, L3.arch, and L4.arch coefficients have the constrained relative sizes. We can also recover the α parameter from the original specification by using lincom.

```
. lincom [ARCH]l1.arch/.4

 ( 1)   2.5 [ARCH]L.arch = 0.0
```

D.ln_wpi	Coef.	Std. Err.	z	P>|z|	[95% Conf. Interval]	
(1)	.5450344	.1844468	2.95	0.003	.1835253	.9065436

Any of the `arch` parameters could be used to produce an identical estimate.

◁

Saved Results

`arch` saves in `e()`:

Scalars

`e(N)`	number of observations	`e(ic)`	number of iterations
`e(k)`	number of variables	`e(rank)`	rank of `e(V)`
`e(k_eq)`	number of equations	`e(power)`	φ for power arch terms
`e(k_dv)`	number of dependent variables	`e(tmin)`	minimum time
`e(df_m)`	model degrees of freedom	`e(tmax)`	maximum time
`e(ll)`	log likelihood	`e(N_gaps)`	number of gaps
`e(rc)`	return code	`e(archi)`	$\sigma_0^2 = \epsilon_0^2$, priming values
`e(chi2)`	χ^2	`e(condobs)`	# of conditioning observations
`e(p)`	significance		

Macros

`e(cmd)`	arch	`e(archm)`	ARCH-in-mean lags
`e(depvar)`	name of dependent variable	`e(archmexp)`	ARCH-in-mean exp
`e(title)`	title in estimation output	`e(mhet)`	1 if multiplicative heteroskedasticity
`e(title2)`	secondary title in estimation output	`e(earch)`	lags for EARCH terms
`e(eqnames)`	names of equations	`e(egarch)`	lags for EGARCH terms
`e(wtype)`	weight type	`e(aarch)`	lags for AARCH terms
`e(wexp)`	weight expression	`e(narch)`	lags for NARCH terms
`e(vcetype)`	covariance estimation method	`e(aparch)`	lags for APARCH terms
`e(user)`	name of likelihood-evaluator program	`e(nparch)`	lags for NPARCH terms
`e(opt)`	type of optimization	`e(saarch)`	lags for SAARCH terms
`e(chi2type)`	Wald; type of model χ^2 test	`e(parch)`	lags for PAARCH terms
`e(tech)`	maximization technique	`e(tparch)`	lags for TPARCH terms
`e(ma)`	lags for moving average terms	`e(abarch)`	lags for ABARCH terms
`e(ar)`	lags for autoregressive terms	`e(tarch)`	lags for TARCH terms
`e(tmins)`	formatted minimum time	`e(sdgarch)`	lags for SDGARCH terms
`e(tmaxs)`	formatted maximum time	`e(pgarch)`	lags for PGARCH terms
`e(predict)`	program used to implement `predict`	`e(garch)`	lags for GARCH terms
`e(cnslist)`	constraint numbers	`e(arch)`	lags for ARCH terms
`e(cond)`	flag if called by `arima`		

Matrices

`e(b)`	coefficient vector	`e(V)`	variance–covariance matrix of
`e(ilog)`	iteration log (up to 20 iterations)		the estimators

Functions

`e(sample)`	marks estimation sample

Methods and Formulas

`arch` is implemented as an ado-file using the `ml` commands; see [R] **ml**. The robust variance computation is performed by `_robust`; see [P] **_robust**.

The mean equation for the model estimated by `arch` and with ARMA terms can be written as

$$y_t = \mathbf{x_t}\boldsymbol{\beta} + \sum_{i=1}^{p} \psi_i g(\sigma^2_{t-i}) + \sum_{j=1}^{p} \rho_j \left\{ y_{t-j} - x_{t-j}\boldsymbol{\beta} - \sum_{i=1}^{p} \psi_i g(\sigma^2_{t-j-i}) \right\}$$

$$+ \sum_{k=1}^{q} \theta_k \epsilon_{t-k} + \epsilon_t \qquad\qquad \text{(conditional mean)}$$

where

$\boldsymbol{\beta}$ are the regression parameters

ψ are the ARCH-in-mean parameters

ρ are the autoregression parameters

$\boldsymbol{\theta}$ are the moving average parameters

$g()$ is a general function, see option `archmexp()`

Any or all of the parameters in this full specification of the conditional mean may be zero. For example, the model need not have moving average parameters ($\boldsymbol{\theta} = 0$), or ARCH-in-mean parameters ($\psi = 0$).

The variance equation will be one of the following:

$$\sigma^2 = \gamma_0 + A(\boldsymbol{\sigma}, \boldsymbol{\epsilon}) + B(\boldsymbol{\sigma}, \boldsymbol{\epsilon})^2 \tag{1}$$

$$\ln \sigma_t^2 = \gamma_0 + C(\ln \boldsymbol{\sigma}, \mathbf{z}) + A(\boldsymbol{\sigma}, \boldsymbol{\epsilon}) + B(\boldsymbol{\sigma}, \boldsymbol{\epsilon})^2 \tag{2}$$

$$\sigma_t^{\varphi} = \gamma_0 + D(\boldsymbol{\sigma}, \boldsymbol{\epsilon}) + A(\boldsymbol{\sigma}, \boldsymbol{\epsilon}) + B(\boldsymbol{\sigma}, \boldsymbol{\epsilon})^2 \tag{3}$$

where $A(\boldsymbol{\sigma}, \boldsymbol{\epsilon})$, $B(\boldsymbol{\sigma}, \boldsymbol{\epsilon})$, $C(\ln \boldsymbol{\sigma}, \mathbf{z})$, and $D(\boldsymbol{\sigma}, \boldsymbol{\epsilon})$ are just linear sums of the appropriate ARCH terms; see *Details of syntax*. Equation (1) is used if no EGARCH or power ARCH terms are included in the model, equation (2) if EGARCH terms are included, and equation (3) if any power ARCH terms are included; again, see *Details of syntax*.

Priming values

The above model is recursive with potentially long memory. It is necessary to assume pre-estimation sample values for ϵ_t, ϵ_t^2, and σ_t^2 to begin the recursions and the remaining computations are therefore conditioned on these priming values. These priming values can be controlled using the `arch0()` and `arma0()` options and most of the computations used to compute these priming values are presented in *Options affecting conditioning (priming) values*.

The `arch0(xb0wt)` and `arch0(xbwt)` options compute a weighted sum of estimated disturbances with more weight on the early observations. With either of these options

$$\sigma^2_{t_0-i} = \epsilon^2_{t_0-i} = (1 - .7) \sum_{t=0}^{T-1} .7^{T-t-1} \epsilon^2_{T-t} \qquad \forall i$$

where t_0 is the first observation for which the likelihood is computed; see *Options affecting conditioning (priming) values*. The ϵ_t^2 are all computed from the conditional mean equation. If `arch0(xb0wt)` is specified, β, ψ_i, ρ_j, and θ_k are taken from initial regression estimates and held constant during optimization. If `arch0(xbwt)` is specified, the current estimates of β, ψ_i, ρ_j, and θ_k are used to compute ϵ_t^2 on every iteration. Note that if any ψ_i is in the mean equation (ARCH-in-mean is specified), the estimates of ϵ_t^2 from the initial regression estimates are not consistent.

Likelihood from prediction error decomposition

The likelihood function for ARCH has a particularly simple form. Given priming (or conditioning) values of ϵ_t, ϵ_t^2, and σ_t^2, the mean equation above can be solved recursively for every ϵ_t (prediction error decomposition). Likewise, the conditional variance can be computed recursively for each observation by using the variance equation. Using these predicted errors, their associated variances, and the assumption that $\epsilon_t \sim N(0, \sigma_t^2)$, the log likelihood for each observation t is

$$\ln L_t = -\frac{1}{2} w_t \left\{ \ln(2\pi\sigma_t^2) + \sum_{t=t_0}^{T} \frac{\epsilon_t^2}{\sigma_t^2} \right\}$$

where $w_t = 1$ if weights are not specified.

Missing data

ARCH will allow missing data or missing observations, but makes no attempt to condition on the surrounding data. If a dynamic component cannot be computed—ϵ_t, ϵ_t^2, and/or σ_t^2—its priming value is substituted. If a covariate, the dependent variable, or entire observation is missing, the observation does not enter the likelihood and its dynamic components are set to their priming values for that observation. This is only acceptable asymptotically and should not be used with large amounts of missing data.

References

Baum, C. F. 2000. sts15: Tests for stationarity of a time series. *Stata Technical Bulletin* 57: 36–39.

Baum, C. F. and V. Wiggins. 2000. sts16: Tests for long memory in a time series. *Stata Technical Bulletin* 57: 39–44.

Berndt, E. K., B. H. Hall, R. E. Hall, and J. A. Hausman. 1974. Estimation and inference in nonlinear structural models. *Annals of Economic and Social Measurement* 3/4: 653–665.

Black, F. 1976. Studies of stock price volatility changes. *Proceedings from the American Statistical Association, Business and Economics Statistics*, 653–665.

Bollerslev, T. 1986. Generalized autoregressive conditional heteroskedasticity. *Journal of Econometrics* 31: 307–327.

Bollerslev, T., R. Y. Chou, and K. F. Kroner. 1992. ARCH modeling in finance. *Journal of Econometrics* 52: 5–59.

Bollerslev, T., R. F. Engle, and D. B. Nelson. 1994. ARCH models. In *Handbook of Econometrics, Volume IV*, ed. R. F. Engle and D. L. McFadden. New York: Elsevier.

Bollerslev, T. and J. M. Wooldridge. 1992. Quasi maximum likelihood estimation and inference in dynamic models with time varying covariances. *Econometric Reviews* 11: 143–172.

Davidson, R. and J. G. MacKinnon. 1993. *Estimation and Inference in Econometrics*. Oxford: Oxford University Press.

Ding, Z., C. W. J. Granger, and R. F. Engle. 1993. A long memory property of stock market returns and a new model. *Journal of Empirical Finance* 1: 83–106.

Enders, W. 1995. *Applied Econometric Time Series*. New York: John Wiley & Sons.

Engle, R. F. 1982. Autoregressive conditional heteroskedasticity with estimates of the variance of U.K. inflation. *Econometrica* 50: 987–1008.

———. 1990. Discussion: Stock market volatility and the crash of 87. *Review of financial studies* 3: 103–106.

Engle, R. F., D. M. Lilien, and R. P. Robins. 1987. Estimating time varying risk premia in the term structure: the ARCH-M model. *Econometrica* 55: 391–407.

Glosten, L. R., R. Jagannathan, and D. Runkle. 1993. On the relation between the expected value and the volatility of the nominal excess return on stocks. *Journal of Finance* 48: 1779–1801.

Greene, W. H. 2000. *Econometric Analysis*. 4th ed. Upper Saddle River, NJ: Prentice–Hall.

Hamilton, J. D. 1994. *Time Series Analysis*. Princeton: Princeton University Press.

Harvey, A. C. 1989. *Forecasting, structural time series models and the Kalman filter*. Cambridge: Cambridge University Press.

———. 1990. *The Econometric Analysis of Time Series*. 2d ed. Cambridge, MA: MIT Press.

Higgins, M. L. and A. K. Bera. 1992. A class of nonlinear ARCH models. *International Economic Review* 33: 137–158.

Judge, G. G., W. E. Griffiths, R. C. Hill, H. Lütkepohl, and T.-C. Lee. 1985. *The Theory and Practice of Econometrics*. 2d ed. New York: John Wiley & Sons.

Johnston, J. and J. DiNardo. 1997. *Econometric Methods*. 3d ed. New York: McGraw–Hill.

Kmenta, J. 1997. *Elements of Econometrics*. 2d ed. Ann Arbor: University of Michigan Press.

Nelson, D. B. 1991. Conditional heteroskedasticity in asset returns: a new approach. *Econometrica* 59: 347–370.

Press, W. H., S. A. Teukolsky, W. T. Vetterling, and B. P. Flannery. 1992. *Numerical Recipes in C: The Art of Scientific Computing*. 2d ed. Cambridge: Cambridge University Press.

Wooldridge, J. M. 2000. *Introductory Econometrics: A Modern Approach*. Cincinnati, OH: South-Western College Publishing.

Zakoian, J. M. 1990. Threshold heteroskedastic models. Unpublished manuscript. *CREST, INSEE*.

Also See

Complementary:	[R] **adjust**, [R] **lincom**, [R] **mfx**, [R] **predict**, [R] **test**, [R] **testnl**, [R] **tsset**, [R] **vce**, [R] **xi**
Related:	[R] **arima**, [R] **prais**, [R] **regress**
Background:	[U] **14.4.3 Time-series varlists**,
	[U] **16.5 Accessing coefficients and standard errors**,
	[U] **23 Estimation and post-estimation commands**,
	[U] **23.11 Obtaining robust variance estimates**,
	[U] **23.12 Obtaining scores**,
	[U] **27.3 Time-series dates**

Title

> **areg** — Linear regression with a large dummy-variable set

Syntax

> areg *depvar* $[$*indepvars*$]$ $[$*weight*$]$ $[$if *exp*$]$ $[$in *range*$]$, <u>a</u>bsorb(*varname*$_1$)
>
> $[$ <u>l</u>evel(*#*) <u>r</u>obust <u>cl</u>uster(*varname*$_2$) $]$

by ... : may be used with areg; see [R] **by**.

aweights, fweights, and pweights are allowed; see [U] **14.1.6 weight**.

areg shares the features of all estimation commands; see [U] **23 Estimation and post-estimation commands**.

Syntax for predict

> predict $[$*type*$]$ *newvarname* $[$if *exp*$]$ $[$in *range*$]$ $[$, *statistic* $]$

where $y_j = \mathbf{x}_j\mathbf{b} + d_{\text{absorbvar}} + e_j$ and *statistic* is

xb	$\mathbf{x}_j\mathbf{b}$, fitted values (the default)
stdp	standard error of the prediction
<u>d</u>residuals	$d_{\text{absorbvar}} + e_j = y_j - \mathbf{x}_j\mathbf{b}$
* xbd	$\mathbf{x}_j\mathbf{b} + d_{\text{absorbvar}}$
* d	$d_{\text{absorbvar}}$
* <u>r</u>esiduals	residual

Unstarred statistics are available both in and out of sample; type predict ... if e(sample) ... if wanted only for the estimation sample. Starred statistics are calculated only for the estimation sample even when if e(sample) is not specified.

Description

areg estimates a linear regression absorbing one categorical factor; that is, it estimates a fixed-effects model.

Note: See the command xtreg, fe in [R] **xtreg** for an improved version of areg.

Options

absorb(*varname*$_1$) specifies the categorical variable which is to be included in the regression as if it were specified by dummy variables. absorb() is not optional.

level(*#*) specifies the confidence level, in percent, for confidence intervals. The default is level(95) or as set by set level; see [U] **23.5 Specifying the width of confidence intervals**.

robust specifies that the Huber/White/sandwich estimator of variance is to be used in place of the traditional calculation. This alternative variance estimator produces consistent standard errors even if the data are weighted or the residuals are not identically distributed. robust combined with cluster() further allows residuals which are not independent within cluster (although they must be independent between clusters).

If you specify pweights, robust is implied; see [U] **23.11 Obtaining robust variance estimates**.

cluster(*varname₂*) specifies that the observations are independent across groups (clusters) but not necessarily within groups. *varname₂* specifies to which group each observation belongs. cluster() affects the estimated standard errors and variance–covariance matrix of the estimators (VCE), but not the estimated coefficients. cluster() can be used with pweights to produce estimates for unstratified cluster-sampled data, but see [R] **svy estimators** for a command designed especially for survey data.

cluster() implies robust; that is, specifying robust cluster() is equivalent to typing cluster() by itself.

Note: Exercise caution when using the cluster() option with areg. The effective number of degrees of freedom for the robust variance estimator is $n_g - 1$, where n_g is the number of clusters. Thus, the number of levels of the absorb() variable should not exceed the number of clusters.

Options for predict

xb, the default, calculates the prediction of $\mathbf{x}_j\mathbf{b}$, the fitted values, using the average effect of the absorbed variable. Also see xbd below.

stdp calculates the standard error of $\mathbf{x}_j\mathbf{b}$.

dresiduals calculates $y_j - \mathbf{x}_j\mathbf{b}$, which are the residuals plus the effect of the absorbed variable.

xbd calculates $\mathbf{x}_j\mathbf{b} + d_{\text{absorbvar}}$, which are the fitted values including the individual effects of the absorbed variable.

d calculates $d_{\text{absorbvar}}$, the individual coefficients for the absorbed variable.

residuals calculates the residuals; that is, $y_j - (\mathbf{x}_j\mathbf{b} + d_{\text{absorbvar}})$.

Remarks

Suppose you have a regression model that includes among the explanatory variables a large number k of mutually exclusive and exhaustive dummies:

$$\mathbf{y} = \mathbf{X}\boldsymbol{\beta} + \mathbf{d}_1\gamma_1 + \mathbf{d}_2\gamma_2 + \cdots + \mathbf{d}_k\gamma_k + \boldsymbol{\epsilon}$$

For instance, the dummy variables $\mathbf{d}_i$ might indicate countries in the world or states of the United States. One solution would be to estimate the model using regress, but this solution is only possible if k is small enough so that the total number of variables (the number of columns of $\mathbf{X}$ plus the number of $\mathbf{d}_i$'s plus one for $\mathbf{y}$) is sufficiently small—meaning less than matsize (see [R] **matsize**). For problems with more variables than the largest possible value of matsize (40 for Small Stata and 800 for Intercooled Stata), regress will not work. areg provides a way of obtaining estimates of $\boldsymbol{\beta}$—but not the γ_i's—in these cases. The effects of the dummy variables are said to be absorbed.

▷ Example

So that we can compare the results produced by areg with Stata's other regression commands, we will estimate a model where k is small. It should be understood, however, that areg's real use is when k is large.

In our automobile data, we have a variable called rep78 that is coded 1, 2, 3, 4, and 5 where 1 means poor and 5 excellent. Let us assume that we wish to estimate a regression of mpg on weight, gear_ratio, and rep78 (parameterized as a set of dummies). Since rep78 assumes only 5 values, we can estimate this model using regress. We first use tabulate to generate the dummies (see [R] **tabulate** and [U] **28.2 Using indicator variables in estimation**).

```
. tab rep78, gen(r)
```

Repair Record 1978	Freq.	Percent	Cum.
1	2	2.90	2.90
2	8	11.59	14.49
3	30	43.48	57.97
4	18	26.09	84.06
5	11	15.94	100.00
Total	69	100.00	

```
. regress mpg weight gear_ratio r1-r4
```

Source	SS	df	MS
Model	1575.97621	6	262.662702
Residual	764.226686	62	12.3262369
Total	2340.2029	68	34.4147485

Number of obs = 69
F(6, 62) = 21.31
Prob > F = 0.0000
R-squared = 0.6734
Adj R-squared = 0.6418
Root MSE = 3.5109

mpg	Coef.	Std. Err.	t	P>|t|	[95% Conf. Interval]	
weight	-.0051031	.0009206	-5.54	0.000	-.0069433	-.003263
gear_ratio	.901478	1.565552	0.58	0.567	-2.228015	4.030971
r1	-2.036937	2.740728	-0.74	0.460	-7.515574	3.4417
r2	-2.419822	1.764338	-1.37	0.175	-5.946682	1.107039
r3	-2.557432	1.370912	-1.87	0.067	-5.297846	.1829814
r4	-2.788389	1.395259	-2.00	0.050	-5.577472	.0006939
_cons	36.23782	7.01057	5.17	0.000	22.22389	50.25175

To estimate the `areg` equivalent, we type

```
. areg mpg weight gear_ratio, absorb(rep78)
```

Number of obs = 69
F(2, 62) = 41.64
Prob > F = 0.0000
R-squared = 0.6734
Adj R-squared = 0.6418
Root MSE = 3.5109

mpg	Coef.	Std. Err.	t	P>|t|	[95% Conf. Interval]	
weight	-.0051031	.0009206	-5.54	0.000	-.0069433	-.003263
gear_ratio	.901478	1.565552	0.58	0.567	-2.228015	4.030971
_cons	34.05889	7.056383	4.83	0.000	19.95338	48.1644
rep78	F(4,62) =	1.117	0.356		(5 categories)	

Note that both **regress** and **areg** display the same R^2 values, root mean square error, and, for **weight** and **gear_ratio**, the same parameter estimates, standard errors, t statistics, significance levels, and confidence intervals. **areg**, however, does not report the coefficients for **rep78** and, in fact, they are not even calculated. It is this computational trick that makes the problem manageable when k is large. **areg** does report a test that the coefficients associated with **rep78** are jointly zero. In this case, this test has a significance level of 35.6%. This F test for **rep78** is the same as we would obtain after **regress** if we were to specify **test r1 r2 r3 r4** or, equivalently, **testparm r1-r4**; see [R] **test**.

The model F tests reported by **regress** and **areg** also differ. The **regress** command reports a test that all coefficients except that of the constant are equal to zero; thus, the dummies are included in this test. The `areg` output shows a test that all coefficients excluding the dummies and the constant are equal to zero. This is the same test that can be obtained after `regress` by typing `test weight gear_ratio`.

◁

❏ **Technical Note**

The intercept reported by `areg` deserves some explanation because, given k mutually exclusive and exhaustive dummies, it is arbitrary. `areg` identifies the model by choosing the intercept that makes the prediction calculated at the means of the independent variables equal to the mean of the dependent variable: $\overline{y} = \overline{x}\,\widehat{\beta}$.

```
. predict yhat
(option xb assumed; fitted values)

. summarize mpg yhat if rep78~=.
```

Variable	Obs	Mean	Std. Dev.	Min	Max
mpg	69	21.28986	5.866408	12	41
yhat	69	21.28986	4.383224	11.58643	28.07367

We had to include `if rep78~=.` in our `summarize` command because we have missing values in our data. `areg` automatically dropped those missing values (as it should) in forming the estimates, but `predict` with the `xb` option is quite willing to make predictions for cases with missing `rep78` because it does not know that `rep78` is really part of our model.

Note that these predicted values do not include the absorbed effects (i.e., the $d_i\gamma_i$). For predicted values that include these effects, you could use the `xbd` option of `predict` or see [R] **xtreg**.

❏

▷ **Example**

`areg, robust` is a Huberized version of `areg`; see [P] **_robust**. Just as `areg` is equivalent to using `regress` with dummies, `areg, robust` is equivalent to using `regress, robust` with dummies. You can use `areg, robust` when you expect heteroskedastic or nonnormal errors. `areg, robust`, like ordinary regression, does assume that the observations are independent unless the `cluster()` option is specified. If the `cluster(`*varname₂*`)` option is specified, this independence assumption is relaxed and only the clusters identified by equal values of *varname₂* are assumed to be independent.

Assume we were to collect data by randomly sampling 10,000 doctors (from 1,000 hospitals) and then sampling 10 of each of their patients, yielding a total dataset of 100,000 patients in a cluster sample. If, in some regression, we wished to include effects of the hospitals to which the doctors belonged, we would want to include a dummy variable for each hospital, adding 1,000 variables to our model. `regress` would not be able to estimate such a model, but `areg` could.

```
. areg depvar patient_vars, absorb(hospital) cluster(doctor)
```

◁

Saved Results

areg saves in e():

Scalars
e(N)	number of observations	e(ar2)	adjusted R-squared
e(tss)	total sum of squares	e(F)	F statistic
e(df_m)	model degrees of freedom	e(F_absorb)	F statistic for absorbed effect
e(rss)	residual sum of squares		(only when robust is not specified)
e(df_r)	residual degrees of freedom	e(df_a)	degrees of freedom for absorbed effect
e(r2)	R-squared		

Macros
e(cmd)	areg	e(wexp)	weight expression
e(depvar)	name of dependent variable	e(absvar)	name of absorb variable
e(wtype)	weight type	e(predict)	program used to implement predict

Matrices
e(b)	coefficient vector	e(V)	variance–covariance matrix of the estimators

Functions
e(sample)	marks estimation sample

Methods and Formulas

areg is implemented as an ado-file.

areg begins by recalculating *depvar* and *indepvars* to have mean 0 within the groups specified by absorb(). The overall mean of each variable is then added back in. The adjusted *depvar* is then regressed on the adjusted *indepvars* using regress, yielding the coefficient estimates. The variance–covariance matrix of the coefficients is then adjusted to account for the absorbed variables—this calculation yields the same results (up to numerical round-off error) as if the matrix had been calculated directly by the formulas given in [R] **regress**.

areg works similarly, calling _robust after regress to produce the robust variance estimates; see [P] **_robust**. The model F test uses the robust variance estimates. There is, however, no simple computational means of obtaining a robust test of the absorbed dummies; thus, this test is not displayed when the robust option is specified.

Also See

Complementary:	[R] **lincom**, [R] **mfx**, [R] **predict**, [R] **test**, [R] **testnl**, [R] **vce**, [R] **xi**
Related:	[R] **regress**, [R] **xtreg**, [R] **xtregar**, [P] **_robust**
Background:	[U] **16.5 Accessing coefficients and standard errors**, [U] **23 Estimation and post-estimation commands**, [U] **23.11 Obtaining robust variance estimates**, [U] **28.2 Using indicator variables in estimation**

Title

> **arima** — Autoregressive integrated moving average models

Syntax

Basic syntax for a regression/structural model with ARMA *disturbances*

> arima *depvar* [*varlist*] , ar(*numlist*) ma(*numlist*)

Basic syntax for an ARIMA(*p,d,q*) *model*

> arima *depvar*, arima($\#_p$,$\#_d$,$\#_q$)

Full syntax

> arima *depvar* [*varlist*] [*weight*] [if *exp*] [in *range*] [, ar(*numlist*) ma(*numlist*)
>
> arima($\#_p$,$\#_d$,$\#_q$) noconstant constraints(*numlist*) hessian opg robust
>
> score(*newvarlist* | *stub**) diffuse p0($\#$|*matname*) state0($\#$|*matname*)
>
> condition savespace detail level($\#$)
>
> *maximize_options* from(*initial_values*) gtolerance($\#$)
>
> bhhh dfp bfgs nr bhhhbfgs($\#$,$\#$) bhhhdfp($\#$,$\#$)]

You must tsset your data before using arima; see [R] **tsset**.
depvar and *varlist* may contain time-series operators; see [U] **14.4.3 Time-series varlists**.
iweights are allowed; see [U] **14.1.6 weight**.
arima shares the features of all estimation commands; see [U] **23 Estimation and post-estimation commands**.

Syntax for predict

> predict [*type*] *newvarname* [if *exp*] [in *range*] [, *statistic*
>
> structural dynamic(*time_constant*) t0(*time_constant*)]

where *statistic* is

xb	predicted values for the model—the differenced series; the default
y	fitted values in *y*—the undifferenced series
mse	mean square error of the prediction xb
residuals	residuals or predicted innovations
yresiduals	residuals or predicted innovations in *y*—the undifferenced series

and *time_constant* is a # or a time literal such as d(1jan1995) or q(1995q1), etc.

These statistics are available both in and out of sample; type predict ... if e(sample) ... if wanted only for
the estimation sample.

Description

arima estimates a model of *depvar* on *varlist* where the disturbances are allowed to follow a linear autoregressive moving-average (ARMA) specification. The dependent and independent variables may be differenced or seasonally differenced to any degree. When independent variables are not specified, these models reduce to autoregressive integrated moving average (ARIMA) models in the dependent variable. Missing data are allowed and are handled using the Kalman filter and methods suggested by Harvey (1989 and 1993); see *Methods and Formulas*.

Referring to the full syntax, *depvar* is the variable being modeled and the structural or regression part of the model is specified in *varlist*. The options ar() and ma() are used to specify the lags of autoregressive and moving average terms respectively.

arima allows time-series operators in the dependent variable and independent variable lists and it is often convenient to make extensive use of these operators; see [U] **27.3 Time-series dates** for an extended discussion of time-series operators.

arima typed without arguments redisplays the previous estimates.

Options

Material in the *Remarks* section may be helpful for understanding some of the options.

ar(*numlist*) specifies the autoregressive terms to be included in the model. These are the autoregressive terms of the structural model disturbance. For example, ar(1/3) specifies that lags of 1, 2, and 3 of the structural disturbance are included in the model; ar(1 4) specifies that lags 1 and 4 are included; possibly to account for quarterly effects.

If the model does not contain any regressors, these terms can also be considered autoregressive terms for the dependent variable.

ma(*numlist*) specifies the moving average terms to be included in the model. These are the terms for the lagged innovations—white noise disturbances.

arima($\#_p$,$\#_d$,$\#_q$) is an alternate, shorthand notation for specifying models that are autoregressive in the dependent variable. The dependent variable and any independent variables are differenced $\#_d$ times, 1 through $\#_p$ lags of autocorrelations are included, and 1 through $\#_q$ lags of moving averages are included. For example, the specification

. arima D.y, ar(1/3) ma(1/3)

is equivalent to

. arima y, arima(2,1,3)

The latter is easier to write for "classic" ARIMA models but is not nearly as expressive as the former. If gaps in the AR or MA lags are to be modeled, or if different operators are to be applied to independent variables, the first syntax will generally be required.

noconstant suppresses the constant term (intercept) in the structural model.

constraints(*numlist*) specifies the constraint numbers of the linear constraints to be applied during estimation. The default is to perform unconstrained estimation. Constraints are specified using the constraint command; see [R] **constraint** (also see [R] **reg3** for use of constraint in multiple-equation contexts).

If constraints are placed between structural model parameters and ARMA terms, it is not uncommon for the first few iterations to attempt steps into nonstationary areas. This can be ignored if the final solution is well within the bounds of stationary solutions.

hessian and opg specifies how standard errors are to be calculated. The default is opg unless one of the options bfgs, dfp, or nr is specified, in which case the default is hessian.

hessian specifies that the standard errors and coefficient covariance matrix be estimated from the full Hessian—the matrix of negative second derivatives of the log-likelihood function. These are the estimates produced by most of Stata's maximum likelihood estimators.

opg specifies that the standard errors and coefficient covariance matrix be estimated using the outer product of the coefficient gradients with respect to the observation likelihoods.

hessian and opg provide asymptotically equivalent estimates of the standard errors and covariance matrix and there is no theoretical justification for preferring either estimate.

robust specifies that the Huber/White/sandwich estimator of variance is to be used in place of the traditional calculation; see [U] **23.11 Obtaining robust variance estimates**.

For state-space models in general and ARIMA in particular, the robust or quasi-maximum likelihood estimates (QMLE) of variance are robust to symmetric nonnormality in the disturbances—including, as a special case, heteroskedasticity. The robust variance estimates are not generally robust to functional misspecification of the structural or ARMA components of the model; see Hamilton (1994, 389) for a brief discussion.

score(*newvarlist* | *stub**) creates a new variable for each parameter in the model. Each new variable contains the derivative of the model log-likelihood with respect to the parameter for each observation in the estimation sample: $\partial L_t / \partial \beta_k$, where L_t is the log likelihood for observation t and β_k is the kth parameter in the model.

If score(*newvarlist*) is specified, the *newvarlist* must contain a new variable for each parameter in the model. If score(*stub**) is specified, variables named *stub#* are created for each parameter in the model. The *newvarlist* is filled, or the #'s in *stub#* are created, in the order in which the estimated parameters are reported in the estimation results table.

Unlike scores for most other models, the scores from arima are individual gradients of the log likelihood with respect to the variables, not with respect to $\mathbf{x}_t\beta$. Since the general ARIMA model is inherently nonlinear, especially when it includes MA terms, the scores with respect to $\mathbf{x}_t\beta$ could not be used to reconstruct the gradients for the individual parameters.

diffuse specifies that a diffuse prior (see Harvey 1989 or 1993) be used as a starting point for the Kalman filter recursions. Using diffuse, nonstationary models may be estimated with arima (also see option p0() below; diffuse is equivalent to specifying p0(1e9)).

By default, arima uses the unconditional expected value of the state vector ξ_t (see *Methods and Formulas*) and the mean square error (MSE) of the state vector to initialize the filter. When the process is stationary, this corresponds to the expected value and expected variance of a random draw from the state vector and produces unconditional maximum likelihood estimates of the parameters. This default is not appropriate, however, and the unconditional MSE cannot be computed when the process is not stationary. For a nonstationary process, an alternate starting point must be used for the recursions.

In the absence of nonsample or pre-sample information, diffuse may be specified to start the recursions from a state vector of zero and a state MSE matrix corresponding to an effectively infinite variance on this initial state. This amounts to an uninformative and improper prior that is updated to a proper MSE as data from the sample become available; see Harvey (1989).

Note that nonstationary models may also correspond to models with infinite variance given a particular specification. This and other problems with nonstationary series make convergence difficult and sometimes impossible.

diffuse can also be useful if a model contains one or more long AR or MA lags. Computation of the unconditional MSE of the state vector (see *Methods and Formulas*) requires construction and inversion of a square matrix that is of dimension $\max(p, q + 1)$, where p and q are the maximum AR and MA lags respectively. For a maximum lag of 28, this would require a 784 by 784 matrix. Estimation with `diffuse` does not require this matrix.

For large samples, there is little difference between using the default starting point and the `diffuse` starting point. Unless the series has a very long memory, the initial conditions affect the likelihood of only the first few observations.

p0(#|*matname*) is a rarely specified option that can be used for nonstationary series or when an alternate prior for starting the Kalman recursions is desired (see `diffuse` above for a discussion of the default starting point and *Methods and Formulas* for background).

If *matname* is given, it specifies a matrix to be used as the MSE of the state vector for starting the Kalman filter recursions—$\mathbf{P}_{1|0}$. Alternately, a single number, *#*, may be supplied and the MSE of the initial state vector $\mathbf{P}_{1|0}$ will have this number on its diagonal and all off-diagonal values set to zero.

This option may be used with nonstationary series to specify a larger or smaller diagonal for $\mathbf{P}_{1|0}$ than that supplied by `diffuse`. It may also be used in conjunction with `state0()` when the user believes they have a better prior for the initial state vector and its MSE.

state0(#|*matname*) is a rarely used option that specifies an alternate initial state vector, $\boldsymbol{\xi}_{1|0}$ (see *Methods and Formulas*), for starting the Kalman filter recursions. If *#* is specified, all elements of the vector are taken to be *#*. The default initial state vector is `state0(0)`.

condition specifies that conditional rather than full maximum likelihood estimates be produced. The pre-sample values for ϵ_t and μ_t are taken to be their expected value of zero and the estimate of the variance of ϵ_t is taken to be constant over the entire sample; see Hamilton (1994, 132). This estimation method is not appropriate for nonstationary series, but may be preferable for long series or for models that have one or more long AR or MA lags. `diffuse`, `p0()`, and `state0()` have no meaning for models estimated from the conditional likelihood and may not be specified with `condition`.

If the series is long and stationary and if the underlying data generating process does not have a long memory, then estimates will be similar whether estimated by unconditional maximum likelihood (the default), conditional maximum likelihood (`condition`), or maximum likelihood from a diffuse prior (`diffuse`).

In small samples, however, results of conditional vs. unconditional maximum likelihood may differ substantially; see Ansley and Newbold (1980). Whereas the default unconditional maximum likelihood estimates make the most use of sample information when all the assumptions of the model are met, Harvey (1989) and Ansley and Kohn (1985) argue for diffuse priors in many cases, particularly in ARIMA models corresponding to an underlying structural model.

The `condition` or `diffuse` options may also be preferred when the model contains one or more long AR or MA lags; this avoids inverting potentially large matrices (see `diffuse` above).

When `condition` is specified, estimation is performed by the `arch` command (see [R] **arch**), and more control of the estimation process can be obtained by using `arch` directly.

savespace specifies that memory use be conserved by retaining only those variables required for estimation. The original dataset is restored after estimation. This option is rarely used and should be used only if there is insufficient space to estimate a model without the option. Note, however, that `arima` requires considerably more temporary storage during estimation than most estimation commands in Stata.

detail specifies that a detailed list of any gaps in the series be reported. These include gaps due to missing observations or missing data for the dependent variable or independent variables.

level(#) specifies the confidence level in percent for confidence intervals of the coefficients.

maximize_options control the maximization process; see [R] **maximize**. These options are sometimes more important for ARIMA models than most maximum likelihood models because of potential convergence problems with ARIMA models, particularly if the specified model combined with the sample data imply a nonstationary model.

Several alternate optimization methods such as Berndt–Hall–Hall–Hausman (BHHH) and Boyd–Fletcher–Goldfarb–Shanno (BFGS) are provided for arima models. Whereas arima models are not as difficult to optimize as ARCH models, their likelihoods are generally not quadratic and often pose optimization difficulties; this is particularly true if a model is nonstationary or nearly nonstationary. Since each method attacks the optimization differently, some problems can be successfully optimized by an alternate method when one method fails.

The default optimization method for arima is a hybrid method combining BHHH and BFGS iterations. This hybrid method has been found operationally to provide good convergence properties on difficult likelihoods.

The following options are all related to maximization and are either particularly important in estimating ARIMA models or not available for most other estimators.

from(*initial_values*) allows the starting values of the model coefficients to be set by the user; see [R] **maximize** for a general discussion and syntax options.

The standard syntax for from() accepts a matrix, a list of values, or coefficient name value pairs; see [R] **maximize**. In addition, arima accepts from(armab0) and this specifies that the starting value for all ARMA parameters in the model be set to zero prior to optimization.

ARIMA models may be sensitive to initial conditions and may have coefficient values that correspond to local maxima. The default starting values for arima are generally very good, particularly in large samples for stationary series.

gtolerance(#) is a rarely used maximization option that specifies a threshold for the relative size of the gradient; see [R] **maximize**. The default gradient tolerance for arima is .05.

gtolerance(999) may be specified to effectively disable the gradient criterion when convergence is difficult to achieve. If the optimizer becomes stuck with repeated "(backed up)" messages, it is likely that the gradient still contains substantial values, but an uphill direction cannot be found for the likelihood. Using gtolerance(999), results will often be obtained, but it is unclear whether the global maximum likelihood has been found. It is usually better to set the maximum number of iterations (see [R] **maximize**) to the point where the optimizer appears to be stuck and then inspect the estimation results.

bhhh, dfp, bfgs, nr, bhhhbfgs(), bhhhdfp() specify how the likelihood function is to be maximized. bhhhbfgs(5,10) is the default.

bhhh specifies that the Berndt–Hall–Hall–Hausman (BHHH, Berndt et al. 1974) method be used. While it is difficult to make general statements about convergence properties of nonlinear optimization methods, BHHH tends to do well in areas far from the maximum, but does not have quadratic convergence in areas near the maximum.

dfp specifies that the Davidon–Fletcher–Powell (DFP) method be used; see Press et al. (1992). As currently implemented, dfp requires substantially less temporary storage space than the other methods (with the exception of bfgs) and this may be an advantage for models with many parameters.

bfgs specifies that the Boyd–Fletcher–Goldfarb–Shanno (BFGS) method be used; see Press et al. (1992). BFGS optimization is similar to DFP with second-order terms included when updating the Hessian. bfgs, just as dfp, requires little memory.

nr specifies that Stata's modified Newton–Raphson method be used. Since all derivatives for arima are taken numerically, this method may be very slow for models with many parameters.

bhhhbfgs($\#_1$,$\#_2$) specifies BHHH and BFGS be combined. $\#_1$ designates the number of BHHH steps and $\#_2$ designates the number of BFGS steps. Optimization alternates between these sets of BHHH and BFGS steps until convergence is achieved. The default optimization method is bhhhbfgs(5, 10).

bhhhdfp($\#_1$,$\#_2$) specifies that BHHH and DFP be combined. $\#_1$ designates the number of BHHH steps and $\#_2$ designates the number of DFP steps. The optimization alternates between these sets of BHHH and DFP steps until convergence is achieved.

Options for predict

Five statistics can be computed by using predict after arima: the predictions from the model (the default also given by option xb), the undifferenced predictions (option y), the MSE of xb (option mse), the predictions of residuals or innovations (option residual), and the predicted residuals or innovations in terms of y (option yresiduals). Given the dynamic nature of the ARMA component and that the dependent variable might be differenced, there are alternate ways of computing each. We can use all the data on the dependent variable available right up to the time of each prediction (the default, which is often called a one-step prediction), or we can use the data up to a particular time, after which the predicted value of the dependent variable is used recursively to make subsequent predictions (option dynamic()). Either way, we can consider or ignore the ARMA disturbance component (the component is considered by default and ignored if you specify option structural).

All calculations can be made in or out of sample.

xb (the default) calculates the predictions from the model. If D.*depvar* is the dependent variable, these predictions are of D.*depvar* and not of *depvar* itself.

y specifies that predictions of *depvar* are to be made even if the model was specified in terms of, say, D.*depvar*.

mse calculates the MSE of xb.

residuals calculates the residuals. If no other options are specified, these are the predicted innovations ϵ_t, i.e., they include the ARMA component. If option structural is specified, these are the residuals μ_t from the structural equation; see structural below.

yresiduals calculates the residuals in terms of *depvar*, even if the model was specified in terms of, say, D.*depvar*. As with residuals, the yresiduals are computed from the model including any ARMA component. If option structural is specified, any ARMA component is ignored and yresiduals are the residuals from the structural equation; see structural below.

structural specifies that the calculation is to be made considering the structural component only, ignoring the ARMA terms, thus producing the steady-state equilibrium predictions.

dynamic(*time_constant*) specifies how lags of y_t in the model are to be handled. If dynamic() is not specified, actual values are used everywhere lagged values of y_t appear in the model to produce one-step ahead forecasts.

dynamic(*time_constant*) produces dynamic (also known as recursive) forecasts. *time_constant* specifies when the forecast is to switch from one-step ahead to dynamic. In dynamic forecasts, references to y evaluate to the prediction of y for all periods at or after *time_constant*; they evaluate to the actual value of y for all prior periods.

`dynamic(10)` would calculate predictions where any reference to y_t with $t < 10$ evaluates to the actual value of y_t and any reference to y_t with $t \geq 10$ evaluates to the prediction of y_t. This means that one-step ahead predictions are calculated for $t < 10$ and dynamic predictions thereafter. Depending on the lag structure of the model, the dynamic predictions might still reference some actual values of y_t.

In addition, you may specify `dynamic(.)` to have `predict` automatically switch from one-step to dynamic predictions at $p + q$, where p is the maximum AR lag and q is the maximum MA lag.

`t0`(*time_constant*) specifies the starting point for the recursions to compute the predicted statistics; disturbances are assumed to be 0 for $t < $ `t0()`. The default is to set `t0()` to the minimum t observed in the estimation sample, meaning that observations prior to that are assumed to have disturbances of 0.

`t0()` is irrelevant if `structural` is specified because in that case all observations are assumed to have disturbances of 0.

`t0(5)` would begin recursions at $t = 5$. If you were quarterly, you might instead type `t0(q(1961q2))` to obtain the same result.

Note that the ARMA component of `arima` models is recursive and depends on the starting point of the predictions. This includes one-step ahead predictions.

Remarks

`arima` estimates both standard ARIMA models that are autoregressive in the dependent variable and structural models with ARMA disturbances. Good introductions to the former models can be found in Box, Jenkins, and Reinsel (1994), Hamilton (1994), Harvey (1993), Newton (1988), Diggle (1990), and many others. The latter models are developed fully in Hamilton (1994) and Harvey (1989), both of which provide extensive treatment of the Kalman filter (Kalman 1960) and the state-space form used by `arima` to estimate the models.

Considering a first-order autoregressive AR(1) and a moving average MA(1) process, `arima` estimates all of the parameters in the model

$$y_t = \mathbf{x_t}\beta + \mu_t \qquad\qquad \textit{structural equation}$$
$$\mu_t = \rho\mu_{t-1} + \theta\epsilon_{t-1} + \epsilon_t \qquad\qquad \textit{disturbance, ARMA}(1,1)$$

where

ρ	is the first-order autocorrelation parameter
θ	is the first-order moving average parameter
ϵ_t	$\sim i.i.d.\ N(0, \sigma^2)$; which is to say ϵ_t is taken to be a white-noise disturbance

We can combine the two equations and write a general ARMA(p, q) in the disturbances process as

$$y_t = \mathbf{x_t}\beta + \rho_1(y_{t-1} - \mathbf{x}_{t-1}\beta) + \rho_2(y_{t-2} - \mathbf{x}_{t-2}\beta) + \cdots + \rho_p(y_{t-p} - \mathbf{x}_{t-p}\beta)$$
$$+ \theta_1\epsilon_{t-1} + \theta_2\epsilon_{t-2} + \cdots + \theta_q\epsilon_{t-q} + \epsilon_t$$

It is also common to write the general form of the ARMA model succinctly using lag operator notation

$$\boldsymbol{\rho}(L^p)(y_t - \mathbf{x_t}\beta) = \boldsymbol{\theta}(L^q)\epsilon_t \qquad\qquad \text{ARMA}(p, q)$$

where

$$\boldsymbol{\rho}(L^p) = 1 - \rho_1 L - \rho_2 L^2 - \cdots - \rho_2 L^p$$
$$\boldsymbol{\theta}(L^q) = 1 + \theta_1 L + \theta_2 L^2 + \cdots + \theta_2 L^q$$

For stationary series, full or unconditional maximum likelihood estimates are obtained via the Kalman filter. For nonstationary series, if some prior information is available, initial values for the filter can be specified using state0() and p0() as suggested by Hamilton (1994), or an uninformative prior can be assumed using the option diffuse as suggested by Harvey (1989).

Time-series models without a structural component do not have the $\mathbf{x}_t\beta$ terms and are often written as autoregressions in the dependent variable, rather than autoregressions in the disturbances from a structural equation. Other than a scale factor for the constant, these models are exactly equivalent to the ARMA in the disturbances formulation estimated by arima, but the latter are more flexible and allow a wider class of models.

❑ Technical Note

Proof: Without loss of generality consider a model that is ARMA(1, 1) in the dependent variable

$$y_t = \alpha + \rho y_{t-1} + \theta \epsilon_{t-1} + \epsilon_t \tag{1a}$$

We can combine the structural and disturbance equations of the ARMA(1,1) in the disturbances formulation and replace the structural $\mathbf{x}_t\beta$ with the constant β_0, by writing

$$y_t = \beta_0 + \rho \mu_{t-1} + \theta \epsilon_{t-1} + \epsilon_t \tag{1b}$$

From the simplified structural equation we have $\mu_t = y_t - \beta_0$, so 1b can be rewritten as

$$y_t = \beta_0 + \rho(y_t - \beta_0) + \theta \epsilon_{t-1} + \epsilon_t$$

or,

$$y_t = (1 - \rho)\beta_0 + \rho y_t + \theta \epsilon_{t-1} + \epsilon_t \tag{1c}$$

Equations $(1a)$ and $(1b)$ are equivalent with the constant in $(1b)$ scaled by $(1 - \rho)$. arima estimates models as autoregressive in the disturbances, and we have just seen that these subsume models that are autoregressive in the dependent variable.

❑

▷ Example

Enders (1995, 106–110) considers an ARIMA model of the US Wholesale Price Index (WPI) using quarterly data over the period 1960q1 through 1990q4. The simplest ARIMA model that includes differencing, autoregressive, and moving average components is the ARIMA(1,1,1) specification. We can estimate this model using arima by typing

```
. arima wpi, arima(1,1,1)

(setting optimization to BHHH)
Iteration 0:    log likelihood = -139.80133
Iteration 1:    log likelihood =  -135.6278
Iteration 2:    log likelihood = -135.41838
Iteration 3:    log likelihood = -135.36691
Iteration 4:    log likelihood = -135.35892
(switching optimization to BFGS)
Iteration 5:    log likelihood = -135.35471
Iteration 6:    log likelihood = -135.35135
Iteration 7:    log likelihood = -135.35132
Iteration 8:    log likelihood = -135.35131

ARIMA regression

Sample:  1960q2 to 1990q4                   Number of obs    =        123
                                            Wald chi2(2)     =     310.64
Log likelihood = -135.3513                  Prob > chi2      =     0.0000
```

D.wpi	Coef.	OPG Std. Err.	z	P>|z|	[95% Conf. Interval]	
wpi _cons	.7498197	.3340968	2.24	0.025	.0950019	1.404637
ARMA ar L1	.8742288	.0545435	16.03	0.000	.7673256	.981132
ma L1	-.4120458	.1000284	-4.12	0.000	-.6080979	-.2159938
/sigma	.7250436	.0368065	19.70	0.000	.6529042	.7971829

Examining the estimation results, we see that the AR(1) coefficient is .87 and the MA(1) coefficient is −.41 and both are highly significant. The estimated variance of the white-noise disturbance ϵ is .73.

This model could also have been estimated by typing

```
. arima D.wpi, ar(1) ma(1)
```

The D. placed in front of the dependent variable `wpi` is the Stata time-series operator for differencing. Thus we would be modeling the first difference in WPI from 2nd quarter 1960 through 4th quarter 1990. The advantage of this second syntax is that it allows a richer choice of models. The `arima`($\#_p$, $\#_d$, $\#_q$) option does not provide for seasonal differencing or seasonal AR and MA terms.

◁

▷ Example

After examining first differences of WPI, Enders chose a model of differences in the natural logarithms to stabilize the variance in the differenced series. The raw data and first difference of the logarithms are graphed below.

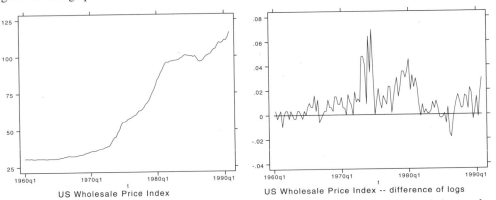

US Wholesale Price Index   US Wholesale Price Index -- difference of logs

On the basis of the autocorrelations, partial autocorrelations (see graphs below) and the results of preliminary estimations, Enders identified an ARMA model in the log-differenced series.

```
. ac D.ln_wpi, needle

. pac D.ln_wpi, needle
```

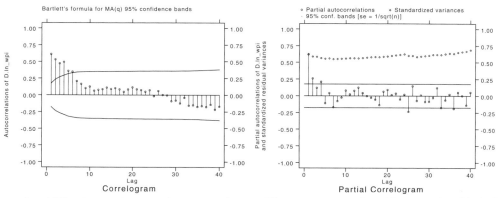

Correlogram   Partial Correlogram

In addition to an autoregressive term and an MA(1) term, a seasonal MA(4) term at lag 4 is included to account for a remaining quarterly effect. Thus, the model to be estimated is

$$\Delta \ln(wpi_t) = \beta_0 + \rho\{\Delta \ln(wpi_{t-1}) - \beta_0\} + \theta_1 \epsilon_{t-1} + \theta_4 \epsilon_{t-4} + \epsilon_t$$

where $\Delta x \equiv x_t - x_{t-1}$ or, using lag operators $\Delta x \equiv (1 - L)x$.

We can estimate this model using **arima** and Stata's standard difference operator:

```
. arima D.ln_wpi, ar(1) ma(1 4)

(setting optimization to BHHH)
Iteration 0:    log likelihood =  382.67447
Iteration 1:    log likelihood =  384.80754
Iteration 2:    log likelihood =  384.84749
Iteration 3:    log likelihood =  385.39213
Iteration 4:    log likelihood =  385.40983
(switching optimization to BFGS)
Iteration 5:    log likelihood =   385.9021
Iteration 6:    log likelihood =  385.95646
Iteration 7:    log likelihood =  386.02979
Iteration 8:    log likelihood =  386.03326
Iteration 9:    log likelihood =  386.03354
Iteration 10:   log likelihood =  386.03357

ARIMA regression

Sample:  1960q2 to 1990q4                  Number of obs    =       123
                                           Wald chi2(3)     =    333.60
Log likelihood =  386.0336                 Prob > chi2      =    0.0000
```

D.ln_wpi	Coef.	OPG Std. Err.	z	P>|z|	[95% Conf. Interval]
ln_wpi					
_cons	.0110493	.0048349	2.29	0.022	.0015731 .0205255
ARMA					
ar					
L1	.7806991	.0944946	8.26	0.000	.5954931 .965905
ma					
L1	-.3990039	.1258753	-3.17	0.002	-.6457149 -.1522928
L4	.3090813	.1200945	2.57	0.010	.0737003 .5444622
/sigma	.0104394	.0004702	22.20	0.000	.0095178 .0113609

In this final specification, the log-differenced series is still highly autocorrelated at a level of .78, while innovations have a negative impact in the ensuing quarter $(-.40)$ and a positive seasonal impact of .31 in the following year.

◁

❑ Technical Note

We also note one item where the results differ from most of Stata's estimation commands—the standard error of the coefficients is reported as OPG Std. Err. As noted in the *Options* section, the default standard errors and covariance matrix for arima estimates are derived from the outer product of gradients (OPG). This is one of three asymptotically equivalent methods of estimating the covariance matrix of the coefficients (only two of which are usually tractable to derive). Discussions and derivations of all three estimates can be found in Davidson and MacKinnon (1993), Greene (2000), and Hamilton (1994). Bollerslev, Engle, and Nelson (1994) suggest that the OPG estimates may be more numerically stable in time series regressions when the likelihood and its derivatives depend on recursive computations, certainly the case for the Kalman filter. To date, we have not found any numerical instabilities in either estimate of the covariance matrix—subject to the stability and convergence of the overall model.

Most of Stata's estimation commands provide covariance estimates derived from the Hessian of the likelihood function. These alternate estimates can also be obtained from arima by specifying the hessian option.

❑

▷ Example

As a simple example of a model including covariates we can estimate an update of Friedman and Meiselman's (1963) equation representing the quantity theory of money. They postulated a straightforward relationship between personal consumption expenditures (consump) and the money supply as measured by M2 (m2).

$$\text{consump}_t = \beta_0 + \beta_1 m2_t + \mu_t$$

Friedman and Meiselman estimated the model over a period ending in 1956; we will re-estimate the model over the period 1959q1 through 1981q4. We restrict our attention to the period prior to 1982 because the Federal Reserve manipulated the money supply extensively in the latter 1980s to control inflation and the relationship between consumption and the money supply becomes much more complex during the latter part of the decade.

Since our purpose is to demonstrate arima we will include both an autoregressive and a moving average term for the disturbances in the model; the original estimates included neither. Thus, we model the disturbance of the structural equation as

$$\mu_t = \rho\mu_{t-1} + \theta\epsilon_{t-1} + \epsilon_t$$

Following the original authors, the relationship is estimated on seasonally adjusted data so there is no need to explicitly include seasonal effects. It might be preferable to obtain seasonally unadjusted data and simultaneously model the structural and seasonal effects.

The estimation will be restricted to the desired sample by using the tin() function in an if expression; see [U] **16.3.4 Time-series functions** and [U] **27.3 Time-series dates**. By leaving the first argument of tin() blank, we are including all available data up to and including the second date (1981q4). We estimate the model by typing

```
. arima consump m2, ar(1) ma(1), if tin( , 1981q4)
```

(output omitted)

```
Iteration 10:  log likelihood = -340.50774
```

ARIMA regression

Sample: 1959q1 to 1981q4

	Number of obs	=	92
	Wald chi2(3)	=	4394.80
Log likelihood = -340.5077	Prob > chi2	=	0.0000

consump	Coef.	OPG Std. Err.	z	P>|z|	[95% Conf. Interval]	
consump						
m2	1.122029	.0363563	30.86	0.000	1.050772	1.193286
_cons	-36.09872	56.56703	-0.64	0.523	-146.9681	74.77062
ARMA						
ar						
L1	.9348486	.0411323	22.73	0.000	.8542308	1.015467
ma						
L1	.3090592	.0885883	3.49	0.000	.1354293	.4826891
/sigma	9.655308	.5635157	17.13	0.000	8.550837	10.75978

We find a relatively small money velocity with respect to consumption (1.122029) over this period, although consumption is only one facet of the income velocity. We also note a very large first-order autocorrelation in the disturbances as well as a statistically significant first-order moving average.

We might be concerned that our specification has led to disturbances that are heteroskedastic or non-Gaussian. We re-estimate the model using the robust option.

```
. arima consump m2, ar(1) ma(1) robust, if tin( , 1981q4)
```

(output omitted)

```
Iteration 10:  log likelihood = -340.50774
```

ARIMA regression

Sample: 1959q1 to 1981q4

	Number of obs	=	92
	Wald chi2(3)	=	1176.26
Log likelihood = -340.5077	Prob > chi2	=	0.0000

consump	Coef.	Semi-robust Std. Err.	z	P>|z|	[95% Conf. Interval]	
consump						
m2	1.122029	.0433302	25.89	0.000	1.037103	1.206954
_cons	-36.09872	28.10478	-1.28	0.199	-91.18307	18.98563
ARMA						
ar						
L1	.9348486	.0493428	18.95	0.000	.8381385	1.031559
ma						
L1	.3090592	.1605359	1.93	0.054	-.0055854	.6237038
/sigma	9.655308	1.082639	8.92	0.000	7.533375	11.77724

We do note a substantial increase in the estimated standard errors, and our once clearly significant moving average term is now only marginally significant.

◁

Saved Results

arima saves in e():

Scalars

e(N)	number of observations	e(ic)	number of iterations
e(k)	number of variables	e(rank)	rank of e(V)
e(k_eq)	number of equations	e(sigma)	standard error of the disturbance
e(k_dv)	number of dependent variables	e(tmin)	minimum time
e(df_m)	model degrees of freedom	e(tmax)	maximum time
e(ll)	log likelihood	e(N_gaps)	number of gaps
e(rc)	return code	e(ar_max)	maximum AR lag
e(chi2)	χ^2	e(ma_max)	maximum MA lag
e(p)	significance		

Macros

e(cmd)	arima	e(chi2type)	Wald; type of model χ^2 test
e(depvar)	name of dependent variable	e(tech)	maximization technique
e(title)	title in estimation output	e(ma)	lags for moving average terms
e(eqnames)	names of equations	e(ar)	lags for autoregressive terms
e(wtype)	weight type	e(unsta)	unstationary or blank
e(wexp)	weight expression	e(tmins)	formatted minimum time
e(vcetype)	covariance estimation method	e(tmaxs)	formatted maximum time
e(user)	name of likelihood-evaluator program	e(predict)	program used to implement predict
e(opt)	type of optimization		

Matrices

e(b)	coefficient vector	e(V)	variance–covariance matrix of
e(ilog)	iteration log (up to 20 iterations)		the estimators

Functions

e(sample)	marks estimation sample

Methods and Formulas

arima is implemented as an ado-file.

Estimation is by maximum likelihood using the Kalman filter via the prediction error decomposition; see Hamilton (1994), Gourieroux and Monfort (1997) or, in particular, Harvey (1989). Any of these sources will serve as excellent background for the estimation of these models using the state-space form; each also provides considerable detail on the method outlined below.

ARIMA model

The model to be estimated is

$$y_t = \boldsymbol{\xi}_t \boldsymbol{\beta} + \mu_t \tag{1}$$

$$\mu_t = \sum_{i=1}^{p} \rho_i \mu_{t-i} + \sum_{j=1}^{q} \theta_j \epsilon_{t-j} + \epsilon_t \tag{2}$$

which can be written as the single equation:

$$y_t = \mathbf{x_t} \boldsymbol{\beta} + \sum_{i=1}^{p} \rho_i (y_{t-i} - x_{t-i} \boldsymbol{\beta}) + \sum_{j=1}^{q} \theta_j \epsilon_{t-j} + \epsilon_t \tag{3}$$

Kalman filter equations

We will roughly follow Hamilton's (1994) notation and write the Kalman filter

$$\boldsymbol{\xi}_t = \mathbf{F}\boldsymbol{\xi}_{t-1} + \mathbf{v}_t \qquad (\textit{state equation})$$
$$\mathbf{y}_t = \mathbf{A}'\mathbf{x}_t + \mathbf{H}'\boldsymbol{\xi}_t + \mathbf{w}_t \qquad (\textit{observation equation})$$

and

$$\begin{pmatrix} \mathbf{v}_t \\ \mathbf{w}_t \end{pmatrix} \sim N\left\{ \mathbf{0}, \begin{pmatrix} \mathbf{Q} & \mathbf{0} \\ \mathbf{0} & \mathbf{R} \end{pmatrix} \right\} \qquad (6)$$

We maintain the standard Kalman filter matrix and vector notation, although for univariate models $\mathbf{y}_t$, $\mathbf{w}_t$, and $\mathbf{R}$ are scalars.

Kalman filter or state-space representation of the ARIMA model

A univariate ARIMA model can be cast in state-space form by defining the Kalman filter matrices as follows (see Hamilton 1994, or Gourieroux and Monfort 1997, for details):

$$F = \begin{bmatrix} \rho_1 & \rho_2 & \cdots & \rho_{p-1} & \rho_p \\ 1 & 0 & \cdots & 0 & 0 \\ 0 & 1 & \cdots & 0 & 0 \\ 0 & 0 & \cdots & 1 & 0 \end{bmatrix}$$

$$\mathbf{v}_t = \begin{bmatrix} \epsilon_{t-1} \\ 0 \\ \cdots \\ \cdots \\ \cdots \\ 0 \end{bmatrix}$$

$$\mathbf{A}' = \boldsymbol{\beta}$$
$$\mathbf{H}' = \begin{bmatrix} 1 & \theta_1 & \theta_2 & \cdots & \theta_q \end{bmatrix}$$
$$\mathbf{w}_t = 0$$

Note that the Kalman filter representation does not require that the moving average terms be invertible.

Kalman filter recursions

In order to see how missing data are handled, the updating recursions for the Kalman filter will be left in two steps. It is also common to write the updating equations as a single step using the gain matrix $\mathbf{K}$. We will provide the updating equations with little justification; see the sources listed above for details.

As a linear combination of a vector of random variables, the state $\boldsymbol{\xi}_t$ can be updated to its expected value based on the prior state as

$$\boldsymbol{\xi}_{t|t-1} = \mathbf{F}\boldsymbol{\xi}_{t-1} + \mathbf{v}_{t-1} \qquad (7)$$

and this state is a quadratic form that has the covariance matrix

$$\mathbf{P}_{t|t-1} = \mathbf{F}\mathbf{P}_{t-1}\mathbf{F}' + \mathbf{Q} \qquad (8)$$

and the estimator of $\mathbf{y}_t$ is

$$\widehat{\mathbf{y}}_{t|t-1} = \mathbf{x}_t\boldsymbol{\beta} + \mathbf{H}'\boldsymbol{\xi}_{t|t-1} \tag{9}$$

which implies an innovation or prediction error

$$\widehat{\boldsymbol{\iota}}_t = \mathbf{y}_t - \widehat{\mathbf{y}}_{t|t-1} \tag{10}$$

and this value or vector has mean square error (MSE)

$$\mathbf{M}_t = \mathbf{H}'\mathbf{P}_{t|t-1}\mathbf{H} + \mathbf{R} \tag{11}$$

Now, the expected value of $\boldsymbol{\xi}_t$ conditional on a realization of $\mathbf{y}_t$ is

$$\boldsymbol{\xi}_t = \boldsymbol{\xi}_{t|t-1} + \mathbf{P}_{t|t-1}\mathbf{H}\mathbf{M}_t^{-1}\widehat{\boldsymbol{\iota}}_t \tag{12}$$

with MSE

$$\mathbf{P}_t = \mathbf{P}_{t|t-1} - \mathbf{P}_{t|t-1}\mathbf{H}\mathbf{M}_t^{-1}\mathbf{H}'\mathbf{P}_{t|t-1} \tag{13}$$

This gives the full set of Kalman filter recursions.

Kalman filter initial conditions

When the series, conditional on $\mathbf{x}_t\boldsymbol{\beta}$, is stationary, the initial conditions for the filter can be considered a random draw from the stationary distribution of the state equation. The initial values of the state and the state MSE will be the expected values from this stationary distribution. For an ARIMA model, these can be written as

$$\xi_{1|0} = \mathbf{0} \tag{14}$$

and

$$\text{vec}(\mathbf{P}_{1|0}) = (\mathbf{I}_{r^2} - \mathbf{F} \otimes \mathbf{F})^{-1}\text{vec}(\mathbf{Q}) \tag{15}$$

where vec() is an operator representing the column matrix resulting from stacking each successive column of the target matrix.

If the series is not stationary, the above does not constitute a random draw from a stationary distribution and some other values must be chosen for initial state conditions. Hamilton (1994) suggests they be specified based on prior expectations, while Harvey suggests a diffuse and improper prior having a state vector of $\mathbf{0}$ and with an infinite variance. This corresponds to $\mathbf{P}_{1|0}$ with diagonal elements of ∞. Stata allows either approach to be taken for nonstationary series—initial priors may be specified with state0() and p0(), and a diffuse prior may be specified with diffuse.

Likelihood from prediction error decomposition

Given the outputs from the Kalman filter recursions and the assumption that the state and observation vectors are Gaussian, the likelihood for the state space model follows directly from the resulting multivariate normal in the predicted innovations. The log likelihood for observation t is

$$\ln L_t = -\frac{1}{2}\left\{ \ln(2\pi) + \ln(|\mathbf{M}_t|) - \boldsymbol{\iota}_t'\mathbf{M}_t^{-1}\boldsymbol{\iota}_t \right\} \tag{16}$$

Missing data

Missing data, whether a missing dependent variable y_t, one or more missing covariates $\mathbf{x}_t$, or completely missing observations, are handled by continuing the state updating equations without any contribution from the data; see Harvey (1989 and 1993). That is to say, equations (7) and (8) are iterated for every missing observation while equations (12) and (13) are ignored. Thus, for observations with missing data, $\boldsymbol{\xi}_t = \boldsymbol{\xi}_{t|t-1}$ and $\mathbf{P}_t = \mathbf{P}_{t|t-1}$. In the absence of any information from the sample, this effectively assumes the prediction error for the missing observations is 0. Alternate methods of handling missing data based on the EM algorithm have been suggested; e.g., Shumway (1984, 1988).

References

Ansley, C. F. and R. Kohn. 1985. Estimation, filtering and smoothing in state space models with incompletely specified initial conditions. *Annals of Statistics* 13: 1286–1316.

Ansley, C. F. and P. Newbold. 1980. Finite sample properties of estimators for auto-regressive moving average processes. *Journal of Econometrics* 13: 159–184.

Baum, C. F. 2000. sts15: Tests for stationarity of a time series. *Stata Technical Bulletin* 57: 36–39.

Baum, C. F. and V. Wiggins. 2000. sts16: Tests for long memory in a time series. *Stata Technical Bulletin* 57: 39–44.

Berndt, E. K., B. H. Hall, R. E. Hall, and J. A. Hausman. 1974. Estimation and inference in nonlinear structural models. *Annals of Economic and Social Measurement* 3/4: 653–665.

Bollerslev, T., R. F. Engle, D. B. Nelson. 1994. ARCH Models. In *Handbook of Econometrics, Volume IV*, ed. R. F. Engle and D. L. McFadden. New York: Elsevier.

Box, G. E. P., G. M. Jenkins, G. C. Reinsel. 1994. *Time Series Analysis: Forecasting and Control.* 3d ed. Englewood Cliffs, NJ: Prentice–Hall.

David, J. S. 1999. sts14: Bivariate Granger causality test. *Stata Technical Bulletin* 51: 40–41. Reprinted in *Stata Technical Bulletin Reprints*, vol. 9, pp. 350–351.

Davidson, R. and J. G. MacKinnon. 1993. *Estimation and Inference in Econometrics.* Oxford: Oxford University Press.

Diggle, P. J. 1990. *Time Series: A Biostatistical Introduction.* Oxford: Oxford University Press.

Enders, W. 1995. *Applied Econometric Time Series.* New York: John Wiley & Sons.

Friedman, M. and D. Meiselman. 1963. The relative stability of monetary velocity and the investment multiplier in the United States, 1987–1958. In *Stabilization Policies*, Commission on Money and Credit. Englewood Cliffs, NJ: Prentice–Hall.

Gourieroux, C. and A. Monfort. 1997. *Time Series and Dynamic Models.* Cambridge: Cambridge University Press.

Greene, W. H. 2000. *Econometric Analysis.* 4th ed. Upper Saddle River, NJ: Prentice–Hall.

Hamilton, J. D. 1994. *Time Series Analysis.* Princeton: Princeton University Press.

Harvey, A. C. 1989. *Forecasting, structural time series models and the Kalman filter.* Cambridge: Cambridge University Press.

———. 1993. *Time Series Models.* Cambridge, MA: MIT Press.

Hipel, K. W. and A. I. McLeod. 1994. *Time Series Modelling of Water Resources and Environmental Systems.* Amsterdam: Elsevier.

Kalman, R. E. 1960. A new approach to linear filtering and prediction problems. *Journal of Basic Engineering, Transactions of the ASME* Series D, 82: 35–45.

Newton, H. J. 1988. *TIMESLAB: A Time Series Analysis Laboratory.* Belmont, CA: Wadsworth & Brooks/Cole.

Press, W. H., S. A. Teukolsky, W. T. Vetterling, B. P. Flannery. 1992. *Numerical Recipes in C: The Art of Scientific Computing.* 2d ed. Cambridge: Cambridge University Press.

Shumway, R. H. 1984. Some applications of the EM algorithm to analyzing incomplete time series data. In *Time Series Analysis of Irregularly Observed Data*, ed. E. Parzen, 290–324. New York: Springer-Verlag.

———. 1988. *Applied Statistical Time Series Analysis.* Upper Saddle River, NJ: Prentice–Hall.

Also See

Complementary:	[R] adjust, [R] lincom, [R] mfx, [R] predict, [R] test, [R] testnl, [R] tsset, [R] vce, [R] xi
Related:	[R] arch, [R] prais, [R] regress
Background:	[U] 14.4.3 Time-series varlists,
	[U] 16.5 Accessing coefficients and standard errors,
	[U] 23 Estimation and post-estimation commands,
	[U] 23.11 Obtaining robust variance estimates,
	[U] 23.12 Obtaining scores,
	[U] 27.3 Time-series dates

Title

> **binreg** — Generalized linear models: extensions to the binomial family

Syntax

> binreg *depvar* [*varlist*] [*weight*] [if *exp*] [in *range*] [, <u>nocon</u>stant ml
>
> <u>sca</u>le(x2|dev|#) [<u>ln</u>]<u>off</u>set(*varname*) disp(#) coeff [or|rr|hr|rd]
>
> <u>level</u>(#) <u>iter</u>ate(#) <u>ltol</u>erance(#) <u>init</u>(*varname*) n(*varname*|#) <u>nolog</u>
>
> *glm_options*]

by ... : may be used with binreg; see [R] **by**.

fweights, aweights, iweights, and pweights are allowed; see [U] **14.1.6 weight**.

This command shares the features of all estimation commands; see [U] **23 Estimation and post-estimation commands**.

Syntax for predict

> predict [*type*] *newvarname* [if *exp*] [in *range*] [, *statistic* <u>nooff</u>set <u>stan</u>dardized
>
> <u>stud</u>entized <u>mod</u>ified <u>adj</u>usted

where *statistic* is one of

> <u>mu</u> | xb | <u>eta</u> | <u>stdp</u> | <u>ans</u>combe | <u>cook</u>sd | <u>deviance</u> | <u>hat</u> | <u>likelihood</u> |
>
> <u>pearson</u> | <u>response</u> | <u>score</u> | <u>working</u>

These statistics are available both in and out of sample; type predict ... if e(sample) ... if wanted only for the estimation sample.

Description

binreg fits generalized linear models for the binomial family. It estimates odds ratios, risk ratios, health ratios, and risk differences. The available links are

Option	Implied link	Parameter
or	logit	Odds ratios = $\exp(\beta)$
rr	log	Risk ratios = $\exp(\beta)$
hr	log complement	Health ratios = $\exp(\beta)$
rd	identity	Risk differences = β

Note that estimates of odds, risk, and health ratios are obtained by exponentiating the appropriate coefficients. The option or produces the same results as Stata's logistic command, and or coeff yields the same results as the logit command. When no link is specified/implied, or is assumed (the logit link is implied).

Options

noconstant specifies that the linear predictor has no intercept term, thus forcing it through the origin on the scale defined by the link function.

ml requests the ML Newton–Raphson optimization of the log-likelihood instead of the MQL IRLS optimization of the deviance.

scale(x2|dev|#) overrides the default scale parameter. By default, scale(1) is assumed for discrete distributions (binomial, Poisson, and negative binomial), and scale(x2) for continuous distributions (Gaussian, gamma, and inverse Gaussian).

scale(x2) specifies that the scale parameter be set to the Pearson chi-squared (or generalized chi-squared) statistic divided by the residual degrees of freedom.

scale(dev) sets the scale parameter to the deviance divided by the residual degrees of freedom. This provides an alternative to scale(x2) for continuous distributions and over- or under-dispersed discrete distributions.

scale(#) sets the scale parameter to #.

[ln]offset(*varname*) specifies an offset to be added to the linear predictor. offset() specifies the values directly: $g(E(y)) = xB+varname$. lnoffset() specifies exponentiated values: $g(E(y)) = xB+\ln(varname)$.

disp(#) multiplies the variance of y by # and divides the deviance by #. The resulting distributions are members of the quasi-likelihood family.

coeff displays the nonexponentiated coefficients and corresponding standard errors and confidence intervals. This has no effect when the rd option is specified, as it always presents the nonexponentiated coefficients.

or requests the logit link and results in odds ratios if coeff is not specified.

rr requests the log link and results in risk ratios if coeff is not specified.

hr requests the log complement link and results in health ratios if coeff is not specified.

rd requests the identity link and results in risk differences if coeff is not specified.

level(#) specifies the confidence level, in percent, for confidence intervals. The default is level(95) or as set by set level; see [U] **23.5 Specifying the width of confidence intervals**.

iterate(#) specifies the maximum number of iterations allowed in estimating the model; iterate(50) is the default.

ltolerance(#) specifies the convergence criterion for the change in deviance between iterations; ltolerance(1e-6) is the default.

init(*varname*) specifies *varname* containing an initial estimate for the mean of *depvar*. This can be useful if you encounter convergence difficulties.

n(*varname*|#) specifies either a constant integer to use as the denominator for the binomial family, or a variable which holds the denominator for each observation.

nolog suppresses the iteration log.

glm_options are the options allowed with glm, family(binomial); see [R] **glm**.

Options for predict

mu, the default, specifies that predict is to calculate $g^{-1}(\mathbf{x}\widehat{\beta})$, the inverse link of the linear prediction.

xb calculates the linear prediction $\eta = \mathbf{x}\widehat{\beta}$.

eta is a synonym for xb.

stdp calculates the standard error of the linear prediction.

anscombe calculates the Anscombe (1972) residuals. The aim here is to produce residuals that closely follow a normal distribution.

cooksd calculates Cook's distance, which measures the aggregate change in the estimated coefficients when each observation is left out of the estimation.

deviance calculates the deviance residuals. Deviance residuals are recommended by McCullagh and Nelder (1989) and by others as having the best properties for examining goodness of fit of a GLM. They are approximately normally distributed if the model is correct. They may be plotted against the fitted values or against a covariate to inspect the model's fit. Also see the pearson option below.

hat calculates the diagonals of the "hat" matrix as an analog to simple linear regression.

likelihood calculates a weighted average of the standardized deviance and standardized Pearson (described below) residuals.

pearson calculates the Pearson residuals. Be aware that Pearson residuals often have markedly skewed distributions for non-normal family distributions. Also see the deviance option above.

response calculates the differences between the observed and fitted outcomes.

score calculates the scores used in calculating the sandwich estimate of variance. See the score() entry in the *Options* section above.

working calculates the working residuals, which are response residuals weighted according to the derivative of the link function.

nooffset is relevant only if you specified offset(*varname*) for binreg. It modifies the calculations made by predict so that they ignore the offset variable; the linear prediction is treated as $\mathbf{x}_j\mathbf{b}$ rather than $\mathbf{x}_j\mathbf{b} + \text{offset}_j$.

standardized requests that the residual be multiplied by the factor $(1-h)^{-1/2}$, where h is the diagonal of the hat matrix. This is done to take the correlation between *depvar* and its predicted value into account.

studentized requests that the residual be multiplied by one over the square root of the estimated scale parameter.

modified requests that the denominator of the residual be modified to be a reasonable estimate of the variance of *depvar*. The base residual is multiplied by the factor $(k/w)^{-1/2}$, where k is either one or the user-specified dispersion parameter, and w is the specified weight (or one if left unspecified).

adjusted adjusts the deviance residual to make the convergence to the limiting normal distribution faster. The adjustment deals with adding to the deviance residual a higher-order term which depends on the variance function family. This option is only allowed when deviance is specified.

Remarks

Wacholder (1986) suggests methods for estimating risks ratios and risk differences from prospective binomial data. These estimates are obtained by selecting the proper link functions in the generalized linear model framework. (See *Methods and Formulas* for details, also see [R] **glm**).

▷ Example

Wacholder (1986) presents an example, utilizing data from Wright et al. (1983), of an investigation of the relationship between alcohol consumption and the risk of a low birth weight baby. Covariates examined included whether the mother smoked (yes or no), mother's social class (three levels) and drinking frequency (light, moderate or heavy). The data for the 18 possible categories determined by the covariates are illustrated below.

Let's first describe the data and list a few observations.

```
. list, noobs
      cat        d        n      alc      smo      soc
       1       11       84        3        1        1
       2        5       79        2        1        1
       3       11      169        1        1        1
       4        6       28        3        2        1
       5        3       13        2        2        1
       6        1       26        1        2        1
       7        4       22        3        1        2
       8        3       25        2        1        2
       9       12      162        1        1        2
      10        4       17        3        2        2
      11        2        7        2        2        2
      12        6       38        1        2        2
      13        0       14        3        1        3
      14        1       18        2        1        3
      15       12       91        1        1        3
      16        7       19        3        2        3
      17        2       18        2        2        3
      18        8       70        1        2        3
```

Each observation corresponds to one of the 18 covariate structures. The number of low birth babies out of n in each category is given by the variable d.

We will begin by estimating risk ratios:

(Continued on next page)

```
. xi: binreg d I.soc I.alc I.smo, n(n) rr
I.soc             _Isoc_1-3          (naturally coded; _Isoc_1 omitted)
I.alc             _Ialc_1-3          (naturally coded; _Ialc_1 omitted)
I.smo             _Ismo_1-2          (naturally coded; _Ismo_1 omitted)

Iteration 1 : deviance =   14.2879
Iteration 2 : deviance =   13.6070
Iteration 3 : deviance =   13.6050
Iteration 4 : deviance =   13.6050

Residual df  =        12                    No. of obs =        18
Pearson X2   =  11.51517                    Deviance   =  13.60503
Dispersion   =  .9595976                    Dispersion =  1.133752

Binomial (N=n) distribution, log link
```

		EIM				
d	Risk Ratio	Std. Err.	z	P>|z|	[95% Conf. Interval]	
_Isoc_2	1.340001	.3127382	1.25	0.210	.848098	2.11721
_Isoc_3	1.349487	.3291488	1.23	0.219	.8366715	2.176619
_Ialc_2	1.191157	.3265354	0.64	0.523	.6960276	2.038503
_Ialc_3	1.974078	.4261751	3.15	0.002	1.293011	3.013884
_Ismo_2	1.648444	.332875	2.48	0.013	1.109657	2.448836

By default, the program outputs the risk ratios (the exponentiated regression coefficients) estimated by the model. We can see that the risk ratio comparing heavy drinkers with light drinkers, after adjusting for smoking and social class, is $\exp(0.6801017) = 1.9740785$. That is, mothers who drink heavily during their pregnancy have approximately twice the risk of delivering low weight babies than mothers who are light drinkers.

The nonexponentiated coefficients can be obtained via the coeff option.

```
. xi: binreg d I.smo I.soc I.alc, n(n) rr coeff
I.smo             _Ismo_1-2          (naturally coded; _Ismo_1 omitted)
I.soc             _Isoc_1-3          (naturally coded; _Isoc_1 omitted)
I.alc             _Ialc_1-3          (naturally coded; _Ialc_1 omitted)

Iteration 1 : deviance =   14.2879
Iteration 2 : deviance =   13.6070
Iteration 3 : deviance =   13.6050
Iteration 4 : deviance =   13.6050

Residual df  =        12                    No. of obs =        18
Pearson X2   =  11.51517                    Deviance   =  13.60503
Dispersion   =  .9595976                    Dispersion =  1.133752

Binomial (N=n) distribution, log link
Risk ratio coefficients
```

		EIM				
d	Coef.	Std. Err.	z	P>|z|	[95% Conf. Interval]	
_Ismo_2	.4998317	.2019329	2.48	0.013	.1040505	.8956129
_Isoc_2	.2926702	.2333866	1.25	0.210	-.1647591	.7500994
_Isoc_3	.2997244	.2439066	1.23	0.219	-.1783238	.7777726
_Ialc_2	.1749248	.274133	0.64	0.523	-.362366	.7122156
_Ialc_3	.6801017	.2158856	3.15	0.002	.2569737	1.10323
_cons	-2.764079	.2031606	-13.61	0.000	-3.162266	-2.365891

Risk differences are obtained using the rd option:

```
. xi: binreg d I.soc I.alc I.smo, n(n) rd
I.soc            _Isoc_1-3          (naturally coded; _Isoc_1 omitted)
I.alc            _Ialc_1-3          (naturally coded; _Ialc_1 omitted)
I.smo            _Ismo_1-2          (naturally coded; _Ismo_1 omitted)
Iteration 1 : deviance =    18.6728
Iteration 2 : deviance =    14.9436
Iteration 3 : deviance =    14.9185
Iteration 4 : deviance =    14.9176
Iteration 5 : deviance =    14.9176
Iteration 6 : deviance =    14.9176
Iteration 7 : deviance =    14.9176
```

Residual df = 12			No. of obs = 18			
Pearson X2 = 12.60353			Deviance = 14.91758			
Dispersion = 1.050294			Dispersion = 1.243132			

```
Binomial (N=n) distribution, identity link
Risk difference coefficients
```

d	Coef.	EIM Std. Err.	z	P>|z|	[95% Conf. Interval]	
_Isoc_2	.0263817	.0232124	1.14	0.256	-.0191137	.0718771
_Isoc_3	.0365553	.0268668	1.36	0.174	-.0161026	.0892132
_Ialc_2	.0122539	.0257713	0.48	0.634	-.0382569	.0627647
_Ialc_3	.0801291	.0302878	2.65	0.008	.020766	.1394921
_Ismo_2	.0542415	.0270838	2.00	0.045	.0011582	.1073248
_cons	.059028	.0160693	3.67	0.000	.0275327	.0905232

The risk difference between the heavy drinkers and the light drinkers is simply the value of the coefficient for _Ialc_3 = 0.0801291. Because the risk differences are obtained directly from the coefficients estimated using the identity link, the coeff option has no effect in this case.

Health ratios are obtained using the hr option. The health ratios (exponentiated coefficients for the log complement link) are reported directly.

```
. xi: binreg d I.soc I.alc I.smo, n(n) hr
I.soc            _Isoc_1-3          (naturally coded; _Isoc_1 omitted)
I.alc            _Ialc_1-3          (naturally coded; _Ialc_1 omitted)
I.smo            _Ismo_1-2          (naturally coded; _Ismo_1 omitted)
Iteration 1 : deviance =    21.1523
Iteration 2 : deviance =    15.1647
Iteration 3 : deviance =    15.1320
Iteration 4 : deviance =    15.1311
Iteration 5 : deviance =    15.1311
Iteration 6 : deviance =    15.1311
Iteration 7 : deviance =    15.1311
```

Residual df = 12			No. of obs = 18			
Pearson X2 = 12.84204			Deviance = 15.13111			
Dispersion = 1.07017			Dispersion = 1.260925			

```
Binomial (N=n) distribution, log-complement link
Health ratio (HR)
```

d	HR	EIM Std. Err.	z	P>|z|	[95% Conf. Interval]	
_Isoc_2	.9720541	.024858	-1.11	0.268	.9245342	1.022017
_Isoc_3	.9597182	.0290412	-1.36	0.174	.9044535	1.01836
_Ialc_2	.9871517	.0278852	-0.46	0.647	.9339831	1.043347
_Ialc_3	.9134243	.0325726	-2.54	0.011	.8517631	.9795493
_Ismo_2	.9409983	.0296125	-1.93	0.053	.8847125	1.000865

To see the nonexponentiated coefficients we can specify the `coeff` option.

◁

Saved Results

`binreg` saves in `e()`:

Scalars

`e(N)`	number of observations	`e(N_clust)`	number of clusters
`e(k)`	number of parameters	`e(ll)`	log-likelihood, if ML
`e(df)`	residual degrees of freedom	`e(deviance)`	deviance
`e(phi)`	scale parameter	`e(deviance_p)`	Pearson deviance
`e(disp)`	dispersion parameter	`e(dispers)`	dispersion
`e(rc)`	return code	`e(dispers_p)`	Pearson dispersion
`e(df_m)`	model degrees of freedom	`e(disp)`	dispersion parameter
`e(aic)`	model AIC, if ML	`e(vf)`	factor set by `vfactor()`, 1 if not set
`e(bic)`	model BIC		

Macros

`e(cmd)`	`binreg`	`e(offset)`	offset
`e(depvar)`	name of dependent variable	`e(predict)`	program used to implement `predict`
`e(link)`	name of link function used by `glm`		
`e(m)`	number of binomial trials	`e(clustvar)`	cluster variable
`e(se1)`	std. error header, line 1	`e(cons)`	set if `noconstant` specified
`e(se2)`	std. error header, line 2	`e(linkt)`	link title
`e(wtype)`	weight type	`e(linkf)`	link form
`e(wexp)`	weight expression	`e(title_fl)`	family–link title

Matrices

`e(b)`	coefficient vector	`e(V)`	variance–covariance matrix of the estimators
`e(ilog)`	iteration log (up to 20 iterations)		

Functions

`e(sample)`	marks estimation sample

Methods and Formulas

`binreg` is implemented as an ado-file.

Let π_i be the probability of success for the i observation, $i = 1, \ldots, N$, and $X\beta$ the linear predictor. Then the link function relates the covariates of each observation to its respective probability through the linear predictor.

In logistic regression the logit link is used:

$$\ln\left(\frac{\pi}{1-\pi}\right) = X\beta$$

The regression coefficient β_k represents the change in the logarithm of the odds associated with a one unit change in the value of X_k covariate; thus, $\exp(\beta_k)$ is the ratio of the odds associated with a change of one unit in X_k.

For risk differences, the identity link $\pi = X\beta$ is used. The regression coefficient β_k represents the risk difference associated with a change of one unit in X_k. When using the identity link, it is possible to obtain fitted probabilities outside of the interval $(0, 1)$. As suggested by Wacholder, at each iteration fitted probabilities are checked for range conditions (and put back in range if necessary). For example, if the identity link results in a fitted probability that is smaller than $1e - 4$, the probability is replaced with $1e - 4$ before the link function is calculated.

A similar adjustment is made for the logarithmic link, which is used for estimating the risk ratio, $\ln(\pi) = X\beta$, where $\exp(\beta_k)$ is the risk ratio associated with a change of one unit in X_k, and for the log complement link used to estimate the probability of no disease or health, where $\exp(\beta_k)$ represents the "health ratio" associated with a change of one unit in X_k.

References

Hardin, J. and M. Cleves. 1999. sbe29: Generalized linear models: extensions to the binomial family. *Stata Technical Bulletin* 50: 21–25.

Wacholder, S. 1986. Binomial regression in GLIM: estimating risk ratios and risk differences. *American Journal of Epidemiology* 123: 174–184.

Wright, J. T., I. G. Barrison, I. G. Lewis et al. 1983. Alcohol consumption, pregnancy and low birthweight. *Lancet* 1: 663–665.

Also See

Complementary:	[R] **adjust**, [R] **lincom**, [R] **linktest**, [R] **mfx**, [R] **predict**, [R] **test**, [R] **testnl**, [R] **vce**, [R] **xi**
Related:	[R] **glm**
Background:	[U] **16.5 Accessing coefficients and standard errors**, [U] **23 Estimation and post-estimation commands**, [U] **23.11 Obtaining robust variance estimates**

Title

> **biprobit** — Bivariate probit models

Syntax

Bivariate probit model

> biprobit *depvar_1* *depvar_2* [*varlist*] [*weight*] [if *exp*] [in *range*] [, <u>r</u>obust
>
>   <u>cl</u>uster(*varname*) <u>score</u>(*newvarlist*) <u>partial</u> <u>nocon</u>stant <u>constraints</u>(*numlist*)
>
>   noskip <u>l</u>evel(#) offset1(*varname*) offset2(*varname*) *maximize_options*]

Seemingly unrelated bivariate probit model

> biprobit *equation1* *equation2* [*weight*] [if *exp*] [in *range*] [, <u>r</u>obust
>
>   <u>cl</u>uster(*varname*) <u>score</u>(*newvarlist*) <u>partial</u> <u>constraints</u>(*numlist*) noskip
>
>   <u>l</u>evel(#) *maximize_options*]

where *equation1* and *equation2* are specified as

> ([*eqname*:] *depvar* [=] [*varlist*] [, <u>off</u>set(*varname*) <u>nocon</u>stant])

by ... : may be used with biprobit; see [R] **by**.

pweights, fweights, and iweights are allowed; see [U] **14.1.6 weight**.

biprobit shares the features of all estimation commands; see [U] **23 Estimation and post-estimation commands**.

Syntax for predict

> predict [*type*] *newvarname* [if *exp*] [in *range*] [, *statistic* <u>nooff</u>set]

where *statistic* is

<u>p11</u>	$\Phi_2(\mathbf{x}_j\mathbf{b}, \mathbf{z}_j\mathbf{g}, \rho)$, predicted probability $\Pr(y_{1j}=1, y_{2j}=1)$ (the default)
p10	$\Phi_2(\mathbf{x}_j\mathbf{b}, -\mathbf{z}_j\mathbf{g}, -\rho)$, predicted probability $\Pr(y_{1j}=1, y_{2j}=0)$
p01	$\Phi_2(-\mathbf{x}_j\mathbf{b}, \mathbf{z}_j\mathbf{g}, -\rho)$, predicted probability $\Pr(y_{1j}=0, y_{2j}=1)$
p00	$\Phi_2(-\mathbf{x}_j\mathbf{b}, -\mathbf{z}_j\mathbf{g}, \rho)$, predicted probability $\Pr(y_{1j}=0, y_{2j}=0)$
pmarg1	$\Phi(\mathbf{x}_j\mathbf{b})$, marginal success probability for equation 1
pmarg2	$\Phi(\mathbf{z}_j\mathbf{g})$, marginal success probability for equation 2
pcond1	$\Phi_2(\mathbf{x}_j\mathbf{b}, \mathbf{z}_j\mathbf{g}, \rho)/\Phi(\mathbf{z}_j\mathbf{g})$, conditional probability of success for equation 1
pcond2	$\Phi_2(\mathbf{x}_j\mathbf{b}, \mathbf{z}_j\mathbf{g}, \rho)/\Phi(\mathbf{x}_j\mathbf{b})$, conditional probability of success for equation 2
xb1	$\mathbf{x}_j\mathbf{b}$, fitted values for equation 1
xb2	$\mathbf{z}_j\mathbf{g}$, fitted values for equation 2
stdp1	standard error of fitted values for equation 1
stdp2	standard error of fitted values for equation 2

where $\Phi()$ is the standard normal distribution function and $\Phi_2()$ is the bivariate standard normal distribution function.

These statistics are available both in and out of sample; type predict ... if e(sample) ... if wanted only for the estimation sample.

Description

biprobit estimates maximum-likelihood two-equation probit models—either a bivariate probit or a seemingly unrelated probit (limited to two equations).

Options

robust specifies that the Huber/White/sandwich estimator of the variance is to be used in place of the conventional MLE variance estimator. robust combined with cluster() further allows observations which are not independent within cluster (although they must be independent between clusters).

If you specify pweights, robust is implied; see [U] **23.11 Obtaining robust variance estimates**.

cluster(*varname*) specifies that the observations are independent across groups (clusters) but not necessarily within groups. *varname* specifies to which group each observation belongs. cluster() affects the estimated standard errors and variance–covariance matrix of the estimators (VCE), but not the estimated coefficients. cluster() can be used with pweights to produce estimates for unstratified cluster-sampled data.

cluster() implies robust; that is, specifying robust cluster() is equivalent to typing cluster() by itself.

score(*newvarlist*) creates a new variable, or a set of new variables, containing the contributions to the scores for each equation and ancillary parameter in the model.

The first new variable specified will contain $u_{1j} = \partial \ln L_j / \partial(\mathbf{x}_j\boldsymbol{\beta})$ for each observation j in the sample, where $\ln L_j$ is the jth observation's contribution to the log likelihood.
The second new variable: $u_{2j} = \partial \ln L_j / \partial(\mathbf{z}_j\boldsymbol{\gamma})$
The third: $u_{3j} = \partial \ln L_j / \partial(\text{atanh}\,\rho)$
If only one variable is specified, only the first score is computed; if two variables are specified, only the first two scores are computed; and so on.

The jth observation's contribution to the score vector is

$$\left\{\, \partial \ln L_j / \partial\boldsymbol{\beta} \;\; \partial \ln L_j / \partial\boldsymbol{\gamma} \;\; \partial \ln L_j / \partial(\text{atanh}\,\rho) \,\right\} = \left(\, u_{1j}\mathbf{x}_j \;\; u_{2j}\mathbf{z}_j \;\; u_{3j} \,\right)$$

The score vector can be obtained by summing over j. See [U] **23.12 Obtaining scores**.

partial specifies that the partial observability model should be estimated. Note that this particular model commonly has poor convergence properties and we recommend that you use the difficult option if you want to estimate the Poirier partial observability model; see [R] **ml**.

Note that this model computes the product of the two dependent variables such that you do not have to replace each with the product.

noconstant omits the constant term from the equation. This option may be specified on the regression equation, the selection equation, or both.

constraints(*numlist*) specifies by number the linear constraints to be applied during estimation. The default is to perform unconstrained estimation. Constraints are specified using the constraint command; see [R] **constraint**. See [R] **reg3** for the use of constraints in multiple-equation contexts.

noskip specifies that a full maximum-likelihood model with only a constant for the regression equation be estimated. This model is not displayed but is used as the base model to compute a likelihood-ratio test for the model test statistic displayed in the estimation header. By default, the overall model test statistic is an asymptotically equivalent Wald test of all the parameters in the regression equation being zero (except the constant). For many models, this option can substantially increase estimation time.

level(*#*) specifies the confidence level, in percent, for confidence intervals. The default is level(95) or as set by set level; see [U] **23.5 Specifying the width of confidence intervals**.

offset(*varname*) is a rarely used option that specifies a variable to be added directly to **Xb**. This option may be specified on either the regression or the selection equation (or both). In the seemingly unrelated model syntax, it is clear to which equation this option applies. In the bivariate probit syntax, use the offset1(*varname*) and offset2(*varname*) options to be clear.

maximize_options control the maximization process; see [R] **maximize**. With the possible exception of iterate(0) and trace, you should never have to specify them.

Options for predict

p11, the default, calculates the bivariate predicted probability $\Pr(y_{1j} = 1, y_{2j} = 1)$.

p10 calculates the bivariate predicted probability $\Pr(y_{1j} = 1, y_{2j} = 0)$.

p01 calculates the bivariate predicted probability $\Pr(y_{1j} = 0, y_{2j} = 1)$.

p00 calculates the bivariate predicted probability $\Pr(y_{1j} = 0, y_{2j} = 0)$.

pmarg1 calculates the univariate (marginal) predicted probability of success $\Pr(y_{1j} = 1)$.

pmarg2 calculates the univariate (marginal) predicted probability of success $\Pr(y_{2j} = 1)$.

pcond1 calculates the conditional (on success in equation 2) predicted probability of success $\Pr(y_{1j} = 1, y_{2j} = 1)/\Pr(y_{2j} = 1)$.

pcond2 calculates the conditional (on success in equation 1) predicted probability of success $\Pr(y_{1j} = 1, y_{2j} = 1)/\Pr(y_{1j} = 1)$.

xb1 calculates the probit linear prediction $\mathbf{x}_j\mathbf{b}$.

xb2 calculates the probit linear prediction $\mathbf{z}_j\mathbf{g}$.

stdp1 calculates the standard error of the linear prediction of equation 1.

stdp2 calculates the standard error of the linear prediction of equation 2.

nooffset is relevant only if you specified offset(*varname*) for biprobit. It modifies the calculations made by predict so that they ignore the offset variable; the linear prediction is treated as $\mathbf{x}_j\mathbf{b}$ rather than $\mathbf{x}_j\mathbf{b} + \text{offset}_j$.

Remarks

For a good introduction to the bivariate probit models, see Greene (2000, 849–855) and Pindyck and Rubinfeld (1998). Poirier (1980) explains the partial observability model. Van de Ven and Van Pragg (1981) explain the probit model with sample selection; see [R] **heckprob** for details.

▷ Example

We use the data from Pindyck and Rubinfeld (1998, 332). In this dataset, the variables are whether children attend private school (**private**), number of years the family has been at the present residence (**years**), log of property tax (**logptax**), log of income (**loginc**), and whether one voted for an increase in property taxes (**vote**).

We wish to model the bivariate outcomes of whether children attend private school and whether the head of the household voted for an increase in property tax based on the other covariates.

```
. biprobit private vote years logptax loginc

Fitting comparison equation 1:

Iteration 0:    log likelihood = -31.967097
Iteration 1:    log likelihood = -31.454068
Iteration 2:    log likelihood = -31.448959
Iteration 3:    log likelihood = -31.448958

Fitting comparison equation 2:

Iteration 0:    log likelihood = -63.036914
Iteration 1:    log likelihood = -58.581911
Iteration 2:    log likelihood = -58.497419
Iteration 3:    log likelihood = -58.497288

Comparison:     log likelihood = -89.946246

Fitting full model:

Iteration 0:    log likelihood = -89.946246
Iteration 1:    log likelihood = -89.258897
Iteration 2:    log likelihood = -89.254028
Iteration 3:    log likelihood = -89.254028
```

Bivariate probit regression				Number of obs	=	95
				Wald chi2(6)	=	9.59
Log likelihood = -89.254028				Prob > chi2	=	0.1431

	Coef.	Std. Err.	z	P>|z|	[95% Conf. Interval]	
private						
years	-.0118884	.0256778	-0.46	0.643	-.0622159	.0384391
logptax	-.1066962	.6669782	-0.16	0.873	-1.413949	1.200557
loginc	.3762037	.5306484	0.71	0.478	-.663848	1.416255
_cons	-4.184694	4.837817	-0.86	0.387	-13.66664	5.297253
vote						
years	-.0168561	.0147834	-1.14	0.254	-.0458309	.0121188
logptax	-1.288707	.5752266	-2.24	0.025	-2.416131	-.1612839
loginc	.998286	.4403565	2.27	0.023	.1352031	1.861369
_cons	-.5360573	4.068509	-0.13	0.895	-8.510188	7.438073
/athrho	-.2764525	.2412099	-1.15	0.252	-.7492153	.1963102
rho	-.2696186	.2236753			-.6346806	.1938267

Likelihood ratio test of rho=0:   chi2(1) = 1.38444   Prob > chi2 = 0.2393

The output shows several iteration logs. The first iteration log corresponds to running the univariate probit model for the first equation and the second log corresponds to running the univariate probit for the second model. If $\rho = 0$, then the sum of the log likelihoods from these two models will equal the log likelihood of the bivariate probit model; this sum is printed in the iteration log as the comparison log likelihood.

The final iteration log is for estimating the full bivariate probit model. A likelihood-ratio test of the log likelihood for this model and the comparison log likelihood is presented at the end of the output. If we had specified the robust option, then this test would be presented as a Wald test instead of as a likelihood-ratio test.

Note that we could have estimated the same model using the seemingly unrelated syntax as

```
. biprobit (private=years logptax loginc) (vote=years logptax loginc)
```

Saved Results

biprobit saves in e():

Scalars

e(N)	number of observations		e(rc)	return code
e(k)	number of variables		e(chi2)	χ^2
e(k_eq)	number of equations		e(chi2_c)	χ^2 for comparison test
e(k_dv)	number of dependent variables		e(p)	significance
e(df_m)	model degrees of freedom		e(rho)	ρ
e(ll)	log likelihood		e(ic)	number of iterations
e(ll_0)	log likelihood, constant-only model		e(rank)	rank of e(V)
e(ll_c)	log likelihood, comparison model		e(rank0)	rank of e(V) for constant-only
e(N_clust)	number of clusters			model

Macros

e(cmd)	biprobit		e(opt)	type of optimization
e(depvar)	name(s) of dependent variable(s)		e(chi2type)	Wald or LR; type of model χ^2 test
e(title)	title in estimation output		e(chi2_ct)	Wald or LR; type of model χ^2 test
e(wtype)	weight type			corresponding to e(chi2_c)
e(wexp)	weight expression		e(offset1)	offset for first equation
e(clustvar)	name of cluster variable		e(offset2)	offset for second equation
e(vcetype)	covariance estimation method		e(predict)	program used to implement predict
e(user)	name of likelihood-evaluator		e(cnslist)	constraint numbers
	program			

Matrices

e(b)	coefficient vector		e(V)	variance–covariance matrix of
e(ilog)	iteration log (up to 20 iterations)			the estimators

Functions

e(sample)	marks estimation sample

Methods and Formulas

biprobit is implemented as an ado-file.

The log likelihood, L, is given by

$$\xi_i^{\beta} = x_i\beta + \text{offset}_i^{\beta}$$

$$\xi_i^{\gamma} = z_i\gamma + \text{offset}_i^{\gamma}$$

$$q_{1i} = \begin{cases} 1 & \text{if } y_{1i} \neq 0 \\ -1 & \text{otherwise} \end{cases}$$

$$q_{2i} = \begin{cases} 1 & \text{if } y_{2i} \neq 0 \\ -1 & \text{otherwise} \end{cases}$$

$$\rho_i^* = q_{1i}q_{2i}\rho$$

$$L = \sum_{i=1}^{n} w_i \ln \Phi_2\left(q_{1i}\xi_i^{\beta}, q_{2i}\xi_i^{\gamma}, \rho_i^*\right)$$

where $\Phi_2()$ is the cumulative bivariate normal distribution function (with mean $\begin{bmatrix} 0 & 0 \end{bmatrix}'$) and w_i is an optional weight for observation i. This derivation assumes that

$$y_{1i}^* = x_i\beta + \epsilon_{1i} + \text{offset}_i^\beta$$
$$y_{2i}^* = z_i\gamma + \epsilon_{2i} + \text{offset}_i^\gamma$$
$$E(\epsilon_1) = E(\epsilon_2) = 0$$
$$\text{Var}(\epsilon_1) = \text{Var}(\epsilon_2) = 1$$
$$\text{Cov}(\epsilon_1, \epsilon_2) = \rho$$

where y_{1i}^* and y_{2i}^* are the unobserved latent variables; instead we observe only $y_{ji} = 1$ if $y_{ji}^* > 0$ and $y_{ji} = 0$ otherwise (for $j = 1, 2$).

In the maximum likelihood estimation, ρ is not directly estimated. Directly estimated is atanh ρ:

$$\text{atanh}\,\rho = \frac{1}{2}\ln\left(\frac{1+\rho}{1-\rho}\right)$$

From the form of the likelihood, it is clear that if $\rho = 0$, then the log likelihood for the bivariate probit models is equal to the sum of the log likelihoods of the two univariate probit models. A likelihood-ratio test may therefore be performed by comparing the likelihood of the full bivariate model with the sum of the log likelihoods for the univariate probit models.

References

Greene, W. H. 2000. *Econometric Analysis*. 4th ed. Upper Saddle River, NJ: Prentice–Hall.

Hardin, J. W. 1996. sg61: Bivariate probit models. *Stata Technical Bulletin* 33: 15–20. Reprinted in *Stata Technical Bulletin Reprints*, vol. 6, pp. 152–158.

Heckman, J. 1979. Sample selection bias as a specification error. *Econometrica* 47: 153–161.

Pindyck, R. and D. Rubinfeld. 1998. *Econometric Models and Economic Forecasts*. 4th ed. New York: McGraw–Hill.

Poirier, D. 1981. Partial observability in bivariate probit models. *Journal of Econometrics* 12: 209–217.

Van de Ven, W. P. M. M. and B. M. S. Van Pragg. 1981. The demand for deductibles in private health insurance: A probit model with sample selection. *Journal of Econometrics* 17: 229–252.

Also See

Complementary:	[R] **adjust**, [R] **constraint**, [R] **lincom**, [R] **lrtest**, [R] **mfx**, [R] **predict**, [R] **test**, [R] **testnl**, [R] **vce**, [R] **xi**
Related:	[R] **heckman**, [R] **probit**
Background:	[U] **16.5 Accessing coefficients and standard errors**, [U] **23 Estimation and post-estimation commands**, [U] **23.11 Obtaining robust variance estimates**, [U] **23.12 Obtaining scores**

Title

> **bitest** — Binomial probability test

Syntax

> **bitest** *varname* = #$_p$ $\left[weight\right]$ $\left[\text{if } exp\right]$ $\left[\text{in } range\right]$ $\left[, \underline{\text{detail}}\right]$
>
> **bitesti** #$_N$ #$_{\text{succ}}$ #$_p$ $\left[, \underline{\text{detail}}\right]$

by ... : may be used with **bitest** (but not with **bitesti**); see [R] **by**.
bitest allows fweights; see [U] **14.1.6 weight**.

Description

bitest performs exact hypothesis tests for binomial random variables. The null hypothesis is that the probability of a success on a single trial is #$_p$. The total number of trials is the number of nonmissing values of *varname* (in **bitest**) or #$_N$ (in **bitesti**). The number of observed successes is the number of 1s in *varname* (in **bitest**) or #$_{\text{succ}}$ (in **bitesti**). *varname* must contain only 0s, 1s, and missing.

bitesti is the immediate form of **bitest**; see [U] **22 Immediate commands** for a general introduction to immediate commands.

Options

detail shows the probability of the observed number k_{obs} of successes, the probability of the number k_{opp} of successes on the opposite tail of the distribution that is used to compute the two-sided p-value, and the probability of the point next to k_{opp}. This information can be safely ignored. See the technical note below for details.

Remarks

▷ Example

You test 15 university students for high levels of one measure of visual quickness which, from other evidence, you believe is present in 30% of the nonuniversity population. Included in your data is quick, taking on the values 1 ("success") or 0 ("failure") depending on the outcome of the test.

```
. bitest quick = 0.3
```

Variable	N	Observed k	Expected k	Assumed p	Observed p
quick	15	7	4.5	0.30000	0.46667

```
Pr(k >= 7)              = 0.131143  (one-sided test)
Pr(k <= 7)              = 0.949987  (one-sided test)
Pr(k <= 1 or k >= 7)   = 0.166410  (two-sided test)
```

The first part of the output reveals that, assuming a true probability of success of 0.3, the expected number of successes is 4.5 and you observed 7. Said differently, the assumed frequency under the null hypothesis H_0 is 0.3 and the observed frequency is 0.47.

The first line under the table is a one-sided test; it is the probability of observing 7 or more successes conditional on $p = 0.3$. It is a test of $H_0: p = 0.3$ versus the alternative hypothesis $H_A: p > 0.3$. Said in English, the alternative hypothesis is that more than 30% of university students score at high levels on this test of visual quickness. The p-value for this hypothesis test is 0.13.

The second line under the table is a one-sided test of H_0 versus the opposite alternative hypothesis $H_A: p < 0.3$.

The third line is the two-sided test. It is a test of H_0 versus the alternative hypothesis $H_A: p \neq 0.3$.

◁

❑ Technical Note

The p-value of a hypothesis test is the probability (calculated assuming H_0 is true) of observing any outcome as extreme or more extreme than the observed outcome. "Extreme" means in the direction of the alternative hypothesis. In the previous example, the outcomes $k = 8, 9, \ldots, 15$ are clearly "more extreme" than the observed outcome $k_{obs} = 7$ when considering the alternative hypothesis $H_A: p \neq 0.3$. However, outcomes with only a few successes are also in the direction of this alternative hypothesis. For two-sided hypotheses, outcomes with k successes are considered "as extreme or more extreme" than the observed outcome k_{obs} if $\Pr(k) \leq \Pr(k_{obs})$. Here, $\Pr(k = 0)$ and $\Pr(k = 1)$ are both less than $\Pr(k = 7)$, so they are included in the two-sided p-value.

The **detail** option allows you to see the probability (calculated assuming H_0 is true) of the observed successes ($k = 7$) and the probability of the boundary point ($k = 1$) of the opposite tail used for the two-sided p-value.

```
. bitest quick = 0.3, detail
          Variable |      N   Observed k   Expected k   Assumed p   Observed p
    --------------+------------------------------------------------------------
             quick |     15          7          4.5       0.30000     0.46667

    Pr(k >= 7)               = 0.131143  (one-sided test)
    Pr(k <= 7)               = 0.949987  (one-sided test)
    Pr(k <= 1 or k >= 7)     = 0.166410  (two-sided test)

    Pr(k == 7)               = 0.081130  (observed)
    Pr(k == 2)               = 0.091560
    Pr(k == 1)               = 0.030520  (opposite extreme)
```

Also shown is the probability of the point next to the boundary point. This probability, namely $\Pr(k = 2) = 0.092$, is certainly close to the probability of the observed outcome $\Pr(k = 7) = 0.081$, so some people might argue that $k = 2$ should be included in the two-sided p-value. Statisticians (at least some that we know) would reply that the p-value is a precisely defined concept and that this is an arbitrary "fuzzification" of its definition. When you compute exact p-values according to the precise definition of a p-value, your Type I error is never more than what you say it is—so no one can criticize you for being anticonservative. Including the point $k = 2$ is being overly conservative since it makes the p-value larger yet. But it is your choice; being overly conservative, at least in statistics, is always safe. Know that **bitest** and **bitesti** always keep to the precise definition of a p-value, so if you wish to include this extra point, you must do so by hand or by using the **r()** saved results; see *Saved Results* below.

❑

Immediate form

▷ Example

The binomial test is a function of two statistics and one parameter: N the number of observations, k_{obs} the number of observed successes, and p the assumed probability of a success on a single trial. For instance, in a city of $N = 2{,}500{,}000$ you observe $k_{obs} = 36$ cases of a particular disease when the population rate for the disease is $p = 0.00001$.

```
. bitesti 2500000 36 .00001
         N    Observed k   Expected k   Assumed p   Observed p

   2500000          36           25       0.00001      0.00001
   Pr(k >= 36)           = 0.022458  (one-sided test)
   Pr(k <= 36)           = 0.985448  (one-sided test)
   Pr(k <= 14 or k >= 36) = 0.034859  (two-sided test)
```
◁

▷ Example

Boice and Monson (1977) present data on breast cancer cases and person-years of observations for women with tuberculosis who were repeatedly exposed to multiple x-ray fluoroscopies, and women with tuberculosis who were not. The data are

	Exposed	Not Exposed	Total
Breast cancer	41	15	56
Person-years	28,010	19,017	47,027

We can thus test whether x-ray fluoroscopic examinations are associated with breast cancer; the assumed rate of exposure is $p = 28010/47027$.

```
. bitesti 56 41 28010/47027
         N    Observed k   Expected k   Assumed p   Observed p

        56          41      33.35446     0.59562      0.73214
   Pr(k >= 41)           = 0.023830  (one-sided test)
   Pr(k <= 41)           = 0.988373  (one-sided test)
   Pr(k <= 25 or k >= 41) = 0.040852  (two-sided test)
```
◁

Saved Results

`bitest` and `bitesti` save in `r()`:

Scalars

r(N)	number N of trials	r(k_opp)	opposite extreme k
r(P_p)	assumed probability p of success	r(P_k)	probability of observed k (**detail** only)
r(k)	observed number k of successes	r(P_oppk)	probability of opposite extreme k (**detail** only)
r(p_l)	lower one-sided p-value	r(k_nopp)	k next to opposite extreme (**detail** only)
r(p_u)	upper one-sided p-value	r(P_nopp k)	probability of k next to opposite extreme
r(p)	two-sided p-value		(**detail** only)

Methods and Formulas

bitest and bitesti are implemented as ado-files.

Let N, k_{obs}, and p be, respectively, the number of observations, the observed number of successes, and the assumed probability of success on a single trial. The expected number of successes is Np, and the observed probability of success on a single trial is k_{obs}/N.

bitest and bitesti compute exact p-values based on the binomial distribution. The upper one-sided p-value is

$$\Pr(k \geq k_{obs}) = \sum_{m=k_{obs}}^{N} \binom{N}{m} p^m (1-p)^{N-m}$$

The lower one-sided p-value is

$$\Pr(k \leq k_{obs}) = \sum_{m=0}^{k_{obs}} \binom{N}{m} p^m (1-p)^{N-m}$$

If $k_{obs} \geq Np$, the two-sided p-value is

$$\Pr(k \leq k_{opp} \text{ or } k \geq k_{obs})$$

where k_{opp} is the largest number $\leq Np$ such that $\Pr(k = k_{opp}) \leq \Pr(k = k_{obs})$. If $k_{obs} < Np$, the two-sided p-value is

$$\Pr(k \leq k_{obs} \text{ or } k \geq k_{opp})$$

where k_{opp} is the smallest number $\geq Np$ such that $\Pr(k = k_{opp}) \leq \Pr(k = k_{obs})$.

References

Boice, J. D. and R. R. Monson. 1977. Breast cancer in women after repeated fluoroscopic examinations of the chest. *Journal of the National Cancer Institute* 59: 823–832.

Hoel, P. G. 1984. *Introduction to Mathematical Statistics*. 5th ed. New York: John Wiley & Sons.

Also See

Complementary:	[R] **ci**, [R] **prtest**
Background:	[U] **22 Immediate commands**

Title

Syntax

boxcox *depvar* [*indepvars*] [*weight*] [if *exp*] [in *range*]

    [, model(<u>lhs</u>only | <u>rhs</u>only | <u>lam</u>bda | theta) <u>notrans</u>(*varlist*) lrtest

    from(*init_specs*) <u>nocon</u>stant <u>nolog</u> nologlr <u>iter</u>ate(#) <u>level</u>(#)]

by ... : may be used with boxcox; see [R] **by**.

fweights and iweights are allowed; see [U] **14.1.6 weight**.

boxcox shares the features of all estimation commands; see [U] **23 Estimation and post-estimation commands**.

boxcox, model(lhs) is the model that was estimated by boxcox in versions before Stata 7.

Syntax for predict

predict [*type*] *newvarname* [if *exp*] [in *range*]

    [, { xbt | yhat | <u>res</u>iduals } <u>nooff</u>set]

These statistics are available both in and out of sample; type predict ... if e(sample) ... if wanted only for the estimation sample.

Description

boxcox finds the maximum likelihood estimates of the parameter(s) of the Box–Cox transform, the coefficients on the independent variables, and the standard deviation of the normally distributed errors for a model in which *depvar* is regressed on *indepvars*. The user has the option of estimating the following models:

Option	Estimates
lhsonly	$y_j^{(\theta)} = \beta_1 x_{1j} + \beta_2 x_{2j} + \cdots + \beta_k x_{kj} + \epsilon_j$
rhsonly	$y_j = \beta_1 x_{1j}^{(\lambda)} + \beta_2 x_{2j}^{(\lambda)} + \cdots + \beta_k x_{kj}^{(\lambda)} + \epsilon_j$
rhsonly notrans()	$y_j = \beta_1 x_{1j}^{(\lambda)} + \beta_2 x_{2j}^{(\lambda)} + \cdots + \beta_k x_{kj}^{(\lambda)} + \gamma_1 z_{1j} + \cdots + \gamma_l z_{lj} + \epsilon_j$
lambda	$y_j^{(\lambda)} = \beta_1 x_{1j}^{(\lambda)} + \beta_2 x_{2j}^{(\lambda)} + \cdots + \beta_k x_{kj}^{(\lambda)} + \epsilon_j$
lambda notrans()	$y_j^{(\lambda)} = \beta_1 x_{1j}^{(\lambda)} + \beta_2 x_{2j}^{(\lambda)} + \cdots + \beta_k x_{kj}^{(\lambda)} + \gamma_1 z_{1j} + \cdots + \gamma_l z_{lj} + \epsilon_j$
theta	$y_j^{(\theta)} = \beta_1 x_{1j}^{(\lambda)} + \beta_2 x_{2j}^{(\lambda)} + \cdots + \beta_k x_{kj}^{(\lambda)} + \epsilon_j$
theta notrans()	$y_j^{(\theta)} = \beta_1 x_{1j}^{(\lambda)} + \beta_2 x_{2j}^{(\lambda)} + \cdots + \beta_k x_{kj}^{(\lambda)} + \gamma_1 z_{1j} + \cdots + \gamma_l z_{lj} + \epsilon_j$

Any variable to be transformed must be strictly positive.

Options

model(lhsonly | rhsonly | lambda | theta) specifies which of the four models to fit.

>   model(lhsonly) applies the Box–Cox transform to *depvar* only. model(lhsonly) is the default value.

>   model(rhsonly) causes the transform to be applied to the *indepvars* only.

>   model(lambda) causes the transform to be applied to both *depvar* and *indepvars*, and they are transformed by the same parameter.

>   model(theta) causes the transform to be applied to both *depvar* and *indepvars*, but this time each side is transformed by a separate parameter.

notrans(*varlist*) specifies that the variables in *varlist* are to be included as nontransformed independent variables.

lrtest specifies that a likelihood-ratio test of significance is to be performed and reported for each independent variable.

from() allows the user to specify the initial values for Box–Cox transformation parameter(s); see [R] **maximize**.

Model	Initial value specification
lhsonly	from(θ_0, copy)
rhsonly	from(λ_0, copy)
lambda	from(λ_0, copy)
theta	from(λ_0 θ_0, copy)

noconstant suppresses the constant term (intercept) in the model.

nolog suppresses the iteration log when estimating the full model.

nologlr suppresses the iteration log when estimating the restricted models required by the lrtest option. If nologlr is specified when lrtest is not, then it is ignored.

iterate(#) specifies the maximum number of iterations that the maximum likelihood optimizer will undertake in search of a solution.

level(#) specifies the confidence level, in percent, for confidence intervals. The default is level(95) or as set by set level; see [U] **23.5 Specifying the width of confidence intervals**.

Options for predict

xbt, the default, calculates the "linear" prediction. For all the models except model(lhsonly), all the *indepvars* are transformed.

yhat calculates the predicted value of y.

residuals calculates the residuals after the predicted value of y has been subtracted from the actual value.

nooffset is relevant only if you specified offset(*varname*) for boxcox. It modifies the calculations made by predict so that they ignore the offset variable; the linear prediction is treated as $x_j b$ rather than $x_j b + \text{offset}_j$.

Remarks

The Box–Cox transform

$$y^{(\lambda)} = \frac{y^\lambda - 1}{\lambda}$$

has been widely used in applied data analysis. Box and Cox (1964) developed the transformation and argued that the transformation could make the residuals more closely normal and less heteroskedastic. Cook and Weisberg (1982) discuss the transform in this light. Since the transform embeds several popular functional forms, it has received some attention as a method for testing functional forms, in particular,

$$y^{(\lambda)} = \begin{cases} y - 1 & \text{if } \lambda = 1 \\ \ln(y) & \text{if } \lambda = 0 \\ 1 - 1/y & \text{if } \lambda = -1 \end{cases}$$

Davidson and MacKinnon (1993) discuss this use of the transform. Atkinson (1985) also gives a good general treatment.

Theta model

`boxcox` obtains the maximum likelihood estimates of the parameters for four different models. The most general of the models, the `theta` model, is

$$y_j^{(\theta)} = \beta_0 + \beta_1 x_{1j}^{(\lambda)} + \beta_2 x_{2j}^{(\lambda)} + \cdots + \beta_k x_{kj}^{(\lambda)} + \gamma_1 z_{1j} + \gamma_2 z_{2j} + \cdots + \gamma_l z_{lj} + \epsilon_j$$

where $\epsilon \sim N(0, \sigma^2)$. Here the dependent variable y is subject to a Box–Cox transform with parameter θ. Each of the *indepvars* $x_1, x_2, \ldots, x_k$ is transformed by a Box–Cox transform with parameter λ. The $z_1, z_2, \ldots, z_l$ specified in the `notrans()` option are independent variables that are not transformed.

Box and Cox (1964) argued that this transformation would leave behind residuals that more closely follow a normal distribution than those produced by a simple linear regression model. Users should bear in mind that the normality of ϵ is assumed and that `boxcox` obtains maximum likelihood estimates of the $k + l + 4$ parameters under this assumption. `boxcox` does not choose λ and θ so that the residuals are approximately normally distributed. Users interested in this type of transformation to normality should see the official Stata commands `lnskew0` and `bcskew0` in [R] **lnskew0**. However, those commands work on a more restrictive model in which none of the independent variables are transformed.

▷ Example

Consider an example using the auto data.

```
. boxcox mpg weight price, notrans(foreign) model(theta) lrtest
Estimating comparison model

Iteration 0:    log likelihood = -234.39434
Iteration 1:    log likelihood = -228.26891
Iteration 2:    log likelihood = -228.26777
Iteration 3:    log likelihood = -228.26777

Estimating full model

Iteration 0:    log likelihood = -194.13727
```

```
Iteration 1:   log likelihood = -184.34212
Iteration 2:   log likelihood = -177.87944
Iteration 3:   log likelihood =  -175.7193
Iteration 4:   log likelihood = -175.67343
Iteration 5:   log likelihood = -175.67343

Estimating comparison models for LR tests

Iteration 0:   log likelihood = -179.58214
Iteration 1:   log likelihood = -177.59036
Iteration 2:   log likelihood = -177.58739
Iteration 3:   log likelihood = -177.58739

Iteration 0:   log likelihood = -203.92855
Iteration 1:   log likelihood = -201.30202
Iteration 2:   log likelihood = -201.18334
Iteration 3:   log likelihood = -201.18233
Iteration 4:   log likelihood = -201.18233

Iteration 0:   log likelihood = -178.83799
Iteration 1:   log likelihood = -175.98405
Iteration 2:   log likelihood = -175.97931
Iteration 3:   log likelihood = -175.97931
```

		Number of obs	=	74
		LR chi2(4)	=	105.19
Log likelihood = -175.67343		Prob > chi2	=	0.000

mpg	Coef.	Std. Err.	z	P>|z|	[95% Conf. Interval]	
/lambda	.7601689	.6289991	1.21	0.227	-.4726467	1.992984
/theta	-.7189314	.3244439	-2.22	0.027	-1.35483	-.0830331

Estimates of scale-variant parameters

	Coef.	chi2(df)	P>chi2(df)	df of chi2
Notrans				
foreign	-.0114338	3.828	0.050	1
_cons	1.3774			
Trans				
weight	-.000239	51.018	0.000	1
price	-6.18e-06	0.612	0.434	1
/sigma	.0138489			

Test HO:	Restricted log likelihood	chi2	Prob > chi2
theta=lambda = -1	-181.64479	11.94	0.001
theta=lambda = 0	-178.2406	5.13	0.023
theta=lambda = 1	-194.13727	36.93	0.000

The output is composed of the iteration logs and three distinct tables. The first table contains a standard header for a maximum likelihood estimator and a standard output table for the Box–Cox transform parameters. The second table contains the estimates of the scale-variant parameters. The third table contains the output from likelihood-ratio tests on three standard functional form specifications.

If we were to interpret this output, the right-hand-side transformation would not significantly add to the regression, while the left-hand-side transformation would make the 5% but not the 1% cutoff. `price` is certainly not significant and `foreign` lies right on the 5% cutoff. `weight` is clearly significant. The output also says that the linear and multiplicative inverse specifications are both strongly rejected. A natural log specification can be rejected at the 5% but not the 1% level.

◁

❏ Technical Note

Spitzer (1984) showed that the Wald statistics of whether the coefficients of the right-hand-side variables, transformed or untransformed, are significantly different from zero are not invariant to changes in the scale of the transformed dependent variable. Davidson and MacKinnon (1993) also discuss this point. It is worth noting that this problem is an example of the manipulability of Wald statistics in nonlinear models. Lafontaine and White (1986) analyze this problem numerically, and Phillips and Park (1988) analyze it using Edgeworth expansions. See Drukker (2000b) for a more detailed discussion of this issue. Since the parameter estimates and their Wald tests are not scale invariant, no Wald tests or confidence intervals are reported for these parameters. However, when the `lrtest` option is specified, likelihood-ratio tests are performed and reported. Schlesselman (1971) showed that, if a constant is included in the model, then the parameter estimates of the Box–Cox transforms are scale invariant. For this reason, it is highly recommended that the `noconstant` option not be used.

The `lrtest` option does not perform a likelihood-ratio test on the constant. Hence, no value for this statistic is reported. Unless the data are properly scaled, the restricted model frequently does not converge. For this reason, no likelihood-ratio test on the constant is performed by the `lrtest` option. However, if a user has a special interest in performing this test, then it can be done by estimating the constrained model separately. If problems with convergence are encountered, rescaling the data by their means may help.

❏

Lambda model

A less general model than the one above is called the `lambda` model. It specifies that the same parameter be used in both the left-hand side and right-hand side transformations. Specifically,

$$y_j^{(\lambda)} = \beta_0 + \beta_1 x_{1j}^{(\lambda)} + \beta_2 x_{2j}^{(\lambda)} + \cdots + \beta_k x_{kj}^{(\lambda)} + \gamma_1 z_{1j} + \gamma_2 z_{2j} + \cdots + \gamma_l z_{lj} + \epsilon_j$$

where $\epsilon \sim N(0, \sigma^2)$. Here the *depvar* variable y and each of the *indepvars* $x_1, x_2, \ldots, x_k$ are transformed by a Box–Cox transform with the common parameter λ. Again, the $z_1, z_2, \ldots, z_l$ are independent variables that are not transformed.

Left-hand-side only model

Even more restrictive than a common transformation parameter is transforming the dependent variable only. Since the dependent variable is on the left-hand side of the equation, this model is known as the `lhsonly` model. In this case, one is estimating the parameters of the model

$$y_j^{(\theta)} = \beta_0 + \beta_1 x_{1j} + \beta_2 x_{2j} + \cdots + \beta_k x_{kj} + \epsilon_j$$

where $\epsilon \sim N(0, \sigma^2)$. In this case only the *depvar*, y, is transformed by a Box–Cox transform with the parameter θ.

This is the model that was estimated by Stata 6.0 and earlier versions. Even so, this implementation offers some advantages over the previous one. In particular, one can easily obtain likelihood-ratio tests of the significance of the independent variables. In contrast, the previous **boxcox** offers Wald statistics that use variance estimates of the coefficients which are conditional on θ. This difference is important. Spitzer (1984) shows that the variance estimates conditional on θ will underestimate the true variance.

▷ Example

In this example, mpg is again hypothesized to be a function of weight, price, and foreign in a Box–Cox model in which only mpg is subject to the transform.

```
. boxcox mpg weight price foreign, model(lhs) lrtest  nolog nologlr
Estimating comparison model

Estimating full model

Estimating comparison models for LR tests
```

		Number of obs	=	74
		LR chi2(3)	=	105.04
Log likelihood = -175.74705		Prob > chi2	=	0.000

mpg	Coef.	Std. Err.	z	P>|z|	[95% Conf. Interval]
/theta	-.7826999	.281954	-2.78	0.006	-1.33532 -.2300802

Estimates of scale-variant parameters

	Coef.	chi2(df)	P>chi2(df)	df of chi2
Notrans				
weight	-.0000294	58.056	0.000	1
price	-4.66e-07	0.469	0.493	1
foreign	-.0097564	4.644	0.031	1
_cons	1.249845			
/sigma	.0132444			

Test HO:	Restricted log likelihood	LR statistic chi2	P-Value Prob > chi2
theta = -1	-176.04312	0.59	0.442
theta = 0	-179.54104	7.59	0.006
theta = 1	-194.13727	36.78	0.000

It is worth noting that this model rejects both linear and log specifications of mpg but fails to reject the hypothesis that $1/\text{mpg}$ is linear in the independent variables. These findings are in line with what an engineer would have expected. In engineering terms, gallons per mile represent actual energy consumption, and energy consumption should be approximately linear in weight.

◁

Right-hand-side only model

The fourth model leaves the *depvar* alone and transforms a subset of the *indepvars* using the parameter λ. This is the `rhsonly` model. In this model the *depvar*, y, is given by

$$y_j = \beta_0 + \beta_1 x_{1j}^{(\lambda)} + \beta_2 x_{2j}^{(\lambda)} + \cdots + \beta_k x_{kj}^{(\lambda)} + \gamma_1 z_{1j} + \gamma_2 z_{2j} + \cdots + \gamma_l z_{lj} + \epsilon_j$$

where $\epsilon \sim N(0, \sigma^2)$. Here each of the *indepvars* $x_1, x_2, \ldots, x_k$ are transformed by a Box–Cox transform with the parameter λ. Again, the $z_1, z_2, \ldots, z_l$ are independent variables that are not transformed.

▷ Example

Here is an example with the `rhsonly` model. In this example, `price` and `foreign` are not included in the list of covariates. (You are invited to use the auto data and check that they fare no better here than above.)

```
. boxcox mpg weight, model(rhs) lrtest  nolog nologlr
Estimating full model

Estimating comparison models for LR tests

Comparison model for LR test on weight is a linear regression
Lambda is not identified in the restricted model
```

		Number of obs	=	74
		LR chi2(2)	=	82.90
Log likelihood = -192.94368		Prob > chi2	=	0.000

mpg	Coef.	Std. Err.	z	P>|z|	[95% Conf. Interval]
/lambda	-.4460916	.6551107	-0.68	0.496	-1.730085 .8379018

Estimates of scale-variant parameters

	Coef.	chi2(df)	P>chi2(df)	df of chi2
Notrans				
_cons	1359.092			
Trans				
weight	-614.3876	82.901	0.000	1
/sigma	3.281854			

Test HO:	Restricted log likelihood	LR statistic chi2	P-Value Prob > chi2
lambda = -1	-193.2893	0.69	0.406
lambda = 0	-193.17892	0.47	0.493
lambda = 1	-195.38869	4.89	0.027

The interpretation of the output is similar to all the cases above, except for one caveat. As requested, a likelihood-ratio test was performed on the lone independent variable. However, when it is dropped to form the constrained model, the comparison model is not a right-hand-side only

Box–Cox model, but rather a simple linear regression on a constant model. When weight is dropped, there are no longer any transformed variables. Hence, λ is not identified and it must also be dropped. This process leaves a linear regression on a constant as the "comparison model". It also implies that the test statistic has 2 degrees of freedom instead of 1. At the top of the output, a more concise warning informs the user of this point.

A similar identification issue can also arise in the `lambda` and `theta` models when only one independent variable is specified. In these cases, warnings also appear on the output.

◁

Saved Results

boxcox saves in `e()`:

Scalars

`e(N)`	number of observations	`e(ll_tm1)`	log likelihood of model $\lambda=\theta=-1$
`e(ll)`	log likelihood	`e(chi2_tm1)`	LR of $\lambda=\theta=-1$ vs. full model
`e(chi2)`	LR statistic of full vs. comparison	`e(p_tm1)`	p-value of $\lambda=\theta=-1$ vs. full model
`e(df_m)`	full model degrees of freedom	`e(ll_t0)`	log likelihood of model $\lambda=\theta=0$
`e(ll0)`	log likelihood of the restricted model	`e(chi2_t0)`	LR of $\lambda=\theta=0$ vs. full model
`e(df_r)`	restricted model degrees of freedom	`e(p_t0)`	p-value of $\lambda=\theta=0$ vs. full model
`e(ll_t1)`	log likelihood of model $\lambda=\theta=1$	`e(rc)`	return code
`e(chi2_t1)`	LR of $\lambda=\theta=1$ vs. full model	`e(ic)`	number of iterations
`e(p_t1)`	p-value of $\lambda=\theta=1$ vs. full model		

Macros

`e(cmd)`	boxcox	`e(wexp)`	weight expression
`e(depvar)`	name of dependent variable	`e(chi2type)`	LR; type of model χ^2 test
`e(model)`	lhsonly, rhsonly, lambda, or theta	`e(lrtest)`	lrtest if requested
`e(ntrans)`	yes if nontransformed *indepvars*	`e(predict)`	program used to implement
`e(wtype)`	weight type		predict

Matrices

`e(b)`	coefficient vector	`e(df)`	degrees of freedom of LR tests on
`e(V)`	variance–covariance matrix of		*indepvars*
	the estimators (see note below)	`e(chi2m)`	LR statistics for tests on *indepvars*
`e(pm)`	p-values for LR tests on *indepvars*		

Functions

`e(sample)`	marks estimation sample

Note that `e(V)` contains all zeros except for the element(s) that correspond to the parameter(s) of the Box–Cox transform.

Methods and Formulas

boxcox is implemented as an ado-file.

In the internal computations,

$$y^{(\lambda)} = \begin{cases} \frac{y^{\lambda}-1}{\lambda} & \text{if } |\lambda| > 10^{-10} \\ \\ \ln(y) & \text{otherwise} \end{cases}$$

The unconcentrated log likelihood for the theta model is

$$\ln L = \left(\frac{-N}{2}\right)\left\{\ln(2\pi) + \ln(\sigma^2)\right\} + (\theta - 1)\sum_{i=1}^{N}\ln(y_i) - \left(\frac{1}{2\sigma^2}\right)\text{SSR}$$

where

$$\text{SSR} = \sum_{i=1}^{N}(y_i^{(\theta)} - \beta_0 + \beta_1 x_{i1}^{(\lambda)} + \beta_2 x_{i2}^{(\lambda)} + \cdots + \beta_k x_{ik}^{(\lambda)} + \gamma_1 z_{i1} + \gamma_2 z_{i2} + \cdots + \gamma_l z_{il})^2$$

Writing the SSR in matrix form,

$$\text{SSR} = (\mathbf{Y}^{(\theta)} - \mathbf{X}^{(\lambda)}\mathbf{b}' - \mathbf{Zg}')'(\mathbf{Y}^{(\theta)} - \mathbf{X}^{(\lambda)}\mathbf{b}' - \mathbf{Zg}')$$

where $\mathbf{Y}^{(\theta)}$ is an $N \times 1$ vector of elementwise transformed data, $\mathbf{X}^{(\lambda)}$ is an $N \times k$ matrix of elementwise transformed data, $\mathbf{Z}$ is an $N \times l$ matrix of untransformed data, $\mathbf{b}$ is a $1 \times k$ vector of coefficients, and $\mathbf{g}$ is a $1 \times l$ vector of coefficients. Letting

$$\mathbf{W}_\lambda = \left(\mathbf{X}^{(\lambda)}\ \mathbf{Z}\right)$$

be the horizontal concatenation of $\mathbf{X}^{(\lambda)}$ and $\mathbf{Z}$ and

$$\mathbf{d}' = \begin{pmatrix} \mathbf{b}' \\ \mathbf{g}' \end{pmatrix}$$

be the vertical concatenation of the coefficients yields

$$\text{SSR} = (\mathbf{Y}^{(\theta)} - \mathbf{W}_\lambda\mathbf{d}')'(\mathbf{Y}^{(\theta)} - \mathbf{W}_\lambda\mathbf{d}')$$

For given values of λ and θ, the solutions for $\mathbf{d}'$ and σ^2 are

$$\widehat{\mathbf{d}}' = (\mathbf{W}_\lambda'\mathbf{W}_\lambda)^{-1}\mathbf{W}_\lambda'\mathbf{Y}^{(\theta)}$$

and

$$\widehat{\sigma}^2 = \frac{1}{N}\left(\mathbf{Y}^{(\theta)} - \mathbf{W}_\lambda\widehat{\mathbf{d}}'\right)'\left(\mathbf{Y}^{(\theta)} - \mathbf{W}_\lambda\widehat{\mathbf{d}}'\right)$$

Substituting these solutions into the log-likelihood function yields the concentrated log-likelihood function

$$\ln L_c = \left(-\frac{N}{2}\right)\left\{\ln(2\pi) + 1 + \ln(\widehat{\sigma}^2)\right\} + (\theta - 1)\sum_{i=1}^{N}\ln(y_i)$$

Similar calculations yield the concentrated log-likelihood function for the lambda model:

$$\ln L_c = \left(-\frac{N}{2}\right)\left\{\ln(2\pi) + 1 + \ln(\widehat{\sigma}^2)\right\} + (\lambda - 1)\sum_{i=1}^{N}\ln(y_i)$$

the `lhsonly` model:

$$\ln L_c = \left(-\frac{N}{2}\right)\left\{\ln(2\pi) + 1 + \ln(\widehat{\sigma}^2)\right\} + (\theta - 1)\sum_{i=1}^{N}\ln(y_i)$$

and the `rhsonly` model:

$$\ln L_c = \left(-\frac{N}{2}\right)\left\{\ln(2\pi) + 1 + \ln(\widehat{\sigma}^2)\right\}$$

where $\widehat{\sigma}^2$ is specific to each model and is defined analogously to that in the `theta` model.

References

Atkinson, A. C. 1985. *Plots, Transformations and Regression*. Oxford: Oxford University Press.

Box, G. E. P. and D. R. Cox. 1964. An analysis of transformations. *Journal of the Royal Statistical Society*, Series B 26: 211–243.

Carroll, R. J. and D. Ruppert. 1988. *Transformation and Weighting in Regression*. New York: Chapman & Hall.

Cook, R. D. and S. Weisberg. 1982. *Residuals and Influence in Regression*. New York: Chapman & Hall.

Davidson, R. and J. G. MacKinnon. 1993. *Estimation and Inference in Econometrics*. Oxford: Oxford University Press.

Drukker, D. M. 2000a. sg130: Box–Cox regression models. *Stata Technical Bulletin* 54: 27–36. Reprinted in *Stata Technical Bulletin Reprints*, vol. 9, pp. 307–319.

——. 2000b. sg131: On the manipulability of Wald statistics in Box–Cox regression models. *Stata Technical Bulletin* 54: 36–42. Reprinted in *Stata Technical Bulletin Reprints*, vol. 9, pp. 319–327.

Lafontaine, F. and K. J. White. 1986. Obtaining any Wald statistic you want. *Economics Letters* 21: 35–40.

Phillips, P. C. B. and J. Y. Park. 1988. On the formulation of Wald tests of nonlinear restrictions. *Econometrica* 56: 1065–1083.

Schlesselman, J. 1971. Power families: A note on the Box and Cox transformation. *Journal of the Royal Statistical Society*, Series B 33: 307–311.

Spitzer, J. J. 1984. Variance estimates in models with the Box–Cox transformation: Implications for estimation and hypothesis testing. *The Review of Economics and Statistics* 66: 645–652.

Also See

Complementary:	[R] **lincom**, [R] **mfx**, [R] **predict**, [R] **regress**, [R] **test**, [R] **testnl**
Related:	[R] **lnskew0**
Background:	[U] **16.5 Accessing coefficients and standard errors**,
	[U] **23 Estimation and post-estimation commands**

Title

> **brier** — Brier score decomposition

Syntax

> brier *outcome*$_{\text{var}}$ *forecast*$_{\text{var}}$ $\left[\text{if } exp\right]$ $\left[\text{in } range\right]$ $\left[,\ \underline{\text{g}}\text{roup}(\#)\ \right]$

by ... : may be used with brier; see [R] **by**.

Description

> brier computes the Yates, Sanders, and Murphy decompositions of the Brier Mean Probability Score. *outcome*$_{\text{var}}$ contains 0/1 values reflecting the actual outcome of the experiment and *forecast*$_{\text{var}}$ contains the corresponding probabilities as predicted by, say, logit, probit, or a human forecaster.

Options

> group(#) specifies the number of groups that will be used to compute the decomposition. group(10) is the default.

Remarks

> You have a binary (0/1) response and a formula that predicts the corresponding probabilities of having observed a positive outcome (1). If the probabilities were obtained from logistic regression, there are numerous methods that assess goodness of fit (see, for instance, lfit in [R] **logistic**). However, the probabilities might be computed from a published formula or from a model estimated on another sample, both completely unrelated to the data at hand, or perhaps the forecasts are not from a formula at all. In any case, you now have a *test dataset* consisting of the forecast probabilities and observed outcomes. Your test dataset might, for instance, record predictions made by a meteorologist on the probability of rain along with a variable recording whether it actually rained.

> The Brier score is an aggregate measure of disagreement between the observed outcome and a prediction—the average squared error difference. The Brier score decomposition is a partition of the Brier score into components that suggest reasons for discrepancy. These reasons fall roughly into three groups: (1) lack of overall calibration between the average predicted probability and the actual probability of the event in your data; (2) misfit of the data in groups defined within your sample; and (3) inability to match actual 0 and 1 responses.

> (1) refers to simply overstating or understating the probabilities.

> (2) refers to what is standardly called a goodness-of-fit test: the data are grouped and the predictions for the group are compared with the outcomes.

> (3) refers to an individual-level measure of fit. Imagine that the grouped outcomes are predicted on average correctly but that, within the group, the outcomes are poorly predicted.

> Using logit or probit analysis to fit your data will guarantee that there is no lack of fit due to (1) and a good model fitter will be able to avoid problem (2). Problem (3) is inherent in any prediction exercise.

▷ Example

You have data on the outcomes of 20 basketball games (`win`) and the probability of victory predicted by a local pundit (`for`).

```
. summarize win for
    Variable |       Obs        Mean    Std. Dev.        Min         Max
-------------+--------------------------------------------------------------
         win |        20         .65    .4893605           0           1
         for |        20       .4785    .2147526         .15          .9

. brier win for, group(5)
Mean probability of outcome   0.6500
                of forecast   0.4785

Correlation                   0.5907
ROC area                      0.8791  p = 0.0030

Brier score                   0.1828
Spiegelhalter's z-statistic  -0.6339  p = 0.7369
Sanders-modified Brier score  0.1861
Sanders resolution            0.1400
Outcome index variance        0.2275
Murphy resolution             0.0875
Reliability-in-the-small      0.0461
Forecast variance             0.0438
Excess forecast variance      0.0285
Minimum forecast variance     0.0153
Reliability-in-the-large      0.0294
2*Forecast-Outcome-Covar      0.1179
```

The mean probabilities of forecast and outcome are simply the mean of the predicted probabilities and the actual outcomes (win/losses). The correlation is the product-moment correlation between them.

The Brier score measures the total difference between the event (winning) and the forecast probability of that event as an average squared difference. As a benchmark, a perfect forecaster would have a Brier score of 0, a perfect misforecaster (predicts probability of win is 1 when loses and 0 when wins) would have a Brier score of 1; a fence-sitter (forecasts every game as 50/50) would have a Brier score of .25. Our pundit is doing reasonably well.

Spiegelhalter's Z statistic is a standard normal test statistic for testing whether an individual Brier score is extreme. The ROC area is the area under the receiver operating curve and the associated test is a test of whether it is greater than 0.5. The more accurate are the forecast probabilities, the larger is the ROC area.

The Sanders-modified Brier score measures the difference between a grouped forecast measure and the event, where the data are grouped by sorting the sample on the forecast and dividing it into approximately equally sized groups. The difference between the modified and the unmodified score is typically minimal. In order that this and the other statistics which require grouping, the Sanders and Murphy resolutions and Reliability-in-the-small, be well-defined, group boundaries are chosen so as not to allocate observations with the same forecast probability to different groups. This is done by grouping on the forecast using `xtile, n(#)` with # being the number of groups; see [R] **pctile**.

Sanders resolution measures error that arises from statistical considerations in evaluating the forecast for a group. A group with all positive or all negative outcomes would have a Sanders resolution of 0: it would most certainly be feasible to predict exactly what happened to each member of the group. If the group had 40% positive responses, on the other hand, a forecast that assigned $p = .4$ to each member of the group would be a good one and yet, there would be "errors" in the squared difference sense. (The "error" would be $(1 - .4)^2$ or $(0 - .4)^2$ for each member.) The Sanders resolution is the average across groups of such "expected" errors. The .1400 value in our data out of an overall Brier score of .1828 or .1861 suggests that a substantial portion of the "error" in our data is inherent.

Outcome index variance is just the variance of the outcome variable. This is the expected value of the Brier score if all the forecast probabilities were merely the average observed outcome. Remember that a fence-sitter has an expected Brier score of .25; a smarter fence sitter (who would guess $p = .65$ for this data) would have a Brier score of .2275.

The Murphy resolution measures the variation in the average outcomes across groups. If all groups have the same frequency of positive outcomes, little information in any forecast is possible and the Murphy resolution is 0. If groups differ markedly, the Murphy resolution is as large as .25. The .0875 means there is some, but not a lot of variation, and .0875 is probably higher than in most real cases. If you had groups in your data that varied between 40% and 60% positive outcomes, the Murphy resolution would be .01; between 30% and 70%, .04.

Reliability-in-the-small measures the error that comes from the average forecast within group not measuring the average outcome within group—a classical goodness-of-fit measure, 0 meaning a perfect fit and 1 meaning a complete lack of fit. The calculated value of 0.0461 shows some amount of lack of fit. Remember, the number is squared, and we are saying that probabilities could be just more than $\sqrt{.0461} = .215$ or 21.5% off.

Forecast variance measures the amount of discrimination being attempted—that is, the variation in the forecasted probabilities. A small number indicates a fence-sitter making constant predictions. If the forecasts were from a logistic regression model, forecast variance would tend to increase with the amount of information available. Our pundit shows considerable forecast variance of .0438 (standard deviation $\sqrt{.0438} = .2093$), which is in line with the reliability-in-the-small, suggesting that the forecaster is attempting as much variation as is available in this data.

Excess forecast variance is the amount of actual forecast variance over a theoretical minimum. The theoretical minimum—called the minimum forecast variance—corresponds to forecasts of p_0 for observations ultimately observed to be negative responses and p_1 for observations ultimately observed to be positive outcomes. Moreover, p_0 and p_1 are set to the average forecasts made for the ultimate negative and positive outcomes. These predictions would be just as good as the predictions the forecaster did make and any variation in the actual forecast probabilities above this is useless. If this number is large, above $1-2$ percent, then the forecaster may be attempting more than is possible. The .0285 in our data suggests this possibility.

Reliability-in-the-large measures the discrepancy between the mean forecast and the observed fraction of positive outcomes. This will be 0 for forecasts made by most statistical models—at least when measured on the same sample used for estimation—since they, by design, reproduce sample means. For our human pundit, the .0294 says that there is a $\sqrt{.0294}$ or 17 percentage point difference. (This difference can also be found by calculating the difference in the averages of the observed outcomes and forecast probabilities: $.65 - .4785 = .17$.) That difference, however, is not significant, as we would see if we typed **ttest win=for**; see [R] **ttest**. If this data were larger and the bias persisted, this would be a critical shortcoming of the forecast.

Twice the forecast-outcome covariance is a measure of how accurately the forecast corresponds to the outcome. It is similar in concept to R-squared in linear regression.

◁

Methods and Formulas

brier is implemented as an ado-file.

See Wilks (1995, 259–263) or Schmidt and Griffith (1998) for a discussion of the Brier score.

Let d_j, $j = 1, \ldots, N$, be the observed outcomes, $d_j = 0$ or $d_j = 1$, and let f_j be the corresponding forecasted probabilities that d_j is 1, $0 \leq f_j \leq 1$. Assume the data are ordered so that $f_{j+1} \geq f_j$ (brier sorts the data to obtain this order). Divide the data into K nearly equally sized groups, group 1 containing observations 1 through $j_2 - 1$, group 2 observations j_2 through $j_3 - 1$, and so on.

Define

$$\overline{f}_0 = \text{average } f_j \text{ among } d_j = 0$$
$$\overline{f}_1 = \text{average } f_j \text{ among } d_j = 1$$
$$\overline{f} = \text{average } f_j$$
$$\overline{d} = \text{average } d_j$$
$$\widetilde{f}_k = \text{average } f_j \text{ in group } k$$
$$\widetilde{d}_k = \text{average } d_j \text{ in group } k$$
$$\widetilde{n}_k = \text{number of observations in group } k$$

The Brier score is $\sum_j (d_j - f_j)^2 / N$.

The Sanders-modified Brier score is $\sum_j (d_j - \widetilde{f}_{k(j)})^2 / N$.

Let p_j denote the true but unknown probability that $d_j = 1$. Under the null hypothesis that $p_j = f_j$ for all j, Spiegelhalter (1986) determined that the expectation and variance of the Brier score is given by the following:

$$E(\text{Brier}) = \frac{1}{N} \sum_{j=1}^{N} f_j (1 - f_j)$$

$$\text{Var}(\text{Brier}) = \frac{1}{N^2} \sum_{j=1}^{N} f_j (1 - f_j)(1 - 2f_j)^2$$

Denoting the observed value of the Brier score by O(Brier), Spiegelhalter's Z statistic is given by

$$Z = \frac{O(\text{Brier}) - E(\text{Brier})}{\sqrt{\text{Var}(\text{Brier})}}$$

The corresponding p-value is given by the upper-tail probability of Z under the standard normal distribution.

The area under the ROC curve is estimated by applying the trapezoidal rule to the empirical ROC curve. This area is Wilcoxon's test statistic, so the corresponding p-value is just that of a one-sided Wilcoxon test of the null hypothesis that the distribution of predictions is constant across the two outcomes.

The Sanders resolution is $\sum_k \widetilde{n}_k \{\widetilde{d}_k (1 - \widetilde{d}_k)\} / N$.

The outcome index variance is $\overline{d}(1 - \overline{d})$.

The Murphy resolution is $\sum_k \widetilde{n}_k (\widetilde{d}_k - \overline{d})^2 / N$.

Reliability-in-the-small is $\sum_k \widetilde{n}_k (\widetilde{d}_k - \widetilde{f}_k)^2 / N$.

The forecast variance is $\sum_j (f_j - \overline{f})^2 / N$.

The minimum forecast variance is $\left\{ \sum_{j \in F} (f_j - \overline{f}_0)^2 + \sum_{j \in S} (f_j - \overline{f}_1)^2 \right\} / N$, where F is the set of observations for which $d_j = 0$ and S is the complement.

The excess forecast variance is the difference between the forecast variance and the minimum forecast variance.

Reliability-in-the-large is $(\overline{f} - \overline{d})^2$.

Twice the outcome covariance is $2(\overline{f}_1 - \overline{f}_0)\overline{d}(1 - \overline{d})$.

Acknowledgment

We would like to thank Richard Goldstein for his contributions to this improved version of `brier`.

References

Brier, G. W. 1950. Verification of forecasts expressed in terms of probability. *Monthly Weather Review* 78: 1–3.

Goldstein, R. 1996. sg55: Extensions to the brier command. *Stata Technical Bulletin* 32: 21–22. Reprinted in *Stata Technical Bulletin Reprints*, vol. 6, pp. 133–134.

Hadorn, D., E. B. Keeler, W. H. Rogers, and R. Brook. 1993. *Assessing the Performance of Mortality Prediction Models*. N-3599-HCFA. Santa Monica, CA: The Rand Corporation.

Holloway, L. and P. Mielke. 1998. Glenn Wilson Brier 1913–1998. *Bulletin of the American Meteorological Society* 79: 1438–1439.

Murphy, A. H. 1973. A new vector partition of the probability score. *Journal of Applied Meteorology* 12: 595–600.

———. 1997. Forecast verification. In *Economic Value of Weather and Climate Forecasts*, ed. R. W. Katz and A. H. Murphy, 19–74. Cambridge: Cambridge University Press.

Redelmeier, D. A., D. A. Bloch, and D. H. Hickam. 1991. Assessing predictive accuracy: how to compare Brier scores. *Journal of Clinical Epidemiology* 44: 1141–1146.

Rogers, W. H. 1992. sbe9: Brier score decomposition. *Stata Technical Bulletin* 10: 20–22. Reprinted in *Stata Technical Bulletin Reprints*, vol. 2, pp. 92–94.

Sanders, F. 1963. On subjective probability forecasting. *Journal of Applied Meteorology* 2: 191–201.

Schmidt, C. H. and J. L. Griffith. 1998. Multivariate classification rules: calibration and discrimination. In *Encyclopedia of Biostatistics*, ed. P. Armitage and T. Colton, 2844–2850. New York: John Wiley & Sons.

Spiegelhalter, D. J. 1986. Probabilistic prediction in patient management and clinical trials. *Statistics in Medicine* 5: 421–433.

Wilks, D. S. 1995. *Statistical Methods in the Atmospheric Sciences*. San Diego: Academic Press.

Yates, J. F. 1982. External correspondence: Decompositions of the mean probability score. *Organizational Behavior and Human Performance* 30: 132–156.

Also See

Complementary: [R] **logistic**, [R] **logit**, [R] **predict**, [R] **probit**

Title

bstrap — Bootstrap sampling and estimation

Syntax

bstrap *progname* $\big[$, <u>r</u>eps(#) <u>s</u>ize(#) <u>d</u>ots <u>arg</u>s(...) <u>l</u>evel(#) <u>cl</u>uster(*varnames*)

    <u>id</u>cluster(*newvarname*) <u>sa</u>ving(*filename*) <u>doub</u>le <u>e</u>very(#) replace <u>no</u>isily $\big]$

bs "*command*" "*exp_list*" $\big[$, *bstrap_options* $\big]$

bstat $\big[$*varlist*$\big]$ $\big[$, <u>s</u>tat(#) <u>l</u>evel(#) $\big]$

bsample $\big[$*exp*$\big]$ $\big[$, <u>cl</u>uster(*varnames*) <u>id</u>cluster(*newvarname*) $\big]$

Description

    bstrap runs the user-defined program *progname* reps() times on bootstrap samples of size size().

    bs runs the user-specified *command* bootstrapping the statistics specified in *exp_list*. The expressions in *exp_list* must be separated by spaces, and there must be no spaces within each expression. Note that *command* and *exp_list* must both be enclosed in double quotes. *exp_list* can contain saved results (such as e(F) or r(mean)) but these should *not* be enclosed in single left and right quotes. Similarly, S_# global macros are allowed but the $ sign should not be placed in front of the macro; see the last two technical notes in *The bs command* section below. bs takes the same options as bstrap except for args().

    bstat displays bootstrap estimates of standard error and bias, and calculates confidence intervals using three different methods: normal approximation, percentile, and bias-corrected. bstrap and bs automatically run bstat after completing all the bootstrap replications. If the user specifies the saving(*filename*) option with bstrap or bs, then bstat can be run on the data in *filename* to view the bootstrap estimates again.

    bsample is a low-level utility for do-it-yourselfers who prefer not to use bstrap or bs. bsample draws a sample with replacement from the existing data; the sample replaces the dataset in memory. *exp* specifies that the size of the sample and must be less than or equal to _N. If *exp* is not specified, a sample of size _N is drawn (or size n_c when the cluster() option is specified, where n_c is the number of clusters).

    Since bootstrapping is a random process, persons interested in reproducibility of results should first set the random number seed by typing set seed # before running bstrap, bs, or bsample; see [R] **generate**.

Options

reps(#) specifies the number of bootstrap replications to be performed. The default is 50. How many replications should be specified? The conventional wisdom, summarized for instance in Mooney and Duval (1993, 11), is that 50–200 replications are generally adequate for estimates of standard error, and thus are adequate for normal-approximation confidence intervals, which are based on the standard error estimates. For estimates of confidence intervals using the percentile or bias-corrected methods, you should use 1,000 or more replications.

size(#) specifies the size of the samples to be drawn. The default is _N unless cluster() is specified. If cluster() is specified, the default is the number of clusters in the original dataset. Unless all the clusters contain the same number of observations, the bootstrap sample sizes will differ between replications. If size(#) is specified, # must be less than or equal to the number of observations, or if clustered, the number of clusters.

dots requests that a dot be placed on the screen at the beginning of each replication, thus providing entertainment if a large number of reps() are requested.

args(...) (bstrap only) specifies any arguments to be passed to *progname*. The first query call to *progname* is then of the form '*progname* ? ...' and subsequent calls are of the form '*progname postname* ...'.

level(#) specifies the confidence level, in percent, for confidence intervals. The default is level(95) or as set by set level; see [R] **level**.

cluster(*varnames*) specifies the variable(s) identifying resampling clusters. If specified, the sample drawn during each replication is a bootstrap sample of clusters.

idcluster(*newvarname*) creates a new variable containing a unique identifier for each resampled cluster.

saving(*filename*) creates a Stata data file (.dta file) containing the bootstrap distribution for each user-specified statistic.

double specifies that the bootstrap results for each replication are to be stored as doubles, meaning 8-byte reals. By default, they are stored as floats, meaning 4-byte reals.

every(#) specifies that results are to be written to disk every #th replication. every() should only be specified in conjunction with saving() when performing bootstraps that take a long time. This will allow recovery of partial results should some other software crash your computer. See [P] **postfile**.

replace indicates that the file specified by saving() may already exist and, if it does, it should be overwritten.

noisily requests that any output from the user-defined program be displayed.

stat(#) (bstat only) allows the user to specify the observed value of the statistic (i.e., the value of the statistic computed using the original dataset). Specifying this option is not necessary when using a dataset created using the saving() option with bstrap or bs. In these cases, the observed value of the statistic is stored with the dataset as a characteristic (see [P] **char**) and is automatically retrieved by bstat when needed.

Remarks

With few assumptions, bootstrapping provides a way of estimating standard errors and other measures of statistical precision (Efron 1979, Efron and Stein 1981, Efron 1982, Efron and Tibshirani 1986, Efron and Tibshirani 1993; also see Davison and Hinkley 1997, Mooney and Duval 1993, and

Stine 1990). It provides a way to obtain such measures when no formula is otherwise available, or when available formulas make assumptions that are not tenable.

Mechanically, the procedure is this: One has a dataset containing N observations and an estimator which, when applied to the data, produces certain statistics. One draws, with replacement, N observations from the N observation dataset. In this random drawing, some of the original observations will appear once, some more than once, and some not at all. Using that dataset, one applies the estimator and estimates the statistics. One then does it again, drawing a new random sample and re-estimating, and again, and keeps track of the estimated statistics at each step of the way (called a replication).

Thus, one builds a dataset of estimated statistics. From this data, one can calculate the standard deviation using the standard formula: $\{\sum (\theta_i^* - \overline{\theta^*})^2 / (k-1)\}^{1/2}$, where θ_i^* is the statistic calculated using the ith bootstrap sample and k the number of replications. This formula gives an estimate of the standard error of the statistic. Note that although the average $\overline{\theta^*}$ of the bootstrapped statistic is used in the calculation of the standard deviation, it is not used as the estimated value of the statistic itself. The point estimate used is the original observed statistic θ_{obs}; i.e., the value of the statistic computed using the original N observations.

Researchers new to bootstrapping may think that the average $\overline{\theta^*}$ is somehow a better estimate of the parameter than the observed value θ_{obs}, but it is not. If the statistic is biased in some way, $\overline{\theta^*}$ exaggerates the bias. In fact, the bias can be estimated as $\overline{\theta^*} - \theta_{\mathrm{obs}}$ (Efron 1982, 33). Knowing this, one might be tempted to subtract this estimate of bias from θ_{obs} to produce an unbiased statistic. The bootstrap bias estimate has, however, an indeterminate amount of random error. Thus, this unbiased estimator may have greater mean square error than the biased estimator (Mooney and Duval 1993, Hinkley 1978), so it is best to stick with θ_{obs} as the point estimate of the statistic.

❑ Technical Note

The logic behind the bootstrap is this: All measures of precision come from a statistic's sampling distribution. The sampling distribution tells you, when the statistic is estimated on a sample of size N from some population, the relative frequencies of the values of the statistic. The sampling distribution, in turn, is determined by the distribution of the population and the formula used to estimate the statistic.

In some cases, the sampling distribution can be derived analytically. For instance, if the underlying population is distributed normally and one calculates means, the sampling distribution for the mean is distributed as t with $N-1$ degrees of freedom. In other cases, deriving the sampling distribution is too hard, as in the case of means calculated from nonnormal populations. Sometimes, as in the case of means, it is not too difficult to derive the sampling distribution as $N \to \infty$. The distribution of means converges to a normal. We will then use that asymptotic result to calculate some measure of statistical precision on a finite sample of size N even though we know it is incorrect.

As a mechanical matter, if we knew the population distribution, we could obtain the sampling distribution by simulation: we would draw random samples of size N, calculate the statistic, and make a tally. Bootstrapping does precisely this, but it uses the observed distribution of the sample in place of the true population distribution. Thus, the bootstrap procedure hinges on the assumption that the observed distribution is a good estimate of the underlying population distribution. In return, the bootstrap produces an estimate, called the bootstrap distribution, of the sampling distribution. From this, one can estimate the standard error of the statistic, produce confidence intervals, or calculate an estimate of any other function of the statistic.

The accuracy with which the bootstrap distribution estimates the sampling distribution depends on the number of observations in the original sample and the number of replications in the bootstrap. A crudely estimated sampling distribution is quite adequate if one is only going to extract, say, the standard deviation. A better estimate is needed if one is going to use the 2.5th and 97.5th percentiles of the distribution to produce a 95% confidence interval. If one is going to extract many features simultaneously about the distribution, an even better estimate is needed. It is generally believed that replications on the order of 1,000 produce very good estimates, but that for estimates of standard errors only 50–200 replications are needed.

❑

The bs command

We first describe the bs command because it is much simpler to use, although more limited, than bstrap.

▷ Example

Let's say that we wish to compute bootstrap estimates for the standard errors of the coefficients for the following regression.

```
. reg mpg weight gear foreign
```

Source	SS	df	MS
Model	1629.67805	3	543.226016
Residual	813.781411	70	11.6254487
Total	2443.45946	73	33.4720474

```
Number of obs =      74
F(  3,    70) =   46.73
Prob > F      =  0.0000
R-squared     =  0.6670
Adj R-squared =  0.6527
Root MSE      =  3.4096
```

mpg	Coef.	Std. Err.	t	P>|t|	[95% Conf. Interval]	
weight	-.006139	.0007949	-7.72	0.000	-.0077245	-.0045536
gear_ratio	1.457113	1.541286	0.95	0.348	-1.616884	4.53111
foreign	-2.221682	1.234961	-1.80	0.076	-4.684734	.2413715
_cons	36.10135	6.285984	5.74	0.000	23.56435	48.63835

To run the bootstrap, we put the command in double quotes and give a list of the coefficients (see [U] **16.5 Accessing coefficients and standard errors** and [U] **16.6 Accessing results from Stata commands**) that we wish to bootstrap, enclosing this list in double quotes as well.

```
. bs "reg mpg weight gear foreign" "_b[weight] _b[gear_ratio] _b[foreign]", reps(100)
command:     reg mpg weight gear foreign
statistics:  _b[weight] _b[gear_ratio] _b[foreign]
(obs=74)

Bootstrap statistics
```

Variable	Reps	Observed	Bias	Std. Err.	[95% Conf. Interval]	
bs1	100	-.006139	.0000414	.0005756	-.0072812	-.0049969 (N)
					-.007267	-.0049173 (P)
					-.007267	-.0049173 (BC)
bs2	100	1.457113	-.004336	1.407497	-1.335665	4.249892 (N)
					-1.240059	4.321906 (P)
					-1.883508	3.452275 (BC)
bs3	100	-2.221682	.1992346	1.330934	-4.862543	.41918 (N)
					-4.622502	.3200419 (P)
					-4.640817	.0877294 (BC)

```
N = normal, P = percentile, BC = bias-corrected
```

The table of bootstrap statistics is produced by the `bstat` command, which is automatically called by `bs` after it finishes all the replications.

The first confidence interval is based on the assumption of approximate normality of the sampling (and hence bootstrap) distribution (see *Methods and Formulas* below). Since it is based on the standard error, it is a reasonable estimate if normality is approximately true even for this small number of replications. For the percentile and bias-corrected confidence intervals, we should have many more replications, so let's run it again.

This time we will set the random number seed in case we wish to reproduce the results, and we will save the bootstrap distribution as a dataset called `bsauto.dta`.

```
. set seed 1
. bs "reg mpg weight gear foreign" "_b[weight] _b[gear_ratio] _b[foreign]", reps(1000)
> saving (bsauto)
command:    reg mpg weight gear foreign
statistics: _b[weight] _b[gear_ratio] _b[foreign]
(obs=74)
```

Bootstrap statistics

Variable	Reps	Observed	Bias	Std. Err.	[95% Conf. Interval]		
bs1	1000	-.006139	.0000567	.000628	-.0073714	-.0049067	(N)
					-.0073044	-.0048548	(P)
					-.0074355	-.004928	(BC)
bs2	1000	1.457113	.1051695	1.455478	-1.399032	4.313259	(N)
					-1.262111	4.585372	(P)
					-1.523927	4.174376	(BC)
bs3	1000	-2.221682	-.019636	1.202329	-4.581061	.1376977	(N)
					-4.442199	.2677989	(P)
					-4.155504	.6170642	(BC)

N = normal, P = percentile, BC = bias-corrected

The estimated standard errors here differ from our previous estimates using only 100 replications by, respectively, 8%, 3%, and 11%. So much for our advice that 50–200 replications are good enough to estimate standard errors! Well, the more replications the better—that advice you should believe.

Note that the bias for the coefficient of `foreign` went from 15% of the standard error to 1% and flipped sign. Efron (1982, 8) comments that when the estimated bias is less than 25% of the standard error, bias should not be a serious concern. So, in this case, the estimated biases are nothing to take note of.

Which of the three methods to compute confidence intervals should we use? If the statistic is unbiased, then the percentile and bias-corrected methods should give similar results. From a computational standpoint, the bias-corrected confidence interval will be the same as the percentile confidence interval when the observed value of the statistic is equal to the median of the bootstrap distribution. Thus, for unbiased statistics, the two methods should give similar results as the number of replications becomes large. For biased statistics, the bias-corrected method should yield confidence intervals with better coverage probability (i.e., closer to the nominal value of 95% or whatever was specified) than the percentile method.

When the bootstrap distribution is approximately normal, all three methods should give similar confidence intervals as the number of replications becomes large. If we examine the normality of these bootstrap distributions using, say, the `pnorm` command (see [R] **diagplots**), we see that they very closely follow a normal distribution. Thus, in this case, the normal-approximation would also be a valid choice. The chief advantage of the normal-approximation method is that it (supposedly) requires fewer replications than the other methods. Of course, it should only be used when the bootstrap distribution exhibits normality.

We can load `bsauto.dta` containing the bootstrap distributions for these three coefficients:

```
. use bsauto, clear
(bs: reg mpg weight gear foreign)
. describe

Contains data from bsauto.dta
  obs:         1,000                        bs: reg mpg weight gear foreign
  vars:            3                        14 Sep 2000 16:07
  size:       16,000 (96.7% of memory free)
```

variable name	storage type	display format	value label	variable label
bs1	float	%9.0g		_b[weight]
bs2	float	%9.0g		_b[gear_ratio]
bs3	float	%9.0g		_b[foreign]

```
Sorted by:
```

We can now run other commands, such as **pnorm**, on the bootstrap distributions. If we want to see the bootstrap statistics again, we can simply type

```
. bstat
```

The output will be the same as before. To see the statistics for `bs1` only, we could type `bstat bs1`. The `bs` command names variables `bs1`, `bs2`, ..., and labels them with the expression that produced them; obviously, you can rename them if you wish (see [R] **rename**).

◁

❑ Technical Note

If you have two datasets from separate runs of **bs** (assuming the random number seed was set to different values), you can combine them using **append** (see [R] **append**) and then get the bootstrap statistics for the combined datasets by running **bstat**.

❑

❑ Technical Note

When using **bs**, do not forget to enclose the command and list of statistics in double quotes. The list of statistics can contain complex expressions as long as each expression contains no spaces. For example, to bootstrap the range of a variable **x**, we could type

```
. bs "summarize x" "r(max)-r(min)", reps(1000)
```

Of course, we could also bootstrap the minimum and maximum and later compute the range.

```
. bs "summarize x" "r(max) r(min)", reps(1000) saving(mybs)
(output omitted)
. use mybs, clear
(bs: summarize x)
. gen range = bs1 - bs2
. bstat range, stat(19.5637501)
(output omitted)
```

The `stat()` option in `bstat` specifies the observed value of the range.

❑

❑ Technical Note

In the previous technical note, we had the command

```
. bs "summarize x" "r(max) r(min)", reps(1000) saving(mybs)
```

Note that we did not enclose r(max) and r(min) in single quotes as we would in most other contexts. The following would be incorrect:

```
. bs "summarize x" "`r(max)´ `r(min)´", reps(1000) saving(mybs)
```

This would cause an error because `r(max)´ refers to the contents of r(max) which is a number, but bs wants to see a name.

❑

❑ Technical Note

User-written commands previous to version 6.0 saved results in S_# macros. You can use bs on these commands, but do not place a $ in front of the S_# macro in the *exp_list*. For instance, if you want bootstrapped estimates of the values saved in $S_1 and $S_2 by *oldcmd*, type

```
.bs "oldcmd oldcmd-args" "S_1 S_2"
```

Note that the following would produce an error:

```
.bs "oldcmd oldcmd-args" "$S_1 $S_2"
```

The reason is the same as discussed in the previous technical note.

Also note that bs allows only global macros that begin with S_. In fact, anything beginning with S_ in the list of statistics will be interpreted as a global macro.

❑

The bstrap command

bstrap calls the user-defined ado program *progname* in two ways. At the outset, bstrap issues '*progname* ?' and expects *progname* to set the global macro S_1 to contain a list of variable names under which results are to be stored. Thereafter, bstrap issues '*progname postname*' calls, each time with a bootstrap sample in memory, and expects *progname* to calculate the statistics and store the results using post *postname*. Details of post can be found in [P] **postfile**, but enough information is provided below to use post successfully.

progname must have the following outline:

```
program define progname
        if "`1´" == "?" {
                global S_1 "variable names"
                exit
        }
        perform calculation of statistic(s) on data in memory
        post `1´ (result1) (result2) ...
end
```

There must be the same number of results following post `1´ as there are variable names following global S_1.

▷ Example

Suppose that we wish to produce a bootstrap estimate of the ratio of two means. Since `summarize` only saves results for one variable, we must call `summarize` twice to compute the means. Thus, we cannot use `bs` for this problem. (Actually, we could. We could use `collapse` to compute the means in a single call, but calling `summarize` twice is much faster.)

We write the program below and save it as a text file called `ratio.ado` (see [U] **20 Ado-files**). Our program computes the single statistic mean of `price` divided by mean of `weight`.

```
program define ratio
        version 7.0
        if "`1'" == "?" {
                global S_1 "ratio"
                exit
        }
        tempname y
        summarize price, meanonly
        scalar `y' = r(mean)
        summarize weight, meanonly
        post `1' (`y'/`r(mean)')
end
```

The result of running our program is

```
. use auto, clear
(1978 Automobile Data)

. set seed 10001

. bstrap ratio, reps(1000)
(obs=74)

Bootstrap statistics
```

Variable	Reps	Observed	Bias	Std. Err.	[95% Conf. Interval]	
ratio	1000	2.041841	.0014779	.0962384	1.852989	2.230694 (N)
					1.862993	2.251586 (P)
					1.878892	2.254994 (BC)

N = normal, P = percentile, BC = bias-corrected

As with the `bs` command, we should specify the `saving()` option if we want to save the bootstrap distribution.

◁

❏ Technical Note

`bstrap`, `bs`, and `bsample` do not know which variables of the dataset in memory matter to the calculation at hand. You can speed their execution by dropping unnecessary variables because otherwise they are included in each bootstrap sample.

By the same token, you should drop observations with missing values. If you do not, this causes no problem in one sense because all Stata commands deal with missing values gracefully.

It does, however, cause a statistical problem. Bootstrap sampling is defined as drawing, with replacement, resamples of size N from a sample of size N. `bstrap`, `bs`, and `bsample` determine N by counting the number of observations in memory, not counting the number of nonmissing values on the relevant variables. The result is that too many observations are resampled and, moreover, the resulting resamples, since drawn from a population with missing values, are of unequal sizes.

If the number of missing values relative to sample size is small, this will make little difference. If you have a large number of missing values, however, you should first drop the missing values.

❑

▷ Example

We can improve our ratio program and, in the process, demonstrate the use of bstrap's args() option. We do not have to write our program to produce a statistic for two particular variables. We can make it work for any two variables, and then specify the variable names in the args() option when we run bstrap. Here is this more general version:

```
program define ratio
        version 7.0
        if "`1'" == "?" {
                global S_1 "ratio"
                exit
        }
        tempname y
        summarize `2', meanonly
        scalar `y' = r(mean)
        summarize `3', meanonly
        post `1' (`y'/`r(mean)')
end
```

We call bstrap using

```
. bstrap ratio, reps(1000) args(price weight)
```

When bstrap calls ratio after drawing a bootstrap sample, it will pass the arguments *postname* price weight. These arguments can be accessed via the local macros `1' `2' `3'; see [U] **21 Programming Stata** for more information. The args command (see [P] **syntax**) allows you to use named arguments instead of numbered local macros.

◁

Saved Results

bstat saves in r():

Scalars

r(reps)	number of replications	r(ub_n)	normal-approx. upper confidence bound
r(stat)	observed value of statistic	r(lb_p)	percentile lower confidence bound
r(bias)	estimated bias	r(ub_p)	percentile upper confidence bound
r(se)	estimated standard error	r(lb_bc)	bias-corrected lower confidence bound
r(lb_n)	normal-approx. lower confidence bound	r(ub_bc)	bias-corrected upper confidence bound

Methods and Formulas

bstrap, bs, bstat and bsample are implemented as ado-files.

Let θ_{obs} be the observed value of the statistic; i.e., the value of the statistic calculated using the original dataset. Let $i = 1, 2, \ldots, k$ denote the bootstrap samples, and let θ_i^* be the values of the statistic computed using each of these samples.

The standard error is estimated as

$$\widehat{se} = \left\{ \frac{1}{k-1} \sum_{i=1}^{k} (\theta_i^* - \overline{\theta^*})^2 \right\}^{1/2}$$

where

$$\overline{\theta^*} = \frac{1}{k} \sum_{i=1}^{k} \theta_i^*$$

The bias is estimated as

$$\widehat{bias} = \overline{\theta^*} - \theta_{obs}$$

Confidence intervals with nominal coverage rates $1 - \alpha$ are calculated according to the following formulas. The normal-approximation method yields confidence intervals:

$$\left[\theta_{obs} - t_{1-\alpha/2,k-1} \, \widehat{se}, \; \theta_{obs} + t_{1-\alpha/2,k-1} \, \widehat{se} \right]$$

where $t_{1-\alpha/2,k-1}$ is the $(1 - \alpha/2)$th quantile of the t distribution with $k - 1$ degrees of freedom.

The percentile method yields confidence intervals:

$$\left[\theta_{\alpha/2}^*, \, \theta_{1-\alpha/2}^* \right]$$

where θ_p^* is the pth quantile (the $100p$th percentile) of the bootstrap distribution $(\theta_1^*, \ldots, \theta_k^*)$.

Let

$$z_0 = \Phi^{-1} \{ \#(\theta_i^* \le \theta_{obs})/k \}$$

where $\#(\theta_i^* \le \theta_{obs})$ is the number of elements of the bootstrap distribution that are less than or equal to the observed statistic, and Φ is the standard cumulative normal. Let

$$p_1 = \Phi(2z_0 - z_{1-\alpha/2})$$
$$p_2 = \Phi(2z_0 + z_{1-\alpha/2})$$

where $z_{1-\alpha/2}$ is the $(1 - \alpha/2)$th quantile of the normal distribution. The bias-corrected method yields confidence intervals

$$\left[\theta_{p_1}^*, \, \theta_{p_2}^* \right]$$

where θ_p^* is the pth quantile of the bootstrap distribution as defined previously.

References

Davison, A. C. and D. V. Hinkley. 1997. *Bootstrap Methods and their Application*. Cambridge: Cambridge University Press.

Efron, B. 1979. Bootstrap methods: Another look at the jackknife. *Annals of Statistics* 7: 1–26.

——. 1982. *The Jackknife, the Bootstrap and Other Resampling Plans*. Philadelphia: Society for Industrial and Applied Mathematics.

Efron, B. and C. Stein. 1981. The jackknife estimate of variance. *Annals of Statistics* 9: 586–596.

Efron, B. and R. Tibshirani. 1986. Bootstrap measures for standard errors, confidence intervals, and other measures of statistical accuracy. *Statistical Science* 1: 54–77.

——. 1993. *An Introduction to the Bootstrap*. New York: Chapman & Hall.

Gleason, J. R. 1997. ip18: A command for randomly resampling a dataset. *Stata Technical Bulletin* 37: 17–22. Reprinted in *Stata Technical Bulletin Reprints*, vol. 7, pp. 77–83.

——. 1999. ip18.1: Update to resample. *Stata Technical Bulletin* 52: 9–10. Reprinted in *Stata Technical Bulletin Reprints*, vol. 9, p. 119.

Gould, W. 1994. ssi6.2: Faster and easier bootstrap estimation. *Stata Technical Bulletin* 21: 24–33. Reprinted in *Stata Technical Bulletin Reprints*, vol. 4, pp. 211–223.

Hamilton, L. C. 1991. ssi2: Bootstrap programming. *Stata Technical Bulletin* 4: 18–27. Reprinted in *Stata Technical Bulletin Reprints*, vol. 1, pp. 208–220.

——. 1992. *Regression with Graphics*. Pacific Grove, CA: Brooks/Cole Publishing Company.

——. 1998. *Statistics with Stata 5*. Pacific Grove, CA: Brooks/Cole Publishing Company.

Hinkley, D. V. 1978. Improving the jackknife with special reference to correlation estimation. *Biometrika* 65: 13–22.

Mooney, C. Z. and R. D. Duval. 1993. *Bootstrapping: A Nonparametric Approach to Statistical Inference*. Newbury Park, CA: Sage Publications.

Stine, R. 1990. An introduction to bootstrap methods: examples and ideas. In *Modern Methods of Data Analysis*, ed. J. Fox and J. S. Long, 353–373. Newbury Park, CA: Sage Publications.

Also See

Complementary:	[P] **postfile**
Related:	[R] **jknife**, [R] **sample**, [R] **simul**
Background:	[U] **16.5 Accessing coefficients and standard errors**,
	[U] **16.6 Accessing results from Stata commands**,
	[U] **21 Programming Stata**

Title

> **by** — Repeat Stata command on subsets of the data

Syntax

> by *varlist* :   *stata_cmd*
>
> by<u>sort</u> *varlist* :   *stata_cmd*

The above diagrams show by and bysort as they are typically used.
The full syntax of the commands is

> by *varlist$_1$* $\left[\,(varlist_2)\,\right]$ $\left[\,,\ \underline{s}ort\ rc0\ \right]$:   *stata_cmd*
>
> by<u>sort</u> *varlist$_1$* $\left[\,(varlist_2)\,\right]$ $\left[\,,\ rc0\ \right]$:   *stata_cmd*

Description

Most Stata commands allow the by prefix, which repeats the command for each group of observations for which the values of the variables in *varlist* are the same. by without the sort option requires that the data be sorted by *varlist*; see [R] **sort**.

Stata commands that work with the by prefix indicate this immediately following their syntax diagram by reporting, for example, "by ... : may be used with logistic; see [R] **by**".

by and bysort are really the same command; bysort is just by with the sort option.

The *varlist$_1$* (*varlist$_2$*) syntax is of special use to programmers. It verifies that the data are sorted by *varlist$_1$* *varlist$_2$* and then performs a by as if only *varlist$_1$* were specified. For instance,

> by pid (time): gen growth = (bp - bp[_n-1])/bp

performs the generate by values of pid, but first verifies that the data are sorted by pid and time within pid.

Options

sort specifies that if the data are not already sorted by *varlist*, by is to sort them.

rc0 specifies that even if the *stata_cmd* produces an error in one of the by-groups, then by ... : is still to run the *stata_cmd* on the remaining by-groups. The default action is to stop when an error occurs. rc0 is especially useful when *stata_cmd* is an estimation command and some by-groups have insufficient observations.

Remarks

▷ Example

```
. by foreign : regress mpg weight displ
not sorted
r(5);
. sort foreign
. by foreign : regress mpg weight displ
```

-> foreign = Domestic

Source	SS	df	MS
Model	880.666134	2	440.333067
Residual	266.776174	49	5.44441171
Total	1147.44231	51	22.4988688

Number of obs = 52
F(2, 49) = 80.88
Prob > F = 0.0000
R-squared = 0.7675
Adj R-squared = 0.7580
Root MSE = 2.3333

mpg	Coef.	Std. Err.	t	P>|t|	[95% Conf. Interval]	
weight	-.005813	.0008759	-6.64	0.000	-.0075732	-.0040528
displacement	-.0015662	.0071435	-0.22	0.827	-.0159216	.0127892
_cons	39.47539	1.773799	22.25	0.000	35.91081	43.03998

-> foreign = Foreign

Source	SS	df	MS
Model	524.521708	2	262.260854
Residual	393.341928	19	20.7022067
Total	917.863636	21	43.7077922

Number of obs = 22
F(2, 19) = 12.67
Prob > F = 0.0003
R-squared = 0.5715
Adj R-squared = 0.5263
Root MSE = 4.55

mpg	Coef.	Std. Err.	t	P>|t|	[95% Conf. Interval]	
weight	.0047562	.0073953	0.64	0.528	-.0107224	.0202348
displacement	-.2779164	.1287029	-2.16	0.044	-.5472947	-.0085382
_cons	44.6697	5.745669	7.77	0.000	32.64388	56.69552

Note that by requires that the data be sorted. In the above example, we could have typed 'by foreign, sort: regress mpg weight displ' or 'bysort foreign: regress mpg weight displ' rather than the separate sort; all would yield the same results.

◁

For more examples, see [U] **14.1.2 by varlist:**, [U] **14.5 by varlist: construct**, and [U] **31.2 The by construct**.

Also See

Related: [R] **for**, [R] **sort**,
[P] **foreach**, [P] **forvalues**, [P] **while**

Background: [U] **14.1.2 by varlist:**,
[U] **14.4 varlists**,
[U] **14.5 by varlist: construct**,
[U] **31.2 The by construct**

Title

> **canon** — Canonical correlations

Syntax

> canon (*varlist₁*) (*varlist₂*) $[weight]$ $[if\ exp]$ $[in\ range]$ $\left[\ ,\ \text{lc}(\#)\ \underline{\text{noc}}\text{onstant}\ \underline{\text{level}}(\#)\ \right]$

by ... : may be used with canon; see [R] **by**.

aweights and fweights are allowed; see [U] **14.1.6 weight**.

canon shares the features of all estimation commands; see [U] **23 Estimation and post-estimation commands**.

Syntax for predict

> predict $[type]$ *newvarname* $[if\ exp]$ $[in\ range]$, $\{\ \text{u}\ |\ \text{v}\ |\ \text{stdu}\ |\ \text{stdv}\ \}$

Note that one of the statistics must be specified.

These statistics are available both in and out of sample; type predict ... if e(sample) ... if wanted only for the estimation sample.

Description

canon estimates canonical correlations and provides the loadings for calculating the appropriate linear combinations corresponding to those correlations.

canon typed without arguments redisplays previous estimation results.

Options

lc(#) specifies that linear combinations for the #th canonical correlation are to be displayed. lc(1) is the default.

noconstant specifies that means are not to be subtracted when calculating correlations.

level(#) specifies the confidence level, in percent, for confidence intervals for the coefficients in the reported linear combination. The default is level(95) or as set by set level; see [U] **23.5 Specifying the width of confidence intervals**. These "confidence intervals" are the result of an approximate and aggressive calculation; see the technical note below.

Options for predict

Note that there is not a default statistic for predict after canon; that is, you must specify one of the options.

u and v calculate the linear combinations of *varlist₁* and *varlist₂*, respectively. For the first canonical correlation (lc(1)), u and v are the linear combinations having maximal correlation. For the second canonical correlation (lc(2)), u and v have maximal correlation subject to the constraints that u is orthogonal to the lc(1) u, and v is orthogonal to the lc(1) v. The third and higher are defined similarly.

stdu and stdv calculate the standard errors of the respective linear combinations.

Remarks

Canonical correlations (Hotelling 1935, 1936) attempt to describe the relationships between two sets of variables. Given two sets of variables $\mathbf{X} = (x_1, x_2, \ldots, x_K)$ and $\mathbf{Y} = (y_1, y_2, \ldots, y_L)$, the goal is to find linear combinations of $\mathbf{X}$ and $\mathbf{Y}$ so that the correlation between the linear combinations is as high as possible. That is, letting $\widehat{x}_1$ and $\widehat{y}_1$ be the linear combinations

$$\widehat{x}_1 = \beta_{11}x_1 + \beta_{12}x_2 + \cdots + \beta_{1K}x_K$$

$$\widehat{y}_1 = \gamma_{11}y_1 + \gamma_{12}y_2 + \cdots + \gamma_{1L}y_L$$

we wish to find the maximum correlation between $\widehat{x}_1$ and $\widehat{y}_1$. The second canonical correlation coefficient is defined as the ordinary correlation between

$$\widehat{x}_2 = \beta_{21}x_1 + \beta_{22}x_2 + \cdots + \beta_{2K}x_K$$

$$\widehat{y}_2 = \gamma_{21}y_1 + \gamma_{22}y_2 + \cdots + \gamma_{2L}y_L$$

This correlation is maximized subject to the constraints that $\widehat{x}_1$ and $\widehat{x}_2$ along with $\widehat{y}_1$ and $\widehat{y}_2$ are orthogonal, and $\widehat{x}_1$ and $\widehat{y}_2$ along with $\widehat{x}_2$ and $\widehat{y}_1$ are also orthogonal. The third, and so on, are defined similarly. There are $m = \min(K, L)$ such correlations.

▷ Example

Consider two scientists trying to describe how "big" a car is. The first scientist takes physical measurements—the length, weight, headroom, and trunk space—whereas the second takes mechanical measurements—the engine displacement, mileage rating, gear ratio, and turning circle. Can they agree on a conceptual framework?

```
. canon (length weight headroom trunk) (displ mpg gear_ratio turn)
Linear combinations for canonical correlation 1        Number of obs =      74
```

	Coef.	Std. Err.	t	P>|t|	[95% Conf. Interval]	
u						
length	.0094779	.0060748	1.56	0.123	-.0026292	.021585
weight	.0010162	.0001615	6.29	0.000	.0006943	.0013381
headroom	.0351132	.0641755	0.55	0.586	-.0927884	.1630148
trunk	-.0022823	.0158555	-0.14	0.886	-.0338823	.0293176
v						
displacement	.0053704	.0009541	5.63	0.000	.0034688	.007272
mpg	-.0461481	.0107324	-4.30	0.000	-.0675377	-.0247585
gear_ratio	.0329583	.1598716	0.21	0.837	-.2856654	.3515821
turn	.0793927	.0158975	4.99	0.000	.0477091	.1110762

```
                                          (Std. Errors estimated conditionally)
Canonical correlations:
  0.9476   0.3400   0.0634   0.0447
```

canon reported the linear combinations corresponding to the first canonical correlation along with all four of the correlations. We find that the two views are closely related: the best linear combination of the physical measurements is correlated at almost 0.95 with the best linear combination of the mechanical measurements.

We can prove that the first canonical correlation is correct by calculating the reported linear combinations and then calculating the ordinary correlation:

```
. predict physical, u
. predict mechanical, v
. correlate mechanical physical
(obs=74)
```

	mechan~l physical
mechanical	1.0000
physical	0.9476 1.0000

◁

❏ Technical Note

canon reports standard errors for the coefficients in the linear combinations; most other software does not. You should view these standard errors as lower bounds for the true standard errors: the calculation is quite aggressive. It is based on the assumption that the coefficients for one set of measurements are correct for the purpose of calculating the coefficients and standard errors of the other relationship based on a linear regression.

❏

Saved Results

canon saves in e():

Scalars

e(N)	number of observations	e(df_r)	residual degrees of freedom
e(df)	degrees of freedom	e(n_lc)	number of linear combinations

Macros

e(cmd)	canon	e(wexp)	weight expression
e(wtype)	weight type	e(predict)	program used to implement predict

Matrices

e(b)	coefficient vector	e(V)	variance–covariance matrix of the
e(ccorr)	canonical correlation coefficients		estimators

Functions

e(sample)	marks estimation sample

Methods and Formulas

canon is implemented as an ado-file.

Let the correlation matrix between the two sets of variables be

$$\begin{pmatrix} \mathbf{A} & \mathbf{B} \\ \mathbf{B}' & \mathbf{C} \end{pmatrix}$$

That is, $\mathbf{A}$ is the correlation matrix of the first set of variables with themselves, $\mathbf{C}$ is the correlation matrix of the second set of variables with themselves, and $\mathbf{B}$ contains the cross-correlations.

The squared canonical correlations are then the eigenvalues of $\mathbf{V} = \mathbf{B}'\mathbf{A}^{-1}\mathbf{B}\mathbf{C}^{-1}$ or $\mathbf{W} = \mathbf{B}\mathbf{C}^{-1}\mathbf{B}'\mathbf{A}^{-1}$ (either will work), both nonsymmetric matrices (Wilks 1962, 587–592). The corresponding left eigenvectors are the linear combinations for the two sets of variables in standardized (variance 1) form.

To calculate standard errors in this form, assume that the left eigenvectors of $\mathbf{V}$ are fixed and write $\mathbf{V} = (\mathbf{v}_1, \mathbf{v}_2, \ldots, \mathbf{v}_m)$. The left eigenvector of $\mathbf{W}$ corresponding to $\mathbf{v}_k$ is proportional to $\mathbf{v}_k \mathbf{B}' \mathbf{C}^{-1}$, which has variance $(1 - r_k^2)\mathbf{C}^{-1}$, where r_k is the corresponding canonical correlation. These answers are then scaled to have mean 0 and variance 1 and are in terms of the original scale of the variables.

References

Hotelling, H. 1935. The most predictable criterion. *Journal of Educational Psychology* 26: 139–142.

——. 1936. Relations between two sets of variates. *Biometrika* 28: 321–377.

Wilks, S. S. 1962. *Mathematical Statistics*. New York: John Wiley & Sons.

Also See

Complementary:	[R] **adjust**, [R] **lincom**, [R] **predict**, [R] **test**, [R] **testnl**, [R] **vce**
Related:	[R] **correlate**, [R] **factor**, [R] **pcorr**, [R] **regress**
Background:	[U] **23 Estimation and post-estimation commands**

Title

> **cd** — Change directory

Syntax

Stata for Windows:

cd

cd ["]*directory_name*["]

cd ["]*drive*:["]

cd ["]*drive*:*directory_name*["]

pwd

Stata for Macintosh:

cd

cd ["]*folder_name*["]

cd ["]:*drive_name*["]

cd ["]:*drive_name*:*folder_name*["]

pwd

Stata for Unix:

cd [*directory_name*]

pwd

Note for Stata for Windows and Stata for Macintosh users: If your *directory_name* contains embedded spaces, remember to enclose it in double quotes.

Description

Stata for Windows: cd changes the working directory to the specified drive and directory. pwd is equivalent to typing cd without arguments; both display the name of the current working directory. Note: Users can shell out to a DOS window; see [R] **shell**. However, typing !cd *directory_name* will not change Stata's current directory; use the cd command to change directories.

Stata for Macintosh: cd changes the current working folder to *folder_name* or, if *folder_name* is not specified, displays the path name of the current folder. pwd displays the path of the current working folder.

Stata for Unix: cd changes the current working directory to *directory_name* or, if *directory_name* is not specified, the home directory. pwd displays the path of the current working directory.

Remarks

Stata for Windows

When you start Stata for Windows, your working directory is set to the *Start in* directory specified in the **Properties**. You can change this; see [GSW] **A.4 The Windows Properties Sheet**. You can always see what your working directory is by looking at the status bar at the bottom of the Stata window.

Once you are in Stata, you can change your directory with the cd command.

```
. cd
c:\data
. cd city
c:\data\city
. cd d:
D:\
. cd kande
D:\kande
. cd "additional detail"
D:\kande\additional detail
. cd c:
C:\
. cd data\city
C:\data\city
. cd \a\b\c\d\e\f\g
C:\a\b\c\d\e\f\g
. cd ..
C:\a\b\c\d\e\f
. cd ...
C:\a\b\c\d
. cd ....
C:\a
```

When we typed 'cd d:', we changed to the current directory of the D drive. We navigated our way to d:\kande\additional detail with three commands: cd d:, then cd kande, then cd "additional detail". Note the double quotes around "additional detail"—they are necessary because of the space in the directory name. We could have changed to this directory in a single command: cd "d:\kande\additional detail".

Notice the last three cd commands in the example above. You are probably familiar with the cd .. syntax to move up one directory from where you are. The last two cd commands above let you take advantage of a feature of Windows to let you move up more than one directory. cd ... is shorthand for 'cd ..\..'. cd .... is shorthand for 'cd ..\..\..'. Note that these shorthand cd commands are not limited to Stata—they will work in your DOS windows under Windows as well.

❑ Technical Note

Note that when you type cd d: to change to the current directory of the D drive, Windows changes to the current directory of the process that started Stata.

A better way to understand this is to think about starting Stata from a DOS window under Windows. Pretend that in your DOS window, the current directory on the C drive is C:\WINDOWS, and the current directory on the D drive is D:\KANDE. Imagine starting Stata from the DOS prompt by typing c:\stata\wstata.exe. Inside Stata, you could type cd "d:\kande\additional detail" to change your current directory. You could then type cd c: to change to the current directory on the C drive—C:\WINDOWS. If you then typed 'cd d:', you would switch to what Windows 95 remembers as the current directory on the D drive—D:\KANDE!

No matter where you cd to inside Stata, if you cd away from the D drive and then cd back to the D drive without specifying a path, your current directory will be the current directory of the D drive in DOS before you started Stata.

❑

Stata for Macintosh

Macintosh users should read [U] **14.6 File-naming conventions** for a description of how filenames are written in a command language before reading this entry.

Invoking an application and then changing folders is an action foreign to most Macintosh users. If it is foreign to you, you can ignore cd and pwd. However, they can be useful. You can see the current folder (where Stata saves files and looks for files) by typing pwd. You can change the current folder by using cd or by selecting **Set Current Folder...** from the **File** menu.

```
. pwd
:Macintosh HD:Analysis:First Results

cd "~:Analysis:Second Results"
:Macintosh HD:Analysis:Second Results

. _
```

If you now wanted to change to :Macintosh HD:Analysis:Second Results:Stage 1, you could type 'cd "Stage 1"'. If you wanted instead to change to :Macintosh HD:Analysis, you could type 'cd ..'.

Stata for Unix

cd and pwd are equivalent to Unix's cd and pwd commands. Like csh, Stata's cd understands '~' as an abbreviation for the home directory $HOME, so you can type things like cd ~/data; see [U] **14.6 File-naming conventions**.

```
. pwd
/usr/bill/proj
. cd ~/data/city
/usr/bill/data/city

. _
```

If you now wanted to change to /usr/bill/data/city/ny, you could type cd ny. If you wanted instead to change to /usr/bill/data, you could type 'cd ..'.

Also See

Complementary:	[R] **shell**
Related:	[R] **copy**, [R] **dir**, [R] **erase**, [R] **mkdir**, [R] **shell**, [R] **type**
Background:	[U] **14.6 File-naming conventions**

Title

centile — Report centile and confidence interval

Syntax

centile $\left[\textit{varlist}\right]$ $\left[\texttt{if } \textit{exp}\right]$ $\left[\texttt{in } \textit{range}\right]$ $\left[\texttt{, } \underline{\texttt{c}}\texttt{entile}(\textit{numlist}) \underline{\texttt{cci}} \underline{\texttt{n}}\texttt{ormal} \underline{\texttt{m}}\texttt{eansd}\right.$

$\underline{\texttt{l}}\texttt{evel}(\#)$ $\Big]$

by ... : may be used with centile; see [R] **by**.

Description

centile estimates specified centiles and calculates confidence intervals. If no *varlist* is specified, centile calculates centiles for all the variables in the dataset. If centile() is not specified, medians (centile(50)) are reported.

Options

centile(*numlist*) specifies the centiles to be reported. The default is to display the 50th centile. Specifying centile(5) requests that the 5th centile be reported. Specifying centile(5 50 95) requests that the 5th, 50th, and 95th centiles be reported. Specifying centile(10(10)90) requests that the 10th, 20th, ..., 90th centiles be reported; see [P] **numlist**.

cci (conservative confidence interval) forces the confidence limits to fall exactly on sample values. Confidence intervals displayed with the cci option are slightly wider than those with the default (nocci) option.

normal causes the confidence interval to be calculated using a formula for the standard error of a normal-distribution quantile given by Kendall and Stuart (1969, 237). The normal option is useful when you want empirical centiles—that is, centiles based on sample order statistics rather than on the mean and standard deviation—and are willing to assume normality.

meansd causes the centile and confidence interval to be calculated based on the sample mean and standard deviation and assumes normality.

level(#) specifies the confidence level, in percent, for confidence intervals. The default is level(95) or as set by set level; see [R] **level**.

Remarks

The qth centile of a continuous random variable X is defined as the value of C_q which fulfills the condition $\Pr(X \leq C_q) = q/100$. The value of q must be in the range $0 < q < 100$, though q is not necessarily an integer. By default, centile estimates C_q for the variables in *varlist* and for the value(s) of q given in centile(*numlist*). It makes no assumptions as to the distribution of X and, if necessary, uses linear interpolation between neighboring sample values. Extreme centiles (for example, the 99th centile in samples smaller than 100) are fixed at the minimum or maximum sample value. An "exact" confidence interval for C_q is also given, using the binomial-based method described below in *Methods and Formulas*. The detailed theory is given by Conover (1999, 143–148). Again, linear interpolation is employed to improve the accuracy of the estimated confidence limits, but extremes are fixed at the minimum or maximum sample value.

You can prevent `centile` from interpolating when calculating binomial-based confidence intervals by specifying `cci`. The resulting intervals are generally wider than with the default, that is, the coverage (confidence level) tends to be greater than the nominal value (given as usual by `level(#)`, by default 95%).

If the data are believed to be normally distributed (a common case), there are two alternative methods for estimating centiles. If `normal` is specified, C_q is calculated as just described, but its confidence interval is based on a formula for the standard error (s.e.) of a normal-distribution quantile given by Kendall and Stuart (1969, 237). If `meansd` is alternatively specified, C_q is estimated as $\overline{x} + z_q \times s$, where $\overline{x}$ and s are the sample mean and standard deviation and z_q is the qth centile of the standard normal distribution (e.g., $z_{95} = 1.645$). The confidence interval is derived from the s.e. of the estimate of C_q.

▷ Example

Using the `auto.dta`, we estimate the 5th, 50th and 95th centiles of the variable `price`:

```
. format price %8.2fc
. centile price, centile(5 50 95)
```

Variable	Obs	Percentile	Centile	— Binom. Interp. — [95% Conf. Interval]	
price	74	5	3,727.75	3,291.23	3,914.16
		50	5,006.50	4,593.57	5,717.90
		95	13,498.00	11,061.53	15,865.30

`summarize` produces somewhat different results from `centile`; see *Methods and Formulas*.

```
. summarize price, detail
```

Price

	Percentiles	Smallest		
1%	3291	3291		
5%	3748	3299		
10%	3895	3667	Obs	74
25%	4195	3748	Sum of Wgt.	74
50%	5006.5		Mean	6165.257
		Largest	Std. Dev.	2949.496
75%	6342	13466		
90%	11385	13594	Variance	8699526
95%	13466	14500	Skewness	1.653434
99%	15906	15906	Kurtosis	4.819188

The confidence limits produced using the `cci` option are slightly wider than those produced without this option:

```
. centile price, c(5 50 95) cci
```

Variable	Obs	Percentile	Centile	— Binomial Exact — [95% Conf. Interval]	
price	74	5	3,727.75	3,291.00	3,955.00
		50	5,006.50	4,589.00	5,719.00
		95	13,498.00	10,372.00	15,906.00

If we are willing to assume `price` is normally distributed, we could include either the `normal` or the `meansd` option:

```
. centile price, c(5 50 95) normal
```

Variable	Obs	Percentile	— Normal, based on observed centiles —	
			Centile	[95% Conf. Interval]
price	74	5	3,727.75	3,211.19 4,244.31
		50	5,006.50	4,096.68 5,916.32
		95	13,498.00	5,426.81 21,569.19

```
. centile price, c(5 50 95) meansd
```

Variable	Obs	Percentile	— Normal, based on mean and std. dev.—	
			Centile	[95% Conf. Interval]
price	74	5	1,313.77	278.93 2,348.61
		50	6,165.26	5,493.24 6,837.27
		95	11,016.75	9,981.90 12,051.59

With the `normal` option, the centile estimates are by definition the same as before. The confidence intervals for the 5th and 50th centiles are similar to the previous ones, but the interval for the 95th centile is very different. The results using the `meansd` option are also very different from both previous sets of estimates.

We can use `sktest` (see [R] **sktest**) to check the correctness of the normality assumption:

```
. sktest price
```

Skewness/Kurtosis tests for Normality

Variable	Pr(Skewness)	Pr(Kurtosis)	——— joint ———	
			adj chi2(2)	Prob>chi2
price	0.000	0.013	21.77	0.0000

`sktest` reveals that `price` is definitely not normally distributed, so the normal assumption is not reasonable and the `normal` and `meansd` options are not appropriate for these data. We should rely on the results from the default choice, which does not assume normality. If the data are normally distributed, however, the precision of the estimated centiles and their confidence intervals will be ordered (best) `meansd` > `normal` > [default] (worst). The `normal` option is useful when we really do want empirical centiles (that is, centiles based on sample order statistics rather than on the mean and standard deviation) but are willing to assume normality.

◁

Saved Results

`centile` saves in `r()`:

Scalars

`r(N)`	number of observations	`r(lb_#)`	#-requested centile lower confidence bound
`r(n_cent)`	number of centiles requested	`r(ub_#)`	#-requested centile upper confidence bound
`r(c_#)`	value of # centile		

Macros

`r(centiles)`	centiles requested

Methods and Formulas

`centile` is implemented as an ado-file.

Default case

The calculation is based on the method of Mood and Graybill (1963, 408). Let $x_1 \leq x_2 \leq \cdots \leq x_n$ be a sample of size n arranged in ascending order. Denote the estimated qth centile of the x's as c_q. We require that $0 < q < 100$. Let $R = (n + 1)q/100$ have integer part r and fractional part f, that is, $r = \text{int}(R)$ and $f = R - r$. (If R is itself an integer, then $r = R$ and $f = 0$.) Note that $0 \leq r \leq n$. For convenience, define $x_0 = x_1$ and $x_{n+1} = x_n$. C_q is estimated by

$$c_q = x_r + f \times (x_{r+1} - x_r)$$

that is, c_q is a weighted average of x_r and x_{r+1}. Loosely speaking, a (conservative) $p\%$ confidence interval for C_q involves finding the observations ranked t and u which correspond respectively to the $\alpha = (100 - p)/200$ and $1 - \alpha$ quantiles of a binomial distribution with parameters n and $q/100$, i.e., $\text{B}(n, q/100)$. More precisely, define the ith value $(i = 0, \ldots, n)$ of the cumulative binomial distribution function as $F_i = \Pr(S \leq i)$, where S has distribution $\text{B}(n, q/100)$. For convenience, let $F_{-1} = 0$ and $F_{n+1} = 1$. t is found such that $F_t \leq \alpha$ and $F_{t+1} > \alpha$, and u is found such that $1 - F_u \leq \alpha$ and $1 - F_{u-1} > \alpha$.

With the `cci` option in force, the (conservative) confidence interval is (x_{t+1}, x_{u+1}) and its actual coverage probability is $F_u - F_t$.

The default case uses linear interpolation on the F_i as follows. Let

$$g = (\alpha - F_t)/(F_{t+1} - F_t)$$
$$h = \{\alpha - (1 - F_u)\}/\{(1 - F_{u-1}) - (1 - F_u)\}$$
$$= (\alpha - 1 + F_u)/(F_u - F_{u-1})$$

The interpolated lower and upper confidence limits (c_{qL}, c_{qU}) for C_q are

$$c_{qL} = x_{t+1} + g \times (x_{t+2} - x_{t+1})$$
$$c_{qU} = x_{u+1} - h \times (x_{u+1} - x_u)$$

For example, suppose we want a 95% confidence interval for the median of a sample of size 13. $n = 13$, $q = 50$, $p = 95$, $\alpha = .025$, $R = 14 \times 50/100 = 7$, and $f = 0$. The median is therefore the 7th observation. Some example data x_i and the values of F_i are as follows:

i	F_i	$1 - F_i$	x_i	i	F_i	$1 - F_i$	x_i
0	0.0001	0.9999	–	7	0.7095	0.2905	33
1	0.0017	0.9983	5	8	0.8666	0.1334	37
2	0.0112	0.9888	7	9	0.9539	0.0461	45
3	0.0461	0.9539	10	10	0.9888	0.0112	59
4	0.1334	0.8666	15	11	0.9983	0.0017	77
5	0.2905	0.7095	23	12	0.9999	0.0001	104
6	0.5000	0.5000	28	13	1.0000	0.0000	211

The median is $x_7 = 33$. Also, $F_2 \leq .025$ and $F_3 > .025$ so $t = 2$; $1 - F_{10} \leq .025$ and $1 - F_9 > .025$ so $u = 10$. The conservative confidence interval is therefore

$$(c_{50L}, c_{50U}) = (x_{t+1}, x_{u+1}) = (x_3, x_{11}) = (10, 77)$$

with actual coverage $F_{10} - F_2 = .9888 - .0112 = .9776$ (97.8% confidence). For the interpolation calculation, we have

$$g = (.025 - .0112)/(.0461 - .0112) = .395$$
$$h = (.025 - 1 + .9888)/(.9888 - .9539) = .395$$

So
$$c_{50L} = x_3 + .395 \times (x_4 - x_3) = 10 + .395 \times 5 = 11.98$$
$$c_{50U} = x_{11} - .395 \times (x_{11} - x_{10}) = 77 - .395 \times 18 = 69.89$$

normal case

The value of c_q is as above. Its s.e. is given by the formula

$$s_q = \sqrt{q(100 - q)} \Big/ \Big\{ 100 n Z(c_q; \overline{x}, s) \Big\}$$

where $\overline{x}$ and s are the mean and s.d. of the x_i and

$$Z(Y; \mu, \sigma) = \left(1/\sqrt{2\pi\sigma^2} \right) e^{-(Y-\mu)^2/2\sigma^2}$$

is the density function of a normally distributed variable Y with mean μ and s.d. σ. The confidence interval for C_q is $(c_q - z_{100(1-\alpha)} s_q, c_q + z_{100(1-\alpha)} s_q)$.

meansd case

The value of c_q is $\overline{x} + z_q \times s$. Its s.e. is given by the formula

$$s_q^\star = s \sqrt{1/n + z_q^2/(2n - 2)}.$$

The confidence interval for C_q is $(c_q - z_{100(1-\alpha)} \times s_q^\star, c_q + z_{100(1-\alpha)} \times s_q^\star)$.

Acknowledgment

centile was written by Patrick Royston of the MRC Clinical Trials Unit, London.

References

Conover, W. J. 1999. *Practical Nonparametric Statistics*. 3d ed. New York: John Wiley & Sons.

Kendall, M. G. and A. Stuart. 1969. *The Advanced Theory of Statistics, Vol. I.* 3d ed. London: Griffin.

Mood, A. M. and F. A. Graybill. 1963. *Introduction to the Theory of Statistics*. 2d ed. New York: McGraw–Hill.

Royston, P. 1992. sg7: Centile estimation command. *Stata Technical Bulletin* 8: 12–15. Reprinted in *Stata Technical Bulletin Reprints*, vol. 2, pp. 122–125.

Also See

Related: [R] **ci**, [R] **pctile**, [R] **summarize**

Title

cf — Compare two datasets

Syntax

cf *varlist* using *filename* [, _verbose_]

Description

cf compares *varlist* of the dataset in memory (master dataset) with the corresponding variables in *filename* (using dataset). cf returns nothing (i.e., a return code of 0) if the specified variables are identical and a return code of 9 if there are any differences.

Options

verbose mentions the result of the comparison variable-by-variable. Unless verbose is specified, only the differences are mentioned.

Remarks

The messages produced by cf are of the form:

```
varname: does not exist in using
varname: ___ in master but ___ in using
varname: ___ mismatches
varname: match
```

An example of the second message is "str4 in master but float in using". Unless verbose is specified, the fourth message does not appear—silence indicates matches.

▷ Example

You think the dataset in memory is identical to mydata.dta, but you are unsure. If there are differences, you want to understand them before continuing:

```
. cf _all using mydata

. _
```

In this case, all of the variables that are in the master dataset are in mydata.dta, and these variables are the same in both datasets. Alternatively, you might see

```
. cf _all using mydata
          mpg:  2 mismatches
     headroom:  does not exist in using
 displacement:  does not exist in using
    gear_ratio:  does not exist in using
r(9);
```

189

Two changes were made to the mpg variable, and the variables headroom, displacement, and gear_ratio do not exist in mydata.dta.

◁

Methods and Formulas

cf is implemented as an ado-file. If you are using Small Stata, you may get the error "too many variables" when you stipulate _all and have many variables in your dataset. (This will not happen if you are using Intercooled Stata.) If this happens, you will have to perform the comparison with groups of variables.

References

Gleason, J. R. 1995. dm36: Comparing two Stata data sets. *Stata Technical Bulletin* 28: 10–13. Reprinted in *Stata Technical Bulletin Reprints*, vol. 5, pp. 39–43.

Also See

Related: [R] **compare**

Title

checksum — Calculate checksum of file

Syntax

<u>checksum</u> *filename* [, save <u>sav</u>ing(*filename2* [, replace]) replace]

<u>set</u> checksum { on | off }

Description

checksum creates *filename*.sum files for later use by Stata when it reads files over a network. These optional files are used to reduce the chances of corrupted files going undetected. Whenever Stata reads file *filename.suffix* over a network, whether it be by **use**, **net**, **update**, etc., it also looks for *filename*.sum. If Stata finds that file, Stata reads it, too, and then uses its contents to verify that the first file was received without error. If there are errors, Stata informs the user that the file could not be read.

set checksum on, which is the default, tells Stata to verify that files downloaded over a network have been received without error.

set checksum off tells Stata to bypass the file verification.

❑ Technical Note

checksum calculates a CRC checksum following the POSIX 1003.2 specification and displays the file size in bytes. **checksum** produces the same results as the Unix **cksum** command. Comparing the checksum of the original file with the received file guarantees the integrity of the received file.

When comparing Stata's **checksum** results with those of Unix, do not confuse Unix's **sum** and **cksum** commands. Unix's **cksum** and Stata's **checksum** use a more robust algorithm than that used by Unix's **sum**, and on some Unixes, there is no **cksum** command and the more robust algorithm is obtained by specifying an option with **sum**.

❑

Options

save saves the output of the **checksum** command to the ASCII file *filename*.sum. The default is to display a report but not create a file.

replace is for use with **save**; it permits Stata to overwrite an existing *filename*.sum file.

saving(*filename2* [, replace]) is an alternative to **save**. It saves the output in the specified filename. You must supply a file extension if you want one, as none is assumed.

Remarks

Say you wish to put a dataset on your homepage so that colleagues can use it over the Internet by typing

```
. use http://www.myuni.edu/department/~joe/mydata
```

`mydata.dta` is important and, even though the chances of the file `mydata.dta` being corrupted by the Internet are small, you wish to guard against that. The solution is to create the checksum file named `mydata.sum` and also place that on your homepage. Your colleagues will need type nothing different, but now Stata will verify that all goes well. When they `use` the file, they will see either

```
. use http://www.myuni.edu/department/~joe/mydata
(important data from joe)
```

or

```
. use http://www.myuni.edu/department/~joe/mydata
file transmission error (checksums do not match)
http://www.myuni.edu/department/~joe/mydata.dta not downloaded
r(639);
```

To make the checksum file, change to the directory where the file is located and type

```
. checksum mydata.dta, save
Checksum for mydata.dta = 263508742, size = 4052
file mydata.sum saved
```

Saved Results

`checksum` saves in `r()`:

Scalars

r(version)	checksum version number
r(filelen)	length of file, in bytes
r(checksum)	checksum value

Also See

Complementary: [R] **net**, [R] **save**

Title

> **ci** — Confidence intervals for means, proportions, and counts

Syntax

> ci [*varlist*] [*weight*] [if *exp*] [in *range*] [, level(*#*) binomial poisson
>
>   exposure(*varname*) total]

cii #_{obs}	#_{mean} #_{sd} [, level(*#*)]		(normal variable)

ci #$_{obs}$ #$_{mean}$ #$_{sd}$ [, level(*#*)]   (normal variable)

cii #$_{obs}$ #$_{succ}$ [, level(*#*)]   (binomial variable)

cii #$_{exposure}$ #$_{events}$, poisson [level(*#*)]   (Poisson variable)

by ... : may be used with ci (but not with cii); see [R] **by**.
aweights and fweights are allowed; see [U] **14.1.6 weight**.

Description

ci computes standard errors and confidence intervals for each of the variables in *varlist*.

cii is the immediate form of ci; see [U] **22 Immediate commands** for a general discussion of immediate commands.

Options

level(*#*) specifies the confidence level, in percent, for confidence intervals. The default is level(95) or as set by **set level**; see [R] **level**.

binomial tells ci that the variables are 0/1 binomial variables and that exact binomial confidence intervals will be calculated. (cii produces binomial confidence intervals when only two numbers are specified.)

poisson specifies that the variables are Poisson-distributed counts; exact confidence intervals will be calculated.

exposure(*varname*) is used only with poisson. It is not necessary to also specify poisson if exposure() is specified; poisson is assumed. *varname* contains the total exposure (typically a time or an area) during which the number of events recorded in *varlist* were observed.

total is for use with the by ... : prefix. It requests that, in addition to output for each by-group, output be added for all groups combined.

Remarks

Remarks are presented under the headings

> *Ordinary confidence intervals*
> *Binomial confidence intervals*
> *Poisson confidence intervals*
> *Immediate form*

Ordinary confidence intervals

▷ Example

Without the `binomial` or `poisson` options, `ci` produces "ordinary" confidence intervals, which is to say, confidence intervals that are correct if the variable is distributed normally.

```
. ci mpg price
```

Variable	Obs	Mean	Std. Err.	[95% Conf.	Interval]
mpg	74	21.2973	.6725511	19.9569	22.63769
price	74	6165.257	342.8719	5481.914	6848.6

The standard error of the mean of `mpg` is 0.67, and the 95% confidence interval is $[19.96, 22.64]$. We can obtain wider, 99% confidence intervals by typing

```
. ci mpg price, level(99)
```

Variable	Obs	Mean	Std. Err.	[99% Conf.	Interval]
mpg	74	21.2973	.6725511	19.51849	23.07611
price	74	6165.257	342.8719	5258.405	7072.108

◁

▷ Example

`by()` breaks out the confidence intervals according to by-group; `total` adds an overall summary. For instance,

```
. ci mpg, by(foreign) total
```

-> foreign = Domestic

Variable	Obs	Mean	Std. Err.	[95% Conf.	Interval]
mpg	52	19.82692	.657777	18.50638	21.14747

-> foreign = Foreign

Variable	Obs	Mean	Std. Err.	[95% Conf.	Interval]
mpg	22	24.77273	1.40951	21.84149	27.70396

-> Total

Variable	Obs	Mean	Std. Err.	[95% Conf.	Interval]
mpg	74	21.2973	.6725511	19.9569	22.63769

◁

❑ Technical Note

You can control the formatting of the numbers in the output by attaching a display format to the variable; see [U] **15.5 Formats: controlling how data are displayed**. For instance,

```
. format mpg %9.2f
. ci mpg
```

Variable	Obs	Mean	Std. Err.	[95% Conf.	Interval]
mpg	74	21.30	0.67	19.96	22.64

❑

Binomial confidence intervals

▷ Example

You have data on employees including a variable marking whether the employee was promoted last year.

. ci promoted, binomial

Variable	Obs	Mean	Std. Err.	— Binomial Exact — [95% Conf. Interval]	
promoted	20	.1	.067082	.0123474	.31698

The interpretation is as follows: If the true probability of being promoted were 0.012, the chances of observing a result as extreme or more extreme than the result observed $(20 \cdot 0.1 = 2$ or more promotions) would be 2.5%. If the true probability of being promoted were 0.317, the chances of observing a result as extreme or more extreme than observed (2 or fewer promotions) would be 2.5%.

◁

❑ Technical Note

Binomial confidence intervals can differ markedly from ordinary confidence intervals when sample sizes are small or when the probability of a positive outcome is extreme. In the above case, `ci` without the `binomial` option reports the confidence interval $[-.048, .248]$. As sample sizes increase, the binomial and ordinary confidence intervals become virtually identical, but it is always better to use the binomial calculation when the underlying variable follows the binomial distribution.

❑

❑ Technical Note

Let us repeat the promotion example, but this time, with data in which there are no promotions over the observed period:

. ci promoted, binomial

Variable	Obs	Mean	Std. Err.	— Binomial Exact — [95% Conf. Interval]	
promoted	20	0	0	0	.1684265*

(*) one-sided, 97.5% confidence interval

The confidence interval is $[0, .168]$ and this is the confidence interval most books publish. It is not, however, a true 95% confidence interval because the lower tail has vanished. As Stata notes, it is a one-sided, 97.5% confidence interval. If you wanted to put 5% in the right tail, you could type `ci promoted, binomial level(90)`.

❑

❑ Technical Note

`ci` with the `binomial` option ignores any variables that do not take on the values 0 and 1 exclusively. For instance, with our automobile dataset:

```
. ci mpg foreign, binomial
```

Variable	Obs	Mean	Std. Err.	— Binomial Exact — [95% Conf. Interval]	
foreign	74	.2972973	.0531331	.1965893	.4148362

Note that we also requested the confidence interval for mpg but Stata ignored us. It does that so you can type ci, binomial and obtain correct confidence intervals for all the variables that are 0/1 in your data.

❏

Poisson confidence intervals

▷ Example

You have data on the number of bacterial colonies on a Petri dish. The dish has been divided into 36 small squares and the number of colonies in each square has been counted. Each observation in your dataset represents a square on the dish. The variable count records the number of colonies in each square counted, which varies from 0 to 5.

```
. ci count, poisson
```

Variable	Exposure	Mean	Std. Err.	— Poisson Exact — [95% Conf. Interval]	
count	36	2.333333	.2545875	1.861159	2.888813

ci reports the average number of colonies per square is 2.33. If the expected number of colonies per square were as low as 1.86, the probability of observing 2.33 or more colonies per square would be 2.5%. If the expected number were as large as 2.89, the probability of observing $36 \cdot 2.33 = 84$ or fewer colonies per square would be 2.5%.

◁

❏ Technical Note

The number of "observations"—how finely the Petri dish is divided—makes no difference. The Poisson distribution is a function only of the count. In our example above, we observed a total of $2.33 \cdot 36 = 84$ colonies and a confidence interval of $[1.86 \cdot 36, 2.89 \cdot 36] = [67, 104]$. We would obtain the same $[67, 104]$ confidence interval if our dish were divided into, say, 49 squares rather than 36.

In terms of the counts, it is not even important that all the squares be of the same size. In terms of *rates*, however, such differences do matter, but in an easy-to-calculate way. Rates are obtained from counts by dividing by exposure, which is typically a number multiplied by either time or an area. In the case of our Petri dishes, we divide by an area to obtain a rate, but if our example were cast in terms of being infected by a disease, we might divide by person-years to obtain the rate. Rates are convenient because they are easier to compare: we might have 2.3 colonies per square inch or .0005 infections per person-year.

So let us assume that we wish to obtain the number of colonies per square inch and, moreover, that not all the "squares" on our dish are of equal size. We have a variable called **area** which records the area of each "square":

```
. ci count, exposure(area)
```

Variable	Exposure	Mean	Std. Err.	— Poisson Exact — [95% Conf. Interval]	
count	3	28	3.055051	22.33391	34.66575

The rates are now in more familiar terms. In our sample, there are 28 colonies per square inch and the 95% confidence interval is $[22.3, 34.7]$. When we did not specify exposure(), ci assumed that each observation contributed 1 to exposure.

❏

❏ Technical Note

As with the binomial option, had there been no colonies on our dish, ci would calculate a one-sided confidence interval:

```
. ci count, poisson
```

Variable	Exposure	Mean	Std. Err.	— Poisson Exact — [95% Conf. Interval]	
count	36	0	0	0	.102434*

(*) one-sided, 97.5% confidence interval

❏

Immediate form

▷ Example

You are reading a soon-to-be-published paper by a colleague. In it is a table showing the number of observations, mean, and standard deviation of 1980 median family income for the Northeast and West. You correctly feel that the paper would be much improved if it included the confidence intervals. The paper claims that for 166 cities in the Northeast, the average of median family income is $19,509 with a standard deviation of $4,379:

```
. cii 166 19509 4379
```

Variable	Obs	Mean	Std. Err.	[95% Conf. Interval]	
	166	19509	339.8763	18837.93	20180.07

For the West:

```
. cii 256 22557 5003
```

Variable	Obs	Mean	Std. Err.	[95% Conf. Interval]	
	256	22557	312.6875	21941.22	23172.78

◁

▷ Example

You flip a coin 10 times and it comes up heads only once. You are shocked and decide to obtain a 99% confidence interval for this coin:

```
. cii 10 1, level(99)
```

Variable	Obs	Mean	Std. Err.	— Binomial Exact —[99% Conf. Interval]	
	10	.1	.0948683	.0005005	.5442871

◁

▷ Example

The number of reported traffic accidents in Santa Monica over a 24-hour period is 27. You need know nothing else:

```
. cii 1 27, poisson
```

Variable	Exposure	Mean	Std. Err.	— Poisson Exact —[95% Conf. Interval]	
	1	27	5.196152	17.79773	39.28305

◁

Saved Results

ci and cii saves in r():

Scalars

r(N)	number of observations or exposure		r(lb)	lower bound of confidence interval
r(mean)	mean		r(ub)	upper bound of confidence interval
r(se)	estimate of standard error			

Methods and Formulas

ci and cii are implemented as ado-files.

Ordinary

Define n, $\overline{x}$, and s^2 as the number of observations, (weighted) average, and (unbiased) estimated variance of the variable in question; see [R] **summarize**.

The standard error of the mean s_μ is defined as $\sqrt{s^2/n}$.

Let α be $1 - l/100$, where l is the significance level specified by the user. Define t_α as the two-sided t statistic corresponding to a significance level of α with $n - 1$ degrees of freedom; t_α is obtained from Stata as invttail(n-1,0.5*α). The lower and upper confidence bounds are, respectively, $\overline{x} - s_\mu t_\alpha$ and $\overline{x} + s_\mu t_\alpha$.

Binomial

Given k successes out of n trials, the mean probability is $p = k/n$ with standard error $\sqrt{p(1-p)/n}$. ci calculates the exact confidence interval $[k_1, k_2]$ such that $\Pr(K \leq k_1) \leq \alpha/2$ and $\Pr(K \geq k_2) \leq \alpha/2$. Solution is by bisection. If $k = 0$ or $k = n$, the calculation of the appropriate tail is skipped.

Poisson

Given a count k, the expected count is k and the standard deviation is $\sqrt{k}$. ci calculates the exact confidence interval $[k_1, k_2]$ such that $\Pr(K \leq k_1) \leq \alpha/2$ and $\Pr(K \geq k_2) \leq \alpha/2$. Solution is by Newton's method. If $k = 0$, the calculation of k_1 is skipped. All values are reported as rates, which are the above numbers divided by the total exposure.

References

Feller, W. 1968. *An Introduction to Probability Theory and Its Applications*, vol. 1. 3d ed. New York: John Wiley & Sons.

Gleason, J. R. 1999. sg119: Improved confidence intervals for binomial proportions. *Stata Technical Bulletin* 52: 16–18. Reprinted in *Stata Technical Bulletin Reprints*, vol. 9, pp. 208–211.

Hamilton, L. C. 1996. *Data Analysis for Social Scientists*. Belmont, CA: Duxbury Press.

Hoel, P. G. 1984. *Introduction to Mathematical Statistics*. 5th ed. New York: John Wiley & Sons.

Rothman, K. J. and S. Greenland. 1998. *Modern Epidemiology*. 2d ed. Philadelphia: Lippincott–Raven.

Also See

Complementary: [R] **bitest**, [R] **ttest**

Related: [R] **centile**, [R] **means**, [R] **pctile**, [R] **st stci**, [R] **summarize**

Background: [U] **22 Immediate commands**

Title

> **clogit** — Conditional (fixed-effects) logistic regression

Syntax

> **clogit** *depvar* [*indepvars*] [*weight*] [**if** *exp*] [**in** *range*] ,
>
> **group**(*varname*) [**level**(*#*) **or** **offset**(*varname*) *maximize_options*]

by ...: may be used with **clogit**; see [R] **by**.

fweights and **iweights** are allowed (see [U] **14.1.6 weight**), but they are interpreted to apply to groups as a whole, not to individual observations. See *Use of weights* below.

clogit shares the features of all estimation commands; see [U] **23 Estimation and post-estimation commands**.

clogit may be used with **sw** to perform stepwise estimation; see [R] **sw**.

Syntax for predict

> **predict** [*type*] *newvarname* [**if** *exp*] [**in** *range*] [, { **pc1** | **pu0** | **xb** | **stdp** }
>
> **nooffset**]

These statistics are available both in and out of sample; type **predict** ... **if e(sample)** ... if wanted only for the estimation sample.

Description

clogit estimates what biostatisticians and epidemiologists call conditional logistic regression for matched case–control groups (see, for example, Hosmer and Lemeshow 1989, chapter 7), and what economists and other social scientists call fixed-effects logit for panel data (see, for example, Chamberlain 1980). It also estimates McFadden's choice model (McFadden 1974). Computationally, these models are exactly the same.

See [R] **logistic** for a list of related estimation commands.

Options

group(*varname*) is not optional; it specifies an identifier variable (numeric or string) for the matched groups. **strata**(*varname*) is a synonym for **group**().

level(*#*) specifies the confidence level, in percent, for confidence intervals. The default is **level(95)** or as set by **set level**; see [U] **23.5 Specifying the width of confidence intervals**.

or reports the estimated coefficients transformed to odds ratios; i.e., e^b rather than b. Standard errors and confidence intervals are similarly transformed. This option affects how results are displayed and not how they are estimated. **or** may be specified at estimation or when replaying previously estimated results.

offset(*varname*) specifies that *varname* is to be included in the model with coefficient constrained to be 1.

maximize_options control the maximization process; see [R] **maximize**. You should never have to specify them.

Options for predict

pc1, the default, calculates the probability of a positive outcome conditional on one positive outcome within group.

pu0 calculates the probability of a positive outcome, assuming that the fixed effect is zero.

xb calculates the linear prediction.

stdp calculates the standard error of the linear prediction.

nooffset is relevant only if you specified **offset**(*varname*) for **clogit**. It modifies the calculations made by **predict** so that they ignore the offset variable; the linear prediction is treated as $\mathbf{x}_j \mathbf{b}$ rather than $\mathbf{x}_j \mathbf{b} + \text{offset}_j$.

Remarks

Remarks are presented under the headings

> *Matched case–control data*
> *Use of weights*
> *Fixed-effects logit*
> *McFadden's choice model*
> *Predictions*

clogit performs maximum likelihood estimation of models with a dichotomous dependent variable coded as 0/1 (more precisely, **clogit** interprets 0 and not 0 to indicate the dichotomy). Conditional logistic analysis differs from regular logistic regression in that the data are grouped and the likelihood is calculated relative to each group; i.e., a conditional likelihood is used; see *Methods and Formulas* at the end of this entry.

Biostatisticians and epidemiologists estimate these models when analyzing matched case–control studies with $1:1$ matching, $1:k_{2i}$ matching, or $k_{1i}:k_{2i}$ matching, where i denotes the ith matched group for $i = 1, 2, \ldots, n$, where n is the total number of groups. **clogit** estimates a model appropriate for all these matching schemes or for any mix of the schemes, since the matching $k_{1i}:k_{2i}$ can vary from group to group. Note that **clogit** always uses the true conditional likelihood, not an approximation. (Using the true likelihood for $k_{1i}:k_{2i}$ matching when $k_{1i} > 1$ was introduced in Stata version 5.) Biostatisticians and epidemiologists sometimes refer to the matched groups as "strata", but we will stick to the more generic term "group".

Economists and other social scientists estimating fixed-effects logit models have data that look exactly like the data biostatisticians and epidemiologists call $k_{1i}:k_{2i}$ matched case–control data. In terms of how the data are arranged, $k_{1i}:k_{2i}$ matching means that in the ith group the dependent variable is 1 a total of k_{1i} times and 0 a total of k_{2i} times. There are a total of $T_i = k_{1i} + k_{2i}$ observations for the ith group. This data arrangement is what economists and other social scientists call "panel data" or "cross-sectional time-series data".

McFadden's choice model (McFadden 1974) in its basic form is simply an application of conditional logistic regression with $1:k_{2i}$ matching. The only new wrinkle here is how you set up the variables in your dataset. We discuss this in detail in the section *McFadden's choice model* below.

So no matter what terminology you use, the computation and the use of the **clogit** command is the same. The following example shows how your data should be arranged to use **clogit**.

▷ **Example**

Suppose we have grouped data with the variable **id** containing a unique identifier for each group. Our outcome variable **y** contains 0s and 1s. If we were biostatisticians, $\mathbf{y} = 1$ would indicate a case, $\mathbf{y} = 0$ would be a control, and **id** would be an identifier variable that indicates the groups of matched case–controls.

If we were economists, $y = 1$ might indicate, for example, that a person was unemployed at any time during a year, $y = 0$ that a person was employed all year, and id would be an identifier variable for persons.

If we list the first few observations of this dataset, it looks like

```
. list y x1 x2 id in 1/11
             y       x1       x2       id
  1.         0        0        4     1014
  2.         0        1        4     1014
  3.         0        1        6     1014
  4.         1        1        8     1014
  5.         0        0        1     1017
  6.         0        0        7     1017
  7.         1        1       10     1017
  8.         0        0        1     1019
  9.         0        1        7     1019
 10.         1        1        7     1019
 11.         1        1        9     1019
```

Pretending we are biostatisticians, we describe our data as follows: The first group (id = 1014) consists of 4 matched persons: 1 case ($y = 1$) and 3 controls ($y = 0$); i.e., 1 : 3 matching. The second group has 1 : 2 matching and the third 2 : 2.

Pretending we are economists, we describe our data as follows: The first group consists of 4 observations (one per year) for person 1014. This person had a period of unemployment during 1 year out of 4. The second person had a period of unemployment during 1 year out of 3, and the third 2 years out of 4.

Our independent variables are x1 and x2. To estimate the conditional (fixed-effects) logistic model, we type

```
. clogit y x1 x2, group(id)
note: multiple positive outcomes within groups encountered.
Iteration 0:    log likelihood = -126.34772
Iteration 1:    log likelihood =  -123.4154
Iteration 2:    log likelihood = -123.41386

Conditional (fixed-effects) logistic regression    Number of obs   =       369
                                                    LR chi2(2)      =      9.07
                                                    Prob > chi2     =    0.0107
Log likelihood = -123.41386                         Pseudo R2       =    0.0355
```

y	Coef.	Std. Err.	z	P>|z|	[95% Conf. Interval]	
x1	.653363	.2875214	2.27	0.023	.0898313	1.216895
x2	.0659169	.0449555	1.47	0.143	-.0221942	.154028

◁

❏ Technical Note

Note the message "note: multiple positive outcomes within groups encountered" at the top of the clogit output for the previous example. This is merely informing you that you have $k_{1i} : k_{2i}$ matching with $k_{1i} > 1$ for at least one group. If your data should be 1 : k_{2i} matched, then there is an error in it somewhere.

We can see the distribution of k_{1i} and $T_i = k_{1i} + k_{2i}$ for the data of the previous example by the following steps.

```
. by id, sort: gen k1 = sum(y)
. by id: replace k1 = . if _n < _N
(303 real changes made, 303 to missing)
. by id: gen T = sum(y~=.)
. by id: replace T = . if _n < _N
(303 real changes made, 303 to missing)
. tab k1
```

k1	Freq.	Percent	Cum.
1	48	72.73	72.73
2	12	18.18	90.91
3	4	6.06	96.97
4	2	3.03	100.00
Total	66	100.00	

```
. tab T
```

T	Freq.	Percent	Cum.
2	5	7.58	7.58
3	5	7.58	15.15
4	12	18.18	33.33
5	11	16.67	50.00
6	13	19.70	69.70
7	8	12.12	81.82
8	3	4.55	86.36
9	7	10.61	96.97
10	2	3.03	100.00
Total	66	100.00	

So we see that k_{1i} ranges from 1 to 4 and T_i ranges from 2 to 10 for this data.

❑

❑ Technical Note

In the case of $k_{1i} : k_{2i}$ matching (and hence in the general case of fixed-effects logit), clogit uses a recursive algorithm to compute the likelihood. This means that there are no limits on the size of T_i. However, computation time is proportional to $\sum T_i \min(k_{1i}, k_{2i})$, so clogit will take roughly 10 times longer to estimate a model with 10 : 10 matching than one with 1 : 10. But clogit is very fast, so computation time only becomes an issue when $\min(k_{1i}, k_{2i})$ is around 100 or more. See *Methods and Formulas* at the end of this entry for details.

❑

Matched case–control data

Here we give a more detailed example of matched case–control data.

▷ Example

Hosmer and Lemeshow (1989, 262–265) present data on matched pairs of infants, one with low birth weight and another with regular birth weight. The data are matched on age of the mother. Several possible maternal exposures are considered: race (three categories), smoking status, presence of hypertension, presence of uterine irritability, previous preterm delivery, and weight at the last menstrual period.

```
. describe
Contains data from lowbirth.dta
  obs:           112                          Applied Logistic Regression,
                                                Hosmer & Lemeshow, pp. 262-265
  vars:           11                          6 Jul 2000 13:14
  size:        1,792 (99.5% of memory free)
```

variable name	storage type	display format	value label	variable label
pairid	byte	%8.0g		Case-control pair id
low	byte	%8.0g		Baby has low birth weight
age	byte	%8.0g		Age of mother
lwt	int	%8.0g		Mother's last menstrual weight
smoke	byte	%8.0g		Mother smoked during pregnancy
ptd	byte	%8.0g		Mother had previous preterm baby
ht	byte	%8.0g		Mother has hypertension
ui	byte	%8.0g		Uterine irritability
race1	byte	%8.0g		mother is white
race2	byte	%8.0g		mother is black
race3	byte	%8.0g		mother is other

```
Sorted by:  pairid
```

We list the case–control indicator variable low, the match identifier variable pairid, and a couple of the covariates, lwt and smoke, for the first 10 observations.

```
. list low lwt smoke pairid in 1/10
         low      lwt    smoke    pairid
  1.       0      135        0         1
  2.       1      101        1         1
  3.       0       98        0         2
  4.       1      115        0         2
  5.       0       95        0         3
  6.       1      130        0         3
  7.       0      103        0         4
  8.       1      130        1         4
  9.       0      122        1         5
 10.       1      110        1         5
```

We estimate a conditional logistic model of low birth weight on mother's weight, race, smoking behavior, and history.

```
. clogit low lwt smoke ptd ht ui race2 race3, strata(pairid) nolog
Conditional (fixed-effects) logistic regression   Number of obs   =       112
                                                  LR chi2(7)      =     26.04
                                                  Prob > chi2     =    0.0005
Log likelihood = -25.794271                       Pseudo R2       =    0.3355
```

low	Coef.	Std. Err.	z	P>|z|	[95% Conf. Interval]	
lwt	-.0183757	.0100806	-1.82	0.068	-.0381333	.0013819
smoke	1.400656	.6278396	2.23	0.026	.1701131	2.631199
ptd	1.808009	.7886502	2.29	0.022	.2622829	3.353735
ht	2.361152	1.086128	2.17	0.030	.2323797	4.489924
ui	1.401929	.6961585	2.01	0.044	.0374836	2.766375
race2	.5713643	.6896449	0.83	0.407	-.7803149	1.923044
race3	-.0253148	.6992044	-0.04	0.971	-1.39573	1.345101

We might prefer to see results presented as odds ratios. We could have specified the or option when we first estimated the model, or we can now redisplay results and specify or:

```
. clogit, or
Conditional (fixed-effects) logistic regression     Number of obs   =       112
                                                    LR chi2(7)      =     26.04
                                                    Prob > chi2     =    0.0005
Log likelihood = -25.794271                         Pseudo R2       =    0.3355
```

low	Odds Ratio	Std. Err.	z	P>|z|	[95% Conf. Interval]	
lwt	.9817921	.009897	-1.82	0.068	.9625847	1.001383
smoke	4.057862	2.547686	2.23	0.026	1.185439	13.89042
ptd	6.098293	4.80942	2.29	0.022	1.299894	28.60938
ht	10.60316	11.51639	2.17	0.030	1.261599	89.11467
ui	4.06303	2.828513	2.01	0.044	1.038195	15.90088
race2	1.770681	1.221141	0.83	0.407	.4582617	6.84175
race3	.975003	.6817263	-0.04	0.971	.2476522	3.838573

Smoking, previous preterm delivery, hypertension, uterine irritability, and possibly the mother's weight all contribute to low birth weight. race2 (mother black) and race3 (mother other) are statistically insignificant when compared with the race1 (mother white) omitted group, although the race2 effect is large. We can test the joint statistical significance of race2 and race3 using test:

```
. test race2 race3
 ( 1)  race2 = 0.0
 ( 2)  race3 = 0.0
          chi2(  2) =      0.88
        Prob > chi2 =    0.6436
```

For a more complete description of test, see [R] test. Note that test presents results in terms of coefficients rather than odds ratios. Jointly testing that the coefficients on race2 and race3 are zero is equivalent to jointly testing that the odds ratios are 1.

In this example, one case was matched to one control, so-called 1 : 1 matching. From clogit's point-of-view, that was not important—k_1 cases could have been matched to k_2 controls ($k_1 : k_2$ matching) and we would have estimated the model in the same way. Furthermore, the matching can change from group to group, which we have denoted as $k_{1i} : k_{2i}$ matching, where i denotes the group. clogit does not care. To estimate the conditional logistic regression model, we specified the group(*varname*) option, in our case, group(pairid). The case and control are stored in separate observations. clogit knew they were linked (in the same group) because the related observations share the same value of pairid.

◁

❑ Technical Note

clogit provides a way to extend McNemar's test to multiple controls per case ($1 : k_{2i}$ matching) and to multiple controls matched with multiple cases ($k_{1i} : k_{2i}$ matching).

In Stata, McNemar's test is calculated by the mcc command; see [R] epitab. The mcc command, however, requires that the matched case and control appear in a single observation, so the data will need to be manipulated from one to two observations per stratum before using clogit. Alternatively, if you begin with clogit's two-observations-per-group organization, you will have to change it to one observation per group if you wish to use mcc. In either case, reshape provides an easy way to change the organization of the data. We will demonstrate its use below, but we direct you to [R] reshape for a more thorough discussion.

In the above example, we used `clogit` to analyze the relationship between low birth weight and various characteristics of the mother. Assume we now want to assess the relationship between low birth weight and smoking ignoring the mother's other characteristics. Using `clogit`, we obtain the following results:

```
. clogit low smoke, strata(pairid) or

Iteration 0:   log likelihood = -37.257978
Iteration 1:   log likelihood = -35.431994
Iteration 2:   log likelihood = -35.419285
Iteration 3:   log likelihood = -35.419282
```

Conditional (fixed-effects) logistic regression

Number of obs	=	112
LR chi2(1)	=	6.79
Prob > chi2	=	0.0091
Pseudo R2	=	0.0875

Log likelihood = -35.419282

low	Odds Ratio	Std. Err.	z	P>|z|	[95% Conf. Interval]
smoke	2.75	1.135369	2.45	0.014	1.224347 6.176763

Let us compare our estimated odds ratio and 95% confidence interval with that produced by `mcc`. We begin by reshaping the data:

```
. keep low smoke pairid

. reshape wide smoke, i(pairid) j(low 0 1)
```

Data	long	->	wide
Number of obs.	112	->	56
Number of variables	3	->	3
j variable (2 values)	low	->	(dropped)
xij variables:			
	smoke	->	smoke0 smoke1

We now have the variables `smoke0` (formed from `smoke` and `low = 0`), recording 1 if the control mother smoked and 0 otherwise; and `smoke1` (formed from `smoke` and `low = 1`), recording 1 if the case mother smoked and 0 otherwise. We can now use `mcc`:

```
. mcc smoke1 smoke0
```

	Controls		
Cases	Exposed	Unexposed	Total
Exposed	8	22	30
Unexposed	8	18	26
Total	16	40	56

```
McNemar's chi2(1) =      6.53    Prob > chi2 = 0.0106
Exact McNemar significance probability     = 0.0161
```

Proportion with factor

Cases	.5357143	
Controls	.2857143	[95% Conf. Interval]

difference	.25	.0519726	.4480274
ratio	1.875	1.148685	3.060565
rel. diff.	.35	.1336258	.5663742
odds ratio	2.75	1.17909	7.144221 (exact)

Note that both methods estimated the same odds ratio and that the 95% confidence intervals are similar. `clogit` produced a confidence interval of $[1.22, 6.18]$ while `mcc` produced a confidence interval of $[1.18, 7.14]$.

❑

Use of weights

With `clogit`, weights apply to groups as a whole, not to individual observations. For example, if there is a group in your dataset with a frequency weight of 3, it means that there are a total of 3 groups in your sample with the same values of the dependent and independent variables as this one group. Weights must have the same value for all observations belonging to the same group; otherwise, an error message will be displayed.

▷ Example

We use the example from the above discussion of the `mcc` command. Here, we had a total of 56 matched case–control groups, each with one case matched to one control. We had 8 matched pairs in which both the case and the control are exposed, 22 pairs in which the case is exposed and the control is unexposed, 8 pairs in which the case is unexposed and the control is exposed, and 18 pairs in which they are both unexposed.

Using weights, it is easy to enter these data into Stata and run `clogit`.

```
. input id case exposed weight

           id        case     exposed      weight
  1. 1 1 1 8
  2. 1 0 1 8
  3. 2 1 1 22
  4. 2 0 0 22
  5. 3 1 0 8
  6. 3 0 1 8
  7. 4 1 0 18
  8. 4 0 0 18
  9. end
. clogit case exposed [w=weight], strata(id) or
(frequency weights assumed)
Iteration 0:   log likelihood = -37.257978
Iteration 1:   log likelihood = -35.431994
Iteration 2:   log likelihood = -35.419285
Iteration 3:   log likelihood = -35.419282
```

Conditional (fixed-effects) logistic regression

			Number of obs	=	112
			LR chi2(1)	=	6.79
			Prob > chi2	=	0.0091
Log likelihood = -35.419282			Pseudo R2	=	0.0875

case	Odds Ratio	Std. Err.	z	P>|z|	[95% Conf. Interval]
exposed	2.75	1.135369	2.45	0.014	1.224347 6.176763

◁

Fixed-effects logit

The fixed-effects logit model can be written as

$$\Pr(y_{it} = 1 \mid \mathbf{x}_{it}) = F(\alpha_i + \mathbf{x}_{it}\boldsymbol{\beta})$$

where F is the cumulative logistic distribution

$$F(z) = \frac{\exp(z)}{1 + \exp(z)}$$

and $i = 1, 2, \ldots, n$ denotes the independent units (called "groups" by clogit), and $t = 1, 2, \ldots, T_i$ denotes the observations for the ith unit (group).

Estimating this model using a full maximum-likelihood approach leads to difficulties, however. When T_i is fixed, the maximum likelihood estimates for α_i and $\boldsymbol{\beta}$ are inconsistent (Andersen 1970 and Chamberlain 1980). This difficulty can be circumvented by looking at the probability of $\mathbf{y}_i = (y_{i1}, \ldots, y_{iT_i})$ conditional on $\sum_{t=1}^{T_i} y_{it}$. This conditional probability does not involve the α_i, so they are never estimated when the resulting conditional likelihood is used. See Hamerle and Ronning (1995) for a succinct and lucid development. See *Methods and Formulas* for the estimation equation.

To demonstrate fixed-effects logit, we use the same dataset that was used in [R] **probit** to illustrate probit, robust cluster() and in [R] **xtprobit** to illustrate xtprobit.

▷ Example

We are studying unionization of women in the United States and are using the union dataset; see [R] **xt**. We estimate the fixed-effects logit model:

```
. clogit union age grade not_smsa south black, group(idcode)
note: multiple positive outcomes within groups encountered.
note: 2744 groups (14165 obs) dropped due to all positive or
      all negative outcomes.
note: black omitted due to no within-group variance.
Iteration 0:   log likelihood = -4540.1394
Iteration 1:   log likelihood =   -4516.15
Iteration 2:   log likelihood = -4516.1385
```

Conditional (fixed-effects) logistic regression			Number of obs	=	12035
			LR chi2(4)	=	68.09
			Prob > chi2	=	0.0000
Log likelihood = -4516.1385			Pseudo R2	=	0.0075

union	Coef.	Std. Err.	z	P>|z|	[95% Conf. Interval]	
age	.0170301	.004146	4.11	0.000	.0089042	.0251561
grade	.0853572	.0418781	2.04	0.042	.0032777	.1674367
not_smsa	.0083678	.1127962	0.07	0.941	-.2127087	.2294444
south	-.748023	.1251749	-5.98	0.000	-.9933613	-.5026848

We received three messages at the top of the output. The first one, "multiple positive outcomes within groups encountered", we expected. Our data do indeed have multiple positive outcomes (union = 1) in many groups. (Here, of course, a group consists of all the observations for a particular individual.)

The second message tells us that 2744 groups were "dropped" by clogit. When either union = 0 or union = 1 for all observations for an individual, then this individual's contribution to the log-likelihood is zero. Although these are perfectly valid observations in every sense, they have no effect on the estimation, and so they are not included in the total "Number of obs". Hence, the reported "Number of obs" gives the effective sample size of the estimation. Here it is 12,035 observations—only 46% of the total 26,200.

It is easy to check that there are indeed 2744 groups with union either all 0 or all 1. We will generate a variable that contains the fraction of observations for each individual that has union = 1.

```
. by idcode: gen fraction = sum(union)/sum(union~=.)

. by idcode: replace fraction = . if _n < _N
(21766 real changes made, 21766 to missing)

. tab fraction
```

fraction	Freq.	Percent	Cum.
0	2481	55.95	55.95
.0833333	30	0.68	56.63
.0909091	33	0.74	57.37
.1	53	1.20	58.57
(output omitted)			
.9	10	0.23	93.59
.9090909	11	0.25	93.84
.9166667	10	0.23	94.07
1	263	5.93	100.00
Total	4434	100.00	

Since $2481 + 263 = 2744$, we confirm what clogit did.

The third warning message from clogit said "black omitted due to no within-group variance". Obviously, race stays constant for an individual across time. Any such variables are collinear with the α_i (i.e., the fixed effects), and just as the α_i drop out of the conditional likelihood, so do all variables that are unchanging within groups. Thus, they cannot be estimated with the conditional fixed-effects model.

There are several alternative estimators implemented in Stata that you could conceivably use with this data:

```
cloglog ... ,  robust cluster(...)
logit ... ,  robust cluster(...)
probit ... ,  robust cluster(...)
scobit ... ,  robust cluster(...)
xtclog ... ,  i(...)
xtgee ... ,  i(...) family(binomial) link(logit) corr(exchangeable)
xtlogit ... ,  i(...)
xtprobit ... ,  i(...)
```

See [R] **cloglog**, [R] **logit**, [R] **probit**, [R] **scobit**, [R] **xtclog**, [R] **xtgee**, [R] **xtlogit**, and [R] **xtprobit** for details.

◁

McFadden's choice model

clogit can also be used to estimate McFadden's choice model (McFadden 1974; for a brief introduction see, for example, Greene 2000, Section 19.7).

For such models, we have a set of unordered choices, say, $1, 2, \ldots, T$. Let y_{it} be an indicator variable for the choice actually chosen by the ith individual. That is, $y_{it} = 1$ if individual i chose choice t, and $y_{it'} = 0$ for $t' \neq t$. We write the independent variables of the model as $\mathbf{z}_{it} = [\,\mathbf{x}_{it}\ \mathbf{w}_i\,]$, where $\mathbf{x}_{it}$ are attributes of the choices for the ith individual and $\mathbf{w}_i$ are attributes of the individual.

▷ Example

We have data on 295 consumers and their choice of automobile. We have a three-category choice car, which represents the nationality of the manufacturer of the consumer's car, whether American, Japanese, or European. We want to explore the relationship of the choice of car to dealer, the number of dealerships of each nationality in the consumer's city, and to the sex (variable sex) and income (variable income in 1000s of dollars) of the consumer. dealer is obviously an attribute of the choice ($\mathbf{x}_{it}$ in our previous notation), and sex and income attributes of the individual ($\mathbf{w}_i$). The consumer's choice of car is indicated by the variable choice (y_{it}).

Let's list some of the data.

```
. list id car choice dealer sex income in 1/12
         id        car   choice   dealer      sex   income
  1.      1   American        0       18     male     46.7
  2.      1      Japan        0        8     male     46.7
  3.      1     Europe        1        5     male     46.7
  4.      2   American        1       17     male     26.1
  5.      2      Japan        0        6     male     26.1
  6.      2     Europe        0        2     male     26.1
  7.      3   American        1       12     male     32.7
  8.      3      Japan        0        6     male     32.7
  9.      3     Europe        0        2     male     32.7
 10.      4   American        0       18   female     49.2
 11.      4      Japan        1        7   female     49.2
 12.      4     Europe        0        4   female     49.2
```

Since we want to examine how the consumer's attributes apply to the choices, we must interact the attributes with dummy variables for the choices. Here's how we do it:

```
. gen japan  = (car==2)
. gen europe = (car==3)
. gen sexJap = sex*japan
. gen sexEur = sex*europe
. gen incJap = income*japan
. gen incEur = income*europe
```

We can now run our model.

```
. clogit choice japan europe sexJap sexEur incJap incEur dealer, group(id)
Iteration 0:  log likelihood = -284.51561
Iteration 1:  log likelihood = -251.47313
Iteration 2:  log likelihood = -250.78678
Iteration 3:  log likelihood =  -250.7794
Iteration 4:  log likelihood =  -250.7794
```

```
Conditional (fixed-effects) logistic regression    Number of obs   =      885
                                                   LR chi2(7)      =   146.62
                                                   Prob > chi2     =   0.0000
Log likelihood =  -250.7794                        Pseudo R2       =   0.2262
```

choice	Coef.	Std. Err.	z	P>|z|	[95% Conf. Interval]	
japan	-1.352189	.6911829	-1.96	0.050	-2.706882	.0025049
europe	-2.355249	.8526681	-2.76	0.006	-4.026448	-.6840502
sexJap	-.5346039	.3141564	-1.70	0.089	-1.150339	.0811314
sexEur	.5704111	.4540247	1.26	0.209	-.319461	1.460283
incJap	.0325318	.012824	2.54	0.011	.0073973	.0576663
incEur	.032042	.0138676	2.31	0.021	.004862	.0592219
dealer	.0680938	.0344465	1.98	0.048	.00058	.1356076

Displaying the results as odds ratios makes them easier to interpret.

```
. clogit, or
Conditional (fixed-effects) logistic regression    Number of obs   =      885
                                                   LR chi2(7)      =   146.62
                                                   Prob > chi2     =   0.0000
Log likelihood =  -250.7794                        Pseudo R2       =   0.2262
```

choice	Odds Ratio	Std. Err.	z	P>|z|	[95% Conf. Interval]	
japan	.2586735	.1787907	-1.96	0.050	.0667446	1.002508
europe	.0948699	.0808925	-2.76	0.006	.0178376	.5045692
sexJap	.5859013	.1840647	-1.70	0.089	.3165294	1.084513
sexEur	1.768994	.803167	1.26	0.209	.7265405	4.307179
incJap	1.033067	.013248	2.54	0.011	1.007425	1.059361
incEur	1.032561	.0143191	2.31	0.021	1.004874	1.061011
dealer	1.070466	.0368737	1.98	0.048	1.00058	1.145232

We see, for example, that in this sample men (sex = 1) are less likely to own Japanese cars than women (odds ratio 0.59), but that men are more likely to own European cars (odds ratio 1.77).

◁

❑ Technical Note

McFadden's choice model is closely related to multinomial logistic regression (mlogit). If all independent variables are attributes of the individual, then the model is exactly the same as multinomial logit. Let's try running the previous example with just the attributes of the individual, omitting dealer, the attribute of the choice.

```
. clogit choice sexJap incJap japan sexEur incEur europe, group(id)
Iteration 0:   log likelihood = -284.66485
Iteration 1:   log likelihood = -253.31044
Iteration 2:   log likelihood =  -252.7268
Iteration 3:   log likelihood = -252.72012
Iteration 4:   log likelihood = -252.72012
```

```
Conditional (fixed-effects) logistic regression   Number of obs   =        885
                                                  LR chi2(6)      =     142.74
                                                  Prob > chi2     =     0.0000
Log likelihood = -252.72012                       Pseudo R2       =     0.2202
```

choice	Coef.	Std. Err.	z	P>|z|	[95% Conf. Interval]
sexJap	-.4694799	.3114939	-1.51	0.132	-1.079997 .141037
incJap	.0276854	.0123666	2.24	0.025	.0034472 .0519236
japan	-1.962652	.6216804	-3.16	0.002	-3.181123 -.7441806
sexEur	.5388442	.4525278	1.19	0.234	-.348094 1.425782
incEur	.0273669	.013787	1.98	0.047	.000345 .0543889
europe	-3.180029	.7546837	-4.21	0.000	-4.659182 -1.700876

To run `mlogit`, we must rearrange the dataset. `mlogit` requires a dependent variable that indicates the choice—1, 2, or 3—for each individual. This is just our variable `car` for those observations that represent the choice actually chosen.

```
. keep if choice == 1
(590 observations deleted)

. mlogit car sex income

Iteration 0:   log likelihood =  -259.1712
Iteration 1:   log likelihood = -252.81165
Iteration 2:   log likelihood = -252.72014
Iteration 3:   log likelihood = -252.72012

Multinomial regression                            Number of obs   =        295
                                                  LR chi2(4)      =      12.90
                                                  Prob > chi2     =     0.0118
Log likelihood = -252.72012                       Pseudo R2       =     0.0249
```

car	Coef.	Std. Err.	z	P>|z|	[95% Conf. Interval]
Japan					
sex	-.4694799	.3114939	-1.51	0.132	-1.079997 .141037
income	.0276854	.0123666	2.24	0.025	.0034472 .0519236
_cons	-1.962652	.6216803	-3.16	0.002	-3.181123 -.7441807
Europe					
sex	.5388442	.4525278	1.19	0.234	-.3480941 1.425783
income	.0273669	.013787	1.98	0.047	.000345 .0543889
_cons	-3.180029	.7546837	-4.21	0.000	-4.659182 -1.700876

(Outcome car==American is the comparison group)

The results are exactly the same.

❑

Predictions

`predict` may be used after `clogit` to obtain predicted values of the index $\mathbf{x}_{it}\beta$. Predicted probabilities for conditional logistic regression must be interpreted carefully. Probabilities are estimated for each group as a whole, not for individual observations. Furthermore, the probabilities are conditional on the number of positive outcomes in the group (i.e., the number of cases and the number of controls), or it is assumed that the fixed effect is zero.

predict produces probabilities of a positive outcome within group conditional on there being one positive outcome:

$$\Pr(y_{it} = 1) = \frac{\exp(\mathbf{x}_{it}\boldsymbol{\beta})}{\sum_{t=1}^{T_i} \exp(\mathbf{x}_{it}\boldsymbol{\beta})}$$

or predict calculates pu0:

$$\Pr(y_{it} = 1) = \frac{\exp(\mathbf{x}_{it}\boldsymbol{\beta})}{1 + \exp(\mathbf{x}_{it}\boldsymbol{\beta})}$$

predict may be used for both within-sample and out-of-sample predictions.

▷ Example

Suppose that you have $1 : k_{2i}$ matched data and that you have previously estimated the model

    . clogit y x1 x2 x3, group(id)

To obtain the predicted values of the index, you could type predict idx, xb to create a new variable called idx. From idx, you could then calculate the predicted probabilities. Easier, however, would be to type

    . predict phat
    (option pc1 assumed; conditional probability for single outcome within group)

phat would then contain the predicted probabilities.

It is important to say again that the predicted probabilities are really predicted probabilities for the group as a whole (i.e., they are the predicted probability of observing $y_{it} = 1$ *and* $y_{it'} = 0$ for all $t' \neq t$). Thus, if you want to obtain the predicted probabilities for the estimation sample, it is important that when you make the calculation, predictions be restricted to the same sample on which you estimated the data. You cannot predict the probabilities and then just keep the relevant ones because the entire sample determines each probability. Thus, assuming that you are not attempting to make out-of-sample predictions, you type

    . predict phat if e(sample)
    (option pc1 assumed; conditional probability for single outcome within group)

◁

Saved Results

clogit saves in e():

Scalars

e(N)	number of observations	e(ll)	log likelihood
e(df_m)	model degrees of freedom	e(ll_0)	log likelihood, constant-only model
e(r2_p)	pseudo R-squared	e(chi2)	χ^2

Macros

e(cmd)	clogit	e(wexp)	weight expression
e(depvar)	name of dependent variable	e(chi2type)	LR; type of model χ^2 test
e(group)	name of group() variable	e(offset)	offset
e(wtype)	weight type	e(predict)	program used to implement predict

Matrices

e(b)	coefficient vector	e(V)	variance–covariance matrix of the estimators

Functions

e(sample)	marks estimation sample

Methods and Formulas

Breslow and Day (1980, 247–279), Collett (1991, 262–276), and Hosmer and Lemeshow (1989, 187–215) provide a biostatistical point of view on conditional logistic regression. Hamerle and Ronning (1995) give a succinct and lucid review of fixed-effects logit; Chamberlain (1980) is a standard reference for this model. Greene (2000, chapter 19) provides a straightforward textbook description of conditional logistic regression from an economist's point of view, as well as a brief description of choice models.

Let $i = 1, 2, \ldots, n$ denote the groups and $t = 1, 2, \ldots, T_i$ the observations for the ith group. Let y_{it} be the dependent variable taking on values 0 or 1. Let $\mathbf{y}_i = (y_{i1}, \ldots, y_{iT_i})$ be the outcomes for the ith group as a whole. Let $\mathbf{x}_{it}$ be a row vector of covariates. Let

$$k_{1i} = \sum_{t=1}^{T_i} y_{it}$$

be the observed number of ones for the dependent variable in the ith group. Biostatisticians would say that there are k_{1i} cases matched to $k_{2i} = T_i - k_{1i}$ controls in the ith group.

We consider the probability of a possible value of $\mathbf{y}_i$ conditional on $\sum_{t=1}^{T_i} y_{it} = k_{1i}$ (Hamerle and Ronning 1995, equation 8.33; Hosmer and Lemeshow 1989, equation 7.3):

$$\Pr\left(\mathbf{y}_i \mid \sum_{t=1}^{T_i} y_{it} = k_{1i}\right) = \frac{\exp\left(\sum_{t=1}^{T_i} y_{it}\mathbf{x}_{it}\boldsymbol{\beta}\right)}{\sum_{\mathbf{d}_i \in S_i} \exp\left(\sum_{t=1}^{T_i} d_{it}\mathbf{x}_{it}\boldsymbol{\beta}\right)}$$

where d_{it} is equal to 0 or 1 with $\sum_{t=1}^{T_i} d_{it} = k_{1i}$, and S_i is the set of all possible combinations of k_{1i} ones and k_{2i} zeros. Clearly, there are $\binom{T_i}{k_{1i}}$ such combinations. But one does not have to enumerate all these combinations to compute the denominator of the above equation. It can be computed recursively.

Denote the denominator by

$$f_i(T_i, k_{1i}) = \sum_{\mathbf{d}_i \in S_i} \exp\left(\sum_{t=1}^{T_i} d_{it}\mathbf{x}_{it}\boldsymbol{\beta}\right)$$

Consider, computationally, how f_i changes as we go from a total of one observation in the group to two observations to three, etc. Doing this, we derive the recursive formula

$$f_i(T, k) = f_i(T - 1, k) + f_i(T - 1, k - 1)\,\exp(\mathbf{x}_{iT}\boldsymbol{\beta})$$

where we define $f_i(T, k) = 0$ if $T < k$ and $f_i(T, 0) = 1$.

The conditional log-likelihood is

$$L = \sum_{i=1}^{n} \left\{ \sum_{t=1}^{T_i} y_{it}\mathbf{x}_{it}\boldsymbol{\beta} - \log f_i(T_i, k_{1i}) \right\}$$

The derivatives of the conditional log-likelihood can also be computed recursively by taking derivatives of the recursive formula for f_i.

Computation time is roughly proportional to

$$p^2 \sum_{i=1}^{n} T_i \min(k_{1i}, k_{2i})$$

where p is the number of independent variables in the model. If $\min(k_{1i}, k_{2i})$ is small, computation time is not an issue. But if it is large, say 100 or more, patience may be required.

Note that if T_i is large for all groups, the bias of the unconditional fixed-effects estimator is not a concern, and one can confidently use logit with an indicator variable for each group (provided, of course, that the number of groups does not exceed matsize; see [R] **matsize**).

References

Andersen, E. B. 1970. Asymptotic properties of conditional maximum likelihood estimators. *Journal of the Royal Statistical Society* B 32: 283–301.

Breslow, N. E. and N. E. Day. 1980. *Statistical Methods in Cancer Research*, vol. 1. Lyon: International Agency for Research on Cancer.

Chamberlain, G. 1980. Analysis of covariance with qualitative data. *Review of Economic Studies* 47: 225–238.

Collett, D. 1991. *Modelling Binary Data*. London: Chapman & Hall.

Greene, W. H. 2000. *Econometric Analysis*. 4th ed. Upper Saddle River, NJ: Prentice–Hall.

Hamerle, A. and G. Ronning. 1995. Panel analysis for qualitative variables. In *Handbook of Statistical Modeling for the Social and Behavioral Sciences*, ed. G. Arminger, C. C. Clogg, and M. E. Sobel, 401–451. New York: Plenum Press.

Hosmer, D. W., Jr., and S. Lemeshow. 1989. *Applied Logistic Regression*. New York: John Wiley & Sons. (*Second edition forthcoming in 2001*.)

McFadden, D. 1974. Conditional logit analysis of qualitative choice behavior. In *Frontiers in Econometrics*, ed. P. Zarembka, 105–142. New York: Academic Press.

Also See

Complementary:	[R] **adjust**, [R] **lincom**, [R] **linktest**, [R] **lrtest**, [R] **predict**, [R] **sw**, [R] **test**, [R] **testnl**, [R] **vce**, [R] **xi**
Related:	[R] **cloglog**, [R] **logistic**, [R] **logit**, [R] **mlogit**, [R] **nlogit**, [R] **ologit**, [R] **oprobit**, [R] **probit**, [R] **scobit**, [R] **xtclog**, [R] **xtlogit**, [R] **xtgee**, [R] **xtprobit**
Background:	[U] **16.5 Accessing coefficients and standard errors**, [U] **23 Estimation and post-estimation commands**, [R] **maximize**

Title

> **cloglog** — Maximum-likelihood complementary log-log estimation

Syntax

> **cloglog** *depvar* [*indepvars*] [*weight*] [**if** *exp*] [**in** *range*] [, **level**(*#*)]
>
> **noconstant** **robust** **cluster**(*varname*) **score**(*newvarname*) **offset**(*varname*)
>
> **constraints**(*numlist*) **asis** **nolog** *maximize_options*]

by ... : may be used with **cloglog**; see [R] **by**.

fweights, **iweights**, and **pweights** are allowed; see [U] **14.1.6 weight**.

This command shares the features of all estimation commands; see [U] **23 Estimation and post-estimation commands**.

cloglog may be used with **sw** to perform stepwise estimation; see [R] **sw**.

Syntax for predict

> **predict** [*type*] *newvarname* [**if** *exp*] [**in** *range*] [, { **p** | **xb** | **stdp** } **nooffset**]

These statistics are available both in and out of sample; type **predict** ... **if e(sample)** ... if wanted only for the estimation sample.

Description

cloglog estimates a maximum-likelihood complementary log-log model.

See [R] **logistic** for a list of related estimation commands.

Options

level(*#*) specifies the confidence level, in percent, for confidence intervals. The default is **level**(95) or as set by **set level**; see [U] **23.5 Specifying the width of confidence intervals**.

noconstant suppresses the constant term (intercept) in the model.

robust specifies that the Huber/White/sandwich estimator of variance is to be used in place of the traditional calculation; see [U] **23.11 Obtaining robust variance estimates**. **robust** combined with **cluster**() allows observations which are not independent within cluster (although they must be independent between clusters).

If you specify **pweights**, **robust** is implied; see [U] **23.13 Weighted estimation**.

cluster(*varname*) specifies that the observations are independent across groups (clusters) but not necessarily within groups. *varname* specifies to which group each observation belongs; e.g., **cluster**(personid) in data with repeated observations on individuals. **cluster**() affects the estimated standard errors and variance–covariance matrix of the estimators (VCE), but not the estimated coefficients; see [U] **23.11 Obtaining robust variance estimates**. **cluster**() can be used with **pweights** to produce estimates for unstratified cluster-sampled data.

cluster() implies **robust**; specifying **robust cluster**() is equivalent to typing **cluster**() by itself.

score(*newvar*) creates *newvar* containing $u_j = \partial \ln L_j / \partial (\mathbf{x}_j \mathbf{b})$ for each observation j in the sample. The score vector is $\sum \partial \ln L_j / \partial \mathbf{b} = \sum u_j \mathbf{x}_j$; i.e., the product of *newvar* with each covariate summed over observations. See [U] **23.12 Obtaining scores**.

offset(*varname*) specifies that *varname* is to be included in the model with coefficient constrained to be 1.

constraints(*numlist*) specifies by number the linear constraints to be applied during estimation. The default is to perform unconstrained estimation. Constraints are specified using the constraint command; see [R] **constraint**.

asis forces retention of perfect predictor variables and their associated perfectly predicted observations and may produce instabilities in maximization; see [R] **probit**.

nolog suppresses the iteration log.

maximize_options control the maximization process; see [R] **maximize**. You should never have to specify them.

Options for predict

p, the default, calculates the probability of a positive outcome.

xb calculates the linear prediction.

stdp calculates the standard error of the linear prediction.

nooffset is relevant only if you specified offset(*varname*) for cloglog. It modifies the calculations made by predict so that they ignore the offset variable; the linear prediction is treated as $\mathbf{x}_j \mathbf{b}$ rather than $\mathbf{x}_j \mathbf{b} + \text{offset}_j$.

Remarks

cloglog performs maximum likelihood estimation of models with dichotomous dependent variables coded as 0/1 (or, more precisely, coded as 0 and not 0).

▷ Example

You have data on the make, weight, and mileage rating of 22 foreign and 52 domestic automobiles. You wish to estimate a model explaining whether a car is foreign based on its weight and mileage. Here is an overview of your data:

```
. describe

Contains data from auto.dta
  obs:            74                          1978 Automobile Data
  vars:            4                          7 Jul 2000 13:51
  size:        1,998 (99.7% of memory free)

              storage  display     value
variable name   type   format      label       variable label

make           str18   %-18s                   Make and Model
mpg            int     %8.0g                   Mileage (mpg)
weight         int     %8.0gc                  Weight (lbs.)
foreign        byte    %8.0g       origin      Car type

Sorted by:  foreign
     Note:  dataset has changed since last saved
```

```
. inspect foreign
foreign:  Car type                      Number of Observations
                                                           Non-
                                       Total   Integers   Integers
  |  #                   Negative        -         -          -
  |  #                   Zero           52        52          -
  |  #                   Positive       22        22          -
  |  #
  |  #    #              Total          74        74          -
  |  #    #              Missing         -
  +---------------                      ----
  0              1                       74
     (2 unique values)
        foreign is labeled and all values are documented in the label.
```

The variable **foreign** takes on two unique values, 0 and 1. The value 0 denotes a domestic car and 1 denotes a foreign car.

The model you wish to estimate is

$$\Pr(\texttt{foreign} = 1) = F(\beta_0 + \beta_1\texttt{weight} + \beta_2\texttt{mpg})$$

where $F(z) = 1 - \exp\left\{-\exp(z)\right\}$.

To estimate this model, you type

```
. cloglog foreign weight mpg
Iteration 0:   log likelihood = -33.526894
Iteration 1:   log likelihood = -27.868343
Iteration 2:   log likelihood =  -27.74293
Iteration 3:   log likelihood = -27.742769
Iteration 4:   log likelihood = -27.742769

Complementary log-log regression          Number of obs    =         74
                                          Zero outcomes    =         52
                                          Nonzero outcomes =         22

                                          LR chi2(2)       =      34.58
Log likelihood = -27.742769               Prob > chi2      =     0.0000
```

foreign	Coef.	Std. Err.	z	P>|z|	[95% Conf. Interval]	
weight	-.0029153	.0006974	-4.18	0.000	-.0042823	-.0015483
mpg	-.1422911	.076387	-1.86	0.062	-.2920069	.0074247
_cons	10.09694	3.351841	3.01	0.003	3.527448	16.66642

You find that heavier cars are less likely to be foreign and that cars yielding better gas mileage are also less likely to be foreign, at least holding the weight of the car constant.

See [R] **maximize** for an explanation of the output.

◁

❏ Technical Note

Stata interprets a value of 0 as a negative outcome (failure) and treats all other values (except missing) as positive outcomes (successes). Thus, if your dependent variable takes on the values 0 and 1, 0 is interpreted as failure and 1 as success. If your dependent variable takes on the values 0, 1, and 2, 0 is still interpreted as failure, but both 1 and 2 are treated as successes.

If you prefer a more formal mathematical statement, when you type `cloglog y x`, Stata estimates the model

$$\Pr(y_j \neq 0 \mid \mathbf{x}_j) = 1 - \exp\Big\{ -\exp(\mathbf{x}_j\boldsymbol{\beta}) \Big\}.$$

❑

Robust standard errors

If you specify the `robust` option, `cloglog` reports robust standard errors as described in [U] **23.11 Obtaining robust variance estimates**. In the case of the model of `foreign` on `weight` and `mpg`, the robust calculation increases the standard error of the coefficient on `mpg` by 44 percent:

```
. cloglog foreign weight mpg, robust
Iteration 0:   log likelihood = -33.526894
Iteration 1:   log likelihood = -27.868343
Iteration 2:   log likelihood =  -27.74293
Iteration 3:   log likelihood = -27.742769
Iteration 4:   log likelihood = -27.742769
Complementary log-log regression
```

					Number of obs	=	74
					Zero outcomes	=	52
					Nonzero outcomes	=	22
					Wald chi2(2)	=	29.74
Log likelihood = -27.742769					Prob > chi2	=	0.0000

foreign	Coef.	Robust Std. Err.	z	P>|z|	[95% Conf. Interval]	
weight	-.0029153	.0007484	-3.90	0.000	-.0043822	-.0014484
mpg	-.1422911	.1102466	-1.29	0.197	-.3583704	.0737882
_cons	10.09694	4.317305	2.34	0.019	1.635174	18.5587

Without `robust`, the standard error for the coefficient on `mpg` was reported to be .076 with a resulting confidence interval of $[-.29, .01]$.

`robust` with the `cluster()` option has the ability to relax the independence assumption required by the complementary log-log estimator to being just independence between clusters. To demonstrate this, we will switch to a different dataset.

You are studying unionization of women in the United States and are using the `union` dataset; see [R] **xt**. You estimate the following model ignoring that women are observed an average of 5.9 times each in this dataset:

```
. cloglog union age grade not_smsa south southXt
Iteration 0:   log likelihood = -13609.987
Iteration 1:   log likelihood = -13544.321
Iteration 2:   log likelihood = -13544.202
Iteration 3:   log likelihood = -13544.202
Complementary log-log regression
```

	Number of obs	=	26200
	Zero outcomes	=	20389
	Nonzero outcomes	=	5811
	LR chi2(5)	=	640.06
Log likelihood = -13544.202	Prob > chi2	=	0.0000

union	Coef.	Std. Err.	z	P>|z|	[95% Conf. Interval]	
age	.0085897	.0023034	3.73	0.000	.0040752	.0131043
grade	.0447187	.0057069	7.84	0.000	.0335334	.0559039
not_smsa	-.1906552	.0317663	-6.00	0.000	-.252916	-.1283943
south	-.6446647	.0557644	-11.56	0.000	-.7539609	-.5353684
southXt	.0068271	.0047297	1.44	0.149	-.0024428	.0160971
_cons	-1.966755	.0991779	-19.83	0.000	-2.16114	-1.77237

The reported standard errors in this model are probably meaningless. Women are observed repeatedly and so the observations are not independent. Looking at the coefficients, you find a large southern effect against unionization and little time trend. The `robust` and `cluster()` options provide a way to estimate this model and obtain correct standard errors:

```
. cloglog union age grade not_smsa south southXt, robust cluster(id) nolog
```

Complementary log-log regression		Number of obs	=	26200
		Zero outcomes	=	20389
		Nonzero outcomes	=	5811
		Wald chi2(5)	=	160.78
Log likelihood = -13544.202		Prob > chi2	=	0.0000

(standard errors adjusted for clustering on idcode)

union	Coef.	Robust Std. Err.	z	P>|z|	[95% Conf. Interval]	
age	.0085897	.0033831	2.54	0.011	.0019591	.0152204
grade	.0447187	.0125927	3.55	0.000	.0200375	.0693999
not_smsa	-.1906552	.064189	-2.97	0.003	-.3164632	-.0648471
south	-.6446647	.0833807	-7.73	0.000	-.8080878	-.4812415
southXt	.0068271	.0063038	1.08	0.279	-.0055282	.0191824
_cons	-1.966755	.186019	-10.57	0.000	-2.331346	-1.602165

These standard errors are roughly 50% larger than those reported by the inappropriate conventional calculation. By comparison, another way we could estimate this model is with an equal-correlation population-averaged complementary log-log model:

```
. xtclog union age grade not_smsa south southXt, i(id) pa nolog
```

GEE population-averaged model		Number of obs	=	26200
Group variable:	idcode	Number of groups	=	4434
Link:	cloglog	Obs per group: min =		1
Family:	binomial	avg =		5.9
Correlation:	exchangeable	max =		12
		Wald chi2(5)	=	232.44
Scale parameter:	1	Prob > chi2	=	0.0000

union	Coef.	Std. Err.	z	P>|z|	[95% Conf. Interval]	
age	.0045777	.0021754	2.10	0.035	.0003139	.0088415
grade	.0544267	.0095097	5.72	0.000	.035788	.0730654
not_smsa	-.1051731	.0430512	-2.44	0.015	-.189552	-.0207943
south	-.6578891	.061857	-10.64	0.000	-.7791266	-.5366515
southXt	.0142329	.004133	3.44	0.001	.0061325	.0223334
_cons	-2.074687	.1358008	-15.28	0.000	-2.340851	-1.808522

The coefficient estimates are similar but these standard errors are smaller than those produced by `cloglog, robust cluster()`. This is as we would expect. If the within-panel correlation assumptions are valid, the population-averaged estimator should be more efficient.

In addition to this estimator, we may use the `xtgee` command to fit a panel estimator (with complementary log-log link) and any number of assumptions on the within-idcode correlation.

What is important to understand is that `cloglog, robust cluster()` is robust to assumptions about within-cluster correlation. That is, it inefficiently sums within cluster for the standard error calculation rather than attempting to exploit what might be assumed about the within-cluster correlation (as do the `xtgee` population-averaged models).

Obtaining predicted values

Once you have estimated a model, you can obtain the predicted probabilities using the `predict` command for both the estimation sample and other samples; see [U] **23 Estimation and post-estimation commands** and [R] **predict.** Here we will make only a few additional comments.

`predict` without arguments calculates the predicted probability of a positive outcome. With the `xb` option, it calculates the linear combination $x_j b$, where x_j are the independent variables in the jth observation and b is the estimated parameter vector.

With the `stdp` option, `predict` calculates the standard error of the prediction, which is *not* adjusted for replicated covariate patterns in the data.

▷ Example

In a previous example, we estimated the complementary log-log model `cloglog foreign mpg weight`. To obtain predicted probabilities,

```
. predict p
(option p assumed; Pr(foreign))

. summarize foreign p
```

Variable	Obs	Mean	Std. Dev.	Min	Max
foreign	74	.2972973	.4601885	0	1
p	74	.2928348	.29732	.0032726	.9446067

◁

(Continued on next page)

Saved Results

cloglog saves in e():

Scalars

e(N)	number of observations	e(ll_0)	log likelihood, constant-only model
e(k)	number of variables	e(N_clust)	number of clusters
e(k_eq)	number of equations	e(rc)	return code
e(k_dv)	number of dependent variables	e(chi2)	χ^2
e(N_f)	number of zero outcomes	e(p)	significance
e(N_s)	number of nonzero outcomes	e(ic)	number of iterations
e(df_m)	model degrees of freedom	e(rank)	rank of e(V)
e(ll)	log likelihood		

Macros

e(cmd)	cloglog	e(user)	name of likelihood-evaluator program
e(depvar)	name of dependent variable	e(opt)	type of optimization
e(title)	title in estimation output	e(chi2type)	Wald or LR; type of model χ^2 test
e(wtype)	weight type	e(offset)	offset
e(wexp)	weight expression	e(predict)	program used to implement **predict**
e(clustvar)	name of cluster variable	e(cnslist)	constraint numbers
e(vcetype)	covariance estimation method		

Matrices

e(b)	coefficient vector	e(V)	variance–covariance matrix of
e(ilog)	iteration log (up to 20 iterations)		the estimators

Functions

e(sample)	marks estimation sample

Methods and Formulas

Complementary log-log analysis (related to the gompit model, so-named due to its relationship to the Gompertz distribution) is an alternative to logit and probit analysis, but it is unlike these other estimators in that the transformation is not symmetric. Typically this model is used when the positive (or negative) outcome is rare.

The log-likelihood function for complementary log-log is

$$\ln L = \sum_{j \in S} w_j \ln F(\mathbf{x}_j \mathbf{b}) + \sum_{j \notin S} w_j \ln \left\{ 1 - F(\mathbf{x}_j \mathbf{b}) \right\}$$

where S is the set of all observations j such that $y_j \neq 0$, $F(z) = 1 - \exp\left\{ -\exp(z) \right\}$, and w_j denotes the optional weights. $\ln L$ is maximized as described in [R] **maximize**.

One can fit a gompit model by reversing the success–failure sense of the dependent variable and using cloglog.

If robust standard errors are requested, the calculation described in *Methods and Formulas* of [R] **regress** is carried forward with $\mathbf{u}_j = [\exp(\mathbf{x}_j \mathbf{b}) \exp\left\{ -\exp(\mathbf{x}_j \mathbf{b}) \right\} / F(\mathbf{x}_j \mathbf{b})] \mathbf{x}_j$ for the positive outcomes and $\left\{ -\exp(\mathbf{x}_j \mathbf{b}) \right\} \mathbf{x}_j$ for the negative outcomes.

Acknowledgment

We would like to thank Joseph Hilbe of Arizona State University for providing the inspiration for the `cloglog` command (Hilbe 1996, 1998).

References

Clayton, D. and M. Hills. 1993. *Statistical Models in Epidemiology*. Oxford: Oxford University Press.

Hilbe, J. 1996. sg53: Maximum-likelihood complementary log-log regression. *Stata Technical Bulletin* 32: 19–20. Reprinted in *Stata Technical Bulletin Reprints*, vol. 6, pp. 129–131.

———. 1998. sg53.2: Stata-like commands for complementary log-log regression. *Stata Technical Bulletin* 41: 23. Reprinted in *Stata Technical Bulletin Reprints*, vol. 7, pp. 166–167.

Long, J. S. 1997. *Regression Models for Categorical and Limited Dependent Variables*. Thousand Oaks, CA: Sage Publications.

Also See

Complementary:	[R] **adjust**, [R] **constraint**, [R] **lincom**, [R] **linktest**, [R] **lrtest**, [R] **mfx**, [R] **predict**, [R] **sw**, [R] **test**, [R] **testnl**, [R] **vce**, [R] **xi**
Related:	[R] **biprobit**, [R] **clogit**, [R] **cusum**, [R] **glm**, [R] **glogit**, [R] **hetprob**, [R] **logistic**, [R] **logit**, [R] **mlogit**, [R] **ologit**, [R] **probit**, [R] **scobit**, [R] **xtclog**, [R] **xtprobit**
Background:	[U] **16.5 Accessing coefficients and standard errors**, [U] **23 Estimation and post-estimation commands**, [U] **23.11 Obtaining robust variance estimates**, [U] **23.12 Obtaining scores**, [R] **maximize**

Title

cluster — Introduction to cluster analysis commands

Syntax

`cluster` *subcommand* ···

Description

Stata's cluster analysis routines give you a choice of several hierarchical and partition clustering methods. Post clustering summarization methods as well as cluster management tools are also provided. This entry provides an overview of cluster analysis, the `cluster` command, and Stata's cluster analysis management tools. The similarity and dissimilarity measures available for use with the cluster analysis methods are also explained.

The `cluster` command has the following *subcommand*s, which are detailed in their respective manual entries.

Partition clustering methods

kmeans	[R] **cluster kmeans**	Kmeans cluster analysis
kmedians	[R] **cluster kmedians**	Kmedians cluster analysis

Hierarchical clustering methods

singlelinkage	[R] **cluster singlelinkage**	Single linkage cluster analysis
averagelinkage	[R] **cluster averagelinkage**	Average linkage cluster analysis
completelinkage	[R] **cluster completelinkage**	Complete linkage cluster analysis

Post clustering commands

dendrogram	[R] **cluster dendrogram**	Dendrograms for hierarchical cluster analysis
generate	[R] **cluster generate**	Generate summary and grouping variables from a cluster analysis

User utilities

notes	[R] **cluster notes**	Place notes in cluster analyses
dir	[R] **cluster utility**	Directory list of cluster analyses
list	[R] **cluster utility**	List cluster analyses
drop	[R] **cluster utility**	Drop cluster analyses
rename	[R] **cluster utility**	Rename cluster analyses
renamevar	[R] **cluster utility**	Rename cluster analysis variables

Programmer utilities

	[P] **cluster subroutines**	Add cluster analysis routines
query	[P] **cluster utilities**	Obtain cluster analysis attributes
set	[P] **cluster utilities**	Set cluster analysis attributes
delete	[P] **cluster utilities**	Delete cluster analysis attributes
parsedistance	[P] **cluster utilities**	Parse (dis)similarity measure names
measures	[P] **cluster utilities**	Compute (dis)similarity measures

Remarks

Remarks are presented under the headings

> *Introduction to cluster analysis*
> *Stata's cluster analysis system*
> *Stata's cluster analysis methods*
> > *Partition cluster analysis methods*
> > *Hierarchical cluster analysis methods*
> > *Data transformations and variable selection*
> *Similarity and dissimilarity measures*
> > *Similarity and dissimilarity measures for continuous data*
> > *Similarity measures for binary data*
> > *Binary similarity measures applied to averages*
> *Post clustering commands*
> *Cluster management tools*

Introduction to cluster analysis

Cluster analysis attempts to determine the natural groupings (or clusters) of observations. Sometimes it is called "classification", but this term is used by others to mean discriminant analysis which, while related to cluster analysis, is not the same. To avoid confusion, we will use "cluster analysis" or "clustering" when referring to finding groups in data. It is difficult (maybe impossible) to give a definition of cluster analysis. Kaufman and Rousseeuw (1990) start their book by saying that "Cluster analysis is the art of finding groups in data". Everitt (1993) uses the terms "cluster", "group", and "class", and says concerning a formal definition for these terms that "In fact it turns out that such formal definition is not only difficult but may even be misplaced".

Who uses cluster analysis and why? Everitt (1993) and Gordon (1999) provide examples of the use of cluster analysis. These include the refining or redefining of diagnostic categories in psychiatry, the detection of similarities in artifacts by archaeologists to study the spatial distribution of artifact types, the discovery of hierarchical relationships in the field of taxonomy, and the identification of sets of similar cities so that one city from each class can be sampled in a market research task. In addition, the activity that is now called "data mining" relies extensively on cluster analysis methods.

We view cluster analysis as an exploratory data analysis technique. This view is shared by Everitt (1993). He says, speaking of cluster analysis techniques, "Many of these have taken their place alongside other exploratory data analysis techniques as tools of the applied statistician. The term exploratory is important here since it explains the largely absent 'p-value', ubiquitous in many other areas of statistics". He then says, "clustering methods are intended largely for generating rather than testing hypotheses." This states the case very well.

It has been said that there are as many cluster analysis methods as there are people performing cluster analysis. This is a gross understatement! There are infinitely more ways to perform a cluster analysis than people who perform them.

There are several general types of cluster analysis methods, and within each of these there are numerous specific methods. Additionally, most cluster analysis methods allow a variety of distance measures for determining the similarity or dissimilarity between observations. Some of the measures do not meet the requirements to be called a distance metric, so the more general term "dissimilarity measure" is used in place of distance. Similarity measures may also be used in place of dissimilarity measures. There are an infinite number of (dis)similarity measures. For instance, there are an infinite number of Minkowski distance metrics, with the familiar Euclidean, absolute value, and maximum value distances being special cases.

In addition to cluster method and (dis)similarity measure choice, someone performing a cluster analysis might decide to perform data transformations before clustering. Then, there is the determining of how many clusters there really are in the data. Looking at all of these choices, you can see why there are more cluster analysis methods than people performing cluster analysis.

Stata's cluster analysis system

Stata's `cluster` command was designed to allow you to keep track of the various cluster analyses performed on your data. The main clustering subcommands `singlelinkage`, `averagelinkage`, `completelinkage`, `kmeans`, and `kmedians` create named Stata cluster objects that keep track of the variables these methods create and hold other identifying information for the cluster analysis. These cluster objects become part of your dataset. They are saved with your data when your data are `saved` and are retrieved when you again `use` your dataset; see [R] **save**.

Post cluster analysis subcommands are also available with the `cluster` command to help examine the created clusters. Cluster management tools are also provided that allow you to add information to the cluster objects as well as manipulate them as needed.

The main clustering subcommands, available similarity and dissimilarity measures, post clustering subcommands, and cluster management tools are discussed in the following sections. Stata's cluster analysis system is extendable in many ways. Programmers wishing to add to the cluster system should see [P] **cluster subroutines**.

Stata's cluster analysis methods

Stata's clustering methods fall into two general types: partition and hierarchical. These two types are discussed below. There exist other types, such as fuzzy partition (where observations can belong to more than one group). Stata's `cluster` command is designed so that programmers can add more methods of whatever type they desire; see [P] **cluster subroutines** and [P] **cluster utilities** for details.

❑ Technical Note

For those familiar with Stata's large array of estimation commands, we warn you not to get confused between cluster analysis (the `cluster` command) and the `cluster()` option allowed with many estimation commands. Cluster analysis finds groups in data. The `cluster()` option allowed with various estimation commands indicates that the observations are independent across the groups defined by the option, but not necessarily independent within those groups. A grouping variable produced by the `cluster` command will seldom satisfy the assumption behind the use of the `cluster()` option.

❑

Partition cluster analysis methods

Partition methods break the observations into a distinct number of nonoverlapping groups. There are many different partition methods. Stata has implemented two of them, kmeans and kmedians.

One of the more commonly used partition clustering methods is called kmeans cluster analysis. In kmeans clustering, the user specifies the number of clusters to create. These k clusters are formed by an iterative process. Each observation is assigned to the group whose mean is closest, and then based on that categorization new group means are determined. These steps continue until no observations change groups. The algorithm begins with k seed values which act as the k group means. There are many ways to specify the beginning seed values. See [R] **cluster kmeans** for the details of the `cluster kmeans` command.

A variation of kmeans clustering is kmedians clustering. The same process is followed in kmedians as in kmeans, with the exception that medians instead of means are computed to represent the group centers at each step; see [R] **cluster kmedians** for details.

These partition clustering methods will generally be quicker and will allow larger datasets than the hierarchical clustering methods outlined below. However, if you wish to examine clustering to various numbers of clusters, you will need to execute `cluster` numerous times with the partition methods. Clustering to various numbers of groups using a partition method will typically not produce clusters that are hierarchically related. If this is important for your application, consider using one of the hierarchical methods.

Hierarchical cluster analysis methods

Hierarchical clustering methods are generally of two types: agglomerative or divisive. Hierarchical clustering creates (by either dividing or combining) hierarchically related sets of clusters.

Agglomerative hierarchical clustering methods begin with each observation being considered as a separate group (N groups each of size 1). The closest two groups are combined ($N - 1$ groups, one of size 2 and the rest of size 1) and this process continues until all observations belong to the same group. This process creates a hierarchy of clusters. In addition to choosing the similarity or dissimilarity measure to use in comparing two observations, there is the choice of what should be compared between groups that contain more than one observation. Three popular choices are single linkage, complete linkage, and average linkage. These three hierarchical agglomerative clustering methods are available with the `cluster` command.

Single linkage clustering computes the (dis)similarity between two groups as the (dis)similarity between the closest pair of observations between the two groups. Complete linkage clustering, on the other hand, uses the farthest pair of observations between the two groups to determine the (dis)similarity of the two groups. Average linkage clustering uses the average (dis)similarity of observations between the groups as the measure between the two groups.

The `cluster singlelinkage` command implements single linkage hierarchical agglomerative clustering; see [R] **cluster singlelinkage** for details. Single linkage clustering suffers (or benefits, depending on your point of view) from what is called chaining. Since the closest points between two groups determine the next merger, long, thin clusters can result. If this chaining feature is not what you desire, then consider using either complete linkage or average linkage. Single linkage clustering is faster and uses less memory than complete or average linkage due to special properties of the method that can be exploited computationally.

Complete linkage hierarchical agglomerative clustering is implemented by the `cluster completelinkage` command; see [R] **cluster completelinkage** for details. Complete linkage clustering is at the other extreme from single linkage clustering. Complete linkage produces spatially compact clusters. Complete linkage clustering is not the best method for recovering elongated cluster structures. Several sources, including Kaufman and Rousseeuw (1990), discuss the chaining of single linkage and the clumping of complete linkage.

Average linkage hierarchical agglomerative cluster analysis has properties that are intermediate of single and complete linkage clustering. The `cluster averagelinkage` command provides average linkage clustering; see [R] **cluster averagelinkage**.

There are numerous other hierarchical agglomerative clustering methods outlined in the cluster analysis literature. Single, complete, and average linkage were selected for implementation in Stata because they span a wide range of attributes, from the chaining of single linkage to the compactness of complete linkage, and because these three methods are among the best known.

Unlike the hierarchical agglomerative clustering methods, in divisive hierarchical clustering you begin with all observations belonging to one group. This group is then split in some fashion to create two groups. One of these two groups is then split to create three groups. One of these three groups is split to create four groups, and so on, until all observations are in their own separate group. Stata does not currently have any divisive hierarchical clustering commands. There are relatively few mentioned in the literature, and they tend to be particularly time consuming to compute.

To appreciate the underlying computational complexity of both agglomerative and divisive hierarchical clustering, consider the following information paraphrased from Kaufman and Rousseeuw (1990). The first step of an agglomerative algorithm considers $N(N-1)/2$ possible fusions of observations to find the closest pair. This number grows quadratically with N. For divisive hierarchical clustering, the first step would attempt to find the best split into two nonempty subsets, and if all possibilities were considered, it would amount to $2^{(N-1)} - 1$ comparisons. This number grows exponentially in N.

Data transformations and variable selection

Stata's `cluster` command does not have any built-in data transformations, but, since Stata has full data management and statistical capabilities, you can use other Stata commands to transform your data before calling the `cluster` command. In some cases, standardization of the variables is important to keep a variable with high variance from dominating the cluster analysis. In other cases, standardization of variables acts to hide the true groupings present in the data. The decision to standardize or perform other data transformations depends heavily on the type of data you are analyzing and on the nature of the groups you are trying to discover.

A related topic is the selection of variables to use in the cluster analysis. Data transformations (such as standardization of variables) and the variables selected for use in clustering can have a large impact on the groupings that are discovered. These, and other, cluster analysis data issues are covered in many of the cluster analysis books, including Anderberg (1973), Gordon (1999), Everitt (1993), and Späth (1980).

Similarity and dissimilarity measures

A variety of similarity and dissimilarity measures have been implemented for Stata's clustering commands. Some of these measures were designed for continuous variables, while others were designed for binary variables. In the formulas below, x_{ab} is the value of variable a and observation b. All summations and maximums are over the p variables involved in the cluster analysis for the two observations in the (dis)similarity comparison. Do not confuse this with most other contexts, where the summations and maximums are over the observations. For clustering, we compare two observations across their variables.

Similarity and dissimilarity measures for continuous data

The similarity and dissimilarity measures for continuous data available in Stata include the following:

L2 (alias <u>Euclidean</u>)
requests the Minkowski distance metric with argument 2

$$\sqrt{\sum_{k=1}^{p}(x_{ki} - x_{kj})^2}$$

which is best known as Euclidean distance. This is the default dissimilarity measure for the `cluster` command.

L1 (aliases <u>abs</u>olute, cityblock, and <u>manhattan</u>)
  requests the Minkowski distance metric with argument 1

$$\sum_{k=1}^{p} |x_{ki} - x_{kj}|$$

  which is best known as absolute value distance.

<u>Linf</u>inity (alias <u>maximum</u>)
  requests the Minkowski distance metric with infinite argument

$$\max_{k=1,...,p} |x_{ki} - x_{kj}|$$

  and is best known as maximum value distance.

L(#)
  requests the Minkowski distance metric with argument #:

$$\left(\sum_{k=1}^{p} |x_{ki} - x_{kj}|^{\#}\right)^{1/\#} \qquad \# \geq 1$$

  We discourage the use of extremely large values for #. Since the absolute value of the difference is being raised to the value of #, depending on the nature of your data, you could experience numeric overflow or underflow. With a large value of #, the L() option will produce similar cluster results to the Linf option. Use the numerically more stable Linf option instead of a large value for # in the L() option.

  See Anderberg (1973) for a discussion of the Minkowski metric and its special cases.

Canberra
  requests the following distance metric

$$\sum_{k=1}^{p} \frac{|x_{ki} - x_{kj}|}{|x_{ki}| + |x_{kj}|}$$

  which ranges from 0 to p, the number of variables used in the cluster analysis; see Gordon (1999) and Gower (1985). Gordon (1999) explains that the Canberra distance is very sensitive to small changes near zero.

(Continued on next page)

`correlation`
   requests the correlation coefficient similarity measure

$$\frac{\sum_{k=1}^{p}(x_{ki} - \overline{x}_{.i})(x_{kj} - \overline{x}_{.j})}{\sqrt{\sum_{k=1}^{p}(x_{ki} - \overline{x}_{.i})^2 \sum_{l=1}^{p}(x_{lj} - \overline{x}_{.j})^2}}$$

where $\overline{x}_{.j}$ is the mean for observation j over the p variables in the cluster analysis.

The correlation similarity measure takes values between -1 and 1. With this measure, the relative direction of the two observation vectors is important. The correlation similarity measure is related to the angular separation similarity measure (described next). The correlation similarity measure gives the cosine of the angle between the two observation vectors measured from the mean; see Gordon (1999).

`angular` (alias `angle`)
   requests the angular separation similarity measure

$$\frac{\sum_{k=1}^{p} x_{ki} x_{kj}}{\sqrt{\sum_{k=1}^{p} x_{ki}^2 \sum_{l=1}^{p} x_{lj}^2}}$$

which is the cosine of the angle between the two observation vectors measured from zero and takes values from -1 to 1; see Gordon (1999).

Similarity measures for binary data

Similarity measures for binary data are based on the four values from the cross tabulation of the two observations.

		obs. j	
		1	0
obs. i	1	a	b
	0	c	d

a is the number of variables where observations i and j both had ones, and d is the number of variables where observations i and j both had zeros. The number of variables where observation i is one and observation j is zero is b, and the number of variables where observation i is zero and observation j is one is c.

The `cluster` command follows Stata's general practice of treating nonzero values as a one when a binary variable is expected. Specifying one of the binary similarity measures imposes this behavior.

Gower (1985) gives an extensive list of fifteen binary similarity measures. Fourteen of these are implemented in Stata. (The excluded measure has many cases where the quantity is undefined and so was not implemented.) Anderberg (1973) gives an interesting table where many of these measures are compared based on whether the zero–zero matches are included in the numerator, whether these matches are included in the denominator, and how the weighting of matches and mismatches is handled.

The formulas for some of these binary similarity measures are undefined when either one or both of the observations are all zeros (or, in some cases, all ones). Gower (1985) says concerning these cases, "These coefficients are then conventionally assigned some appropriate value, usually zero."

The following binary similarity coefficients are available in the `cluster` command. Unless stated otherwise, the similarity measures range from 0 to 1.

matching
  requests the simple matching binary similarity coefficient

$$\frac{a+d}{a+b+c+d}$$

  which is the proportion of matches between the two observations.

Jaccard
  requests the Jaccard binary similarity coefficient

$$\frac{a}{a+b+c}$$

  which is the proportion of matches when at least one of the observations had a one. In the case where both observations are all zeros, this measure is undefined. In this case, Stata declares the answer to be one, meaning perfect agreement. This is a reasonable choice for cluster analysis and will cause an all zero observation to have similarity of one only with another all zero observation. In all other cases, an all zero observation will have Jaccard similarity of zero to the other observation.

Russell
  requests the Russell & Rao binary similarity coefficient

$$\frac{a}{a+b+c+d}$$

Hamman
  requests the Hamman binary similarity coefficient

$$\frac{(a+d)-(b+c)}{a+b+c+d}$$

  which is the number of agreements minus disagreements divided by the total. The Hamman coefficient ranges from -1, perfect disagreement, to 1, perfect agreement. The Hamman coefficient is equal to twice the simple matching coefficient minus 1.

Dice
  requests the Dice binary similarity coefficient

$$\frac{2a}{2a+b+c}$$

  suggested by Sorenson, Dice, and Czekanowski. The Dice coefficient is similar to the Jaccard similarity coefficient, but gives twice the weight to agreements. Like the Jaccard coefficient, the Dice coefficient is declared by Stata to be one if both observations are all zero, thus avoiding the case where the formula is undefined.

antiDice
   requests the following binary similarity coefficient

$$\frac{a}{a + 2(b + c)}$$

   which is credited to Anderberg (1973). Stata did not call this the Anderberg coefficient, since there
   is another coefficient better known by that name; see the Anderberg option. The name antiDice
   is our creation. This coefficient takes the opposite view from the Dice coefficient and gives double
   weight to disagreements. As with the Jaccard and Dice coefficients, the antiDice coefficient is
   declared to be one if both observations are all zeros.

Sneath
   requests the Sneath & Sokal binary similarity coefficient

$$\frac{2(a + d)}{2(a + d) + (b + c)}$$

   which is similar to the simple matching coefficient, but gives double weight to matches. Also
   compare the Sneath & Sokal coefficient to the Dice coefficient, which differs only in whether it
   includes d.

Rogers
   requests the Rogers & Tanimoto binary similarity coefficient

$$\frac{a + d}{(a + d) + 2(b + c)}$$

   which takes the opposite approach from the Sneath & Sokal coefficient and gives double weight
   to disagreements. Also compare the Rogers & Tanimoto coefficient to the antiDice coefficient,
   which differs only in whether it includes d.

Ochiai
   requests the Ochiai binary similarity coefficient

$$\frac{a}{\sqrt{(a + b)(a + c)}}$$

   The formula for the Ochiai coefficient is undefined when one or both of the observations being
   compared is all zeros. If both are all zeros, Stata declares the measure to be one, and if only one
   of the two observations is all zeros the measure is declared to be zero.

Yule
   requests the Yule binary similarity coefficient

$$\frac{ad - bc}{ad + bc}$$

   which ranges from -1 to 1. The formula for the Yule coefficient is undefined when one or both of
   the observations are either all zeros or all ones. Stata declares the measure to be 1 when $b + c = 0$,
   meaning there is complete agreement. Stata declares the measure to be -1 when $a + d = 0$,
   meaning there is complete disagreement. Otherwise, if $ad - bc = 0$, Stata declares the measure
   to be 0. These rules, applied before using the Yule formula, avoid the cases where the formula
   would produce an undefined result.

Anderberg

requests the Anderberg binary similarity coefficient

$$\left(\frac{a}{a+b} + \frac{a}{a+c} + \frac{d}{c+d} + \frac{d}{b+d} \right) \bigg/ 4$$

The Anderberg coefficient is undefined when one or both observations are either all zeros or all ones. This difficulty is overcome by first applying the rule that if both observations are all ones (or both observations are all zeros), then the similarity measure is declared to be one. Otherwise, if any of the marginal totals ($a + b$, $a + c$, $c + d$, $b + d$) are zero, then the similarity measure is declared to be zero.

Kulczynski

requests the Kulczynski binary similarity coefficient

$$\left(\frac{a}{a+b} + \frac{a}{a+c} \right) \bigg/ 2$$

The formula for this measure is undefined when one or both of the observations are all zeros. If both observations are all zeros, Stata declares the similarity measure to be one. If only one of the observations is all zeros, the similarity measure is declared to be zero.

Gower2

requests the following binary similarity coefficient

$$\frac{ad}{\sqrt{(a+b)(a+c)(d+b)(d+c)}}$$

which, presumably, was first presented by Gower (1985). Stata uses the name `Gower2` to avoid confusion with the better known Gower coefficient (not currently in Stata), which is used to combine continuous and categorical (dis)similarity measures computed on a dataset into one measure.

The formula for this similarity measure is undefined when one or both of the observations are all zeros or all ones. This is overcome by first applying the rule that if both observations are all ones (or both observations are all zeros), then the similarity measure is declared to be one. Otherwise, if $ad = 0$, then the similarity measure is declared to be zero.

Pearson

requests Pearson's ϕ binary similarity coefficient

$$\frac{ad - bc}{\sqrt{(a+b)(a+c)(d+b)(d+c)}}$$

which ranges from -1 to 1. The formula for this coefficient is undefined when one or both of the observations are either all zeros or all ones. Stata declares the measure to be 1 when $b + c = 0$, meaning there is complete agreement. Stata declares the measure to be -1 when $a + d = 0$, meaning there is complete disagreement. Otherwise, if $ad - bc = 0$, Stata declares the measure to be 0. These rules, applied before using Pearson's ϕ coefficient formula, avoid the cases where the formula would produce an undefined result.

Binary similarity measures applied to averages

With single, average, and complete linkage hierarchical clustering, (dis)similarities are always computed between observations. With kmeans clustering, (dis)similarities are computed between observations and group averages. With binary data, a group average is interpreted as a proportion. With kmedians clustering, when there are an equal number of zeros and ones within a group for a particular variable, Stata calls the median 0.5, which can also be interpreted as a proportion and indicates that half the observations in that group for that variable were zero while the other half were one.

Stata's `cluster kmeans` and `cluster kmedians` commands allow the use of the binary similarity measures; see [R] **cluster kmeans** and [R] **cluster kmedians**. The values of a, b, c, and d, in the case of comparing a binary observation to a group proportion, are obtained by assigning the appropriate fraction of the count to these values. In our earlier table showing the relationship of a, b, c, and d in the cross-tabulation of observation i and observation j, if we replace observation j by the group proportions vector, then when observation i is 1 we add the corresponding proportion to a, and add one minus that proportion to b. When observation i is 0, we add the corresponding proportion to c, and add one minus that proportion to d. After the values of a, b, c, and d are computed in this way, the binary similarity measures are computed using the formulas as already described.

Post clustering commands

Stata's `cluster dendrogram` command presents the dendrogram (cluster tree) after a hierarchical cluster analysis; see [R] **cluster dendrogram**. Options allow you to view the top portion of the tree or the portion of the tree associated with a group. These options are important with larger datasets, since the full dendrogram cannot be presented.

The `cluster generate` command produces grouping variables after hierarchical clustering; see [R] **cluster generate**. These variables can then be used in other Stata commands, such as those that tabulate, summarize, and provide graphs. For instance, you might use `cluster generate` to create a grouping variable. You then might use the `factor` and `score` commands (see [R] **factor**) to obtain the first two principal components of the data, and follow that with a `graph` command (see [G] **graph**) to plot the principal components, using the grouping variable from the `cluster generate` command to control the point labeling of the graph. This would allow you to get one type of view into the clustering behavior of your data.

Cluster management tools

You may add notes to your cluster analysis with the `cluster notes` command; see [R] **cluster notes**. This command also allows you to view and delete notes attached to the cluster analysis.

The `cluster dir` and `cluster list` commands allow you to list the cluster objects and attributes currently defined for your dataset. `cluster drop` lets you remove a cluster object. See [R] **cluster utility** for details.

Cluster objects are referenced by name. Many of the `cluster` commands will, by default, use the cluster object from the most recently performed cluster analysis if no name is provided. The `cluster use` command tells Stata to set a particular cluster object as the latest. The name attached to a cluster object may be changed with the `cluster rename` command, and the variables associated with a cluster analysis may be renamed with the `cluster renamevar` command. See [R] **cluster utility** for details.

Programmers, and regular users if they desire, can exercise fine control over the attributes that are stored with a cluster object; see [P] **cluster utilities**.

References

Anderberg, M. R. 1973. *Cluster Analysis for Applications*. New York: Academic Press.

Day, W. H. E. and H. Edelsbrunner. 1984. Efficient algorithms for agglomerative hierarchical clustering methods. *Journal of Classification* 1: 7–24.

Everitt, B. S. 1993. *Cluster Analysis*. 3d ed. London: Edward Arnold.

Gordon, A. D. 1999. *Classification*. 2d ed. Boca Raton, FL: CRC Press.

Gower, J. C. 1985. Measures of similarity, dissimilarity, and distance. In *Encyclopedia of Statistical Sciences*, Vol. 5, ed. S. Kotz, N. L. Johnson, and C. B. Read, 397–405. New York: John Wiley & Sons.

Kaufman, L. and P. J. Rousseeuw. 1990. *Finding Groups in Data*. New York: John Wiley & Sons.

Rohlf, F. J. 1982. Single-link clustering algorithms. In *Handbook of Statistics*, Vol. 2, ed. P. R. Krishnaiah and L. N. Kanal, 267–284. Amsterdam: North–Holland Publishing Company.

Sibson, R. 1973. SLINK: An optimally efficient algorithm for the single-link cluster method. *Computer Journal* 16: 30–34.

Späth, H. 1980. *Cluster Analysis Algorithms for Data Reduction and Classification of Objects*. Chichester, England: Ellis Horwood.

Also See

Complementary:	[R] **cluster averagelinkage**, [R] **cluster completelinkage**, [R] **cluster dendrogram**, [R] **cluster generate**, [R] **cluster kmeans**, [R] **cluster kmedians**, [R] **cluster notes**, [R] **cluster singlelinkage**, [R] **cluster utility**
Related:	[P] **cluster subroutines**, [P] **cluster utilities**

Title

cluster averagelinkage — Average linkage cluster analysis

Syntax

> cluster averagelinkage [*varlist*] [if *exp*] [in *range*] [, name(*clname*)
>
> *distance_option* generate(*stub*)]

Description

The cluster averagelinkage command performs hierarchical agglomerative average linkage cluster analysis. See [R] **cluster** for a general discussion of cluster analysis and a description of the other cluster commands. The cluster dendrogram command (see [R] **cluster dendrogram**) will display the resulting dendrogram, and the cluster generate command (see [R] **cluster generate**) will produce grouping variables.

Options

name(*clname*) specifies the name to attach to the resulting cluster analysis. If name() is not specified, Stata finds an available cluster name, displays it for your reference, and then attaches the name to your cluster analysis.

distance_option is one of the similarity or dissimilarity measures allowed within Stata. Capitalization of the option does not matter. See [R] **cluster** for a discussion of these measures.

The available measures designed for continuous data are: L2 (synonym Euclidean) which is the default; L1 (synonyms absolute, cityblock, and manhattan); Linfinity (synonym maximum); L(#); Canberra; correlation; and angular (synonym angle).

The available measures designed for binary data are: matching, Jaccard, Russell, Hamman, Dice, antiDice, Sneath, Rogers, Ochiai, Yule, Anderberg, Kulczynski, Gower2, and Pearson.

generate(*stub*) provides a prefix for the variable names created by cluster averagelinkage. By default, the variable name prefix will be the name specified in name(). Three variables are created and attached to the cluster analysis results, with the suffixes _id, _ord, and _hgt. Users generally will not need to access these variables directly.

Remarks

An example using the default L2 (Euclidean) distance on continuous data and an example using the matching coefficient on binary data illustrate the cluster averagelinkage command. These are the same datasets used as examples in [R] **cluster singlelinkage** and [R] **cluster completelinkage** so that you can compare the results from using different hierarchical clustering methods.

▷ Example

As explained in the first example of [R] **cluster singlelinkage**, as the senior data analyst for a small biotechnology firm, you are given a dataset with four chemical laboratory measurements on 50 different samples of a particular plant gathered from the rain forest. The head of the expedition that gathered the samples thinks, based on information from the natives, that an extract from the plant might reduce negative side effects from your company's best-selling nutritional supplement.

While the company chemists and botanists continue exploring the possible uses of the plant and plan future experiments, the head of product development asks you to take a look at the preliminary data and report anything that might be helpful to the researchers.

While all 50 of the plants are supposed to be of the same type, you decide to perform a cluster analysis to see if there are subgroups or anomalies among them. Single linkage clustering helped you discover an anomaly in the data. You now wish to see if you discover the same thing using average linkage clustering with the default Euclidean distance.

You first call `cluster averagelinkage` and use the `name()` option to attach the name `L2alnk` to the resulting cluster analysis. The `cluster list` command (see [R] **cluster utility**) is then applied to list the components of your cluster analysis. The `cluster dendrogram` command then graphs the dendrogram; see [R] **cluster dendrogram**. As described in the [R] **cluster singlelinkage** example, the `labels()` option is used instead of the default action of showing the observation number to identify which laboratory technician produced the data.

```
. cluster averagelinkage x1 x2 x3 x4, name(L2alnk)
. cluster list L2alnk
L2alnk  (type: hierarchical,  method: average,  dissimilarity: L2)
      vars: L2alnk_id (id variable)
            L2alnk_ord (order variable)
            L2alnk_hgt (height variable)
      other: range: 0 .
            cmd: cluster averagelinkage x1 x2 x3 x4, name(L2alnk)
. cluster dendrogram L2alnk, vertlab ylab labels(labtech)
```

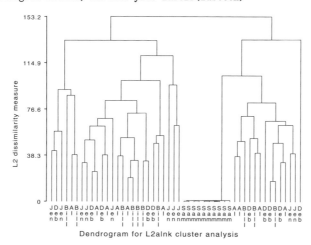

Dendrogram for L2alnk cluster analysis

As with single linkage clustering, you see that the samples analyzed by Sam, the lab technician, cluster together closely (dissimilarity measures near zero) and are separated from the rest of the data by a large dissimilarity gap (the long vertical line going up from Sam's cluster to eventually combine with other observations). When you examined the data, you discovered that Sam's data are all between zero and one, while the other four technicians have data that range from zero up to near 150. It appears that Sam has made a mistake.

If you compare the dendrogram from this average linkage clustering to those from single linkage clustering and complete linkage clustering, you will notice that the y axis range is intermediate of these two other methods. This is a property of these linkage methods. With average linkage, it is the average of the (dis)similarities between the two groups that determines the distance between the groups. This is in contrast to the smallest distance and largest distance that define single linkage and complete linkage clustering.

◁

▷ Example

This example analyzes the same data as introduced in the second example of [R] **cluster singlelinkage**. The sociology professor of your graduate level class gives, as homework, a dataset containing 30 observations on 60 binary variables, with the assignment to tell him something about the 30 subjects represented by the observations.

In addition to examining single linkage clustering of these data, you decide to see what average linkage clustering shows. As with the single linkage clustering, you pick the simple matching binary coefficient to measure the similarity between groups. The `name()` option is used to attach the name `alink` to the cluster analysis. `cluster list` displays the details; see [R] **cluster utility**. `cluster tree`, which is a synonym for `cluster dendrogram`, then displays the cluster tree (dendrogram); see [R] **cluster dendrogram**.

```
. cluster a a1-a60, match name(alink)
. cluster list alink
alink  (type: hierarchical,  method: average,  similarity: matching)
       vars: alink_id (id variable)
             alink_ord (order variable)
             alink_hgt (height variable)
      other: range: 1 0
             cmd: cluster averagelinkage a1-a60, match name(alink)
. cluster tree
```

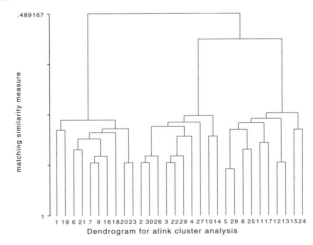

Dendrogram for alink cluster analysis

Since, by default, Stata uses the most recently performed cluster analysis, you do not need to type in the cluster name when calling `cluster tree`.

As with single linkage clustering, the dendrogram from average linkage clustering seems to indicate the presence of three groups among the 30 observations. Later you receive another variable called `truegrp` that identifies the groups the teacher believes are in the data. You use the `cluster generate` command (see [R] **cluster generate**) to create a grouping variable, based on your average linkage clustering, to compare with `truegrp`. You do a cross tabulation of `truegrp` and `agrp3`, your grouping variable, to see if your conclusions match those of the teacher.

```
. cluster gen agrp3 = group(3)
. table agrp3 truegrp
```

	truegrp		
agrp3	1	2	3
1		10	
2	10		
3			10

Other than the numbers arbitrarily assigned to the three groups, your teacher's conclusions and the results from the average linkage clustering are in agreement.

◁

❏ Technical Note

`cluster averagelinkage` requires more memory and execution time than `cluster singlelinkage`. With a large number of observations the execution time may be significant.

❏

Methods and Formulas

[R] **cluster** discusses hierarchical clustering and places average linkage clustering in this general framework. It compares the typical behavior of average linkage with single and complete linkage.

Conceptually, hierarchical agglomerative average linkage clustering proceeds as follows. The N observations start out as N separate groups, each of size one. The two closest observations are merged into one group, producing $N - 1$ total groups. The closest two groups are then merged, so that there are $N - 2$ total groups. This process continues until all the observations are merged into one large group. This produces a hierarchy of groupings from one group to N. For average linkage clustering, the decision of closest groups for merging is based on the average (dis)similarity between the observations of the two groups.

The average linkage clustering algorithm produces two variables that act as a pointer representation of a dendrogram. To this Stata adds a third variable used to restore the sort order, as needed, so that the two variables of the pointer representation remain valid. The first variable of the pointer representation gives the order of the observations. The second variable has one less element, and gives the height in the dendrogram at which the adjacent observations in the order variable join.

See [R] **cluster** for the details and formulas of the available *distance_options*, which include (dis)similarity measures for continuous and binary data.

Also See

Complementary:	[R] **cluster dendrogram**, [R] **cluster generate**, [R] **cluster notes**, [R] **cluster utility**
Related:	[R] **cluster completelinkage**, [R] **cluster singlelinkage**
Background:	[R] **cluster**

Title

> **cluster completelinkage** — Complete linkage cluster analysis

Syntax

> cluster completelinkage [*varlist*] [if *exp*] [in *range*] [, name(*clname*)
>
> *distance_option* generate(*stub*)]

Description

The cluster completelinkage command performs hierarchical agglomerative complete linkage cluster analysis, which is also known as the farthest neighbor technique. See [R] **cluster** for a general discussion of cluster analysis and a description of the other cluster commands. The cluster dendrogram command (see [R] **cluster dendrogram**) will display the resulting dendrogram, and the cluster generate command (see [R] **cluster generate**) will produce grouping variables.

Options

name(*clname*) specifies the name to attach to the resulting cluster analysis. If name() is not specified, Stata finds an available cluster name, displays it for your reference, and then attaches the name to your cluster analysis.

distance_option is one of the similarity or dissimilarity measures allowed within Stata. Capitalization of the option does not matter. See [R] **cluster** for a discussion of these measures.

The available measures designed for continuous data are: L2 (synonym Euclidean), which is the default; L1 (synonyms absolute, cityblock, and manhattan); Linfinity (synonym maximum); L(#); Canberra; correlation; and angular (synonym angle).

The available measures designed for binary data are: matching, Jaccard, Russell, Hamman, Dice, antiDice, Sneath, Rogers, Ochiai, Yule, Anderberg, Kulczynski, Gower2, and Pearson.

generate(*stub*) provides a prefix for the variable names created by cluster completelinkage. By default, the variable name prefix will be the name specified in name(). Three variables are created and attached to the cluster analysis results, with the suffixes _id, _ord, and _hgt. Users generally will not need to access these variables directly.

Remarks

An example using the default L2 (Euclidean) distance on continuous data and an example using the matching coefficient on binary data illustrate the cluster completelinkage command. These are the same datasets used as examples in [R] **cluster singlelinkage** and [R] **cluster averagelinkage** so that you can compare the results from using different hierarchical clustering methods.

▷ Example

As explained in the first example of [R] **cluster singlelinkage**, as the senior data analyst for a small biotechnology firm, you are given a dataset with four chemical laboratory measurements on 50 different samples of a particular plant gathered from the rain forest. The head of the expedition that gathered the samples thinks, based on information from the natives, that an extract from the plant might reduce negative side effects from your company's best-selling nutritional supplement.

While the company chemists and botanists continue exploring the possible uses of the plant and plan future experiments, the head of product development asks you to take a look at the preliminary data and report anything that might be helpful to the researchers.

While all 50 of the plants are supposed to be of the same type, you decide to perform a cluster analysis to see if there are subgroups or anomalies among them. Single linkage clustering helped you discover an anomaly in the data. You now wish to see if you discover the same thing using complete linkage clustering with the default Euclidean distance.

You first call `cluster completelinkage` and use the `name()` option to attach the name `L2clnk` to the resulting cluster analysis. The `cluster list` command (see [R] **cluster utility**) is then applied to list the components of your cluster analysis. The `cluster dendrogram` command then graphs the dendrogram; see [R] **cluster dendrogram**. As described in the [R] **cluster singlelinkage** example, the `labels()` option is used instead of the default action of showing the observation number to identify which laboratory technician produced the data.

```
. cluster completelinkage x1 x2 x3 x4, name(L2clnk)

. cluster list L2clnk
L2clnk  (type: hierarchical,  method: complete,  dissimilarity: L2)
      vars: L2clnk_id (id variable)
            L2clnk_ord (order variable)
            L2clnk_hgt (height variable)
     other: range: 0 .
            cmd: cluster completelinkage x1 x2 x3 x4, name(L2clnk)

. cluster dendrogram L2clnk, vertlab ylab labels(labtech)
```

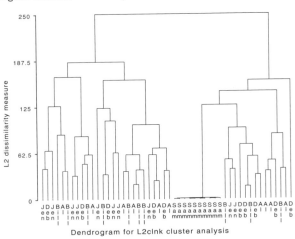

Dendrogram for L2clnk cluster analysis

As with single linkage clustering, you see that the samples analyzed by Sam, the lab technician, cluster together closely (dissimilarity measures near zero) and are separated from the rest of the data by a large dissimilarity gap (the long vertical line going up from Sam's cluster to eventually combine with other observations). When you examined the data, you discovered that Sam's data are all between zero and one, while the other four technicians have data that range from zero up to near 150. It appears that Sam has made a mistake.

If you compare the dendrogram from this complete linkage clustering to those from single linkage clustering and average linkage clustering, you will notice that the vertical lines at the top of the tree are relatively longer and the y axis range is larger. This is a property of these linkage methods. The distance between groups is larger for complete linkage, since, by definition, with complete linkage the distance between two groups is the distance between their farthest members.

◁

▷ Example

This example analyzes the same data as introduced in the second example of [R] **cluster singlelinkage**. The sociology professor of your graduate level class gives, as homework, a dataset containing 30 observations on 60 binary variables, with the assignment to tell him something about the 30 subjects represented by the observations.

In addition to examining single linkage clustering of these data, you decide to see what complete linkage clustering shows. As with the single linkage clustering, you pick the simple matching binary coefficient to measure the similarity between groups. The `name()` option is used to attach the name `clink` to the cluster analysis. `cluster list` displays the details; see [R] **cluster utility**. `cluster tree`, which is a synonym for `cluster dendrogram`, then displays the cluster tree (dendrogram); see [R] **cluster dendrogram**.

```
. cluster c a1-a60, match name(clink)
. cluster list clink
clink  (type: hierarchical,  method: complete,  similarity: matching)
      vars: clink_id (id variable)
            clink_ord (order variable)
            clink_hgt (height variable)
     other: range: 1 0
            cmd: cluster completelinkage a1-a60, match name(clink)
. cluster tree
```

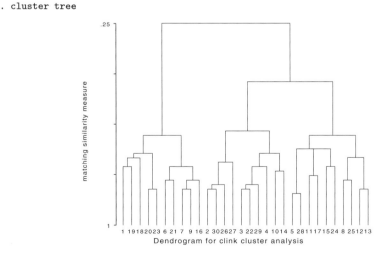

Dendrogram for clink cluster analysis

Since, by default, Stata uses the most recently performed cluster analysis, you do not need to type in the cluster name when calling `cluster tree`.

As with single linkage clustering, the dendrogram from complete linkage clustering seems to indicate the presence of three groups among the 30 observations. Later you receive another variable called `truegrp` that identifies the groups the teacher believes are in the data. You use the `cluster generate` command (see [R] **cluster generate**) to create a grouping variable, based on your complete linkage clustering, to compare with `truegrp`. You do a cross tabulation of `truegrp` and `cgrp3`, your grouping variable, to see if your conclusions match those of the teacher.

```
. cluster gen cgrp3 = group(3)
. table cgrp3 truegrp
```

cgrp3	truegrp 1	2	3
1		10	
2	10		
3			10

Other than the numbers arbitrarily assigned to the three groups, your teacher's conclusions and the results from the complete linkage clustering are in agreement.

◁

❑ Technical Note

`cluster completelinkage` requires more memory and execution time than `cluster singlelinkage`. With a large number of observations the execution time may be significant.

❑

Methods and Formulas

[R] **cluster** discusses hierarchical clustering and places complete linkage clustering in this general framework. It compares the typical behavior of complete linkage with single and average linkage.

Conceptually, hierarchical agglomerative complete linkage clustering proceeds as follows. The N observations start out as N separate groups each of size one. The two closest observations are merged into one group, producing $N - 1$ total groups. The closest two groups are then merged, so that there are $N - 2$ total groups. This process continues until all the observations are merged into one large group. This produces a hierarchy of groupings from one group to N. For complete linkage clustering, the decision of closest groups for merging is based on the farthest observations between the two groups.

The complete linkage clustering algorithm produces two variables that act as a pointer representation of a dendrogram. To this Stata adds a third variable used to restore the sort order, as needed, so that the two variables of the pointer representation remain valid. The first variable of the pointer representation gives the order of the observations. The second variable has one less element, and gives the height in the dendrogram at which the adjacent observations in the order variable join.

See [R] **cluster** for the details and formulas of the available *distance_options*, which include (dis)similarity measures for continuous and binary data.

Also See

Complementary:	[R] **cluster dendrogram**, [R] **cluster generate**, [R] **cluster notes**, [R] **cluster utility**
Related:	[R] **cluster averagelinkage**, [R] **cluster singlelinkage**
Background:	[R] **cluster**

Title

cluster dendrogram — Dendrograms for hierarchical cluster analysis

Syntax

cluster <u>dend</u>rogram [*clname*] [if *exp*] [in *range*] [, quick <u>labels</u>(*varname*)

<u>vertl</u>abels <u>cutn</u>umber(*#*) <u>cutv</u>alue(*#*) <u>labc</u>utn <u>sav</u>ing(*filename*[, replace])

title_options   axes_options]

Note: cluster <u>tree</u> is a synonym for cluster dendrogram.

In addition to the restrictions imposed by if and in, the observations are automatically restricted to those that were used in the formation of the cluster analysis.

Description

cluster dendrogram produces dendrograms (also called cluster trees) from a hierarchical clustering. See [R] **cluster** for discussion of cluster analysis, hierarchical clustering, and the available cluster commands.

Dendrograms graphically present the information concerning which observations are grouped together at various levels of (dis)similarity. At the bottom of the dendrogram, each observation is considered its own cluster. Vertical lines extend up for each observation, and at various (dis)similarity values these lines are connected to the lines from other observations with a horizontal line. The observations continue to combine until, at the top of the dendrogram, all observations are grouped together.

The height of the vertical lines and the range of the (dis)similarity axis give visual clues about the strength of the clustering. Long vertical lines indicate more distinct separation between the groups. Long vertical lines at the top of the dendrogram indicate that the groups represented by those lines are well separated from one another. Shorter lines indicate groups that are not as distinct.

Options

quick switches to a different style of dendrogram where the vertical lines only go straight up from the observations, instead of the default action of recentering the lines after each merge of observations in the dendrogram hierarchy. Some people prefer this representation, and it is quicker to render.

labels(*varname*) indicates that *varname* is to be used in place of observation numbers for labeling the observations at the bottom of the dendrogram.

vertlabels indicates that the labeling for the observations at the bottom of the dendrogram is to be presented vertically instead of horizontally. This is helpful when the labels have several characters and there are enough observations in the dendrogram to cause the labels to overlap.

cutnumber(*#*) displays only the top *#* branches of the dendrogram. With large dendrograms, the lower levels of the tree become too crowded. With cutnumber(), you can limit your view to the upper portion of the dendrogram. Also see the cutvalue() and labcutn options.

cutvalue(#) displays only the top portion of the dendrogram. Only those branches of the dendrogram that are above the # (dis)similarity measure are presented. With large dendrograms, the lower levels of the tree become too crowded. With cutvalue(), you can limit your view to the upper portion of the dendrogram. Also see the cutnumber() and labcutn options.

labcutn requests that the number of observations associated with each branch be displayed below the branches. labcutn is allowed only with cutnumber() or cutvalue() since, otherwise, the number of observations for each branch is one.

saving(*filename*[, replace]) saves the graph in a file that can be reviewed by graph using (see [G] **graph**) and printed by pulling down the **File** menu and choosing **Print Graph**. If you do not specify an extension, .gph will be assumed.

Allowed *title_options* are
    title("*text*"),
    t1title("*text*"), t2title("*text*"),   b1title("*text*"), b2title("*text*"),
    l1title("*text*"), l2title("*text*"),   r1title("*text*"), and r2title("*text*").
    See [G] **graph options** for details.

Allowed *axes_options* are
    noaxis, gap(#),
    ylabel[(*numlist*)], rlabel[(*numlist*)],   ytick(*numlist*), and rtick(*numlist*).
    See [G] **graph options** for details.

Remarks

Examples of the cluster dendrogram command can be found in [R] **cluster singlelinkage**, [R] **cluster completelinkage**, [R] **cluster averagelinkage**, and [R] **cluster generate**. Here we illustrate some of the additional options available with cluster dendrogram.

▷ Example

In the first example of [R] **cluster completelinkage**, the dendrogram for the complete linkage clustering of 50 observations on four variables was illustrated with the following dendrogram:

    . cluster dendrogram L2clnk, vertlab ylab labels(labtech)

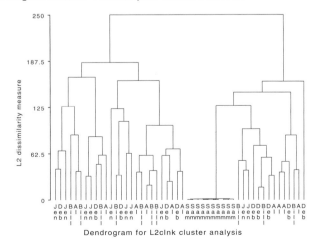

Dendrogram for L2clnk cluster analysis

This same dendrogram can be rendered in a slightly different format with the `quick` option:

```
. cluster dendrogram L2clnk, vertlab ylab labels(labtech) quick
```

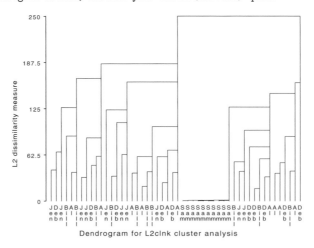

Dendrogram for L2clnk cluster analysis

Some people prefer this style of dendrogram. The option name `quick` comes from the fact that this style of dendrogram is quicker to render.

To display the dendrogram for one subgroup, use the `if` and `in` conditions to restrict to the subgroup observations. This is usually accomplished with the `cluster generate` command, which creates a grouping variable; see [R] **cluster generate**.

Here we show the third of three groups in the dendrogram by first generating the grouping variable for three groups and then using `if` in the command for `cluster dendrogram` to restrict to the third of those three groups.

```
. cluster gen g3 = group(3)
. cluster tree if g3==3, ylab
```

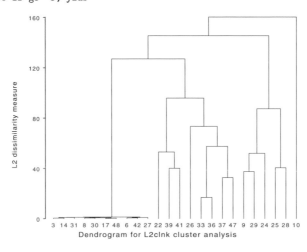

Dendrogram for L2clnk cluster analysis

Since we find it easier to type, we used the synonym `tree` instead of `dendrogram`. We did not specify the cluster name, instead allowing it to default to the latest performed cluster analysis. We also omitted the `vertlabels` and `labels()` options, which bring us back to the default action of showing, horizontally, the observation numbers.

This example has only 50 observations. When there are a large number of observations, the dendrogram becomes too busy. You will need to limit which part of the dendrogram you display. One way to view a subpart of the dendrogram is to use `if` and `in` to limit to one particular group, as we did above.

The other way you can limit your view of the dendrogram is to specify that you only wish to view the top portion of the tree. The `cutnumber()` and `cutvalue()` options allow you to do this:

```
. cluster tree, cutn(15) labcutn rlabel
```

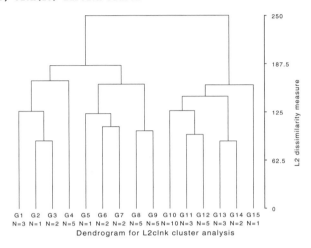

Dendrogram for L2clnk cluster analysis

We limited our view to the top 15 branches of the dendrogram with `cutn(15)`. By default, the 15 branches were labeled `G1` through `G15`. The `labcutn` option provided, below these branch labels, the number of observations in each of the 15 groups. And, just for variety, we specified the `rlabel` option to place the dissimilarity measure axis on the right instead of the left.

The `cutvalue()` option provides another method of limiting the view to the top branches of the dendrogram. With this option, you specify the similarity or dissimilarity value at which to trim the tree.

(Continued on next page)

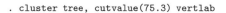

. cluster tree, cutvalue(75.3) vertlab

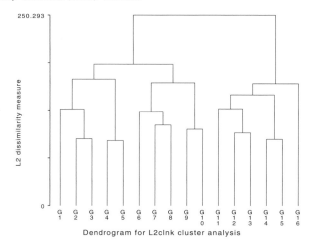

Dendrogram for L2clnk cluster analysis

This time we limited the dendrogram to those branches with dissimilarity greater than 75.3 by using the cutvalue(75.3) option. There were 16 branches (groups) that met that restriction. We also specified the vertlabels option, but did not specify the labcutn option. This listed the 16 group labels vertically and omitted the number of observations in each group.

The various title options allow you to add titles to the four sides of the dendrogram. The allowed axis options give you control over how, if at all, the (dis)similarity axis is to be displayed. You can experiment with these options to find the look you like best.

◁

❏ Technical Note

Programmers can exercise control over what graphical procedure is executed when **cluster dendrogram** is called. This will be helpful to programmers adding new hierarchical clustering methods that require a different dendrogram algorithm. See [P] **cluster subroutines** for details.

❏

Also See

Complementary: [R] **cluster averagelinkage**, [R] **cluster completelinkage**,
[R] **cluster generate**, [R] **cluster singlelinkage**,
[P] **cluster subroutines**

Background: [R] **cluster**,
[G] **graph options**

Title

cluster generate — Generate summary and grouping variables from a cluster analysis

Syntax

cluster generate {*newvarname* | *stub*} = $\underline{\text{gro}}$ups(*numlist*) $\Big[$, $\underline{\text{n}}$ame(*clname*)

     $\underline{\text{t}}$ies($\underline{\text{e}}$rror | $\underline{\text{s}}$kip | $\underline{\text{l}}$ess | $\underline{\text{m}}$ore) $\Big]$

cluster generate *newvarname* = cut(*#*) $\Big[$, $\underline{\text{n}}$ame(*clname*) $\Big]$

Description

The cluster generate command generates summary or grouping variables from a cluster analysis. What is produced depends on the function. See [R] **cluster** for information on available cluster analysis commands.

The groups(*numlist*) function generates grouping variables, giving the grouping for the specified number(s) of clusters from a hierarchical cluster analysis. If a single number is given, *newvarname* is produced with group numbers going from 1 to the number of clusters requested. If more than one number is specified, a new variable is generated for each number using the provided *stub* name appended with the number. For instance,

        cluster gen xyz = groups(5/7), name(myclus)

creates variables xyz5, xyz6, and xyz7, giving the five, six, and seven groups obtained from the cluster analysis named myclus.

The cut(*#*) function generates a grouping variable corresponding to cutting the dendrogram (see [R] **cluster dendrogram**) of a hierarchical cluster analysis at the specified (dis)similarity value.

Additional cluster generate functions may be added; see [P] **cluster subroutines**.

Options

name(*clname*) specifies the name of the cluster analysis to use in producing the new variables. The default is the latest performed cluster analysis, which can be reset using the cluster use command; see [R] **cluster utility**.

ties(error | skip | less | more) indicates what to do in the case of ties with the groups() function. A hierarchical cluster analysis has ties when multiple groups are generated at a particular (dis)similarity value. For example, you might have the case where you can uniquely create two, three, and four groups, but the next possible grouping produces eight groups due to ties.

ties(error), the default, produces an error message and does not generate the requested variables.

ties(skip) indicates that the offending requests are to be ignored. No error message is produced, and only the requests that produce unique groupings will be honored. With multiple values specified in the groups() function, ties(skip) allows the processing of those that produce unique groupings, ignoring the rest.

251

ties(less) produces the results for the largest number of groups less than or equal to your request. In the example above with groups(6) and using ties(less), you would get the same result as you would by using groups(4).

ties(more) produces the results for the smallest number of groups greater than or equal to your request. In the example above with groups(6) and using ties(more), you would get the same result as you would by using groups(8).

Remarks

Examples of the use of the groups() function of cluster generate can be found in [R] **cluster singlelinkage**, [R] **cluster completelinkage**, [R] **cluster averagelinkage**, and [R] **cluster dendrogram**. Additional examples of the groups() and cut() functions of cluster generate are provided here.

Visually, these functions are best understood with a reference to the dendrogram from a hierarchical cluster analysis. The cluster dendrogram command produces dendrograms (cluster trees) from a hierarchical cluster analysis; see [R] **cluster dendrogram**.

▷ Example

The first example of [R] **cluster completelinkage** performs a complete linkage cluster analysis on 50 observations with four variables. The dendrogram presented there was labeled at the bottom by the name of the laboratory technician responsible for the data. Here we reproduce that same dendrogram, but use the default action of placing observation numbers as labels. We then use the groups() function of cluster generate to produce a grouping variable, splitting the data into two groups.

```
. cluster dendrogram L2clnk, vertlab ylab
```

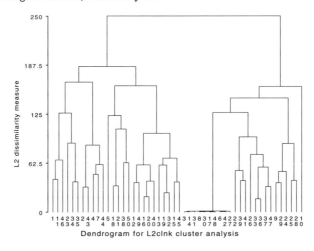

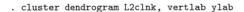

```
. cluster generate g2 = group(2), name(L2clnk)
```

```
. codebook g2
```

```
g2 ─────────────────────────────────────────────────── (unlabeled)
                    type:  numeric (byte)

                   range:  [1,2]                     units:  1
           unique values:  2              coded missing:  0 / 50

               tabulation:  Freq.  Value
                              26   1
                              24   2
. bysort g2 : summarize x*
```

```
-> g2 = 1
```

Variable	Obs	Mean	Std. Dev.	Min	Max
x1	26	91.5	37.29432	17.4	143
x2	26	74.58077	41.19319	4.8	142.1
x3	26	101.0077	36.95704	16.3	147.9
x4	26	71.77308	43.04107	6.6	146.1

```
-> g2 = 2
```

Variable	Obs	Mean	Std. Dev.	Min	Max
x1	24	18.8	23.21742	0	77
x2	24	30.05833	37.66979	0	143.6
x3	24	18.54583	21.68215	.2	69.7
x4	24	41.89167	43.62025	.1	130.9

The group() function of cluster generate created a grouping variable named g2, with ones indicating the 26 observations belonging to the left main branch of the dendrogram, and twos indicating the 24 observations belonging to the right main branch of the dendrogram. The summary of the x variables used in the cluster analysis for each group shows that the second group is characterized by lower values.

We could have obtained the same grouping variable by using the cut() function of cluster generate.

```
. cluster gen g2cut = cut(200)
. table g2 g2cut
```

	g2cut	
g2	1	2
1	26	
2		24

Looking at the y axis of the dendrogram, we decide to cut the tree at the dissimilarity value of 200. We did not specify the name() option. Instead, since this was the latest cluster analysis performed, we let it default to this latest cluster analysis. The table output shows that we obtained the same result with cut(200) as with group(2) for this example.

How many groups are produced if we cut the tree at the value 105.2?

```
. cluster gen z = cut(105.2)

. codebook z, tabulate(20)
```

```
z ─────────────────────────────────────────────────── (unlabeled)
                       type:  numeric (byte)
                      range:  [1,11]                      units:  1
              unique values:  11               coded missing:  0 / 50

                  tabulation:  Freq.  Value
                                  3   1
                                  3   2
                                  5   3
                                  1   4
                                  2   5
                                  2   6
                                 10   7
                                 10   8
                                  8   9
                                  5   10
                                  1   11
```

The `codebook` command shows that the result of cutting the dendrogram at the value 105.2 produced eleven groups, ranging in size from one to ten observations.

The `group()` function of `cluster generate` may be used to create multiple grouping variables with a single call. Here we create the grouping variables for groups of size three to twelve:

```
. cluster gen gp = gr(3/12)

. summarize gp*
```

Variable	Obs	Mean	Std. Dev.	Min	Max
gp3	50	2.26	.8033095	1	3
gp4	50	3.14	1.030356	1	4
gp5	50	3.82	1.438395	1	5
gp6	50	3.84	1.461897	1	6
gp7	50	3.96	1.603058	1	7
gp8	50	4.24	1.911939	1	8
gp9	50	5.18	2.027263	1	9
gp10	50	5.94	2.385415	1	10
gp11	50	6.66	2.781939	1	11
gp12	50	7.24	3.197959	1	12

In this case, we used abbreviations for `generate` and `group()`. The `group()` function takes a numlist; see [U] **14.1.8 numlist**. We specified 3/12, which indicates the numbers 3 to 12. `gp`, the stub name we provide, is appended with the number as the variable name for each group variable produced.

◁

▷ Example

The second example of [R] **cluster singlelinkage** shows the following dendrogram from the single linkage clustering of 30 observations on 60 variables. In that example, we used the `group()` function of `cluster generate` to produce a grouping variable for three groups. What happens when we try to obtain four groups from this clustering?

(Continued on next page)

```
. cluster tree
```

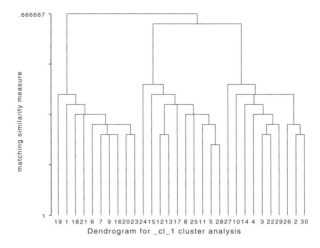

Dendrogram for _cl_1 cluster analysis

```
. cluster gen g4 = group(4)
cannot create 4 groups due to ties
r(198);
```

Stata complains that it cannot create four groups from this cluster analysis.

The ties() option gives us control over this situation. We just need to decide whether we want more or less groups than we asked for when faced with ties. We demonstrate both ways.

```
. cluster gen more4 = gr(4) , ties(more)
. cluster gen less4 = gr(4) , ties(less)
. summarize more4 less4
```

Variable	Obs	Mean	Std. Dev.	Min	Max
more4	30	2.933333	1.638614	1	5
less4	30	2	.8304548	1	3

For this cluster analysis, ties(more) with group(4) produces five groups, while ties(less) with group(4) produces three groups.

The ties(skip) option is convenient when we want to produce a range of grouping variables.

```
. cluster gen group = gr(4/20) , ties(skip)
. summarize group*
```

Variable	Obs	Mean	Std. Dev.	Min	Max
group5	30	2.933333	1.638614	1	5
group9	30	4.866667	2.622625	1	9
group13	30	7.066667	3.92106	1	13
group18	30	9.933333	5.419844	1	18

With this cluster analysis, the only unique groupings available are 5, 9, 13, and 18 within the range 4 to 20.

◁

Also See

Complementary:	[R] **cluster averagelinkage**, [R] **cluster completelinkage**, [R] **cluster dendrogram**, [R] **cluster singlelinkage**, [P] **cluster subroutines**
Related:	[R] **egen**, [R] **generate**
Background:	[R] **cluster**

Title

> **cluster kmeans** — Kmeans cluster analysis

Syntax

cluster $\underline{\text{k}}$means $\big[$*varlist*$\big]$ $\big[$**if** *exp*$\big]$ $\big[$**in** *range*$\big]$, k(#) $\big[$ $\underline{\text{n}}$ame(*clname*)

    distance_option $\underline{\text{s}}$tart(*start_option*) $\underline{\text{gen}}$erate(*groupvar*) $\underline{\text{iter}}$ate(#) $\underline{\text{keepc}}$enters $\big]$

Description

cluster kmeans performs kmeans partition cluster analysis. See [R] **cluster** for a general discussion of cluster analysis and a description of the other **cluster** commands. See [R] **cluster kmedians** for an alternative that uses medians instead of means.

Options

k(#) is required, and indicates that # groups are to be formed by the cluster analysis.

name(*clname*) specifies the name to attach to the resulting cluster analysis. If name() is not specified, Stata finds an available cluster name, displays it for your reference, and then attaches the name to your cluster analysis.

distance_option is one of the similarity or dissimilarity measures allowed within Stata. Capitalization of the option does not matter. See [R] **cluster** for a discussion of these measures.

The available measures designed for continuous data are: L2 (synonym $\underline{\text{Eucl}}$idean) which is the default; L1 (synonyms $\underline{\text{abs}}$olute, cityblock, and $\underline{\text{man}}$hattan); $\underline{\text{Linf}}$inity (synonym $\underline{\text{max}}$imum); L(#); $\underline{\text{Can}}$berra; $\underline{\text{corr}}$elation; and $\underline{\text{ang}}$ular (synonym $\underline{\text{ang}}$le).

The available measures designed for binary data are: $\underline{\text{mat}}$ching, $\underline{\text{Jac}}$card, $\underline{\text{Russ}}$ell, Hamman, Dice, antiDice, Sneath, Rogers, Ochiai, Yule, Anderberg, Kulczynski, Gower2, and Pearson.

start(*start_option*) indicates how the k initial group centers are to be obtained. The available *start_options* are: $\underline{\text{kr}}$andom$\big[$(*seed#*)$\big]$, $\underline{\text{f}}$irstk$\big[$, $\underline{\text{ex}}$clude$\big]$, $\underline{\text{l}}$astk$\big[$, $\underline{\text{ex}}$clude$\big]$, $\underline{\text{pr}}$andom$\big[$(*seed#*)$\big]$, $\underline{\text{ev}}$erykth, $\underline{\text{seg}}$ments, group(*varname*), and $\underline{\text{r}}$andom$\big[$(*seed#*)$\big]$.

krandom$\big[$(*seed#*)$\big]$, the default, indicates that k unique observations are to be chosen at random, from among those to be clustered, as starting centers for the k groups. Optionally, a random number seed may be specified to cause the command **set seed** *seed#* (see [R] **generate**) to be applied before the k random observations are chosen.

firstk$\big[$, exclude$\big]$ indicates that the first k observations, from among those to be clustered, are to be used as the starting centers for the k groups. With the addition of the **exclude** option, these first k observations are then not included among the observations to be clustered.

lastk$\big[$, exclude$\big]$ indicates that the last k observations, from among those to be clustered, are to be used as the starting centers for the k groups. With the addition of the **exclude** option, these last k observations are then not included among the observations to be clustered.

prandom$\big[(seed\#)\big]$ indicates that k partitions are to be formed randomly among the observations to be clustered. The group means from the k groups defined by this partitioning are used as the starting group centers. Optionally, a random number seed may be specified to cause the command set seed *seed#* (see [R] **generate**) to be applied before the k partitions are chosen.

everykth indicates that k partitions are to be formed by assigning observations 1, $1 + k$, $1 + 2k$, ..., to the first group; assigning observations 2, $2 + k$, $2 + 2k$, ..., to the second group; and so on, to form k groups. The group means from these k groups are used as the starting group centers.

segments indicates that k nearly equal partitions are to be formed from the data. Approximately the first N/k observations are assigned to the first group, the second N/k observations are assigned to the second group, and so on. The group means from these k groups are used as the starting group centers.

group(*varname*) provides an initial grouping variable, *varname*, that defines k groups among the observations to be clustered. The group means from these k groups are used as the starting group centers.

random$\big[(seed\#)\big]$ indicates that k random initial group centers are to be generated. The values are randomly chosen from a uniform distribution over the range of the data. Optionally, a random number seed may be specified to cause the command set seed *seed#* (see [R] **generate**) to be applied before the k group centers are generated.

generate(*groupvar*) provides the name of the grouping variable to be created by cluster kmeans. By default, it will be the name specified in name().

iterate(*#*) specifies the maximum number of iterations to allow in the kmeans clustering algorithm. The default is iterate(10000).

keepcenters indicates that the group means, from the k groups that are produced, are to be appended to the data.

Remarks

Two examples of using cluster kmeans are presented, one using continuous data and the other using binary data. See [R] **cluster kmedians** to see these same two datasets examined using kmedians clustering.

▷ Example

You have measured the flexibility, speed, and strength of the 80 students in your physical education class. You want to split the class into four groups, based on their physical attributes, so that they can receive the mix of flexibility, strength, and speed training that will best help them improve.

Here is a summary of the data and a matrix graph showing the data:

```
. summarize flex speed strength
```

Variable	Obs	Mean	Std. Dev.	Min	Max
flexibility	80	4.402625	2.788541	.03	9.97
speed	80	3.875875	3.121665	.03	9.79
strength	80	6.439875	2.449293	.05	9.57

. graph flex speed strength, lab mat

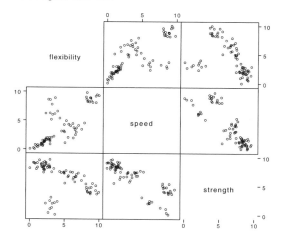

As you expected, based on what you saw the first day of class, the data indicate a wide range of levels of performance for the students. The graph seems to indicate that there are some distinct groups, which leads you to believe that your plan will work well.

You decide to do a cluster analysis to create four groups, one for each of your class assistants. You have had good experience with kmeans clustering in the past, and generally like the behavior of the absolute value distance.

You don't really care what starting values are used in the cluster analysis, but you do want to be able to reproduce the same results if you ever decide to rerun your analysis. You decide to use the krandom() option to pick k of the observations at random as the initial group centers. You supply a random number seed for reproducibility. You also add the keepcenters option so that the means of the four groups will be added to the bottom of your dataset.

```
. cluster k flex speed strength, k(4) name(g4abs) start(kr(385617)) abs keepcen
. cluster list g4abs
g4abs  (type: partition,  method: kmeans,  dissimilarity: L1)
      vars: g4abs (group variable)
     other: k: 4
            start: krandom(385617)
            range: 0 .
            cmd: cluster kmeans flex speed strength, k(4) name(g4abs)
                 start(kr(385617)) abs keepcen
. table g4abs
```

g4abs	Freq.
1	15
2	20
3	35
4	10

```
. list flex speed strength in 81/1
      flexibi~y      speed    strength
81.      8.852    8.743334       4.358
82.      5.9465     3.4485      6.8325
83.    1.969429   1.144857    8.478857
84.      3.157       6.988       1.641

. drop in 81/1
(4 observations deleted)

. tabstat flex speed strength, by(g4abs) stat(min mean max)

Summary statistics: min, mean, max
  by categories of: g4abs
```

g4abs	flexib~y	speed	strength
1	8.12	8.05	3.61
	8.852	8.743333	4.358
	9.97	9.79	5.42
2	4.32	1.05	5.46
	5.9465	3.4485	6.8325
	7.89	5.32	7.66
3	.03	.03	7.38
	1.969429	1.144857	8.478857
	3.48	2.17	9.57
4	2.29	5.11	.05
	3.157	6.988	1.641
	3.99	8.87	3.02
Total	.03	.03	.05
	4.402625	3.875875	6.439875
	9.97	9.79	9.57

After looking at the last four observations (which are the group means since you specified **keepcenters**), you decided that what you really wanted to see was the minimum and maximum values and the mean for the four groups. You removed the last four observations and then used the **tabstat** command to view the desired statistics.

Group 1, with 15 students, is already doing very well in flexibility and speed, but will need extra strength training. Group 2, with 20 students, needs to emphasize speed training, but could use some improvement in the other categories as well. Group 3, the largest, with 35 students, has serious problems with both flexibility and speed, though they did very well in the strength category. Group 4, the smallest, with 10 students, needs help with flexibility and strength.

Since you like looking at graphs, you decide to view the matrix graph again, but with the addition of group numbers as plotting symbols.

(*Continued on next page*)

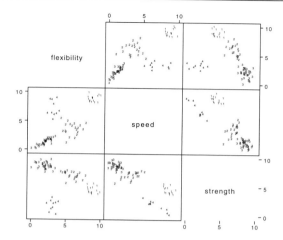

The groups, as shown in the graph, do appear reasonably distinct. However, you had hoped to have groups that were about the same size. You are curious what clustering to three or five groups would produce. For no good reason, you decide to use the first k observations as initial group centers for clustering to three groups, and random numbers within the range of the data for clustering to five groups.

```
. cluster k flex speed strength, k(3) name(g3abs) start(firstk) abs
. cluster k flex speed strength, k(5) name(g5abs) start(random(33576)) abs
. table g3abs g4abs, col
```

g3abs	1	2	3	4	Total
		g4abs			
1				10	10
2		18	35		53
3	15	2			17

```
. table g5abs g4abs, col
```

g5abs	1	2	3	4	Total
		g4abs			
1		20			20
2	15				15
3				6	6
4				4	4
5			35		35

With three groups, the unequal group size problem gets worse. With five groups, the smallest group gets split. Four groups seem like the best option for this class. You will try to help the assistant assigned to group 3 in dealing with the larger group.

◁

▷ Example

You have just started a women's club. Thirty women, from throughout the community, have sent in their requests to join. You have them fill out a questionnaire with 35 yes/no questions relating to sports, music, reading, and hobbies. Here is a description of the dataset:

```
. describe

Contains data
  obs:           30
  vars:          35
  size:       1,170 (99.5% of memory free)
```

variable name	storage type	display format	value label	variable label
bike	byte	%8.0g		enjoy bicycle riding Y/N
bowl	byte	%8.0g		enjoy bowling Y/N
swim	byte	%8.0g		enjoy swimming Y/N
jog	byte	%8.0g		enjoy jogging Y/N
hock	byte	%8.0g		enjoy watching hockey Y/N
foot	byte	%8.0g		enjoy watching football Y/N
base	byte	%8.0g		enjoy baseball Y/N
bask	byte	%8.0g		enjoy basketball Y/N
arob	byte	%8.0g		participate in aerobics Y/N
fshg	byte	%8.0g		enjoy fishing Y/N
dart	byte	%8.0g		enjoy playing darts Y/N
clas	byte	%8.0g		enjoy classical music Y/N
cntr	byte	%8.0g		enjoy country music Y/N
jazz	byte	%8.0g		enjoy jazz music Y/N
rock	byte	%8.0g		enjoy rock and roll music Y/N
west	byte	%8.0g		enjoy reading western novels Y/N
romc	byte	%8.0g		enjoy reading romance novels Y/N
scif	byte	%8.0g		enjoy reading sci. fiction Y/N
biog	byte	%8.0g		enjoy reading biographies Y/N
fict	byte	%8.0g		enjoy reading fiction Y/N
hist	byte	%8.0g		enjoy reading history Y/N
cook	byte	%8.0g		enjoy cooking Y/N
shop	byte	%8.0g		enjoy shopping Y/N
soap	byte	%8.0g		enjoy watching soap operas Y/N
sew	byte	%8.0g		enjoy sewing Y/N
crft	byte	%8.0g		enjoy craft activities Y/N
auto	byte	%8.0g		enjoy automobile mechanics Y/N
pokr	byte	%8.0g		enjoy playing poker Y/N
brdg	byte	%8.0g		enjoy playing bridge Y/N
kids	byte	%8.0g		have children Y/N
hors	byte	%8.0g		have a horse Y/N
cat	byte	%8.0g		have a cat Y/N
dog	byte	%8.0g		have a dog Y/N
bird	byte	%8.0g		have a bird Y/N
fish	byte	%8.0g		have a fish Y/N

```
Sorted by:
    Note:  dataset has changed since last saved
```

Now you are trying to plan the first club meeting. You decide to have a lunch along with the business meeting that will officially organize the club and ratify its charter. You want the club to get off to a good start, so you worry about the best way to seat the guests. You decide to use kmeans clustering on the yes/no data from the questionnaires to put people with similar interests at the same tables.

You have five tables that can each seat up to eight comfortably. You request clustering to five groups and hope that the group sizes will fall under this table size limit.

You really want people placed together based on shared positive interests, instead of on shared non-interests. From among all the available binary similarity measures, you decide to use the Jaccard coefficient, since it does not include jointly zero comparisons in its formula; see [R] **cluster**. The Jaccard coefficient is also easy to understand.

```
. cluster kmeans bike-fish, k(5) Jaccard st(firstk) name(gr5)
. cluster list gr5
gr5 (type: partition,  method: kmeans,  similarity: Jaccard)
      vars: gr5 (group variable)
     other: k: 5
            start: firstk
            range: 1 0
            cmd: cluster kmeans bike-fish, k(5) Jaccard st(firstk) name(gr5)

. table gr5
```

gr5	Freq.
1	7
2	7
3	5
4	5
5	6

You get lucky; the groups are reasonably close in size. You will seat yourself at one of the tables with only five people, and your sister, who did not fill out a questionnaire, at the other table with only five people to make things as even as possible.

Now, you wonder, what are the characteristics of these five groups? You decide to use the `tabstat` command to view the proportion answering yes to each question for each of the five groups.

```
. tabstat bike-fish, by(gr5) format(%4.3f)
Summary statistics: mean
  by categories of: gr5
```

gr5	bike	bowl	swim	jog	hock	foot
1	0.714	0.571	0.714	0.571	0.143	0.143
2	0.286	0.143	0.571	0.714	0.143	0.143
3	0.400	0.200	0.600	0.200	0.200	0.400
4	0.200	0.000	0.200	0.200	0.000	0.400
5	0.000	0.500	0.000	0.000	0.333	0.167
Total	0.333	0.300	0.433	0.367	0.167	0.233

gr5	base	bask	arob	fshg	dart	clas
1	0.429	0.571	0.857	0.429	0.571	0.429
2	0.571	0.286	0.714	0.429	0.857	0.857
3	0.600	0.400	0.000	0.800	0.200	0.000
4	0.200	0.600	0.400	0.000	0.000	0.800
5	0.167	0.333	0.000	0.500	0.167	0.000
Total	0.400	0.433	0.433	0.433	0.400	0.433

gr5	cntr	jazz	rock	west	romc	scif
1	0.857	0.571	0.286	0.714	0.571	0.286
2	0.571	0.857	0.429	0.143	0.143	0.857
3	0.200	0.200	0.600	0.000	0.000	0.200
4	0.200	0.400	0.400	0.200	0.400	0.000
5	0.833	0.167	0.667	0.500	0.667	0.000
Total	0.567	0.467	0.467	0.333	0.367	0.300

gr5	biog	fict	hist	cook	shop	soap
1	0.429	0.429	0.571	0.714	0.571	0.571
2	0.429	0.571	0.571	0.000	0.429	0.143
3	0.000	0.200	0.000	0.600	1.000	0.600
4	1.000	1.000	1.000	0.600	0.600	0.200
5	0.000	0.167	0.000	0.333	1.000	0.667
Total	0.367	0.467	0.433	0.433	0.700	0.433

gr5	sew	crft	auto	pokr	brdg	kids
1	0.429	0.571	0.143	0.571	0.429	0.714
2	0.143	0.714	0.429	0.286	0.714	0.143
3	0.400	0.200	0.600	1.000	0.200	0.600
4	0.800	0.800	0.000	0.000	0.000	1.000
5	0.000	0.000	0.333	0.667	0.000	0.500
Total	0.333	0.467	0.300	0.500	0.300	0.567

gr5	hors	cat	dog	bird	fish
1	0.571	0.571	1.000	0.286	0.429
2	0.143	0.571	0.143	0.429	0.143
3	0.000	0.200	0.200	0.400	0.800
4	0.000	0.400	0.000	0.000	0.200
5	0.167	0.167	0.833	0.167	0.167
Total	0.200	0.400	0.467	0.267	0.333

It appears that group 1 likes participating in most sporting activities, prefers country music, likes reading western and romance novels, enjoys cooking, and is more likely to have kids and various animals, including horses.

Group 2 likes some sports (swimming, jogging, aerobics, baseball, and darts), prefers classical and jazz music, prefers science fiction (but also enjoys biography, fiction and history), dislikes cooking, enjoys playing bridge, is not likely to have children, and is more likely to have a cat than any other animal.

Group 3 seems to enjoy swimming, baseball, and fishing (but dislikes aerobics), prefers rock and roll music (disliking classical), does not enjoy reading, prefers poker over bridge, and is more likely to own a fish than any other animal.

Group 4 dislikes many of the sports, prefers classical music, likes reading biographies, fiction, and history, enjoys sewing and crafts, dislikes card games, has kids, and not likely to have pets.

Group 5 dislikes sports, prefers country and rock and roll music, will pick up romance and western novels on occasion, dislikes sewing and crafts, prefers poker instead of bridge, and is most likely to have a dog.

◁

Methods and Formulas

Kmeans cluster analysis is discussed in most cluster analysis books; see the references in [R] **cluster**. [R] **cluster** also provides a general discussion of cluster analysis, including kmeans clustering, and discusses the available `cluster` subcommands.

Kmeans clustering is an iterative procedure that partitions the data into k groups or clusters. The procedure begins with k initial group centers. Observations are assigned to the group with the closest center. The mean of the observations assigned to each of the groups is computed, and the process is repeated. These steps continue until all observations remain in the same group from the previous iteration.

To avoid endless loops, an observation will only be reassigned to a different group if it is closer to the other group center. In the case of a tied distance between an observation and two or more group centers, the observation is assigned to its current group if that is one of the closest, and to the lowest numbered group otherwise.

The `start()` option provides many ways of specifying the beginning group centers. These include methods that specify the actual starting centers, as well as methods that specify initial partitions of the data from which the beginning centers are computed.

Some kmeans clustering algorithms recompute the group centers after each reassignment of an observation. Other kmeans clustering algorithms, including Stata's `cluster kmeans` command, recompute the group centers only after a complete pass through the data. A disadvantage of this method is that orphaned group centers can occur. An orphaned center is one which has no observations that are closest to it. The advantage of recomputing means only at the end of each pass through the data is that the sort order of the data does not potentially change your final result.

Stata deals with orphaned centers by finding the observation that is farthest from its center and using that as a new group center. The observations are then reassigned to the closest groups, including this (these) new center(s).

Continuous or binary data are allowed with `cluster kmeans`. The mean of a group of binary observations for a variable is the proportion of ones for that group of observations and variable. The binary similarity measures can accommodate the comparison of a binary observation to a binary mean (proportion). See [R] **cluster** for details on this subject and the formulas for all the available (dis)similarity measures.

Also See

Complementary:	[R] **cluster notes**, [R] **cluster utility**
Related:	[R] **cluster kmedians**
Background:	[R] **cluster**

Title

cluster kmedians — Kmedians cluster analysis

Syntax

cluster <u>kmed</u>ians [*varlist*] [if *exp*] [in *range*] , k(*#*) [<u>n</u>ame(*clname*)

　　distance_option <u>s</u>tart(*start_option*) <u>gen</u>erate(*groupvar*) <u>iter</u>ate(*#*) <u>keepc</u>enters]

Description

cluster kmedians performs kmedians partition cluster analysis. See [R] **cluster** for a general discussion of cluster analysis and a description of the other cluster commands. See [R] **cluster kmeans** for an alternative that uses means instead of medians.

Options

k(*#*) is required, and indicates that *#* groups are to be formed by the cluster analysis.

name(*clname*) specifies the name to attach to the resulting cluster analysis. If name() is not specified, Stata finds an available cluster name, displays it for your reference, and then attaches the name to your cluster analysis.

distance_option is one of the similarity or dissimilarity measures allowed within Stata. Capitalization of the option does not matter. See [R] **cluster** for a discussion of these measures.

　The available measures designed for continuous data are: L2 (synonym <u>Euclid</u>ean) which is the default; L1 (synonyms <u>absolute</u>, cityblock, and <u>manhat</u>tan); <u>Linf</u>inity (synonym <u>max</u>imum); L(*#*); <u>Canberra</u>; <u>correl</u>ation; and angular (synonym <u>angl</u>e).

　The available measures designed for binary data are: <u>match</u>ing, <u>Jaccard</u>, <u>Russell</u>, Hamman, Dice, antiDice, Sneath, Rogers, Ochiai, Yule, Anderberg, Kulczynski, Gower2, and Pearson.

start(*start_option*) indicates how the *k* initial group centers are to be obtained. The available *start_option*s are: <u>krandom</u>[(*seed#*)], <u>firstk</u>[, exclude], <u>lastk</u>[, exclude], <u>prandom</u>[(*seed#*)], everykth, segments, group(*varname*), and <u>r</u>andom[(*seed#*)].

　krandom[(*seed#*)], the default, indicates that *k* unique observations are to be chosen at random, from among those to be clustered, as starting centers for the *k* groups. Optionally, a random number seed may be specified to cause the command set seed *seed#* (see [R] **generate**) to be applied before the *k* random observations are chosen.

　firstk[, exclude] indicates that the first *k* observations, from among those to be clustered, are to be used as the starting centers for the *k* groups. With the addition of the exclude option, these first *k* observations are then not included among the observations to be clustered.

　lastk[, exclude] indicates that the last *k* observations, from among those to be clustered, are to be used as the starting centers for the *k* groups. With the addition of the exclude option, these last *k* observations are then not included among the observations to be clustered.

prandom $\lceil (seed\#) \rceil$ indicates that k partitions are to be formed randomly among the observations to be clustered. The group medians from the k groups defined by this partitioning are used as the starting group centers. Optionally, a random number seed may be specified to cause the command set seed *seed#* (see [R] **generate**) to be applied before the k partitions are chosen.

everykth indicates that k partitions are to be formed by assigning observations 1, $1 + k$, $1 + 2k$, ..., to the first group; assigning observations 2, $2 + k$, $2 + 2k$, ..., to the second group; and so on, to form k groups. The group medians from these k groups are used as the starting group centers.

segments indicates that k nearly equal partitions are to be formed from the data. Approximately the first N/k observations are assigned to the first group, the second N/k observations are assigned to the second group, and so on. The group medians from these k groups are used as the starting group centers.

group(*varname*) provides an initial grouping variable, *varname*, that defines k groups among the observations to be clustered. The group medians from these k groups are used as the starting group centers.

random $\lceil (seed\#) \rceil$ indicates that k random initial group centers are to be generated. The values are randomly chosen from a uniform distribution over the range of the data. Optionally, a random number seed may be specified to cause the command set seed *seed#* (see [R] **generate**) to be applied before the k group centers are generated.

generate(*groupvar*) provides the name of the grouping variable to be created by cluster kmedians. By default, it will be the name specified in name().

iterate(*#*) specifies the maximum number of iterations to allow in the kmedians clustering algorithm. The default is iterate(10000).

keepcenters indicates that the group medians, from the k groups that are produced, are to be appended to the data.

Remarks

The data from the two examples introduced in [R] **cluster kmeans** are presented here to demonstrate the use of cluster kmedians. The first dataset contains continuous data, and the second dataset contains binary data.

▷ Example

You have measured the flexibility, speed, and strength of the 80 students in your physical education class. You want to split the class into four groups, based on their physical attributes, so that they can receive the mix of flexibility, strength, and speed training that will best help them improve.

The data are summarized and graphed in [R] **cluster kmeans**. You previously performed a kmeans clustering on these data to obtain four groups. You now wish to see if kmedians clustering will produce the same grouping for this dataset. Again you will specify four groups, absolute value distance, and k random observations as beginning centers (but using a different random number seed).

```
. cluster kmed flex speed strength, k(4) name(kmed4) abs start(kr(11736))
. cluster list kmed4
kmed4  (type: partition,  method: kmedians,  dissimilarity: L1)
     vars: kmed4 (group variable)
    other: k: 4
           start: krandom(11736)
           range: 0 .
           cmd: cluster kmedians flex speed strength, k(4) name(kmed4) abs
               start(kr(11736))

. table g4abs kmed4
```

		kmed4		
g4abs	1	2	3	4
1		15		
2			20	
3	35			
4				10

Other than a difference in how the groups are numbered, kmedians clustering and kmeans clustering produced the same results for this dataset.

In [R] **cluster kmeans**, you checked the results from clustering to three groups and to five groups. Now you want to see what happens with kmedians clustering for three groups and five groups.

```
. cluster kmed flex speed strength, k(3) name(kmed3) abs start(lastk)
. cluster kmed flex speed strength, k(5) name(kmed5) abs start(prand(8723))
. cluster list kmed3 kmed5
kmed3  (type: partition,  method: kmedians,  dissimilarity: L1)
     vars: kmed3 (group variable)
    other: k: 3
           start: lastk
           range: 0 .
           cmd: cluster kmedians flex speed strength, k(3) name(kmed3) abs
               start(lastk)
kmed5  (type: partition,  method: kmedians,  dissimilarity: L1)
     vars: kmed5 (group variable)
    other: k: 5
           start: prandom(8723)
           range: 0 .
           cmd: cluster kmedians flex speed strength, k(5) name(kmed5) abs
               start(prand(8723))

. table g3abs kmed3, row
```

		kmed3	
g3abs	1	2	3
1	6		4
2	18	35	
3	2		15
Total	26	35	19

. table g5abs kmed5, row

			kmed5		
g5abs	1	2	3	4	5
1		20			
2	15				
3				6	
4				4	
5			20		15
Total	15	20	20	10	15

Kmeans and kmedians clustering produced different groups for three groups and five groups.

Since one of your concerns was having a better balance in the group sizes, you decide to look a little bit closer at the five-group solution produced by kmedians clustering.

. table g4abs kmed5, row col

			kmed5			
g4abs	1	2	3	4	5	Total
1	15					15
2		20				20
3			20		15	35
4				10		10
Total	15	20	20	10	15	80

. tabstat flex speed strength, by(kmed5) stat(min mean max)

Summary statistics: min, mean, max
  by categories of: kmed5

kmed5	flexib~y	speed	strength
1	8.12	8.05	3.61
	8.852	8.743333	4.358
	9.97	9.79	5.42
2	4.32	1.05	5.46
	5.9465	3.4485	6.8325
	7.89	5.32	7.66
3	1.85	1.18	7.38
	2.4425	1.569	8.2775
	3.48	2.17	9.19
4	2.29	5.11	.05
	3.157	6.988	1.641
	3.99	8.87	3.02
5	.03	.03	7.96
	1.338667	.5793333	8.747333
	2.92	.99	9.57
Total	.03	.03	.05
	4.402625	3.875875	6.439875
	9.97	9.79	9.57

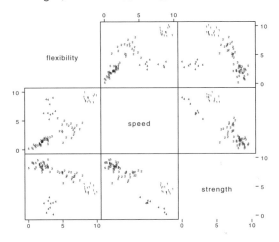

The five-group kmedians clustering split the group with 35 students from the four-group clustering into groups of size 20 and size 15. Looking at the output from `tabstat` you see that this group was broken up so that the 15 slowest students are split apart from the other 20 (who are still slower than the remaining groups).

The characteristics of the five groups are as follows: Group 1, with 15 students, is already doing very well in flexibility and speed, but will need extra strength training. Group 2, with 20 students, needs to emphasize speed training, but could use some improvement in the other categories as well. Group 3, which used to have 35 students, now has 20 students, and has serious problems with both flexibility and speed, though they did very well in the strength category. Group 4, with 10 students, needs help with flexibility and strength. Group 5, which was split off of Group 3, has the 15 slowest students.

Even though the matrix graph showing the five groups does not indicate that groups 3 and 5 are very distinct, you decide to go with five groups anyway to even out the group sizes. You will take the slowest group and work with them directly, since they will need a lot of extra help, while your four class assistants take care of the other four groups.

◁

▷ Example

As explained in the second example of [R] **cluster kmeans**, you have just started a women's club. Thirty women, from throughout the community, have sent in their requests to join. You have them fill out a questionnaire with 35 yes/no questions relating to sports, music, reading, and hobbies. A description of the data is found in [R] **cluster kmeans**.

In planning the first meeting of the club, you are trying to assign seats at the five lunch tables based on shared interests among the women. Kmeans clustering gave you five groups that are each about the right size and seem to make sense in terms of each groups common characteristics; see [R] **cluster kmeans**. Now you want to see if kmedian clustering suggests a better solution.

As before, you select the Jaccard coefficient as the binary similarity measure, and the first k observations as starting centers.

```
. cluster kmed bike-fish, k(5) Jaccard st(firstk) name(kmedian5)
```

```
. cluster list kmedian5
kmedian5 (type: partition,  method: kmedians,  similarity: Jaccard)
       vars: kmedian5 (group variable)
      other: k: 5
             start: firstk
             range: 1 0
             cmd: cluster kmedians bike-fish, k(5) Jaccard st(firstk)
                  name(kmedian5)

. table gr5 kmedian5, row col
```

			kmedian5			
gr5	1	2	3	4	5	Total
1	7					7
2	1	6				7
3			5			5
4				5		5
5	1		1		4	6
Total	9	6	6	5	4	30

The resulting groups are similar. Three ladies are grouped differently with this kmedian clustering compared to the kmeans clustering. However, there is a more even distribution of women to the five groups of the kmeans clustering. Since the five lunch tables can seat only eight comfortably, and the kmedians clustering produces one group of size 9, you decide to stick with the groups produced by kmeans clustering.

◁

Methods and Formulas

Kmedians cluster analysis is a variation of the standard kmeans clustering discussed in most cluster analysis books; see the references in [R] **cluster**. [R] **cluster** also provides a general discussion of cluster analysis, including kmeans and kmedians clustering, and discusses the available `cluster` subcommands.

Kmedians clustering is an iterative procedure that partitions the data into k groups or clusters. The procedure begins with k initial group centers. Observations are assigned to the group with the closest center. The median of the observations assigned to each of the groups is computed, and the process is repeated. These steps continue until all observations remain in the same group from the previous iteration.

To avoid endless loops, an observation will only be reassigned to a different group if it is closer to the other group center. In the case of a tied distance between an observation and two or more group centers, the observation is assigned to its current group if that is one of the closest, or to the lowest numbered group otherwise.

The `start()` option provides many ways of specifying the beginning group centers. These include methods that specify the actual starting centers, as well as methods that specify initial partitions of the data from which the beginning centers are computed.

Stata's `cluster kmedians` command recomputes the group centers only after a complete pass through the data. A disadvantage of this method is that orphaned group centers can occur. An orphaned center is one which has no observations that are closest to it. The advantage of recomputing means only at the end of each pass through the data, instead of after each reassignment, is that the sort order of the data does not potentially change your final result.

Stata deals with orphaned centers by finding the observation that is farthest from its center and using that as a new group center. The observations are then reassigned to the closest groups, including this (these) new center(s).

Continuous or binary data are allowed with `cluster kmedians`. The median of a group of binary observations for a variable is almost always either zero or one. However, if there are an equal number of zeros and ones for a group, then the median is 0.5, which is treated as a proportion (just as with kmeans clustering). The binary similarity measures can accommodate the comparison of a binary observation to a proportion. See [R] **cluster** for details on this subject and the formulas for all the available (dis)similarity measures.

Also See

Complementary:	[R] **cluster notes**, [R] **cluster utility**
Related:	[R] **cluster kmeans**
Background:	[R] **cluster**

Title

> **cluster notes** — Place notes in cluster analysis

Syntax

cluster <u>note</u>s *clname* : *text*

cluster <u>note</u>s

cluster <u>note</u>s *clnamelist*

cluster <u>note</u>s drop *clname* $\big[$in *numlist* $\big]$

Description

The `cluster notes` command attaches notes to a previously run cluster analysis. The notes become part of the data and are saved when the data is saved and retrieved when the data is used; see [R] **save**.

To add a note to a cluster analysis, type `cluster notes`, the cluster analysis name, a colon, and the text.

Typing `cluster notes` by itself will list all cluster notes associated with all defined cluster analyses. `cluster notes` followed by one or more cluster names lists the notes for those cluster analyses.

`cluster notes drop` allows you to drop cluster notes.

Remarks

The cluster analysis system in Stata has many features that allow you to manage the various cluster analyses that you perform. See [R] **cluster** for information on all the available cluster analysis commands, and, in particular, see [R] **cluster utility** for other `cluster` commands, including `cluster list`, that help you manage your analyses. The `cluster notes` command is modeled after Stata's `notes` command (see [R] **notes**), but realize that they are different systems and do not interact.

▷ Example

We illustrate the `cluster notes` command starting with three cluster analyses having already been performed. The `cluster dir` command shows us the names of all the existing cluster analyses; see [R] **cluster utility**.

```
. cluster dir
sngeuc
sngabs
kmn3abs
. cluster note sngabs : I used single linkage with absolute value distance
. cluster note sngeuc : Euclidean distance and single linkage
. cluster note kmn3abs : This has the 3 group kmeans cluster results
```

273

```
. cluster notes
sngeuc
    notes:   1. Euclidean distance and single linkage
sngabs
    notes:   1. I used single linkage with absolute value distance
kmn3abs
    notes:   1. This has the kmeans cluster results for 3 groups
```

After adding a note to each of the three cluster analyses we used the `cluster notes` command without arguments to list all the notes for all the cluster analyses.

The * and ? characters may be used when referring to cluster names; see [U] **14.2 Abbreviation rules**.

```
. cluster note k* : Verify that observation 5 is correct.  I am suspicious that
>  there was a typographical error or instrument failure in recording the infor
>  mation.
. cluster notes kmn3abs
kmn3abs
    notes:   1. This has the kmeans cluster results for 3 groups
             2. Verify that observation 5 is correct. I am suspicious that
                there was a typographical error or instrument failure in
                recording the information.
```

`cluster notes` expanded `k*` to `kmn3abs` the only cluster name that begins with a `k`. Notes that extend to multiple lines are automatically wrapped when displayed. When entering long notes you just continue to type until your note is finished. Pressing return signals that you are done with that note.

After examining the dendrogram (see [R] **cluster dendrogram**) for the `sngeuc` single linkage cluster analysis and seeing one small group of data that split off from the main body of data at a very large distance you investigate further and find data problems. You decide to add some notes to the `sngeuc` analysis.

```
. cluster note *euc : All of Sam's data looks wrong to me.
. cluster note *euc : I think Sam should be fired.
. cluster notes sng?*
sngeuc
    notes:   1. Euclidean distance and single linkage
             2. All of Sam's data looks wrong to me.
             3. I think Sam should be fired.
sngabs
    notes:   1. I used single linkage with absolute value distance
```

Sam, one of the lab technicians, who happens to be the owners nephew and is paid more than you, really messed up. After adding these notes, you get second thoughts about keeping the notes attached to the cluster analysis (and the data). You decide you really want to delete those notes and add a more politically correct note.

```
. cluster note sngeuc : Ask Jennifer to help Sam reevaluate his data.
. cluster note sngeuc
sngeuc
    notes:   1. Euclidean distance and single linkage
             2. All of Sam's data looks wrong to me.
             3. I think Sam should be fired.
             4. Ask Jennifer to help Sam reevaluate his data.
. cluster note drop sngeuc in 2/3
```

```
. cluster notes kmn3abs s*
kmn3abs
     notes:   1. This has the kmeans cluster results for 3 groups
              2. Verify that observation 5 is correct. I am suspicious that
                 there was a typographical error or instrument failure in
                 recording the information.
sngeuc
     notes:   1. Euclidean distance and single linkage
              2. Ask Jennifer to help Sam reevaluate his data.
sngabs
     notes:   1. I used single linkage with absolute value distance
```

Just for illustration purposes the new note was added before deleting the two offending notes. **cluster notes drop** can take an **in** argument followed by a list of note numbers. The numbers correspond to those shown in the listing provided by the **cluster notes** command. After the deletions the note numbers are reassigned to remove gaps. So, **sngeuc** note 4 becomes note 2 after the deletion of notes 2 and 3 as shown above.

Without an **in** argument the **cluster notes drop** command drops all notes associated with the named cluster.

◁

Remember that the cluster notes are stored with the data and, as with other updates you make to the data, the additions and deletions are not permanent until you save the data; see [R] **save**.

❑ Technical Note

Programmers can access the notes (and all the other cluster attributes) using the **cluster query** command; see [P] **cluster utilities**.

❑

Also See

Complementary:	[R] **cluster utility**, [R] **save**, [P] **cluster utilities**
Related:	[R] **notes**
Background:	[R] **cluster**

Title

| **cluster singlelinkage** — Single linkage cluster analysis |

Syntax

cluster <u>s</u>inglelinkage [*varlist*] [if *exp*] [in *range*] [, <u>n</u>ame(*clname*)

    distance_option <u>gene</u>rate(*stub*)]

Description

The cluster singlelinkage command performs hierarchical agglomerative single linkage cluster analysis which is also known as the nearest neighbor technique. See [R] **cluster** for a general discussion of cluster analysis and a description of the other cluster commands. The cluster dendrogram command (see [R] **cluster dendrogram**) will display the resulting dendrogram, and the cluster generate command (see [R] **cluster generate**) will produce grouping variables.

Options

name(*clname*) specifies the name to attach to the resulting cluster analysis. If name() is not specified, Stata finds an available cluster name, displays it for your reference, and then attaches the name to your cluster analysis.

distance_option is one of the similarity or dissimilarity measures allowed within Stata. Capitalization of the option does not matter. See [R] **cluster** for a discussion of these measures.

The available measures designed for continuous data are: L2 (synonym <u>Eucl</u>idean) which is the default; L1 (synonyms <u>abs</u>olute, cityblock, and <u>manhat</u>tan); <u>Linf</u>inity (synonym <u>max</u>imum); L(*#*); <u>Can</u>berra; <u>corr</u>elation; and <u>ang</u>ular (synonym <u>angl</u>e).

The available measures designed for binary data are: <u>mat</u>ching, <u>J</u>accard, <u>Russ</u>ell, Hamman, Dice, antiDice, Sneath, Rogers, Ochiai, Yule, Anderberg, Kulczynski, Gower2, and Pearson.

generate(*stub*) provides a prefix for the variable names created by cluster singlelinkage. By default, the variable name prefix will be the name specified in name(). Three variables are created and attached to the cluster analysis results, with the suffixes _id, _ord, and _hgt. Users generally will not need to access these variables directly.

Remarks

An example using the default L2 (Euclidean) distance on continuous data and an example using the matching coefficient on binary data illustrate the cluster singlelinkage command. The data from these two examples are also used in [R] **cluster completelinkage** and [R] **cluster averagelinkage** so that you can compare different hierarchical clustering methods.

▷ Example

As the senior data analyst for a small biotechnology firm, you are given a dataset with four chemical laboratory measurements on 50 different samples of a particular plant gathered from the rain forest. The head of the expedition that gathered the samples thinks, based on information from the natives, that an extract from the plant might reduce negative side effects from your company's best-selling nutritional supplement.

While the company chemists and botanists continue exploring the possible uses of the plant, and plan future experiments, the head of product development asks you to take a look at the preliminary data and report anything that might be helpful to the researchers.

While all 50 of the plants are supposed to be of the same type, you decide to perform a cluster analysis to see if there are subgroups or anomalies among them. You arbitrarily decide to use single linkage clustering with the default Euclidean distance.

```
. cluster singlelinkage x1 x2 x3 x4, name(sngeuc)
. cluster list sngeuc
sngeuc  (type: hierarchical,  method: single,  dissimilarity: L2)
       vars: sngeuc_id (id variable)
             sngeuc_ord (order variable)
             sngeuc_hgt (height variable)
      other: range: 0 .
             cmd: cluster singlelinkage x1 x2 x3 x4, name(sngeuc)
```

The `cluster singlelinkage` command generated some variables and created a cluster object with the name `sngeuc`, which you supplied as an argument. `cluster list` provides details about the cluster object; see [R] **cluster utility**.

What you really want to see is the dendrogram for this cluster analysis; see [R] **cluster dendrogram**.

```
. cluster dendrogram sngeuc, vertlab ylab
```

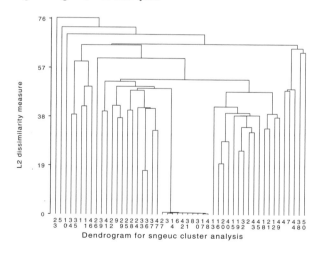

Dendrogram for sngeuc cluster analysis

From your experience with looking at dendrograms, two things jump out at you about this cluster analysis. The first is the observations showing up in the middle of the dendrogram that are all very close to each other (very short vertical bars) and are far from any other observations (the long vertical bar connecting them to the rest of the dendrogram). Next you notice that if you ignore those ten observations, the rest of the dendrogram does not indicate strong clustering as evidenced by the relatively short vertical bars in the upper portion of the dendrogram.

You start to look for clues as to why these ten observations are so peculiar. Looking at scatter plots is usually helpful and so you examine the matrix of scatter plots.

```
. graph x1 x2 x3 x4, matrix label
```

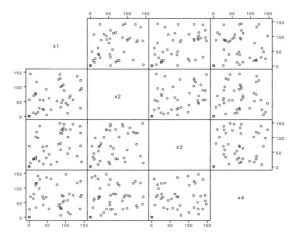

Unfortunately, these scatterplots do not indicate what might be going on.

Suddenly, based on your past experience with the laboratory technicians, you have an idea of what to check next. Because of past data mishaps, the company started the policy of placing within each dataset a variable giving the name of the technician who produced the measurement. You decide to view the dendrogram, using the technician's name as the label instead of the default observation number.

```
. cluster dendrogram sngeuc, vertlab ylab labels(labtech)
```

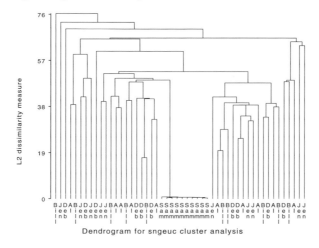

Your suspicions are confirmed. Sam, one of the laboratory technicians, has messed up once again. You list the data and see that all of his observations are between zero and one, while the other four technicians' data range up to about 150, as expected. It looks like Sam forgot, once again, to calibrate his sensor before analyzing his samples. You decide to save a note of your findings with this cluster analysis (see [R] **cluster notes** for the details) and send the data back to the laboratory to be fixed.

◁

▷ Example

The sociology professor of your graduate level class gives, as homework, a dataset containing 30 observations on 60 binary variables, with the assignment to tell him something about the 30 subjects represented by the observations. You feel that this assignment is too vague, but, since your grade depends on it, you get to work trying to figure something out.

Among the analyses you try is the following cluster analysis. You decide to use single linkage clustering with the simple matching binary coefficient, since it is easy to understand. Just for fun, though it makes no difference to you, you specify the **generate()** option to force the generated variables to have **zstub** as a prefix. You let Stata pick a name for your cluster analysis by not specifying the **name()** option.

```
. cluster s a1-a60, matching gen(zstub)
cluster name: _cl_1
. cluster list
_cl_1  (type: hierarchical,  method: single,  similarity: matching)
       vars: zstub_id (id variable)
             zstub_ord (order variable)
             zstub_hgt (height variable)
      other: range: 1 0
             cmd: cluster singlelinkage a1-a60, matching gen(zstub)
```

Stata selected _cl_1 as the cluster name, and created the variables zstub_id, zstub_ord, and zstub_hgt.

You display the dendrogram using the **cluster tree** command, which is a synonym for **cluster dendrogram**. Since Stata uses the most recently performed cluster analysis by default, you do not need to type in the name.

(Continued on next page)

. cluster tree

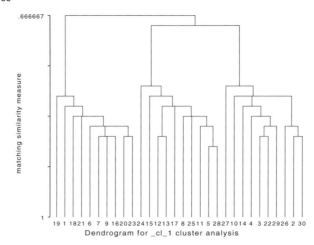

The dendrogram seems to indicate the presence of three groups among the 30 observations. You decide that this is probably the structure your teacher wanted you to find, and you begin to write up your report. You want to examine the three groups further, so you use the `cluster generate` command (see [R] **cluster generate**) to create a grouping variable to make the task easier. You examine various summary statistics and tables for the three groups and finish your report.

After the assignment is turned in, your professor gives you the identical dataset with the addition of one more variable, `truegrp`, which indicates the groupings he feels are in the data. You do a cross tabulation of the `truegrp` and `grp3`, your grouping variable, to see if you are going to get a good grade on the assignment.

. cluster gen grp3 = group(3)

. table grp3 truegrp

	truegrp		
grp3	1	2	3
1		10	
2			10
3	10		

Other than the numbers arbitrarily assigned to the three groups, both you and your professor are in agreement. You rest easier that night knowing that you may survive one more semester.

◁

Methods and Formulas

[R] **cluster** discusses hierarchical clustering and places single linkage clustering in this general framework. It compares the typical behavior of single linkage with complete and average linkage.

Conceptually, hierarchical agglomerative single linkage clustering proceeds as follows. The N observations start out as N separate groups, each of size one. The two closest observations are merged into one group, producing $N - 1$ total groups. The closest two groups are then merged, so that there are $N - 2$ total groups. This process continues until all the observations are merged into one large group. This produces a hierarchy of groupings from one group to N. For single linkage clustering, the decision of closest groups for merging is based on closest observations between the two groups.

Stata's implementation of single linkage clustering is modeled after the algorithm presented in Sibson (1973) and mentioned in Rohlf (1982). This algorithm produces two variables that act as a pointer representation of a dendrogram. To this Stata adds a third variable used to restore the sort order, as needed, so that the two variables of the pointer representation remain valid. The first variable of the pointer representation gives the order of the observations. The second variable has one less element, and gives the height in the dendrogram at which the adjacent observations in the order variable join.

See [R] **cluster** for the details and formulas of the available *distance_option*s, which include (dis)similarity measures for continuous and binary data.

References

See [R] **cluster** for references related to cluster analysis, including single linkage clustering. The following references are especially important in terms of the implementation of single linkage clustering:

Day, W. H. E. and H. Edelsbrunner. 1984. Efficient algorithms for agglomerative hierarchical clustering methods. *Journal of Classification* 1: 7–24.

Rohlf, F. J. 1982. Single-link clustering algorithms. In *Handbook of Statistics*, Vol. 2, ed. P. R. Krishnaiah and L. N. Kanal, 267–284. Amsterdam: North Holland Publishing Company.

Sibson, R. 1973. SLINK: An optimally efficient algorithm for the single-link cluster method. *Computer Journal* 16: 30–34.

Also See

Complementary:	[R] **cluster dendrogram**, [R] **cluster generate**, [R] **cluster notes**, [R] **cluster utility**
Related:	[R] **cluster averagelinkage**, [R] **cluster completelinkage**
Background:	[R] **cluster**

Title

cluster utility — List, rename, use, and drop cluster analyses

Syntax

cluster dir

cluster list [*clnamelist*] [, <u>a</u>ll <u>n</u>otes <u>t</u>ype <u>m</u>ethod <u>d</u>issimilarity <u>s</u>imilarity
    <u>v</u>ars <u>c</u>hars <u>o</u>ther]

cluster drop { *clnamelist* | _all }

cluster use *clname*

cluster rename *oldclname newclname*

cluster renamevar *oldvarname newvarname* [, <u>n</u>ame(*clname*)]

cluster renamevar *oldstub newstub* , <u>p</u>refix [<u>n</u>ame(*clname*)]

Description

These cluster utility commands allow you to view and manipulate the cluster objects you have
created. See [R] **cluster** for an overview of cluster analysis and the available cluster commands.
If you desire even more control over your cluster objects, or if you are programming new cluster
subprograms, there are additional cluster programmer utilities available; see [P] **cluster utilities**
for details.

The cluster dir command provides a directory style listing of all the currently defined clusters.
cluster list provides a detailed listing of the specified clusters, or all current clusters if no cluster
names are specified. The default action is to list all the information attached to the cluster(s). You
may limit the type of information listed by specifying particular options.

The cluster drop command removes the named clusters. The keyword _all specifies that all
current cluster analyses are to be dropped.

Stata cluster analyses are referenced by name. Many of the cluster commands default to using
the most currently defined cluster analysis if no cluster name is provided. The cluster use command
places the named cluster analysis as if it were the latest executed cluster analysis so that, by default,
this cluster analysis will be used if the cluster name is omitted from many of the cluster commands.
Also realize that you may use the * and ? name matching characters to shorten the typing of cluster
names; see [U] **14.2 Abbreviation rules**.

cluster rename allows you to rename a cluster analysis. This only changes the cluster name. It
does not change any of the variable names attached to the cluster analysis. The cluster renamevar
command, on the other hand, allows you to rename the variables attached to a cluster analysis and to
update the cluster object with the new variable name(s). You do not want to use the rename command
(see [R] **rename**) to rename variables attached to a cluster analysis, since this would invalidate the
cluster object. Use the cluster renamevar command instead.

Options

all, the default, specifies that all items and information attached to the cluster(s) are to be listed. You may instead pick among the notes, type, method, dissimilarity, similarity, vars, chars, and other options to limit what is presented.

notes specifies that cluster notes are to be listed.

type specifies that the type of cluster analysis is to be listed.

method specifies that the cluster analysis method is to be listed.

dissimilarity specifies that the dissimilarity measure is to be listed.

similarity specifies that the similarity measure is to be listed.

vars specifies that the variables attached to the cluster(s) are to be listed.

chars specifies that any Stata characteristics attached to the cluster(s) are to be listed.

other specifies that information attached to the cluster(s) under the heading 'other' are to be listed.

name(*clname*), for use with cluster renamevar, indicates the cluster analysis within which the variable renaming is to take place. If name() is not specified, the most recently performed cluster analysis (or the one specified by cluster use) will be used.

prefix, for use with cluster renamevar, indicates that all variables attached to the cluster analysis that have *oldstub* as the beginning of their name are to be renamed, with *newstub* replacing *oldstub*.

Remarks

▷ Example

We demonstrate these cluster utility commands by beginning with four already defined cluster analyses. The dir and list subcommands provide listings of the cluster analyses.

```
. cluster dir
bcx3kmed
ayz5kmeans
abc_clink
xyz_slink
. cluster list xyz_slink
xyz_slink  (type: hierarchical,  method: single,  dissimilarity: L2)
        vars: xyz_slink_id (id variable)
              xyz_slink_ord (order variable)
              xyz_slink_hgt (height variable)
       other: range: 0 .
              cmd: cluster singlelinkage x y z, name(xyz_slink)
. cluster list
bcx3kmed  (type: partition,  method: kmedians,  dissimilarity: L2)
        vars: bcx3kmed (group variable)
       other: k: 3
              start: krandom
              range: 0 .
              cmd: cluster kmedians b c x, k(3) name(bcx3kmed)
```

```
ayz5kmeans  (type: partition,  method: kmeans,  dissimilarity: L2)
       vars: ayz5kmeans (group variable)
      other: k: 5
             start: krandom
             range: 0 .
             cmd: cluster kmeans a y z, k(5) name(ayz5kmeans)
 abc_clink  (type: hierarchical,  method: complete,  dissimilarity: L2)
       vars: abc_clink_id (id variable)
             abc_clink_ord (order variable)
             abc_clink_hgt (height variable)
      other: range: 0 .
             cmd: cluster completelinkage a b c, name(abc_clink)
 xyz_slink  (type: hierarchical,  method: single,  dissimilarity: L2)
       vars: xyz_slink_id (id variable)
             xyz_slink_ord (order variable)
             xyz_slink_hgt (height variable)
      other: range: 0 .
             cmd: cluster singlelinkage x y z, name(xyz_slink)

. cluster list a*, vars
ayz5kmeans
       vars: ayz5kmeans (group variable)

abc_clink
       vars: abc_clink_id (id variable)
             abc_clink_ord (order variable)
             abc_clink_hgt (height variable)
```

cluster dir listed the names of the four currently defined cluster analyses. cluster list followed by the name of one of the cluster analyses listed the information attached to that cluster analysis. The cluster list command, without an argument, listed the information for all currently defined cluster analyses. We demonstrated the vars option of cluster list to show that you can restrict the information that is listed. Notice also the use of a* as the cluster name. The *, in this case, indicates that any ending is allowed. For these four cluster analyses, it matches the names ayz5kmeans and abc_clink.

We now demonstrate the use of the renamevar subcommand.

```
. cluster renamevar ayz5kmeans g5km
variable ayz5kmeans not found in bcx3kmed
r(198);

. cluster renamevar ayz5kmeans g5km, name(ayz5kmeans)

. cluster list ayz5kmeans
ayz5kmeans  (type: partition,  method: kmeans,  dissimilarity: L2)
       vars: g5km (group variable)
      other: k: 5
             start: krandom
             range: 0 .
             cmd: cluster kmeans a y z, k(5) name(ayz5kmeans)
```

The first use of cluster renamevar failed because we did not specify which cluster object to use (with the name() option), and the most recent cluster object, bcx3kmed, was not the appropriate one. After specifying the name() option with the appropriate cluster name, the renamevar subcommand changed the name as shown in the cluster list command that followed.

The cluster use command places a particular cluster object to be the one used by default. We show this in conjunction with the prefix option of the renamevar subcommand.

```
. cluster use ayz5kmeans
. cluster renamevar g grp, prefix
. cluster renamevar xyz_slink_ wrk, prefix name(xyz*)
. cluster list ayz* xyz*
ayz5kmeans  (type: partition,  method: kmeans,  dissimilarity: L2)
       vars: grp5km (group variable)
      other: k: 5
             start: krandom
             range: 0 .
             cmd: cluster kmeans a y z, k(5) name(ayz5kmeans)
xyz_slink  (type: hierarchical,  method: single,  dissimilarity: L2)
       vars: wrkid (id variable)
             wrkord (order variable)
             wrkhgt (height variable)
      other: range: 0 .
             cmd: cluster singlelinkage x y z, name(xyz_slink)
```

The `cluster use` command placed **ayz5kmeans** as the current cluster object. The `cluster re-namevar` command that followed capitalized on this by leaving off the `name()` option. The `prefix` option allowed the changing of the variable names, as demonstrated in the `cluster list` of the two changed cluster objects.

`cluster rename` changes the name of cluster objects. `cluster drop` allows you to drop some or all of the cluster objects.

```
. cluster rename xyz_slink bob
. cluster rename ayz* sam
. cluster list, type method vars
sam  (type: partition,  method: kmeans)
       vars: grp5km (group variable)
bob  (type: hierarchical,  method: single)
       vars: wrkid (id variable)
             wrkord (order variable)
             wrkhgt (height variable)
bcx3kmed  (type: partition,  method: kmedians)
       vars: bcx3kmed (group variable)
abc_clink  (type: hierarchical,  method: complete)
       vars: abc_clink_id (id variable)
             abc_clink_ord (order variable)
             abc_clink_hgt (height variable)
. cluster drop bcx3kmed abc_clink
. cluster dir
sam
bob
. cluster drop _all
. cluster dir
```

We used options with `cluster list` to limit what was presented. The `_all` keyword with `cluster drop` removed all currently defined cluster objects.

◁

Also See

Related: [R] **cluster notes**, [R] **notes**,
                 [P] **cluster utilities**; [P] **char**

Background: [R] **cluster**

Title

cnsreg — Constrained linear regression

Syntax

cnsreg *depvar indepvars* [*weight*] [if *exp*] [in *range*] , constraints(*numlist*)

[level(#)]

by ... : may be used with cnsreg; see [R] **by**.

aweights and fweights are allowed; see [U] **14.1.6 weight**.

cnsreg shares the features of all estimation commands; see [U] **23 Estimation and post-estimation commands**.

Syntax for predict

predict [*type*] *newvarname* [if *exp*] [in *range*] [, *statistic*]

where *statistic* is

xb	$x_j b$, fitted values (the default)
residuals	residuals
pr(*a*,*b*)	$\Pr(a < y_j < b)$
e(*a*,*b*)	$E(y_j \mid a < y_j < b)$
ystar(*a*,*b*)	$E(y_j^*)$, $y_j^* = \max(a, \min(y_j, b))$
stdp	standard error of the prediction
stdf	standard error of the forecast

where *a* and *b* may be numbers or variables; *a* equal to '.' means $-\infty$; *b* equal to '.' means $+\infty$.

These statistics are available both in and out of sample; type predict ... if e(sample) ... if wanted only for the estimation sample.

Description

cnsreg estimates constrained linear regression models. cnsreg typed without arguments redisplays the previous cnsreg results.

Options

constraints(*numlist*) specifies the constraint numbers of the constraints to be applied and is not optional.

level(#) specifies the confidence level, in percent, for confidence intervals. The default is level(95) or as set by set level; see [U] **23.5 Specifying the width of confidence intervals**.

286

Options for predict

xb, the default, calculates the linear prediction.

residuals calculates the residuals; that is, $y_j - \mathbf{x}_j\mathbf{b}$.

pr(a,b) calculates $\Pr(a < \mathbf{x}_j\mathbf{b} + u_j < b)$, the probability that $y_j|\mathbf{x}_j$ would be observed in the interval (a, b).

a and b may be specified as numbers or variable names; lb and ub are variable names;
pr(20,30) calculates $\Pr(20 < \mathbf{x}_j\mathbf{b} + u_j < 30)$;
pr(lb,ub) calculates $\Pr(lb < \mathbf{x}_j\mathbf{b} + u_j < ub)$;
and pr(20,ub) calculates $\Pr(20 < \mathbf{x}_j\mathbf{b} + u_j < ub)$.

$a = .$ means $-\infty$; pr(.,30) calculates $\Pr(\mathbf{x}_j\mathbf{b} + u_j < 30)$;
pr(lb,30) calculates $\Pr(\mathbf{x}_j\mathbf{b} + u_j < 30)$ in observations for which $lb = .$
(and calculates $\Pr(lb < \mathbf{x}_j\mathbf{b} + u_j < 30)$ elsewhere).

$b = .$ means $+\infty$; pr(20,.) calculates $\Pr(\mathbf{x}_j\mathbf{b} + u_j > 20)$;
pr(20,ub) calculates $\Pr(\mathbf{x}_j\mathbf{b} + u_j > 20)$ in observations for which $ub = .$
(and calculates $\Pr(20 < \mathbf{x}_j\mathbf{b} + u_j < ub)$ elsewhere).

e(a,b) calculates $E(\mathbf{x}_j\mathbf{b} + u_j \mid a < \mathbf{x}_j\mathbf{b} + u_j < b)$, the expected value of $y_j|\mathbf{x}_j$ conditional on $y_j|\mathbf{x}_j$ being in the interval (a, b), which is to say, $y_j|\mathbf{x}_j$ is censored.
a and b are specified as they are for pr().

ystar(a,b) calculates $E(y_j^*)$ where $y_j^* = a$ if $\mathbf{x}_j\mathbf{b} + u_j \le a$, $y_j^* = b$ if $\mathbf{x}_j\mathbf{b} + u_j \ge b$, and $y_j^* = \mathbf{x}_j\mathbf{b} + u_j$ otherwise, which is to say, y_j^* is truncated. a and b are specified as they are for pr().

stdp calculates the standard error of the prediction. It can be thought of as the standard error of the predicted expected value or mean for the observation's covariate pattern. This is also referred to as the standard error of the fitted value.

stdf calculates the standard error of the forecast. This is the standard error of the point prediction for a single observation. It is commonly referred to as the standard error of the future or forecast value. By construction, the standard errors produced by stdf are always larger than those by stdp; see [R] **regress** *Methods and Formulas*.

Remarks

▷ Example

In principle, constrained linear regression estimates can be obtained by modifying the list of independent variables. For instance, if you wanted to estimate the model

$$\texttt{mpg} = \beta_0 + \beta_1\,\texttt{price} + \beta_2\,\texttt{weight} + u$$

and constrain $\beta_1 = \beta_2$, you could write

$$\texttt{mpg} = \beta_0 + \beta_1(\texttt{price} + \texttt{weight}) + u$$

and run a regression of mpg on price + weight. The estimated coefficient on the sum would be the constrained estimate of β_1 and β_2. Using **cnsreg**, however, is easier:

```
. constraint define 1 price = weight

. cnsreg mpg price weight, constraint(1)
```

Constrained linear regression

```
                                          Number of obs =        74
                                          F(  1,     72) =     37.59
                                          Prob > F       =    0.0000
                                          Root MSE       =     4.722
```

(1)   price - weight = 0.0

mpg	Coef.	Std. Err.	t	P>|t|	[95% Conf.	Interval]
price	-.0009875	.0001611	-6.13	0.000	-.0013086	-.0006664
weight	-.0009875	.0001611	-6.13	0.000	-.0013086	-.0006664
_cons	30.36718	1.577958	19.24	0.000	27.22158	33.51278

You define constraints using the **constraint** command; see [R] **constraint**. You estimate the model using **cnsreg** and specify the constraint number or numbers in the **constraints()** option.

Just to show that the results above are correct, here is the result of applying the constraint by hand:

```
. gen x = price + weight

. regress mpg x
```

Source	SS	df	MS
Model	838.065767	1	838.065767
Residual	1605.39369	72	22.2971346
Total	2443.45946	73	33.4720474

```
                                          Number of obs =        74
                                          F(  1,     72) =     37.59
                                          Prob > F       =    0.0000
                                          R-squared      =    0.3430
                                          Adj R-squared  =    0.3339
                                          Root MSE       =     4.722
```

mpg	Coef.	Std. Err.	t	P>|t|	[95% Conf.	Interval]
x	-.0009875	.0001611	-6.13	0.000	-.0013086	-.0006664
_cons	30.36718	1.577958	19.24	0.000	27.22158	33.51278

◁

▷ Example

Models can be estimated subject to multiple simultaneous constraints. You simply define the constraints and then include the constraint numbers in the **constraints()** option. For instance, assume you wish to estimate the model

$$\text{mpg} = \beta_0 + \beta_1 \text{price} + \beta_2 \text{weight} + \beta_3 \text{displ} + \beta_4 \text{gear\_ratio} + \beta_5 \text{foreign} + \beta_6 \text{length} + u$$

subject to the constraints

$$\beta_1 = \beta_2 = \beta_3 = \beta_6$$
$$\beta_4 = -\beta_5 = \beta_0/20$$

(This model, like the one in the previous example, is admittedly senseless.) You estimate the model by typing

```
. constraint def 1 price=weight

. constraint def 2 displ=weight
```

```
. constraint def 3 length=weight
. constraint def 5 gear_ratio = -foreign
. constraint def 6 gear_ratio = _cons/20
. cnsreg mpg price weight displ gear_ratio foreign length, c(1-3,5-6)
```

Constrained linear regression

```
                                        Number of obs =      74
                                        F(  2,    72) =  785.20
                                        Prob > F      =  0.0000
                                        Root MSE      =  4.6823
```

```
( 1)   price - weight = 0.0
( 2) - weight + displacement = 0.0
( 3) - weight + length = 0.0
( 4)   gear_ratio + foreign = 0.0
( 5)   gear_ratio - .05 _cons = 0.0
```

mpg	Coef.	Std. Err.	t	P>|t|	[95% Conf. Interval]	
price	-.000923	.0001534	-6.02	0.000	-.0012288	-.0006172
weight	-.000923	.0001534	-6.02	0.000	-.0012288	-.0006172
displacement	-.000923	.0001534	-6.02	0.000	-.0012288	-.0006172
gear_ratio	1.326114	.0687589	19.29	0.000	1.189046	1.463183
foreign	-1.326114	.0687589	-19.29	0.000	-1.463183	-1.189046
length	-.000923	.0001534	-6.02	0.000	-.0012288	-.0006172
_cons	26.52229	1.375178	19.29	0.000	23.78092	29.26365

There are many ways we could have specified the constraints() option (which we abbreviated c() above). We typed c(1-3,5-6), meaning we want constraints 1 through 3 and 5 and 6; those numbers correspond to the constraints we defined. The only reason we did not use the number 4 was to emphasize that constraints do not have to be consecutively numbered. We typed c(1-3,5-6), but we could have typed c(1,2,3,5,6) or c(1-3,5,6) or c(1-2,3,5,6) or even c(1-6), which would have worked as long as constraint 4 is not defined. If we had previously defined a constraint 4, c(1-6) would have included it.

◁

Saved Results

cnsreg saves in e():

Scalars

e(N)	number of observations	e(F)	*F* statistic
e(df_m)	model degrees of freedom	e(rmse)	root mean square error
e(df_r)	residual degrees of freedom	e(ll)	log likelihood

Macros

e(cmd)	cnsreg	e(wexp)	weight expression
e(depvar)	name of dependent variable	e(predict)	program used to implement predict
e(wtype)	weight type		

Matrices

e(b)	coefficient vector	e(V)	variance–covariance matrix of the estimators

Functions

e(sample)	marks estimation sample

Methods and Formulas

cnsreg is implemented as an ado-file.

Let n be the number of observations, p the total number of parameters (prior to restrictions and including the constant), and c the number of constraints. The coefficients are calculated as $\mathbf{b}' = \mathbf{T}\{(\mathbf{T}'\mathbf{X}'\mathbf{W}\mathbf{X}\mathbf{T})^{-1}(\mathbf{T}'\mathbf{X}'\mathbf{W}\mathbf{y} - \mathbf{T}'\mathbf{X}'\mathbf{W}\mathbf{X}\mathbf{a}')\} + \mathbf{a}'$, where $\mathbf{T}$ and $\mathbf{a}$ are as defined in [P] **matrix constraint**. $\mathbf{W} = \mathbf{I}$ if no weights are specified. If weights are specified, let $\mathbf{v}: 1 \times n$ be the specified weights. If fweight frequency weights are specified, $\mathbf{W} = \text{diag}(\mathbf{v})$. If aweight analytic weights are specified, then $\mathbf{W} = \text{diag}[\mathbf{v}/(\mathbf{1}'\mathbf{v})(\mathbf{1}'\mathbf{1})]$, which is to say, the weights are normalized to sum to the number of observations.

The mean square error is $s^2 = (\mathbf{y}'\mathbf{W}\mathbf{y} - 2\mathbf{b}'\mathbf{X}'\mathbf{W}\mathbf{y} + \mathbf{b}'\mathbf{X}'\mathbf{W}\mathbf{X}\mathbf{b})/(n - p + c)$. The variance–covariance matrix is $s^2\mathbf{T}(\mathbf{T}'\mathbf{X}'\mathbf{W}\mathbf{X}\mathbf{T})^{-1}\mathbf{T}'$.

Also See

Complementary:	[R] **adjust**, [R] **constraint**, [R] **lincom**, [R] **linktest**, [R] **mfx**, [R] **predict**, [R] **test**, [R] **testnl**,[R] **vce**, [R] **xi**
Related:	[R] **reg3**, [R] **regress**
Background:	[U] **16.5 Accessing coefficients and standard errors**, [U] **23 Estimation and post-estimation commands**

Title

codebook — Produce a codebook describing the contents of data

Syntax

codebook [*varlist*] [, all header notes mv tabulate(*#*)]

Description

codebook examines the variable names, labels, and data to produce a code book describing the dataset.

Options

all is equivalent to specifying options header and notes. It provides a complete report, which excludes only performing mv.

header adds a header to the top of the output that lists the dataset name, the date that the dataset was last saved, etc.

notes list any notes attached to the variables; see [R] notes.

mv specifies that codebook is to search the data to determine the pattern of missing values. This is a cpu-intensive task.

tabulate(*#*) specifies the number of unique values of the variables to use to determine whether a variable is categorical or continuous. The default is 9; meaning that when there are more than 9 unique values, the variable is classified as continuous.

Remarks

codebook, without arguments, is most usefully combined with log to produce a printed listing for enclosure in a notebook documenting the data; see [U] **18 Printing and preserving output**. codebook is, however, also useful interactively, since you can specify one or a few variables.

▷ Example

codebook examines the data in producing its results. For variables that codebook thinks are continuous, it presents the mean, standard deviation, and the 10th, 25th, 50th, 75th, and 90th percentiles. For variables that it thinks are categorical, it presents a tabulation. In part, codebook makes this determination by counting the number of unique values of the variable. If the number is 9 or fewer, codebook reports a tabulation; otherwise, it reports summary statistics.

(Continued on next page)

```
. codebook fips division, all

                   Dataset:  educ.dta
                Last saved:  22 Jun 2000 10:13
                             DATA HAVE CHANGED SINCE LAST SAVED

                     Label:  ccdb46, 52-54
       Number of variables:  42
    Number of observations:  956
                      Size:  149,136 bytes ignoring labels, etc.

  _dta:
    1.  confirmed data with steve on 7/22

fips ─────────────────────────────────────────────── state/place code
                      type:  numeric (long)

                     range:  [10060,560050]             units:  1
             unique values:  956             coded missing:  0 / 956

                      mean:     256495
                  std. dev:     156998

               percentiles:        10%      25%      50%      75%      90%
                                  61462   120426   252848   391360   482530

division ──────────────────────────────────────────── Census Division
                      type:  numeric (int)
                     label:  division

                     range:  [1,9]                      units:  1
             unique values:  9               coded missing:  0 / 956

                tabulation:  Freq.   Numeric  Label
                               69          1  N. Eng.
                               97          2  Mid Atl
                              206          3  E.N.C.
                               78          4  W.N.C.
                              115          5  S. Atl.
                               46          6  E.S.C.
                               89          7  W.S.C.
                               61          8  Mountain
                              195          9  Pacific
```

Since division has 9 unique values, codebook reported a tabulation. If division had one more unique value, codebook would have switched to reporting summary statistics unless we had included the tabulate(#) option.

◁

▷ Example

The mv option is quite useful. It instructs codebook to search the data to determine the pattern of missing values.

(Continued on next page)

```
. codebook cooldd heatdd tempjan tempjuly, mv

cooldd ─────────────────────────────────────────── Cooling degree days
                     type:  numeric (int)

                    range:  [0,4389]                 units:  1
            unique values:  438            coded missing:  3 / 956

                     mean:  1240.41
                std. dev:  937.668

              percentiles:         10%      25%      50%      75%      90%
                                   411      615      940     1566     2761

           missing values:      heatdd==. <-> cooldd==.
                                tempjan==. --> cooldd==.
                                tempjuly==. --> cooldd==.

heatdd ─────────────────────────────────────────── Heating degree days
                     type:  numeric (int)

                    range:  [0,10816]                units:  1
            unique values:  471            coded missing:  3 / 956

                     mean:  4425.53
                std. dev:  2199.6

              percentiles:         10%      25%      50%      75%      90%
                                  1510     2460     4950     6232     6919

           missing values:      cooldd==. <-> heatdd==.
                                tempjan==. --> heatdd==.
                                tempjuly==. --> heatdd==.

tempjan ────────────────────────────────────── Average January temperature
                     type:  numeric (float)

                    range:  [2.2,72.6]               units:  .1
            unique values:  310            coded missing:  2 / 956

                     mean:  35.749
                std. dev:  14.1881

              percentiles:         10%      25%      50%      75%      90%
                                  20.2     25.1     31.3     47.8     55.1

           missing values:   tempjuly==. <-> tempjan==.

tempjuly ────────────────────────────────────── Average July temperature
                     type:  numeric (float)

                    range:  [58.1,93.6]              units:  .1
            unique values:  196            coded missing:  2 / 956

                     mean:  75.0538
                std. dev:  5.49504

              percentiles:         10%      25%      50%      75%      90%
                                  68.8     71.8    74.25     78.7     82.3

           missing values:   tempjan==. <-> tempjuly==.
```

codebook reports that if `tempjan` is missing, `tempjuly` is missing and vice versa. In the output for the `cooldd` variable, `codebook` also reports that the pattern of missing values is the same for `cooldd` and `heatdd`. In both cases, the correspondence is indicated with "`<->`".

For `cooldd`, `codebook` also states that "`tempjan==. --> cooldd==.`". The one-way arrow means that a missing `tempjan` value implies a missing `cooldd` value, but a missing `cooldd` value does not necessarily imply a missing `tempjan` value.

◁

Another feature of `codebook`—this one for numeric variables—is to determine the units of the variable. For instance, in the example above, `tempjan` and `tempjuly` both have units of .1, meaning that temperature is recorded to tenths of a degree. `codebook` handles precision considerations in making this determination (note that `tempjan` and `tempjuly` are `floats` and see [U] **16.10 Precision and problems therein**). If we had a variable in our dataset recorded in 100s (e.g., 21,500, 36,800, etc.), `codebook` would have reported the units as 100. If we had a variable that took on only values divisible by 5 (5, 10, 15, etc.), `codebook` would have reported the units as 5.

▷ Example

When `codebook` determines that neither a tabulation nor a listing of summary statistics is appropriate, for instance, in the case of a string variable or in the case of a numeric variable taking on many labeled values, it reports a few examples instead.

```
. codebook name

name ─────────────────────────────────────────────────────── City name
                  type:  string (str30)

         unique values:  956                coded missing:  0 / 956

              examples:  "Corona, CA"
                         "Huntington Beach, CA"
                         "Muskegon, MI"
                         "Salinas, CA"

               warning:  variable has embedded blanks
```

`codebook` is also on the lookout for common problems that might cause you to make errors when dealing with the data. In the case of string variables, this includes leading, embedded, and trailing blanks. `codebook` informed us that `name` includes embedded blanks. If `name` ever had leading or trailing blanks, it would have mentioned that, too.

◁

Methods and Formulas

`codebook` is implemented as an ado-file.

Also See

Related: [R] **describe**, [R] **inspect**, [R] **notes**

Background: [U] **18 Printing and preserving output**

Title

collapse — Make dataset of means, medians, etc.

Syntax

collapse *clist* [*weight*] [if *exp*] [in *range*] [, by(*varlist*) cw fast]

where *clist* is either

[(*stat*)] *varlist* [[(*stat*)] ...]

[(*stat*)] *target_var=varname* [*target_var=varname* ...] [[(*stat*)] ...]

or any combination of the *varlist* and *target_var* forms, and *stat* is one of

mean	means (default)	median	medians
sd	standard deviations	p1	1st percentile
sum	sums	p2	2nd percentile
rawsum	sums ignoring optionally specified weight	...	3rd–49th percentiles
count	number of nonmissing observations	p50	50th percentile (same as median)
max	maximums	...	51st–97th percentiles
min	minimums	p98	98th percentile
iqr	interquartile range	p99	99th percentile

If *stat* is not specified, mean is assumed.

aweights, fweights, pweights, and iweights are allowed; see [U] **14.1.6 weight**, and see the *Weights* section below. pweights may not be used with statistic sd.

Examples:

. collapse age educ income, by(state)

. collapse (mean) age educ (median) income, by(state)

. collapse (mean) age educ income (median) medinc=income, by(state)

. collapse (p25) gpa [fw=number], by(year)

Description

collapse converts the dataset in memory into a dataset of means, sums, medians, etc. *clist* must refer to numeric variables exclusively.

Note: See [R] **contract** if you want to collapse to a dataset of frequencies.

Options

by(*varlist*) specifies the groups over which the means, etc., are to be calculated. If not specified, the resulting dataset will contain one observation. If specified, *varlist* may refer to either string or numeric variables.

cw specifies casewise deletion. If not specified, all possible observations are used for each calculated statistic.

fast specifies that collapse not go to extra work so that it can restore the original dataset should the user press *Break*. fast is intended for use by programmers.

Remarks

collapse takes the dataset in memory and creates a new dataset containing summary statistics of the original data. Since the syntax diagram for collapse makes using it appear more complicated than it is, collapse is best explained with examples.

▷ Example

Consider the following artificial data on the grade-point average (gpa) of college students:

```
. describe

Contains data from college.dta
  obs:            12
  vars:            4                           6 Jul 2000 14:17
  size:          168 (99.9% of memory free)

              storage  display    value
variable name   type    format    label    variable label

gpa            float   %9.0g               gpa for this year
hour           int     %9.0g               Total academic hours
year           int     %9.0g               1 = freshman, 2 = sophomore, 3
                                              = junior, 4 = senior
number         int     %9.0g               number of students

Sorted by:  year

. list

        gpa     hour    year   number
 1.     3.2      30       1       3
 2.     3.5      34       1       2
 3.     2.8      28       1       9
 4.     2.1      30       1       4
 5.     3.8      29       2       3
 6.     2.5      30       2       4
 7.     2.9      35       2       5
 8.     3.7      30       3       4
 9.     2.2      35       3       2
10.     3.3      33       3       3
11.     3.4      32       4       5
12.     2.9      31       4       2

. collapse (p25) gpa [fw=number], by(year)

. list

        year     gpa
 1.      1       2.8
 2.      2       2.5
 3.      3       3.3
 4.      4       2.9

. use college, clear

. collapse gpa hour [fw=number], by(year)

. list

        year       gpa       hour
 1.      1      2.788889   29.44444
 2.      2      2.991667   31.83333
 3.      3      3.233333   32.11111
 4.      4      3.257143   31.71428

. use college, clear

. collapse (mean) gpa hour (median) medgpa=gpa medhour=hour [fw=num], by(year)
```

```
. list
```

	year	gpa	hour	medgpa	medhour
1.	1	2.788889	29.44444	2.8	29
2.	2	2.991667	31.83333	2.9	30
3.	3	3.233333	32.11111	3.3	33
4.	4	3.257143	31.71428	3.4	32

```
. use college, clear
. collapse (count) gpa hour (min) mingpa=gpa minhour=hour [fw=num], by(year)
. list
```

	year	gpa	hour	mingpa	minhour
1.	1	18	18	2.1	28
2.	2	12	12	2.5	29
3.	3	9	9	2.2	30
4.	4	7	7	2.9	31

```
. use college, clear
. replace gpa = . in 2/4
(3 real changes made, 3 to missing)
. list
```

	gpa	hour	year	number
1.	3.2	30	1	3
2.	.	34	1	2
3.	.	28	1	9
4.	.	30	1	4
5.	3.8	29	2	3
6.	2.5	30	2	4
7.	2.9	35	2	5
8.	3.7	30	3	4
9.	2.2	35	3	2
10.	3.3	33	3	3
11.	3.4	32	4	5
12.	2.9	31	4	2

```
. collapse gpa hour [fw=num], by(year)
. list
```

	year	gpa	hour
1.	1	3.2	29.44444
2.	2	2.991667	31.83333
3.	3	3.233333	32.11111
4.	4	3.257143	31.71428

```
. use college, clear
. replace gpa = . in 2/4
(3 real changes made, 3 to missing)
. collapse (mean) gpa hour [fw=num], by(year) cw
. list
```

	year	gpa	hour
1.	1	3.2	30
2.	2	2.991667	31.83333
3.	3	3.233333	32.11111
4.	4	3.257143	31.71428

◁

▷ Example

We have individual-level data from the Census in which each observation is a person. Among other variables, the dataset contains the numeric variables **age**, **educ**, and **income** and the string variable **state**. We want to create a 50-observation dataset containing the means of age, education, and income for each state.

```
. collapse age educ income, by(state)
```

The resulting dataset contains means because `collapse` assumes you want means if you do not specify otherwise. To make this explicit, we could have typed

```
. collapse (mean) age educ income, by(state)
```

Had we wanted the mean for `age` and `educ`, but the median for `income`, we could have typed

```
. collapse (mean) age educ (median) income, by(state)
```

Or, if we wanted the mean for `age` and `educ`, but both the mean and the median for `income`,

```
. collapse (mean) age educ income (median) medinc=income, by(state)
```

This last dataset will contain three variables containing means—`age`, `educ`, and `income`—and one variable containing the median of income—`medinc`.

◁

Variable-wise or casewise deletion

▷ Example

Let us assume that in our Census data, we have 25,000 persons for whom age is recorded but only 15,000 for whom income is recorded; that is, `income` is missing for 10,000 observations. If you wanted summary statistics for `age` and `income`, by default, `collapse` will use all 25,000 observations when calculating the summary statistics for `age`. If you prefer that `collapse` use only the 15,000 observations for which `income` is not missing, specify the `cw` (casewise) option:

```
. collapse (mean) age income (median) medinc=income, by(state) cw
```

◁

Weights

`collapse` allows all four weight types and defaults to `aweight`s. Weight normalization only impacts the `sum`, `count`, and `sd` statistics.

Here are the definitions for `count` and `sum` with weights:

count:
    unweighted: $\_N$, the number of physical observations
    `aweight`: $\_N$, the number of physical observations
    `fweight, iweight, pweight`: $W = \sum w_j$, the sum of the user-specified weights
sum:
    unweighted: $\sum x_j$, the sum of the variable
    `aweight`: $\sum v_j x_j$; $v_j = (w_j$ normalized to sum to $\_N)$
    `fweight, iweight, pweight`: $\sum w_j x_j$

The `sd` statistic with weights returns the bias-corrected standard deviation, which is based on the factor $\sqrt{N/(N-1)}$, where N is the number of observations. `sd` is not allowed with `pweight`ed data. Otherwise `sd` is changed by the weights through the computation of the count (N) as outlined above.

For instance, consider a case where there are 25 physical observations in the dataset and a weighting variable that sums to 57. In the unweighted case, the weight is not specified and $N = 25$. In the analytically weighted case, N is still 25; the scale of the weight is irrelevant. In the frequency-weighted case, however, $N = 57$, the sum of the weights.

▷ Example

Using our same Census data, suppose that instead of starting with individual-level data and aggregating to state level, we started with state-level data and wanted to aggregate to the region level. Also assume that our dataset contains pop, the population of each state.

To obtain unweighted means and medians of age and income, by region, along with total population,

```
. collapse (mean) age income (median) medage=age medinc=income (sum) pop, by(region)
```

To obtain weighted means and medians of age and income, by region, along with total population and using frequency weights:

```
. collapse (mean) age income (median) medage=age medinc=income (count) pop
            [fweight=pop], by(region)
```

Note: Specifying (sum) pop would not have worked because that would have yielded the pop-weighted sum of pop. Specifying (count) age would have worked as well as (count) pop because count merely counts the number of nonmissing observations. The counts here, however, are frequency-weighted and equal the sum of pop.

Same as above, but using analytic weights:

```
. collapse (mean) age income (median) medage=age medinc=income (rawsum) pop
            [aweight=pop], by(region)
```

Note: Specifying (count) pop would not have worked because, with analytic weights, count would count numbers of physical observations. Specifying (sum) pop would not have worked because sum would calculate weighted sums (with a normalized weight). The rawsum function, however, ignores the weights and just sums the specified variable. rawsum would have worked as the solution to all three cases.

◁

A final example

▷ Example

We have state data containing information on each state's median age, marriage rate, and divorce rate. We want to form a new dataset containing various summary statistics, by region, of the variables:

```
. use census5
(1980 Census data by state)
```

```
. describe

Contains data from census5.dta
    obs:             50                          1980 Census data by state
   vars:              6                          6 Jul 2000 14:22
   size:          1,800 (98.6% of memory free)

              storage  display    value
variable name   type   format     label    variable label

state          str14   %14s                State
region         int     %8.0g      cenreg   Census region
pop            long    %10.0g              Population
median_age     float   %9.2f               Median age
marriage_rate  float   %9.0g               Marriage rate
divorce_rate   float   %9.0g               Divorce rate

Sorted by:  region

. collapse (median) median_age marriage divorce (mean) avgmrate=marriage
> avgdrate=divorce [aw=pop], by(region)

. list

         region  median_~e  marriag~e  divorce~e    avgmrate    avgdrate
  1.        NE     31.90    .0080657   .0035295    .0081472    .0035359
  2.  N Cntrl     29.90    .0093821   .0048636    .0096701    .004961
  3.    South     29.60    .0112609   .0065792    .0117082    .0059439
  4.     West     29.90    .0089093   .0056423    .0125199    .0063464

. describe

Contains data
    obs:              4                          1980 Census data by state
   vars:              6
   size:            104 (98.8% of memory free)

              storage  display    value
variable name   type   format     label    variable label

region         int     %8.0g      cenreg   Census region
median_age     float   %9.2f               (p 50) median_age
marriage_rate  float   %9.0g               (p 50) marriage_rate
divorce_rate   float   %9.0g               (p 50) divorce_rate
avgmrate       float   %9.0g               (mean) marriage_rate
avgdrate       float   %9.0g               (mean) divorce_rate

Sorted by:  region
     Note:  dataset has changed since last saved
```
◁

Methods and Formulas

collapse is implemented as an ado-file.

References

Gould, W. W. 1995. dm27: An improved collapse, with weights. *Stata Technical Bulletin* 24: 5–8. Reprinted in *Stata Technical Bulletin Reprints*, vol. 4, pp. 40–43.

Also See

Related: [R] **contract**, [R] **egen**, [R] **summarize**

Title

> **compare** — Compare two variables

Syntax

> compare *varname*$_1$ *varname*$_2$ $\left[\texttt{if } exp\right]$ $\left[\texttt{in } range\right]$

> by ... : may be used with compare; see [R] **by**.

Description

> compare reports the differences and similarities in *varname*$_1$ and *varname*$_2$.

Remarks

▷ Example

> One of the more useful accountings made by compare is the pattern of missing values:

```
. compare rep77 rep78
```

	count	minimum	———— difference ———— average	maximum
rep77<rep78	16	-3	-1.3125	-1
rep77=rep78	43			
rep77>rep78	7	1	1	1
jointly defined	66	-3	-.2121212	1
rep77 missing only	3			
jointly missing	5			
total	74			

> We see that in 5 observations both **rep77** and **rep78** are missing and that in 3 more observations, **rep77** is also missing.

◁

❑ Technical Note

> compare may be used with numeric variables, string variables, or both. When used with string variables, the summary of the differences (minimum, average, maximum) is not reported. When used with string and numeric variables, the breakdown by <, =, and > is also suppressed.

> For strings, both "" and "." are treated as missing values. Stata does not normally attach any special meaning to the string ".", but some Stata users use the string "." to mean missing value.

❑

Methods and Formulas

compare is implemented as an ado-file.

Also See

Related: [R] **codebook**, [R] **inspect**

Title

compress — Compress data in memory

Syntax

compress [*varlist*]

Description

compress attempts to reduce the amount of memory used by your data.

Remarks

compress reduces the size of your dataset by considering demoting

doubles	to	longs, ints, or bytes
floats	to	ints or bytes
longs	to	ints or bytes
ints	to	bytes
strings	to	shorter strings

compress leaves your data logically unchanged but (probably) appreciably smaller. compress never makes a mistake, results in loss of precision, or hacks off strings.

▷ Example

If you do not specify a *varlist*, compress considers all the variables in your dataset, so typing compress by itself is enough:

```
. compress
mpg was float now byte
price was long now int
yenprice was double now long
weight was double now int
make was str26 now str18

.
```

If there are no compression possibilities, compress does nothing. For instance, typing compress again:

```
. compress

.
```

◁

Also See

Related: [R] **recast**

Title

constraint — Define and list constraints

Syntax

constraint <u>def</u>ine # [*exp=exp* | *coefficientlist*]

constraint <u>dir</u> [*numlist* | _all]

constraint drop { *numlist* | _all }

constraint <u>l</u>ist [*numlist* | _all]

where *coefficientlist* is as defined in [R] **test**.

is restricted to the range 1 to 999, inclusive.

Description

constraint defines, lists, and drops linear constraints. Constraints are for use by models that allow constrained estimation.

Remarks

The use of constraints is discussed in [R] **cnsreg**, [R] **mlogit**, and [R] **reg3**; this entry is concerned only with practical aspects of defining and manipulating constraints.

Constraints are defined by the constraint define command. The currently defined constraints can be listed by either constraint list or constraint dir; both do the same thing. Existing constraints can be eliminated by constraint drop.

▷ Example

Constraints are numbered from 1 to 999 and you assign the number when you define the constraint:

```
. constraint define 2 [Insured]site2 = 0
```

The currently defined constraints can be listed by constraint list:

```
. constraint list
      2:   [Insured]site2 = 0
```

constraint drop is used to drop constraints:

```
. constraint drop 2
. constraint list
```

304

The empty list after `constraint list` indicates that no constraints are defined. Below, we demonstrate the various syntaxes allowed by `constraint`:

```
. constraint define 1 [Insured]
. constraint define 10 [Insured]: site1 site2
. constraint define 11 [Insured]: site3 site4
. constraint define 20 [Prepay=Unins]: site1 site2 site3 site4
. constraint define 21 [Prepay=Unins]: race
. constraint define 30 [Prepay]
. constraint define 31 [Insure]
. constraint list
      1:   [Insured]
     10:   [Insured]: site1 site2
     11:   [Insured]: site3 site4
     20:   [Prepay=Unins]: site1 site2 site3 site4
     21:   [Prepay=Unins]: race
     30:   [Prepay]
     31:   [Insure]
. constraint drop 20-25, 31
. constraint list
      1:   [Insured]
     10:   [Insured]: site1 site2
     11:   [Insured]: site3 site4
     30:   [Prepay]
. constraint drop _all
. constraint list
```

◁

❏ Technical Note

The syntax of the constraint itself is not checked by the `constraint` command because a constraint can only be interpreted in the context of a model. Thus, `constraint` is willing to define constraints that subsequently will not make sense. Any errors in the constraints will be detected, and mentioned, at the time of estimation.

❏

References

Weesie, J. 1999. sg100: Two-stage linear constrained estimation. *Stata Technical Bulletin* 47: 24–30. Reprinted in *Stata Technical Bulletin Reprints*, vol. 8, pp. 217–225.

Also See

Complementary: [R] **cnsreg**, [R] **ml**, [R] **mlogit**

Title

> **contract** — Make dataset of frequencies

Syntax

> contract *varlist* [*weight*] [if *exp*] [in *range*] [, freq(*varname*) zero nomiss]

fweights are allowed; see [U] **14.1.6 weight**.

Description

> contract replaces the dataset in memory with a new dataset consisting of all combinations of *varlist* that exist in the data and a new variable that contains the frequency of each combination.

Options

> freq(*varname*) specifies a name for the frequency variable. If not specified, _freq is used. The name must be new.

> zero specifies that combinations with frequency zero are wanted.

> nomiss specifies that observations with missing values on any of the variables in *varlist* will be dropped. If nomiss is not specified, all observations possible are used.

Remarks

> contract takes the dataset in memory and creates a new dataset containing all combinations of *varlist* that exist in the data and a new variable that contains the frequency of each combination.

> Sometimes it is desirable to collapse a dataset into frequency form. Several observations identical on one or more variables will be replaced by one such observation together with the frequency of the corresponding set of values. For example, in certain generalized linear models the frequency of some combination of values is the response variable, so we need to produce that response variable. The set of covariate values associated with each frequency is sometimes called a covariate class or covariate pattern. Such collapsing is reversible for the variables concerned, as the original dataset could be reconstituted by using expand (see [R] **expand**) with the variable containing the frequencies of each covariate class.

▷ Example

> Suppose we wish to collapse the auto dataset to a set of frequencies of the two variables rep78, which takes values 1, 2, 3, 4 and 5, and foreign, which takes values labeled 'Domestic' and 'Foreign'.

```
. contract rep78 foreign
. list

        rep78    foreign      _freq
  1.        1    Domestic         2
  2.        2    Domestic         8
```

```
3.        3 Domestic        27
4.        3  Foreign         3
5.        4 Domestic         9
6.        4  Foreign         9
7.        5 Domestic         2
8.        5  Foreign         9
9.        . Domestic         4
10.       .  Foreign         1
```

By default, `contract` uses the variable name `_freq` for the new variable that contains the frequencies. If `_freq` is in use, then the user is reminded to specify a new variable name via the `freq( )` option.

Specifying the `zero` option requests that combinations with frequency zero also be listed.

```
. contract rep78 foreign, zero
. list
        rep78    foreign        _freq
1.         1 Domestic           2
2.         1  Foreign           0
3.         2 Domestic           8
4.         2  Foreign           0
5.         3 Domestic          27
6.         3  Foreign           3
7.         4 Domestic           9
8.         4  Foreign           9
9.         5 Domestic           2
10.        5  Foreign           9
11.        . Domestic           4
12.        .  Foreign           1
```

◁

Methods and Formulas

`contract` is implemented as an ado-file.

Acknowledgment

`contract` was written by Nicholas J. Cox of the University of Durham (Cox 1998).

References

Cox, N. J. 1998. dm59: Collapsing datasets to frequencies. *Stata Technical Bulletin* 44: 2–3. Reprinted in *Stata Technical Bulletin Reprints*, vol. 8, pp. 20–21.

Also See

Complementary:	[R] **expand**
Related:	[R] **collapse**

Title

> **copy** — Copy file from disk or URL

Syntax

> copy *filename_1 filename_2* [, <u>pub</u>lic <u>t</u>ext replace]

filename_1 may be a filename or a URL. *filename_2* may *not* be a URL.

Double quotes may be used to enclose the filenames and the quotes must be used if the filename contains embedded blanks.

Description

> copy copies *filename_1* to *filename_2*.

Options

> public specifies that *filename_2* is to be readable by everyone; otherwise, the file will be created according to the default permissions of your operating system.

> text specifies that *filename_1* is to be interpreted as a text file and is to be translated to the native form of text files on your computer. Computers differ on how end-of-line is recorded: Unix systems record a single linefeed character, Windows computers record a carriage-return/linefeed combination, and Macintosh computers record just a carriage return. text specifies that *filename_1* is to be examined to determine how it has end-of-line recorded and then the line-end characters are to be switched to whatever is appropriate for your computer when the copy is made.

> There is no reason to specify text when copying a file already on your computer to a different location because the file would already be in your computer's format.

> Do not specify text unless you know the file is a text file; if the file is binary and you specify text, the copy will be useless. Be warned that most word processors produce binary, not text files. The term text, as it is used here, specifies a particular ASCII way of recording textual information.

> When other parts of Stata read text files, they do not care how lines are terminated, so there is no reason to translate end-line characters on that score. You specify text because you may want to look at the file using other software.

> replace specifies that *filename_2* may already exist and, if so, it is to be replaced.

Remarks

> Examples:

> Windows:

```
. copy orig.dta newcopy.dta
. copy "my document" "copy of document"
. copy ..\mydir\doc.txt document\doc.tex
. copy http://www.stata.com/examples/simple.dta simple.dta
. copy http://www.stata.com/examples/simple.txt simple.txt, text
```

Unix:

. copy orig.dta newcopy.dta

. copy ../mydir/doc.txt document/doc.tex

. copy http://www.stata.com/examples/simple.dta simple.dta

. copy http://www.stata.com/examples/simple.txt simple.txt, text

Macintosh:

. copy orig.dta newcopy.dta

. copy "my document" "copy of document"

. copy ..:mydir:doc.txt document:doc.tex

. copy http://www.stata.com/examples/simple.dta simple.dta

. copy http://www.stata.com/examples/simple.txt simple.txt, text

Also See

Related:	[R] **cd**, [R] **dir**, [R] **erase**, [R] **mkdir**, [R] **shell**, [R] **type**
Background:	[U] **14.6 File-naming conventions**

Title

> **copyright** — Display copyright information

Syntax

```
copyright
```

Description

copyright presents copyright notifications concerning tools, libraries, and the like used in the construction of Stata.

Remarks

The correct form for a copyright notice is

Copyright *dates* by *author/owner*

Note that the word "copyright" is spelled out. You can use the © symbol, but (C) has never been given legal recognition. The phrase "All Rights Reserved" was historically required but is no longer needed.

Currently, most works are copyrighted from the moment they are written, and no copyright notice is required. Copyright concerns the protection of the expression and structure of facts and ideas, not the facts and ideas themselves. Also note that copyright concerns the ownership of the expression and not the name given to the expression, which is covered under trademark law.

Copyright law as it exists today began in England in 1710 with the Statute of Anne, *An Act for the Encouragement of Learning by Vesting the Copies of Printed Books in the Authors or Purchases of Such Copies, during the Times therein mentioned*. In 1672, Massachusetts introduced the first copyright law in what was to become the United States. After the Revolutionary War, copyright was introduced into the U.S. Constitution in 1787 and went into effect on 31may1790. On 9jun1790, the first copyright in the U.S. was registered for *The Philadelphia Spelling Book* by John Barry.

There are significant differences in the understanding of copyright in the English- and non-English-speaking world. The Napoleonic or Civil Code, the dominant legal system in the non-English-speaking world, splits the rights into two classes: the author's economic rights and the author's moral rights. Moral rights are available only to "natural persons". Legal persons (corporations) have economic rights, but not moral rights.

Also See

Related: Copyright page of this book

310

Title

---

corr2data — Create a dataset with a specified correlation structure

---

Syntax

corr2data *newvarlist* [, n(*#*) m̲eans(*vector*) corr(*matname*) cov(*matname*)

s̲ds(*vector*) d̲ouble clear]

Description

corr2data can be used to add new variables with specified correlation structures to the existing dataset or to create a dataset with a specified correlation structure.

Options

n(*#*) specifies the number of observations to be generated. Default is the current number of observations. If n(*#*) is not specified or is the same as the current number of observations, corr2data will add the new variables to the existing dataset; otherwise, corr2data will replace the dataset in memory.

means(*vector*) specifies the means of the generated variables. The default is means(0).

corr(*matname*) specifies the correlation matrix. cov() and corr() may not be specified together. If neither corr() nor cov() is specified, the default is orthogonal data.

cov(*matname*) specifies the covariance matrix. cov() and corr() may not be specified together. If neither corr() nor cov() is specified, the default is orthogonal data.

sds(*vector*) specifies the standard deviations of the generated variables. sds() and cov() may not be specified together.

double specifies that the new variables are to be stored as Stata doubles, meaning 8-byte reals. If double is not specified, variables are stored as floats, meaning 4-byte reals. See [R] **data types**.

clear specifies that it is okay to replace the dataset in memory even though the current dataset has not been saved on disk.

Remarks

▷ Example

We first run a factor analysis using the auto dataset.

```
. factor weight length  trunk
(obs=74)
            (principal factors; 2 factors retained)
    Factor    Eigenvalue    Difference    Proportion    Cumulative

      1        2.37834        2.36209        1.0184        1.0184
      2        0.01625        0.07536        0.0070        1.0253
      3       -0.05911           .          -0.0253        1.0000
```

| | Factor Loadings | | |
Variable	1	2	Uniqueness
weight	0.95026	-0.07919	0.09073
length	0.97237	0.00264	0.05448
trunk	0.72789	0.09986	0.46020

Suppose for some reason, we no longer have the `auto` dataset. Instead we know the covariance matrix of `weight`, `length` and `trunk`, and we want to do the same factor analysis again. The covariance matrix is

```
. mat list V

symmetric V[3,3]
            weight      length       trunk
weight   604029.84
length   16370.922   495.78989
 trunk   2234.6612   69.202518   18.296187
```

In order to do the factor analysis in Stata, we need to create a dataset that has the specified correlation structure.

```
. corr2data x y z, n(74) cov(V)
(obs 74)

. factor x y z
(obs=74)
```

| | (principal factors; 2 factors retained) | | | |
Factor	Eigenvalue	Difference	Proportion	Cumulative
1	2.37834	2.36209	1.0184	1.0184
2	0.01625	0.07536	0.0070	1.0253
3	-0.05911	.	-0.0253	1.0000

| | Factor Loadings | | |
Variable	1	2	Uniqueness
x	0.95026	-0.07919	0.09073
y	0.97237	0.00264	0.05448
z	0.72789	0.09986	0.46020

Note that the results from the factor analysis based on the generated data are the same as those based on the real data.

◁

Methods and Formulas

`corr2data` is implemented as an ado-file. Two steps are involved in generating the desire dataset. The first step is to generate a zero mean, zero correlated dataset. The second step is to apply the desired correlation structure and the means to the zero mean, zero correlated dataset. In both steps, we take into account the fact that given any matrix $\mathbf{A}$ and any vector of variables $\mathbf{X}$, $\mathrm{Var}(\mathbf{A}'\mathbf{X}) = \mathbf{A}'\mathrm{Var}(\mathbf{X})\mathbf{A}$.

Also See

Related: [R] **drawnorm**

Background: [R] **data types**

Title

> **correlate** — Correlations (covariances) of variables or estimators

Syntax

<u>cor</u>relate [*varlist*] [*weight*] [if *exp*] [in *range*] [, <u>m</u>eans <u>nof</u>ormat <u>c</u>ovariance

   _coef <u>wr</u>ap]

pwcorr [*varlist*] [*weight*] [if *exp*] [in *range*] [, <u>o</u>bs sig <u>p</u>rint(#) <u>st</u>ar(#)

   <u>b</u>onferroni <u>sid</u>ak]

by ... : may be used with correlate and pwcorr; see [R] **by**.
aweights and fweights are allowed; see [U] **14.1.6 weight**.
The *varlist* following correlate may contain time-series operators; see [U] **14.4.3 Time-series varlists**.

Description

The correlate command displays the correlation matrix or covariance matrix for a group of variables or for the coefficients of the most recent estimation. Also see [R] **vce**.

pwcorr displays all the pairwise correlation coefficients between the variables in *varlist* or, if *varlist* is not specified, all the variables in the dataset.

Options

means causes summary statistics (means, standard deviations, minimums, and maximums) to be displayed with the matrix.

noformat displays the summary statistics requested by the means option in g format regardless of the display formats associated with the variables.

covariance displays the covariances rather than the correlation coefficients.

_coef displays the correlations (or covariances if covariance is also specified) between the coefficients of the last estimation.

wrap requests that no action be taken on wide correlation matrices to make them readable. It prevents Stata from breaking wide matrices into pieces to enhance readability. You might want to specify this option if you are displaying results in a window wider than 80 characters. In that case, you may need to set linesize to however many characters you can display across a single line; see [R] **log**.

obs adds a line to each row of the matrix reporting the number of observations used to calculate the correlation coefficient.

sig adds a line to each row of the matrix reporting the significance level of each correlation coefficient.

print(#) specifies the significance level of correlation coefficients to be printed. Correlation coefficients with larger significance levels are left blank in the matrix. Typing pwcorr, print(.10) would list only correlation coefficients significant at the 10% level or better.

`star(#)` specifies the significance level of correlation coefficients to be starred. Typing `pwcorr, star(.05)` would star all correlation coefficients significant at the 5% level or better.

`bonferroni` makes the Bonferroni adjustment to calculated significance levels. This affects printed significance levels and the `print()` and `star()` options. Thus, `pwcorr, print(.05)` bonferroni prints coefficients with Bonferroni-adjusted significance levels of .05 or less.

`sidak` makes the Šidák adjustment to calculated significance levels. This affects printed significance levels and the `print()` and `star()` options. Thus, `pwcorr, print(.05)` sidak prints coefficients with Šidák-adjusted significance levels of .05 or less.

Remarks

correlate

Typing `correlate` by itself produces a correlation matrix for all the variables in the dataset. If you specify the *varlist*, a correlation matrix for just those variables is displayed.

▷ Example

You have state data on demographic characteristics of the population. To obtain a correlation matrix, type `correlate`:

```
. correlate
(obs=50)
```

	state	brate	pop	medage	division	region	mrgrate
state	1.0000						
brate	0.0208	1.0000					
pop	-0.0540	-0.2830	1.0000				
medage	-0.0624	-0.8800	0.3294	1.0000			
division	-0.1345	0.6356	-0.1081	-0.5207	1.0000		
region	-0.1339	0.6086	-0.1515	-0.5292	0.9688	1.0000	
mrgrate	0.0509	0.0677	-0.1502	-0.0177	0.2280	0.2490	1.0000
dvcrate	-0.0655	0.3508	-0.2064	-0.2229	0.5522	0.5682	0.7700
medage2	-0.0621	-0.8609	0.3324	0.9984	-0.5162	-0.5239	-0.0202

	dvcrate	medage2
dvcrate	1.0000	
medage2	-0.2192	1.0000

Since you did not specify the `wrap` option, Stata did its best to make the result readable by breaking the table into two parts.

To obtain the correlations between `mrgrate`, `dvcrate`, and `medage`, type `correlate mrgrate dvcrate medage`:

```
. correlate mrgrate dvcrate medage
(obs=50)
```

	mrgrate	dvcrate	medage
mrgrate	1.0000		
dvcrate	0.7700	1.0000	
medage	-0.0177	-0.2229	1.0000

◁

▷ Example

The variable pop in our previous example represents the total population of the state. Thus, to obtain population-weighted correlations between mrgrate, dvcrate, and medage, type

```
. correlate mrgrate dvcrate medage [w=pop]
(analytic weights assumed)
(sum of wgt is    2.2591e+08)
(obs=50)
              mrgrate  dvcrate   medage

    mrgrate    1.0000
    dvcrate    0.5854   1.0000
     medage   -0.1316  -0.2833   1.0000
```

◁

With the covariance option, correlate can be used to obtain covariance matrices as well as correlation matrices. This can be done for both weighted and unweighted data.

▷ Example

To obtain the matrix of covariances between mrgrate, dvcrate, and medage, type correlate mrgrate dvcrate medage, covariance:

```
. correlate mrgrate dvcrate medage, covariance
(obs=50)
              mrgrate  dvcrate   medage

    mrgrate   .000662
    dvcrate   .000063   1.0e-05
     medage  -.000769  -.001191  2.86775
```

You could have obtained the pop-weighted covariance matrix by typing correlate mrgrate dvcrate medage [w=pop], covariance.

◁

By specifying the _coef option, you can use correlate to display the correlation or covariance matrix for the coefficients from the last estimated model. You may not specify a *varlist*, in *range*, or if *exp* since the sample was determined by the most recent estimation command. You may not specify a weight, either. If the most recent estimates were weighted, the correlation (covariance) matrix displayed is correctly weighted already.

▷ Example

The only possible forms of correlate with the _coef option are correlate, _coef and correlate, _coef covariance. Before you can use one of these two forms, you must estimate a model—here we will use regression—but we emphasize that you can use correlate after any estimation procedure, even maximum likelihood procedures such as clogit, logistic, logit, ologit, and mlogit. We run a regression of mrgrate on medage and medage2, excluding Nevada from the data:

```
. regress mrgrate medage medage2 if state~="Nevada"
```

Source	SS	df	MS
Model	.000179759	2	.00008988
Residual	.00034728	46	7.5496e-06
Total	.000527039	48	.00001098

```
Number of obs =      49
F(  2,     46) =   11.91
Prob > F       =  0.0001
R-squared      =  0.3411
Adj R-squared  =  0.3124
Root MSE       =  .00275
```

mrgrate	Coef.	Std. Err.	t	P>|t|	[95% Conf. Interval]	
medage	-.0041675	.0040848	-1.02	0.313	-.0123899	.0040548
medage2	.0000518	.0000692	0.75	0.459	-.0000876	.0001911
_cons	.0928522	.0602392	1.54	0.130	-.0284031	.2141075

To obtain the correlation matrix of the coefficients, we now type `correlate, _coef`:

```
. correlate, _coef
```

	medage	medage2	_cons
medage	1.0000		
medage2	-0.9984	1.0000	
_cons	-0.9983	0.9935	1.0000

The results show a large amount of collinearity among the explanatory variables.

We did not have to type the `correlate` command immediately after running the regression. We could have gone on to do other things—retrieving the residuals, plotting them, and so on—before requesting to see the correlation matrix. Stata never forgets the most recent estimates (unless you explicitly eliminate them by typing `discard`).

We can obtain the covariance matrix of the estimators by typing `correlate, _coef covariance`:

```
. correlate, _coef covariance
```

	medage	medage2	_cons
medage	.000017		
medage2	-2.8e-07	4.8e-09	
_cons	-.000246	4.1e-06	.003629

◁

pwcorr

`correlate` calculates correlation coefficients using casewise deletion: when you request correlations of variables $x_1, x_2, \ldots, x_k$, any observation for which any of $x_1, x_2, \ldots, x_k$ is missing is not used. Thus, if x_3 and x_4 have no missing values, but x_2 is missing for half the data, the correlation between x_3 and x_4 is calculated using only the half of the data for which x_2 is not missing. Of course, you can obtain the correlation between x_3 and x_4 using all the data by typing `correlate` x_3 x_4.

`pwcorr` makes obtaining such pairwise correlation coefficients easier.

▷ Example

Using the `auto.dta`, we investigate the correlation between several of the variables.

```
. pwcorr mpg price rep78 foreign, obs sig
```

	mpg	price	rep78	foreign
mpg	1.0000			
	74			
price	-0.4594	1.0000		
	0.0000			
	74	74		
rep78	0.3739	0.0066	1.0000	
	0.0016	0.9574		
	69	69	69	
foreign	0.3613	0.0487	0.5922	1.0000
	0.0016	0.6802	0.0000	
	74	74	69	74

```
. pwcorr mpg price headroom rear_seat trunk rep78 foreign, print(.05) star(.01)
```

	mpg	price	headroom	rear_s~t	trunk	rep78	foreign
mpg	1.0000						
price	-0.4594*	1.0000					
headroom	-0.4220*		1.0000				
rear_seat	-0.5213*	0.4194*	0.5238*	1.0000			
trunk	-0.5703*	0.3143*	0.6620*	0.6480*	1.0000		
rep78	0.3739*					1.0000	
foreign	0.3613*		-0.2939	-0.2409	-0.3594*	0.5922*	1.0000

```
. pwcorr mpg price headroom rear_seat trunk rep78 foreign, print(.05) bon
```

	mpg	price	headroom	rear_s~t	trunk	rep78	foreign
mpg	1.0000						
price	-0.4594	1.0000					
headroom	-0.4220		1.0000				
rear_seat	-0.5213	0.4194	0.5238	1.0000			
trunk	-0.5703		0.6620	0.6480	1.0000		
rep78	0.3739					1.0000	
foreign	0.3613				-0.3594	0.5922	1.0000

◁

❑ Technical Note

The **correlate** command will report the correlation matrix of the data, but there are occasions when you need the matrix stored as a Stata matrix so you can further manipulate it. You can obtain it by typing

```
. matrix accum R = varlist, nocons dev
. matrix R = corr(R)
```

The first line places the cross-product matrix of the data in matrix R. The second line converts that to a correlation matrix. See also [P] **matrix define** and [P] **matrix accum**.

❑

Saved Results

correlate saves in r():

Scalars

r(N)	number of observations	r(Var_1)	variance of first variable (covariance only)
r(rho)	ρ (first and second variables)	r(Var_2)	variance of second variable (covariance only)
r(cov_12)	covariance (covariance only)		

Note that pwcorr will leave in its wake only the results of the last call that it makes internally to correlate, for the correlation between the last variable and itself. Only rarely is this useful.

Methods and Formulas

pwcorr is implemented as an ado-file.

For a discussion of correlation, see, for instance, Snedecor and Cochran (1989, 177–195); for a more introductory explanation, see Edwards (1984).

According to Snedecor and Cochran (1989, 180), the term "co-relation" was first proposed by Galton (1888). The product-moment correlation coefficient is often called the Pearson product-moment correlation coefficient because Pearson (1896, 1898) was partially responsible for popularizing its use. See Stigler (1986) for information on the history of correlation.

The estimate of the product-moment correlation coefficient ρ is

$$\widehat{\rho} = \frac{\sum_{i=1}^{n} w_i (x_i - \overline{x})(y_i - \overline{y})}{\sqrt{\sum_{i=1}^{n} w_i (x_i - \overline{x})^2} \sqrt{\sum_{i=1}^{n} w_i (y_i - \overline{y})^2}}$$

where w_i are the weights if specified, or $w_i = 1$ if weights are not specified. $\overline{x} = (\sum w_i x_i)/(\sum w_i)$ is the mean of x, and $\overline{y}$ is similarly defined.

The unadjusted significance level is calculated by pwcorr as

$$p = 2 * \texttt{ttail}(n - 2, \widehat{\rho}\sqrt{n - 2}/\sqrt{1 - \widehat{\rho}^2})$$

Let v be the number of variables specified so that $k = v(v-1)/2$ correlation coefficients are to be estimated. If bonferroni is specified, the adjusted significance level is $p' = \min(1, kp)$. If sidak is specified, $p' = \min\left\{1, 1 - (1 - p)^n\right\}$. In both cases, see *Methods and Formulas* in [R] **oneway** for a more complete description of the logic behind these adjustments.

As for the correlation or covariance matrix of estimators, see the appropriate estimation command. When correlate is used after a maximum likelihood procedure, it obtains the covariance matrix from the inverse of the information matrix.

References

Edwards, A. L. 1984. *An Introduction to Linear Regression and Correlation.* 2d ed. New York: W. H. Freeman and Company.

Galton, F. 1888. Co-relations and their measurement, chiefly from anthropometric data. *Proceedings of the Royal Society of London* 45: 135–145.

Gleason, J. R. 1996. sg51: Inference about correlations using the Fisher z-transform. *Stata Technical Bulletin* 32: 13–18. Reprinted in *Stata Technical Bulletin Reprints*, vol. 6, pp. 121–128.

Goldstein, R. 1996. sg52: Testing dependent correlation coefficients. *Stata Technical Bulletin* 32: 18. Reprinted in *Stata Technical Bulletin Reprints*, vol. 6, pp. 128–129.

Pearson, K. 1896. Mathematical contributions to the theory of evolution.—III. Regression, heredity, and panmixia. *Philosophical Transactions of the Royal Society of London*, A, 187: 253–318.

Pearson, K. and L. N. G. Filon. 1898. Mathematical contributions to the theory of evolution.—IV. On the probable errors of frequency constants and on the influence of random selection on variation and correlation. *Philosophical Transactions of the Royal Society of London*, A, 191: 229–311.

Snedecor, G. W. and W. G. Cochran. 1989. *Statistical Methods.* 8th ed. Ames, IA: Iowa State University Press.

Stigler, S. M. 1986. *The History of Statistics.* Cambridge, MA: The Belknap Press of Harvard University Press.

Wolfe, F. 1997. sg64: pwcorrs: An enhanced correlation display. *Stata Technical Bulletin* 35: 22–25. Reprinted in *Stata Technical Bulletin Reprints*, vol. 6, pp. 163–167.

——. 1999. sg64.1: Update to pwcorrs. *Stata Technical Bulletin* 49: 17. Reprinted in *Stata Technical Bulletin Reprints*, vol. 9, p. 159.

Also See

Complementary: [R] **matsize**, [R] **vce**

Related: [R] **pcorr**, [R] **spearman**, [R] **summarize**

Title

corrgram — Correlogram

Syntax

corrgram *varname* [**if** *exp*] [**in** *range*] [**,** <u>nopl</u>ot <u>lags</u>(#)]

ac *varname* [**if** *exp*] [**in** *range*] [**,** <u>lags</u>(#) **fft needle** <u>gen</u>erate(*newvarname*)

    <u>l</u>evel(#) *graph_options*]

pac *varname* [**if** *exp*] [**in** *range*] [**,** <u>lags</u>(#) **needle** <u>gen</u>erate(*newvarname*)

    <u>l</u>evel(#) *graph_options*]

These commands are for use with time-series data; see [R] **tsset**. You must **tsset** your data before using **corrgram**, **ac**, or **pac**. In addition, the time series must be dense (nonmissing and no gaps in the time variable) in the sample if you specify the **fft** option.

varname may contain time-series operators; see [U] **14.4.3 Time-series varlists**.

Description

corrgram lists a table of the autocorrelations, partial autocorrelations, and Q statistics. It will also list a character-based plot of the autocorrelations and partial autocorrelations.

The **ac** command produces a correlogram (the autocorrelations) with pointwise confidence intervals obtained from the Q statistic; see [R] **wntestq**.

The **pac** command produces a graph of the partial correlogram (the partial autocorrelations) with confidence intervals calculated using a standard error of $1/\sqrt{n}$. The residual variances for each lag are also included on the graph.

Options

noplot prevents the character-based plots from being in the listed table of autocorrelations and partial autocorrelations.

lags(#) specifies the number of autocorrelations to calculate. The default is to use $\min([n/2]-2, 40)$ where $[n/2]$ is the greatest integer less than or equal to $n/2$.

fft specifies that the autocorrelations should be calculated using two Fourier transforms. This technique can be faster than simply iterating over the requested number of lags.

needle specifies that the graph should be drawn using vertical lines from zero to the calculated correlations instead of lines that connect the calculated correlations.

generate(*newvarname*) specifies a new variable to contain the autocorrelation (**ac** command) or partial autocorrelation (**pac** command) values.

level(#) specifies the confidence level, in percent, for the confidence bands in the **ac** or **pac** graph. The default is **level(95)** or as set by **set level**; see [R] **level**.

graph_options are any of the options allowed with `graph, twoway`; see [G] **graph options**.

Remarks

The Q statistics provided in the output are the same statistics that you would get by running the `wntestq` command for each of the lags in the table; see [R] **wntestq**.

`corrgram` provides an easy means to obtain lists of autocorrelations and partial autocorrelations. By default, character-based plots of these values are provided, but if you are going to cut and paste these values to a report, you may want to use the `noplot` option to suppress these character-based plots.

▷ Example

Here, we use the international airline passengers dataset (Box, Jenkins, and Reinsel 1994, Series G). This dataset has 144 observations on the monthly number of international airline passengers from 1949 through 1960. We can list the autocorrelations and partial autocorrelations using

```
. corrgram air, lags(20)
```

					-1 0 1	-1 0 1
LAG	AC	PAC	Q	Prob>Q	[Autocorrelation]	[Partial Autocor]
1	0.9480	0.9589	132.14	0.0000	|———	|———
2	0.8756	-0.3298	245.65	0.0000	|———	—|
3	0.8067	0.2018	342.67	0.0000	|———	|-
4	0.7526	0.1450	427.74	0.0000	|———	|-
5	0.7138	0.2585	504.8	0.0000	|———	|—
6	0.6817	-0.0269	575.6	0.0000	|———	|
7	0.6629	0.2043	643.04	0.0000	|———	|-
8	0.6556	0.1561	709.48	0.0000	|———	|-
9	0.6709	0.5686	779.59	0.0000	|———	|———
10	0.7027	0.2926	857.07	0.0000	|———	|—
11	0.7432	0.8402	944.39	0.0000	|———	|———
12	0.7604	0.6127	1036.5	0.0000	|———	|———
13	0.7127	-0.6660	1118	0.0000	|———	———|
14	0.6463	-0.3846	1185.6	0.0000	|———	—|
15	0.5859	0.0787	1241.5	0.0000	|———	|
16	0.5380	-0.0266	1289	0.0000	|———	|
17	0.4997	-0.0581	1330.4	0.0000	|——	|
18	0.4687	-0.0435	1367	0.0000	|——	|
19	0.4499	0.2773	1401.1	0.0000	|——	|—
20	0.4416	-0.0405	1434.1	0.0000	|——	|

If we wished to produce a high-quality graph instead of the character-based plot, we could type

(Graph on next page)

. ac air, lags(20)

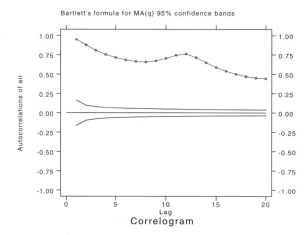

We can emphasize the discrete nature of the autocorrelations using the **needle** option.

. ac air, lags(20) needle

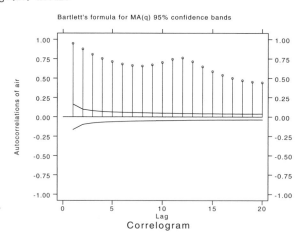

In the preceding examples, we have not removed the trend or annual cycle from the data. We can do that by taking first and twelfth differences. Below we plot the partial autocorrelations of the transformed data:

(Graph on next page)

```
. pac DS12.air, lags(20) needle
```

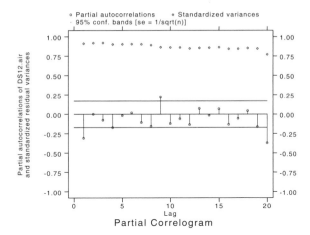

Partial Correlogram

◁

Saved Results

corrgram saves in r():

Scalars
r(lags)   number of lags

Matrices
r(AC)   vector of autocorrelations
r(PAC)   vector of partial autocorrelations
r(Q)   vector of Q statistics

Methods and Formulas

corrgram, ac, and pac are implemented as ado-files.

Box, Jenkins, and Reinsel (1994), Newton (1988), Chatfield (1996), and Hamilton (1994) provide excellent descriptions of correlograms. Newton (1988) provides additional discussion on the calculation of the various quantities.

The autocovariance function for a time series $x_1, x_2, \ldots, x_n$ is defined for $|v| < n$ as

$$\widehat{R}(v) = \frac{1}{n} \sum_{i=1}^{n-|v|} (x_i - \overline{x})(x_{i+v} - \overline{x})$$

where $\overline{x}$ is the sample mean, and the autocorrelation function is then defined as

$$\widehat{\rho}(v) = \frac{\widehat{R}(v)}{\widehat{R}(0)}$$

The partial autocorrelation of lag v is the autocorrelation between $x(t)$ and $x(t + v)$ after having removed the common linear effect of the data in between; the lag-1 partial autocorrelation is then asymptotically the same as the lag-1 autocorrelation.

The residual variances (which appear on the graph produced with the `pac` command) are the sample multiple correlation coefficients of the decomposition of the overall variability due to the autocovariance at the various lags.

In other words, for a given lag v, we regress x on lags 1 through v of x. The partial autocorrelation coefficient $\widehat{\theta}(v)$ is the coefficient on lag v of x in the regression and the residual variance is the estimated variance of the regression—these residual variances are then standardized by dividing them by the sample variance, $\widehat{R}(0)$, of the time series.

Acknowledgment

The `ac` and `pac` commands are based on the `ac` and `pac` commands written by Sean Becketti (1992), a past editor of the *Stata Technical Bulletin*.

References

Becketti, S. 1992. sts1: Autocorrelation and partial autocorrelation graphs. *Stata Technical Bulletin* 5: 27–28. Reprinted in *Stata Technical Bulletin Reprints*, vol. 1, pp. 221–223.

Box, G. E. P., G. M. Jenkins, and G. C. Reinsel. 1994. *Time Series Analysis: Forecasting and Control*. 3d ed. Englewood Cliffs, NJ: Prentice–Hall.

Chatfield, C. 1996. *The Analysis of Time Series: An Introduction*. 5th ed. London: Chapman & Hall.

Hamilton, J. D. 1994. *Time Series Analysis*. Princeton: Princeton University Press.

Newton, H. J. 1988. *TIMESLAB: A Time Series Laboratory*. Pacific Grove, CA: Wadsworth & Brooks/Cole.

Also See

Complementary:	[R] **tsset**, [R] **wntestq**
Related:	[R] **pergram**
Background:	*Stata Graphics Manual*

Title

---
count — Count observations satisfying specified condition

Syntax

<u>cou</u>nt [if *exp*] [in *range*]

by ... : may be used with count; see [R] **by**.

Description

count counts the number of observations that satisfy the specified conditions. If no conditions are specified, count displays the number of observations in the data.

Remarks

count may strike you as an almost useless command, but it can be one of Stata's handiest.

▷ Example

How many times have you obtained a statistical result and then asked yourself how it was possible? You think a moment, and then mutter aloud "Wait a minute. Is income ever *negative* in this data?" or "Is sex ever equal to *3*?" count can quickly answer those questions:

```
. count
  641
. count if income<0
    0
. count if sex==3
    1
. by division: count if sex==3
-> division=        1        1
-> division=        2        0
-> division=        3        0
```

We have 641 observations. income is never negative. sex, however, takes on the value 3 once. When we decompose the count by division, we see that it takes on that odd value in division 1.

◁

Saved Results

count saves in r():

> Scalars
>   r(N)   number of observations

Also See

Related: [R] **tabulate**

Title

> **cox** — Estimate Cox proportional hazards model

Syntax

> cox *timevar* $\big[$*varlist*$\big]$ $\big[$*weight*$\big]$ $\big[$if *exp*$\big]$ $\big[$in *range*$\big]$ $\big[$, hr <u>d</u>ead(*failvar*)
>
> t0(*varname*) <u>str</u>ata(*varnames*) <u>r</u>obust <u>cl</u>uster(*varname*) <u>off</u>set(*varname*)
>
> tvc(*varlist*) texp(*exp*) basehc(*newvar*) <u>basec</u>hazard(*newvar*)
>
> <u>bases</u>urv(*newvar*) <u>mg</u>ale(*newvar*) esr(*newvar(s)*) <u>sch</u>oenfeld(*newvar(s)*)
>
> <u>scaleds</u>ch(*newvar(s)*) nocoef <u>noh</u>eader
>
> $\big[$ <u>bres</u>low | <u>ef</u>ron | exactm | exactp $\big]$ <u>l</u>evel(*#*) *maximize_options* $\big]$

by ... : may be used with cox; see [R] **by**.

fweights, iweights, and pweights are allowed; see [U] **14.1.6 weight**. No weights are allowed if you use the exactp or efron options for handling ties.

cox shares the features of all estimation commands; see [U] **23 Estimation and post-estimation commands**.

cox may be used with sw to perform stepwise estimation; see [R] **sw**.

Syntax for predict

> predict $\big[$*type*$\big]$ *newvarname* $\big[$if *exp*$\big]$ $\big[$in *range*$\big]$ $\big[$, { hr | xb | stdp } <u>nooff</u>set $\big]$

These statistics are available both in and out of sample; type predict ... if e(sample) ... if wanted only for the estimation sample. Note that a richer set of statistics is available from predict following stcox estimation; see [R] **st stcox**.

Description

cox estimates maximum-likelihood proportional hazards models. The regressors may be either fixed or time-varying (fixed within intervals); delayed entry (left truncation) is allowed, as are gaps and (right) censoring. The failure event may be unique or recurring.

We advise use of stcox over cox but only because we think using stcox is easier; the choice is yours. If you take our advice, see [R] **st stcox** and skip reading this entry.

cox and stcox produce the same results and, as a matter of fact, this is assured because stcox calls cox to produce results.

Options

hr reports the estimated coefficients transformed to hazard ratios, i.e., e^b rather than b. Standard errors and confidence intervals are similarly transformed. This option affects how results are displayed, not how they are estimated. hr may be specified at estimation or when replaying previously estimated results.

dead(*failvar*) specifies the name of a variable recording 0 if censored and nonzero—typically 1—if failure. If *failvar* contains missing, the observation is not used in estimation. If dead() is not specified, all observations are assumed to have failed at *timevar*.

t0(*varname*) specifies the variable that indicates when the observation became at risk. t0() can be used to handle left truncation, gaps, time-varying covariates, and recurring failures.

In the following data, each subject has only one record, but the third subject was observed starting at time 5, not 0:

id	t0	t	d	x1	x2
55	0	12	0	3	0
56	0	30	1	2	1
57	5	22	1	1	0
58	0	16	0	2	0

The interpretation of these data is that subject 55 had $x1 = 3$ and $x2 = 0$ over the interval $(0, 12]$ and then, at time 12, was lost due to censoring; subject 56 had $x1 = 2$ and $x2 = 1$ over the interval $(0, 30]$ and then, at time 30, failed; subject 57 had $x1 = 1$ and $x2 = 0$ over the interval $(5, 22]$ and then, at time 22, failed.

The id variable is listed merely for your information. You would estimate a Cox regression on these data by typing

```
. cox t x1 x2, dead(d) t0(t0)
```

In the following data, covariate x1 varies over time:

id	t0	t	d	x1	x2
91	0	15	0	2	1
91	15	22	0	1	1
91	22	31	1	3	1
92	0	11	0	3	0
92	11	52	0	.	0
92	52	120	1	2	0

The interpretation here is that subject 91 had $x1 = 2$ over the interval $(0, 15]$, $x1 = 1$ over the interval $(15, 22]$, and $x1 = 3$ over the interval $(22, 31]$; the value of x2 never varied from 1; and at time 31 a failure was observed. (If subject 91 were instead censored at time 31, the value of d in the subject's last observation would be 0 rather than 1.)

As before, id is listed merely for your information. The command for estimating a Cox model is the same as before,

```
. cox t x1 x2, dead(d) t0(t0)
```

although we would recommend

```
. cox t x1 x2, dead(d) t0(t0) robust cluster(id)
```

but that is a different issue altogether; see cluster() below.

Note that there are many ways the same history can be recorded. The history on subject 91 could just as well be recorded

id	t0	t	d	x1	x2
91	0	15	0	2	1
91	15	20	0	1	1
91	20	22	0	1	1
91	22	31	1	3	1

and it would make no difference.

Note the missing value of x1 in subject 92's second record. That causes no difficulty. Subject 92 will be included in risk pools between $(0, 11]$ and between $(52, 120]$.

In the following data, some subjects fail more than once (and have time-varying regressors):

id	t0	t	d	x1	x2
23	0	12	1	2	1
23	12	18	0	1	1
23	18	22	1	3	1
24	0	8	1	3	0
24	8	22	1	1	0
24	22	31	1	2	0

Subject 23 has x2 $= 1$ at all times. Between $(0, 12]$, x1 $= 2$ and a failure is observed at time 12. Between $(12, 18]$, x1 $= 1$ and no failure is observed. Between $(18, 22]$, x1 $= 3$ and another failure is observed at time 22.

Again, the estimation command is the same

    . cox t x1 x2, dead(d) t0(t0)

and again, we would recommend

    . cox t x1 x2, dead(d) t0(t0) robust cluster(id)

strata(*varnames*) specifies up to 5 strata variables. Observations with equal values of the strata variables are assumed to be in the same stratum. Stratified estimates (equal coefficients across strata but baseline hazard unique to each stratum) are then estimated.

robust specifies that the robust method of calculating the variance–covariance matrix (Lin and Wei 1989) is to be used instead of the conventional inverse-matrix-of-second-derivatives method.

cluster(*varname*) implies robust and specifies a variable on which clustering is to be based. By default, each observation in the data is assumed to represent a cluster. Consider the following data:

t0	t	d	x1	x2
0	15	0	2	1
15	22	0	1	1
22	31	1	3	1

Does this represent three subjects or just one? Perhaps three subjects were observed: one over $(0, 15]$, another over $(15, 22]$, and a third over $(22, 31]$. In that case, the survival times should be independent and, if you want robust standard errors, you specify the robust option but not the cluster() option.

On the other hand, if the data are

id	t0	t	d	x1	x2
91	0	15	0	2	1
91	15	22	0	1	1
91	22	31	1	3	1

that is, if the data represent the same subject, then these records do not amount to independent observations and, if you wanted robust standard errors, you would specify robust and cluster(id), although you could omit the robust because it is implied by cluster().

offset(*varname*) specifies that *varname* is to be included in the model with coefficient constrained to be 1.

tvc(*varlist*) is used to specify those variables that vary continuously with respect to time, i.e., time-varying covariates. This is a convenience option used to speed up calculations and to avoid the need to have to stsplit the data over many failure times.

texp(*exp*) is used in conjunction with tvc(*varlist*) to specify which function of analysis time should be multiplied by the time-varying covariates. For example, specifying texp(ln(*timevar*)) would cause the time-varying covariates to be multiplied by the logarithm of analysis time. If tvc(*varlist*) is used without texp(*exp*), then it is understood that you mean texp(*timevar*) and thus the time-varying covariates are multiplied by the analysis time.

Please see [R] **st stcox** for more information on using time-varying covariates.

basehc(*newvar*) adds *newvar* to the data containing the estimated baseline hazard contributions (Kalbfleisch & Prentice 1980, 85). If strata() is also specified, baseline estimates for each stratum are provided.

basechazard(*newvar*) adds *newvar* to the data containing the estimated cumulative baseline hazard. If strata() is also specified, cumulative baseline estimates for each stratum are provided.

basesurv(*newvar*) adds *newvar* to the data containing the estimated baseline survival function. Note that, in the null model, this is equivalent to the Kaplan–Meier product-limit estimate. If strata() is also specified, baseline estimates for each stratum are provided.

mgale(*newvar*) adds *newvar* containing the partial martingale residuals, which are fully described in [R] **st stcox** under *Methods and Formulas*. If each observation in your data represents a different subject, then the partial martingale residuals are the martingale residuals.

If you have repeated observations on subjects, the value mgale() saves in each observation is the observation's contribution to the martingale residual and these partial residuals can be summed within subject to obtain the subject's martingale residual. Say you specify mgale(pmr) and variable patid in your data records the subject id. Then egen mr = sum(pmr), by(patid) would create each subject's martingale residual.

esr(*newvar(s)*) adds *newvar(s)* containing the partial efficient score residuals, which are fully described in [R] **st stcox** under *Methods and Formulas*. If each observation in your data represents a different subject, the partial efficient score residuals are the efficient score residuals.

If you have repeated observations on subjects, the values esr() stores in each observation are the observation's contribution to the score residuals and these partial residuals can be summed within subject to obtain the subject's efficient score residuals. This could be accomplished as noted under mgale() above.

One efficient score residual variable is created for each regressor in the model; the first new variable corresponds to the first regressor, the second to the second, and so on.

schoenfeld(*newvar(s)*) adds *newvar(s)* containing the Schoenfeld residuals, which are fully described in [R] **st stcox** under *Methods and Formulas*. Schoenfeld residuals are calculated and reported only at failure times.

One Schoenfeld residual variable is created for each regressor in the model; the first new variable corresponds to the first regressor, the second to the second, and so on.

scaledsch(*newvar(s)*) adds *newvar(s)* containing the scaled Schoenfeld residuals, which are fully described in [R] **st stcox** under *Methods and Formulas*. Scaled Schoenfeld residuals are calculated and reported only at failure times.

One scaled Schoenfeld residual variable is created for each regressor in the model; the first new variable corresponds to the first regressor, the second to the second, and so on.

NOTE: The easiest way to specify the preceding three options is (for example) esr(*stub**), where *stub* is a (short) name of your choosing. Stata then creates variables *stub*1, *stub*2, etc. Alternatively, you may specify each variable name explicitly, in which case there must be as many (and no more) variables specified in esr() as regressors in the model.

One caution is necessary for the preceding three options. `cox` will drop variables from the model due to collinearity. This is a desirable feature. A side-effect is that the score residual variable, Schoenfeld residual variable, and scaled Schoenfeld residual variable may not align with the regressors in the way you expect. Say you estimate a model by typing

    . cox time x1 x2 x3, dead(fail) esr(r1 r2 r3)

Usually, `r1` will contain the residual associated with `x1`, `r2` the residual associated with `x2`, and so on.

Now assume that `x2` is dropped due to collinearity. In that case, `r1` will correspond to `x1`, `r2` to `x3`, and `r3` will contain 0. This happens because, after omitting the collinear variables, there are only two variables in the model: `x1` and `x3`.

`nocoef` is for use by programmers. It prevents `cox` from displaying results but still allows it to display the iteration log.

`noheader` is for use by programmers. It causes `cox` to display the coefficient table only; the table above the coefficients reporting chi-squared tests and the like is suppressed. The code for `stcox`, for instance, uses this option, since `stcox` wants to substitute its own (more informative) header.

`breslow`, `efron`, `exactm`, and `exactp` each specify a method for handling tied failure times in the calculation of the model (and residuals). `breslow` is the default. Each method is fully described in [R] **st stcox** under *Methods and Formulas*. Note that `efron` and the exact methods require substantially more computer time than the default `breslow` option. `exactm` and `exactp` may not be specified with `robust` or `cluster()`, or with `tvc()`.

`level(#)` specifies the confidence level, in percent, for confidence intervals. The default is `level(95)` or as set by `set level`; see [U] **23.5 Specifying the width of confidence intervals**.

maximize_options control the maximization process; see [R] **maximize**. You should never have to specify them.

Options for predict

`hr`, the default, calculates the relative hazard (hazard ratio); that is, the exponentiated linear prediction.

`xb` calculates the linear prediction.

`stdp` calculates the standard error of the linear prediction.

`nooffset` is relevant only if you specified `offset()` with `cox`. It modifies the calculations made by `predict` so that they ignore the offset variable; the linear prediction is treated as $\mathbf{X}_j\mathbf{b}$ rather than $\mathbf{X}_j\mathbf{b} + \text{offset}_j$.

Remarks

`cox` is related to the `stcox` command. In fact, `stcox` constructs a `cox` command (based on what the user types) and runs it, so most everything said about `stcox` in [R] **st stcox** is relevant here. The syntaxes of `cox` and `stcox` are nearly the same. In [R] **st stcox**, when you see an example such as

    . stcox drug age

the equivalent `cox` command might be

    . cox *timevar* drug age

or

    . cox *timevar* drug age, dead(*failvar*)

or

> . cox *timevar* drug age, dead(*failvar*) t0(*t0var*)

depending on the context of stcox.

stcox fills in the identities of the time of censoring or failure variable (*timevar*), the outcome variable (*failvar*), and the entry-time variable (*t0var*) for you. Users of stcox first stset their data and that is how stcox knows what to fill in.

The other difference between these commands concerns an implied cluster() option when you specify robust. With cox, it is your responsibility to specify clustering if you want it. With stcox, specifying robust implies cluster() if a subject-id variable has been set.

Saved Results

cox saves in e():

Scalars
e(N)	number of observations	e(ll_0)	log likelihood, constant-only model
e(df_m)	model degrees of freedom	e(N_clust)	number of clusters
e(r2_p)	pseudo R-squared	e(chi2)	χ^2
e(ll)	log likelihood		

Macros
e(cmd)	cox	e(method)	requested estimation method
e(depvar)	name of dependent variable	e(ties)	method used for handling ties
e(wtype)	weight type	e(vcetype)	covariance estimation method
e(wexp)	weight expression	e(chi2type)	Wald or LR; type of model χ^2 test
e(clustvar)	name of cluster variable	e(offset)	offset
e(t0)	name of variable marking entry time	e(predict)	program used to implement predict
e(texp)	function of analysis time used with tvc()		

Matrices
e(b)	coefficient vector	e(V)	variance–covariance matrix of the estimators

Functions
e(sample)	marks estimation sample

Methods and Formulas

See [R] **st stcox**.

References

See the references in [R] **st stcox**.

Also See

Complementary:	[R] **adjust**, [R] **lincom**, [R] **linktest**, [R] **lrtest**, [R] **mfx**, [R] **predict**, [R] **sw**, [R] **test**, [R] **testnl**, [R] **vce**
Related:	[R] **st stcox**; [R] **ltable**, [R] **st streg**, [R] **weibull**
Background:	[U] **16.5 Accessing coefficients and standard errors**, [U] **23 Estimation and post-estimation commands**, [U] **23.11 Obtaining robust variance estimates**, [R] **maximize**

Title

cross — Form every pairwise combination of two datasets

Syntax

cross using *filename*

Description

cross forms every pairwise combination of the data in memory with the data in *filename*. If *filename* is specified without a suffix, .dta is assumed.

Remarks

This is a rarely used command; also see [R] **joinby**, [R] **merge**, and [R] **append**.

Crossing refers to the operation of merging two datasets in every way possible. That is, the first observation of the data in memory is merged with every observation of *filename*, followed by the second, and so on. Thus, the result will have $N_1 N_2$ observations, where N_1 and N_2 are the number of observations in memory and in *filename*, respectively.

Typically, the datasets will have no common variables. If they do, such variables will take on only the values of the data in memory.

▷ Example

You wish to form a dataset containing all combinations of three age categories and two sexes to serve as a stub. The three age categories are 20, 30, and 40. The two sexes are male and female:

```
. input str6 sex
            sex
  1. male
  2. female
  3. end
. save sex
file sex.dta saved
. drop _all
. input agecat
        agecat
  1. 20
  2. 30
  3. 40
  4. end
. cross using sex
. list
```

	agecat	sex
1.	20	male
2.	30	male
3.	40	male
4.	20	female
5.	30	female
6.	40	female

◁

Methods and Formulas

cross is implemented as an ado-file.

Also See

Complementary: [R] **save**

Related: [R] **append**, [R] **fillin**, [R] **joinby**, [R] **merge**

Title

---

ct — Count-time data

Description

The term ct refers to count-time data and the commands—all of which begin with the letters ct—for analyzing them. If you have data on populations, whether people or generators, with observations recording the number of units under test at time t (subjects alive) and the number of subjects that failed or were lost due to censoring, you have what we call count-time data.

If, on the other hand, you have data on individual subjects with observations recording that this subject came under observation at time t_0 and then, later, at t_1, a failure or censoring was observed, you have what we call survival-time data. If you have survival-time data, you are in the wrong place; see [R] **st**.

Do not confuse count-time data with counting-process data which can be analyzed using the st commands; see [R] **st**.

There are two ct commands:

ctset	[R] **ct ctset**	Declare data to be count-time data
cttost	[R] **ct cttost**	Convert count-time data to survival-time data

The key is the cttost command. Once you have converted your count-time data to survival-time data, you can use the st commands to analyze the data. The entire process is

1. ctset your data so that Stata knows it is count-time data; see [R] **ct ctset**.

2. Type cttost to convert your data to survival-time data. You can see [R] **ct cttost** but it is not necessary; you just have to type cttost.

3. Use the st commands; see [R] **st**.

Also See

Complementary: [R] **ct ctset**, [R] **ct cttost**, [R] **st**

336

Title

> **ct ctset** — Declare data to be count-time data

Syntax

ctset *timevar nfailvar* $\big[$*ncensvar* $\big[$*nentvar*$\big]\big]$ $\big[$, by(*varlist*) <u>nos</u>how $\big]$

ctset, $\big\{$ <u>s</u>how | <u>nos</u>how $\big\}$

ctset, clear

$\big\{$ ctset | ct $\big\}$

Description

ct refers to count-time data and is described in [R] **ct** and below. Do not confuse count-time data with counting-process data, which can be analyzed using the st commands; see [R] **st**.

In the first syntax, **ctset** declares the data in memory to be ct data, informing Stata of the key variables. When you **ctset** your data, **ctset** also runs various checks to ensure that what you have declared makes sense.

In the second syntax, **ctset** changes the value of **show/noshow**. In **show** mode—the default—the other ct commands display the identities of the key ct variables before their normal output. If you **ctset, noshow**, they will not do this. If you do that and then wish to restore their default behavior, type **ctset, show**.

In the third syntax, **ctset, clear** causes Stata to forget the ct markers; it makes the data no longer ct data to Stata. The dataset itself remains unchanged. It is not necessary to **ctset, clear** before doing another **ctset**. **ctset, clear** is used mostly by programmers.

In the fourth syntax, **ctset**—which can be abbreviated **ct** in this case—displays the identities of the key ct variables *and* it reruns the checks on your data. Thus, **ct** is useful to remind you of what you have **ctset** (especially if you have **ctset, noshow**) and to reverify your data if you make changes to it.

In the above syntax diagrams, *timevar* refers to the time of failure, censoring, or entry. It should contain times ≥ 0.

nfailvar records the number failing at time *timevar*.

The optional *ncensvar* records the number censored at time *timevar*.

The optional *nentvar* records the number entering at time *timevar*.

Stata sequences events at the same time as

at *timevar*	*nfailvar* failures occurred,
then at *timevar* $+ 0$	*ncensvar* censorings occurred,
finally at *timevar* $+ 0 + 0$	*nentvar* subjects entered the data.

Options

by(*varlist*) indicates that counts are provided by group. For instance, consider data containing records such as

t	fail	cens	sex	agecat
5	10	2	0	1
5	6	1	1	1
5	12	0	0	2

These data indicate that, in the category sex = 0 and agecat = 1, 10 failed and 2 were censored at time 5; for sex = 1, 1 was censored and 6 failed; and so on.

The above data would be declared

```
. ctset t fail cens, by(sex agecat)
```

The order of the records is not important.

That there be a record at every time for every group is not important.

That there be only a single record for a time and group is not important.

All that is important is that the data contain the full table of events.

noshow and show specify whether the identities of the key ct variables be displayed at the start of every ct command. Some users find the report reassuring; others find it repetitive. In any case, you can set and unset show, and you can always type ct to see the summary.

clear makes Stata forget that this is ct data.

Remarks

About all you can do with ct data in Stata is convert it to survival-time (st) data, which is enough. All survival-analysis commands can be run on st data. To analyze count-time data with Stata,

```
. ctset ...
. cttost
. ( now use any of the st commands )
```

Example 1: Simple ct data

Generators are run until they fail. Here is your data:

```
. list
      failtime      fail
  1.         22         1
  2.         30         1
  3.         40         2
  4.         52         1
  5.         54         4
  6.         55         2
  7.         85         7
  8.         97         1
  9.        100         3
 10.        122         2
 11.        140         1
```

For instance, at time 54, 4 generators failed. The `ctset` for these data is

```
. ctset failtime fail
          time:  failtime
      no. fail:  fail
      no. lost:  --              (meaning 0 lost)
     no. enter:  --              (meaning all enter at time 0)
```

It is not important that there be only one observation per failure time. For instance, according to our data, at time 85 there were 7 failures. We could remove that observation and substitute two in its place—one stating that at time 85 there were 5 failures and another that at time 85 there were 2 more failures. `ctset` would interpret that data just as it did the previous data.

In more realistic examples, the generators might differ from one another. For instance, the following data shows the number failing with old-style (`bearings` = 0) and new-style (`bearings` = 1) bearings:

```
. list
        bearings   failtime     fail
  1.           0         22        1
  2.           0         40        2
  3.           0         54        1
  4.           0         84        2
  5.           0         97        2
  6.           0        100        1
  7.           1         30        1
  8.           1         52        1
  9.           1         55        1
 10.           1        100        3
 11.           1        122        2
 12.           1        140        1
```

That the data are sorted on bearings is not important. The `ctset` command for these data is

```
. ctset failtime fail, by(bearings)
          time:  failtime
      no. fail:  fail
      no. lost:  --              (meaning 0 lost)
     no. enter:  --              (meaning all enter at time 0)
            by:  bearings
```

Example 2: ct data with censoring

In real data, not all units fail in the time alloted. Say the generator experiment was stopped after 150 days. The data might be

```
. list
        bearings   failtime     fail   censored
  1.           0         22        1          0
  2.           0         40        2          0
  3.           0         54        1          0
  4.           0         84        2          0
  5.           1         97        2          0
  6.           0        100        1          0
  7.           0        150        0          2
  8.           1         30        1          0
  9.           1         52        1          0
 10.           1         55        1          0
 11.           1        122        2          0
 12.           1        140        1          0
 13.           1        150        0          3
```

The `ctset` for this data is

```
. ctset failtime fail censored, by(bearings)
        time:  failtime
    no. fail:  fail
    no. lost:  censored
   no. enter:  --                      (meaning all enter at time 0)
          by:  bearings
```

In some other data, observations might also be censored along the way; that is, the value of censored would not be 0 before time 150. For instance, a record might read

bearings	failtime	fail	censored
0	84	2	1

The would mean that at time 84, 2 failed and 1 was lost due to censoring. The failure and censoring occurred at the same time and, when you analyze these data, Stata will assume that the censored observation could have failed; that is, that the censoring occurred after the two failures.

Example 3: ct data with delayed entry

Data on survival time of patients with a particular kind of cancer are collected. Time is measured as time since diagnosis. After data collection started, the sample was enriched with some patients from hospital records who had been previously diagnosed. Some of the data are

time	die	cens	ent	other variables
0	0	0	50	
1	0	0	5	. . .
⋮				
30	0	0	3	. . .
31	0	1	2	. . .
32	1	0	1	. . .
⋮				
100	1	1	0	. . .
⋮				

50 patients entered at time 0 (time of diagnosis); 5 patients entered 1 day after diagnosis; 3, 2, and 1 entered 30, 31, and 32 days after diagnosis; and, on the 32nd day, one of the previously entering patients died.

If the other variables are named `sex` and `agecat`, the `ctset` command for this data is

```
. ctset time die cens ent, by(sex agecat)
        time:  time
    no. fail:  die
    no. lost:  cens
   no. enter:  ent
          by:  sex agecat
```

The count-time format is an inferior way to record data like these—data in which every subject does not enter at time 0—because some information is already lost. When did the patient who died on the 32nd day enter? There is no way of telling.

For traditional survival-analysis calculations, it does not matter. More modern methods of estimating standard errors, however, seek to account for which patient is which, and these data will not support the use of such methods.

This issue concerns the robust estimates of variance and the `robust` options on some of the st analysis commands. After converting the data, you must not use the `robust` option even if an st command allows it because the identities of the subjects—tying together when a subject starts and ceases to be at risk—are assigned randomly by `cttost` when you convert your ct to st data. When did the patient who died on the 32nd day enter? For conventional calculations, it does not matter, and `cttost` chooses a time randomly from the available entry times.

Data errors flagged by ctset

`ctset` requires only two things of your data: that the counts all be positive or zero and, if you specify an entry variable, that the entering and exiting (failure + censored) balance.

If all subjects enter at time 0, we recommend you do not specify a number-that-enter variable. `ctset` can determine for itself the number who enter at time 0 by summing the failures and censorings.

Also See

Complementary:	[R] **ct cttost**, [R] **st**
Background:	[R] **ct**

Title

> **ct cttost** — Convert count-time data to survival-time data

Syntax

cttost $\left[\,,\ \text{t0}(t0var)\ \text{w}(wvar)\ \text{clear}\ \underline{\text{nopreserve}}\,\right]$

cttost is for use with count-time data; see [R] **ct**. You must have **ctset** your data before using this command.

Description

cttost converts count-time data to their survival-time format. This is the way count-time data are analyzed with Stata. Do not confuse count-time data with counting-process data, which can be analyzed with the st commands; see [R] **ct ctset** for a definition and examples of count data.

Options

t0(t0var) specifies the name of the new variable to create that records entry time should such a variable be necessary. (For most ct data, no entry-time variable is necessary because everyone enters at time 0.)

Even if an entry-time variable is necessary, you need not specify this option. cttost will, by default, choose t0, time0, or etime according to which name does not already exist in the data.

w(wvar) specifies the name of the new variable to be created that records the frequency weights for the new pseudo-observations. Count-time data are actually converted to frequency-weighted st data and a variable is needed to record the weights. This sounds more complicated than it is. Understand that cttost needs a new variable name, which will become a permanent part of the st data.

If you do not specify w(), cttost will, by default, choose w, pop, weight, or wgt according to which name does not already exist in the data.

clear specifies that it is okay to proceed with the transformation even through the current dataset has not been saved on disk.

nopreserve speeds the transformation by not saving the original data, from which it can be restored should things go wrong or should the user press *Break*. nopreserve is intended for use by programmers using cttost as a subroutine. Programmers can specify this option if they have already preserved the original data. nopreserve changes nothing about the transformation that is made.

Remarks

There is nothing to converting ct to st data. We have some count-time data,

342

```
. ct
           time:  time
       no. fail:  ndead
       no. lost:  ncens
      no. enter:  --                    (meaning all enter at time 0)
             by:  agecat treat
. list in 1/5
        agecat      treat       time      ndead      ncens
  1.         2          1        464          4          0
  2.         3          0        268          3          1
  3.         2          0        638          2          0
  4.         1          0        803          1          4
  5.         1          0        431          2          0
```

and, to convert it, we type `cttost`:

```
. cttost
(data is now st)
      failure event:  ndead ~= 0 & ndead ~= .
 obs. time interval:  (0, time]
 exit on or before:  failure
             weight:  [fweight=w]
```

```
         33  total obs.
          0  exclusions

         33  physical obs. remaining, equal to
         82  weighted obs., representing
         39  failures in single record/single failure data
      48726  total analysis time at risk, at risk from t =          0
                                earliest observed entry t =          0
                                 last observed exit t =           1227
```

Now that it is converted, we can use any of the st commands:

```
. sts test treat, logrank
         failure _d:  ndead
    analysis time _t:  time
             weight:  [fweight=w]
```

Log-rank test for equality of survivor functions

treat	Events observed	Events expected
0	22	17.05
1	17	21.95
Total	39	39.00

```
            chi2(1) =       2.73
            Pr>chi2 =     0.0986
```

Also See

Complementary: [R] **ct ctset**, [R] **st**

Background: [R] **ct**

Title

cumsp — Cumulative spectral distribution

Syntax

cumsp *varname* [if *exp*] [in *range*] [, generate(*newvarname*) *graph_options*]

cumsp is for use with time-series data; see [R] **tsset**. You must tsset your data before using cumsp. In addition, the time series must be dense (nonmissing and no gaps in the time variable) in the sample specified.

varname may contain time-series operators; see [U] **14.4.3 Time-series varlists**.

Description

cumsp plots the cumulative sample spectral distribution function evaluated at the natural frequencies for a (dense) time series.

Options

gen(*newvarname*) specifies a new variable to contain the log periodogram values.

graph_options are the usual graph options for graph, twoway; see [G] **graph options**.

Remarks

▷ Example

Here, we use the international airline passengers dataset (Box, Jenkins, and Reinsel 1994, Series G). This dataset has 144 observations on the monthly number of international airline passengers from 1949 through 1960. In the cumulative sample spectral distribution function for these data, we also request a vertical line at frequency 1/12. Since the data are monthly, there will be a pronounced jump in the cumulative sample spectral distribution plot at the 1/12 value if there is an annual cycle in the data.

. cumsp air, xline(.083333333)

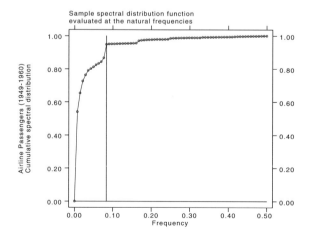

The cumulative sample spectral distribution function clearly illustrates the annual cycle.

◁

Methods and Formulas

A time series of interest is decomposed into a unique set of sinusoids of various frequencies and amplitudes.

A plot of the sinusoidal amplitudes versus the frequencies for the sinusoidal decomposition of a time series gives us the spectral density of the time series. If we calculate the sinusoidal amplitudes for a discrete set of "natural" frequencies $(1/n, 2/n, \ldots, q/n)$, then we obtain the periodogram.

Let $x(1), \ldots, x(n)$ be a time series and let $\omega_k = (k-1)/n$ denote the natural frequencies for $k = 1, \ldots, [n/2] + 1$ where $[\,]$ indicates the greatest integer function. Define

$$C_k^2 = \frac{1}{n^2} \left| \sum_{t=1}^{n} x(t) e^{2\pi i (t-1) \omega_k} \right|^2$$

A plot of nC_k^2 versus ω_k is then called the periodogram.

The sample spectral density may then be defined as $\widehat{f}(\omega_k) = nC_k^2$.

If we let $\widehat{f}(\omega_1), \ldots, \widehat{f}(\omega_Q)$ be the sample spectral density function of the time series evaluated at the frequencies $\omega_j = (j-1)/Q$ for $j = 1, \ldots, Q$ and we let $q = [Q/2] + 1$, then

$$\widehat{F}(\omega_k) = \frac{\displaystyle\sum_{i=1}^{k} \widehat{f}(\omega_j)}{\displaystyle\sum_{i=1}^{q} \widehat{f}(\omega_j)}$$

is the sample spectral distribution function of the time series.

References

Box, G. E. P., G. M. Jenkins, and G. C. Reinsel. 1994. *Time Series Analysis: Forecasting and Control*. 3d ed. Englewood Cliffs, NJ: Prentice–Hall.

Newton, H. J. 1988. *TIMESLAB: A Time Series Laboratory*. Pacific Grove, CA: Wadsworth & Brooks/Cole.

Also See

Complementary:	[R] **tsset**
Related:	[R] **corrgram**, [R] **pergram**
Background:	*Stata Graphics Manual*

Title

cumul — Cumulative distribution

Syntax

cumul *varname* [*weight*] [if *exp*] [in *range*], generate(*newvar*) [freq]

by ... : may be used with cumul; see [R] by.

fweights and aweights are allowed; see [U] **14.1.6 weight**.

Description

cumul creates *newvar* defined as the empirical cumulative distribution function (e.c.d.f.) of *varname*.

Options

generate(*newvar*) is not optional. It specifies the name of the new variable to be created.

freq specifies the cumulative be in frequency units; otherwise it is normalized so that *newvar* is 1 for the largest value of *varname*.

Remarks

▷ Example

cumul is most often used with **graph** to graph the empirical cumulative distribution. For instance, you have data on the median family income of 957 U.S. cities:

```
. cumul faminc, gen(cum)
. gr cum faminc, c(1) s(i) border ylab(0(.25)1) xlab yline(.25,.5,.75)
        xline(20000,30000,40000) t2("1980 Census, 957 U.S. Cities")
        t1(Cumulative of median family income)
```

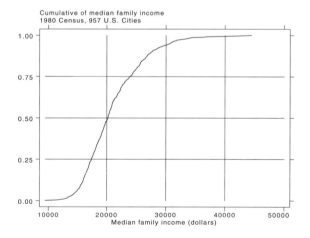

It would have been enough to type graph cum faminc, c(l) s(i), but we wanted to make the graph look better; see [G] **graph options**.

If you had wanted a weighted cumulative, you would have typed cumul faminc [w=pop] at the first step.

◁

▷ Example

To graph two (or more) cumulatives on the same graph, use cumul and stack; see [R] **stack**. For instance, you have data on the average January and July temperature of 956 U.S. cities:

```
. cumul tempjan, gen(cjan)
. cumul tempjuly, gen(cjuly)
. stack  cjan tempjan  cjuly tempjuly, into(c temp) wide clear
. gr cjan cjuly temp, c(ll) s(ii) sort ylab(0(.25)1) border
                xlab(0(20)100) xline(20(20)80)
                yline(.25,.5,.75)
                t1("Cumulatives: Average January and July Temperatures")
                t2("956 U.S. Cities")
```

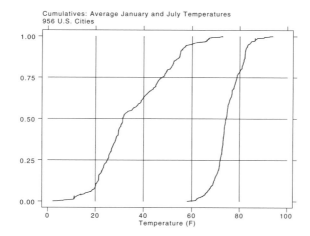

As before, it would have been enough to type graph cjan cjuly temp, c(ll) s(ii) sort. See [R] **stack** for an explanation of how this works.

◁

❑ Technical Note

According to Beniger and Robyn (1978), Fourier (1821) published the first graph of a cumulative frequency distribution, which was later given the name "ogive" by Galton (1875).

❑

Methods and Formulas

cumul is implemented as an ado-file.

References

Beniger, J. R. and D. L. Robyn. 1978. Quantitative graphics in statistics: a brief history. *The American Statistician* 32: 1–11.

Clayton, D. and M. Hills. 1999. gr37: Cumulative distribution function plots. *Stata Technical Bulletin* 49: 10–12. Reprinted in *Stata Technical Bulletin Reprints*, vol. 9, pp. 96–98.

Cox, N. J. 1999. gr41: Distribution function plots. *Stata Technical Bulletin* 51: 12–16. Reprinted in *Stata Technical Bulletin Reprints*, vol. 9, pp. 108–112.

Fourier, J. B. J. 1821. Notions générales, sur la population. *Recherches Statistiques sur la Ville de Paris et le Département de la Seine* 1: 1–70.

Galton, F. 1875. Statistics by intercomparison, with remarks on the law of frequency of error. *Philosophical Magazine* 49: 33–46.

Wilk, M. B. and R. Gnanadesikan. 1968. Probability plotting methods for the analysis of data. *Biometrika* 55: 1–17.

Also See

Complementary:	[R] **stack**
Related:	[R] **diagplots**, [R] **kdensity**
Background:	*Stata Graphics Manual*

Title

cusum — Cusum plots and tests for binary variables

Syntax

cusum *yvar xvar* [if *exp*] [in *range*] [, yfit(*fitvar*) nograph nocalc

generate(*newvar*) *graph_options*]

Description

cusum graphs the cumulative sum (cusum) of a binary (0/1) variable *yvar* against a (usually) continuous variable *xvar*.

Options

yfit(*fitvar*) calculates a cusum against *fitvar*, that is, the running sums of the "residuals" *fitvar* minus *yvar*. Typically, *fitvar* is the predicted probability of a positive outcome obtained from a logistic regression analysis.

nograph suppresses the plot.

nocalc suppresses calculation of the cusum test statistics.

generate(*newvar*) saves the cusum in *newvar*.

graph_options are any of the options allowed with graph, twoway; see [G] **graph options**.

Remarks

The cusum is the running sum of the proportion of ones in the sample, a constant number, minus *yvar*:

$$ c_j = \sum_{k=1}^{j} f - yvar_{(k)}, \qquad 1 \le j \le N $$

where $f = (\sum yvar)/N$ and $yvar_{(k)}$ refers to the corresponding value of *yvar* when *xvar* is placed in ascending order: $xvar_{(k+1)} \ge xvar_{(k)}$. Tied values of *xvar* are broken at random. If you want them broken the same way in two runs, you must set the random number seed to the same value before giving the cusum command; see [R] **generate**.

A U-shaped or inverted U-shaped cusum indicates respectively a negative or a positive trend of *yvar* with *xvar*. A sinusoidal shape is evidence of a nonmonotonic (for example, quadratic) trend. cusum displays the maximum absolute cusum for monotonic and nonmonotonic trends of *yvar* on *xvar*. These are nonparametric tests of departure from randomness of *yvar* with respect to *xvar*. Approximate values for the tests are given.

▷ Example

For the automobile dataset, `auto.dta`, we wish to investigate the relationship between `foreign` (0 = domestic, 1 = foreign) and car weight as follows:

```
. cusum foreign weight
```

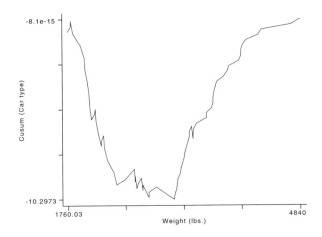

Variable	Obs	Pr(1)	CusumL	zL	Pr>zL	CusumQ	zQ	Pr>zQ
foreign	74	0.2973	10.30	3.963	0.000	3.32	0.469	0.320

The resulting plot, which is U-shaped, suggests a negative monotonic relationship. The trend is confirmed by a highly significant linear cusum statistic, labeled CusumL in the output above.

Some 29.73% of the cars are foreign (coded 1). The proportion of foreign cars diminishes with increasing weight. Stated crudely, the domestic cars are heavier than the foreign ones. We could have discovered that by typing `table foreign, stats(mean weight)`, but such an approach does not give the full picture of the relationship. The quadratic cusum (CusumQ) is not significant, so we do not suspect any tendency for the very heavy cars to be foreign rather than domestic. A slightly enhanced version of the plot shows the preponderance of domestic (coded 0) cars at the heavy end of the weight axis:

```
. label drop origin
. cusum foreign weight, xlabel ylabel connect(.) symbol([foreign])
```

(Graph on next page)

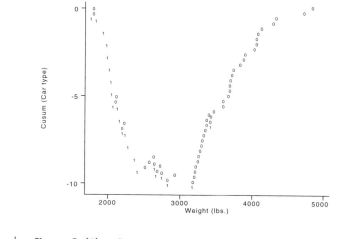

Variable	Obs	Pr(1)	CusumL	zL	Pr>zL	CusumQ	zQ	Pr>zQ
foreign	74	0.2973	10.30	3.963	0.000	2.92	0.064	0.475

The example is, of course, artificial as we would not really try to model the probability of a car being foreign given its weight!

◁

Saved Results

cusum saves in r():

Scalars

r(N)	number of observations	r(P_zl)	*p*-value for test (linear)
r(prop1)	proportion of positive outcomes	r(cusumq)	quadratic cusum
r(cusuml)	cusum	r(zq)	test (quadratic)
r(zl)	test (linear)	r(P_zq)	*p*-value for test (quadratic)

Methods and Formulas

cusum is implemented as an ado-file.

Acknowledgment

cusum was written by Patrick Royston of the MRC Clinical Trials Unit, London.

References

Royston, P. 1992. The use of cusums and other techniques in modelling continuous covariates in logistic regression. *Statistics in Medicine* 11: 1115–1129.

——. 1993. sqv7: Cusum plots and tests for binary variables. *Stata Technical Bulletin* 12: 16–17. Reprinted in *Stata Technical Bulletin Reprints*, vol. 2, pp. 175–177.

Also See

Complementary:	[R] **logistic**, [R] **logit**, [R] **probit**
Background:	*Stata Graphics Manual*

Title

data types — Quick reference for data types

Description

This entry provides a quick reference for data types allowed by Stata. See [U] **15 Data** for details.

Remarks

Storage Type	Minimum	Maximum	Closest to 0 without being 0	missing	bytes
byte	-127	126	± 1	127	1
int	$-32{,}767$	$32{,}766$	± 1	$32{,}767$	2
long	$-2{,}147{,}483{,}647$	$2{,}147{,}483{,}646$	± 1	$2{,}147{,}483{,}647$	4
float	-10^{36}	10^{36}	$\pm 10^{-36}$	2^{128}	4
double	-10^{308}	10^{308}	$\pm 10^{-323}$	2^{1023}	8

Precision for `float` is 6×10^{-8}

Precision for `double` is 2×10^{-16}

String Storage Type	Maximum Length	Bytes
str1	1	1
str2	2	2
...	.	.
...	.	.
...	.	.
str80	80	80

Also See

Complementary: [R] **compress**, [R] **destring**, [R] **encode**, [R] **format**, [R] **recast**

Background: [U] **15.2.2 Numeric storage types**,
[U] **15.4.4 String storage types**,
[U] **15.5 Formats: controlling how data are displayed**,
[U] **16.10 Precision and problems therein**

Title

> **describe** — Describe contents of data in memory or on disk

Syntax

<u>d</u>escribe [*varlist*] [, <u>s</u>hort <u>d</u>etail <u>f</u>ullnames <u>n</u>umbers]

<u>d</u>escribe using *filename* [, <u>s</u>hort <u>d</u>etail]

ds [*varlist*]

lookfor *string* [*string* [...]]

Description

describe produces a summary of the contents of the dataset in memory or the data stored in a Stata-format dataset.

ds lists variable names in a compact format.

lookfor helps in finding variables by searching for *string* among all variable names and labels.

Options

short suppresses the specific information for each variable. Only the general information (number of observations, number of variables, size, and sort order) is displayed.

detail includes information on the width of a single observation; the maximum number of observations holding the number of variables constant; the maximum number of variables holding the number of observations constant; the maximum width for a single observation; and the maximum size of the dataset.

fullnames specifies that **describe** is to display the full name of the variables. The default is to present an abbreviation when the variable name is longer than 15 characters. **describe using** always shows the full names of the variables, so **fullnames** may not be specified with **describe using**.

numbers specifies that **describe** is to present the variable number with the variable name. If **numbers** is specified, variable names are abbreviated when the name is longer than 8 characters. Options **numbers** and **fullnames** may not be specified together. **numbers** may not be specified with **describe using**.

Remarks

describe

If `describe` is typed without any operands, then the contents of the dataset currently in memory are described.

▷ Example

The basic description includes some general information on the number of variables and observations along with a description of every variable in the dataset:

```
. describe, numbers
Contains data from states.dta
  obs:            50                          State data
  vars:            5                          6 Jul 2000 16:39
  size:        1,300 (99.7% of memory free)   (_dta has notes)

          variable  storage  display   value
            name     type    format    label    variable label

        1. state     str8     %9s
        2. region    int      %8.0g     reg      Census Region
        3. median~e  float    %9.0g              Median Age
        4. marria~e  long     %12.0g             Marriages per 100,000
        5. divorc~e  long     %12.0g             Divorces per 100,000

Sorted by:  region
```

In this example, the dataset in memory came from the file `states.dta` and contains 50 observations on 5 variables. This dataset occupies only a small portion of the available memory, leaving 99.7% of memory free. The dataset is labeled "State data" and was last modified on July 6, 2000 at 16:39 (4:39 p.m.). The "_dta has notes" indicates that a note is attached to the dataset; see [U] **15.7 Notes attached to data**.

The first variable is named `state`. It is stored as a `str8` and has a display format of `%9s`.

The next variable, `region`, is stored as an `int` and has a display format of `%8.0g`. This variable has associated with it a *value label* called `reg`, and the variable is labeled `Census Region`.

The third variable, which is abbreviated `median~e`, is stored as a `float`, has a display format of `%9.0g`, has no value label, and has a variable label of `Median Age`. The variables that are abbreviated `marria~e` and `divorc~e` are both stored as `long`s and have display formats of `%12.0g`. These last two variables are labeled `Marriages per 100,000` and `Divorces per 100,000`, respectively.

The data are sorted by `region`.

Since we specified the `numbers` option, the variables are numbered; e.g., `region` is variable 2 in this dataset.

◁

▷ Example

To view the full variable names, we could omit the `numbers` option and specify the `fullnames` option.

```
. describe, fullnames
Contains data from states.dta
  obs:           50                          State data
  vars:           5                          6 Jul 2000 16:39
  size:       1,300 (99.7% of memory free)   (_dta has notes)
```

variable name	storage type	display format	value label	variable label
state	str8	%9s		
region	int	%8.0g	reg	Census Region
median_age	float	%9.0g		Median Age
marriage_rate	long	%12.0g		Marriages per 100,000
divorce_rate	long	%12.0g		Divorces per 100,000

```
Sorted by:  region
```

In this case, we did not need to specify the **fullnames** option to see the unabbreviated variable names since the longest variable name is 13 characters. Omitting the **numbers** option results in 15-character variable names being displayed.

◁

❏ Technical Note

The above **describe** listing also shows that the size of the dataset is 1,300. In case you are curious,

$$\{(8 + 2 + 4 + 4 + 4) + 4\} \times 50 = 1300$$

The 8, 2, 4, 4, and 4 are the storage requirements for a **str8**, **int**, **float**, **long**, and **long**, respectively; see [U] **15.2.2 Numeric storage types**. The extra 4 is needed for pointers, etc. The 50 is the number of observations in the dataset.

❏

▷ Example

If you specify the **short** option, only general information about the data is presented:

```
. describe, short
Contains data from states.dta
  obs:           50                          State data
  vars:           5                          6 Jul 2000 16:39
  size:       1,300 (99.7% of memory free)
Sorted by:  region
```

◁

If you specify a *varlist*, only the variables in that *varlist* are described.

▷ Example

The **detail** option is useful for determining how many observations or variables you can add to your dataset:

```
. describe, detail
Contains data from states.dta
   obs:           50 (max=      34,869)    State data
  vars:            5 (max=       2,047)    6 Jul 2000 16:39
 width:           22 (max=       8,192)
  size:        1,300 (max=   1,046,728)    (_dta has notes)
```

variable name	storage type	display format	value label	variable label
state	str8	%9s		
region	int	%8.0g	reg	Census Region
median_age	float	%9.0g		Median Age
marriage_rate	long	%12.0g		Marriages per 100,000
divorce_rate	long	%12.0g		Divorces per 100,000

```
Sorted by:  region
```

If you did not increase the number of variables in this dataset, you could have a maximum of 34,869 observations. The maximum number of variables is 2,047, which is the maximum for Intercooled Stata. The 8,192 is the maximum width allowed by Intercooled Stata. The 1,046,728 is the maximum size for the dataset. The maximum dataset size could possibly be increased since many operating systems allow you to change the size of memory; see [U] **7 Setting the size of memory** and [R] **memory**.

◁

▷ Example

Let's change datasets. The `describe` *varlist* command is particularly useful when combined with the '*' abbreviation character. For instance, we can describe all the variables whose names start with `pop` by typing `describe pop*`:

```
. describe pop*
```

variable name	storage type	display format	value label	variable label
pop	long	%12.0gc		Population
poplt5	long	%12.0gc		Pop, < 5 year
pop5_17	long	%12.0gc		Pop, 5 to 17 years
pop18p	long	%12.0gc		Pop, 18 and older
pop65p	long	%12.0gc		Pop, 65 and older
popurban	long	%12.0gc		Urban population

We can describe the variables `state`, `region`, and `pop18p` by specifying them:

```
. describe state region pop18p
```

variable name	storage type	display format	value label	variable label
state	str14	%-14s		State
region	int	%-8.0g	cenreg	Census region
pop18p	long	%12.0gc		Pop, 18 and older

◁

Typing `describe using` *filename* describes the data stored in *filename*. If an extension is not specified, `.dta` is assumed.

▷ Example

We can describe the contents of states.dta without disturbing the data we currently have in memory by typing

```
. describe using states
Contains data                               State data
  obs:            50                        6 Jul 2000 16:39
  vars:            5
  size:        1,300
```

variable name	storage type	display format	value label	variable label
state	str8	%9s		
region	int	%8.0g	reg	Census Region
median_age	float	%9.0g		Median Age
marriage_rate	long	%12.0g		Marriages per 100,000
divorce_rate	long	%12.0g		Divorces per 100,000

```
Sorted by:  region
```
◁

ds

If ds is typed without any operands, then a compact list of the variable names for the data currently in memory is displayed.

▷ Example

ds can be especially useful for Intercooled Stata users who can have datasets with up to 2,047 variables, but even if you have considerably fewer variables you may find it convenient.

```
. ds
fips        hhsamp      hh10t19     hh20t29     hh30t39     hh40t49     hh50txx     medhhinc
medfinc     famsamp     femfam      rnkhhinc    mincpc      povfam      povfamf     povper
povperd     povchld     povchldd    genrev      igrev       igrevfs     cgtaxes     cgptaxes
cgstaxes
```
◁

▷ Example

You might wonder why you would ever specify a *varlist* with this command. Remember that a *varlist* understands the '*' abbreviation character and '−' dash notation; see [U] **14.4 varlists**.

```
. ds p*
povfam      povfamf     povper      povperd     povchld     povchldd

. ds povfam-cgtaxes
povfam      povfamf     povper      povperd     povchld     povchldd    genrev      igrev
igrevfs     cgtaxes
```
◁

lookfor

▷ Example

lookfor finds variables by searching for *string*, ignoring case, among the variable names and labels.

```
. lookfor tax

              storage  display   value
variable name  type    format    label    variable label
─────────────────────────────────────────────────────────────────────
cgtaxes        long    %12.0gc            Taxes of city government
cgptaxes       long    %12.0gc            Property taxes of city
                                            government
cgstaxes       long    %12.0gc            Sales taxes of city government

. lookfor median

              storage  display   value
variable name  type    format    label    variable label
─────────────────────────────────────────────────────────────────────
medhhinc       long    %12.0gc            Median household income 1979
medfinc        long    %12.0gc            Median family money income
rnkhhinc       int     %8.0g             Rank of median household income
```

lookfor median found rnkhhinc because the word median was in the variable label.

◁

▷ Example

If multiple strings are specified, variable names or labels containing any of the strings are listed.

```
. lookfor median tax

              storage  display   value
variable name  type    format    label    variable label
─────────────────────────────────────────────────────────────────────
medhhinc       long    %12.0gc            Median household income 1979
medfinc        long    %12.0gc            Median family money income
rnkhhinc       int     %8.0g             Rank of median household income
cgtaxes        long    %12.0gc            Taxes of city government
cgptaxes       long    %12.0gc            Property taxes of city
                                            government
cgstaxes       long    %12.0gc            Sales taxes of city government
```

◁

Saved Results

describe saves in r():

Scalars

r(N)	number of observations	r(k_max)	maximum number of variables
r(k)	number of variables	r(widthmax)	maximum width of dataset
r(width)	width of dataset	r(changed)	data-have-changed-since-last-saved flag
r(N_max)	maximum number of observations		

Methods and Formulas

ds and `lookfor` are implemented as ado-files.

References

Cox, N. J. 1999. dm67: Numbers of missing and present values. *Stata Technical Bulletin* 49: 7–8. Reprinted in *Stata Technical Bulletin Reprints*, vol. 9, pp. 26–27.

——. 2000. dm78: Describing variables in memory. *Stata Technical Bulletin* 56: 2–4.

Gleason, J. R. 1998. dm61: A tool for exploring Stata datasets (Windows and Macintosh only). *Stata Technical Bulletin* 45: 2–5. Reprinted in *Stata Technical Bulletin Reprints*, vol. 8, pp. 22–27.

——. 1999. dm61.1: Update to varxplor. *Stata Technical Bulletin* 51: 2. Reprinted in *Stata Technical Bulletin Reprints*, vol. 9, p. 15.

Also See

Complementary:	[R] **compress**, [R] **format**, [R] **label**, [R] **notes**, [R] **order**, [R] **rename**
Related:	[R] **cf**, [R] **codebook**, [R] **compare**
Background:	[U] **7 Setting the size of memory**, [U] **15 Data**, [R] **memory**

Title

destring — Change string variables to numeric

Syntax

destring [*varlist*], { generate(*newvarlist*) | replace } [ignore("*chars*") force

float percent]

Description

destring converts variables in *varlist* from string to numeric. If *varlist* is not specified, destring will attempt to convert all variables in the dataset from string to numeric. Characters listed in ignore() are removed. Variables in *varlist* that are already numeric will not be changed. destring treats both empty strings "" and "." as indicating missing values. Note that destring also ignores any leading or trailing spaces so that, for example, " " is equivalent to "" and " . " is equivalent to ".".

Options

Either generate() or replace must be specified. With either option, if any string variable contains nonnumeric values not specified with ignore(), no variable will be generated or replaced unless force is specified.

generate(*newvarlist*) specifies that a new variable is to be created for each variable in *varlist*. *newvarlist* must contain the same number of new variable names as there are variables in *varlist*. If *varlist* is not specified, destring attempts to generate a numeric variable for each variable in the dataset; *newvarlist* must then contain the same number of new variable names as there are variables in the dataset.

Any variable labels or characteristics will be copied to the new variables created.

replace specifies that the variables in *varlist* should be converted to numeric variables. If *varlist* is not specified, destring attempts to convert all variables from string to numeric.

Any variable labels or characteristics will be retained.

ignore("*chars*") specifies nonnumeric characters to be removed. If any string variable contains any nonnumeric characters other than those specified with ignore(), no action will take place for that variable unless force is also specified.

force specifies that any string values containing nonnumeric characters, in addition to any specified with ignore(), are treated as indicating missing numeric values.

float specifies that any new numeric variables should be created initially as type float. The default is type double. destring attempts automatically to compress each new numeric variable after creation.

percent is to be used with percent variables. If any percent signs are found in the values of a variable, they are removed and all values of that variable are divided by 100 to convert it to fractional form. percent by itself implies that the percent sign "%" is an argument to ignore(), but the converse is not true.

Remarks

▷ Example

You read in a dataset, but somehow all variables were created as strings. The variables do not contain any nonnumeric characters, and you want to convert them all from string to numeric data types.

```
. describe id num code total income
    1. id        str3   %9s
    2. num       str3   %9s
    3. code      str4   %9s
    4. total     str5   %9s
    5. income    str5   %9s
. list
```

	id	num	code	total	income
1.	111	243	1234	543	23423
2.	111	123	2345	67854	12654
3.	111	234	3456	345	43658
4.	222	345	4567	57	23546
5.	333	456	5678	23	21432
6.	333	567	6789	23465	12987
7.	333	678	7890	65	9823
8.	444	789	8976	23	32980
9.	444	901	7654	23	18565
10.	555	890	6543	423	19234

```
. destring, replace
id has all characters numeric; replaced as int
num has all characters numeric; replaced as int
code has all characters numeric; replaced as int
total has all characters numeric; replaced as long
income has all characters numeric; replaced as long

. describe id num code total income
    1. id        int    %10.0g
    2. num       int    %10.0g
    3. code      int    %10.0g
    4. total     long   %10.0g
    5. income    long   %10.0g
. list
```

	id	num	code	total	income
1.	111	243	1234	543	23423
2.	111	123	2345	67854	12654
3.	111	234	3456	345	43658
4.	222	345	4567	57	23546
5.	333	456	5678	23	21432
6.	333	567	6789	23465	12987
7.	333	678	7890	65	9823
8.	444	789	8976	23	32980
9.	444	901	7654	23	18565
10.	555	890	6543	423	19234

◁

▷ Example

Your dataset contains the variable date, which was accidentally recorded as a string because of spaces after the year and month. You want to remove the spaces. destring will convert it to numeric and remove the spaces.

```
. describe date
    1. date        str10   %10s
. list date
            date
 1. 1999 12 10
 2. 2000 07 09
 3. 1997 03 02
 4. 1999 09 01
 5. 1998 10 03
 6. 2000 03 29
 7. 2000 08 08
 8. 1997 10 20
 9. 1998 01 17
10. 1999 11 13
. destring date, replace ignore(" ")
date: characters space removed; replaced as long
. describe date
    1. date        long    %10.0g
. list date
            date
 1.    19991210
 2.    20000708
 3.    19970302
 4.    19990900
 5.    19981004
 6.    20000328
 7.    20000808
 8.    19971020
 9.    19980116
10.    19991112
```

◁

▷ Example

Your dataset contains the variables **date**, **price**, and **percent**. These variables were accidentally read into Stata as string variables because they contain spaces, dollar signs, commas, and percent signs. You want to remove all of these characters and create new variables for **date**, **price**, and **percent** containing numeric values. After removing the percent sign, you want to convert the variable **percent** to decimal form.

```
. describe date price percent
    1. date        str14   %10s
    2. price       str11   %11s
    3. percent     str3    %9s
. list date price percent
            date          price    percent
 1. 1999 12 10      $2,343.68        34%
 2. 2000 07 08      $7,233.44        86%
 3. 1997 03 02     $12,442.89        12%
 4. 1999 09 00    $233,325.31         6%
 5. 1998 10 04      $1,549.23        76%
 6. 2000 03 28     $23,517.03        35%
 7. 2000 08 08          $2.43        69%
 8. 1997 10 20      $9,382.47        32%
 9. 1998 01 16    $289,209.32        45%
10. 1999 11 12      $8,282.49         1%
```

```
. destring date price percent, generate(date2 price2 percent2) ignore("$ ,%") percent
date: characters space removed; date2 generated as long
price: characters $ , removed; price2 generated as double
percent: characters % removed; percent2 generated as double
```

```
. describe date date2 price price2 percent percent2
```

```
    1. date       str10   %10s
    2. date2      long    %10.0g
    3. price      str11   %11s
    4. price2     double  %10.0g
    5. percent    str3    %9s
    6. percent2   double  %10.0g
```

```
. list date date2 price price2 percent percent2
```

	date	date2	price	price2	percent	percent2
1.	1999 12 10	19991210	$2,343.68	2343.68	34%	.34
2.	2000 07 08	20000708	$7,233.44	7233.44	86%	.86
3.	1997 03 02	19970302	$12,442.89	12442.89	12%	.12
4.	1999 09 00	19990900	$233,325.31	233325.31	6%	.06
5.	1998 10 04	19981004	$1,549.23	1549.23	76%	.76
6.	2000 03 28	20000328	$23,517.03	23517.03	35%	.35
7.	2000 08 08	20000808	$2.43	2.43	69%	.69
8.	1997 10 20	19971020	$9,382.47	9382.47	32%	.32
9.	1998 01 16	19980116	$289,209.32	289209.32	45%	.45
10.	1999 11 12	19991112	$8,282.49	8282.49	1%	.01

◁

Saved characteristics

Each time the destring command is issued, an entry will be made in the characteristics list of each converted variable. You can type char list to view these characteristics.

After the last example given above, we could use char list to find out what characters were removed by the destring command.

```
. char list
     date2[destring]    :  Characters removed were: space
     price2[destring]   :  Characters removed were: $ ,
     percent2[destring] :  Characters removed were: %
```

Acknowledgment

destring was originally written by Nicholas J. Cox of the University of Durham, U.K.

References

Cox, N. J. 1999a. dm45.2: Changing string variables to numeric: correction. *Stata Technical Bulletin* 52: 2. Reprinted in *Stata Technical Bulletin Reprints*, vol. 9, p. 14.

——. 1999b. dm45.1: Changing string variables to numeric: update. *Stata Technical Bulletin* 49: 2. Reprinted in *Stata Technical Bulletin Reprints*, vol. 9, p. 14.

Cox, N. J. and W. Gould. 1997. dm45: Changing string variables to numeric. *Stata Technical Bulletin* 37: 4–6. Reprinted in *Stata Technical Bulletin Reprints*, vol. 7, pp. 34–37.

Cox, N. J. and J. Wernow. 2000a. dm80.1: Update to changing numeric variables to string. *Stata Technical Bulletin* 57: 2.

——. 2000b. dm80: Changing numeric variables to string. *Stata Technical Bulletin* 56: 8.

Also See

Complementary: [R] **generate**

Related: [R] **egen**, [R] **encode**, [R] **functions**

Title

> **dfuller** — Augmented Dickey–Fuller test for unit roots

Syntax

> dfuller *varname* $\begin{bmatrix} \text{if } exp \end{bmatrix}$ $\begin{bmatrix} \text{in } range \end{bmatrix}$ $\begin{bmatrix} , \underline{\text{nocon}}\text{stant} \underline{\text{lags}}(\#) \underline{\text{tr}}\text{end} \underline{\text{regress}} \end{bmatrix}$

dfuller is for use with time-series data; see [R] **tsset**. You must tsset your data before using dfuller. *varname* may contain time-series operators; see [U] **14.4.3 Time-series varlists**.

Description

dfuller performs the augmented Dickey–Fuller test for unit roots on a variable. The user may optionally exclude the constant, include a trend term, and/or include lagged values of the difference of the variable in the regression.

Options

noconstant suppresses the constant term (intercept) in the model.

lags(#) specifies the number of lagged difference terms to include in the covariate list.

trend specifies that a trend term should be included in the associated regression. This option may not be used with the noconstant option.

regress specifies that the associated regression table should appear in the output. By default, the regression table is not produced.

Remarks

Hamilton (1994) and Fuller (1976) give excellent overviews of this topic; see especially Chapter 17 of the former. Dickey and Fuller (1979) proposed a collection of tests for unit roots that relied on the derived asymptotic distributions of test statistics for AR(1) random walks (standard Brownian motion). See their paper for details.

▷ Example

In this example, we examine the international airline passengers dataset from Box, Jenkins, and Reinsel (1994, Series G). This dataset has 144 observations on the monthly number of international airline passengers from 1949 through 1960.

```
. dfuller air
Dickey-Fuller test for unit root                   Number of obs   =       143

                           ——————— Interpolated Dickey-Fuller ———————
                  Test         1% Critical      5% Critical     10% Critical
               Statistic          Value           Value            Value
————————————————————————————————————————————————————————————————————————————
   Z(t)          -1.748          -3.496          -2.887           -2.577
————————————————————————————————————————————————————————————————————————————
* MacKinnon approximate p-value for Z(t) = 0.4065
```

If we wanted to see the associated regression, we could type

```
. dfuller air, regress
Dickey-Fuller test for unit root                    Number of obs    =      143
```

	Test Statistic	1% Critical Value	Interpolated Dickey-Fuller 5% Critical Value	10% Critical Value
Z(t)	-1.748	-3.496	-2.887	-2.577

```
* MacKinnon approximate p-value for Z(t) = 0.4065
```

D.air	Coef.	Std. Err.	t	P>|t|	[95% Conf. Interval]
air						
L1	-.041068	.023493	-1.75	0.083	-.0875122	.0053761
_cons	13.7055	7.133673	1.92	0.057	-.3972779	27.80829

Note that we fail to reject the hypothesis that there is a unit root in this time series by looking either at the MacKinnon approximate asymptotic *p*-value or the interpolated Dickey–Fuller critical values.

◁

▷ Example

In this example, we examine the Canadian lynx data from Newton (1988, 587). Here we include a time trend and two lags of the differenced time series in the calculation of the statistic.

```
. dfuller lynx, lags(2) trend
Augmented Dickey-Fuller test for unit root          Number of obs    =      111
```

	Test Statistic	1% Critical Value	Interpolated Dickey-Fuller 5% Critical Value	10% Critical Value
Z(t)	-6.388	-4.036	-3.449	-3.149

```
* MacKinnon approximate p-value for Z(t) = 0.0000
```

We reject the hypothesis that there is a unit root in this time series.

◁

Saved Results

dfuller saves in r():

Scalars

r(N)	number of observations	r(Zt)	Dickey–Fuller test statistic
r(lags)	Number of lagged differences	r(p)	MacKinnon approximate *p*-value (if there is a constant or trend in associated regression)

Methods and Formulas

In the OLS estimation of an AR(1) process with Gaussian errors,

$$y_i = \rho y_{i-1} + \epsilon_i$$

where ϵ_i are independent and identically distributed as $N(0, \sigma^2)$ and $y_0 = 0$, the OLS estimate (based on an n-observation time series) of the autocorrelation parameter ρ is given by

$$\widehat{\rho}_n = \frac{\sum\limits_{i=1}^{n} y_{i-1} y_i}{\sum\limits_{i=1}^{n} y_i^2}$$

We know that if $|\rho| < 1$, then

$$\sqrt{n}(\widehat{\rho}_n - \rho) \to N(0, 1 - \rho^2)$$

If this result is valid when $\rho = 1$, then the resulting distribution collapses to a point mass (the variance is zero).

It is this motivation that drives one to check for the possibility of a unit root in an autoregressive process.

In order to compute the test statistics, we compute the Dickey–Fuller regression

$$y_i = \alpha + \rho y_{i-1} + \epsilon_i$$

where we may exclude the constant or include a trend term (i).

The augmented Dickey–Fuller regression instead uses the differenced time series d_i where $d_i = y_i - y_{i-1}$ and fits the regression

$$d_i = \alpha + \rho y_{i-1} + \beta_1 d_{i-1} + \cdots + \beta_k d_{i-k} + \epsilon_i$$

where again we may exclude the constant or include a trend term (i). We also, in this case, specify the number of lagged difference terms to include in the list of covariates. The lagged differences are included in order to eliminate any serial correlation in the ϵ_i values.

The critical values included in the output are linearly interpolated from the table of values that appears in Fuller (1976), and the MacKinnon approximate p-values use the regression surface published in MacKinnon (1994).

References

Box, G. E. P., G. M. Jenkins, and G. C. Reinsel. 1994. *Time Series Analysis: Forecasting and Control*. 3d ed. Englewood Cliffs, NJ: Prentice–Hall.

Dickey, D. A. and W. A. Fuller. 1979. Distribution of the estimators for autoregressive time series with a unit root. *Journal of the American Statistical Association* 74: 427–431.

Fuller, W. A. 1976. *Introduction to Statistical Time Series*. New York: John Wiley & Sons.

Hamilton, J. D. 1994. *Time Series Analysis*. Princeton: Princeton University Press.

MacKinnon, J. G. 1994. Approximate asymptotic distribution functions for unit-root and cointegration tests. *Journal of Business and Economic Statistics* 12: 167–176.

Newton, H. J. 1988. *TIMESLAB: A Time Series Laboratory*. Pacific Grove, CA: Wadsworth & Brooks/Cole.

Also See

Complementary:	[R] **tsset**
Related:	[R] **pperron**

Title

```
diagplots — Distributional diagnostic plots
```

Syntax

symplot *varname* [if *exp*] [in *range*] [, *graph_options*]

quantile *varname* [if *exp*] [in *range*] [, *graph_options*]

qnorm *varname* [if *exp*] [in *range*] [, grid *graph_options*]

pnorm *varname* [if *exp*] [in *range*] [, grid *graph_options*]

qchi *varname* [if *exp*] [in *range*] [, df(*#*) grid *graph_options*]

pchi *varname* [if *exp*] [in *range*] [, df(*#*) grid *graph_options*]

qqplot *varname*$_1$ *varname*$_2$ [if *exp*] [in *range*] [, *graph_options*]

Description

symplot graphs a symmetry plot of *varname*.

quantile plots the ordered values of *varname* against the quantiles of a uniform distribution.

qnorm plots the quantiles of *varname* against the quantiles of the normal distribution (Q–Q plot).

pnorm graphs a standardized normal probability plot (P–P plot).

qchi plots the quantiles of *varname* against the quantiles of a χ^2 distribution (Q–Q plot).

pchi graphs a χ^2 probability plot (P–P plot).

qqplot plots the quantiles of *varname*$_1$ against the quantiles of *varname*$_2$ (Q–Q plot).

See [R] **regression diagnostics** for regression diagnostic plots and [R] **logistic** for logistic regression diagnostic plots.

Options

grid adds grid lines at the .05, .10, .25, .50, .75, .90, and .95 quantiles when specified with qnorm or qchi. With pnorm and pchi, grid is equivalent to yline(.25,.5,.75) xline(.25,.5,.75).

df(*#*) specifies the degrees of freedom of the χ^2 distribution. The default is 1.

graph_options are any of the options allowed with graph, twoway; see [G] **graph options**.

Remarks

▷ Example

You have data on 74 automobiles. To make a symmetry plot of the variable `price`, type

`. symplot price, ylabel xlabel border`

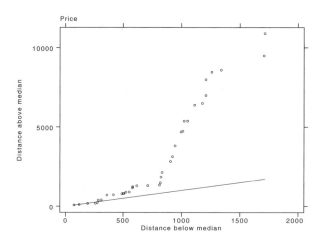

All points would lie along the reference line (defined as $y = x$) if car prices were symmetrically distributed. The points in this plot lie above the reference line, indicating that the distribution of car prices is skewed to the right—the most expensive cars are far more expensive than the least expensive cars are inexpensive.

The logic works as follows: A variable z is distributed symmetrically if

$$\text{median} - z_{(i)} = z_{(N+1-i)} - \text{median}$$

where $z_{(i)}$ indicates the ith order statistic of z. `symplot` graphs $y_i = \text{median} - z_{(i)}$ versus $x_i = z_{(N+1-i)} - \text{median}$.

For instance, consider the largest and smallest values of `price` in the example above. The most expensive car costs \$15,906, the least expensive \$3,291. Let's compare these two cars with the typical car in the data, and see how much more it costs to buy the most expensive car and compare that with how much less it costs to buy the least expensive car. If the automobile price distribution is symmetric, the price differences would be the same.

Before we can make this comparison, we must agree on a definition for the word "typical". Let's agree that "typical" means median. The price of the median car is \$5,006.50, so the most expensive car costs \$10,899.50 more than the median car, and the least expensive car costs \$1,715.50 less than the median car. We now have one piece of evidence that the car price distribution is not symmetric. We can repeat the experiment for the second most expensive car and the second least expensive car. We find that the second most expensive car costs \$9,494.50 more than the median car, and the second least expensive car costs \$1,707.50 less than the median car. We now have more evidence. We can continue doing this with the third most expensive and the third least expensive, and so on.

Once we have all these numbers, we want to compare each pair and ask how similar, on average, they are. The easiest way to do that is to plot all the pairs.

◁

▷ Example

You have data on the prices of 74 automobiles. To make a quantile plot of `price`, type

`. quantile price, border`

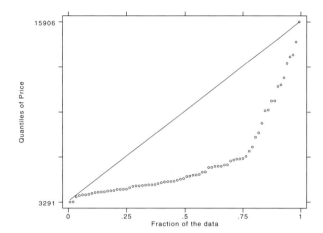

Since we can specify any of the options of **graph**'s **twoway** style, we specified **border**.

In a quantile plot, each value of the variable is plotted against the fraction of the data that has values less than it. The diagonal line is a reference line. If automobile prices were rectangularly distributed, then all the data would be plotted along the line. Since all the points are below the reference line, we know that the price distribution is skewed right.

◁

(Continued on next page)

▷ Example

Continuing with our price data on 74 automobiles, you now wish to compare the distribution of price with the normal distribution:

. qnorm price, grid

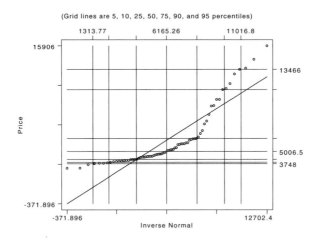

The result shows that the distributions are quite different.

◁

▷ Example

Quantile–normal plots emphasize the tails of the distribution. Normal probability plots put the focus on the center of the distribution:

. pnorm price, grid

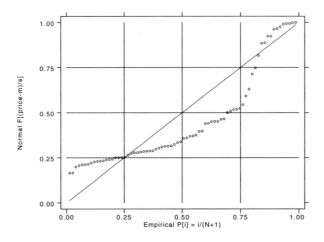

◁

▷ Example

You have data on the weight and country of manufacture of 74 automobiles. You wish to compare the distributions of weights for domestic and foreign automobiles:

```
. generate weightd=weight if ~foreign
(22 missing values generated)
. generate weightf=weight if foreign
(52 missing values generated)
. qqplot weightd weightf, border ylabel xlabel
```

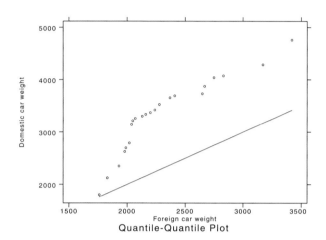

Quantile-Quantile Plot

◁

▷ Example

Suppose we want to examine the distribution of the sum of squares of `price` and `mpg`, standardized for their variances.

```
. egen c1 = std(price)
. egen c2 = std(mpg)
. gen ch = c1^2 + c2^2
. qchi ch, df(2) grid
```

(Graph on next page)

(Grid lines are 5, 10, 25, 50, 75, 90, and 95 percentiles)

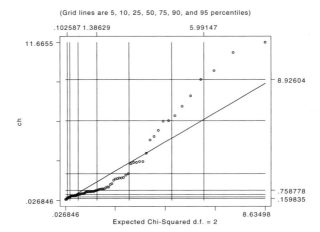

The quadratic form is clearly not χ^2 with 2 degrees of freedom.

◁

▷ Example

We can focus on the center of the distribution by doing a probability plot:

. pchi ch, df(2) grid

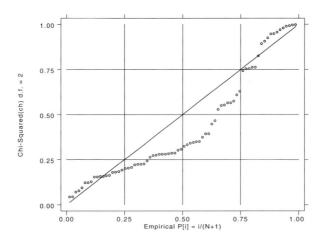

◁

Methods and Formulas

symplot, quantile, qnorm, pnorm, qchi, pchi, and qqplot are implemented as ado-files. Let $x_{(1)}$, $x_{(2)}$, ..., $x_{(N)}$ be the data sorted in ascending order.

If a continuous variable x has a cumulative distribution function $F(x) = P(X \leq x) = p$, the quantiles x_{p_i} are such that $F(x_{p_i}) = p_i$. For example, if $p_i = 0.5$, $x_{0.5}$ is the median. When plotting data, the probabilities p_i are often referred to as plotting positions. There are many different conventions for choice of plotting positions, given $x_{(1)} \leq \ldots \leq x_{(N)}$. Most belong to the family $(i - a)/(N - 2a + 1)$. $a = 0.5$ (suggested by Hazen) and $a = 0$ (suggested by Weibull) are popular choices.

`symplot` plots median $- x_{(i)}$ versus $x_{(N+1-i)} -$ median.

`quantile` plots $x_{(i)}$ versus $(i - 0.5)/N$ (the Hazen position).

`qnorm` plots $x_{(i)}$ against q_i, where $q_i = \Phi^{-1}(p_i)$, Φ is the cumulative normal distribution, and $p_i = i/(N + 1)$ (the Weibull position).

`pnorm` plots $\Phi\{(x_i - \widehat{\mu})/\widehat{\sigma}\}$ versus $p_i = i/(N + 1)$, where $\widehat{\mu}$ is the mean of the data and $\widehat{\sigma}$ is the standard deviation.

`qchi` and `pchi` are similar to `qnorm` and `pnorm`; the cumulative χ^2 distribution is used in place of the cumulative normal distribution.

`qqplot` is just a two-way scatterplot of one variable against the other after both variables have been sorted into ascending order and both variables have the same number of nonmissing observations. If the variables have unequal numbers of nonmissing observations, interpolated values of the variable with more data are plotted against the variable with less.

Acknowledgments

We would like to thank Peter A. Lachenbruch of the Food and Drug Administration (FDA) for writing the original version of `qchi` and `pchi`. Patrick Royston of the MRC Clinical Trials Unit, London also published a very similar command in the *Stata Technical Bulletin* (Royston 1996).

References

Chambers, J. M., W. S. Cleveland, B. Kleiner, and P. A. Tukey. 1983. *Graphical Methods for Data Analysis*. Belmont, CA: Wadsworth International Group.

Cox, N. J. 1999. gr42: Quantile plots, generalized. *Stata Technical Bulletin* 51: 16–18. Reprinted in *Stata Technical Bulletin Reprints*, vol. 9, pp. 113–116.

Daniel, C. and F. S. Wood. 1980. *Fitting Equations to Data*. 2d ed. New York: John Wiley & Sons.

Gan, F. F., K. J. Koehler, and J. C. Thompson. 1991. Probability plots and distribution curves for assessing the fit of probability models. *The American Statistician* 45: 14–21.

Hamilton, L. C. 1992. *Regression with Graphics*, 10–17. Pacific Grove, CA: Brooks/Cole Publishing Company.

———. 1998. *Statistics with Stata 5*. Pacific Grove, CA: Brooks/Cole Publishing Company.

Hoaglin, D. C. 1985. Using quantiles to study shape. In *Exploring Data Tables, Trends, and Shapes*, ed. D. C. Hoaglin, F. Mosteller, and J. W. Tukey, 417–460. New York: John Wiley & Sons.

Royston, P. 1996. sg47: A plot and a test for the χ^2 distribution. *Stata Technical Bulletin* 29: 26–27. Reprinted in *Stata Technical Bulletin Reprints*, vol. 5, pp. 142–144.

Scotto, M. G. 2000. sg140: The Gumbel quantile plot and a test for choice of extreme models. *Stata Technical Bulletin* 55: 23–25.

Wilk, M. B. and R. Gnanadesikan. 1968. Probability plotting methods for the analysis of data. *Biometrika* 55: 1–17.

Also See

Related: [R] **cumul**, [R] **logistic**, [R] **lv**, [R] **regression diagnostics**

Background: *Stata Graphics Manual*

Title

dir — Display filenames

Syntax

$\{\texttt{dir}\,|\,\texttt{ls}\}$ ["] [*filespec*] ["] [, <u>w</u>ide]

Note: On Stata for Windows and Stata for Macintosh, double quotes must be used to enclose *filespec* if the name contains spaces.

Description

dir and ls—they mean the same thing—list the names of files in the specified directory; the names of the commands come from names popular on DOS and Unix computers. *filespec* may be any valid DOS, Unix, or Macintosh file path or file specification (see [U] **14.6 File-naming conventions**) and may include '*' to indicate any string of characters.

Options

<u>w</u>ide under Windows and Macintosh produces an effect similar to specifying /W with the DOS DIR command—it compresses the resulting listing by placing more than one filename on a line. Under Unix, it produces the same effect as typing ls -F -C. Without the wide option, ls is equivalent to typing ls -F -l.

Remarks

Windows: Other than minor differences in presentation format, there is only one difference between the Stata and DOS dir commands. The DOS /P option is unnecessary, since Stata always pauses when the screen is full.

Unix: The only difference between the Stata and Unix ls commands is that piping through the more(1) or pg(1) filter is unnecessary—Stata always pauses when the screen is full.

Macintosh: Macintosh users will, in most cases, use the Finder to see the contents of folders. The DOS- and Unix-like dir command, however, can be useful because it can list only files with a specified suffix.

▷ Example

The only real difference between the Stata dir and DOS and Unix equivalent commands is that output never scrolls off the screen; Stata always pauses when the screen is full.

If you use Stata for Windows and wish to obtain a list of all your Stata-format data files:

```
. dir *.dta
    3.9k   7/07/00 13:51   AUTO.DTA
    0.6k   8/04/00 10:40   CANCER.DTA
    3.5k   7/06/98 17:06   CENSUS.DTA
    3.4k   1/25/98  9:20   HSNG.DTA
    0.3k   1/26/98 16:54   KVA.DTA
    0.7k   4/27/00 11:39   SYSAGE.DTA
    0.5k   5/09/97  2:56   SYSTOLIC.DTA
   10.3k   7/13/98  8:37   Household Survey.dta
```

Or, you could include the **wide** option:

```
. dir *.dta, wide
    3.9k AUTO.DTA           0.6k CANCER.DTA           3.5k CENSUS.DTA
    3.4k HSNG.DTA           0.3k KVA.DTA              0.7k SYSAGE.DTA
    0.5k SYSTOLIC.DTA      10.3k Household Survey.dta
```

Unix users will find it more natural to type

```
. ls *.dta
-rw-r----- 1 roger      2868 Mar  4 15:34 highway.dta
-rw-r----- 1 roger       941 Apr  5 09:43 hoyle.dta
-rw-r----- 1 roger     19312 May 14 10:36 p1.dta
-rw-r----- 1 roger     11838 Apr 11 13:26 p2.dta
```

but they could type `dir` if they preferred. Macintosh users may also type either command.

```
. dir *.dta
07/07/00   13:51      5412   auto.dta
05/21/98   16:22     21210   city.dta
01/21/98    8:52     29719   employee.dta
08/08/98   12:25      5860   empno.dta
```

◁

Also See

Related: [R] **cd**, [R] **copy**, [R] **erase**, [R] **mkdir**, [R] **shell**, [R] **type**

Background: [U] **14.6 File-naming conventions**

Title

> **display** — Substitute for a hand calculator

Syntax

di̲splay *exp*

Description

display displays strings and values of scalar expressions.

display really has many more features and a more complex syntax diagram than the one shown above, but the diagram shown above is adequate for interactive use. For a full discussion of display's capabilities, see [P] **display**.

Remarks

display can be used as a substitute for a hand calculator.

▷ Example

display 2+2 produces the output 4. Stata variables may also appear in the expression, such as in display myvar/2. Since display works only with scalars, the resulting calculation is performed for only the first observation. You could type display myvar[10]/2 to display the calculation for the tenth observation. Here are some more examples:

```
. display sqrt(2)/2
.70710678
. display norm(-1.1)
.13566606
. di (57.2-3)/(12-2)
5.42
. display myvar/10
7
. display myvar[10]/2
3.5
```

◁

Also See

Related: [P] **display**

Background: [U] **16 Functions and expressions**

Title

do — Execute commands from a file

Syntax

$\{\,\texttt{do}\,|\,\underline{\texttt{run}}\,\}$ *filename* [*arguments*] [, nostop]

Description

do and run cause Stata to execute the commands stored in *filename* just as if they were entered from the keyboard. do echoes the commands as it executes them whereas run is silent. If *filename* is specified without an extension, .do is assumed.

Options

nostop allows the do-file to continue executing even if an error occurs. Normally, Stata stops executing the do-file when it detects an error (nonzero return code).

Remarks

You can create *filename* (called a *do-file*) using Stata's do-file editor; see [R] **doedit**. This file will be a standard ASCII (text) file. A complete discussion of do-files can be found in [U] **19 Do-files**.

You can create *filename* using an editor outside of Stata; see [R] **shell** for a way to invoke your favorite editor from inside Stata. Make sure that you save the file in ASCII format.

Also See

Complementary:	[R] **doedit**
Background:	[GSM] **15 Using the Do-file Editor**,
	[GSU] **15 Using the Do-file Editor**,
	[GSW] **15 Using the Do-file Editor**,
	[U] **18 Printing and preserving output**,
	[U] **19 Do-files**

Title

doedit — Edit do-files and other text files

Syntax

<u>doedit</u> [*filename*]

Description

doedit opens a text editor which allows you to edit do-files and other text files.

The do-file editor lets you submit several commands to Stata at once.

Remarks

Pressing Stata's **Do-file Editor** button is equivalent to typing doedit.

doedit, typed by itself, invokes the editor with an empty document. If you specify *filename*, that file is displayed in the editor.

A tutorial discussion of doedit is found in the *Getting Started with Stata* manual. Read [U] **19 Do-files** for an explanation of do-files and then read [GS] **15 Using the Do-file Editor** to learn how to use the do-file editor to create and execute do-files.

Also See

Background: [GSM] **15 Using the Do-file Editor**,
[GSU] **15 Using the Do-file Editor**,
[GSW] **15 Using the Do-file Editor**,
[U] **19 Do-files**

Title

> **dotplot** — Comparative scatterplots

Syntax

dotplot *varname* [if *exp*] [in *range*] [, by(*groupvar*) nx(#) ny(#) <u>center</u>

{ mean | <u>median</u> } <u>bar</u> <u>vert</u> <u>nogroup</u> <u>bounded</u> <u>incr</u>(#) *graph_options*]

dotplot *varlist* [if *exp*] [in *range*] [, nx(#) ny(#) <u>center</u> { mean | <u>median</u> }

<u>bar</u> <u>vert</u> <u>nogroup</u> <u>bounded</u> <u>incr</u>(#) *graph_options*]

Description

   A dotplot is a scatterplot with a grouping of values in the vertical direction ("binning," as in a histogram) and with separation between plotted points in the horizontal direction. The aim is to display all the data for several variables or groups in a single, compact graphic.

   In the first syntax, **dotplot** produces a columnar dotplot of *varname*, with one column per value of *groupvar*. In the second syntax, **dotplot** produces a columnar dotplot for each variable in *varlist*, with one column per variable; by(*groupvar*) is not allowed. In each case, the "dots" are plotted as small circles to increase readability.

Options

by(*groupvar*) identifies the variable for which **dotplot** will display one columnar dotplot for each value of *groupvar*.

nx(#) sets the horizontal dot density. A larger value of # will increase the dot density, reducing the horizontal separation between dots. This will increase the separation between columns if two or more groups or variables are used.

ny(#) sets the vertical dot density (number of "bins" on the *y*-axis). A larger value of # will result in more bins and a plot which is less spread-out in the horizontal direction. # should be determined in conjunction with nx() to give the most pleasing appearance.

center centers the dots for each column on a hidden vertical line.

{ mean | median } plots a horizontal line of pluses at the mean or median of each group.

bar plots horizontal dashed lines at the "shoulders" of each group. The "shoulders" are taken to be the upper and lower quartiles unless **mean** has been specified, in which case they will be the mean plus or minus the standard deviation.

vert when used together with **bar** produces vertical "error bars" instead of horizontal lines. The effect is roughly like a box plot.

nogroup uses the actual values of *yvar* rather than grouping them (the default). This may be useful if *yvar* only takes on a few values.

bounded forces the minimum and maximum of the variable to be used as boundaries of the smallest and largest bins. It is intended for use with a single variable whose support is not the whole of the real line and whose density does not tend to zero at the ends of its support; e.g., a uniform random variable or an exponential random variable.

incr(#) specifies how the x-axis is to be labeled. **incr(1)**, the default, labels all groups. **incr(2)** labels every second group.

graph_options are any of the standard Stata **twoway** graph options except **xscale()**. If you use the **symbol()** option, note that **dotplot** plots the dots, the mean or median, the lower bar, and the upper bar, in that order. If a single symbol is provided by the user, it will be used for the dots and the default symbols will be used for the mean or median and bars. If two or more symbols are provided, they will be followed by the "plus", "dash", "dash". Thus, **s(do) median bar** will use diamonds for the data, small circles for the median, pluses for the lower quartile, and dashes for the upper quartile. See [G] **graph options**.

Remarks

dotplot produces a figure that is a cross between a boxplot, a histogram, and a scatterplot. Like a boxplot, it is most useful for comparing the distributions of several variables or the distribution of a single variable in several groups. Like a histogram, the figure provides a crude estimate of the density and, as with a scatterplot, each symbol (dot) represents a single observation.

▷ Example

dotplot may be used as an alternative to Stata's histogram graph for displaying the distribution of a single variable.

```
. set obs 1000
. gen norm = invnorm(uniform())
. dotplot norm, ylab t1("Normal distribution, sample size 1000")
```

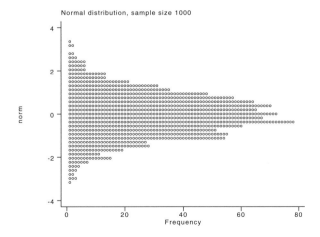

◁

▷ Example

The **by** option enables **dotplot** to be used to compare the distribution of a single variable within different levels of a grouping variable. The options **center**, **median**, and **bar** create a graph that may be compared to Stata's boxplot; see [G] **box**. The next graph illustrates this using Stata's automobile dataset.

. dotplot mpg, by(foreign) nx(20) ny(10) center ylabel median bar

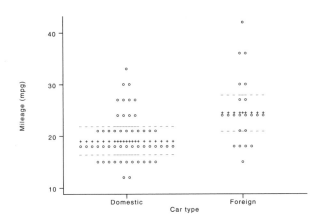

◁

▷ Example

The second version of **dotplot** enables one to compare the distribution of several variables. In the next graph, all ten variables contain measurements on tumor volume.

. dotplot g1r1-g1r10, ylabel l1title("Tumor volume, cu mm")

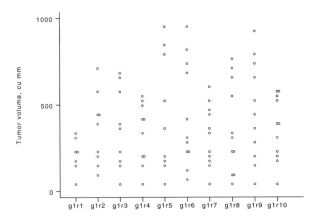

◁

▷ Example

When using the first form with the by option, it is possible to encode a third dimension in a dotplot by using a different plotting symbol for different groups. This will not work with a *varlist*. The example is of a hypothetical matched case–control study. The next graph shows the exposure of each individual in each matched stratum. Cases are marked by the letter 'x' and controls by the letter 'o'.

```
. label define symbol 0 "o" 1 "x"
. label values case symbol
. dotplot dose, by(strata) symbol([case]) center ylab
```

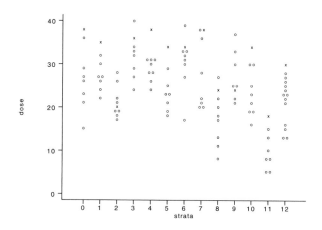

◁

▷ Example

dotplot can also be used with two virtually continuous variables as an alternative to jittering the data to distinguish ties. In this case, one must use the **xlab** option, since otherwise **dotplot** will attempt to label too many points on the *x*-axis. It is often useful in such instances to use a value of **nx** that is smaller than the default. That was not necessary in this example partly because of our choice of symbols.

```
. gen byte hi_price = (price>10000) if price!=.
. label define symbol 0 "|" 1 "o"
. label values hi_price symbol
```

(Graph on next page)

```
. dotplot weight, by(gear_ratio) symbol([hi_price]) center xlab ylab
```

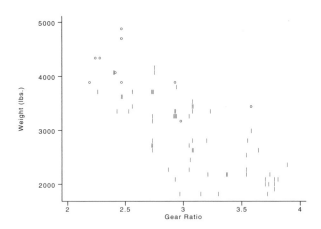

◁

▷ Example

The following figure is included mostly for aesthetic reasons. It also demonstrates `dotplot`'s ability to cope with even very large datasets. The sample size for each variable is 10,000. This may take a long time to print!

```
. set obs 10000
. gen norm0 = invnorm(uniform())
. gen norm1 = invnorm(uniform()) + 1
. gen norm2 = invnorm(uniform()) + 2
. label variable norm0 "N(0,1)"
. label variable norm1 "N(1,1)"
. label variable norm2 "N(2,1)"
```

(*Graph on next page*)

```
. dotplot norm0 norm1 norm2, ylab
```

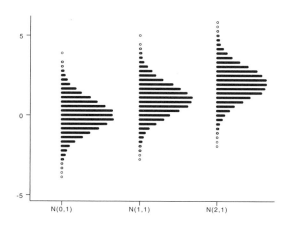

Saved Results

dotplot saves in r():

Scalars
  r(nx) horizontal dot density
  r(ny) vertical dot density

Methods and Formulas

dotplot is implemented as an ado-file.

Acknowledgments

dotplot was written by Peter Sasieni of the Imperial Cancer Research Fund, London, and Patrick Royston of the MRC Clinical Trials Unit, London.

References

Sasieni. P. and P. Royston. 1994. gr14: dotplot: comparative scatterplots. *Stata Technical Bulletin* 19: 8–10. Reprinted in *Stata Technical Bulletin Reprints*, vol. 4, pp. 50–54.

———. 1996. Dotplots. *Applied Statistics* 45: 219–234.

Also See

Background: *Stata Graphics Manual*

Title

> **drawnorm** — Draw a sample from a normal distribution

Syntax

> drawnorm *newvarlist* $\left[\, , \, \text{n}(\#) \; \text{seed}(\#) \; \underline{\text{means}}(row\_vector) \; \text{corr}(matname) \right.$
>
> $\left. \text{cov}(matname) \; \underline{\text{sds}}(row\_vector) \; \underline{\text{d}}\text{ouble clear} \right]$

Description

> **drawnorm** draws a sample from a multivariate normal distribution with desired means and covariance matrix. The default is orthogonal data, mean 0, variance 1. The values generated are a function of the current random number seed or the number specified with **set seed()**; see [R] **generate**.

Options

> **n(#)** specifies the number of observations to be generated. The default is the current number of observations. If **n(#)** is not specified or is the same as the current number of observations, **drawnorm** will add the new variables to the existing dataset; otherwise, **drawnorm** will replace the data in memory.

> **seed(#)** specifies the initial value of the random number seed used by the **uniform()** function. The default is the current random number seed. Specifying **seed(#)** is the same as typing **set seed #** before issuing the **drawnorm** command.

> **means(*vector*)** specifies the means of the generated variables. The default is **means(0)**.

> **corr(*matname*)** specifies the correlation matrix. **cov()** and **corr()** may not be specified together. If neither **corr()** nor **cov()** is specified, the default is orthogonal data.

> **cov(*matname*)** specifies the covariance matrix. **cov()** and **corr()** may not be specified together. If neither **corr()** nor **cov()** is specified, the default is orthogonal data.

> **sds(*vector*)** specifies the standard deviations of the generated variables. **sds()** and **cov()** may not be specified together.

> **double** specifies that the new variables are to be stored as Stata **doubles**, meaning 8-byte reals. If **double** is not specified, variables are stored as **floats**, meaning 4-byte reals. See [R] **data types**.

> **clear** specifies that it is okay to replace the dataset in memory even though the current dataset has not been saved on disk.

Remarks

▷ Example

> Suppose that we want to draw a sample of 1,000 observations from a normal distribution $N(\mathbf{M}, \mathbf{V})$, where $\mathbf{M}$ is the mean matrix and $\mathbf{V}$ is the covariance matrix:

```
. mat list M
M[1,3]
     c1  c2  c3
r1    5  -6  .5
```

```
. mat list V
symmetric V[3,3]
    c1  c2  c3
r1   9
r2   5   4
r3   2   1   1
. drawnorm x y z, n(1000) cov(V) means(M)
(obs 1000)
. summarize
```

Variable	Obs	Mean	Std. Dev.	Min	Max
x	1000	5.001715	3.00608	-4.572042	13.66046
y	1000	-5.980279	2.004755	-12.08166	-.0963039
z	1000	.5271135	1.011095	-2.636946	4.102734

```
. correlate, cov
(obs=1000)
```

	x	y	z
x	9.03652		
y	5.04462	4.01904	
z	2.10142	1.08773	1.02231

◁

❑ Technical Note

The values generated by **drawnorm** are a function of the current random number seed. To reproduce the same dataset each time **drawnorm** is run with the same setup, specify the same seed number in the **seed()** option.

❑

Methods and Formulas

drawnorm is implemented as an ado-file.

Results are asymptotic. The more observations generated, the closer the correlation matrix of the dataset is to the desired correlation structure.

Let $\mathbf{V} = \mathbf{A}'\mathbf{A}$ be the desired covariance matrix and $\mathbf{M}$ be the desired mean matrix. We first generate $\mathbf{X}$, such that $\mathbf{X} \sim N(\mathbf{0}, \mathbf{I})$. Let $\mathbf{Y} = \mathbf{A}'\mathbf{X} + \mathbf{M}$, then $\mathbf{Y} \sim N(\mathbf{M}, \mathbf{V})$.

Also See

Related: [R] **corr2data**, [R] **generate**

Background: [R] **data types**

Title

---
drop — Eliminate variables or observations

Syntax

> drop *varlist*
>
> drop if *exp*
>
> drop in *range* [if *exp*]
>
> keep *varlist*
>
> keep if *exp*
>
> keep in *range* [if *exp*]
>
> clear

by ... : may be used with the second syntax of drop and the second syntax of keep; see [R] **by**.

Description

drop eliminates variables or observations from the data in memory. drop may not be abbreviated.

keep works the same way as drop except that you specify the variables or observations to be kept rather than the variables or observations to be deleted. keep may not be abbreviated.

clear is equivalent to typing

```
. version 7.0
. drop _all
. label drop _all
. matrix drop _all
. scalar drop _all
. constraint drop _all
. cluster drop _all
. eq drop _all
. discard
```

Remarks

The entire dataset can be cleared by typing drop _all. Value labels, macros, and programs are unaffected by this. (Also see [U] **15.6 Dataset, variable, and value labels**, [U] **21.3 Macros**, and [P] **program**.) Alternatively, you can type clear. This does the same as drop _all, but also clears value labels, equations, scalars, and matrices (see [U] **15.6 Dataset, variable, and value labels**, [P] **scalar**, and [P] **matrix utility**).

▷ Example

We will systematically eliminate data until, at the very end, no data are left in memory. We begin by describing the data now in memory:

```
. describe
Contains data from census.dta
    obs:            50                          1980 Census data by state
   vars:            14                          6 Jul 2000 17:06
   size:         3,400 (99.5% of memory free)

              storage  display    value
variable name   type   format     label    variable label

state          str14  %-14s                State
region         int    %-8.0g     cenreg    Census region
pop            long   %12.0gc              Population
poplt5         long   %12.0gc              Pop, < 5 year
pop5_17        long   %12.0gc              Pop, 5 to 17 years
pop18p         long   %12.0gc              Pop, 18 and older
pop65p         long   %12.0gc              Pop, 65 and older
popurban       long   %12.0gc              Urban population
medage         float  %9.2f                Median age
death          long   %12.0gc              Number of deaths
marriage       long   %12.0gc              Number of marriages
divorce        long   %12.0gc              Number of divorces
mrgrate        float  %9.0g
dvcrate        float  %9.0g

Sorted by:  region
     Note:  dataset has changed since last saved
```

We can eliminate all the variables whose names begin with pop by typing drop pop*:

```
. drop pop*
. describe
Contains data from census.dta
    obs:            50                          1980 Census data by state
   vars:             8                          6 Jul 2000 17:06
   size:         2,200 (99.6% of memory free)

              storage  display    value
variable name   type   format     label    variable label

state          str14  %-14s                State
region         int    %-8.0g     cenreg    Census region
medage         float  %9.2f                Median age
death          long   %12.0gc              Number of deaths
marriage       long   %12.0gc              Number of marriages
divorce        long   %12.0gc              Number of divorces
mrgrate        float  %9.0g
dvcrate        float  %9.0g

Sorted by:  region
     Note:  dataset has changed since last saved
```

Let's eliminate more variables and then eliminate observations:

```
. drop marriage divorce mrgrate dvcrate
. describe
```

```
Contains data from census.dta
  obs:           50                        1980 Census data by state
  vars:           4                        6 Jul 2000 17:06
  size:        1,400 (99.7% of memory free)

              storage  display    value
variable name   type    format    label    variable label

state          str14    %-14s               State
region         int      %-8.0g    cenreg    Census region
medage         float    %9.2f               Median age
death          long     %12.0gc             Number of deaths

Sorted by:  region
     Note:  dataset has changed since last saved
```

Next, we will **drop** any observation for which **medage** is greater than 32.

```
. drop if medage>32
(3 observations deleted)
```

Let's drop the first observation in each region:

```
. by region: drop if _n==1
(4 observations deleted)
```

Now we drop all but the last observation in each region:

```
. by region: drop if _n~=_N
(39 observations deleted)
```

Let's now drop the first 2 observations in our dataset:

```
. drop in 1/2
(2 observations deleted)
```

Finally, let's get rid of everything:

```
. drop _all
. describe
Contains data
  obs:            0
  vars:           0
  size:           0 (100.0% of memory free)
Sorted by:
```
◁

Typing **keep in 10/1** is the same as typing **drop in 1/9**.

Typing **keep if x==3** is the same as typing **drop if x~=3**.

keep is especially useful for keeping a few variables from a large dataset. Typing **keep myvar1 myvar2** is the same as typing **drop** followed by all the variables in the dataset *except* **myvar1** and **myvar2**.

Methods and Formulas

clear is implemented as an ado-file.

Also See

Background: [U] **14 Language syntax,**
[U] **16 Functions and expressions**

Title

> **dstdize** — Direct and indirect standardization

Syntax

> dstdize *charvar popvar stratavars* $\begin{bmatrix} \text{if} & exp \end{bmatrix}$ $\begin{bmatrix} \text{in} & range \end{bmatrix}$, by(*groupvars*) $\big[$ <u>us</u>ing(*filename*)
>
> <u>base</u>(# | *string*) <u>saving</u>(*filename*) <u>print</u> <u>f</u>ormat(%*fmt*) <u>level</u>(#) nores $\big]$
>
> istdize *casevar$_s$ popvar$_s$ stratavars* $\begin{bmatrix} \text{if} & exp \end{bmatrix}$ $\begin{bmatrix} \text{in} & range \end{bmatrix}$ <u>us</u>ing(*filename*),
>
> $\Big\{$ <u>pop</u>vars(*casevar$_p$ popvar$_p$*) | rate(*ratevar$_p$* # | *ratevar$_p$ crudevar$_p$*)$\Big\}$
>
> $\big[$ by(*groupvars*) <u>print</u> <u>f</u>ormat(%*fmt*) <u>level</u>(#) $\big]$

Description

dstdize produces standardized rates for *charvar*, which are defined as a weighted average of the stratum-specific rates. These rates can be used to compare the characteristic *charvar* across different populations identified by *groupvars*. Weights used in the standardization are given by *popvar*; the strata across which to average are defined by *stratavars*.

istdize produces indirectly standardized rates for a study population based on a standard population. This standardization method is appropriate when stratum-specific rates for the population being studied either are unavailable or are based on small samples and thus unreliable. The standardization uses the stratum-specific rates of a standard population to calculate the expected number of cases in the study population(s), sums them, and then compares them with the actual number of cases observed. The standard population is specified in another Stata data file named in the **using** option.

In addition to rates, the indirect standardization command produces point estimates and exact confidence intervals of the study population's standardized mortality ratio (SMR), if death is the event of interest, or the standardized incidence ratio (SIR) for studies of incidence. Here we refer to both ratios as SMR.

casevar$_s$ is the variable name for the study population's number of cases (usually deaths). It must contain integers and each subpopulation identified by *groupvar* must have the same values or missing.

popvar$_s$ identifies the number of subjects represented by each observation in the study population.

stratavars define the strata.

Options

by(*groupvars*) is not optional for the **dstdize** command; it specifies the variables identifying the study populations. If **base()** is also specified, there must be only one variable in the **by()** group. If you do not have a variable for this option, you can generate one using something like **gen newvar=1** and then using **newvar** as the argument to this option.

For the **istdize** command **by**(*groupvars*) specifies variables identifying study populations when more than one exist in the data. If this option is not specified the entire study population is treated as one group.

using() or base() may be used to specify the standard population for the dstdize command. You may not specify both options. using(*filename*) supplies the name of a .dta file containing the standard population. The standard population must contain the *popvar* and the *stratavars*. If using() is not specified, the standard population distribution will be obtained from the data. base(# | *string*) allows you to specify one of the values of *groupvar*—either a numeric value or a string—to be used as the standard population. If neither base() nor using() is specified, the entire dataset is used to determine an estimate of the standard population.

saving(*filename*) saves the computed standard population distribution as a Stata dataset that can be used in further analyses.

print outputs a table summary of the standard population before displaying the study population results.

format(%*fmt*) specifies the format in which to display the final summary table. The default is %10.0g.

level(#) specifies the confidence level, in percent, for a confidence interval of the adjusted rate; see [R] **level**.

nores suppresses saving results in r(). This option is seldom specified. Some saved results are stored in matrices. If there are more groups than matsize, dstdize will report " matsize too small". In that case, you can either increase matsize or specify nores. The nores option does not change how results are calculated. nores just specifies that results need not be left behind for use by other programs.

popvars(*casevar_p popvar_p*) or rate(*ratevar_p* # | *ratevar_p crudevar_p*) must be specified with istdize. Only one of these two options is allowed. These options are used to describe the standard population's data.

With popvars(*casevar_p popvar_p*), *casevar_p* records the number of cases (deaths) for each stratum in the standard population and *popvar_p* records the total number of individuals in each stratum (individuals at risk).

With rate(*ratevar_p* #| *ratevar_p crudevar_p*), *ratevar_p* contains the stratum-specific rates. # | *crudevar_p* is used to specify the crude case rate either by a variable name or optionally by the crude case rate value. If a crude rate variable is used, it must be the same for all observations, although it could be missing for some.

Remarks

A frequently recurring problem in epidemiology and other fields is the comparison of rates for some characteristic across different populations. These populations often differ with respect to factors associated with the characteristic under study; thus, the direct comparison of overall rates may be quite misleading.

Direct standardization

The direct method of adjusting for differences among populations involves computing the overall rates that would result if, instead of having different distributions, all populations were to have the same standard distribution. The standardized rate is defined as a weighted average of the stratum-specific rates, with the weights taken from the standard distribution. Direct standardization may be applied only when the specific rates for a given population are available.

dstdize generates adjusted summary measures of occurrence which can be used to compare prevalence, incidence, or mortality rates between populations which may differ with respect to certain characteristics (e.g., age, gender, race). These underlying differences may affect the crude prevalence, mortality, or incidence rates.

▷ Example

We have data (Rothman 1986, 42) on mortality rates for Sweden and Panama for the year 1962, and we wish to compare mortality in these two countries:

```
. use mortality
(1962 Mortality, Sweden & Panama)

. describe

Contains data from mortality.dta
  obs:            6                        1962 Mortality, Sweden & Panama
  vars:           4                        6 Jul 2000 21:35
  size:         114 (99.8% of memory free)
```

variable name	storage type	display format	value label	variable label
nation	str6	%9s		Nation
age_category	byte	%9.0g	age_lbl	Age Category
population	float	%10.0gc		Population in Age Category
deaths	float	%9.0gc		Deaths in Age Category

```
Sorted by:

. list
```

	nation	age_cat~y	population	deaths
1.	Sweden	0 - 29	3145000	3,523
2.	Sweden	30 - 59	3057000	10,928
3.	Sweden	60+	1294000	59,104
4.	Panama	0 - 29	741,000	3,904
5.	Panama	30 - 59	275,000	1,421
6.	Panama	60+	59,000	2,456

When the total number of cases in the population is divided by the population, we obtain the *crude rate*:

```
. collapse (sum) pop deaths, by(nation)

. list
```

	nation	population	deaths
1.	Panama	1075000	7,781
2.	Sweden	7496000	73,555

```
. gen crude = deaths/pop

. list
```

	nation	population	deaths	crude
1.	Panama	1075000	7,781	.0072381
2.	Sweden	7496000	73,555	.0098126

If we examine the total number of deaths in the two nations, it is striking that the total crude mortality rate in Sweden is higher than that of Panama. From the original data, we see one possible explanation: Swedes are older than Panamanians. This makes it difficult to directly compare the mortality rates.

Direct standardization gives us a means of removing the distortion caused by the differing age distributions. The adjusted rate is defined as the weighted sum of the crude rates, where the weights are given by the standard distribution. Suppose we wish to standardize these mortality rates to the following age distribution:

```
. use 1962
(Standard Population Distribution)

. list
```

```
             age_cat~y  populat~n
    1.        0 - 29         .35
    2.       30 - 59         .35
    3.          60+           .3
  . sort age_cat
  . save 1962, replace
  file 1962.dta saved
```

If we multiply the above weights for the age strata by the crude rate for the corresponding age category, the sum gives us the standardized rate.

```
  . use mortality, clear
  (1962 Mortality, Sweden & Panama)
  . gen crude=deaths/pop
  . drop pop
  . sort age_cat
  . merge age_cat using 1962
  age_category was byte now float
  . list
            nation  age_cat~y    deaths      crude  populat~n   _merge
    1.      Sweden     0 - 29     3,523   .0011202        .35        3
    2.      Panama     0 - 29     3,904   .0052686        .35        3
    3.      Panama    30 - 59     1,421   .0051673        .35        3
    4.      Sweden    30 - 59    10,928   .0035747        .35        3
    5.      Panama       60+      2,456   .0416271         .3        3
    6.      Sweden       60+     59,104   .0456754         .3        3
  . gen product = crude*pop
  . by nation, sort: egen adj_rate = sum(product)
  . drop _merge
  . list, noobs nodisplay

    nation  age_cat~y    deaths      crude  populat~n     product   adj_rate
    Sweden     0 - 29     3,523   .0011202        .35    .0003921   .0153459
    Panama     0 - 29     3,904   .0052686        .35     .001844   .0161407
    Panama    30 - 59     1,421   .0051673        .35    .0018085   .0161407
    Sweden    30 - 59    10,928   .0035747        .35    .0012512   .0153459
    Panama       60+      2,456   .0416271         .3    .0124881   .0161407
    Sweden       60+     59,104   .0456754         .3    .0137026   .0153459
```

A comparison of the standardized rates indicates that the Swedes have a slightly lower mortality rate.

To perform the above analysis with `dstdize`,

```
  . use mortality, clear
  (1962 Mortality, Sweden & Panama)
  . dstdize deaths pop age_cat, by(nation) using(1962)
```

```
-> nation= Panama
                              ───Unadjusted───  Std.
                               Pop.  Stratum  Pop.
    Stratum       Pop.   Cases Dist.  Rate[s] Dst[P]    s*P

     0 - 29     741000    3904 0.689  0.0053  0.350  0.0018
    30 - 59     275000    1421 0.256  0.0052  0.350  0.0018
        60+      59000    2456 0.055  0.0416  0.300  0.0125

  Totals:      1075000    7781        Adjusted Cases:   17351.2
                                         Crude Rate:     0.0072
                                      Adjusted Rate:     0.0161
                      95% Conf. Interval: [0.0156, 0.0166]
```

```
-> nation= Sweden
                         ------Unadjusted------  Std.
                             Pop.  Stratum  Pop.
     Stratum      Pop.   Cases  Dist. Rate[s]  Dst[P]   s*P

      0 - 29    3145000    3523  0.420 0.0011  0.350 0.0004
     30 - 59    3057000   10928  0.408 0.0036  0.350 0.0013
        60+     1294000   59104  0.173 0.0457  0.300 0.0137

    Totals:     7496000   73555    Adjusted Cases: 115032.5
                                      Crude Rate:    0.0098
                                   Adjusted Rate:    0.0153
                         95% Conf. Interval: [0.0152, 0.0155]

Summary of Study Populations:
      nation          N     Crude     Adj_Rate      Confidence Interval

     Panama     1075000  0.007238     0.016141   [ 0.015645,    0.016637]
     Sweden     7496000  0.009813     0.015346   [ 0.015235,    0.015457]
```

The summary table above allows us to make a quick inspection of the results within the study populations, and the detail tables give the behavior among the strata within the study populations.

◁

▷ Example

We have individual-level data on persons in four cities over a number of years. Included in the data is a variable indicating whether the person has high blood pressure together with information on the person's age, sex and race. We wish to obtain standardized high blood pressure rates for each city in the years 1990 and 1992 using, as the standard, the age, sex, and race distribution of the four cities and two years combined.

Our dataset contains

```
. describe
Contains data from hbp.dta
  obs:        1,130
  vars:           7                         12 Jul 2000 15:20
  size:      23,730 (96.2% of memory free)

              storage  display    value
variable name   type   format     label      variable label

id              str10  %10s                   Record identification number
city            byte   %8.0g
year            int    %8.0g
sex             byte   %8.0g      sexfmt
age_group       byte   %8.0g      agefmt
race            byte   %8.0g      racefmt
hbp             byte   %8.0g      yn         high blood pressure

Sorted by:
```

The dstdize command is designed to work with aggregate data but will work with individual-level data only if we create a variable recording the population represented by each observation. For individual-level data, this is one:

```
. gen pop = 1
```

Below, we specify `print` to obtain a listing of the standard population and `level(90)` to request 90% rather than 95% confidence intervals. The `if year==1990 | year==1992` restricts the data to the two years for both summary tables and the standard population.

```
. dstdize hbp pop age race sex if year==1990 | year==1992, by(city year) print level(90)
```

```
                          Standard Population
                           Stratum      Pop.    Dist.

       15 - 19    Black   Female         35     0.077
       15 - 19    Black     Male         44     0.097
       15 - 19 Hispanic   Female          5     0.011
       15 - 19 Hispanic     Male         10     0.022
       15 - 19    White   Female          7     0.015
       15 - 19    White     Male          5     0.011
       20 - 24    Black   Female         43     0.095
       20 - 24    Black     Male         67     0.147
       20 - 24 Hispanic   Female         14     0.031
       20 - 24 Hispanic     Male         13     0.029
       20 - 24    White   Female          4     0.009
       20 - 24    White     Male         21     0.046
       25 - 29    Black   Female         17     0.037
       25 - 29    Black     Male         44     0.097
       25 - 29 Hispanic   Female          7     0.015
       25 - 29 Hispanic     Male         13     0.029
       25 - 29    White   Female          9     0.020
       25 - 29    White     Male         16     0.035
       30 - 34    Black   Female         16     0.035
       30 - 34    Black     Male         32     0.070
       30 - 34 Hispanic   Female          2     0.004
       30 - 34 Hispanic     Male          3     0.007
       30 - 34    White   Female          5     0.011
       30 - 34    White     Male         23     0.051

Total:                                  455
(6 observations excluded due to missing values)
```

```
-> city year= 1 1990
                                          ──────Unadjusted──────   Std.
                                            Pop.    Stratum   Pop.
                          Stratum     Pop.  Cases  Dist.  Rate[s] Dst[P]  s*P

       15 - 19    Black   Female        6      2  0.128 0.3333  0.077  0.0256
       15 - 19    Black     Male        6      0  0.128 0.0000  0.097  0.0000
       15 - 19 Hispanic     Male        1      0  0.021 0.0000  0.022  0.0000
       20 - 24    Black   Female        3      0  0.064 0.0000  0.095  0.0000
       20 - 24    Black     Male       11      0  0.234 0.0000  0.147  0.0000
       25 - 29    Black   Female        4      0  0.085 0.0000  0.037  0.0000
       25 - 29    Black     Male        6      1  0.128 0.1667  0.097  0.0161
       25 - 29 Hispanic   Female        2      0  0.043 0.0000  0.015  0.0000
       25 - 29    White   Female        1      0  0.021 0.0000  0.020  0.0000
       30 - 34    Black   Female        1      0  0.021 0.0000  0.035  0.0000
       30 - 34    Black     Male        6      0  0.128 0.0000  0.070  0.0000

Totals:                               47      3    Adjusted Cases:      2.0
                                                      Crude Rate:     0.0638
                                                   Adjusted Rate:     0.0418
                           90% Conf. Interval: [0.0074, 0.0761]
```

   (output omitted)

```
-> city year= 5 1992
```

	Stratum	Pop.	Cases	Unadjusted Pop. Dist.	Stratum Rate[s]	Std. Pop. Dst[P]	s*P
15 - 19 Black	Female	6	0	0.087	0.0000	0.077	0.0000
15 - 19 Black	Male	9	0	0.130	0.0000	0.097	0.0000
15 - 19 Hispanic	Female	1	0	0.014	0.0000	0.011	0.0000
15 - 19 Hispanic	Male	2	0	0.029	0.0000	0.022	0.0000
15 - 19 White	Female	2	0	0.029	0.0000	0.015	0.0000
15 - 19 White	Male	1	0	0.014	0.0000	0.011	0.0000
20 - 24 Black	Female	13	0	0.188	0.0000	0.095	0.0000
20 - 24 Black	Male	10	0	0.145	0.0000	0.147	0.0000
20 - 24 Hispanic	Male	1	0	0.014	0.0000	0.029	0.0000
20 - 24 White	Male	3	0	0.043	0.0000	0.046	0.0000
25 - 29 Black	Female	2	0	0.029	0.0000	0.037	0.0000
25 - 29 Black	Male	2	0	0.029	0.0000	0.097	0.0000
25 - 29 Hispanic	Male	3	0	0.043	0.0000	0.029	0.0000
25 - 29 White	Male	1	0	0.014	0.0000	0.035	0.0000
30 - 34 Black	Female	4	0	0.058	0.0000	0.035	0.0000
30 - 34 Black	Male	5	0	0.072	0.0000	0.070	0.0000
30 - 34 Hispanic	Male	2	0	0.029	0.0000	0.007	0.0000
30 - 34 White	Female	1	0	0.014	0.0000	0.011	0.0000
30 - 34 White	Male	1	1	0.014	1.0000	0.051	0.0505

```
Totals:                          69      1    Adjusted Cases:       3.5
                                                  Crude Rate:    0.0145
                                               Adjusted Rate:    0.0505
                           90% Conf. Interval: [0.0505, 0.0505]
```

Summary of Study Populations:

city year	N	Crude	Adj_Rate	Confidence Interval	
1 1990	47	0.063830	0.041758	[0.007427,	0.076089]
1 1992	56	0.017857	0.008791	[0.000000,	0.022579]
2 1990	64	0.046875	0.044898	[0.009072,	0.080724]
2 1992	67	0.029851	0.014286	[0.002537,	0.026035]
3 1990	69	0.159420	0.088453	[0.050093,	0.126813]
3 1992	37	0.189189	0.046319	[0.025271,	0.067366]
5 1990	46	0.043478	0.022344	[0.002044,	0.042644]
5 1992	69	0.014493	0.050549	[0.050549,	0.050549]

◁

Indirect standardization

Standardization of rates can be performed via the indirect method whenever the stratum-specific rates are either unknown or unreliable. If the stratum-specific rates are known, the direct standardization method is preferred.

In order to apply the indirect method the following must be available:

1. The observed number of cases in each population to be standardized, O. For example, if death rates in two states are being standardized using the US death rate for the same time period, then you must know the total number of deaths in each state.

2. The distribution across the various strata for the population being studied, $n_1, \ldots, n_k$. If you are standardizing the death rate in the two states adjusting for age, then you must know the number of individuals in each of the k age groups.

3. The stratum-specific rates for the standard population, $p_1, \ldots, p_k$. For the example, you must have the US death rate for each stratum (age group).

4. The crude rate of the standard population, C. For the example, you must have the mortality rate for all the US for the year.

The indirect adjusted rate is then

$$R_{\text{indirect}} = C\frac{O}{E}$$

where E is the expected number of cases (deaths) in each population. See the *Methods and Formulas* section for a more detailed description of calculations.

▷ Example

This example is borrowed from Kahn and Sempos (1989, 95–105). We want to compare 1970 mortality rates in California and Maine adjusting for age. Although we have age-specific population counts for the two states, we lack age-specific death rates. In this situation, direct standardization is not feasible. We can use the US population census data for the same year to produce indirectly standardized rates for these two states.

From the United States census, the standard population for this example was entered into Stata and saved in `popkahn.dta`.

```
. use popkahn
. list age pop deaths rate
```

	age	population	deaths	rate
1.	<15	57,900,000	103,062	.00178
2.	15-24	35,441,000	45,261	.00128
3.	25-34	24,907,000	39,193	.00157
4.	35-44	23,088,000	72,617	.00315
5.	45-54	23,220,000	169,517	.0073
6.	55-64	18,590,000	308,373	.01659
7.	65-74	12,436,000	445,531	.03583
8.	75+	7,630,000	736,758	.09656

Note that the standard population contains for each age stratum the total number of individuals (`pop`) and both the age-specific mortality rate (`rate`) and the number of deaths. It is not necessary that the standard population contain all three. If you only have the age-specific mortality rate you can use the `rate(`*ratevar$_p$* *crudevar$_p$*`)` or `rate(`*ratevar$_p$* `#)` options, where *crudevar$_p$* refers to the variable containing the total population's crude death rate or `#` is the total population's crude death rate.

Now let's look at the states' data (study population).

```
. use kahn, clear
```

```
. list

            state        age   population      death
  1. California          <15    5,524,000    166,285
  2. California         15-24   3,558,000    166,285
  3. California         25-34   2,677,000    166,285
  4. California         35-44   2,359,000    166,285
  5. California         45-54   2,330,000    166,285
  6. California         55-64   1,704,000    166,285
  7. California         65-74   1,105,000    166,285
  8. California          75+      696,000    166,285
  9. Maine               <15      286,000     11,051
 10. Maine              15-24     168,000          .
 11. Maine              25-34     110,000          .
 12. Maine              35-44     109,000          .
 13. Maine              45-54     110,000          .
 14. Maine              55-64      94,000          .
 15. Maine              65-74      69,000          .
 16. Maine               75+       46,000          .
```

Note that for each state the number of individuals in each stratum (age group) is contained in the variable pop. The death variable is the total number of deaths observed in the state during the year. It must have the same value for all observations in the group, as for California, or it could be missing in all but one observation per group, as for Maine.

For matching these two datasets, it is important that the strata variables have the same name in both datasets and ideally the same levels. If a level is missing from either dataset, that level will not be included in the standardization.

With the kahn.dta dataset in memory, we now execute the command. We will use the print option to obtain the standard population's summary table, and since we have both the standard population's age-specific count and deaths, we will specify the popvars($casevar_p$ $popvar_p$) option. Alternatively, we could specify the rate(rate 0.00945) option since we know that 0.00945 is the US crude death rate for 1970.

```
. istdize death pop age using popkahn, by(state) pop(deaths pop) print

  ————Standard Population————
    Stratum             Rate
  ————————————————————————————
       <15            0.00178
     15-24            0.00128
     25-34            0.00157
     35-44            0.00315
     45-54            0.00730
     55-64            0.01659
     65-74            0.03583
       75+            0.09656
  ————————————————————————————

Standard population's crude rate:        0.00945
```

(Continued on next page)

```
-> state= California
                    Indirect Standardization
                    Standard
                    Population      Observed        Cases
        Stratum        Rate        Population      Expected
```

Stratum	Standard Population Rate	Observed Population	Cases Expected
<15	0.0018	5524000	9832.72
15-24	0.0013	3558000	4543.85
25-34	0.0016	2677000	4212.46
35-44	0.0031	2359000	7419.59
45-54	0.0073	2330000	17010.10
55-64	0.0166	1704000	28266.14
65-74	0.0358	1105000	39587.63
75+	0.0966	696000	67206.23

```
Totals:                            19953000       178078.73

                               Observed Cases:    166285
                               SMR (Obs/Exp):        0.93
               SMR exact 95% Conf. Interval: [0.9293, 0.9383]
                                   Crude Rate:    0.0083
                                Adjusted Rate:    0.0088
                       95% Conf. Interval: [0.0088, 0.0089]
```

```
-> state= Maine
                    Indirect Standardization
                    Standard
                    Population      Observed        Cases
        Stratum        Rate        Population      Expected
```

Stratum	Standard Population Rate	Observed Population	Cases Expected
<15	0.0018	286000	509.08
15-24	0.0013	168000	214.55
25-34	0.0016	110000	173.09
35-44	0.0031	109000	342.83
45-54	0.0073	110000	803.05
55-64	0.0166	94000	1559.28
65-74	0.0358	69000	2471.99
75+	0.0966	46000	4441.79

```
Totals:                            992000        10515.67

                               Observed Cases:    11051
                               SMR (Obs/Exp):      1.05
               SMR exact 95% Conf. Interval: [1.0314, 1.0707]
                                   Crude Rate:    0.0111
                                Adjusted Rate:    0.0099
                       95% Conf. Interval: [0.0097, 0.0101]
```

Summary of Study Populations (Rates):

state	Cases Observed	Crude	Adj_Rate	Confidence Interval
California	166285	0.008334	0.008824	[0.008782, 0.008866]
Maine	11051	0.011140	0.009931	[0.009747, 0.010118]

Summary of Study Populations (SMR):

state	Cases Observed	Cases Expected	SMR	Exact Confidence Interval
California	166285	178078.73	0.934	[0.929290, 0.938271]
Maine	11051	10515.67	1.051	[1.031405, 1.070687]

Saved Results

dstdize saves in r():

Scalars
    r(k)   number of variables

Macros
    r(by)   variable names specified in by()
    r(c#)   values of r(by) for #th group

Matrices
    r(Nobs)   1 x k vector of number of observations
    r(crude)   1 x k vector of crude rates (*)
    r(adj)   1 x k vector of adjusted rates (*)
                (*) If, in a group, the number of observations is 0, then 9
                is stored for the corresponding crude and adjusted rates.

Methods and Formulas

dstdize and istdize are implemented as ado-files.

The directly standardized rate S_R is defined by

$$S_\mathrm{R} = \frac{\displaystyle\sum_{i=1}^{k} w_i R_i}{\displaystyle\sum_{i=1}^{k} w_i}$$

(Rothman 1986, 44), where R_i is the stratum-specific rate in stratum i, and w_i is the weight for stratum i derived from the standard population.

If n_i is the population of stratum i, the standard error $\mathrm{se}(S_\mathrm{R})$ in stratified sampling for proportions (ignoring the finite population correction) is

$$\mathrm{se}(S_\mathrm{R}) = \frac{1}{\sum w_i} \sqrt{\sum_{i=1}^{k} \frac{w_i^2 R_i(1 - R_i)}{n_i}}$$

(Cochran 1977, 108) from which the confidence intervals are calculated.

For indirect standardization, define O as the observed number of cases in each population to be standardized; $n_1, \ldots, n_k$, the distribution across the various strata for the population being studied; $R_1, \ldots, R_k$, the stratum-specific rates for the standard population; and C, the crude rate of the standard population. Then the expected number of cases (deaths), E, in each population is obtained by applying the standard population stratum-specific rates, $R_1, \ldots, R_k$, to the study populations:

$$E = \sum_{i=1}^{k} n_i R_i$$

The indirectly adjusted rate is then

$$R_\mathrm{indirect} = C \frac{O}{E}$$

and O/E is the study population's standardized mortality ratio (SMR) if death is the event of interest or the standardized incidence ratio (SIR) for studies of disease (or other) incidence.

The exact confidence interval is calculated for each estimated SMR by assuming a Poisson process as described in Breslow and Day (1987, 69–71). These are obtained by first calculating the upper and lower bounds for the confidence interval of the Poisson-distributed observed events, O, say L and U respectively, and then computing $\text{SMR}_L = L/E$ and $\text{SMR}_U = U/E$.

Acknowledgments

We gratefully acknowledge the collaboration of Dr Joel A. Harrison, Cigna Healthcare of Texas; Dr José Maria Pacheco from the Departamento de Epidemiologia, Faculdade de Saúde Pública/USP, Sao Paulo, Brazil; and Dr John L. Moran from The Queen Elizabeth Hospital, Woodville, Australia.

References

Breslow, N. E. and N. E. Day. 1987. *Statistical Methods in Cancer Research*, vol. II. Lyon: International Agency for Research on Cancer.

Cleves, M. 1998. sg80: Indirect standardization. *Stata Technical Bulletin* 42: 43–47. Reprinted in *Stata Technical Bulletin Reprints*, vol. 7, pp. 224–228.

Cochran, W. G. 1977. *Sampling Techniques*. 3d ed. New York: John Wiley & Sons.

Fisher, L. D. and G. van Belle. 1993. *Biostatistics: A Methodology for the Health Sciences*. New York: John Wiley & Sons.

Fleiss, J. L. 1981. *Statistical Methods for Rates and Proportions*. 2d ed. New York: John Wiley & Sons.

Forthofer, R. and E. S. Lee. 1995. *Introduction to Biostatistics: A Guide to Design, Analysis, and Discovery*. New York: Academic Press.

Kahn, H. A. and C. T. Sempos. 1989. *Statistical Methods in Epidemiology*. New York: Oxford University Press.

McGuire, T. and J. A. Harrison. 1994. sbe11: Direct standardization. *Stata Technical Bulletin* 21: 5–9. Reprinted in *Stata Technical Bulletin Reprints*, vol. 4, pp. 88–94.

Pagano, M. and K. Gauvreau. 2000. *Principles of Biostatistics*. 2d ed. Pacific Grove, CA: Brooks/Cole.

Rothman, K. J. 1986. *Modern Epidemiology*. Boston: Little, Brown, and Company.

Wang, D. 2000. sbe40: Modeling mortality data using the Lee–Carter model. *Stata Technical Bulletin* 57: 15–17.

Also See

Related: [R] **epitab**

Title

> **edit** — Edit and list data using Data Editor

Syntax

> <u>edit</u> [*varlist*] [if *exp*] [in *range*] [, <u>nol</u>abel]
>
> <u>brow</u>se [*varlist*] [if *exp*] [in *range*] [, <u>nol</u>abel]

Description

edit brings up a spreadsheet-style data editor for entering new data and editing existing data. edit is a better alternative to input; see [R] **input**.

browse is like edit except that it will not allow you to change the data. browse is a convenient alternative to list; see [R] **list**.

Options

nolabel causes the underlying numeric values rather than the label values (equivalent strings) to be displayed for variables with value labels; see [R] **label**.

Remarks

Remarks are presented under the headings

> *Modes*
> *The current observation and current variable*
> *Double-clicking action*
> *Buttons*
> *Changing values of existing cells*
> *Adding new variables*
> *Adding new observations*
> *Copying and pasting*
> *Exiting*
> *Logging changes*
> *Advice*

A tutorial discussion of edit and browse is found in the *Getting Started with Stata* manual. This entry provides technical details.

Pressing Stata's **Data Editor** button is equivalent to typing edit by itself. Pressing Stata's **Data Browser** button is equivalent to typing browse by itself.

edit, typed by itself, enters the editor with all observations on all variables. If you specify *varlist*, only those variables are displayed in the editor. If you specify one or both of in *range* and if *exp*, only the observations specified are displayed.

Modes

We will refer to the editor in the singular and have it understood that `edit` and `browse` are two aspects of the same thing. In fact, the editor has three modes.

Full-edit mode. This is the editor's mode you enter when you type `edit` or type `edit` followed by a list of variables. All features of the editor are turned on.

Restricted-edit mode. This is the editor's mode you enter when you use `edit`, with or without a list of variables, but include `in` *range*, `if` *exp*, or both. A few of the editor's features are turned off, most notably, the ability to sort data, the ability to delete observations on a data-wide basis, and the ability to paste data into the editor.

Browse mode. This is the editor's mode you enter when you use `browse`. All the editing features are turned off, ensuring that the data cannot be changed. One feature that is left on may surprise you: the ability to sort data. Sorting, in Stata's mind, is not really a change to the dataset. On the other hand, if you enter using `browse` and specify `in` *range* or `if` *exp*, sorting will not be allowed. You can think of this as restricted-browse mode.

Actually, the editor does not set its mode to restricted just because you specify an `in` *range* or `if` *exp*. It sets its mode to restricted if you specify `in` or `if` and if this restriction is effective; that is, if the `in` or `if` actually causes some data to be omitted. For instance, typing `edit if x>0` would result in unrestricted full-edit mode if `x` were greater than zero for all observations.

The current observation and current variable

The bulk of the editor looks like a spreadsheet, with rows corresponding to observations and columns to variables. At all times, one of the cells is highlighted. This is called the current cell. The observation (row) of the current cell is called the current observation. The variable (column) of the current cell is called the current variable.

You change the current cell in the natural way—click with the mouse on another cell, use the arrow keys, or move the scroll bars.

Double-clicking action

When you double-click on a cell, the Variable Information dialog box appears. In edit mode, this allows you to change the variable's name, variable label, and format; see [U] **14.3 Naming conventions**, [U] **15.6.2 Variable labels**, and [U] **15.5 Formats: controlling how data are displayed**.

Buttons

Seven buttons appear at the top of the window.

Preserve updates the backup copy of the data. By default, when you enter the editor, a backup copy is made so that you can abort your changes. (There is a way to vary this; see the technical note below.) If you get to a point where you are satisfied with your changes, but still wish to continue, you do not have to exit and reenter the editor. Press **Preserve**. **Preserve** is grayed out in browse mode.

Restore undoes your changes by restoring the backup copy of your data. Pressing **Restore** does not change the backup copy, so you can press **Restore**, try again, change your mind yet again, and re-press **Restore**. **Restore** is grayed out in browse mode. If you turn off the automatic backup feature (see technical note below), **Restore** is also grayed out in edit mode until you press **Preserve**.

Sort reorders the observations in ascending sequence of the current variable. **Sort** is grayed out in restricted-edit and restricted-browse modes.

≪ shifts the current variable to be the first variable in the dataset. In edit mode, the shift is real. When you exit the editor, the variables will remain in the order you have specified. In browse mode, the shift is cosmetic. While in the editor, it appears as if the variable has been moved but, when you exit, the variables remain in the same order as they were originally.

≫ shifts the current variable to be the last variable in the dataset. In edit mode, the shift is real. When you exit the editor, the variables will remain in the order you have specified. In browse mode, the shift is cosmetic. While in the editor, it appears as if the variable has been moved but, when you exit, the variables remain in the same order as they were originally.

Hide eliminates the variable from the editor. The effect is cosmetic. The variable is not dropped from the dataset; the editor merely stops displaying it.

Delete... brings up a popup window to either (1) delete the current variable, (2) delete the current observation, or (3) delete all observations, data-wide, whose current variable's value is equal to that of the current observation. The third option is not presented in restricted-edit mode. **Delete...** is grayed out in browse mode.

❑ Technical Note

By default, when you enter the editor a backup copy of your data is made on disk. For large datasets, making this copy takes time. If you do not want the backup copy made automatically, pull down **Prefs–General Preferences...** from the Stata menu bar, select **Editor Prefs**, and turn off (uncheck) *Auto-Preserve*. When you enter the editor, **Restore** will now be grayed out until you press **Preserve**, if ever.

❑

Changing values of existing cells

Make the cell you wish to change the current cell. Type the new value and press *Enter*. When updating string variables, do not type double quotes around the string.

❑ Technical Note

Stata experts will wonder about storage types. Say variable `mpg` is stored as an `int` and you want to change the fourth observation to contain 22.5. Just do it. The editor will change the storage type of the variable. Similarly, if the variable is a `str4` and you type `alpha`, it will be promoted to `str5`.

The editor will not, however, change numeric variable types to strings (unless the numeric variable contains only missing values). This is intentional—such a change could result in a loss of data and you probably made a mistake.

❑

Adding new variables

Go to the first empty column and begin entering your data. The first entry you make will create the variable, and it will determine whether that variable is numeric or string. It will be given a name like `var1`, but you can rename it by double-clicking on any cell in the column.

❑ Technical Note

Stata experts: the storage type will be determined automatically. If you type a number, the created variable will be numeric; if you type a string, it will be a string. Thus, if you want a string variable, be sure that your first entry cannot be interpreted as a number: a way to achieve this is to use surrounding quotes, so that "123" will be taken as the string "123", not the number 123. If you want a numeric variable, do not worry about whether it is byte, int, float, etc. If a byte will hold your first number but, to hold your second number, you will need a float, the editor will recast the variable later.

❑

❑ Technical Note

If you do not type in the first empty column but instead type in one to the right of it, the editor will create variables for all the intervening columns.

❑

Adding new observations

Go to the first empty row and begin entering your data. As soon as you add one cell below the last row of the dataset, the observation will be created.

❑ Technical Note

If you do not enter data in the first empty row but instead enter data in a row below it, the editor will create observations for all the intervening rows.

❑

Copying and pasting

You can copy and paste data between Stata's editor and other spreadsheets.

First, select the data you wish to copy. In Stata, click on a cell and drag the mouse across other cells to select a range of cells. If you want to select an entire column, click once on the variable name at the top of that column. If you want to select an entire row, click once on the observation number at the left of that row. You can hold down the mouse button after clicking and drag to select multiple columns or rows.

Once you have selected the data, copy it to the clipboard. In Stata, pull down **Edit** and choose **Copy**.

You can copy data to the clipboard from Stata with or without the variable names at the top of each column. You can access this option by pulling down **Prefs–General Preferences...**, choosing **Editor Prefs**, and checking or unchecking *Include variable names on copy to clipboard*.

If the data you have selected contain any values that have been labeled, you can choose to copy either the value labels or the underlying numeric values. You can access this option by pulling down **Prefs–General Preferences...**, choosing **Editor Prefs**, and checking or unchecking *Copy value labels instead of numbers*. For more information on value labels, see [U] **15.6.3 Value labels** and [R] **label**.

After you have copied data to the clipboard from Stata's editor or another spreadsheet, you can paste it into Stata's editor. First, select the top left cell of the area to which you wish to paste by clicking on it once. Then, pull down **Edit** and choose **Paste**. If you entered Stata's editor in restricted-edit or in browse mode, **Paste** will be grayed out, and you will not be able to paste into Stata's editor.

Stata will paste the data from the clipboard into the editor, overwriting any data below and to the right of the cell you selected as the top left of the paste area.

❑ Technical Note

If you attempt to paste one or more string values into numeric variables, the original numeric values will be left unchanged for those cells. Stata will display a message box to let you know this has happened: "You attempted to paste one or more string values into numeric variables. The contents of these cells, if any, are unchanged."

If you see this message, you should look carefully at the data you pasted into Stata's editor to make sure you pasted into the area you intended. We recommend that you press **Preserve** before pasting into Stata's editor so you can **Restore** the data in case there is a mistake when you paste.

❑

Exiting

If you are using a Macintosh, click on the editor's close box.

If you are using Windows, click on the editor's close box (the box with an **X** at the right of the editor's title bar). You can hold down *Alt* and press *F4* to exit the editor.

Logging changes

When you use `edit` to change existing data (as opposed to entering new data), you will find output in the Stata Results window documenting the changes you made. A line of this output might be

```
- replace mpg=22.5 in 5
```

The syntax is that of a Stata command—the Stata command that could have been typed to achieve the same result as what you did in the editor. The dash in front of the command indicates that the change was done in the editor. If you are logging your results, you will have a permanent record of what you did.

Advice

1. People who care about data integrity know that editors are dangerous—it is too easy to accidentally make changes. Never use `edit` when you mean `browse`.

2. Protect yourself when you edit existing data by limiting exposure. If you need to change `mpg`, and need to see `model` to know which value of `mpg` to change, do not press the **Data Editor** button, type `edit model mpg`. It is now impossible for you to change (damage) variables other than `model` and `mpg`. Furthermore, if you know that you need to change `mpg` only if it is missing, then you can reduce your exposure even more by typing 'edit model mpg if mpg==.'.

3. All of this said, Stata's editor is safer than most because it logs changes to the Results window. Use this feature—look at the log afterwards and verify that the changes you made are the changes you wanted to make.

References

Brady, T. 1998. dm63: Dialog box window for browsing, editing, and entering observations. *Stata Technical Bulletin* 46: 2–6. Reprinted in *Stata Technical Bulletin Reprints*, vol. 8, pp. 28–34.

——. 2000. dm63.1: A new version of winshow for Stata 6. *Stata Technical Bulletin* 53: 3–5. Reprinted in *Stata Technical Bulletin Reprints*, vol. 9, pp. 15–19.

Also See

Related: [R] **input**, [R] **list**

Title

egen — Extensions to generate

Syntax

egen [*type*] *newvar* = *fcn*(*arguments*) [if *exp*] [in *range*] [, *options*]

by ... : may be used with egen unless otherwise noted; see [R] **by**.

Description

egen creates *newvar* of the optionally specified storage type equal to *fcn*(*arguments*). Depending on the *fcn*, *arguments* refers to an expression, *varlist*, or *numlist*, and the *options* are also *fcn* dependent. Note that explicit subscripting (using _N and _n), which is commonly used with generate, should not be used with egen; see [U] **16.7 Explicit subscripting**.

The *fcn*s are

any(*varname*), values(*integer numlist*)
    may not be combined with by. It takes the value of *varname* if *varname* is equal to any of the integer values in a supplied *numlist*, and missing otherwise. See also eqany(*varlist*) and neqany(*varlist*).

count(*exp*)   (allows by *varlist*:)
    creates a constant (within *varlist*) containing the number of nonmissing observations of *exp*. Also see robs() and rmiss().

concat(*varlist*) [, format(*%fmt*) decode maxlength(#) punct(*pchars*)]
    may not be combined with by. It concatenates *varlist* to produce a string variable. Values of string variables are unchanged. Values of numeric variables are converted to string as is, or converted using a format under option format(*%fmt*), or decoded under option decode, in which case maxlength() may also be used to control the maximum label length used. By default, variables are added end-to-end: punct(*pchars*) may be used to specify punctuation, such as a space, punct(" "), or a comma, punct(,).

cut(*varname*), { at(#,#,...,#)|group(#) } [icodes label]
    may not be combined with by. It creates a new categorical variable coded with the left-hand ends of the grouping intervals specified in the at() option, which expects an ascending numlist.

    at(#,#,...,#) supplies the breaks for the groups, in ascending order. The list of break points may be simply a list of numbers separated by commas, but can also include the syntax a(b)c, meaning from a to c in steps of size b. If no breaks are specified, the command expects the option group().

    group(#) specifies the number of equal frequency grouping intervals to be used in the absence of breaks. Specifying this option automatically invokes icodes.

    icodes requests that the codes 0, 1, 2, etc. be used in place of the left-hand ends of the intervals.

    label requests that the integer-coded values of the grouped variable be labeled with the left-hand ends of the grouping intervals. Specifying this option automatically invokes icodes.

412

diff (*varlist*)

may not be combined with **by**. It creates an indicator variable equal to 1 if the variables in *varlist* are not equal, and 0 otherwise.

eqany (*varlist*) , values (*integer numlist*)

may not be combined with **by**. It is 1 if any of the variables in *varlist* are equal to any of the integer values in a supplied *numlist*, and 0 otherwise. See also **any** (*varname*) and **neqany** (*varlist*).

ends (*strvar*) [, punct (*pchars*) <u>tr</u>im { <u>h</u>ead | <u>t</u>ail | <u>l</u>ast }]

may not be combined with **by**. It gives the first "word" or head (with the **head** option), the last "word" (with the **last** option), or the remainder or tail (with the **tail** option) from string variable *strvar*.

head, **last** and **tail** are determined by the occurrence of **pchars**, which is by default a single space " ".

The head is whatever precedes the first occurrence of *pchars*, or the whole of the string if it does not occur. The head of "frog toad" is "frog" and of "frog" is "frog". With **punct(,)**, the head of "frog,toad" is "frog".

The last word is whatever follows the last occurrence of *pchars*, or the whole of the string if it does not occur. The last word of "frog toad newt" is "newt" and of "frog" is "frog". With **punct(,)**, the last word of "frog,toad" is "toad".

The remainder or tail is whatever follows the first occurrence of *pchars*, which will be the empty string "" if it does not occur. The tail of "frog toad newt" is "toad newt" and of "frog" is "". With **punct(,)**, the tail of "frog,toad" is "toad".

The **trim** option trims any leading or trailing spaces.

fill (*numlist*)

may not be combined with **by**. It creates a variable of ascending or descending numbers or complex repeating patterns. *numlist* must contain at least two numbers, and may be specified using standard *numlist* notation; see [U] **14.1.8 numlist**. [if *exp*] and [in *range*] are not allowed with **fill()**.

group (*varlist*) [, <u>m</u>issing <u>l</u>abel <u>tr</u>uncate (*num*)]

may not be combined with **by**. It creates a single variable taking on values 1, 2, ... for the groups formed by *varlist*. *varlist* may contain numeric variables, string variables, or a combination of the two. **missing** indicates that missing values in *varlist* are to be treated like any other number when assigning groups, instead of missing values being assigned to the group missing. The **label** option returns integers from 1 up according to the distinct groups of *varlist* in sorted order. The integers will be labeled with the values of *varlist*, or the value labels if they exist. The **truncate()** option will truncate the values contributed to the label from each variable in *varlist* to the length specified by the integer argument *num*. The **truncate** option cannot be used without specifying the **label** option. The **truncate** option does not change the groups that are formed; it only changes their labels.

iqr (*exp*)   (allows **by** *varlist*:)

creates a constant (within *varlist*) containing the interquartile range of *exp*. Also see **pctile()**.

kurt (*varname*)   (allows **by** *varlist*:)

returns the kurtosis (within *varlist*) of *varname*.

(*Continued on next page*)

ma(*exp*) $\big[$, t(*#*) <u>nomiss</u> $\big]$

may not be combined with **by**. It creates a *#*-period moving average of *exp*. If t() is not specified, t(3) is assumed, producing 3-period moving averages. *#* must be odd and *exp* must not produce missing values. Since moving averages are functions of lags and leads, ma() produces missing where the lags and leads do not exist—at the beginning and end of the series. **nomiss** forces the calculation of shorter, uncentered moving averages for the tails. $\big[$if *exp*$\big]$ is not allowed with ma().

mad(*exp*)   (allows **by** *varlist*:)

returns the median absolute deviation from the median (within *varlist*) of *exp*.

max(*exp*)   (allows **by** *varlist*:)

creates a constant (within *varlist*) containing the maximum value of *exp*. Also see min().

mdev(*exp*)   (allows **by** *varlist*:)

returns the mean absolute deviation from the mean (within *varlist*) of *exp*.

mean(*exp*)   (allows **by** *varlist*:)

creates a constant (within *varlist*) containing the mean of *exp*. Also see sd().

median(*exp*)   (allows **by** *varlist*:)

creates a constant (within *varlist*) containing the median of *exp*. Also see pctile().

min(*exp*)   (allows **by** *varlist*:)

creates a constant (within *varlist*) containing the minimum value of *exp*. Also see max().

mode(*varname*) $\big[$, <u>minmode</u> <u>maxmode</u> <u>nummode</u>(*integer*) <u>missing</u> $\big]$ (allows **by** *varlist*:)

produces the mode (within *varlist*) for *varname*, which may be numeric or string. The mode is the value occurring most frequently. If two or more modes exist, the mode produced will be a missing value. To avoid this, the **minmode**, **maxmode**, or **nummode**() options may be used to specify choices for selecting among the multiple modes. **minmode** returns the lowest value, and **maxmode** returns the highest value. **nummode**(*#*) will return the *#*th mode, counting from the lowest up. Missing values are excluded from determination of the mode unless **missing** is specified. Even so, the value of the mode is recorded for observations for which the values of *varname* are missing unless explicitly excluded, that is, by if *varname* < . or if *varname* != "".

mtr(*year income*)

may not be combined with **by**. It returns the U.S. marginal income tax rate for a married couple with taxable income *income* in year *year*, where $1930 \leq year \leq 1999$. *year* and *income* may be specified as variable names or constants; e.g., mtr(1993 faminc), mtr(surveyyr 28000), or mtr(surveyyr faminc). A blank or comma may be used to separate *income* from *year*.

neqany(*varlist*), <u>values</u>(*integer numlist*)

may not be combined with **by**. It returns the number of variables in *varlist* for which values are equal to any of the integer values in a supplied *numlist*. See also any(*varname*) and eqany(*varlist*).

pc(*exp*) $\big[$, prop $\big]$ (allows **by** *varlist*:)

returns *exp* (within *varlist*) scaled to be a percent of total, between 0 and 100. The **prop** option returns *exp* scaled to be a proportion of total, between 0 and 1.

pctile(*exp*) $\big[$, p(*#*)$\big]$ (allows **by** *varlist*:)

creates a constant (within *varlist*) containing the *#*-th percentile of *exp*. If p(*#*) is not specified, 50 is assumed, meaning medians. Also see median().

rank(*exp*) $\Big[$, $\big\{$ $\underline{\text{f}}$ield | $\underline{\text{t}}$rack | $\underline{\text{un}}$ique $\big\}$ $\Big]$ (allows by *varlist*:)

creates ranks (within *varlist*) of *exp*; by default, equal observations are assigned the average rank. The field option calculates the field rank of *exp*: the highest value is ranked 1, and there is no correction for ties. Two values that are tied for 2nd remain rank 2. The track option calculates the track rank of *exp*: the lowest value is ranked 1, and there is no correction for ties. Two values that are tied for 2nd remain rank 2. The unique option calculates the unique rank of *exp*: values are ranked 1, ..., #, and values and ties are broken arbitrarily. Two values that are tied for 2nd are ranked 2 and 3.

rfirst(*varlist*)

may not be combined with by. It gives the first nonmissing value in *varlist* for each observation (row). If all values in *varlist* are missing for an observation, *newvar* is set to missing.

rlast(*varlist*)

may not be combined with by. It gives the last nonmissing value in *varlist* for each observation (row). If all values in *varlist* are missing for an observation, *newvar* is set to missing.

rmax(*varlist*)

may not be combined with by. It gives the maximum value (ignoring missing values) in *varlist* for each observation (row). If all values in *varlist* are missing for an observation, *newvar* is set to missing.

rmean(*varlist*)

may not be combined with by. It creates the (row) means of the variables in *varlist*, ignoring missing values; for example, if three variables are specified and, in some observations, one of the variables is missing, in those observations *newvar* will contain the mean of the two variables that do exist. Other observations will contain the mean of all three variables. Where none of the variables exist, *newvar* is set to missing.

rmin(*varlist*)

may not be combined with by. It gives the minimum value in *varlist* for each observation (row). If all values in *varlist* are missing for an observation, *newvar* is set to missing.

rmiss(*varlist*)

may not be combined with by. It gives the number of missing values in *varlist* for each observation (row).

robs(*varlist*) $\Big[$, $\underline{\text{s}}$trok $\Big]$

may not be combined with by. It gives the number of nonmissing values in *varlist* for each observation (row)—this is the value used by rmean() for the denominator in the mean calculation.

String variables may not be specified unless option strok is also specified. If strok is specified, string variables will be counted as containing missing values when they contain "". As usual, numeric variables will be counted as containing missing when their value is '.'.

rsd(*varlist*)

may not be combined with by. It creates the (row) standard deviations of the variables in *varlist*, ignoring missing values. Also see rmean().

rsum(*varlist*)

may not be combined with by. It creates the (row) sum of the variables in *varlist*, treating missing as 0.

sd(*exp*)   (allows by *varlist*:)

creates a constant (within *varlist*) containing the standard deviation of *exp*. Also see mean().

seq() $\big[$, <u>f</u>rom(*#*) <u>t</u>o(*#*) <u>b</u>lock(*#*) $\big]$ (allows **by** *varlist*:)

   returns integer sequences. Values start from from (default 1) and increase to to (the default is the maximum number of values) in blocks (default size 1). If to is less than the maximum number, sequences restart at from. Numbering may also be separate within groups defined by *varlist*, or decreasing if to is less than from. Sequences depend on the sort order of observations, following three rules: (1) observations excluded by if or in are not counted, (2) observations are sorted by *varlist*, if specified, and (3) otherwise, the order is that when called. Note that no *arguments* are specified.

skew(*varname*)   (allows **by** *varlist*:)

   returns the skewness (within *varlist*) of *varname*.

std(*exp*) $\big[$, <u>m</u>ean(*#*) <u>s</u>td(*#*) $\big]$

   may not be combined with **by**. It creates the standardized values of *exp*. The options specify the desired mean and standard deviation. The default is mean(0) and std(1), producing a variable with mean 0, standard deviation 1.

sum(*exp*)   (allows **by** *varlist*:)

   creates a constant (within *varlist*) containing the sum of *exp*. Also see mean().

tag(*varlist*) $\big[$, <u>m</u>issing $\big]$

   may not be combined with **by**. It tags just one observation in each distinct group defined by *varlist*. When all observations in a group have the same value for a summary variable calculated for the group, it will be sufficient to use just one such value for many purposes. The result will be 1 or 0, according to whether the observation is tagged, and never missing. Hence, if tag is the variable produced by egen tag = tag(*varlist*), the idiom if tag is always safe. missing specifies that missing values of *varlist* may be included.

Remarks

   Remarks are presented under the headings

> *Summary statistics*
> *Generating patterns*
> *Marking differences among variables*
> *Moving averages*
> *Ranks*
> *Standardized variables*
> *Row functions*
> *Categorical and integer variables*
> *String variables*
> *U.S. marginal income tax rate*

Summary statistics

   The functions count(), iqr(), kurt(), mad(), max(), mdev(), mean(), median(), min(), mode(), pc(), pctile(), sd(), skew(), and sum() create variables containing summary statistics. All functions take a **by** ...: prefix and, if specified, calculate the summary statistics within each by-group.

▷ Example

   Without the **by** ...: prefix, the result produced by these functions is a constant for every observation in the data. For instance, you have data on cholesterol levels (chol) and wish to have a variable that, for each patient, records the deviation from the average across all patients:

```
. egen avg = mean(chol)
. gen dev = chol - avg
```

◁

▷ Example

These functions are most useful when the by ... : prefix is specified. For instance, assume our dataset includes dcode, a hospital-patient diagnostic code, and los, the number of days the patient remained in the hospital. We wish to obtain the deviation in length of stay from the median for all patients within the same diagnostic code:

```
. by dcode, sort: egen medstay = median(los)
. gen deltalos = los - medstay
```

◁

❏ Technical Note

Distinguish carefully between Stata's and egen's sum() functions. Stata's creates the running sum, whereas egen's creates a constant equal to the overall sum; for example,

```
. gen sum1=sum(a)
. egen sum2=sum(a)
. list
```

	a	sum1	sum2
1.	1	1	15
2.	2	3	15
3.	3	6	15
4.	4	10	15
5.	5	15	15

sum(), like the other egen summary statistic functions, can be usefully combined with the by prefix. A common problem in data management is the identification of duplicate (strictly, repeated) values. For example, these may arise from unintentional repetition in data entry or from the combination of datasets known to overlap.

Duplicates with respect to values of a list of variables *varlist* can be identified and counted like this:

```
. by  varlist: egen dups = sum(_N > 1)
```

This adds up _N > 1 within each distinct group defined by *varlist*. This is because under by, _N is the number of observations in each group (not the total number of observations). With unique observations _N == 1 and so _N > 1 is false and is numerically equal to 0. With repeated observations _N > 1 is true and is numerically equal to 1, and adding up those 1s within each group is, naturally, the same as counting them. (See [U] **16.7 Explicit subscripting** for a discussion of the use of _n and _N with by.)

So you can use

```
. tab dups
. list if dups
. drop if dups
```

and so forth. You can vary this idea with

> . by *varlist*: egen unique = sum(_N == 1)

or

> . by *varlist*: egen twos = sum(_N == 2)

if necessary.

❑

❑ Technical Note

The definitions and formulas used by these functions are the same as those used by summarize; see [R] **summarize**. For comparison with summarize, mean() and sd() correspond to the mean and standard deviation. sum() is the numerator of the mean and count() is its denominator. min() and max() correspond to the minimum and maximum. median() or, equally well, pctile() with p(50), is the median. pctile() with p(5) refers to the fifth percentile, and so on. iqr() is the difference between the 75th and 25th percentiles.

❑

▷ Example

The mode is the most common value of a dataset. This idea can be applied to numeric and string variables alike. It is perhaps most useful for categorical variables (whether defined by integers or strings) or for other integer-valued values, but mode() can be applied to variables of any type. Nevertheless, the modes of continuous (or nearly continuous) variables are perhaps better estimated either from inspection of a graph of a frequency distribution or from the results of some density estimation (see [R] **kdensity**).

Missing values need special attention. It is very possible that missing (whether the period . for numeric variables or the empty string "" for string variables) is the most common value in a variable. However, missing values are by default excluded from determination of modes. If you wish to include them, use the missing option.

In contrast, egen mode = mode(*varname*) allows the generation of nonmissing modes for observations for which *varname* is missing. This allows use of the mode as one simple means of imputation for categorical variables. If it is desired that the mode is missing whenever *varname* is missing, that is readily achieved by specifying if *varname* < . or if *varname* != "" or, most generally, if !missing(*varname*).

◁

mad() and mdev() produce alternative measures of spread. The median absolute deviation from the median and even the mean deviation will both be more resistant than the standard deviation to heavy tails or outliers, in particular from distributions with heavier tails than the normal or Gaussian. The first measure was named the MAD by Andrews et al. in 1972, but was already known to K. F. Gauss in 1816, according to Hampel et al. (1986). For further historical and statistical details, see David (1998).

Generating patterns

To create a sequence of numbers, simply "show" the `fill()` function how the sequence should look. It must be a linear progression to produce the expected results. Geometric progressions are not understood. To produce repeating patterns, you present `fill()` with the pattern twice in the *numlist*.

▷ Example

Here are some examples of ascending and descending sequences produced by `fill()`:

```
. egen i=fill(1 2)
. egen w=fill(100 99)
. egen x=fill(22 17)
. egen y=fill(1 1 2 2)
. egen z=fill(8 8 8 7 7 7)
. list
```

	i	w	x	y	z
1.	1	100	22	1	8
2.	2	99	17	1	8
3.	3	98	12	2	8
4.	4	97	7	2	7
5.	5	96	2	3	7
6.	6	95	-3	3	7
7.	7	94	-8	4	6
8.	8	93	-13	4	6
9.	9	92	-18	5	6
10.	10	91	-23	5	5
11.	11	90	-28	6	5
12.	12	89	-33	6	5

◁

▷ Example

Here are examples of patterns produced by `fill()`:

```
. egen a=fill(0 0 1 0 0 1)
. egen b=fill(1 3 8 1 3 8)
. egen c=fill(-3(3)6 -3(3)6)
. egen d=fill(10 20 to 50   10 20 to 50)
. list
```

	a	b	c	d
1.	0	1	-3	10
2.	0	3	0	20
3.	1	8	3	30
4.	0	1	6	40
5.	0	3	-3	50
6.	1	8	0	10
7.	0	1	3	20
8.	0	3	6	30
9.	1	8	-3	40
10.	0	1	0	50
11.	0	3	3	10
12.	1	8	6	20

◁

▷ Example

seq() creates a new variable containing one or more sequences of integers. It is mainly useful for the quick creation of observation identifiers or automatic numbering of levels of factors or categorical variables. seq() is based on the separate command seq (Cox 1997), but one notable detail has been changed, as noted at the end of this section.

In the simplest case,

```
. egen a = seq()
```

is just equivalent to the common idiom

```
. gen a = _n
```

a may also be obtained from

```
. range a 1 _N
```

(the actual value of _N may also be used).

In more complicated cases, seq() with option calls is equivalent to calls to those versatile functions int and mod.

```
. egen b = seq(), b(2)
```

produces integers in blocks of 2, while

```
. egen c = seq(), t(6)
```

restarts the sequence after 6 is reached.

```
. egen d = seq(), f(10) t(12)
```

shows that sequences may start with integers other than 1, and

```
. egen e = seq(), f(3) t(1)
```

shows that they may decrease.

Suppose we have 12 observations in memory. The results of these commands are shown by

```
. list a b c d e
```

	a	b	c	d	e
1.	1	1	1	10	3
2.	2	1	2	11	2
3.	3	2	3	12	1
4.	4	2	4	10	3
5.	5	3	5	11	2
6.	6	3	6	12	1
7.	7	4	1	10	3
8.	8	4	2	11	2
9.	9	5	3	12	1
10.	10	5	4	10	3
11.	11	6	5	11	2
12.	12	6	6	12	1

All these sequences could have been generated in one line with generate and the use of the int and mod functions. The variables b through e are obtained with

```
. gen b = 1 + int((_n - 1)/2)
. gen c = 1 + mod(_n - 1, 6)
. gen d = 10 + mod(_n - 1, 3)
. gen e = 3 - mod(_n - 1, 3)
```

Nevertheless, `seq()` may save users from puzzling out such solutions or from typing in the needed values.

In general, the sequences produced depend on the sort order of observations, following three rules:

1: observations excluded by `if` or `in` are not counted.

2: observations are sorted by *varlist*, if specified.

3: otherwise, the order is that when called.

Note that `seq` (Cox 1997) did not use Rule 3. The consequence was that the result of applying `seq` was not guaranteed to be identical from application to application whenever sorting was required, even with identical data, because of the indeterminacy of sorting. That is, if we sort (say) integer values, it is sufficient that all the 1s are together and are followed by all the 2s. But, there is no guarantee that the order of the 1s, as defined by any other variables, will be identical from sort to sort.

◁

The functions `fill()` and `seq()` are alternatives. In essence, `fill()` requires a minimal example that indicates the kind of sequence required, whereas `seq()` requires that the rule be specified through options. There are sequences that `fill()` can produce that `seq()` cannot, and vice versa. `fill()` cannot be combined with `if` or `in`, in contrast to `seq()`.

Marking differences among variables

▷ Example

You have three measures of respondents' income obtained from different sources. You wish to create the variable `differ` equal to 1 in the case of disagreements:

```
. egen byte differ = diff(inc*)
. list

           inc1        inc2        inc3      differ
   1.      12000       12000       12000          0
   2.      14500       14500           .          1
   3.      17500       17500       18000          1
```

Rather than typing `diff(inc*)`, you could have typed `diff(inc1 inc2 inc3)`.

◁

Moving averages

▷ Example

You have a time-series dataset and want to obtain moving averages. If you do not specify the `t()` option with `ma()`, you will obtain 3-period averages. Below, you obtain 3- and 5-period averages:

```
. egen y3 = ma(y)
(2 missing values generated)
. egen y5 = ma(y), t(5)
(4 missing values generated)
```

```
. list
            time          y          y3         y5
     1.      1980       47.2          .          .
     2.      1981       33.9    35.43333          .
     3.      1982       25.2    29.73334      34.32
     4.      1983       30.1    30.16667      31.52
     5.      1984       35.2    32.83333          .
     6.      1985       33.2          .          .
```

`ma()` assumes that the data are in chronological order. If you had specified the `nomiss` option, the missing values would have been filled in with shorter, uncentered averages.

◁

Ranks

▷ Example

You have a dataset containing eight observations on a variable named x, and these eight observations are divided into two groups of four observations. The eight values are 5, 4, −2, −3, 0, 0, *missing*, and 47. You wish to obtain the rank of the observations both overall and by group.

```
. egen rankx = rank(x)
(1 missing value generated)
. by grp, sort: egen rankx2 = rank(x)
(1 missing value generated)
. list
              x       grp      rankx     rankx2
     1.       5        1          6          4
     2.       4        1          5          3
     3.      -2        1          2          2
     4.      -3        1          1          1
     5.       0        2        3.5        1.5
     6.       0        2        3.5        1.5
     7.       .        2          .          .
     8.      47        2          7          3
```

◁

Standardized variables

▷ Example

You have a variable called age recording the median age in the 50 states. You wish to create the standardized value of age and verify the calculation:

```
. egen stdage = std(age)
. summarize age stdage
    Variable |      Obs        Mean    Std. Dev.        Min        Max
-------------+--------------------------------------------------------
         age |       50       29.54    1.693445       24.2       34.7
      stdage |       50     6.41e-09           1  -3.153336   3.047044
```

```
. correlate age stdage
(obs=50)
                 |      age    stdage
     ------------+-------------------
             age |   1.0000
          stdage |   1.0000    1.0000
```

summarize shows that the new variable has a mean of approximately 0; 10^{-9} is the precision of a float and is close enough to zero for all practical purposes. If we wanted, we could have typed egen double stdage = std(age), making stdage a double-precision variable, and the mean would have been 10^{-16}. In any case, summarize also shows that the standard deviation is 1. correlate shows that the new variable and the original variable are perfectly correlated.

You may optionally specify the mean and standard deviation for the new variable. For instance,

```
. egen newage1 = std(age), std(2)
. egen newage2 = std(age), mean(2) std(4)
. egen newage3 = std(age), mean(2)
. summarize age newage1-newage3
    Variable |       Obs        Mean    Std. Dev.        Min        Max
    ---------+--------------------------------------------------------
         age |        50       29.54    1.693445       24.2       34.7
     newage1 |        50    1.28e-08           2   -6.306671   6.094089
     newage2 |        50           2           4   -10.61334   14.18818
     newage3 |        50           2           1   -1.153336   5.047044
. correlate age newage1-newage3
(obs=50)
                 |      age   newage1   newage2   newage3
     ------------+----------------------------------------
             age |   1.0000
         newage1 |   1.0000    1.0000
         newage2 |   1.0000    1.0000    1.0000
         newage3 |   1.0000    1.0000    1.0000    1.0000
```

◁

Row functions

▷ Example

rsum(). generate's sum() function creates the vertical, running sum of its argument, while egen's sum() function creates a constant equal to the overall sum. egen's rsum() function, however, creates the horizontal sum of its arguments. They all treat missing as zero:

```
. egen hsum = rsum(a b c)
. gen vsum = sum(hsum)
. egen sum = sum(hsum)
. list
              a          b          c       hsum       vsum        sum
   1.         .          2          3          5          5         63
   2.         4          .          6         10         15         63
   3.         7          8          .         15         30         63
   4.        10         11         12         33         63         63
```

◁

▷ Example

rmean(), rsd(), and robs(). summarize displays the mean of a variable across observations; program writers can access the mean in r(mean) (see [R] **summarize**). egen's rmean() function creates the means of observations across variables. rsd() creates the standard deviations of observations across variables. robs() creates a count of the number of nonmissing observations, the denominator of the rmean() calculation:

```
. egen avg = rmean(a b c)
. egen std = rsd(a b c)
. egen n = robs(a b c)
. list
```

	a	b	c	avg	std	n
1.	.	2	3	2.5	.7071068	2
2.	4	.	6	5	1.414214	2
3.	7	8	.	7.5	.7071068	2
4.	10	11	12	11	1	3

◁

▷ Example

rmiss(). rmiss() returns $k - $ robs(), where k is the number of variables specified. rmiss() can be especially useful for finding casewise-deleted observations due to missing values.

```
. corr price weight mpg
(obs=70)
```

	price	weight	mpg
price	1.0000		
weight	0.5309	1.0000	
mpg	-0.4478	-0.7985	1.0000

```
. egen excluded = rmiss(price weight mpg)
. list make price weight mpg if excluded~=0
```

	make	price	weight	mpg
5.	Buick Electra	.	4,080	15
12.	Cad. Eldorado	14,500	3,900	.
40.	Olds Starfire	4,195	.	24
51.	Pont. Phoenix	.	3,420	.

◁

▷ Example

rmin(), rmax(), rfirst(), and rlast(). These return the minimum, maximum, first, or last nonmissing value for the specified variables within an observation (row).

```
. egen min = rmin(x y z)
(1 missing value generated)
. egen max = rmax(x y z)
(1 missing value generated)
. egen first = rfirst(x y z)
(1 missing value generated)
. egen last = rlast(x y z)
(1 missing value generated)
```

```
. list, nodisplay

       x     y     z    min   max  first   last
  1.   -1     2     3    -1     3     -1      3
  2.    .    -6     .    -6    -6     -6     -6
  3.    7     .    -5    -5     7      7     -5
  4.    .     .     .     .     .      .      .
  5.    4     .     .     4     4      4      4
  6.    .     .     8     8     8      8      8
  7.    .     3     7     3     7      3      7
  8.    5    -1     6    -1     6      5      6
```
◁

Categorical and integer variables

▷ Example

any(), eqany(), and neqany() are for categorical or other variables taking integer values. If we define a subset of values specified by an integer *numlist* (see [U] **14.1.8 numlist**), then any() extracts the subset, leaving every other value missing, eqany() defines an indicator variable (1 if in subset, 0 otherwise), and neqany() counts occurrences of the subset across a set of variables. Therefore, with just one variable, eqany(*varname*) and neqany(*varname*) are equivalent.

With the auto dataset, we can generate a variable containing the high values of rep78 and a variable indicating whether rep78 has a high value:

```
. egen hirep = any(rep78), v(3/5)
. egen ishirep = eqany(rep78), v(3/5)
```

In this case, it is easy to produce the same results with official Stata commands:

```
. gen hirep = rep78 if rep78 == 3 | rep78 == 4 | rep78 == 5
. gen byte ishirep = rep78 == 3 | rep78 == 4 | rep78 == 5
```

However, as the specification becomes more complicated, or involves several variables, the egen functions may be more convenient.

◁

▷ Example

group() maps the distinct groups of a *varlist* to a categorical variable that takes on integer values from 1 to the number of groups. The order of the groups is that of the sort order of *varlist*. The *varlist* may be of numeric variables, string variables, or a mixture of the two. The resulting variable can be useful for many purposes, including stepping through the distinct groups in an easy and systematic manner and tidying up an untidy ordering. Suppose the actual (and arbitrary) codes present in the data are 1, 2, 4 and 7, but we desire equally spaced numbers, as when the codes will be values on one axis of a graph. group() will map these to 1, 2, 3 and 4.

You have a variable agegrp that takes on the values 24, 40, 50, and 65, corresponding to age groups 18–24, 25–40, 41–50, and 51 and above. Perhaps you created this coding using the recode() function (see [U] **16.3 Functions** and [U] **28 Commands for dealing with categorical variables**) from another age-in-years variable:

```
. gen agegrp=recode(age,24,40,50,65)
```

You now wish the codes were 1, 2, 3, and 4:

```
. egen agegrp2 = group(agegrp)
```

◁

▷ Example

You have two categorical variables, race and sex, which may be string or numeric. You want to use ir (see [R] **epitab**) to create a Mantel–Haenszel weighted estimate of the incidence rate. ir, however, will allow only one variable to be specified in its by() option. You type

```
. egen racesex = group(race sex)
. ir deaths smokes pyears, by(racesex)
  (output omitted )
```

The new numeric variable racesex will be missing wherever race or sex is missing (meaning . for numeric variables and "" for string variables), so missing values will be handled correctly. When we list some of the data, we see

```
. list race sex racesex

          race       sex    racesex
  1.     black    female          1
  2.     black      male          2
  3.     white    female          3
  4.     white      male          4
  5.     white      male          4
  6.              female          .
  7.     white                    .
```

group() began by putting the data in the order of the grouping variables and then assigned the numeric codes. Note that observations 6 and 7 were assigned to racesex==. because, in one case, race, and in the other sex, were not known. (These observations were then not used by the ir command.)

Had we wanted to treat the unknown groups just as we would any other category, we could have typed

```
. egen rs2=group(race sex), missing
. list race sex rs2

          race       sex        rs2
  1.     black    female          2
  2.     black      male          3
  3.     white    female          5
  4.     white      male          6
  5.     white      male          6
  6.              female          1
  7.     white                    4
```

◁

The resulting variable from group does not have value labels. Therefore, the values from 1 upwards carry no indication of meaning. Interpretation requires comparison with the original *varlist*.

The label option produces a categorical variable with value labels. These value labels are either the actual values of *varname*, or any value labels of *varname*, if they exist. The values of *varname* could be as long as those of a single str80 variable, yet value labels may be no longer than 80 characters.

String variables

Concatenation of string variables is already provided in Stata. In context, Stata understands the addition symbol + as specifying concatenation, or adding strings end to end. "soft" + "ware" produces "software" and, given string variables s1 and s2, s1 + s2 indicates their concatenation.

The complications that may arise in practice include (1) wanting to concatenate the string versions of numeric variables, and (2) wanting to concatenate variables, together with some separator such as a space or a comma. Given numeric variables n1 and n2,

```
. gen str1 newstr = ""
. replace newstr = s1 + string(n1) + string(n2) + s2
```

shows how numeric values may be converted to their string equivalents before concatenation, and

```
. replace newstr = s1 + " " + s2 + " " + s3
```

shows how spaces may be added in between variables. Here, as often happens, it is assumed that we would rather let Stata work out the particular string data type required. That is, we first **generate** a variable of type str1, the most compact string type, and then the **replace** command automatically leads to promotion of the variable to the appropriate data type.

▷ Example

concat() allows you to do everything in one line in a very concise manner.

```
. egen newstr = concat(s1 n1 n2 s2)
```

carries with it an implicit instruction to convert numeric values to their string equivalents, and the appropriate string data type is worked out within concat() by Stata's automatic promotion. Moreover,

```
. egen newstr = concat(s1 s2 s3), p(" ")
```

specifies that spaces are to be used as separators. (The default is no separation of concatenated strings.)

As an example of punctuation other than a space, consider

```
. egen fullname = concat(surname forename), p(", ")
```

Noninteger numerical values can cause difficulties, but

```
. egen newstr = concat(n1 n2), format(%9.3f) p(" ")
```

specifies the use of format %9.3f. In other words, this is equivalent to

```
. gen str1 newstr = ""
. replace newstr = string(n1,"%9.3f") + " " + string(n2,"%9.3f")
```

See [U] **16.3.5 String functions** for more on string().

◁

As a final flourish, the **decode** option instructs concat() to use value labels. With that option, the maxlength() option may also be used. For further details on **decode**, see [R] **encode**. Unlike the **decode** command, however, concat() uses string(*varname*), not "", whenever values of *varname* are not associated with value labels, and the format() option, whenever specified, applies to this use of string().

▷ Example

The function ends(*strvar*) is for subdividing strings. The approach is to find specified separators using the index() string function and then to extract what is desired, which either precedes or follows the separators, using the substr() string function (see [U] **16.3.5 String functions**).

By default, substrings are considered to be separated by individual spaces, so we will give definitions in those terms and then generalize.

The *head* of the string is whatever precedes the first space, or the whole of the string if no space occurs. This could also be called the first 'word'. The *tail* of the string is whatever follows the first space. This could be nothing or one or more words. The *last word* in the string is whatever follows the last space, or the whole of the string if no space occurs.

To make this clear, let us look at some examples. The quotation marks here just mark the limits of each string and are not part of the strings.

	head	tail	last
"frog"	"frog"	""	"frog"
"frog toad"	"frog"	"toad"	"toad"
"frog toad newt"	"frog"	"toad newt"	"newt"
"frog toad newt"	"frog"	" toad newt"	"newt"
"frog toad newt"	"frog"	"toad newt"	"newt"

The main subtlety is that these functions are literal, so the tail of "frog toad newt", in which two spaces follow "frog", includes the second of those spaces, and is thus " toad newt". Therefore, you may prefer to use the trim() option to trim the result of any leading and/or trailing spaces, producing in this instance "toad newt".

The punct(*pchars*) option may be used to specify separators other than spaces. The general definitions of the head, tail, and last options are therefore in terms of whatever separator has been specified; that is, relative to the first or last occurrence of the separator in the string value. Thus, with punct(,) and the string "Darwin, Charles Robert", the head is "Darwin" and the tail and the last are both " Charles Robert". Note again the leading space in this example, which may be trimmed with trim(). The punctuation (here the comma ,) is discarded, just as it is with a single space.

pchars, the argument of punct(), will usually, but not always, be a single character. If two or more characters are specified, then these must occur together; punct(:;) would mean that words are separated by a colon followed by a semi-colon (that is :;). It is not implied, in particular, that the colon and semi-colon are alternatives. For that, the user must modify the programs presented here or resort to first principles using tokenize; see [P] **tokenize**.

With personal names, the options head or last might be applied to extract surnames if strings were like "Darwin, Charles Robert" or "Charles Robert Darwin", with the surname coming first or last. What then happens with surnames like "von Neumann" or "de la Mare"? "von Neumann, John" is no problem, if the comma is specified as a separator, but the option last is not intelligent enough to handle "Walter de la Mare" properly. For that, the best advice is to use programs specially written for person name extraction, such as extrname (Gould 1993).

◁

U.S. marginal income tax rate

mtr(*year income*) (Schmidt 1993, 1994) returns the U.S. marginal income tax rate for a married couple with taxable income *income* in year *year*, $1930 \leq year \leq 1999$.

▷ Example

Schmidt (1993) examines the change in the progressivity of the U.S. tax schedule over the period from 1930 to 1990. As a measure of progressivity, he calculates the difference in the marginal tax rates at the 75th and 25th percentiles of income, using a dataset of percentiles of taxable income developed by Hakkio, Rush, and Schmidt (1993). (Certain aspects of the income distribution were imputed in these data.) A subset of the data contains

```
. use income
(Income distribution, 1930-1990)

. describe

Contains data from income.dta
  obs:            61
  vars:            4                          12 Jul 2000 15:40
  size:         1,220 (99.8% of memory free)

              storage  display    value
variable name   type   format     label      variable label

year            float  %9.0g                 Year
inc25           float  %9.0g                 25th percentile
inc50           float  %9.0g                 50th percentile
inc75           float  %9.0g                 75th percentile

Sorted by:

. summarize
```

Variable	Obs	Mean	Std. Dev.	Min	Max
year	61	1960	17.75293	1930	1990
inc25	61	6948.272	6891.921	819.4	27227.35
inc50	61	11645.15	11550.71	1373.29	45632.43
inc75	61	18166.43	18019.1	2142.33	71186.58

Given the series for income and the (four digit) year, we can generate the marginal tax rates corresponding to the 25th and 75th percentiles of income:

```
. egen mtr25 = mtr(year inc25)

. egen mtr75 = mtr(year inc75)

. summarize mtr25 mtr75
```

Variable	Obs	Mean	Std. Dev.	Min	Max
mtr25	61	.1664898	.0677949	.01125	.23
mtr75	61	.2442053	.1148427	.01125	.424625

A graph of mtr75 − mtr25 vs. year shows the growth of progressivity over time:

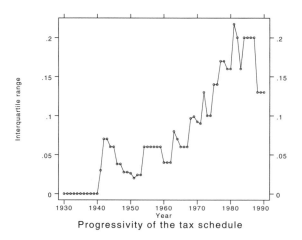

Progressivity of the tax schedule

◁

Methods and Formulas

egen is implemented as an ado-file.

Stata users have written many extra functions for egen. Type `net search egen` to locate Internet sources of programs.

Acknowledgments

The `mtr()` *fcn* of egen was written by Timothy J. Schmidt of the Federal Reserve Bank of Kansas City.

The `cut` *fcn* was written by David Clayton and Michael Hills (1999a, 1999b, 1999c).

Many of the other egen *fcn*s were written by Nicholas J. Cox of the University of Durham.

References

Andrews, D. F., P. J. Bickel, F. R. Hampel, P. J. Huber, W. H. Rogers, and J. W. Tukey. 1972. *Robust estimates of location: survey and advances.* Princeton: Princeton University Press.

Clayton, D. and M. Hills. 1999a. dm66: Recoding variables using grouped values. *Stata Technical Bulletin* 49: 6–7. Reprinted in *Stata Technical Bulletin Reprints*, vol. 9, pp. 23–25.

——. 1999b. dm66.1: Stata 6 version of recoding variables using grouped values. *Stata Technical Bulletin* 50: 3. Reprinted in *Stata Technical Bulletin Reprints*, vol. 9, p. 25.

——. 1999c. dm66.2: Update of cut to Stata 6. *Stata Technical Bulletin* 51: 2–3. Reprinted in *Stata Technical Bulletin Reprints*, vol. 9, pp. 25–26.

Cox, N. J. 1997. dm44: Sequences of integers. *Stata Technical Bulletin* 37: 2–4. Reprinted in *Stata Technical Bulletin Reprints*, vol. 7, pp. 32–33.

——. 1999. dm70: Extensions to generate, extended. *Stata Technical Bulletin* 50: 9–17. Reprinted in *Stata Technical Bulletin Reprints*, vol. 9, pp. 34–45.

——. 2000. dm70.1: Extensions to generate, extended: corrections. *Stata Technical Bulletin* 57: 2.

Cox, N. J. and R. Goldstein. 1999. dm72: Alternative ranking procedures. *Stata Technical Bulletin* 51: 5–7. Reprinted in *Stata Technical Bulletin Reprints*, vol. 9, pp. 48–51.

——. 1999. dm72.1: Alternative ranking procedures: update. *Stata Technical Bulletin* 52: 2. Reprinted in *Stata Technical Bulletin Reprints*, vol. 9, p. 51.

David, H. A. 1998. Early sample measures of variability. *Statistical Science* 13: 368–377.

Esman, R. M. 1998. dm55: Generating sequences and patterns of numeric data: an extension to egen. *Stata Technical Bulletin* 43: 2–3. Reprinted in *Stata Technical Bulletin Reprints*, vol. 8, pp. 4–5.

Gould, W. W. 1993. dm13: Person name extraction. *Stata Technical Bulletin* 13: 6–11. Reprinted in *Stata Technical Bulletin Reprints*, vol. 3, pp. 25–31.

Hakkio, C. S., M. Rush, and T. J. Schmidt. 1993. The marginal income tax rate schedule from 1930 to 1990. Research Working Paper, Federal Reserve Bank of Kansas City.

Hampel, F. R., E. M. Ronchetti, P. J. Rousseeuw, and W. A. Stahel. 1986. *Robust statistics: the approach based on influence functions.* New York: John Wiley & Sons.

Ryan, P. 1999. dm71: Calculating the product of observations. *Stata Technical Bulletin* 51: 3–4. Reprinted in *Stata Technical Bulletin Reprints*, vol. 9, pp. 45–48.

Schmidt, T. J. 1993. sss1: Calculating U.S. marginal income tax rates. *Stata Technical Bulletin* 15: 17–19. Reprinted in *Stata Technical Bulletin Reprints*, vol. 3, pp. 197–200.

——. 1994. sss1.1: Updated U.S. marginal income tax rate function. *Stata Technical Bulletin* 22: 29. Reprinted in *Stata Technical Bulletin Reprints*, vol. 4, p. 224.

Also See

Related: [R] **collapse**, [R] **generate**

Background: [U] **16.3 Functions**

Title

---
eivreg — Errors-in-variables regression

Syntax

> **eivreg** *depvar* [*indepvars*] [*weight*] [**if** *exp*] [**in** *range*] [,
>
>   **reliab**(*indepvar # [indepvar # [...]]*) **level**(*#*)]

by ... : may be used with **eivreg**; see [R] **by**.

aweights and **fweights** are allowed; see [U] **14.1.6 weight**.

eivreg shares the features of all estimation commands; see [U] **23 Estimation and post-estimation commands**.

Syntax for predict

> **predict** [*type*] *newvarname* [**if** *exp*] [**in** *range*] [, *statistic*]

where *statistic* is

xb	$\mathbf{x}_j\mathbf{b}$, fitted values (the default)
residuals	residuals
pr(*a,b*)	$\Pr(a < y_j < b)$
e(*a,b*)	$E(y_j \mid a < y_j < b)$
ystar(*a,b*)	$E(y_j^*)$, $y_j^* = \max(a, \min(y_j, b))$
stdp	standard error of the prediction
stdf	standard error of the forecast

where *a* and *b* may be numbers or variables; *a* equal to '.' means $-\infty$; *b* equal to '.' means $+\infty$.

These statistics are available both in and out of sample; type **predict** ... **if e(sample)** ... if wanted only for the estimation sample.

Description

eivreg estimates errors-in-variables regression models.

Options

reliab(*indepvar # [indepvar # [...]]*) specifies the measurement reliability for each independent variable measured with error. Reliabilities are specified as a pair consisting of an independent variable name (a name that appears in *indepvars*) and the corresponding reliability r, $0 < r \leq 1$. Independent variables for which no reliability is specified are assumed to have reliability 1. If the option is not specified, all variables are assumed to have reliability 1 and the result is thus the same as that produced by **regress** (which is to say, the ordinary least squares results).

level(*#*) specifies the confidence level, in percent, for confidence intervals. The default is **level(95)** or as set by **set level**; see [U] **23.5 Specifying the width of confidence intervals**.

Options for predict

xb, the default, calculates the linear prediction.

residuals calculates the residuals; that is, $y_j - \mathbf{x}_j\mathbf{b}$.

pr(a,b) calculates $\Pr(a < \mathbf{x}_j\mathbf{b} + u_j < b)$, the probability that $y_j|\mathbf{x}_j$ would be observed in the interval (a, b).

a and b may be specified as numbers or variable names; lb and ub are variable names;
pr(20,30) calculates $\Pr(20 < \mathbf{x}_j\mathbf{b} + u_j < 30)$;
pr(lb,ub) calculates $\Pr(lb < \mathbf{x}_j\mathbf{b} + u_j < ub)$;
and pr(20,ub) calculates $\Pr(20 < \mathbf{x}_j\mathbf{b} + u_j < ub)$.

$a = .$ means $-\infty$; pr(.,30) calculates $\Pr(\mathbf{x}_j\mathbf{b} + u_j < 30)$;
pr(lb,30) calculates $\Pr(\mathbf{x}_j\mathbf{b} + u_j < 30)$ in observations for which $lb = .$
(and calculates $\Pr(lb < \mathbf{x}_j\mathbf{b} + u_j < 30)$ elsewhere).

$b = .$ means $+\infty$; pr(20,.) calculates $\Pr(\mathbf{x}_j\mathbf{b} + u_j > 20)$;
pr(20,ub) calculates $\Pr(\mathbf{x}_j\mathbf{b} + u_j > 20)$ in observations for which $ub = .$
(and calculates $\Pr(20 < \mathbf{x}_j\mathbf{b} + u_j < ub)$ elsewhere).

e(a,b) calculates $E(\mathbf{x}_j\mathbf{b} + u_j \mid a < \mathbf{x}_j\mathbf{b} + u_j < b)$, the expected value of $y_j|\mathbf{x}_j$ conditional on $y_j|\mathbf{x}_j$ being in the interval (a, b), which is to say, $y_j|\mathbf{x}_j$ is censored.
a and b are specified as they are for pr().

ystar(a,b) calculates $E(y_j^*)$ where $y_j^* = a$ if $\mathbf{x}_j\mathbf{b} + u_j \leq a$, $y_j^* = b$ if $\mathbf{x}_j\mathbf{b} + u_j \geq b$, and $y_j^* = \mathbf{x}_j\mathbf{b} + u_j$ otherwise, which is to say, y_j^* is truncated. a and b are specified as they are for pr().

stdp calculates the standard error of the prediction. It can be thought of as the standard error of the predicted expected value or mean for the observation's covariate pattern. This is also referred to as the standard error of the fitted value.

stdf calculates the standard error of the forecast. This is the standard error of the point prediction for a single observation. It is commonly referred to as the standard error of the future or forecast value. By construction, the standard errors produced by stdf are always larger than those by stdp; see [R] **regress** *Methods and Formulas*.

Description

Errors-in-variables regression models are useful when one or more of the independent variables is measured with additive noise. Standard regression (as estimated by regress) would underestimate the effect of the variable, and the other coefficients in the model can be biased to the extent they are correlated with the poorly measured variable. One can adjust for the biases if one knows the reliability:

$$r = 1 - \frac{\text{noise variance}}{\text{total variance}}$$

That is, given the model $\mathbf{y} = \mathbf{X}\mathcal{B} + \mathbf{u}$, for some variable $\mathbf{x}_i$ in $\mathbf{X}$, the $\mathbf{x}_i$ is observed with error, $\mathbf{x}_i = \mathbf{x}_i^* + \mathbf{e}$, the noise variance is the variance of $\mathbf{e}$. The total variance is the variance of $\mathbf{x}_i$.

▷ Example

Pretend that in our automobile data the weight of cars was measured with error and pretend that the reliability of our measured weight is 0.85. The result of this would be to underestimate the effect of weight in a regression of, say, price on weight and foreign and it would also bias the estimate of the coefficient on foreign (because being of foreign manufacture is correlated with the weight of cars). We would ignore all of this if we estimated the model with `regress`:

```
. regress price weight foreign
```

Source	SS	df	MS
Model	316859273	2	158429637
Residual	318206123	71	4481776.38
Total	635065396	73	8699525.97

```
Number of obs =      74
F( 2,    71) =   35.35
Prob > F      = 0.0000
R-squared     = 0.4989
Adj R-squared = 0.4848
Root MSE      = 2117.0
```

price	Coef.	Std. Err.	t	P>|t|	[95% Conf. Interval]	
weight	3.320737	.3958784	8.39	0.000	2.531378	4.110096
foreign	3637.001	668.583	5.44	0.000	2303.885	4970.118
_cons	-4942.844	1345.591	-3.67	0.000	-7625.876	-2259.812

With `eivreg`, we can take account of our measurement error:

```
. eivreg price weight foreign, r(weight .85)
```

variable	assumed reliability
weight	0.8500
*	1.0000

```
errors-in-variables regression

Number of obs =      74
F( 2,    71) =   50.37
Prob > F      = 0.0000
R-squared     = 0.6483
Root MSE      = 1773.54
```

price	Coef.	Std. Err.	t	P>|t|	[95% Conf. Interval]	
weight	4.31985	.431431	10.01	0.000	3.459601	5.180099
foreign	4637.32	624.5362	7.43	0.000	3392.03	5882.609
_cons	-8257.017	1452.086	-5.69	0.000	-11152.39	-5361.64

The effect of weight is increased—as we knew it would be—and in this case, the effect of foreign manufacture is also increased. *A priori*, we only knew that the estimate of `foreign` might be biased; we did not know the direction.

◁

❏ Technical Note

Swept under the rug in our example is how one determines the reliability, r. It is not difficult to know that a variable is measured with error, but it is difficult to know the reliability since the ingredients for calculating r depend on the unobserved noise.

For the purposes of our example, we made up a value for r and, in fact, we do not believe that weight is measured with error at all, so the reported `eivreg` results have no validity. The `regress` results were the statistically correct results in this case.

But let's pretend that we do suspect that weight is measured with error and we do not know r. We could, in that case, experiment with various values of r as a way of describing the sensitivity of our estimates to possible error levels. We may not know r, but r does have a simple interpretation and we could probably produce a sensible range for r by thinking about how the data were collected.

If the reliability r is less than the R^2 from a regression of the poorly measured variable on all the other variables, including the dependent variable, the information might as well not have been collected; no adjustment to the final results is possible. In the case of our automobile data, running a regression of `weight` on `foreign` and `price` would result in an R^2 of .6743. Thus, the reliability must be at least .6743 in this case. If you specify a reliability that is too small, `eivreg` will inform you of this and refuse to estimate the model:

```
. eivreg price weight foreign, r(weight .6742)
reliability r too small
r(399);
```

Returning to our problem of how to estimate r, too small or not, if the measurements are summaries of scaled items, the reliability may be estimated using the `alpha` command; see [R] **alpha**. If the score is computed from factor analysis and the data are scored using `score`'s default options (see [R] **factor**), the square of the standard deviation of the score is an estimate of the reliability.

❑

❑ Technical Note

Consider a model with more than one variable measured with error. For instance, say our model is that price is a function of weight, foreign, and mileage rating and that both weight and mileage rating are measured with error.

```
. eivreg price weight foreign mpg, r(weight .85 mpg .9)
```

variable	assumed reliability		errors-in-variables regression
		Number of obs =	74
weight	0.8500	F(3, 70) =	429.14
mpg	0.9000	Prob > F =	0.0000
*	1.0000	R-squared =	0.9728
		Root MSE =	496.41

price	Coef.	Std. Err.	t	P>|t|	[95% Conf. Interval]
weight	12.88302	.6820532	18.89	0.000	11.52271	14.24333
foreign	8268.951	352.8719	23.43	0.000	7565.17	8972.732
mpg	999.2043	73.60037	13.58	0.000	852.413	1145.996
_cons	-56473.19	3710.015	-15.22	0.000	-63872.58	-49073.8

❑

(Continued on next page)

Saved Results

eivreg saves in e():

Scalars

e(N)	number of observations	e(r2)	R-squared
e(df_m)	model degrees of freedom	e(F)	F statistic
e(df_r)	residual degrees of freedom	e(rmse)	root mean square error

Macros

e(cmd)	eivreg	e(rellist)	*indepvars* and associated reliabilities
e(depvar)	name of dependent variable	e(predict)	program used to implement predict

Matrices

e(b)	coefficient vector	e(V)	variance–covariance matrix of the estimators

Functions

e(sample)	marks estimation sample

Methods and Formulas

eivreg is implemented as an ado-file.

Let the model to be estimated be

$$\mathbf{y} = \mathbf{X}^*\mathcal{B} + \mathbf{e}$$

$$\mathbf{X} = \mathbf{X}^* + \mathbf{U}$$

where $\mathbf{X}^*$ are the true values and $\mathbf{X}$ the observed values. Let $\mathbf{W}$ be the user-specified weights. If no weights are specified, $\mathbf{W} = \mathbf{I}$. If weights are specified, let $\mathbf{v}$ be the specified weights. If fweight frequency weights are specified, then $\mathbf{W} = \text{diag}(\mathbf{v})$. If aweight analytic weights are specified, then $\mathbf{W} = \text{diag}\{\mathbf{v}/(\mathbf{1}'\mathbf{v})(\mathbf{1}'\mathbf{1})\}$, which is to say, the weights are normalized to sum to the number of observations.

The estimates $\mathbf{b}$ of $\mathcal{B}$ are obtained as $\mathbf{A}^{-1}\mathbf{X}'\mathbf{W}\mathbf{y}$, where $\mathbf{A} = \mathbf{X}'\mathbf{W}\mathbf{X} - \mathbf{S}$. $\mathbf{S}$ is a diagonal matrix with elements $N(1-r_i)s_i^2$. N is the number of observations, r_i is the user-specified reliability coefficient for the ith explanatory variable or 1 if not specified, and s_i^2 is the (appropriately weighted) variance of the variable.

The variance–covariance matrix of the estimators is obtained as $s^2\mathbf{A}^{-1}\mathbf{X}'\mathbf{W}\mathbf{X}\mathbf{A}^{-1}$, where the root mean square error $s^2 = (\mathbf{y}'\mathbf{W}\mathbf{y} - \mathbf{b}\mathbf{A}\mathbf{b}')/(N-p)$, where p is the number of estimated parameters.

Also See

Complementary:	[R] **adjust**, [R] **lincom**, [R] **linktest**, [R] **mfx**, [R] **predict**, [R] **test**, [R] **testnl**, [R] **vce**, [R] **xi**
Related:	[R] **regress**
Background:	[U] **16.5 Accessing coefficients and standard errors**, [U] **23 Estimation and post-estimation commands**

Title

> **encode** — Encode string into numeric and vice versa

Syntax

<u>enc</u>ode *varname* [if *exp*] [in *range*], <u>g</u>enerate(*newvar*) [<u>l</u>abel(*name*)]

<u>dec</u>ode *varname* [if *exp*] [in *range*], <u>g</u>enerate(*newvar*) [<u>maxl</u>ength(*#*)]

Description

encode creates a new variable named *newvar* based on the string variable *varname*, creating, adding to, or just using (as necessary) the value label *newvar* or, if specified, *name*. Do *not* use **encode** if *varname* contains numbers that merely happen to be stored as strings; instead use **generate** *newvar* =**real**(*varname*) or **destring**; see [U] **26.2 Categorical string variables**, [U] **16.3 Functions**, and [R] **destring**.

decode creates a new string variable named *newvar* based on the "encoded" numeric variable *varname* and its value label.

Options

generate(*newvar*) is not optional. It specifies the name of the variable to be created.

label(*name*) is optional. It specifies the name of the value label to be created or, if the named value label already exists, used and added to as necessary. If **label**() is not specified, **encode** uses the same name for the label as it does for the new variable.

maxlength(*#*) specifies how many characters of the value label to retain; *#* must be between 1 and 80. The default is 80.

Remarks

encode is most useful in making string variables accessible to Stata's statistical routines, most of which can work with only numeric variables. **encode** is also useful in reducing the size of a dataset. If you are not familiar with value labels, read [U] **15.6.3 Value labels**.

The maximum number of associations within each value label is 65,536 (1,000 for Small Stata). Each association in a value label maps a string of up to 80 characters to a number. If your string has entries longer than that, only the first 80 characters are retained and are significant.

▷ Example

You have a dataset on high blood pressure and among the variables is **sex**, a string variable containing either "male" or "female". You wish to run a regression of high blood pressure on race, sex, and age group. You type **regress hbp race sex age_grp** and get the message "no observations".

```
. regress hbp sex race age_grp
no observations
r(2000);
```

Stata's statistical procedures cannot directly deal with string variables; as far as they are concerned, all observations on `sex` are missing. `encode` provides the solution:

```
. encode sex, gen(gender)
. regress hbp gender race age_grp
```

Source	SS	df	MS
Model	2.01013476	3	.67004492
Residual	49.3886164	1117	.044215413
Total	51.3987511	1120	.045891742

```
Number of obs =    1121
F(  3,  1117) =   15.15
Prob > F      =  0.0000
R-squared     =  0.0391
Adj R-squared =  0.0365
Root MSE      =  .21027
```

hbp	Coef.	Std. Err.	t	P>|t|	[95% Conf. Interval]	
gender	.0394747	.0130022	3.04	0.002	.0139633	.0649861
race	-.0409453	.0113721	-3.60	0.000	-.0632583	-.0186322
age_grp	.0241484	.00624	3.87	0.000	.0119049	.0363919
_cons	-.016815	.0389167	-0.43	0.666	-.093173	.059543

`encode` looks at a string variable and makes an internal table of all the values it takes on, in our case "male" and "female". It then alphabetizes that list and assigns numeric codes to each entry. Thus, 1 becomes "female" and 2 becomes "male". It creates a new `int` variable (`gender`) and substitutes a 1 where `sex` is "female", a 2 where `sex` is "male", and a *missing* (`.`) where `sex` is *null* (`""`). It creates a value label (also named `gender`) that records the mapping 1 ↔ `female` and 2 ↔ `male`. Finally, `encode` labels the values of the new variable with the value label.

◁

▷ Example

It is difficult to distinguish the result of `encode` from the original string variable. For instance, in our last two examples we typed `encode sex, gen(gender)`. Let's compare the two variables:

```
. list sex gender in 1/4
        sex    gender
1.   female    female
2.
3.     male      male
4.     male      male
```

They look almost identical, although you should notice the missing value for gender in the second observation.

The difference does show, however, if we tell `list` to ignore the value labels and show how the data really appear:

```
. list sex gender in 1/4, nolabel
        sex    gender
1.   female         1
2.
3.     male         2
4.     male         2
```

We could also ask to see the underlying value label:

```
. label list gender
gender:
           1 female
           2 male
```

gender really is a numeric variable, but since *all* Stata commands understand value labels, the variable displays as "male" and "female" just as would the underlying string variable sex.

◁

▷ Example

You can drastically reduce the size of your dataset by encoding strings and then discarding the underlying string variable. Say you have a string variable that records each person's sex as "male" and "female". "female" has six characters, so at the least you have the variable stored as a str6.

The variable created by encode is an int, which takes only two bytes. Thus, if your dataset contained 1,000 people, the string variable takes (at least) 6,000 bytes whereas the encoded variable takes only 2,000 bytes. Thus, you might

```
. encode sex, gen(gender)
. drop sex
. rename gender sex
```

See decode below for instructions on how to convert an encoded variable back to string form. See [R] **compress** for more ways to compress datasets.

◁

❑ Technical Note

In the examples given above, the value label did not exist before encode created it. That is not required. If the value label does exist, encode will use your encoding as far as it can and add new mappings for anything not found in your value label. For instance, if you wanted "female" to be encoded as 0 rather than 1 (possibly for use in linear regression), you could

```
. label define gender 0 "female"
. encode sex, gen(gender)
```

You can also specify the name of the value label. If you do not, the value label is assumed to have the same name as the newly created variable. For instance:

```
. label define sexlbl 0 "female"
. encode sex, gen(gender) label(sexlbl)
```

❑

decode

decode is used to convert numeric variables with associated value labels into true string variables.

▷ Example

You have a numeric variable named female that records the values 0 and 1. female is associated to a value label named sexlbl that says 0 means male and 1 means female:

```
. describe female

              storage  display   value
variable name  type    format    label      variable label
-----------------------------------------------------------------
female         int     %9.0g     sexlbl
```

```
. label list sexlbl
sexlbl:
           0 male
           1 female
```

We see that **female** is the sixth variable in our dataset and that it is stored as an **int**. It is a numeric variable. Nevertheless, it has an associated value label describing what the numeric codes mean, so if we **tabulate** the variable, for instance, it appears as if it contains the strings "male" and "female":

```
. tabulate female
```

female	Freq.	Percent	Cum.
male	85	55.92	55.92
female	67	44.08	100.00
Total	152	100.00	

We can create a real string variable from this numerically encoded variable using **decode**:

```
. decode female, gen(sex)
. describe sex
```

variable name	storage type	display format	value label	variable label
sex	str6	%9s		

We have a new variable called **sex**. It is a string, and Stata automatically created the shortest possible string. "female" has six characters, so our new variable is a **str6**. **female** and **sex** appear indistinguishable:

```
. list female sex in 1/4
```

	female	sex
1.	male	male
2.	female	female
3.	female	female
4.	female	female

But when we add **nolabel**, the difference is apparent:

```
. list female sex in 1/4, nolabel
```

	female	sex
1.	0	male
2.	1	female
3.	1	female
4.	1	female

◁

▷ Example

decode is most useful in instances where you wish to match merge two datasets on a variable that has been encoded inconsistently.

For instance, you have two datasets on individual states where one of the variables (**state**) takes on values like "CA" and "NY". The state variable was originally a string, but along the way the variable was encoded into an integer with corresponding value label in one or both datasets.

You wish to merge these two datasets, but either (1) one of the datasets has a string variable for state and the other an encoded variable or (2) although both are numeric, you are not certain that the codings are consistent. Perhaps "CA" has been coded 5 in one dataset and 6 in another.

Since `decode` will take an encoded variable and turn it back into a string, `decode` provides the solution:

```
use first                 (load the first dataset)
decode state, gen(st)     (make a string state variable)
drop state                (discard the encoded variable)
sort st                   (sort on string)
save first, replace       (and save it)
use second                (load the second dataset)
decode state, gen(st)     (make a string variable)
drop state                (discard the encoded variable)
sort st                   (sort on string)
merge st using first      (merge the data)
```

Of course, now you should `tabulate _merge` to make sure that the merge went as expected; see [R] **merge**.

◁

References

Cox, N. J. and J. B. Wernow. 2000a. dm80: Changing numeric variables to string. *Stata Technical Bulletin* 56: 8–12.

——. 2000b. dm80.1: Update to changing numeric variables to string. *Stata Technical Bulletin* 57: 2.

Also See

Complementary: [R] **compress**

Background: [U] **15.6.3 Value labels**,
    [U] **26.2 Categorical string variables**

Title

> **epitab** — Tables for epidemiologists

Syntax

Cohort studies

> ir *var*~case~ *var*~exposed~ *var*~time~ [*weight*] [if *exp*] [in *range*] [, by(*varname*)
>
> tb <u>noc</u>rude <u>p</u>ool <u>noh</u>om <u>es</u>tandard <u>is</u>tandard <u>s</u>tandard(*varname*) ird
>
> <u>l</u>evel(*#*)]

> iri *#*~a~ *#*~b~ *#*~N₁~ *#*~N₂~ [, <u>l</u>evel(*#*) tb]

> cs *var*~case~ *var*~exposed~ [*weight*] [if *exp*] [in *range*] [, by(*varlist*) <u>e</u>xact or
>
> tb <u>w</u>oolf <u>noc</u>rude <u>p</u>ool <u>noh</u>om <u>es</u>tandard <u>is</u>tandard <u>s</u>tandard(*varname*) rd
>
> <u>b</u>inomial(*varname*) <u>l</u>evel(*#*)]

> csi *#*~a~ *#*~b~ *#*~c~ *#*~d~ [, <u>e</u>xact or tb <u>w</u>oolf <u>l</u>evel(*#*)]

Case–control studies

> cc *var*~case~ *var*~exposed~ [*weight*] [if *exp*] [in *range*] [, by(*varname*) <u>e</u>xact
>
> <u>cor</u>nfield tb <u>w</u>oolf <u>noc</u>rude <u>p</u>ool <u>noh</u>om bd
>
> <u>es</u>tandard <u>is</u>tandard <u>s</u>tandard(*varname*) <u>b</u>inomial(*varname*) <u>l</u>evel(*#*)]

> cci *#*~a~ *#*~b~ *#*~c~ *#*~d~ [, <u>e</u>xact <u>cor</u>nfield tb <u>w</u>oolf <u>l</u>evel(*#*)]

> tabodds *var*~case~ [*expvar*] [*weight*] [if *exp*] [in *range*] [, or <u>cor</u>nfield tb <u>w</u>oolf
>
> base(*#*) <u>adj</u>ust(*varlist*) <u>b</u>inomial(*varname*) <u>l</u>evel(*#*)
>
> <u>ci</u>plot <u>g</u>raph *graph_options*]

> mhodds *var*~case~ *expvar* [*vars*~adjust~] [*weight*] [if *exp*] [in *range*] [, by(*varlist*)
>
> <u>c</u>ompare(*level₁*, *level₂*) <u>b</u>inomial(*varname*) <u>l</u>evel(*#*)]

Matched case–control studies

> mcc *var*~exposed_case~ *var*~exposed_control~ [*weight*] [if *exp*] [in *range*] [, tb <u>l</u>evel(*#*)]

> mcci *#*~a~ *#*~b~ *#*~c~ *#*~d~ [, tb <u>l</u>evel(*#*)]

fweights are allowed; see [U] **14.1.6 weight**.

Description

ir is used with incidence rate (incidence density or person-time) data. Point estimates and confidence intervals for the incidence rate ratio and difference are calculated along with attributable or prevented fractions for the exposed and total population. iri is the immediate form of ir; see [U] **22 Immediate commands**. Also see [R] **poisson** and [R] **st stcox** for related commands.

cs is used with cohort study data with equal follow-up time per subject and sometimes with cross-sectional data. Risk is then the proportion of subjects who become cases. Point estimates and confidence intervals for the risk difference, risk ratio, and (optionally) the odds ratio are calculated along with attributable or prevented fractions for the exposed and total population. csi is the immediate form of cs; see [U] **22 Immediate commands**. Also see [R] **logistic** and [R] **glogit** for related commands.

cc is used with case–control and cross-sectional data. Point estimates and confidence intervals for the odds ratio are calculated along with attributable or prevented fractions for the exposed and total population. cci is the immediate form of cc; see [U] **22 Immediate commands**. Also see [R] **logistic** and [R] **glogit** for related commands.

tabodds is used with case–control and cross-sectional data. It tabulates the odds of failure against a categorical explanatory variable *expvar*. If *expvar* is specified, tabodds will perform an approximate χ^2 test of homogeneity of odds and a test for linear trend of the log odds against the numerical code used for the categories of *expvar*. Both of these tests are based on the score statistic and its variance; see *Methods and Formulas* below. When *expvar* is absent, the overall odds are reported. The variable var_{case} is coded 0/1 for individual and simple frequency records, and equals the number of cases for binomial frequency records.

Optionally, tabodds will tabulate adjusted or unadjusted odds ratios using either the lowest levels of *expvar* or a user defined level as the reference group. If adjust(*varlist*) is specified, odds ratios adjusted for the variables in *varlist* will be produced along with a (score) test for trend.

mhodds is used with case–control and cross-sectional data. It estimates the ratio of the odds of failure for two categories of *expvar*, controlled for specified confounding variables, $vars_{\text{adjust}}$, and also tests whether this odds ratio is equal to one. When *expvar* has more than two categories but none are specified with the compare option, mhodds assumes that *expvar* is a quantitative variable and calculates a one-degree-of-freedom test for trend. It also calculates an approximate estimate of the rate ratio for a one unit increase in *expvar*. This is a one-step Newton–Raphson approximation to the maximum likelihood estimate calculated as the ratio of the score statistic, U, to its variance, V (Clayton and Hills 1993, 103).

mcc is used with matched case–control data. McNemar's chi-squared, point estimates and confidence intervals for the difference, ratio, and relative difference of the proportion with the factor, along with the odds ratio, are calculated. mcci is the immediate form of mcc; see [U] **22 Immediate commands**. Also see [R] **clogit** and [R] **symmetry** for related commands.

Options

Options are listed in alphabetical order.

adjust(*varlist*) is allowed only with tabodds. It specifies that odds ratios adjusted for the variables in *varlist* be calculated.

base(#) is allowed only with tabodds. It specifies the value of *expvar* to be used as the reference group for calculating odds ratios. If base() is not specified, the minimum value of expvar is used as the reference group.

bd specifies that Breslow and Day's χ^2 test of homogeneity be included in the output of a stratified analysis. This tests whether the exposure effect is the same across strata. bd is relevant only if by() is also specified.

binomial(*varname*) is allowed only with cs, cc, tabodds, and mhodds. It supplies the number of subjects (cases plus controls) for binomial frequency records. For individual and simple frequency records, this option is not used.

by(*varname*) specifies that the tables are stratified on *varname*. Within-stratum statistics are shown and then combined with Mantel–Haenszel weights. If estandard, istandard, or standard() is also specified (see below), the weights specified are used in place of Mantel–Haenszel weights. cs will accept a *varlist*.

ciplot is allowed only with tabodds. It produces the same plot as the graph option, but also includes the confidence intervals. Graph options other than connect() are allowed. This option is not allowed with the or option or the adjust() option.

compare(v_1, v_2) is allowed only with mhodds. It gives the categories of *expvar* to be compared; v_1 defines the numerator and v_2 the denominator. When compare is absent and there are only two categories, the second is compared to the first; when there are more than two categories, an approximate estimate of the odds ratio for a unit increase in *expvar*, controlled for specified confounding variables, is given.

cornfield requests that the Cornfield (1956) approximation be used for calculating the standard error of the odds ratio. Otherwise, standard errors are obtained as the square root of the variance of the score statistic or exactly in the case of cc and cci.

estandard, istandard, and standard(*varname*) request that within-stratum statistics be combined with external, internal, or user-specified weights to produce a standardized estimate. These options are mutually exclusive and can be used only when by() is also specified. (When by() is specified without one of these options, Mantel–Haenszel weights are used.)

estandard external weights are the person-time for the unexposed (ir), the total number of unexposed (cs), or the number of unexposed controls (cc).

istandard internal weights are person-time for the exposed (ir), the total number of exposed (cs), or the number of exposed controls (cc). istandard can be used for producing, among other things, standardized mortality ratios (SMRs).

standard(*varname*) allows user-specified weights. *varname* must contain a constant within stratum and be nonnegative. The scale of *varname* is irrelevant.

exact requests Fisher's exact p be calculated rather than the χ^2 and its significance level. We recommend specifying exact whenever samples are small. A conservative rule-of-thumb for 2×2 tables is to specify exact when the least-frequent cell contains fewer than 1,000 cases. When the least frequent cell contains 1,000 cases or more there will be no appreciable difference between the exact significance level and the significance level based on the χ^2, but the exact significance level will take considerably longer to calculate. Note that exact does *not* affect whether exact confidence intervals are calculated. Commands always calculate exact confidence intervals where they can unless tb or woolf is specified.

graph is allowed only with tabodds. It produces a graph of the odds against the numerical code used for the categories of *expvar*. Graph options other than connect() are allowed. This option is not allowed with the or option or the adjust() option.

ird may be used only with estandard, istandard, or standard(). It requests that ir calculate the standardized incidence rate difference rather than the default incidence rate ratio.

istandard; see estandard, above.

level(#) specifies the confidence level, in percent, for confidence intervals. The default is level(95) or as set by set level; see [R] **level**.

nocrude specifies that in a stratified analysis the crude estimate—the estimate one would obtain without regard to strata—not be displayed. nocrude is relevant only if by() is also specified.

nohom specifies that a χ^2 test of homogeneity not be included in the output of a stratified analysis. This tests whether the exposure effect is the same across strata and can be performed for any pooled estimate—directly pooled or Mantel–Haenszel. nohom is relevant only if by() is also specified.

or is allowed only with cs, csi, and tabodds. For cs and csi, or specified without by() reports the calculation of the odds ratio in addition to the risk ratio. With by(), or specifies that a Mantel–Haenszel estimate of the combined odds ratio be made rather than the Mantel–Haenszel estimate of the risk ratio. In either case, this is the same calculation as would be made by cc and cci. Typically, cc, cci, or tabodds is preferred for calculating odds ratios. For tabodds, or specifies that odds ratios be produced; see base() above for selection of reference category. By default, tabodds will calculate odds.

pool specifies that in a stratified analysis the directly pooled estimate should also be displayed. The pooled estimate is a weighted average of the stratum-specific estimates using inverse-variance weights—weights that are the inverse of the variance of the stratum-specific estimate. pool is relevant only if by() is also specified.

rd may be used only with estandard, istandard, or standard(). It requests that cs calculate the standardized risk difference rather than the default risk ratio.

standard(*varname*); see estandard, above.

tb requests that test-based confidence intervals (Miettinen 1976) be calculated wherever appropriate in place of confidence intervals based on other approximations or exact confidence intervals. We recommend that test-based confidence intervals be used only for pedagogical purposes and never be used for research work.

woolf requests that the Woolf (1955) approximation, also known as the Taylor expansion, be used for calculating the standard error of the odds ratio. Otherwise, with the exception of tabodds and mhodds, the Cornfield (1956) approximation is used. The Cornfield approximation takes substantially longer (a few seconds) to calculate than the Woolf approximation. In the case of tabodds and mhodds standard errors of the odds ratios are obtained as the square root of the variance of the score statistic. This standard error is used in calculating a confidence interval for the odds ratio. (For matched case–control data, exact confidence intervals are always calculated.)

Remarks

Remarks are presented under the headings

> *Incidence rate data*
> *Stratified incidence rate data*
> *Standardized estimates with stratified incidence rate data*
> *Cumulative incidence data*
> *Stratified cumulative incidence data*
> *Standardized estimates with stratified cumulative incidence data*
> *Case–control data*
> *Stratified case–control*
> *Case–control data with multiple levels of exposure*
> *Case–control data with confounders and possibly multiple levels of exposure*
> *Standardized estimates with stratified case–control data*
> *Matched case–control data*

In order to calculate appropriate statistics and suppress inappropriate statistics, the `ir`, `cs`, `cc`, `tabodds`, `mhodds`, and `mcc` commands, along with their immediate counterparts, are organized in the way epidemiologists conceptualize data. `ir` processes incidence rate data from prospective studies; `cs`, cohort study data with equal follow-up time (cumulative incidence); `cc`, `tabodds`, and `mhodds`, case–control or cross-sectional (prevalence) data; and `mcc`, matched case–control data. With the exception of `mcc`, these commands work with both simple and stratified tables.

Epidemiological data are often summarized in a contingency table from which various statistics are calculated. The rows of the table reflect cases and noncases or cases and person-time, and the columns reflect exposure to a *risk factor*. To an epidemiologist, *cases* and *noncases* refer to the outcomes of the process being studied. For instance, a case might be a person with cancer and a noncase a person without cancer.

A *factor* is something that might affect the chances of being ultimately designated a case or a noncase. Thus, a case might be a cancer patient and the factor, smoking behavior. A person is said to be *exposed* or *unexposed* to the factor. Exposure can be classified as a dichotomy, smokes or does not smoke, or at multiple levels such as number of cigarettes smoked per week.

For an introduction to epidemiological methods, see Walker (1991). For an intermediate treatment, see Clayton and Hills (1993) and Lilienfeld and Stolley (1994). For a mathematically intermediate but otherwise advanced discussion, see Kelsey, Thompson, and Evans (1986). For other advanced discussions, see Fisher and van Belle (1993), Kleinbaum, Kupper, and Morgenstern (1982), and Rothman and Greenland (1998). For an anthology of writings on epidemiology since World War II, see Greenland (1987b).

❏ Technical Note

In many of the examples in this section, we provide output having specified the `level(90)` option, obtaining 90% confidence intervals. This was done in order that the results in our examples be the same as those given in various texts, especially Rothman and Greenland (1998). This should not be taken as an endorsement that a 90% confidence interval is somehow appropriate in professional work. ❏

Incidence rate data

In *incidence rate data* from a prospective study, you observe the transformation of noncases into cases. Starting with a group of noncase subjects, you follow them to determine if they become a case (e.g., struck by lightning or, more likely, stricken with cancer). You follow two populations—those exposed and those unexposed to the factor. A summary of the data is

	Exposed	Unexposed	Total
Cases	a	b	$a + b$
Person-time	N_1	N_0	$N_1 + N_0$

▷ Example

It will be easiest to understand these commands if we start with the immediate forms. Remember, in the immediate form, you specify the data on the command line rather than specify names of variables containing the data; see [U] **22 Immediate commands**. You have data (Boice and Monson 1977, reported in Rothman and Greenland 1998, 238) on breast cancer *cases* and person-years of observation for women with tuberculosis repeatedly *exposed* to multiple X-ray fluoroscopies, and those not so exposed:

| | X-ray fluoroscopy | |
	Exposed	Unexposed
Breast cancer cases	41	15
Person-years	28,010	19,017

Using the immediate form of `ir`, you specify the values in the table following the command:

```
. iri 41 15 28010 19017
```

	Exposed	Unexposed		Total
Cases	41	15		56
Person-time	28010	19017		47027

| Incidence Rate | .0014638 | .0007888 | | .0011908 |

	Point estimate	[95% Conf. Interval]		
Inc. rate diff.	.000675	.0000749	.0012751	
Inc. rate ratio	1.855759	1.005722	3.60942	(exact)
Attr. frac. ex.	.4611368	.005689	.7229472	(exact)
Attr. frac. pop	.337618			

(midp) Pr(k>=41) =	0.0177	(exact)
(midp) 2*Pr(k>=41) =	0.0355	(exact)

`iri` shows the table, reports the incidence rates for the exposed and unexposed populations, and then shows the point estimates of the difference and ratio of the two incidence rates along with their confidence intervals. The *incidence rate* is simply the frequency with which noncases are transformed into cases.

Next is reported the attributable fraction among the exposed population, an estimate of the proportion of exposed cases attributable to exposure. We estimate that 46.1% of the 41 breast cancer cases among the exposed were due to exposure. (Had the incidence rate ratio been less than 1, reported would have been the prevented fraction in the exposed population, an estimate of the net proportion of all potential cases in the exposed population that was prevented by exposure; see the following technical note.)

Following that is the attributable fraction in the total population, which is the net proportion of all cases attributable to exposure. This number, of course, depends on the proportion of cases that are exposed in the base population, which here is taken to be $41/56$ and so may not be relevant in all situations. We estimate that 33.8% of the 56 cases were due to exposure. Note that $.338 \times 56 = .461 \times 41 = 18.9$, that is, looked at either way, we estimate that 18.9 cases were caused by exposure.

At the bottom of the table are reported both one- and two-sided exact significance tests. For the one-sided test, the probability that the number of exposed cases is 41 or greater is .0177. This is a "midp" calculation; see *Methods and Formulas* below. The two-sided test is $2 \times .0177 = .0354$.

◁

❏ Technical Note

When the incidence rate is less than 1, `iri` (and `ir`, and `cs` and `csi`, and `cc` and `cci`) substitute the prevented fraction for the attributable fraction. Let us reverse the roles of exposure in the above data, treating as exposed a person who did not receive the X-ray fluoroscopy. You can think of this as a new treatment for preventing breast cancer—the suggested treatment being not to employ fluoroscopy.

```
. iri 15 41 19017 28010
```

	Exposed	Unexposed	Total
Cases	15	41	56
Person-time	19017	28010	47027
Incidence Rate	.0007888	.0014638	.0011908

	Point estimate	[95% Conf. Interval]		
Inc. rate diff.	−.000675	−.0012751	−.0000749	
Inc. rate ratio	.5388632	.2770528	.994311	(exact)
Prev. frac. ex.	.4611368	.005689	.7229472	(exact)
Prev. frac. pop	.1864767			

(midp)	Pr(k<=15) =	0.0177	(exact)
(midp)	2*Pr(k<=15) =	0.0355	(exact)

The prevented fraction among the exposed is the net proportion of all potential cases in the exposed population that were prevented by exposure. We estimate that 46.1% of potential cases among the women receiving the new "treatment" were prevented by the treatment. (Previously, we estimated the same percent of actual cases among women receiving the X-rays were caused by the X-rays.)

The prevented fraction for the population, which is the net proportion of all potential cases in the total population that was prevented by exposure, as with the attributable fraction, depends on the proportion of cases that are exposed in the base population—here taken as 15/56—and so may not be relevant in all situations. We estimate that 18.6% of the potential cases were prevented by exposure.

Also see Greenland and Robins (1988) for a discussion of the interpretation of attributable and prevented fractions.

❑

▷ Example

ir works like iri except that it obtains the entries in the tables by summing data. You specify three variables—the first representing the number of cases represented by this observation, the second whether the observation is for subjects exposed to the factor, and the third recording the total time the subjects in this observation were observed. An observation may reflect a single subject or a group of subjects.

For instance, here is a two-observation dataset for the table in the previous example:

```
. list

        cases    exposed       time
  1.       41          0      28010
  2.       15          1      19017
```

If you typed ir cases exposed time, you would obtain the same output as we obtained above. Another way the data might be recorded is

```
. list

        cases    exposed       time
  1.       20          0      14000
  2.       21          0      14010
  3.       15          1      19017
```

In this case the first two observations will be automatically summed by `ir` since both are exposed. Finally, the data might be individual-level data:

```
. list
        cases    exposed      time
1.          1          1        10
2.          0          1         8
3.          0          0         9
4.          1          0         2
5.          0          1         1
  (output omitted )
```

The first observation represents a woman who got cancer, was exposed, and was observed for 10 years. The second is a woman who did not get cancer, was exposed, and was observed for 8 years, and so on.

◁

❑ Technical Note

`ir` (and all the other commands) assume a subject was exposed if the exposed variable is nonzero and not missing; assume the subject was not exposed if the variable is zero; and ignore the observation if the variable is missing. For `ir`, the case variable and the time variable are restricted to nonnegative integers and are summed within the exposed and unexposed groups to obtain the entries in the table.

❑

Stratified incidence rate data

▷ Example

`ir` can work with stratified as well as single tables. For instance, Rothman (1986, 185) discusses data from Rothman and Monson (1973) on the mortality by sex and age for patients with trigeminal neuralgia:

	Age through 64		Age 65+	
	Males	Females	Males	Females
Deaths	14	10	76	121
Person-years	1516	1701	949	2245

Entering the data into Stata, we have the dataset:

```
. list
        age     male    deaths     pyears
1.      <65        1        14       1516
2.      <65        0        10       1701
3.      65+        1        76        949
4.      65+        0       121       2245
```

And the stratified analysis of the incidence rate ratio is

```
. ir deaths male pyears, by(age) level(90)
    Age category |      IRR      [90% Conf. Interval]   M-H Weight
-----------------+-------------------------------------------------------
             <65 |   1.570844    .7380603   3.431829    4.712465  (exact)
             65+ |   1.485862    1.15357    1.907461   35.95147  (exact)
-----------------+-------------------------------------------------------
           Crude |   1.099794    .8688091   1.388882             (exact)
   M-H combined |   1.49571     1.191914   1.876938
-----------------+-------------------------------------------------------
 Test of homogeneity (M-H)     chi2(1) =      0.02  Pr>chi2 = 0.8992
```

Here we also specified `level(90)` to obtain 90% confidence intervals. The row labeled `M-H combined` reflects the combined Mantel–Haenszel estimates.

As with the previous example, it was not important that each entry in the table correspond to a single observation in the data—`ir` sums the time (`pyears`) and case (`deaths`) variables within the exposure (`male`) category.

From the output, we learn that the Mantel–Haenszel estimate differs from the simple crude estimate—that incidence rates appear to vary by age category—and from the test of homogeneity, we find that the exposure effect (the effect of trigeminal neuralgia) is the same across age categories (i.e., we cannot reject the hypothesis that the effects do not differ). Thus, we are justified in our use of the Mantel–Haenszel estimate.

◁

❑ Technical Note

Stratification is one way to deal with confounding; that is, perhaps sex affects the incidence of trigeminal neuralgia and so does age, so the table was stratified by age in an attempt to uncover the sex effect. (You are concerned that age may confound the true association between sex and the incidence of trigeminal neuralgia because the less-than-65/65+ age distributions are so different for males and females. If age affects incidence, the difference in the age distributions would induce different incidences for males and females and thus confound the true effect of sex.)

One does not, however, have to use tables to uncover effects; the estimation alternative *when you have aggregate data* is Poisson regression and we can use the same data on which we ran `ir` with `poisson`. When you have individual-level data, Poisson regression is an alternative, but so is Cox regression; see below.

(Although `age` in the previous example appears to be a string, it is actually a numeric variable taking on values 0 and 1. We attached a value label to produce the labelings `<65` and `65+` to make `ir`'s output look better; see [U] **15.6.3 Value labels**. Stata's estimation commands will ignore this labeling.)

```
. poisson deaths male age, exposure(pyears) level(90) irr

Iteration 0:    log likelihood = -10.836732
Iteration 1:    log likelihood = -10.734087
Iteration 2:    log likelihood = -10.733944
Iteration 3:    log likelihood = -10.733944

Poisson regression                          Number of obs   =          4
                                            LR chi2(2)      =     164.01
                                            Prob > chi2     =     0.0000
Log likelihood = -10.733944                 Pseudo R2       =     0.8843
```

deaths	IRR	Std. Err.	z	P>|z|	[90% Conf. Interval]	
male	1.495096	.2060997	2.92	0.004	1.191779	1.875611
age	8.888775	1.934943	10.04	0.000	6.213541	12.71583
pyears	(exposure)					

It is worth comparing these results with the Mantel–Haenszel estimates produced by `ir`:

Source	IR Ratio	90% Conf. Int.	
Mantel–Haenszel (`ir`)	1.50	1.19	1.88
`poisson`	1.50	1.19	1.88

Results are identical to two decimal places. Moreover, in addition to obtaining the incidence rate ratio for the `male` exposure variable, we also obtain an estimate and confidence interval for the incidence rate of being 65 and over relative to being less than age 65, although in this case the number is not of much interest since the outcome variable is total mortality and we already knew that older people have a higher mortality rate. In other contexts, however, the number may be of greater interest.

See [R] **poisson** for an explanation of the `poisson` command.

❑

❑ Technical Note

Both the model estimated above and the preceding table asserted that exposure effects are the same across age categories and, if they are not, then both of the previous results are equally inappropriate. The table presented a test of homogeneity, reassuring us that the exposure effects do indeed appear to be constant. The Poisson-regression alternative can be used to reproduce that test by including interactions between the groups and exposure:

```
. gen maleXage = male*age

. poisson deaths male age maleXage, exp(pyears) level(90) irr

Iteration 0:   log likelihood = -10.898799
Iteration 1:   log likelihood = -10.726225
Iteration 2:   log likelihood = -10.725904
Iteration 3:   log likelihood = -10.725904
```

Poisson regression				Number of obs	=	4
				LR chi2(3)	=	164.03
				Prob > chi2	=	0.0000
Log likelihood = -10.725904				Pseudo R2	=	0.8843

deaths	IRR	Std. Err.	z	P>|z|	[90% Conf. Interval]	
male	1.660688	1.396496	0.60	0.546	.4164666	6.622099
age	9.167973	3.01659	6.73	0.000	5.33613	15.75144
maleXage	.9459	.41539	-0.13	0.899	.4593455	1.947829
pyears	(exposure)					

Note that the significance level of the `maleXage` effect is 0.899, the same as previously reported by `ir`.

In this case, forming the male-times-age interaction was easy because there were only two age groups. Had there been more groups, the test would have been slightly more difficult—see the next technical note.

❑

❑ Technical Note

A word of caution is in order when applying `poisson` (or any estimation technique) to more than two age categories. Let's pretend that in our data we had three age categories, which we will call categories 0, 1, and 2, and that they are stored in the variable `agecat`. You might think of the categories as corresponding to age less than 35, 35–64, and 65 and above.

With such data, you might type `ir deaths male pyears, by(agecat)`, but you would *not* type `poisson deaths male agecat, exposure(pyears)` to obtain the equivalent Poisson-regression estimated results. Such a model might be reasonable, but it is not equivalent because you would be constraining the age effect in category 2 to be (multiplicatively) twice the effect in category 1.

To `poisson` (and all of Stata's estimation commands other than `anova`), `agecat` is simply one variable and only one estimated coefficient is associated with it. Thus, the model is

$$\text{Poisson index} = P = \beta_0 + \beta_1 \texttt{male} + \beta_2 \texttt{agecat}$$

Without explanation, the expected number of deaths is then e^P and the incidence rate ratio associated with a variable is e^β; see [R] **poisson**. Thus, the value of the Poisson index when `male==0` and `agecat==1` is $\beta_0 + \beta_2$, and the possibilities are

	male==0	male==1
agecat==0	β_0	$\beta_0 + \beta_1$
agecat==1	$\beta_0 + \beta_2$	$\beta_0 + \beta_2 + \beta_1$
agecat==2	$\beta_0 + 2\beta_2$	$\beta_0 + 2\beta_2 + \beta_1$

What is important to note is that the age effect for `agecat==2` is constrained to be twice the age effect for `agecat==1`—the only difference between lines 3 and 2 of the table is that β_2 is replaced with $2\beta_2$. Under certain circumstances, such a constraint might be reasonable, but it does not correspond to the assumptions made in generating the Mantel–Haenszel combined results.

To obtain results equivalent to the Mantel–Haenszel, you must estimate a separate effect for each age group, meaning replace $2\beta_2$, the constrained effect, with β_3, a new coefficient that is free to take on any value. We can achieve this by creating two new variables and using them in place of `agecat`. `agecat1` will take on the value 1 when `agecat` is 1 and 0 otherwise; `agecat2` will take on the value 1 when `agecat` is 2 and 0 otherwise:

```
. gen agecat1 = (agecat==1)
. gen agecat2 = (agecat==2)
. poisson deaths male agecat1 agecat2 [freq=pop], exposure(pyears) irr
```

In Stata, we do not have to generate these variables for ourselves. We could use Stata's expand-interaction command `xi`:

```
. xi: poisson deaths male i.agecat [freq=pop], exposure(pyears) irr
```

See [R] **xi**. It is also worth reading [U] **28 Commands for dealing with categorical variables**. Although that discussion is in terms of linear regression, what is said there applies equally to Poisson regression.

To reproduce the homogeneity test with multiple age categories, we could type

```
. xi: poisson deaths i.agecat*male [freq=pop], exp(pyears) irr
. testparm _Ia*Xm*
```

Poisson regression combined with `xi` generalizes to multiway tables. For instance, perhaps there are three exposure categories. Assume exposure variable `burn` takes on the values 1, 2, and 3 for first-, second-, and third-degree burns. The table itself is estimated by typing

```
. xi: poisson deaths i.burn i.agecat [freq=pop], exp(pyears) irr
```

and the test of homogeneity by typing

```
. xi: poisson deaths i.burn*i.agecat [freq=pop], exp(pyears) irr
. testparm _Ib*Xa*
```

❏

❑ Technical Note

When you have individual-level data, Cox regression and Poisson regression are alternatives to stratified tables. For instance, if we had the individual-level data for deaths by sex and age for the patients with trigeminal neuralgia, the first few observations might be

```
. list

        patient      male       age      died   studytime
    1.        1         0        64         0           2
    2.        2         1        58         1         3.5
    3.        3         1        44         0           3
    (output omitted)
```

Patient 1 is a female, age 64, who did not die and was followed for 2 years. Patient 2 is a male, age 58, who did die after being followed for 3.5 years. With these data, we could obtain the same incidence-rate table we obtained previously by typing

```
. gen agecat = age>=65
. ir died male studytime, by(agecat)
```

but there would be a problem. We would be assuming that patient 1 contributes 2 person-years to the age 64 group, which is not true. Patient 1 contributes 1 person-year to the age 64 group and 1 more person-year to the age 65 group. We would not have this problem if age did not vary over time, so for the moment, pretend that age is really something else—say race—that does not vary over time. In that case, the Cox regression alternative could be obtained by typing

```
. cox studytime male agecat, dead(died) hr
```

although we prefer the absolutely equivalent stcox to cox and so would type

```
. stset studytime, failure(died)
. stcox male agecat
```

(Yes, it looks like more work to type two commands rather than one, but, in the long run, it is not; see [R] **st**.)

Now let's deal with the fact that age does vary over time. The following commands will transform our data:

```
. expand studytime+cond(int(studytime)==studytime,0,1)
. by patient, sort: gen time=cond(_n~=_N,1,studytime-(_N-1))
. by patient: gen cumtime=sum(time)
. by patient: replace died=0 if _n~=_N
. by patient: replace age=age+_n-1
```

See [R] **expand** and [U] **16 Functions and expressions**, and for an explanation of cond() and sum(), see [U] **16.3 Functions**. After issuing these commands, our data are

```
. list

        patient   male    age   died   studytime    time    cumtime
    1.        1      0      64      0           2       1          1
    2.        1      0      65      0           2       1          2
    3.        2      1      58      0         3.5       1          1
    4.        2      1      59      0         3.5       1          2
    5.        2      1      60      0         3.5       1          3
    6.        2      1      61      1         3.5      .5        3.5
    7.        3      1      44      0           3       1          1
    8.        3      1      45      0           3       1          2
    9.        3      1      46      0           3       1          3
    (output omitted)
```

That is, there are now two observations for patient 1, one at age 64 and another at age 65. In neither case did the patient die. For patient 2, there are now four observations, three corresponding to ages 58–60, during which the patient did not die, and one more (contributing half a year) corresponding to age 61, at which time the patient did die. The variable time records the contribution of the observation to exposure; cumtime records the total time from entry into the study (diagnosis of trigeminal neuralgia) to the end of the observation.

We can obtain our original table from these data by typing

```
. gen agecat = age>=65
. ir died sex time, by(agecat)
```

The corresponding Cox regression model could be estimated by typing

```
. stset cumtime, failure(died) id(patient)
. stcox sex agecat
```

Note that it is with the stset command that we specify that this is a dataset with repeated observations on patients; see [R] st stset. Once the dataset is stset, stcox will know to estimate a time-varying regression. As an aside, it might be better to replace agecat with age since, with Cox regression, one can estimate continuous effects so there is no reason to categorize the data.

So what would happen if we did all of this? We do not have the original data, so results must be speculative. We can make up various datasets that correspond to the aggregate data in the table. One possibility, for instance, is that the 6,411 person-years reported in the aggregate table correspond to 6,411 patients, each observed for 1 year. In that case:

```
. stcox male agecat, level(90)

          failure _d:  dead
    analysis time _t:  cumtime

Iteration 0:   log likelihood = -1937.2353
Iteration 1:   log likelihood = -1858.8456
Iteration 2:   log likelihood = -1855.3196
Iteration 3:   log likelihood = -1855.2292
Iteration 4:   log likelihood = -1855.2291
Refining estimates:
Iteration 0:   log likelihood = -1855.2291

Cox regression -- Breslow method for ties

No. of subjects =        6411          Number of obs   =       6411
No. of failures =         221
Time at risk    =        6411
                                       LR chi2(2)      =     164.01
Log likelihood  =   -1855.2291         Prob > chi2     =     0.0000
```

_t _d	Haz. Ratio	Std. Err.	z	P>|z|	[90% Conf. Interval]	
male	1.495096	.2060997	2.92	0.004	1.191779	1.875611
agecat	8.888775	1.934943	10.04	0.000	6.213541	12.71583

Thus, comparing these results with those previously obtained:

Source	IR Ratio	90% Conf. Int.	
Mantel–Haenszel (ir)	1.50	1.19	1.88
poisson	1.50	1.19	1.88
stcox	1.50	1.19	1.88

Remember, we obtained the Cox regression estimates under the assumption that each patient was observed for only one year (that is, outside of this technical note, we concocted a dataset that would yield the same results as the aggregate data if we ran the `ir` command on them, and we concocted that data assuming that each patient was observed for a single year). If we had the real underlying data, and so knew exactly how long each patient was observed, the `stcox` estimates would be preferable to those of `ir` or `poisson`.   ❑

Standardized estimates with stratified incidence rate data

The `by()` option specifies that the data are stratified and, by default, produce a Mantel–Haenszel combined estimate of the incidence rate ratio. With the `estandard`, `istandard`, or `standard(varname)` options, you can specify your own weights and obtain standardized estimates of the incidence rate ratio or difference.

▷ Example

Rothman and Greenland (1998, 259) report results from Doll and Hill (1966) on age-specific coronary disease deaths among British male doctors by cigarette smoking:

| Age | Smokers | | Nonsmokers | |
	Deaths	Person-years	Deaths	Person-years
35–44	32	52,407	2	18,790
45–54	104	43,248	12	10,673
55–64	206	28,612	28	5,710
65–74	186	12,663	28	2,585
75–84	102	5,317	31	1,462

We have entered these data into Stata:

```
. list

         age    smokes    deaths     pyears
 1.    35-44         1        32      52407
 2.    35-44         0         2      18790
 3.    45-54         1       104      43248
 4.    45-54         0        12      10673
 5.    55-64         1       206      28612
 6.    55-64         0        28       5710
 7.    65-74         1       186      12663
 8.    65-74         0        28       2585
 9.    75-84         1       102       5317
10.    75-84         0        31       1462
```

We can obtain the Mantel–Haenszel combined estimate along with the crude estimate for ignoring stratification of the incidence rate ratio and 90% confidence intervals by typing

```
. ir deaths smokes pyears, by(age) level(90)

         age |      IRR     [90% Conf. Interval]     M-H Weight
-------------+-----------------------------------------------------------
       35-44 |  5.736638    1.704242   33.62016      1.472169   (exact)
       45-54 |  2.138812    1.274529   3.813215      9.624747   (exact)
       55-64 |   1.46824    1.044925   2.110463     23.34176    (exact)
       65-74 |   1.35606    .9625995   1.953472     23.25315    (exact)
       75-84 |  .9047304    .6375086   1.305422     24.31435    (exact)
-------------+-----------------------------------------------------------
       Crude |  1.719823    1.437554   2.068803                 (exact)
 M-H combined|  1.424682    1.194375   1.699399
-------------------------------------------------------------------------
     Test of homogeneity (M-H)     chi2(4) =     10.41  Pr>chi2 = 0.0340
```

Note the presence of heterogeneity revealed by the test; the effect of smoking is not the same across age categories. Moreover, the listed stratum-specific estimates show an effect that appears to be declining with age. (Even if the test of homogeneity was not significant, one should always examine estimates carefully when stratum-specific effects occur on both sides of 1 for ratios and 0 for differences.)

Rothman and Greenland (1998, 264) obtain the standardized incidence rate ratio and 90% confidence intervals weighting each age category by the population of the exposed group, thus producing the standardized mortality ratio (SMR). This calculation can be reproduced by specifying `by(age)` to indicate the table is stratified, and `istandard` to specify we want the internally standardized rate. We may also specify that we would like to see the pooled estimate (weighted average where the weights are based on the variance of the strata calculations):

```
. ir deaths smokes pyears, by(age) level(90) istandard pool
```

age	IRR	[90% Conf. Interval]		Weight	
35-44	5.736638	1.704242	33.62016	52407	(exact)
45-54	2.138812	1.274529	3.813215	43248	(exact)
55-64	1.46824	1.044925	2.110463	28612	(exact)
65-74	1.35606	.9625995	1.953472	12663	(exact)
75-84	.9047304	.6375086	1.305422	5317	(exact)
Crude	1.719823	1.437554	2.068803		(exact)
Pooled (direct)	1.355343	1.134356	1.619382		
I. Standardized	1.417609	1.186541	1.693676		

Test of homogeneity (direct) chi2(4) =   10.20 Pr>chi2 = 0.0372

We obtained the simple pooled results because we specified the `pool` option. Note the significance of the homogeneity test; it provides the motivation for standardizing the rate ratios.

If we wanted the externally standardized ratio (weights proportional to the population of the unexposed group), we would substitute `estandard` for `istandard` in the above command.

Not shown by Rothman and Greenland, but as easily obtained, are the internally and externally weighted standardized incidence rate difference. We will obtain the internally weighted difference:

```
. ir deaths smokes pyears, by(age) level(90) istandard ird
```

age	IRD	[90% Conf. Interval]		Weight
35-44	.0005042	.0002877	.0007206	52407
45-54	.0012804	.0006205	.0019403	43248
55-64	.0022961	.0005628	.0040294	28612
65-74	.0038567	.0000521	.0076614	12663
75-84	-.0020201	-.0090201	.00498	5317
Crude	.0018537	.001342	.0023654	
I. Standardized	.0013047	.001043	.0015664	

◁

▷ Example

In addition to calculating results using internal or external weights, `ir` (and `cs` and `cc`) can calculate results for arbitrary weights. If we wanted to obtain the incidence rate ratio weighting each age category equally:

```
. gen conswgt=1
. ir deaths smokes pyears, by(age) level(90) standard(conswgt)
```

age	IRR	[90% Conf. Interval]		Weight	
35-44	5.736638	1.704242	33.62016	1	(exact)
45-54	2.138812	1.274529	3.813215	1	(exact)
55-64	1.46824	1.044925	2.110463	1	(exact)
65-74	1.35606	.9625995	1.953472	1	(exact)
75-84	.9047304	.6375086	1.305422	1	(exact)
Crude	1.719823	1.437554	2.068803		(exact)
Standardized	1.155026	.9373745	1.423214		

◁

❑ Technical Note

estandard and istandard are convenience features; they do nothing different from what you could accomplish by creating the appropriate weights and using the standard() option. For instance, we could duplicate the previously shown results of istandard (example before last) by typing

```
. sort age smokes
. by age: gen wgt=pyears[_N]
. list in 1/4
```

	age	smokes	deaths	pyears	wgt
1.	35-44	0	2	18790	52407
2.	35-44	1	32	52407	52407
3.	45-54	0	12	10673	43248
4.	45-54	1	104	43248	43248

```
. ir deaths smokes pyears, by(age) level(90) standard(wgt) ird
(output omitted )
```

sort age smokes made the exposed group (smokes = 1) the last observation within each age category. by age: gen wgt=pyears[_N] created wgt equal to the last observation in each age category.

❑

Cumulative incidence data

In cumulative incidence (follow-up or longitudinal) data, rather than using the time a subject was at risk to normalize ratios, you use the number of subjects. A group of noncases is followed for some period of time and during that time some become cases. Each subject is also known to be exposed or unexposed. A summary of the data is

	Exposed	Unexposed	Total
Cases	a	b	$a + b$
Noncases	c	d	$c + d$
Total	$a + c$	$b + d$	$a + b + c + d$

Data of this type are generally summarized using the risk ratio. A ratio of 2 means that an exposed subject is twice as likely to become a case as is an unexposed subject, a ratio of one-half means half as likely, and so on. The "null" value—the number corresponding to no effect—is a ratio of 1. It should be noted that if cross-sectional data are analyzed in this format, a prevalence ratio can be obtained.

▷ Example

You have data on diarrhea during a 10-day follow-up period among 30 breast-fed infants colonized with *Vibrio cholerae* 01 according to antilipopolysaccharide antibody titers in the mother's breast milk (Glass et al. 1983, reported in Rothman and Greenland 1998, 243):

	Antibody Level High	Low
Diarrhea	7	12
No Diarrhea	9	2

The `csi` command works much like the `iri` command. We recommend specifying the `exact` option, however, whenever the least frequent cell contains fewer than 1,000 observations. We have very few observations here:

```
. csi 7 12 9 2, exact
```

	Exposed	Unexposed	Total
Cases	7	12	19
Noncases	9	2	11
Total	16	14	30
Risk	.4375	.8571429	.6333333

	Point estimate	[95% Conf. Interval]	
Risk difference	-.4196429	-.7240828	-.1152029
Risk ratio	.5104167	.2814332	.9257086
Prev. frac. ex.	.4895833	.0742914	.7185668
Prev. frac. pop	.2611111		

```
                1-sided Fisher's exact P = 0.0212
                2-sided Fisher's exact P = 0.0259
```

We find that high antibody levels reduce the risk of diarrhea (the risk falls from .86 to .44). The difference is just significant at the 2.59% two-sided level. (Had we not specified the `exact` option, a χ^2 value and its significance level would have been reported in place of Fisher's exact p. The calculated χ^2 two-sided significance level would have been .0173, but this calculation is inferior for small samples.)

◁

❑ Technical Note

By default, `cs` and `csi` do not report the odds ratio, but they will if you specify the `or` option. If you want odds ratios, however, you should use the `cc` or `cci` commands—the commands appropriate for case–control data—because `cs` and `csi` calculate the attributable (prevented) fraction using the risk ratio even if you specify `or`:

(*Continued on next page*)

```
. csi 7 12 9 2, or exact
```

	Exposed	Unexposed	Total
Cases	7	12	19
Noncases	9	2	11
Total	16	14	30
Risk	.4375	.8571429	.6333333

	Point estimate	[95% Conf. Interval]		
Risk difference	-.4196429	-.7240828	-.1152029	
Risk ratio	.5104167	.2814332	.9257086	
Prev. frac. ex.	.4895833	.0742914	.7185668	
Prev. frac. pop	.2611111			
Odds ratio	.1296296	.0246233	.7180882	(Cornfield)

```
                      1-sided Fisher's exact P = 0.0212
                      2-sided Fisher's exact P = 0.0259
```

Sometimes, the lower or upper confidence bound for the odds ratio will be missing, meaning the Cornfield approximation did not converge. This can occur when the number of observations is quite small. Two other approximations, however, are available—the Woolf confidence intervals (obtained by specifying woolf) and the test-based intervals (obtained by specifying tb).   ❑

❑ Technical Note

As with iri and ir, csi and cs report either the attributable or the prevented fraction for the exposed and total populations; see the discussion under *Incidence rate data* above. In the previous example, we estimated that 49% of potential cases in the exposed population were prevented by exposure. We also estimated that exposure accounted for a 26% reduction in cases over the entire population, but that is based on the exposure distribution of the (small) population (16/30) and probably is of little interest.

Fleiss (1981, 77) reports infant mortality by birth weight for 72,730 live white births in 1974 in New York City:

```
. csi 618 422 4597 67093
```

	Exposed	Unexposed	Total
Cases	618	422	1040
Noncases	4597	67093	71690
Total	5215	67515	72730
Risk	.1185043	.0062505	.0142995

	Point estimate	[95% Conf. Interval]	
Risk difference	.1122539	.1034617	.121046
Risk ratio	18.95929	16.80661	21.38769
Attr. frac. ex.	.9472554	.9404996	.9532441
Attr. frac. pop	.5628883		

```
          chi2(1) =  4327.92  Pr>chi2 = 0.0000
```

In these data, exposed means a premature baby (birth weight 2,500 grams or less) and a case is a dead baby at the end of one year. We find that being premature accounts for 94.7% of deaths among the premature population. We also estimate, paraphrasing from Fleiss (1981, 77), that 56.3% of all white infant deaths in New York City in 1974 could have been prevented if prematurity had been eliminated. (Moreover, Fleiss puts a standard error on the attributable fraction for the population. The formula is given in *Methods and Formulas* but is appropriate only for the population on which the estimates are based.)

❑

▷ Example

cs works like csi except that it obtains its information from the data. The data equivalent to typing csi 7 12 9 2 are

```
. list
          case      exp      pop
1.          1        1        7
2.          1        0       12
3.          0        1        9
4.          0        0        2
```

We could then type cs case exp [freq=pop]. If we had individual-level data, so that each observation reflected a patient and we had 30 observations, we would type cs case exp.

◁

Stratified cumulative incidence data

▷ Example

Rothman and Greenland (1998, 255) reprint the following age-specific information for deaths from all causes for tolbutamide and placebo treatment groups (University Group Diabetes Program 1970):

	Age through 54		Age 55 and above	
	Tolbutamide	Placebo	Tolbutamide	Placebo
Dead	8	5	22	16
Surviving	98	115	76	79

The data corresponding to these results are

```
. list
          age     case    exposed     pop
1.        <55       0        0        115
2.        <55       0        1         98
3.        <55       1        0          5
4.        <55       1        1          8
5.        55+       0        0         69
6.        55+       0        1         76
7.        55+       1        0         16
8.        55+       1        1         22
```

The order of the observations is unimportant. If we were now to type cs case exposed [freq=pop], we would obtain a summary for all the data, ignoring the stratification by age. To incorporate the stratification, we type

```
. cs case exposed [freq=pop], by(age)
    Age category |       RR       [95% Conf. Interval]    M-H Weight
    ─────────────┼─────────────────────────────────────────────────
             <55 |   1.811321     .6112044   5.367898      2.345133
             55+ |   1.192602     .6712664    2.11883      8.568306
    ─────────────┼─────────────────────────────────────────────────
           Crude |   1.435574     .8510221   2.421645
    M-H combined |   1.325555      .797907   2.202132
    ─────────────┴─────────────────────────────────────────────────
  Test of homogeneity (M-H)       chi2(1) =    0.447  Pr>chi2 = 0.5037
```

Mantel–Haenszel weights are appropriate when the risks may differ according to the strata but the risk ratio is believed to be the same (homogeneous across strata). Under these assumptions, Mantel–Haenszel weights are designed to use the information efficiently. They are not intended to measure a composite risk ratio when the within-strata risk ratios differ. In that case, one wants a standardized ratio (see below).

The risk ratios above appear to differ markedly, but the confidence intervals are also broad due to the small sample sizes. The test of homogeneity shows that the differences can be attributed to chance; the use of the Mantel–Haenszel combined is probably justified.

◁

❑ Technical Note

Stratified cumulative incidence tables, as with stratified incidence rate tables, are only one way to control for the effect of a confounding factor. The estimation alternative is logistic regression, although this requires using the odds ratio rather than the risk ratio as the measure of risk. For the above data, the odds ratio is

```
. cs case exposed [freq=pop], by(age) or
    Age category |       OR       [95% Conf. Interval]    M-H Weight
    ─────────────┼─────────────────────────────────────────────────
             <55 |   1.877551     .6238165   5.637046      2.168142 (Cornfield)
             55+ |   1.248355     .6112772   2.547411      6.644809 (Cornfield)
    ─────────────┼─────────────────────────────────────────────────
           Crude |   1.510673     .8381198   2.722012
    M-H combined |   1.403149     .7625152   2.582015
    ─────────────┴─────────────────────────────────────────────────
  Test of homogeneity (M-H)       chi2(1) =    0.347  Pr>chi2 = 0.5556
                    Test that combined OR = 1:
                          Mantel-Haenszel chi2(1) =       1.19
                                           Pr>chi2 =     0.2750
```

In this case the event is sufficiently unlikely to proceed; the risk ratio is 1.33 and the odds ratio is 1.40. We also present the crude estimate obtained for analyzing the data without stratifying.

Recasting the problem in the language of modeling, the outcome variable is **case** and it is to be explained by **age** and **exposed**. (As in the incidence rate example, **age** may appear to be a string variable in our data—we listed the data in the previous example—but it is actually a numeric variable taking on values 0 and 1 with value labels disguising that fact; see [U] **15.6.3 Value labels**.)

```
. logistic case exposed age [freq=pop]
Logit estimates                              Number of obs   =       409
                                             LR chi2(2)      =     22.47
                                             Prob > chi2     =    0.0000
Log likelihood =  -142.6212                  Pseudo R2       =    0.0730
```

case	Odds Ratio	Std. Err.	z	P>|z|	[95% Conf. Interval]	
exposed	1.404674	.4374454	1.09	0.275	.7629451	2.586175
age	4.216299	1.431519	4.24	0.000	2.167361	8.202223

It is worth comparing these results with the Mantel–Haenszel estimates obtained with cs:

Source	Odds Ratio	95% Conf. Int.	
Mantel–Haenszel (cs)	1.40	0.76	2.58
logistic	1.40	0.76	2.59

They are virtually identical.

Logistic regression has advantages over the stratified-table approach. First, we obtained an estimate of the age effect: Being 55 years or over significantly increases the odds of death. In addition to the point estimate, 4.22, we have a confidence interval for the effect: 2.17 to 8.20.

Given the measured age effect, one would expect that it does not apply only to persons on either side of the 55-year cutoff. It would be more reasonable to assume that a 54 year-old patient has a higher probability of death, due merely to age, than a 53 year-old patient; a 53 year-old, a higher probability than a 52; and so on. If we had the underlying data, where each patient's age is presumably known, we could include the actual age in the model and so better control for the age effect. This would improve our estimate of the effect of being exposed to tolbutamide.

See [R] **logistic** for an explanation of the logistic command. Also see the technical note in *Incidence rate data* above; what is said there concerning categorical variables applies to logistic regression as well as Poisson regression.

❏

Standardized estimates with stratified cumulative incidence data

As with ir, cs can produce standardized estimates and the method is basically the same, although the options for which estimates are to be combined or standardized make it confusing. We showed above that cs can produce Mantel–Haenszel weighted estimates of the risk ratio (the default) or the odds ratio (obtained by specifying or). cs can also produce standardized estimates of the risk ratio (the default) or the risk difference (obtained by specifying rd).

▷ Example

To produce an estimate of the internally standardized risk ratio using our age-specific data on deaths from all causes for tolbutamide and placebo treatment groups (example above), we type

```
. cs case exposed [freq=pop], by(age) istandard
```

Age category	RR	[95% Conf. Interval]		Weight
<55	1.811321	.6112044	5.367898	106
55+	1.192602	.6712664	2.11883	98
Crude	1.435574	.8510221	2.421645	
I. Standardized	1.312122	.7889772	2.182147	

We could obtain externally standardized estimates by substituting `estandard` for `istandard`.

If we wish to produce an estimate of the risk ratio weighting each age category equally:

```
. gen wgt=1
. cs case exposed [freq=pop], by(age) standard(wgt)
```

Age category	RR	[95% Conf. Interval]		Weight
<55	1.811321	.6112044	5.367898	1
55+	1.192602	.6712664	2.11883	1
Crude	1.435574	.8510221	2.421645	
Standardized	1.304737	.7844994	2.169967	

If we instead wanted the rate difference:

```
. cs case exposed [freq=pop], by(age) standard(wgt) rd
```

Age category	RD	[95% Conf. Interval]		Weight
<55	.033805	-.0278954	.0955055	1
55+	.0362545	-.0809204	.1534294	1
Crude	.0446198	-.0192936	.1085332	
Standardized	.0350298	-.0311837	.1012432	

If we wanted to weight the less-than-55 age group five times as heavily as the 55-and-over group, we would have created `wgt` to contain 5 for the first age group and 1 for the second (or 10 for the first group and 2 for the second—the scale of the weights does not matter).

◁

Case–control data

In case–control data, one selects a sample on the basis of the outcome under study or, said differently, cases and noncases are sampled at different rates. If one were examining the link between coffee consumption and heart attacks, for instance, one selects a sample of subjects with and without the heart problem and then examines their coffee-drinking behavior. A subject who has suffered a heart attack is called a *case* just as with cohort study data. A subject who has never suffered a heart attack, however, is called a *control* rather than merely a noncase, emphasizing that the sampling was performed with respect to the outcome.

In case–control data, all hope of identifying the risk (i.e., incidence) of the outcome (heart attacks) associated with the factor (coffee drinking) vanishes, at least without information on the underlying sampling fractions, but one can examine the proportion of coffee drinkers among the two populations and reason that, if there is a difference, that coffee drinking may be associated with the risk of heart attacks. Remarkably, even without the underlying sampling fractions, one can also measure the ratio of the odds of heart attacks if one does drink coffee to the odds if one does not—the so-called odds ratio.

What is lost is the ability to compare absolute rates, which is not always the same as comparing relative rates; see Fleiss (1981, 91).

▷ Example

`cci` calculates the odds ratio and the attributable risk associated with a 2×2 table. Rothman et al. (1979) (reprinted in Rothman 1986, 161 and reprinted in Rothman and Greenland 1998, 245) presents case–control data on the history of chlordiazopoxide use in early pregnancy for mothers of children born with and without congenital heart defects:

```
                                        Chlordiazopoxide use
                                             Yes    No
                             Case mothers      4    386
                             Control mothers   4   1250
```

We will use the `level(90)` option to obtain 90% confidence intervals as reported by Rothman and Greenland:

```
. cci 4 386 4 1250, level(90)
                                                                  Proportion
                        |   Exposed   Unexposed  |    Total     Exposed
         ---------------+------------------------+---------------------------
                  Cases |      4          386    |     390        0.0103
               Controls |      4         1250    |    1254        0.0032
         ---------------+------------------------+---------------------------
                  Total |      8         1636    |    1644        0.0049

                           Point estimate            [90% Conf. Interval]
         ---------------+------------------------+---------------------------
             Odds ratio |        3.238342        |    .7698467    13.59663   (exact)
          Attr. frac. ex.|         .6912          |   -.2989599    .9264524   (exact)
          Attr. frac. pop|       .0070892         |
         ---------------+------------------------+---------------------------
                              chi2(1) =     3.07  Pr>chi2 = 0.0799
```

We obtain a point estimate of the odds ratio as 3.24 and a χ^2 value, which is a test that the odds ratio is 1, significant at the 10% level.

◁

❏ Technical Note

Although one tends to think of statistical tests and confidence intervals as being different ways of presenting the same information, that is not exactly true. The statistical test is derived under the assumption of the null hypothesis that the odds ratio is 1. A "test-based" confidence interval is a direct transformation of the statistical test and there can be no disagreement between them. If you specify the `tb` option, `csi` and the other epitab commands will produce test-based confidence intervals. When you do not specify this option, however, either exact or approximate confidence intervals are calculated. Exact confidence intervals are unbeatable—if there is a disagreement between the exact interval and the test statistic, believe the interval. (Within exact results, midp intervals more closely approximate asymptotic test statistics.) All the classical test statistics are derived under various simplifying assumptions, assumptions not present in exact calculations. (The epitab commands always place the word "exact" next to exact calculation results.)

The Cornfield confidence intervals, on the other hand, are an example of an approximation. The Cornfield approximation, along with the other approximations, attempts to produce confidence intervals around a point central to the confidence interval, producing intervals that should more accurately reflect the exact confidence interval when the parameter deviates from the null hypothesis. This serves the purpose of making the confidence interval focus on estimation rather than statistical testing.

In this case, here is the result of calculating the confidence interval for the odds ratio using various methods:

Method	90% Conf. Int.		Source
exact	0.77	13.60	Rothman 1986, 174 or `cci`
Woolf	1.01	10.40	Rothman 1986, 175 or `cci, woolf`
test-based	1.07	9.77	Rothman 1986, 175 or `cci, tb`
Cornfield	1.07	9.83	Rothman 1986, 175 or `cci`

There are only 8 exposed patients in this case and the differences shown above are larger than typically observed. The fact that they are also on both sides of the knife-edge of 1 is (pedagogically speaking) fortuitous. The exact answer, which is just that, includes 1 in the interval and so one cannot reject (at the 10% level) the hypothesis that the odds ratio is 1. That is the "right" answer (but see the next technical note). The Woolf, test-based, and Cornfield intervals exclude 1 and so reassuringly conform to the χ^2 value. In any case, all results are so close to 1 that one should still think about chance as an explanation.

❑

❑ Technical Note

If you specify the **exact** option, **cc** and **cci** will report the exact significance of the table. We could have, and should have, done that above because of the small number of cases. We did not for expositional purposes, but we will do so now:

```
. cci 4 386 4 1250, level(90) exact
```

	Exposed	Unexposed	Total	Proportion Exposed
Cases	4	386	390	0.0103
Controls	4	1250	1254	0.0032
Total	8	1636	1644	0.0049

	Point estimate	[90% Conf. Interval]		
Odds ratio	3.238342	.7698467	13.59663	(exact)
Attr. frac. ex.	.6912	-.2989599	.9264524	(exact)
Attr. frac. pop	.0070892			

```
                    1-sided Fisher's exact P = 0.0964
                    2-sided Fisher's exact P = 0.0964
```

The first thing to note is that in this table the 1- and 2-sided significance values are equal. This is not a mistake, but it does not happen often. Exact significance values are calculated by summing the probabilities for tables that have the same marginals (row and column sums) but that are less likely (given an odds ratio of 1) than the observed table. When considering each possible table, one asks if the table is in the same or opposite tail as the observed table. If it is in the same tail, one counts the table under consideration in the 1-sided test and, either way, one counts it in the 2-sided test. In this case, it just turns out that all the tables more extreme than this table are in the same tail, so the 1- and 2-sided tests are the same.

Note that the exact p is .096 < .100, that is, the table is significant at the 10% level. In the previous example, we said "exact confidence intervals are unbeatable—if there is a disagreement between the exact interval and the test statistic, believe the interval". We also reported (Rothman 1986, 174) that the "exact" confidence interval for the odds ratio is 0.77 to 13.6, which includes 1. How can both statements be true and yet both statistics be "exact"?

Confidence intervals and test statistics measure different things. The .0964 is the fraction of all tables that are less likely than the observed table *conditional on the odds ratio being 1.* The lower bound of the confidence interval 0.77 corresponds to the statement that the probability of observing tables with 4 or more exposed cases *conditional on the odds ratio being .77* is 0.05. The upper bound of the confidence interval 13.6 corresponds to the statement that the probability of observing tables with 4 or less exposed cases *conditional on the odds ratio being 13.6* is 0.05. No two of these are the same question, and there is no reason why the answers to these different questions should somehow agree.

You expect them to agree because you are used to thinking in terms of large-sample approximations. For infinite-sized samples, the answers to the questions above will agree, and for large but finite samples, the answers will tend to agree. If we had a large number of exposed individuals (as we do not), we would not have had this "problem".

❑

❑ Technical Note

The reported value of the attributable or prevented fraction among the exposed is based on using the odds ratio as a proxy for the risk ratio. This can only be justified if the outcome is exceedingly unlikely in the population. The extrapolation to the attributable or prevented fraction for the population assumes the control group is a random sample of the corresponding group in the underlying population.

❑

▷ Example

Equivalent to typing `cci 4 386 4 1250` would be typing `cc case exposed [freq=pop]` with the data:

```
. list

           case    exposed        pop
    1.        1          1          4
    2.        1          0        386
    3.        0          1          4
    4.        0          0       1250
```

◁

Stratified case–control

▷ Example

`cc` has the ability to work with stratified tables. Rothman and Greenland (1998, 273) reprint and discuss data from a case–control study on infants with congenital heart disease and Down's syndrome and healthy controls, according to maternal spermicide use before conception and maternal age at delivery (Rothman 1982):

| | Maternal age to 34 | | Maternal age 35+ | |
	Spermicide used	not used	Spermicide used	not used
Down's syndrome	3	9	1	3
Controls	104	1059	5	86

The data corresponding to these tables are

```
. list

          case    exposed       pop      age
   1.       1          1         3      <35
   2.       1          0         9      <35
   3.       0          1       104      <35
   4.       0          0      1059      <35
   5.       1          1         1      35+
   6.       1          0         3      35+
   7.       0          1         5      35+
   8.       0          0        86      35+
```

The stratified results for the odds ratio are

```
. cc case exposed [freq=pop], by(age) woolf
   Maternal age |      OR       [95% Conf. Interval]    M-H Weight

           <35 |  3.394231     .9048403    12.73242     .7965957 (Woolf)
           35+ |  5.733333     .5016418    65.52706     .1578947 (Woolf)

         Crude |  3.501529     1.110362    11.04208              (Woolf)
  M-H combined |  3.781172     1.18734     12.04142

Test of homogeneity (M-H)      chi2(1) =      0.14  Pr>chi2 = 0.7105
                  Test that combined OR = 1:
                     Mantel-Haenszel chi2(1) =      5.81
                                     Pr>chi2 =    0.0159
```

For no particular reason, we also specified the woolf option to obtain Woolf approximations to the within-strata confidence intervals rather than Cornfield approximations. Had we wanted test-based confidence intervals and the crude estimate, we would have used

```
. cc case exposed [freq=pop], by(age) tb bd
   Maternal age |      OR       [95% Conf. Interval]    M-H Weight

           <35 |  3.394231     .976611     11.79672     .7965957 (tb)
           35+ |  5.733333     .6402941    51.33752     .1578947 (tb)

         Crude |  3.501529     1.189946    10.30358              (tb)
  M-H combined |  3.781172     1.282056    11.15183              (tb)

Test of homogeneity (M-H)      chi2(1) =      0.14  Pr>chi2 = 0.7105
Test of homogeneity (B-D)      chi2(1) =      0.14  Pr>chi2 = 0.7092
                  Test that combined OR = 1:
                     Mantel-Haenszel chi2(1) =      5.81
                                     Pr>chi2 =    0.0159
```

We recommend that test-based confidence intervals only be used for pedagogical reasons and never for research work.

Whatever method is chosen for calculating confidence intervals, also reported is a test of homogeneity, which in our case is $\chi^2(1) = .14$ and "insignificant". That is, the odds of Down's syndrome might vary with maternal age, but we cannot reject the hypothesis that the odds ratios of those exposed to spermicide and those not exposed are the same in the two maternal age strata. This is thus a test to reject the appropriateness of the single, Mantel–Haenszel combined odds ratio—a rejection not justified by these data.

◁

❏ Technical Note

Note that in the last example we requested that Breslow and Day's test of homogeneity be reported by specifying the bd option. For this data, both the Mantel–Haenszel and the Breslow and Day tests produced virtually identical results, but this is not always the case. When data are sparse, you may have strata with zero count in one or more cells. The Mantel–Haenszel test will not include these strata in the homogeneity test because the odds ratios for these strata cannot be estimated. On the other hand, the Breslow and Day homogeneity test includes all strata in its calculation. Note that although Breslow and Day's test of homogeneity is more appropriate when data are sparse, if the number of strata is large and there are few observations per strata, the distribution of the test statistic may not approximate the nominal chi-squared even if the null hypothesis is true.

❏

❏ Technical Note

As with cohort study data, an alternative to stratified tables for uncovering effects is logistic regression. From the logistic point of view, case–control data is no different from cohort study data—one must merely ignore the estimated intercept, which is not reported by `logistic` in any case. (`logit`, on the other hand, makes the same estimates as `logistic` but displays the coefficients rather than transforming them to odds ratios and so does display the estimated intercept. The intercept is meaningless in case–control data because it reflects the baseline prevalence of the outcome which, by sampling, you controlled.)

The data we used with `cs` can be used directly by `logistic`. (The `age` variable, which appears to be a string, is really numeric with an associated value label; see [U] **15.6.3 Value labels**. `age` takes on the value 0 for the age-less-than-35 group and 1 for the 35+ group.)

```
. logistic case exposed age [freq=pop]
Logit estimates                         Number of obs   =       1270
                                        LR chi2(2)      =       8.74
                                        Prob > chi2     =     0.0127
Log likelihood = -81.517532             Pseudo R2       =     0.0509
```

case	Odds Ratio	Std. Err.	z	P>|z|	[95% Conf. Interval]	
exposed	3.787779	2.241922	2.25	0.024	1.187334	12.0836
age	4.582857	2.717351	2.57	0.010	1.433594	14.65029

Comparing the results with those presented by `cc` in the previous example:

Source	Odds Ratio	95% Conf. Int.	
Mantel–Haenszel (cc)	3.78	1.19	12.04
logistic	3.79	1.19	12.08

As with the cohort study data, results are virtually identical and all the same comments we made previously apply once again.

To demonstrate, let us now ask a question that would be difficult to answer on the basis of a stratified table analysis. We now know that spermicide use appears to increase the risk of having a baby with Down's syndrome and we also know that the mother's age also increases the risk. Is the effect of spermicide use statistically different for mothers in the two age groups?

```
. gen ageXex = age*exposed
. logistic case exposed age ageXex [freq=pop]
Logit estimates                         Number of obs   =       1270
                                        LR chi2(3)      =       8.87
                                        Prob > chi2     =     0.0311
Log likelihood = -81.451332             Pseudo R2       =     0.0516
```

case	Odds Ratio	Std. Err.	z	P>|z|	[95% Conf. Interval]	
exposed	3.394231	2.289544	1.81	0.070	.9048403	12.73242
age	4.104651	2.774868	2.09	0.037	1.091034	15.44237
ageXex	1.689141	2.388785	0.37	0.711	.1056563	27.0045

The answer is that the effect is not statistically different. The odds ratio and confidence interval reported for `exposed` now measure the spermicide effect for an `age==0` (age less than 35) mother. The odds ratio and confidence interval reported for `ageXex` are the (multiplicative) difference in the odds ratio for an `age==1` (age 35+) mother relative to a young mother. The point estimate is that the effect is larger for older mothers, suggesting grounds for future research, but the difference is not significant.

See [R] **logistic** for an explanation of the `logistic` command. Also see the technical note under *Incidence rate data* above. What was said there concerning Poisson regression applies equally to logistic regression.

❏

Case–control data with multiple levels of exposure

As previously noted, in a case–control study, subjects with the disease of interest (cases) are compared to disease-free individuals (controls) to assess the relationship between exposure to one or more risk factors and disease incidence. Often, exposure is measured qualitatively at several discrete levels, or measured on a continuous scale and then grouped into 3 or more levels. The data can be summarized as

		Exposure level			
	1	2	...	k	Total
Cases	a_1	a_2	...	a_k	M_1
Controls	c_1	c_2	...	c_k	M_0
Total	N_1	N_2	...	N_k	T

An advantage afforded by having multiple levels of exposure is the ability to examine dose–response relationships. If the association between a risk factor and a disease or outcome is real, we expect the strength of that association to increase with the level and duration of exposure. Demonstrating the existence of a dose–response relationship provides strong support for a direct or even causal relationship between the risk factor and the outcome. On the other hand, the lack of a dose–response is usually seen as an argument against causality.

We can use the `tabodds` command to tabulate and examine the odds of "failure" or odds ratios against a categorical exposure variable. The test for trend calculated by `tabodds` can serve as a test for dose–response if the exposure variable is at least ordinal. Note that if the exposure variable has no natural ordering the trend test is meaningless and should be ignored. See the technical note at the end of this section for more information regarding the test for trend.

Before looking at an example, consider three possible data arrangements for case–control and prevalence studies. The most common data arrangement is individual records, where each subject in the study has his or her own record. Closely related are frequency records where identical individual records are included only once, but with a variable giving the frequency with which the record occurs. The *weight* option is used for this data to specify the frequency variable. Data can also be arranged as binomial frequency records where each record contains a variable D, the number of cases, another variable N, the number of total subject (cases plus controls), and other variables. An advantage of binomial frequency records is that otherwise large datasets can be entered succinctly into a Stata database.

▷ Example

Consider the following data from the Ille-et-Villaine study of esophageal cancer discussed in Breslow and Day (1980, chapter 4):

	Alcohol consumption (g/day)				
	0–39	40–79	80–119	120+	Total
Cases	2	9	9	5	25
Controls	47	31	9	5	92
Total	49	40	18	10	117

corresponding to subjects age 55 to 64 that use from 0 to 9 grams of tobacco per day. There are 24 such tables, each representing one of four levels of tobacco use and one of six age categories. The data can be used to create a binomial frequency record dataset by simply entering each table's data by typing

```
. input alcohol D N agegrp tobacco

         alcohol        D          N      agegrp       tobacco
  1.           1        2         49           4             1
  2.           2        9         40           4             1
  3.           3        9         18           4             1
  4.           4        5         10           4             1
  .
  .
```

where, D is the number of esophageal cancer cases and N is the number of total subjects (cases plus controls) for each combination of six age-groups (agegrp), four levels of alcohol consumption in g/day (alcohol), and four levels of tobacco use in g/day (tobacco).

Both the tabodds and mhodds commands can correctly handle all three data arrangements. Binomial frequency records require that the number of total subjects (cases plus controls) represented by each record N be specified with the binomial() option.

We could also enter the data as frequency-weighted data:

```
. input alcohol case freq agegrp tobacco

         alcohol      case       freq      agegrp       tobacco
  1.           1         1          2           4             1
  2.           1         0         47           4             1
  3.           2         1          9           4             1
  4.           2         0         31           4             1
  5.           3         1          9           4             1
  6.           3         0          9           4             1
  7.           4         1          5           4             1
  8.           4         0          5           4             1
  .
  .
```

If you are planning on using any of the other estimation commands, such as poisson or logistic, we recommend that you enter your data either as individual records or as frequency-weighted records and not as binomial frequency records because the estimation commands currently do not recognize the binomial option.

We have entered all the esophageal cancer data into Stata as a frequency weighted record dataset as previously described. In our data, case indicates the esophageal cancer cases and controls and freq is the number of subjects represented by each record (the weight).

We added value labels to the variables agegrp, alcohol, and tobacco in our dataset to ease interpretation in outputs but note that these variables are numeric.

We are interested in the association between alcohol consumption and esophageal cancer. We first use tabodds to tabulate the odds of esophageal cancer against alcohol consumption:

```
. tabodds case alcohol [fweight=freq]
```

alcohol	cases	controls	odds	[95% Conf. Interval]	
0-39	29	386	0.07513	0.05151	0.10957
40-79	75	280	0.26786	0.20760	0.34560
80-119	51	87	0.58621	0.41489	0.82826
120+	45	22	2.04545	1.22843	3.40587

```
Test of homogeneity (equal odds): chi2(3)  =    158.79
                                   Pr>chi2  =    0.0000

Score test for trend of odds:      chi2(1)  =    152.97
                                   Pr>chi2  =    0.0000
```

The test of homogeneity clearly indicates that the odds of esophageal cancer differ by level of alcohol consumption and the test for trend indicates a significant increase in odds with increasing alcohol use. This is suggestive of a strong dose–response relation. The graph option can be used to study the shape of the relationship of the odds with alcohol consumption. Note that most of the heterogeneity in these data can be "explained" by the linear increase in risk of esophageal cancer with increased dosage (alcohol consumption).

We could also have requested that the odds ratios at each level of alcohol consumption be calculated by specifying the or option. For example, tabodds case alcohol [fweight=freq], or would produce odds ratios using the minimum value of alcohol, i.e., alcohol = 1 (0–39) as the reference group, and the command tabodds case alcohol [fweight=freq], or base(2) would use alcohol = 2 (40–79) as the reference group.

Although our results appear to provide strong evidence in support of an association between alcohol consumption and esophageal cancer, we need to be concerned with the possible existence of confounders, specifically age and tobacco use, in our data. We can again use tabodds to tabulate and examine the odds of esophageal cancer against age and against tobacco use, independently:

```
. tabodds case agegrp [fweight=freq]
```

agegrp	cases	controls	odds	[95% Conf. Interval]	
25-34	1	115	0.00870	0.00121	0.06226
35-44	9	190	0.04737	0.02427	0.09244
45-54	46	167	0.27545	0.19875	0.38175
55-64	76	166	0.45783	0.34899	0.60061
65-74	55	106	0.51887	0.37463	0.71864
75+	13	31	0.41935	0.21944	0.80138

```
Test of homogeneity (equal odds): chi2(5)  =     96.94
                                   Pr>chi2  =    0.0000

Score test for trend of odds:      chi2(1)  =     83.37
                                   Pr>chi2  =    0.0000
```

```
. tabodds case tobacco [fweight=freq]
```

tobacco	cases	controls	odds	[95% Conf. Interval]	
0-9	78	447	0.17450	0.13719	0.22194
10-19	58	178	0.32584	0.24228	0.43823
20-29	33	99	0.33333	0.22479	0.49428
30+	31	51	0.60784	0.38899	0.94983

```
Test of homogeneity (equal odds): chi2(3)  =    29.33
                                   Pr>chi2  =   0.0000
Score test for trend of odds:      chi2(1)  =    26.93
                                   Pr>chi2  =   0.0000
```

We can see that there is evidence to support our concern that both age and tobacco use are potentially important confounders. Clearly, before we can make any statements regarding the association between esophageal cancer and alcohol use, we must examine and, if necessary, adjust for the effect of any confounder. We will return to this example in the following section.

◁

❑ Technical Note

The score test for trend performs a test for linear trend of the log odds against the numerical code used for the exposure variable. The test depends not only on the relationship between dose level and the outcome, but also on the numeric values assigned to each level, or to be more accurate, to the distance between the numeric values assigned. For example, the trend test on a dataset with four exposure levels coded 1, 2, 3, and 4 gives the same results as coding the levels 10, 20, 30, and 40 because the distance between the levels in each case is constant. In the first case, the distance is one unit and in the second case, it is 10 units. However, if we code the exposure levels as 1, 10, 100, and 1000, we would obtain different results because the distance between exposure levels is not constant. Thus, care must be taken when assigning values to exposure levels. You must determine if equally spaced numbers make sense for your data, or if other more meaningful values should be used.

One last comment about the trend test: remember that we are testing whether a log-linear relationship exists between the odds and the outcome variable. For your particular problem, this relationship may not be correct or even make sense, so you must be careful in interpreting the output of this trend test.

❑

Case–control data with confounders and possibly multiple levels of exposure

In the esophageal cancer data example introduced in the previous section, we determined that the apparent association between alcohol consumption and esophageal cancer could be confounded by age and/or tobacco use. The effect of possible confounding factors can be adjusted for by stratifying on these factors. This is the method used by both tabodds and mhodds to adjust for other variables in the dataset. We will compare and contrast these two commands in the following example.

▷ Example

We begin by using tabodds to tabulate unadjusted odd ratios. We do this to compare the adjusted and unadjusted odds ratios.

```
. tabodds case alcohol [fweight=freq], or
```

alcohol	Odds Ratio	chi2	P>chi2	[95% Conf. Interval]	
0-39	1.000000	.	.	.	.
40-79	3.565271	32.70	0.0000	2.237981	5.679744
80-119	7.802616	75.03	0.0000	4.497054	13.537932
120+	27.225705	160.41	0.0000	12.507808	59.262107

```
Test of homogeneity (equal odds): chi2(3) =   158.79
                                   Pr>chi2 =    0.0000
Score test for trend of odds:      chi2(1) =   152.97
                                   Pr>chi2 =    0.0000
```

The alcohol = 1 group (0–39) was used by tabodds as the reference category for calculating the odds ratios. We could have selected a different group by specifying the base() option, however, because the lowest dosage level is most often the adequate reference group, as it is in these data, the base() option is seldom used.

We use tabodds with the adjust() option to tabulate Mantel–Haenszel age-adjusted odds ratios:

```
. tabodds case alcohol [fweight=freq], adjust(age)
Mantel-Haenszel odds ratios adjusted for age
```

alcohol	Odds Ratio	chi2	P>chi2	[95% Conf. Interval]	
0-39	1.000000	.	.	.	.
40-79	4.268155	37.36	0.0000	2.570025	7.088314
80-119	8.018305	59.30	0.0000	4.266893	15.067922
120+	28.570426	139.70	0.0000	12.146409	67.202514

```
Score test for trend of odds: chi2(1) =   135.09
                              Pr>chi2 =    0.0000
```

We observe that the age-adjusted odds ratios are just slightly higher than the unadjusted ones, thus it appears that age is not as strong a confounder as it first appeared. Note that even after adjusting for age, the dose–response relationship, as measured by the trend test, remains strong.

We now perform the same analysis but this time adjust for tobacco use instead of age.

```
. tabodds case alcohol [fweight=freq], adjust(tobacco)
Mantel-Haenszel odds ratios adjusted for tobacco
```

alcohol	Odds Ratio	chi2	P>chi2	[95% Conf. Interval]	
0-39	1.000000	.	.	.	.
40-79	3.261178	28.53	0.0000	2.059764	5.163349
80-119	6.771638	62.54	0.0000	3.908113	11.733306
120+	19.919526	123.93	0.0000	9.443830	42.015528

```
Score test for trend of odds: chi2(1) =   135.04
                              Pr>chi2 =    0.0000
```

Again we observe a significant dose–response relationship and not much difference between the adjusted and unadjusted odds ratios. We could also adjust for the joint effect of both age and tobacco use by specifying adjust(tobacco age), but we will not bother in this case.

◁

A different approach to the analysis of these data may be performed using the mhodds command. As previously mentioned, mhodds estimates the ratio of the odds of failure for two categories of an exposure variable, controlling for any specified confounding variables, and also tests whether this odds ratio is equal to one. In the case of multiple exposures, if two exposure levels are not specified with compare(), mhodds assumes that exposure is quantitative and calculates a one-degree-of-freedom test for trend. This test for trend is the same as tabodds reports.

▷ Example

We first use mhodds to estimate the effect of alcohol controlled for age:

```
. mhodds case alcohol agegrp [fweight=freq]
Score test for trend of odds with alcohol
controlling for agegrp
(The Odds Ratio estimate is an approximation to the odds ratio
for a one unit increase in alcohol)
```

Odds Ratio	chi2(1)	P>chi2	[95% Conf. Interval]	
2.845895	135.09	0.0000	2.385749	3.394792

Because alcohol has more than two levels, mhodds estimated and reported an approximate age adjusted odds ratio for a one unit increase in alcohol consumption. Note that the χ^2 value reported is identical to that reported by tabodds for the score test for trend, on the previous page.

We now use mhodds to estimate the effect of alcohol controlled for age, and while we are at it, we may as well do this by levels of tobacco consumption:

```
. mhodds case alcohol agegrp [fweight=freq], by(tobacco)
Score test for trend of odds with alcohol
controlling for agegrp
by tobacco
note: only 19 of the 24 strata formed in this analysis contribute
      information about the effect of the explanatory variable
(The Odds Ratio estimate is an approximation to the odds ratio
for a one unit increase in alcohol)
```

tobacco	Odds Ratio	chi2(1)	P>chi2	[95% Conf. Interval]	
0-9	3.579667	75.95	0.0000	2.687104	4.768710
10-19	2.303580	25.77	0.0000	1.669126	3.179196
20-29	2.364135	13.27	0.0003	1.488098	3.755890
30+	2.217946	8.84	0.0029	1.311837	3.749921

Mantel-Haenszel estimate controlling for agegrp and tobacco

Odds Ratio	chi2(1)	P>chi2	[95% Conf. Interval]	
2.751236	118.37	0.0000	2.292705	3.301471

```
Test of homogeneity of ORs (approx): chi2(3)  =    5.46
                             Pr>chi2  =  0.1409
```

Again, because alcohol has more than two levels, mhodds estimated and reported an approximate Mantel–Haenszel age and tobacco-use adjusted odds ratio for a one unit increase in alcohol consumption. The χ^2 test for trend reported with the Mantel–Haenszel estimate is again the same as tabodds produces if adjust(agegrp tobacco) is specified.

The results from this analysis also show an effect of alcohol, controlled for age, of about ×2.7, which is consistent across different levels of tobacco consumption. Similarly

```
. mhodds case tobacco agegrp [fweight=freq], by(alcohol)
```

Score test for trend of odds with tobacco
controlling for agegrp
by alcohol

note: only 18 of the 24 strata formed in this analysis contribute
      information about the effect of the explanatory variable

(The Odds Ratio estimate is an approximation to the odds ratio
for a one unit increase in tobacco)

alcohol	Odds Ratio	chi2(1)	P>chi2	[95% Conf. Interval]	
0-39	2.420650	15.61	0.0001	1.561214	3.753197
40-79	1.427713	5.75	0.0165	1.067168	1.910070
80-119	1.472218	3.38	0.0659	0.974830	2.223387
120+	1.214815	0.59	0.4432	0.738764	1.997628

Mantel-Haenszel estimate controlling for agegrp and alcohol

Odds Ratio	chi2(1)	P>chi2	[95% Conf. Interval]	
1.553437	20.07	0.0000	1.281160	1.883580

Test of homogeneity of ORs (approx): chi2(3) =   5.26
                                     Pr>chi2 = 0.1540

shows an effect of tobacco, controlled for age, of about ×1.5, which is consistent across different levels of alcohol consumption.

Comparisons between particular levels of alcohol and tobacco consumption can be made by generating a new variable with levels corresponding to all combinations of alcohol and tobacco, as in

```
. egen alctob = group(alcohol tobacco)
. mhodds case alctob [fweight=freq], compare(16,1)
```

Maximum likelihood estimate of the odds ratio
Comparing alctob==16 vs. alctob==1

Odds Ratio	chi2(1)	P>chi2	[95% Conf. Interval]	
93.333333	103.21	0.0000	14.766136	589.938431

which yields an odds ratio of 93 between subjects with the highest levels of alcohol and tobacco, and those with the lowest levels. Similar results can be obtained simultaneously for all levels of alctob using alctob = 1 as the comparison group by specifying tabodds D alctob , bin(N) or.

◁

Standardized estimates with stratified case–control data

▷ Example

You obtain standardized estimates (in this case, for the odds ratio) using `cc` just as you obtain standardized estimates using `ir` or `cs`. Along with the `by()` option, you specify one of `estandard`, `istandard`, or `standard(`*varname*`)`.

Rothman and Greenland (1998, 272) report the standardized mortality rate (SMR) along with a 90% confidence interval for the case–control study on infants with congenital heart disease and Down's syndrome. We can reproduce his estimates along with the pooled estimates by typing

```
. cc case exposed [freq=pop], by(age) istandard level(90) pool
```

Maternal age	OR	[90% Conf. Interval]		Weight	
<35	3.394231	.7761115	11.5405	104	(exact)
35+	5.733333	.1856098	61.20938	5	(exact)
Crude	3.501529	1.024302	10.04068		(exact)
Pooled (direct)	3.824166	1.442194	10.14028		
I. Standardized	3.779749	1.423445	10.03657		

Test of homogeneity (direct)   chi2(1) =   0.14   Pr>chi2 = 0.7109

Using the distribution of the nonexposed subjects in the source population as the standard, we can obtain an estimate of the standardized risk ratio (SRR):

```
. cc case exposed [freq=pop], by(age) estan level(90)
```

Maternal age	OR	[90% Conf. Interval]		Weight	
<35	3.394231	.7761115	11.5405	1059	(exact)
35+	5.733333	.1856098	61.20938	86	(exact)
Crude	3.501529	1.024302	10.04068		(exact)
E. Standardized	3.979006	1.430689	11.06634		

Finally, if we wanted to weight the two age groups equally, we could type

```
. gen wgt=1
. cc case exposed [freq=pop], by(age) level(90) standard(wgt)
```

Maternal age	OR	[90% Conf. Interval]		Weight	
<35	3.394231	.7761115	11.5405	1	(exact)
35+	5.733333	.1856098	61.20938	1	(exact)
Crude	3.501529	1.024302	10.04068		(exact)
Standardized	5.275104	.8787523	31.66617		

◁

Matched case–control data

Matched case–control studies are performed to gain sample size efficiency and to control for important confounding factors. In a matched case–control design, each case is matched with a control on the basis of demographic characteristics, clinical characteristics, etc. Thus, their difference with respect to the outcome must be due to something other than the matching variables. If the only difference between them was exposure to the factor, one could attribute any difference in outcome to the factor.

A summary of the data is

Cases	Controls Exposed	Unexposed	Total
Exposed	a	b	$a + b$
Unexposed	c	d	$c + d$
Total	$a + c$	$b + d$	$n = a + b + c + d$

Each entry in the table represents the number of case–control pairs. For instance, in a of the pairs both members were exposed; in b of the pairs the case was exposed but the control was not, and so on. In total, n pairs were observed.

▷ Example

Rothman (1986, 257) discusses data from Jick et al. (1973) on a matched case–control study of myocardial infarction and drinking six or more cups of coffee per day (persons drinking from 1 to 5 cups per day were excluded):

Cases	Controls 6+ cups	0 cups
6+ cups	8	8
0 cups	3	8

mcci analyzes matched case–control data:

```
. mcci 8 8 3 8

               | Controls
Cases          | Exposed    Unexposed  |      Total
---------------+------------------------+-----------
      Exposed  |     8           8      |        16
    Unexposed  |     3           8      |        11
---------------+------------------------+-----------
        Total  |    11          16      |        27

McNemar's chi2(1) =      2.27     Prob > chi2 = 0.1317
Exact McNemar significance probability         = 0.2266

Proportion with factor
        Cases       .5925926
        Controls    .4074074      [95% Conf. Interval]
                                  -------------------------
        difference  .1851852      -.0822542     .4526246
        ratio       1.454545       .891101      2.374257
        rel. diff.  .3125         -.0243688      .6493688

        odds ratio  2.666667       .6400699     15.60439   (exact)
```

The relationship is not significant at better than the 13.17% level, but if one justifies a one-sided test, the table is significant at the $13.17/2 = 6.59\%$ level. The point estimate is that drinkers of 6+ cups of coffee per day are 2.67 times more likely to suffer myocardial infarction. The interpretation of the relative difference is that for every 100 controls who fail to have heart attacks, 31.25 might be expected to get heart attacks if they became heavy coffee drinkers.

◁

mcc works like the other nonimmediate commands but does not handle stratified data. If you have stratified matched case–control data, you can use conditional logistic regression to estimate odds ratios; see [R] **clogit**.

Matched case–control studies can also be analyzed using `mhodds` by controlling on the variable used to identify the matched sets. For example, if the variable `set` is used to identify the matched set for each subject,

```
. mhodds fail xvar set
```

will do the job. Note that any attempt to control for further variables will restrict the analysis to the comparison of cases and matched controls that share the same values of these variables. In general, this would lead to the omission of many records from the analysis. Similar considerations usually apply when investigating effect modification using the `by()` option. An important exception to this general rule is that a variable used in matching cases to controls may appear in the `by()` option without loss of data.

▷ Example

Let us use `mhodds` to analyze matched case–control studies using the study of endometrial cancer and exposure to estrogen described in Breslow and Day (1980, chapter 4). In this study, there are four controls matched to each case. Cases and controls were matched on age, marital status, and time living in the community. The data collected included information on the daily dose of conjugated estrogen therapy. Breslow and Day created four levels of the dose variable and began by analyzing the 1:1 study formed by using the first control in each set. We examine the effect of exposure to estrogen:

```
. describe

Contains data from bdendo11.dta
  obs:           126
  vars:           13
  size:         2,898 (99.5% of memory free)
```

variable name	storage type	display format	value label	variable label
set	int	%8.0g		Set number
fail	byte	%8.0g		Case=1/Control=0
gall	byte	%8.0g		Gallbladder dis
hyp	byte	%8.0g		Hypertension
ob	byte	%8.0g		Obesity
est	byte	%8.0g		Estrogen
dos	byte	%8.0g		Ordinal dose
dur	byte	%8.0g		Ordinal duration
non	byte	%8.0g		Non-estrogen drug
duration	int	%8.0g		months
age	int	%8.0g		years
cest	byte	%8.0g		Conjugated est dose
agegrp	float	%9.0g		age group of set

```
Sorted by:  set

. mhodds fail est set

Mantel-Haenszel estimate of the odds ratio
Comparing est==1 vs. est==0, controlling for set

note: only 32 of the 63 strata  formed in this analysis contribute
      information about the effect of the explanatory variable
```

Odds Ratio	chi2(1)	P>chi2	[95% Conf. Interval]	
9.666667	21.12	0.0000	2.944702	31.733072

In the case of the 1:1 matched study, the Mantel–Haenszel methods are equivalent to conditional likelihood methods. The maximum conditional likelihood estimate of the odds ratio is given by the ratio of the off-diagonal frequencies in the following table:

```
. tabulate case control [fweight=freq]

          |     control
     case |      0          1  |     Total
----------+--------------------+----------
        0 |      4          3  |         7
        1 |     29         27  |        56
----------+--------------------+----------
    Total |     33         30  |        63
```

This is $29/3 = 9.67$, which agrees exactly with the value obtained from mhodds and from mcci. In the more general $1:m$ matched study, however, the Mantel–Haenszel methods are no longer equal to the maximum conditional likelihood, although they are usually quite close.

To illustrate the use of the by() option in matched case–control studies, we look at the effect of exposure to estrogen, stratified by age3, which codes the sets into three age groups (55–64, 65–74, and 75+) as follows:

```
. generate age3 =agegrp

. recode age3 1/2=1 3/4=2 5/6=3
(124 changes made)

. mhodds fail est set, by(age3)
Mantel-Haenszel estimate of the odds ratio
Comparing est==1 vs. est==0, controlling for set
by age3
note: only 32 of the 63 strata  formed in this analysis contribute
      information about the effect of the explanatory variable
```

age3	Odds Ratio	chi2(1)	P>chi2	[95% Conf. Interval]	
1	6.000000	3.57	0.0588	0.722351	49.83724
2	15.000000	12.25	0.0005	1.981409	113.5556
3	8.000000	5.44	0.0196	1.000586	63.96252

Mantel-Haenszel estimate controlling for set and age3

Odds Ratio	chi2(1)	P>chi2	[95% Conf. Interval]	
9.666667	21.12	0.0000	2.944702	31.733072

```
Test of homogeneity of ORs (approx): chi2(2)  =    0.41
                                      Pr>chi2  =  0.8128
```

Note that there is no further loss of information when we stratify by age3 because age was one of the matching variables.

The full set of matched controls can be used in the same way. For example, the effect of exposure to estrogen is obtained (using the full dataset) by

```
. use bdendo, clear

. mhodds fail est set

Mantel-Haenszel estimate of the odds ratio
Comparing est==1 vs. est==0, controlling for set

note: only 58 of the 63 strata  formed in this analysis contribute
      information about the effect of the explanatory variable
```

Odds Ratio	chi2(1)	P>chi2	[95% Conf. Interval]
8.461538	31.16	0.0000	3.437773 20.826746

The effect of exposure to estrogen, stratified by **age3**, is obtained by

```
. gen age3 = agegrp

. recode age3 1/2=1 3/4=2 5/6=3
(310 changes made)

. mhodds fail est set, by(age3)

Mantel-Haenszel estimate of the odds ratio
Comparing est==1 vs. est==0, controlling for set
by age3

note: only 58 of the 63 strata  formed in this analysis contribute
      information about the effect of the explanatory variable
```

age3	Odds Ratio	chi2(1)	P>chi2	[95% Conf. Interval]
1	3.800000	3.38	0.0660	0.821651 17.57438
2	10.666667	18.69	0.0000	2.787731 40.81376
3	13.500000	9.77	0.0018	1.598317 114.0262

```
Mantel-Haenszel estimate controlling for set and age3
```

Odds Ratio	chi2(1)	P>chi2	[95% Conf. Interval]
8.461538	31.16	0.0000	3.437773 20.826746

```
Test of homogeneity of ORs (approx): chi2(2)  =    1.41
                                     Pr>chi2  =  0.4943
```

◁

Saved Results

ir and **iri** save in **r()**:

Scalars

r(p)	one-sided p-value	r(afe)	attributable (prev.) fraction among exposed
r(ird)	incidence rate difference	r(lb_afe)	lower bound of CI for **afe**
r(lb_ird)	lower bound of CI for ird	r(ub_afe)	upper bound of CI for **afe**
r(ub_ird)	upper bound of CI for ird	r(afp)	attributable fraction for the population
r(irr)	incidence rate ratio	r(chi2_mh)	Mantel–Haenszel heterogeneity χ^2 (**ir** only)
r(lb_irr)	lower bound of CI for irr	r(chi2_p)	pooled heterogeneity χ^2 (**pool** only)
r(ub_irr)	upper bound of CI for irr	r(df)	degrees of freedom (**ir** only)

cs and csi save in r():

Scalars

r(p)	two-sided p-value	r(ub_or)	upper bound of CI for or
r(rd)	risk difference	r(afe)	attributable (prev.) fraction among exposed
r(lb_rd)	lower bound of CI for rd	r(lb_afe)	lower bound of CI for afe
r(ub_rd)	upper bound of CI for rd	r(ub_afe)	upper bound of CI for afe
r(rr)	risk ratio	r(afp)	attributable fraction for the population
r(lb_rr)	lower bound of CI for rr	r(chi2_mh)	Mantel–Haenszel heterogeneity χ^2 (cs only)
r(ub_rr)	upper bound of CI for rr	r(chi2_p)	pooled heterogeneity χ^2 (pool only)
r(or)	odds ratio	r(df)	degrees of freedom
r(lb_or)	lower bound of CI for or	r(chi2)	χ^2

cc and cci save in r():

Scalars

r(p)	two-sided p-value	r(lb_afe)	lower bound of CI for afe
r(p1_exact)	χ^2 or one-sided exact significance	r(ub_afe)	upper bound of CI for afe
r(p_exact)	two-sided significance (χ^2 or exact)	r(afp)	attributable fraction for the population
		r(chi2_p)	pooled heterogeneity χ^2
r(or)	odds ratio	r(chi2_bd)	Breslow–Day χ^2
r(lb_or)	lower bound of CI for or	r(df_bd)	degrees of freedom for Breslow–Day χ^2
r(ub_or)	upper bound of CI for or	r(df)	degrees of freedom
r(afe)	attributable (prev.) fraction among exposed	r(chi2)	χ^2

tabodds saves in r():

Scalars

r(odds)	odds	r(p_hom)	p-value for test of homogeneity
r(lb_odds)	lower bound for odds	r(df_hom)	degrees of freedom for χ^2 test of homogeneity
r(ub_odds)	upper bound for odds	r(chi2_tr)	χ^2 for score test for trend
r(chi2_hom)	χ^2 test of homogeneity	r(p_trend)	p-value for score test for trend

mhodds saves in r():

Scalars

r(p)	two-sided p-value	r(chi2_hom)	χ^2 test of homogeneity
r(or)	odds ratio	r(df_hom)	degrees of freedom for χ^2 test of homogeneity
r(lb_or)	lower bound of CI for or	r(chi2)	χ^2
r(ub_or)	upper bound of CI for or		

mcc and mcci save in r():

Scalars

r(p_exact)	two-sided significance (χ^2 or exact)	r(R_f)	ratio of proportion with factor
		r(lb_R_f)	lower bound of CI for R_f
r(or)	odds ratio	r(ub_R_f)	upper bound of CI for R_f
r(lb_or)	lower bound of CI for or	r(RD_f)	relative difference in proportion with factor
r(ub_or)	upper bound of CI for or		
r(D_f)	difference in proportion with factor	r(lb_RD_f)	lower bound of CI for RD_f
r(lb_D_f)	lower bound of CI for D_f	r(ub_RD_f)	upper bound of CI for RD_f
r(ub_D_f)	upper bound of CI for D_f	r(chi2)	χ^2

Methods and Formulas

All of the epitab commands are implemented as ado-files.

The notation for incidence-rate data is

	Exposed	Unexposed	Total
Cases	a	b	M_1
Person-time	N_1	N_0	T

The notation for $2 \times k$ tables is

	Exposure level				
	1	2	...	k	Total
Cases	a_1	a_2	...	a_k	M_1
Controls	c_1	c_2	...	c_k	M_0
Total	N_1	N_2	...	N_k	T

If tables are stratified, all quantities are indexed by i, the stratum number.

We will refer to Fleiss (1981), Kleinbaum, Kupper, and Morgenstern (1982), and Rothman (1986) so often that we will adopt the notation F-23 to mean Fleiss (1981) page 23, KKM-52 to mean Kleinbaum et al. (1982) page 52, and R-164 to mean Rothman (1986) page 164.

It is also worth noting that, in all cases, we have avoided making the continuity corrections to χ^2 statistics, following the advice of KKM-292: "[...] the use of a continuity correction has been the subject of considerable debate in the statistical literature [...] On the basis of our evaluation of this debate and other evidence, we do *not* recommend the use of the continuity correction". Breslow and Day (1980, 133), on the other hand, argue for inclusion of the correction, but not strongly. Their summary is that for very small datasets, one should use exact statistics. In practice, we believe the adjustment makes little difference for reasonably sized datasets.

Unstratified incidence rate data

The incidence rate difference is defined $I_d = a/N_1 - b/N_0$ (R-164). The standard error of the incidence rate is $s_{I_d} \approx \sqrt{a/N_1^2 + b/N_0^2}$ (R-170), from which confidence intervals are calculated. For test-based confidence intervals, define

$$\chi = \frac{a - N_1 M_1/T}{\sqrt{M_1 N_1 N_0/T^2}}$$

(R-155). Test-based confidence intervals are $I_d(1 \pm z/\chi)$ (R-171), where z is obtained from the normal distribution.

The incidence rate ratio is defined $I_r = (a/N_1)/(b/N_0)$ (R-164). Let p_l and p_h be the exact confidence interval of the binomial probability for observing a successes out of M_1 trials (obtained from cii, see [R] ci). The exact confidence interval for the incidence ratio is then $(p_l N_0)/\{(1-p_l)N_1\}$ to $(p_u N_0)/\{(1-p_u)N_1\}$ (R-166). Test-based confidence intervals are $I_r^{1 \pm z/\chi}$ (R-172).

The attributable fraction among exposed is defined AFE $= (I_r - 1)/I_r$ for $I_r \geq 1$ (KKM-164, R-38); the confidence interval is obtained by similarly transforming the interval values of I_r. The attributable fraction for the population is AF $=$ AFE $\cdot a/M_1$ (KKM-161); no confidence interval is reported. For $I_r < 1$, the prevented fraction among exposed is defined PFE $= 1 - I_r$ (KKM-166, R-39); the confidence interval is obtained by similarly transforming the interval values of I_r. The prevented fraction for the population is PF $=$ PFE $\cdot N_1/T$ (KKM-165); no confidence interval is reported.

The "midp" one-sided exact significance (R-155) is calculated as the binomial probability (with $n = M_1$ and $p = N_1/T$) $\Pr(k = a)/2 + \Pr(k > a)$ if $I_r >= 1$ and $\Pr(k = a)/2 + \Pr(k < a)$ otherwise. The two-sided significance is twice the one-sided significance (R-155). If preferred, one can obtain non-midp exact probabilities (and, to some ways of thinking, a more reasonable definition of two-sided significance) using `bitest`; see [R] **bitest**.

Unstratified cumulative incidence data

The risk difference is defined $R_d = a/N_1 - b/N_0$ (R-164). Its standard error is

$$s_{R_d} \approx \sqrt{\frac{a(N_1 - a)}{N_1^3} + \frac{b(N_0 - b)}{N_0^3}}$$

(R-172), from which confidence intervals are calculated. For test-based confidence intervals, define

$$\chi = \frac{a - N_1 M_1/T}{\sqrt{(M_1 M_0 N_1 N_0)/\{T^2(T - 1)\}}}$$

(R-163). Test-based confidence intervals are $R_d(1 \pm z/\chi)$ (R-172).

The risk ratio is defined $R_r = (a/N_1)/(b/N_0)$ (R-165). The standard error of $\ln R_r$ is

$$s_{\ln R_r} \approx \sqrt{\frac{c}{aN_1} + \frac{d}{bN_0}}$$

(R-173), from which confidence intervals are calculated. Test-based confidence intervals are $R_r^{1 \pm z/\chi}$ (R-173).

For $R_r \geq 1$, the attributable fraction among the exposed is calculated as AFE $= (R_r - 1)/R_r$ (KKM-164, R-38); the confidence interval is obtained by similarly transforming the interval values for R_r. The attributable fraction for the population is calculated as AF $=$ AFE $\cdot a/M_1$ (KKM-161); no confidence interval is reported, but F-76 provides

$$\sqrt{\frac{c + (a + d)\text{AFE}}{bT}}$$

as the approximate standard error of $\ln(1 - \text{AF})$.

For $R_r < 1$, the prevented fraction among the exposed is calculated as PFE $= 1 - R_r$ (KKM-166, R-39); the confidence interval is obtained by similarly transforming the interval values for R_r. The prevented fraction for the population is calculated as PF $=$ PFE $\cdot N_1/T$; no confidence interval is reported.

The odds ratio is defined $\psi = (ad)/(bc)$ (R-165). The Woolf estimate (Woolf 1955) of the standard error of $\ln \psi$ is

$$s_{\ln \psi} = \sqrt{\frac{1}{a} + \frac{1}{b} + \frac{1}{c} + \frac{1}{d}}$$

(R-173; Schlesselman 1982, 176), from which confidence intervals are calculated. Test-based confidence intervals are $\psi^{1 \pm z/\chi}$ (R-174). Alternatively, the Cornfield (1956) calculation is

$$\psi_l = a_l(M_0 - N_1 + a_l) \Big/ \Big\{ (N_1 - a_l)(M_1 - a_l) \Big\}$$

$$\psi_u = a_u(M_0 - N_1 + a_u) \Big/ \Big\{ (N_1 - a_u)(M_1 - a_u) \Big\}$$

where a_u and a_l are determined iteratively from

$$a_{i+1} = a \pm z_\alpha \left/ \sqrt{\frac{1}{a_i} + \frac{1}{N_1 - a_i} + \frac{1}{M_1 - a_i} + \frac{1}{M_0 - N_1 + a_i}} \right.$$

where z_α is the index from the normal distribution for an α significance level (Schlesselman 1982, 177, but without the continuity correction). a_{i+1} converges to a_u using the plus signs and a_l using the minus signs. a_0 is taken as a. With small numbers, the iterative technique may fail. It is then restarted by decrementing (a_l) or incrementing (a_u) a_0. If that fails, a_0 is again decremented or incremented and iterations restarted, and so on, until a terminal condition is met ($a_0 < 0$ or $a_0 > M_1$), at which point the value is not calculated.

The χ^2 is defined

$$\chi^2 = \sum_{i=1}^{2} \sum_{j=1}^{2} \frac{(p_{ij} - p_i . p_{\cdot j})^2}{p_i . p_{\cdot j}}$$

(F-22, but without the continuity correction) where $p_{11} = a/T$, $p_{12} = b/T$, etc.

Fisher's exact p is calculated as described in [R] **tabulate**.

Unstratified case–control data

Calculation of the odds ratio ψ and χ^2 is as described for unstratified cumulative incidence data. The other calculations described there are inappropriate.

The odds ratio ψ is used as an estimate of the risk ratio in calculating attributable or prevented fractions. For $\psi \geq 1$, the attributable fraction among the exposed is calculated as AFE $= (\psi - 1)/\psi$ (KKM-164); the confidence interval is obtained by similarly transforming the interval values for ψ. The attributable fraction for the population is calculated as AF $=$ AFE $\cdot a/M_1$ (KKM-161). No confidence interval is reported; however, F-94 provides

$$\sqrt{\frac{a}{M_1 b} + \frac{c}{M_0 d}}$$

as the standard error of $\ln(1 - \text{AF})$.

For $\psi < 1$, the prevented fraction among the exposed is calculated as PFE $= 1 - \psi$ (KKM-166); the confidence interval is obtained by similarly transforming the interval values for ψ. The prevented fraction for the population is calculated as PF $= \{(a/M_1)\text{PFE}\}/\{(a/M_1) + \psi\}$ (KKM-164); no confidence interval is reported.

Unstratified matched case–control data

The columns of the 2×2 table reflect controls; the rows, cases. Each entry in the table reflects a pair of a matched case and control.

McNemar's χ^2 (McNemar 1947) is defined as

$$\chi^2 = \frac{(b - c)^2}{b + c}$$

(R-259).

The proportion of controls with the factor is $p_1 = N_1/T$, and the proportion of cases with the factor is $p_2 = M_1/T$.

The difference in the proportions is $P_d = p_2 - p_1$. An estimate of its standard error when the two underlying proportions are *not* hypothesized to be equal is

$$s_{P_d} \approx \frac{\sqrt{(a+d)(b+c)+4bc}}{T\sqrt{T}}$$

(F-117), from which confidence intervals are calculated.

The ratio of the proportions is $P_r = p_2/p_1$ (R-276, R-278). The standard error of $\ln P_r$ is

$$s_{\ln P_r} \approx \sqrt{\frac{b+c}{M_1 N_1}}$$

(R-276), from which confidence intervals are calculated.

The relative difference in the proportions $P_e = (b-c)/(b+d)$ (F-118) is a measure of the relative value of the factor under the assumption that the factor can affect only those patients who are unexposed controls. Its standard error is

$$s_{P_e} \approx \frac{1}{(b+d)^2 \sqrt{(b+c+d)(bc+bd+cd)-bcd}}$$

(F-118), from which confidence intervals are calculated.

The odds ratio is $\psi = b/c$ (F-115), and the exact Fisher confidence interval is obtained by transforming into odds ratios the exact binomial confidence interval for the binomial parameter from observing b successes in $b+c$ trials (R-264). Binomial confidence limits are obtained from `cii` (see [R] **ci**) and are transformed by $p/(1-p)$. Test-based confidence intervals are $\psi^{1\pm z/\chi}$ (R-267) where χ is the square root of McNemar's χ^2, $(b-c)/\sqrt{b+c}$.

Stratified incidence-rate data

Statistics presented for each stratum are calculated independently according to the formulas in *Unstratified incidence-rate data* above. Within strata, the Mantel–Haenszel style weight is $W_i = b_i N_{1i}/T_i$ and the combined incidence rate ratio (Rothman and Boice 1982) is

$$I_{\text{mh}} = \frac{\sum_i a_i N_{0i}/T_i}{\sum_i W_i}$$

(R-196). The standard error is obtained by considering each a_i to be an independent binomial variate conditional on N_{1i} (Greenland and Robins 1985)

$$s_{\ln I_{\text{mh}}} \approx \sqrt{\frac{\sum_i M_{1i} N_{1i} N_{0i}/T_i^2}{\left(\sum_i a_i N_{0i}/T_i\right)\left(\sum_i b_i N_{1i}/T_i\right)}}$$

(R-213), from which confidence intervals are calculated.

For standardized rates, let w_i be the user-specified weight within category i. The standardized rate difference and rate ratio are defined as

$$\text{SRD} = \frac{\sum_i w_i(R_{1i} - R_{0i})}{\sum_i w_i}$$

$$\text{SRR} = \frac{\sum_i w_i R_{1i}}{\sum_i w_i R_{0i}}$$

(R-229). The standard error of SRD is

$$s_{\text{SRD}} \approx \sqrt{\frac{1}{(\sum_i w_i)^2} \sum_i w_i^2 \left(\frac{a_i}{N_{1i}^2} + \frac{b_i}{N_{0i}^2} \right)}$$

(R-231), from which confidence intervals are calculated. The standard error of ln(SRR) is

$$s_{\text{ln(SRR)}} \approx \sqrt{\frac{\sum_i w_i^2 a_i / N_{1i}^2}{(\sum_i w_i R_{1i})^2} + \frac{\sum_i w_i^2 b_i / N_{0i}^2}{(\sum_i w_i R_{0i})^2}}$$

(R-231) from which confidence intervals are calculated.

Internally and externally standardized measures are calculated using $w_i = N_1$ and $w_i = N_0$, respectively.

For directly pooled estimates of risk differences and risk ratios, stratum-specific point estimates and variances are calculated as given in *Unstratified cumulative incidence data*. (Note that for the risk ratio, this calculation is performed in the logs.) Inverse variance weights $w_i = 1/s^2$ are then used to sum the stratum-specific values (which are then exponentiated in the case of the risk ratio). The overall variance of the pooled estimate is calculated as $1/\sum w_i$, from which confidence intervals are calculated (R-183–188).

For risk differences, the χ^2 test of homogeneity is calculated as $(\sum R_{di} - \widehat{R}_d)^2 / \text{var}(R_{di})$ where R_{di} are the stratum-specific rate differences and $\widehat{R}_d$ is the pooled estimate (Mantel–Haenszel or directly pooled). Degrees of freedom are one less than the number of strata (R-222).

For risk ratios, the same calculation is made except that it is made on a logarithmic scale using $\ln(R_{ri})$ (R-222).

Stratified cumulative incidence data

Statistics presented for each stratum are calculated independently according to the formulas in *Unstratified cumulative incidence data* above. The Mantel–Haenszel χ^2 test (Mantel and Haenszel 1959) is

$$\chi_{\text{mh}}^2 = \frac{\left(|\sum_i a_i - N_{1i} M_{1i} / T_i| \right)^2}{\sum_i (N_{1i} N_{0i} M_{1i} M_{0i}) / \{ T_i^2 (T_i - 1) \}}$$

(R-206).

For the odds ratio, the Mantel–Haenszel weight is $W_i = b_i c_i / T_i$ and the combined odds ratio (Mantel and Haenszel 1959) is

$$\psi_{\text{mh}} = \frac{\sum_i a_i d_i / T_i}{\sum_i W_i}$$

(R-195). The standard error (Robins, Breslow, and Greenland 1986) is

$$s_{\ln \psi_{\mathrm{mh}}} \approx \sqrt{\frac{\sum_i P_i R_i}{2 \left(\sum_i R_i\right)^2} + \frac{\sum_i P_i S_i + Q_i R_i}{2 \sum_i R_i \sum_i S_i} + \frac{\sum_i Q_i S_i}{2 \left(\sum_i S_i\right)^2}}$$

where

$$P_i = (a_i + d_i)/T_i$$
$$Q_i = (b_i + c_i)/T_i$$
$$R_i = a_i d_i / T_i$$
$$S_i = b_i c_i / T_i$$

(R-220). Alternatively, test-based confidence intervals are calculated as $\psi_{\mathrm{mh}}^{1 \pm z/\chi}$ (R-220).

For the risk ratio the Mantel–Haenszel style weight is $W_i = b_i N_{1i}/T_i$ and the combined risk ratio (Rothman and Boice 1982) is

$$R_{\mathrm{mh}} = \frac{\sum_i a_i N_{0i}/T_i}{\sum_i W_i}$$

(R-196). The standard error (Greenland and Robins 1985) is

$$s_{\ln R_{\mathrm{mh}}} \approx \frac{\sum_i (M_{1i} N_{1i} N_{0i} - a_i b_i T_i)/T_i^2}{\left(\sum_i a_i N_{0i}/T_i\right)\left(\sum_i b_i N_{1i}/T_i\right)}$$

(R-216) from which confidence intervals are calculated.

For standardized rates, let w_i be the user-specified weight within category. The standardized rate difference (SRD) and rate ratios (SRR) are defined as above (*Stratified incidence rate data*), where the individual risks are defined $R_{1i} = a_i/N_{1i}$ and $R_{0i} = b_i/N_{0i}$. The standard error of SRD is

$$s_{\mathrm{SRD}} \approx \sqrt{\frac{1}{\left(\sum_i w_i\right)^2} \sum_i w_i^2 \left\{ \frac{a_i(N_{1i} - a_i)}{N_{1i}^3} + \frac{b_i(N_{0i} - b_i)}{N_{0i}^3} \right\}}$$

(R-231), from which confidence intervals are calculated. The standard error of ln(SRR) is

$$s_{\ln(\mathrm{SRR})} \approx \sqrt{\frac{\sum_i w_i^2 a_i(N_{1i} - a_i)/N_{1i}^3}{\left(\sum_i w_i R_{1i}\right)^2} + \frac{\sum_i w_i^2 b_i(N_{0i} - b_i)/N_{0i}^3}{\left(\sum_i w_i R_{0i}\right)^2}}$$

(R-231), from which confidence intervals are calculated.

Internally and externally standardized measures are calculated using $w_i = N_1$ and $w_i = N_0$, respectively.

For directly pooled estimates of the odds ratio, stratum-specific odds ratios are summed with stratum-specific inverse variance weights with the calculation performed in the logs and the point estimate and variances being as given in *Unstratified incidence rate data*. The overall variance of the pooled estimate is calculated as the sum of the inverse weights, from which confidence intervals are calculated (R-189–190).

For pooled estimates of risk differences and risk ratios, stratum-specific point estimates and variances are calculated as given in *Unstratified cumulative incidence data*. (Note that for the risk ratio, this calculation is performed in the logs.) Inverse variance weights $w_i = 1/s^2$ are then used to sum the stratum-specific values (which are then exponentiated in the case of the risk ratio). The overall variance of the pooled estimate is calculated as $1/\sum w_i$, from which confidence intervals are calculated (R-183–188).

For risk differences, the χ^2 test of homogeneity is calculated as $(\sum R_{di} - \widehat{R}_d)^2 / \text{var}(R_{di})$ where R_{di} are the stratum-specific rate differences and $\widehat{R}_d$ is the pooled estimate (Mantel–Haenszel or directly pooled). Degrees of freedom are one less than the number of strata (R-222).

For risk and odds ratios, the same calculation is made except that it is made in the logs using $\ln(R_{ri})$ or $\ln(\psi_i)$ (R-222).

Stratified case–control data

Statistics presented for each stratum are calculated independently according to the formulas in *Unstratified cumulative incidence data* above. The combined odds ratio ψ_{mh} and the test that $\psi_{\text{mh}} = 1$ (χ^2_{mh}) are calculated as described in *Stratified cumulative incidence data* above.

For standardized weights, let w_i be the user-specified weight within category. The standardized odds ratio is calculated as

$$\text{SOR} = \frac{\sum_i w_i a_i / c_i}{\sum_i w_i b_i / d_i}$$

(Greenland 1987a). The standard error of $\ln(\text{SOR})$ is

$$s_{\ln(\text{SOR})} = \frac{\sum_i (w_j a_j / c_j)^2 (\frac{1}{a_i} + \frac{1}{b_i} + \frac{1}{c_i} + \frac{1}{d_i})}{\left(\sum_i w_i a_i / c_i\right)^2}$$

(Greenland 1987a), from which confidence intervals are calculated. The internally and externally standardized odds ratios are calculated using $w_i = c_i$ and $w_i = d_i$, respectively.

The directly pooled estimate of the odds ratio is calculated as described in *Stratified cumulative incidence data* above.

The direct and Mantel–Haenszel χ^2 tests of homogeneity are calculated as $\sum \{\ln(R_{ri}) - \ln(\widehat{R}_r)\}^2 / \text{var}\{\ln(R_{ri})\}$ where R_{ri} are the stratum-specific odds ratios and $\widehat{R}_r$ is the pooled estimate (Mantel–Haenszel or directly pooled). The number of degrees of freedom is one less than the number of strata (R-222).

The Breslow–Day χ^2 test of homogeneity is calculated as the sum over all strata of the stratum specific squared deviations of the observed and fitted values based on the overall odds ratio, divided by the variance of the fitted values:

$$\sum_i \frac{\{a_i - A_i(\widehat{\psi})\}^2}{\text{Var}(a_i; \widehat{\psi})}$$

where $A_i(\widehat{\psi})$ is the fitted count for cell a determined as the root of the quadratic equation

$$A(M_0 - N_1 + A) = (\widehat{\psi})(M_1 - A)(N_1 - A)$$

which makes all cell values of the 2×2 table for the ith stratum positive, $\mathrm{Var}(a_i; \widehat{\psi})$ is the variance of the fitted table for the ith stratum, and $\widehat{\psi}$ is the Mantel–Haenszel estimate of the common odds ratio.

By default, both `tabodds` and `mhodds` produce test statistics and confidence intervals based on score statistics (Clayton and Hills, 1993). Using the notation for $2 \times k$ tables, the confidence interval for the odds of the ith exposure level, odds_i, $i = 1, \ldots, k$, is given by

$$\mathrm{odds}_i \cdot \exp\left(\pm z \sqrt{1/a_i + 1/c_i}\right)$$

The score χ^2 test of homogeneity of odds is calculated as

$$\chi^2_{k-1} = \frac{T(T-1)}{M_1 M_0} \sum_{i=1}^{k} \frac{(a_i - E_i)^2}{N_i}$$

where $E_i = (M_1 N_i)/T$.

Let l_i denote the value of the exposure at the ith level. The score χ^2 test for trend of odds is calculated as

$$\chi^2_1 = \frac{U^2}{V}$$

where

$$U = \frac{M_1 M_0}{T} \left(\sum_{i=1}^{k} \frac{a_i l_i}{M_1} - \sum_{i=1}^{k} \frac{c_i l_i}{M_0} \right)$$

and

$$V = \frac{M_1 M_0}{T} \left\{ \frac{\sum_{i=1}^{k} N_i l_i^2 - (\sum_{i=1}^{k} N_i l_i)^2 / T}{T-1} \right\}$$

Acknowledgments

We would like to thank Hal Morgenstern, Department of Epidemiology, UCLA School of Public Health; Ardythe Morrow, Center for Pediatric Research, Norfolk, Virginia; and the late Stewart West, Baylor College of Medicine, for their assistance in designing these commands. We also extend our appreciation to Jonathan Freeman, Department of Epidemiology, Harvard School of Public Health, for encouraging us to extend these commands to include tests for homogeneity, for helpful comments on the default behavior of the commands, and for his comments on an early draft of this section. We would also like to thank David Clayton, MRC Biostatistical Research Unit, Cambridge, and Michael Hills, London School of Hygiene and Tropical Medicine (retired); the original versions of `mhodds` and `tabodds` were written by them. Finally, we would like to thank William Dupont and Dale Plummer for their contribution to the implementation of exact confidence intervals for the odds ratios for `cc` and `cci`.

References

Boice, J. D. and R. R. Monson. 1977. Breast cancer in women after repeated fluoroscopic examinations of the chest. *Journal of the National Cancer Institute* 59: 823–832.

Breslow, N. E. and N. E. Day. 1980. *Statistical Methods in Cancer Research*, vol. 1. Lyon: International Agency for Research on Cancer.

Carlin, J. and S. Vidmar. 2000. sbe35: Menus for epidemiological statistics. *Stata Technical Bulletin* 56: 15–16.

Clayton, D. and M. Hills. 1993. *Statistical Models in Epidemiology*. Oxford: Oxford University Press.

——. 1995. ssa8: Analysis of case–control and prevalence studies. *Stata Technical Bulletin* 27: 26–31. Reprinted in *Stata Technical Bulletin Reprints*, vol. 5, pp. 227–233.

Cornfield, J. 1956. A statistical problem arising from retrospective studies. In *Proceedings of the Third Berkeley Symposium* vol. 4, ed. J. Neyman, 135–148. Berkeley, CA: University of California Press.

Doll, R. and A. B. Hill. 1966. Mortality of British doctors in relation to smoking: observations on coronary thrombosis. In *Epidemiological Approaches to the Study of Cancer and Other Chronic Diseases*, ed. W. Haenszel. *National Cancer Institute Monograph* 19: 205–268.

Dupont, W. D., and D. Plummer. 1999. sbe31: Exact confidence intervals for odds ratios from case–control studies. *Stata Technical Bulletin* 52: 12–16. Reprinted in *Stata Technical Bulletin Reprints*, vol. 9, pp. 150–154.

Fisher, L. D. and G. van Belle. 1993. *Biostatistics: A Methodology for the Health Sciences*. New York: John Wiley & Sons.

Fleiss, J. L. 1981. *Statistical Methods for Rates and Proportions*. 2d ed. New York: John Wiley & Sons.

Glass, R. I., A. M. Svennerholm, B. J. Stoll, M. R. Khan, K. M. B. Hossain, M. I. Huq, and J. Holmgren. 1983. Protection against cholera in breast-fed children by antibodies in breast milk. *New England Journal of Medicine* 308: 1389–1392.

Gleason, J. R. 1999. sbe30: Improved confidence intervals for odds ratios. *Stata Technical Bulletin* 51: 24–27. Reprinted in *Stata Technical Bulletin Reprints*, vol. 9, pp. 146–150.

Greenland, S. 1987a. Interpretation and choice of effect measures in epidemiologic analysis. *American Journal of Epidemiology* 125: 761–768.

——, ed. 1987b. *Evolution of Epidemiologic Ideas: Annotated Readings on Concepts and Methods*. Newton Lower Falls, MA: Epidemiology Resources.

Greenland, S. and J. M. Robins. 1985. Estimation of a common effect parameter from sparse follow-up data. *Biometrics* 41: 55–68.

——. 1988. Conceptual problems in the definition and interpretation of attributable fractions. *American Journal of Epidemiology* 128: 1185–1197.

Jick, H., O. S. Miettinen, R. K. Neff, S. Shapiro, O. P. Heinonen, and D. Slone. 1973. Coffee and myocardial infarction. *New England Journal of Medicine* 289: 63–67.

Kelsey, J. L., W. D. Thompson, and A. S. Evans. 1986. *Methods in Observational Epidemiology*. New York: Oxford University Press.

Kleinbaum, D. G., L. L. Kupper, and H. Morgenstern. 1982. *Epidemiologic Research*. New York: Van Nostrand Reinhold.

Lilienfeld, D. E. and P. D. Stolley. 1994. *Foundations of Epidemiology*. 3d ed. New York: Oxford University Press.

López-Vizcaíno, M. E., S. Pérez-Hoyos, and L. Abraira-García. 2000. sbe32: Automated outbreak detection from public health surveillance data. *Stata Technical Bulletin* 54: 23–25. Reprinted in *Stata Technical Bulletin Reprints*, vol. 9, pp. 154–157.

——. 2000. sbe32.1: Automated outbreak detection from public health surveillance data: errata. *Stata Technical Bulletin* 55: 2.

MacMahon B., S. Yen, D. Trichopoulos, K. Warren and G. Nardi. 1981. Coffee and cancer of the pancreas. *New England Journal of Medicine* 11: 630–633.

Mantel, N. and W. Haenszel. 1959. Statistical aspects of the analysis of data from retrospective studies of disease. *Journal of the National Cancer Institute* 22: 719–748. Reprinted in *Evolution of Epidemiologic Ideas*, ed. S. Greenland, 112–141. Newton Lower Falls, MA: Epidemiology Resources.

McNemar, Q. 1947. Note on the sampling error of the difference between correlated proportions or percentages. *Psychometrika* 12: 153–157.

Miettinen, O. S. 1976. Estimability and estimation in case-referent studies. *American Journal of Epidemiology* 103: 226–235. Reprinted in *Evolution of Epidemiologic Ideas*, ed. S. Greenland, 181–190. Newton Lower Falls, MA: Epidemiology Resources.

Pearce, M. S. and R. Feltbower. 2000. sg149: Tests for seasonal data via the Edwards and Walter & Elwood tests. *Stata Technical Bulletin* 56: 47–49.

Robins, J. M., N. Breslow, and S. Greenland. 1986. Estimators of the Mantel–Haenszel variance consistent in both sparse data and large-strata limiting models. *Biometrics* 42: 311–323.

Rothman, K. J. 1982. Spermicide use and Down's syndrome. *American Journal of Public Health* 72: 399–401.

——. 1986. *Modern Epidemiology*. Boston: Little, Brown and Company.

Rothman, K. J. and J. D. Boice. 1982. *Epidemiologic Analysis with a Programmable Calculator*. Brookline, MA: Epidemiology Resources. (First edition published June 1979 by U.S. Government Printing Office, Washington D.C., NIH Publication No. 79-1649.)

Rothman, K. J., D. C. Fyler, A. Goldblatt, and M. B. Kreidberg. 1979. Exogenous hormones and other drug exposures of children with congenital heart disease. *American Journal of Epidemiology* 109: 433–439.

Rothman, K. J. and S. Greenland. 1998. *Modern Epidemiology*. 2d ed. Philadelphia: Lippincott–Raven.

Rothman, K. J. and R. R. Monson. 1973. Survival in trigeminal neuralgia. *Journal of Chronic Diseases* 26: 303–309.

Schlesselman, J. J. 1982. *Case–Control Studies: Design, Conduct, Analysis*. New York: Oxford University Press.

University Group Diabetes Program. 1970. A study of the effects of hypoglycemic agents on vascular complications in patients with adult onset diabetes. *Diabetes* 19, supplement 2: 747–830.

Walker, A. M. 1991. *Observation and Inference: An Introduction to the Methods of Epidemiology*. Newton Lower Falls, MA: Epidemiology Resources.

Wang, Z. 1999. sbe27: Assessing confounding effects in epidemiological studies. *Stata Technical Bulletin* 49: 12–15. Reprinted in *Stata Technical Bulletin Reprints*, vol. 9, pp. 134–138.

Woolf, B. 1955. On estimating the relation between blood group and disease. *Annals of Human Genetics* 19: 251–253. Reprinted in *Evolution of Epidemiologic Ideas*, ed. S. Greenland, 108–110. Newton Lower Falls, MA: Epidemiology Resources.

Also See

Related:	[R] **bitest**, [R] **ci**, [R] **clogit**, [R] **dstdize**, [R] **logistic**, [R] **poisson**, [R] **st**, [R] **st stcox**, [R] **tabulate**
Background:	[U] **22 Immediate commands**

Title

erase — Erase a disk file

Syntax

$\{$ erase | rm $\}$ $\left[\texttt{"}\right]$ *filename* $\left[\texttt{"}\right]$

Note: In Stata for Windows and Stata for Macintosh, double quotes must be used to enclose *filename* if the name contains spaces.

Description

The erase command erases files stored on disk. Unix users may type erase, but they will probably prefer to type rm. Under Unix, erase is a synonym for rm.

Stata for Macintosh users: Be warned that erase is permanent; the file is not moved to the Trash but is immediately removed from the disk.

Stata for Windows users: Be warned that erase is permanent; the file is not moved to the Recycle Bin, but is immediately removed from the disk.

Remarks

The only difference between Stata's erase (rm) and the DOS DEL or Unix rm(1) is that you may not specify groups of files. Stata requires that you erase files one at a time.

Macintosh users may prefer to discard files by dragging them to the Trash.

Windows users may prefer to discard files by dragging them to the Recycle Bin.

▷ Example

Stata provides six operating-system equivalent commands: cd, copy, dir, erase, mkdir, and type or, from the Unix perspective, cd, copy, ls, rm, mkdir, and cat. These commands are provided for Macintosh users, too, but there is no operating-system equivalent. In addition, Stata for Unix users can issue any operating system command using Stata's shell command, so you should never have to exit Stata to perform some housekeeping detail.

Suppose you have the file mydata.dta stored on disk and you wish to permanently eliminate it:

```
. erase mydata
file mydata not found
r(601);

. erase mydata.dta

. _
```

Our first attempt, erase mydata, was unsuccessful. Although Stata ordinarily supplies the file extension for you, it does not do so when you type erase. You must be explicit. Our second attempt eliminated the file. Unix users could have typed rm mydata.dta if they preferred.

◁

Also See

Related: [R] **cd**, [R] **copy**, [R] **dir**, [R] **mkdir**, [R] **shell**, [R] **type**

Background: [U] **14.6 File-naming conventions**

Title

error messages — Error messages and return codes

Description

Whenever Stata detects that something is wrong—that what you typed is uninterpretable, that you are trying to do something you should not be trying to do, or that you requested the impossible—Stata responds by typing a message describing the problem together with a *return code*. For instance:

```
. lsit
unrecognized command:  lsit
r(199);
. list myvar
variable myvar not found
r(111);
. test a=b
last estimates not found
r(301);
```

In each case, the message is probably sufficient to guide you to a solution. When we typed `lsit`, Stata responded with "unrecognized command". We meant to type `list`. When we typed `list myvar`, Stata responded with "variable myvar not found". There is no variable named `myvar` in our data. When we typed `test a=b`, Stata responded with "last estimates not found". `test` tests hypotheses about previously estimated models, and we have not yet estimated a model.

The numbers in parentheses in the `r(199)`, `r(111)`, and `r(301)` messages are called the *return codes*. To find out more about these messages, type '`search rc #`'.

▷ Example

```
. search rc 301

[R]    error messages . . . . . . . . . . . . . . . . . . . . . . Return code 301
       last estimates not found;
       You typed an estimation command such as regress without arguments
       or attempted to perform a test or typed predict, but there were no
       previous estimation results.
```
                                                                            ◁

Programmers should see [P] **error** for details on programming error messages.

Also See

Complementary: [R] **search**

494

Title

> **estimation commands** — Quick reference for estimation commands

Description

This entry provides a quick reference for Stata's estimation commands. Since enhancements to Stata are continually being added, see the *Stata Technical Bulletin* for possible additions to this list; see [U] **2.4 The Stata Technical Bulletin**.

Remarks

Index to estimation commands

Command	Description	See
anova	Analysis of variance and covariance	[R] **anova**
arch	ARCH family of estimators	[R] **arch**
areg	Linear regression with a large dummy-variable set	[R] **areg**
arima	Autoregressive integrated moving average models	[R] **arima**
binreg	Generalized linear models: extensions to the binomial family	[R] **binreg**
biprobit	Bivariate probit models	[R] **biprobit**
blogit	Maximum likelihood logit on blocked data	[R] **glogit**
boxcox	Box–Cox regression models	[R] **boxcox**
bprobit	Maximum likelihood probit on blocked data	[R] **glogit**
bsqreg	Quantile regression with bootstrapped standard errors	[R] **qreg**
canon	Canonical correlations	[R] **canon**
clogit	Conditional (fixed-effects) logistic regression	[R] **clogit**
cloglog	Maximum-likelihood complementary log-log regression models	[R] **cloglog**
cnreg	Censored-normal regression	[R] **tobit**
cnsreg	Constrained linear regression	[R] **cnsreg**
cox	Maximum-likelihood proportional hazards models	[R] **cox**
dprobit	Maximum likelihood probit with reported coefficients transformed to the change in probability	[R] **probit**
eivreg	Errors-in-variables regression	[R] **eivreg**
ereg	Maximum-likelihood exponential distribution (survival time) models	[R] **weibull**
fracpoly	Fractional polynomial regression	[R] **fracpoly**
gamma	Maximum-likelihood 3-parameter generalized log-gamma distribution (survival time) models	[R] **weibull**
glm	Generalized linear models	[R] **glm**
glogit	Weighted least squares logit estimates on grouped data	[R] **glogit**
gnbreg	Maximum-likelihood generalized negative binomial regression	[R] **nbreg**
gompertz	Maximum-likelihood Gompertz distribution (survival time) models	[R] **weibull**
gprobit	Weighted least squares probit estimates on grouped data	[R] **glogit**

Command	Description	See
heckman	Heckman selection model	[R] **heckman**
heckprob	Probit models with sample selection	[R] **heckprob**
hetprob	Probit models with multiplicative heteroskedasticity	[R] **hetprob**
intreg	Interval regression	[R] **tobit**
iqreg	Interquantile regression	[R] **qreg**
ivreg	Instrumental variables and two-stage least squares regression	[R] **ivreg**
llogistic	Maximum-likelihood log-logistic distribution (survival time) models	[R] **weibull**
lnormal	Maximum-likelihood lognormal distribution (survival time) models	[R] **weibull**
logistic	Logistic regression	[R] **logistic**
logit	Maximum-likelihood logit estimation	[R] **logit**
mlogit	Maximum-likelihood multinomial logit models (polytomous logistic regression)	[R] **mlogit**
mvreg	Multivariate regression	[R] **mvreg**
nbreg	Maximum-likelihood negative binomial regression	[R] **nbreg**
newey	Regression with Newey–West standard errors	[R] **newey**
nl	Nonlinear least squares	[R] **nl**
nlogit	Nested logit	[R] **nlogit**
ologit	Maximum-likelihood ordered logit	[R] **ologit**
oprobit	Maximum-likelihood ordered probit	[R] **oprobit**
poisson	Maximum-likelihood Poisson regression	[R] **poisson**
prais	Prais–Winsten and Cochrane–Orcutt regression	[R] **prais**
probit	Maximum-likelihood probit estimation	[R] **probit**
qreg	Quantile (including median) regression (least absolute-value models—LAV or MAD—or minimum L1-norm models)	[R] **qreg**
reg3	Three-stage least squares regression	[R] **reg3**
regress	Linear regression	[R] **regress**
rreg	Robust regression	[R] **rreg**
scobit	Skewed logit regression	[R] **scobit**
sqreg	Simultaneous quantile regression	[R] **qreg**
stcox	Maximum-likelihood proportional hazards models	[R] **st stcox**
streg	Maximum-likelihood parametric survival models (exponential, Weibull, Gompertz, lognormal, log-logistic, and generalized log-gamma)	[R] **st streg**
sureg	Zellner's seemingly unrelated regression	[R] **sureg**

(Table continued on next page)

Command	Description	See
svyintreg	Pseudo-maximum-likelihood interval regression for complex survey data	[R] **svy estimators**
svyivreg	Instrumental variables regression for complex survey data	[R] **svy estimators**
svylogit	Pseudo-maximum-likelihood logistic regression for complex survey data	[R] **svy estimators**
svymlogit	Pseudo-maximum-likelihood multinomial logistic regression for complex survey data	[R] **svy estimators**
svyologit	Pseudo-maximum-likelihood ordered logit regression for complex survey data	[R] **svy estimators**
svyoprobit	Pseudo-maximum-likelihood ordered probit regression for complex survey data	[R] **svy estimators**
svypois	Pseudo-maximum-likelihood Poisson regression for complex survey data	[R] **svy estimators**
svyprobit	Pseudo-maximum-likelihood probit estimation for complex survey data	[R] **svy estimators**
svyreg	Linear regression for complex survey data	[R] **svy estimators**
sw *cmd*	Stepwise estimation (used with other est. commands)	[R] **sw**
tobit	Tobit regression	[R] **tobit**
treatreg	Treatment effects model	[R] **treatreg**
truncreg	Truncated regression	[R] **truncreg**
vwls	Linear regression using variance-weighted least squares	[R] **vwls**
weibull	Maximum-likelihood Weibull distribution (survival time) models	[R] **weibull**

(Table continued on next page)

Command	Description	See
xtabond	Arellano–Bond linear, dynamic panel-data estimator	[R] **xtabond**
xtclog	Random-effects and population-averaged cloglog models	[R] **xtclog**
xtgee	Generalized estimating equations for population-averaged panel data models	[R] **xtgee**
xtgls	Generalized least squares for panel data	[R] **xtgls**
xtintreg	Random-effects interval data regression models	[R] **xtintreg**
xtivreg	Instrumental variables and two-stage least squares for panel-data models	[R] **xtivreg**
xtlogit	Fixed-effects, random-effects, and population-averaged logit models	[R] **xtlogit**
xtnbreg	Fixed-effects, random-effects, and population-averaged negative binomial models	[R] **xtnbreg**
xtpois	Fixed-effects, random-effects, and population-averaged Poisson models	[R] **xtpois**
xtprobit	Random-effects and population-averaged probit models	[R] **xtprobit**
xtrchh	Hildreth–Houck random coefficients regression models	[R] **xtrchh**
xtreg	Cross-sectional time-series regression models (between-, fixed- GLS random-, and ML random-effects, and population-averaged models)	[R] **xtreg**
xtregar	Fixed- and random-effects linear models with an AR(1) disturbance	[R] **xtregar**
xttobit	Random-effects tobit models	[R] **xttobit**
zinb	Zero-inflated negative binomial models	[R] **zip**
zip	Zero-inflated Poisson models	[R] **zip**

(Summary table begins on next page)

Summary of estimation commands

Guide to Table

Weights: Allowed weights are listed with the default weight listed first. Possibilities are analytic weights (aw), frequency weights (fw), importance weights (iw), and probability weights (pw).

robust: Does the command allow the robust option? Note that if the robust option is specified, aweights are treated as pweights. If the table contains an '(R)' in the robust column, this means that although the command does not take the robust option, the command gives robust estimates of the variance.

sw: Can the command be used with sw to perform stepwise estimation?

adjust: Can adjust be used after the command to obtain adjusted predictions?

lincom: Can lincom be used after the command to form linear combinations of estimators?

linktest: Can linktest be used after the command to perform a specification link test?

lrtest: Can lrtest be used after the command to perform a likelihood-ratio test?

mfx: Can mfx be used after the command to obtain marginal effects or elasticities?

test: Can test be used after the command to test linear hypotheses?

testnl: Can testnl be used after the command to test nonlinear hypotheses?

Command	Weights	robust	sw	adjust	lincom	linktest	lrtest	mfx	test	testnl
anova	aw, fw	no	no	yes	no	yes	no	no	yes	no
arch	iw	yes	no	yes	yes	no	no	yes	yes	yes
areg	aw, fw, pw	yes	no	no	yes	no	no	yes	yes	yes
arima	iw	yes	no	yes	yes	no	no	yes	yes	yes
binreg	fw, aw, iw, pw	yes	no	yes	yes	yes	no	yes	yes	yes
biprobit	pw, fw, iw	yes	no	yes	yes	no	yes	yes	yes	yes
blogit	none	yes	no	yes	yes	no	yes	yes	yes	yes
boxcox	fw, iw	no	no	yes	yes	no	no	yes	yes	yes
bprobit	none	yes	no	yes	yes	no	yes	yes	yes	yes
bsqreg	none	no	no	yes	yes	yes	no	yes	yes	yes
canon	aw, fw	no	no	yes	yes	no	no	no	yes	yes
clogit	fw, iw	no	yes	no	yes	yes	yes	no	yes	yes
cloglog	fw, iw, pw	yes	yes	yes	yes	yes	yes	yes	yes	yes
cnreg	aw, fw	no	yes	yes	yes	yes	yes	yes	yes	yes
cnsreg	aw, fw	no	no	yes	yes	yes	no	yes	yes	yes
cox	fw, iw, pw	yes	yes	yes	yes	yes	yes	yes	yes	yes
dprobit	fw, aw, pw	yes	no	yes	yes	yes	yes	yes	yes	yes
eivreg	aw, fw	no	no	yes	yes	yes	no	yes	yes	yes
ereg	fw, aw, iw, pw	yes	yes	yes	yes	yes	yes	yes	yes	yes
fracpoly	(1)	no	no	(1)	yes	no	(1)	(1)	yes	yes
gamma	fw, iw, pw	yes	yes	yes	yes	yes	yes	yes	yes	yes
glm	fw, aw, iw, pw	yes	yes	yes	yes	yes	no	yes	yes	yes
glogit	none	no	no	yes	yes	no	no	yes	yes	yes
gnbreg	fw, aw, iw, pw	yes	no	yes	yes	no	yes	yes	yes	yes
gompertz	fw, iw, pw	yes	yes	yes	yes	yes	yes	yes	yes	yes
gprobit	none	no	no	yes	yes	no	no	yes	yes	yes

(1) This depends on the command.

Command	Weights	robust	sw	adjust	lincom	linktest	lrtest	mfx	test	testnl
heckman	pw, aw, fw, iw	yes	no	yes	yes	no	yes	yes	yes	yes
heckprob	pw, fw, iw	yes	no	yes	yes	no	yes	yes	yes	yes
hetprob	fw, iw, pw	yes	no	yes	yes	yes	yes	yes	yes	yes
intreg	aw, fw, iw, pw	yes	no	yes	yes	yes	yes	yes	yes	yes
iqreg	none	no	no	yes	yes	yes	no	yes	yes	yes
ivreg	aw, fw, iw, pw	yes	no	yes	yes	yes	no	yes	yes	yes
llogistic	fw, iw, pw	yes	yes	yes	yes	yes	yes	yes	yes	yes
lnormal	fw, iw, pw	yes	yes	yes	yes	yes	yes	yes	yes	yes
logistic	fw, pw	yes	yes	yes	yes	yes	yes	yes	yes	yes
logit	fw, iw, pw	yes	yes	yes	yes	yes	yes	yes	yes	yes
mlogit	fw, iw, pw	yes	no	yes	yes	no	yes	yes	yes	yes
mvreg	aw, fw	no	no	yes	yes	no	no	yes	yes	yes
nbreg	fw, iw, pw	yes	yes	yes	yes	yes	yes	yes	yes	yes
newey	aw	(R)	no	yes	yes	yes	no	yes	yes	yes
nl	aw, fw	no	no	no	no	no	no	no	no	no
nlogit	fw, iw	yes	no	no	yes	no	yes	no	yes	yes
ologit	fw, iw, pw	yes	yes	yes	yes	yes	yes	yes	yes	yes
oprobit	fw, iw, pw	yes	yes	yes	yes	yes	yes	yes	yes	yes
poisson	fw, iw, pw	yes	yes	yes	yes	yes	yes	yes	yes	yes
prais	none	yes	no	yes	yes	no	no	yes	yes	yes
probit	fw, iw, pw	yes	yes	yes	yes	yes	yes	yes	yes	yes
qreg	aw, fw	no	yes	yes	yes	yes	no	yes	yes	yes
reg3	aw, fw	no	no	yes	yes	no	no	yes	yes	yes
regress	aw, fw, iw, pw	yes	yes	yes	yes	yes	yes	yes	yes	yes
rreg	none	no	no	yes	yes	yes	no	yes	yes	yes
scobit	fw, iw, pw	yes	no	yes	yes	yes	yes	yes	yes	yes
sqreg	none	no	no	yes	yes	yes	no	yes	yes	yes
stcox	fw, iw, pw (2)	yes	no	yes	yes	yes	yes	yes	yes	yes
streg	fw, iw, pw (2)	yes	no	yes	yes	yes	yes	yes	yes	yes
sureg	aw, fw	no	no	yes	yes	no	no	yes	yes	yes

(R) The command does not take the `robust` option, but does give robust variance estimates.

(2) Use `stset` to specify the weights; see [R] **st stset**.

(*Table continued on next page*)

Command	Weights	robust	sw	adjust	lincom	linktest	lrtest	mfx	test	testnl
svyintreg	pw, iw	(R)	no	yes	(4)	no	no	yes	(3)	yes
svyivreg	pw, iw	(R)	no	yes	(4)	no	no	yes	(3)	yes
svylogit	pw, iw	(R)	no	yes	(4)	no	no	yes	(3)	yes
svymlogit	pw, iw	(R)	no	yes	(4)	no	no	yes	(3)	yes
svyologit	pw, iw	(R)	no	yes	(4)	no	no	yes	(3)	yes
svyoprobit	pw, iw	(R)	no	yes	(4)	no	no	yes	(3)	yes
svypois	pw, iw	(R)	no	yes	(4)	no	no	yes	(3)	yes
svyprobit	pw, iw	(R)	no	yes	(4)	no	no	yes	(3)	yes
svyreg	pw, iw	(R)	no	yes	(4)	no	no	yes	(3)	yes
tobit	aw, fw	no	yes	yes	yes	yes	yes	yes	yes	yes
treatreg	pw, aw, fw, iw	yes	no	yes	yes	no	yes	yes	yes	yes
truncreg	aw, fw, pw	yes	no	yes	yes	no	yes	yes	yes	yes
vwls	fw	no	no	yes	yes	yes	no	yes	yes	yes
weibull	fw, iw, pw	yes	yes	yes	yes	yes	yes	yes	yes	yes
xtabond	none	yes	no	yes	yes	no	no	yes	yes	yes
xtclog	iw, fw, pw (5)	(6)	no	yes	yes	no	no	yes	yes	yes
xtgee	iw, fw, pw	yes	no	yes	yes	no	no	yes	yes	yes
xtgls	aw	(R)	no	yes	yes	no	no	yes	yes	yes
xtintreg	iw	no	no	yes	yes	no	no	yes	yes	yes
xtivreg	none	no	no	yes	yes	no	no	yes	yes	yes
xtlogit	iw, fw, pw (5)	(6)	no	yes	yes	no	no	yes	yes	yes
xtnbreg	iw, fw, pw (5)	(6)	no	yes	yes	no	(7)	yes	yes	yes
xtpois	iw, fw, pw (5)	(6)	no	yes	yes	no	(7)	yes	yes	yes
xtprobit	iw, fw, pw (5)	(6)	no	yes	yes	no	no	yes	yes	yes
xtrchh	none	no	no	yes	yes	no	no	yes	yes	yes
xtreg	iw, fw, pw (5)	(6)	no	yes	yes	no	(8)	yes	yes	yes
xtregar	none	no	no	yes	yes	no	no	yes	yes	yes
xttobit	iw	no	no	yes	yes	no	no	yes	yes	yes
zinb	fw, iw, pw	yes	no	yes	yes	no	yes	yes	yes	yes
zip	fw, iw, pw	yes	no	yes	yes	no	yes	yes	yes	yes

(R) The command does not take the `robust` option, but does give robust variance estimates.

(3) `svytest` should be used instead of `test`.

(4) `svylc` should be used instead of `lincom`.

(5) Random-effects and fixed-effects models only allow `iw`.

(6) The command allows the `robust` option only with the `pa` option.

(7) Only with the `fe` and `re` options.

(8) Only with the `mle` option.

Also See

Complementary: [R] **adjust**, [R] **lincom**, [R] **linktest**, [R] **lrtest**, [R] **mfx**, [R] **predict**, [R] **sw**, [R] **test**, [R] **testnl**

Background: [U] **14.1.6 weight**,
[U] **23 Estimation and post-estimation commands**,
[U] **23.11 Obtaining robust variance estimates**

Title

> **exit** — Exit Stata

Syntax

> $\underline{e}$xit $\left[\, , \, \text{clear} \, \right]$

Description

Typing `exit` causes Stata to stop processing and return control to the operating system. If the dataset in memory has changed since the last `save` command, you must specify the `clear` option before Stata will let you leave.

`exit` may also be used for exiting do-files or programs; see [P] **exit**.

Stata for Windows users may also exit Stata by clicking on the close box, double-clicking on the system menu box, or by holding down *Alt* and pressing *F4*.

Stata for Macintosh users may also exit Stata by clicking on the close box.

Options

`clear` permits you to `exit` even if the current dataset has not been `saved`.

Remarks

Type `exit` to leave Stata and return to the operating system. If the dataset in memory has changed since the last time it was saved, however, Stata will refuse. At that point, you can either `save` the dataset and then type `exit` or type `exit, clear`:

```
. exit
no; data in memory would be lost
r(4);
. exit, clear
```

Also See

Related: [P] **exit**

Title

> **expand** — Duplicate observations

Syntax

expand [=] *exp* [if *exp*] [in *range*]

Description

expand replaces each observation in the current dataset with *n* copies of the observation, where *n* is equal to the integer part of the required expression. If the expression is less than 1 or equal to *missing*, it is interpreted as if it were 1 and the observation is retained but not duplicated.

Remarks

▷ Example

expand is, admittedly, a strange command. It can, however, be useful in tricky programs or for reformatting data for survival analysis (see examples in [R] **epitab**). Here is a silly use of expand:

```
. list

            n       x
  1.       -1       1
  2.        0       2
  3.        1       3
  4.        2       4
  5.        3       5

. expand n
(3 observations created)

. list

            n       x
  1.       -1       1
  2.        0       2
  3.        1       3
  4.        2       4
  5.        3       5
  6.        2       4
  7.        3       5
  8.        3       5
```

The new observations are added to the end of the dataset. expand informed us that it created 3 observations. The first 3 observations were not replicated since n was less than or equal to 1. n is 2 in the fourth observation, so expand created 1 replication of this observation, bringing the total number of observations of this type to 2. expand created 2 replications of observation 5 since n is 3.

Since there were 5 observations in the original dataset, and since expand adds new observations onto the end of the dataset, you could now undo the expansion by typing drop in 6/l.

◁

Also See

Complementary: [R] **contract**

Related: [R] **fillin**

Title

factor — Principal components and factor analysis

Syntax

<u>fac</u>tor [*varlist*] [*weight*] [if *exp*] [in *range*] [, { pc | pcf | pf | <u>i</u>pf | ml }

   <u>fa</u>ctors(#) <u>mine</u>igen(#) <u>cov</u>ariance <u>me</u>ans <u>pr</u>otect(#) <u>r</u>andom

   maximize_options]

<u>rot</u>ate [, { <u>v</u>arimax | <u>p</u>romax[(#)] } <u>h</u>orst <u>f</u>actors(#)]

<u>sc</u>ore *newvarlist* [if *exp*] [in *range*] [, <u>b</u>artlett <u>nor</u>otate]

greigen [, *graph_options*]

by ... : may be used with factor; see [R] **by**.
aweights and fweights are allowed; see [U] **14.1.6 weight**.

Description

factor performs factor or principal-components analysis of the variables in the *varlist*. factor can produce principal factor, iterated principal factor, principal-components factor, and maximum-likelihood factor analysis in addition to principal components. factor displays the eigenvalues and the factor loadings or eigenvectors.

rotate modifies the results of the last factor command to create a set of loadings that are more interpretable than those produced by factor. Varimax and promax rotations are available.

score creates a set of new variables that are estimates of the factors produced by factor or rotate (i.e., unrotated or rotated factors), or the principal components when factor is used to extract principal components. In the case of factor analysis, both regression and Bartlett scoring are available.

greigen displays a graph of the eigenvalues obtained by factor. Only the first 13 eigenvalues are graphed.

Options

pc, pcf, pf, ipf, and ml indicate the type of estimation to be performed. The default is pf, meaning principal factors; pc estimates principal components; pcf estimates principal-component factors; ipf estimates iterated principal components; ml estimates maximum likelihood factors. Details follow:

pc specifies that principal components be used to analyze the correlation or covariance matrix of the variables. The eigenvectors describe the linear combinations of the variables that produce maximum variance, minimum variance, and other major axes of the correlation or covariance ellipse.

pcf specifies that factor analysis be performed using the principal-components factor method. The communalities are assumed to be 1.

pf specifies that the principal factor method be used to analyze the correlation matrix of the variables. The factor loadings, sometimes called the factor patterns, are computed using the squared multiple correlations as estimates of the communality. pf is the default.

ipf specifies that the iterated principal factor method be used to analyze the correlation matrix of the variables. This re-estimates the communalities iteratively.

ml specifies the maximum-likelihood factor method.

factors(#) and mineigen(#) specify the maximum number of factors to be retained. factors() specifies the number directly and mineigen() specifies it indirectly, saying to keep all factors with eigenvalues greater than the indicated value. The options can be specified individually, together, or not at all. Details follow:

factors(#) sets the maximum number of factors to be retained, which means saved for subsequent use by rotate and score. factor always prints the full set of eigenvalues, but prints the corresponding eigenvectors only for retained factors. Specifying a number larger than the number of variables in the *varlist* is equivalent to specifying the number of variables in the *varlist* and is the default. factors(#) may also be specified with the rotate command. This requests that, even if more factors were previously retained, the rotation should be performed using only the first # factors.

mineigen(#) sets the minimum value of eigenvalues to be retained. For principal components (pc), the default is one, which screens out factors that predict less variance than would be expected from random data. For all factor methods, the default is zero, meaning factors associated with negative eigenvalues will not be printed or retained. Many sources also recommend mineigen(1) in this case, although the justification is more complex and less certain.

covariance may be used only with pc; it requests that principal components be calculated on the covariance matrix rather than on the correlation matrix.

means requests that a table of means be presented before factorization.

protect(#) is used only with ml and requests that # optimizations with random starting values be performed along with squared multiple-correlation coefficient starting values and that the best of the solutions be reported. The output also indicates whether all starting values converged to the same solution. When specified with a large number, such as protect(50), this ensures that the solution found is global and is not just a local maximum. If trace is also specified (see [R] **maximize**), the parameters and likelihoods of each maximization will be printed.

random is used only with ml and requests that random starting values be used. This option is rarely used and should only be used after protect() has shown the presence of multiple maxima.

varimax and promax$\left[(\#)\right]$ specify the type of rotation to be performed. The default is the orthogonal varimax rotation. promax requests an oblique rotation. The optional argument specifies the promax power. Not specifying the argument is equivalent to specifying promax(3). Values less than 4 are recommended, but the choice is yours. Larger promax powers simplify the loading (generate more zeros and ones) at the cost of more correlation between factors. Choosing a value is a matter of trial-and-error, but most sources find values in excess of 4 undesirable in practice. The power must be greater than 1 but is not restricted to integers.

horst requests that the Horst (1965) modification to varimax and promax rotation be made. This modification standardizes the initial factor loadings for each variable to have length 1 before applying the varimax or promax optimizations; see *Methods and Formulas* below.

`bartlett` produces factors scored by the method suggested by Bartlett (1938). This method produces unbiased factors, but they may be less accurate than those produced by the default regression method suggested by Thomson (1951). Regression-scored factors have the smallest mean square error from the true factors but may be biased.

`norotate` specifies that unrotated factors be scored even when you have previously issued a `rotate` command. The default is to use rotated factors from `rotate` if available and unrotated factors otherwise.

maximize_options control the maximization process; see [R] **maximize**. You should never have to specify them. In addition, `rotate` allows the `ltolerance(#)` option to specify its convergence criterion. Its default value is 0.0001.

graph_options are any of the options allowed with `graph`, `twoway`; see [G] **graph options**.

Remarks

Remarks are presented under the headings

> *Principal components analysis*
> *Factor analysis*
> *Rotation*
> *Scoring*

Principal component and factor analysis are statistical techniques for data reduction. They help you reduce the number of variables in an analysis by describing linear combinations of the variables that contain most of the information.

Principal components analysis

Principal component analysis originated with the work of Pearson (1901) and Hotelling (1933). For an introduction, see Rabe-Hesketh and Everitt (2000, chapter 12). In principal component analysis, the objective is to find the unit-length linear combinations of the variables with the greatest variance. If the default (correlation) matrix is used, the variables are scaled to have equal standard deviation before the calculation is undertaken.

▷ Example

You want to compare 74 automobile models on a number of dimensions, including weight, length, engine displacement, and mileage rating. You suspect that these measures are related to each other. `factor` will estimate the principal components, but only if you specify the `pc` option:

```
. factor weight length displ mpg, pc means
(obs=74)
```

Variable	Mean	Std. Dev.	Min	Max
weight	3,019.46	777.1936	1,760	4,840
length	187.9324	22.26634	142	233
displacement	197.2973	91.83722	79	425
mpg	21.43243	6.05473	12	41

(principal components; 4 components retained)

Component	Eigenvalue	Difference	Proportion	Cumulative
1	3.45849	3.11720	0.8646	0.8646
2	0.34129	0.18446	0.0853	0.9499
3	0.15683	0.11344	0.0392	0.9892
4	0.04339	.	0.0108	1.0000

	Eigenvectors			
Variable	1	2	3	4
weight	0.52296	0.22399	0.26009	-0.78019
length	0.51623	0.08354	0.62585	0.57865
displacement	0.49485	0.47169	-0.69026	0.23701
mpg	-0.46383	0.84874	0.25337	0.01723

These results are presented in three panels, although typically there are only two. The first panel shows the table of means produced by the **means** option.

The second panel is a table of components. It lists the eigenvalues of the correlation matrix, ordered from largest to smallest. The third column shows the difference between each eigenvalue and the next smaller eigenvalue. A sudden drop in this number (e.g., from 3.11720 to 0.18446) suggests that subsequent eigenvalues are just sampling noise. Bear in mind that the average of the eigenvalues is always 1.

The third panel displays the eigenvectors associated with each of the components in the second panel. The first eigenvector goes with the first eigenvalue, and so on.

The results confirm that the four measures are strongly related to each other and could be reduced. Looking under the proportion column, we see that the first component accounts for 86.46 percent of the variance in the four variables.

◁

❏ Technical Note

We analyzed the correlation matrix, which is what **factor** does by default, because each of these four variables has different units. This is equivalent to converting all the variables to having mean 0, standard deviation 1, at the outset. Thus, the remainder of the analysis is presented in terms of these "standardized" variables. The first eigenvector tells us that the first component uses roughly equal amounts of each of the variables. The sign on **mpg** is negative because as mileage decreases, weight, length, and displacement increase.

The second component describes the remaining variance after the first component is removed from the data. Interpreting this component is a debatable exercise because its eigenvalue is well below 1 and it is not too much larger than the third eigenvalue. If you do elect to interpret the second component, bear in mind that it is constrained to be orthogonal to the first component. In this case, the second component is associated with high mileage, displacement, and weight. Some analysts might say this describes the performance of the car; others would be more cautious and say it is noise.

Had we specified the **covariance** option in addition to **pc**, the principal components would have been extracted from the unstandardized data. This, however, would not have been a good idea in this case. The standard deviation of weight is much larger than that of the other variables and the first component would load on it heavily.

❏

▷ Example

After principal components or factor analysis, you can graph the eigenvalues with the **greigen** command to help you decide how many components to retain. Up to 13 eigenvalues are plotted.

. greigen

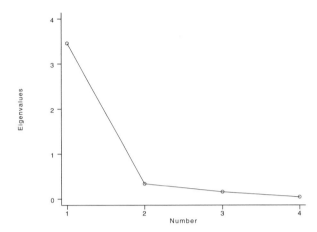

◁

▷ Example

After you decide how many components you wish to retain, `score` will estimate the components. Continuing with our example, we will eschew the interpretation that the second component represents performance and admit that it is only noise. We wish to estimate one component, which we will call `f1`:

. score f1
              (based on unrotated principal components)
              (3 scorings not used)
                    Scoring Coefficients
         Variable | 1
    -------------+------------
           weight | 0.52296
           length | 0.51623
     displacement | 0.49485
              mpg | -0.46383

The table is trying to tell us that `f1` could be obtained by

. egen stdwgt = std(weight)
. egen stdlen = std(length)
. egen stddis = std(displ)
. egen stdmpg = std(mpg)
. gen f1 = .52296*stdwgt + .51623*stdlen + .49485*stddis - .46383*stdmpg

(`egen`'s `std()` function converts a variable to its standardized (mean 0, variance 1) form; see [R] **egen**.)

◁

❑ Technical Note

Had we specified the `covariance` option when we issued the `factor` command, not only would the principal components have been extracted from the unstandardized data, but `score`'s results would then be in terms of the raw variables.

❑

❑ Technical Note

Stata does not allow rotation after using the pc option of **factor** because the definition of "principal components" explicitly indicates that the result is to have axes that are uncorrelated and line up in directions of maximum variance. After a rotation, the result would no longer meet the definition of being principal components.

Rencher (1998, 359–361), Rencher recommends as follows:

> "Since the rotated components are correlated and lack the maximum variance property, their routine use is questionable. If interpretation of the principal components is not satisfactory, one may wish to try factor analysis, in which rotation does not affect any important properties. . . ."

❑

Factor analysis

Factor analysis originated with the work of Spearman (1904). Factor analysis is concerned with finding a small number of common factors (say q of them) that linearly reconstruct the p original variables

$$y_{ij} = z_{i1}b_{1j} + z_{i2}b_{2j} + \cdots + z_{iq}b_{qj} + e_{ij}$$

where y_{ij} is the value of the ith observation on the jth variable, z_{ik} is the ith observation on the kth common factor, b_{kj} is the set of linear coefficients called the factor loadings, and e_{ij} is similar to a residual but known as the jth variable's unique factor. Note that everything except the left-hand-side variable is to be estimated, so the model has an infinite number of solutions. Various constraints are introduced along with a definition of "reconstruct" to make the model determinate.

"Reconstruction" is typically defined in terms of prediction of the covariance matrix of the original variables, unlike principal components where reconstruction means minimum residual variance summed across all equations.

Once the factors and their loadings have been estimated, they are interpreted—an admittedly subjective process. Interpretation typically means examining the b_{kj}'s and assigning names to each factor. Due to the indeterminacy of the factor solution, one is not limited to examining solely the b_{kj}'s. The loadings could be rotated—that is, one could look at another set of b_{kj}'s that, while appearing different, are every bit as good as (and no better than) the original loadings. Such "rotations" come in two flavors—orthogonal and oblique rotations. Since there are an infinite number of potential rotations, different rotations could lead to different interpretations of the same data. These are not to be viewed as conflicting, but instead as two different ways of looking at the same thing.

▷ Example

We wish to analyze physicians' attitudes toward cost and have a dataset of responses to six questions about cost asked of 568 physicians in the Medical Outcomes Study from Tarlov et al. (1989). Factor analysis is often used to validate a combination of questions that looks attractive at first glance. In this case, we wish to create a variable that summarizes the information on each physician's attitude toward cost.

Each of the responses is coded on a 5-point scale, where 1 means agree and 5 means disagree:

```
. describe
Contains data from bg.dta
  obs:            568                        Physician-Cost Data
  vars:             7                        7 Aug 2000 12:42
  size:         7,952 (99.1% of memory free)

              storage  display   value
variable name   type   format    label    variable label

clinid         float   %9.0g              Physician Identifier
bg2cost1       byte    %8.0g              Best health care is expensive
bg2cost2       byte    %8.0g              Cost is a major consideration
bg2cost3       byte    %8.0g              Determine cost of tests first
bg2cost4       byte    %8.0g              Monitor likely complications
                                            only
bg2cost5       byte    %8.0g              Use all means regardless of cost
bg2cost6       byte    %8.0g              Prefer unnecessary tests to
                                            missing tests

Sorted by:  clinid
```

We can perform the factorization on bg2cost1, bg2cost2, ..., bg2cost6 by typing factor bg2cost*, using Stata's shorthand for "all variables that begin with ...":

```
. factor bg2cost*
(obs=527)

               (principal factors; 3 factors retained)
   Factor    Eigenvalue    Difference    Proportion    Cumulative

      1       0.85395       0.31282       1.0309        1.0309
      2       0.54113       0.51787       0.6533        1.6842
      3       0.02326       0.17290       0.0281        1.7123
      4      -0.14964       0.03949      -0.1807        1.5316
      5      -0.18913       0.06211      -0.2283        1.3033
      6      -0.25124           .        -0.3033        1.0000

                        Factor Loadings
        Variable  |      1          2          3       Uniqueness

        bg2cost1  |    0.24703    0.36704   -0.04462    0.80227
        bg2cost2  |   -0.33745    0.33214   -0.07730    0.76983
        bg2cost3  |   -0.37644    0.37557    0.02039    0.71682
        bg2cost4  |   -0.32207    0.19416    0.10352    0.84786
        bg2cost5  |    0.45504    0.24789    0.06415    0.72737
        bg2cost6  |    0.47598    0.23641   -0.00680    0.71751
```

factor retained only the first three factors because the eigenvalues associated with the remaining factors are negative. According to the default mineigen(0) criterion, the factor has to have an eigenvalue greater than 0 to be retained. You can set this threshold higher by specifying mineigen(#) for yourself, causing factor to retain fewer factors automatically. You might want to do this: Although the program elected to retain three factors, only the first two appear to be meaningful.

The first factor seems to describe the physician's average position on cost since it affects the responses to all the questions "positively", as shown by the signs in the first column of the factor-loading table. We say "positively" because, obviously, the signs on three of the loadings are negative. When we look back at the results of describe, however, we find that the sense of the responses on bg2cost2, bg2cost3, and bg2cost4 are reversed. If the physician feels that cost should not be a major influence on medical treatment, he or she is likely to disagree with these three items and agree with the other three.

The second factor loads positively (absolutely, not logically) on all six items and could be interpreted as describing the physician's tendency to agree with any good-sounding idea put forth. Psychologists refer to this as the "positive response set". On statistical grounds we would probably keep this second factor, although on substantive grounds we would be tempted to dump it. We will keep it though, to illustrate the `rotate` command.

◁

❏ Technical Note

Before turning to `rotate`, let us mention the alternative estimation strategies available for the factor model. We specified no options on the `factor` command when we estimated the above model, so we obtained the principal factor solution. The *communalities* (defined as $1 - uniqueness$) were estimated using the squared-multiple correlation coefficients.

We could have instead obtained the estimates from "principal-component factors", treating the communalities as all 1—meaning that there are no unique factors—by specifying the `pcf` option:

```
. factor bg2cost*, pcf
(obs=527)
```

(principal-component factors; 2 factors retained)

Factor	Eigenvalue	Difference	Proportion	Cumulative
1	1.70625	0.30334	0.2844	0.2844
2	1.40291	0.49423	0.2338	0.5182
3	0.90867	0.18568	0.1514	0.6696
4	0.72299	0.05604	0.1205	0.7901
5	0.66695	0.07471	0.1112	0.9013
6	0.59224	.	0.0987	1.0000

Variable	Factor Loadings 1	2	Uniqueness
bg2cost1	0.35804	0.62794	0.47750
bg2cost2	-0.48503	0.52443	0.48972
bg2cost3	-0.53262	0.57249	0.38856
bg2cost4	-0.49188	0.32540	0.65217
bg2cost5	0.62380	0.39624	0.45387
bg2cost6	0.65424	0.37806	0.42903

In this case, we find that the principal-component factor model is inappropriate. We started by assuming that the uniquenesses were 0, and now find that there is considerable uniqueness—there is considerable variance left over after our two factors. We should use some other method.

❏

❏ Technical Note

We could have estimated our model using iterated principal factors by specifying the `ipf` option. In this case, the initial estimates of the communalities would be the squared multiple-correlation coefficients, but the solution would then be iterated to obtain different (better) estimates:

(Continued on next page)

```
. factor bg2cost*, ipf
(obs=527)
```

	(iterated principal factors; 5 factors retained)			
Factor	Eigenvalue	Difference	Proportion	Cumulative
1	1.08374	0.31752	0.5103	0.5103
2	0.76622	0.53817	0.3608	0.8712
3	0.22805	0.19476	0.1074	0.9786
4	0.03328	0.02086	0.0157	0.9942
5	0.01243	0.01260	0.0059	1.0001
6	-0.00017	.	-0.0001	1.0000

	Factor Loadings					
Variable	1	2	3	4	5	Uniqueness
bg2cost1	0.24710	0.40594	-0.13494	-0.13041	0.02887	0.73810
bg2cost2	-0.40415	0.39592	-0.26370	0.03489	0.00398	0.60914
bg2cost3	-0.44801	0.45696	0.12920	0.01364	-0.05645	0.57041
bg2cost4	-0.33266	0.19427	0.26545	0.00912	0.08115	0.77446
bg2cost5	0.52944	0.33390	0.21614	-0.01336	-0.03319	0.56021
bg2cost6	0.51736	0.29434	-0.08016	0.12088	0.02657	0.62396

In this case, we retained too many factors. Unlike principal factors or principal-component factors, we cannot simply ignore the unnecessary factors because the uniquenesses are re-estimated from the data. We need to re-estimate:

```
. factor bg2cost*, ipf factors(2)
(obs=527)
```

	(iterated principal factors; 2 factors retained)			
Factor	Eigenvalue	Difference	Proportion	Cumulative
1	1.03960	0.30810	0.5870	0.5870
2	0.73150	0.60784	0.4130	1.0000
3	0.12366	0.11578	0.0698	1.0698
4	0.00787	0.03654	0.0044	1.0743
5	-0.02867	0.07425	-0.0162	1.0581
6	-0.10291	.	-0.0581	1.0000

	Factor Loadings		
Variable	1	2	Uniqueness
bg2cost1	0.22591	0.39406	0.79368
bg2cost2	-0.35900	0.29732	0.78272
bg2cost3	-0.51895	0.49345	0.48719
bg2cost4	-0.32299	0.16041	0.86994
bg2cost5	0.46677	0.32864	0.67412
bg2cost6	0.51785	0.33254	0.62125

It is instructive to compare the reported uniquenesses for this model and the previous one, where five factors were retained. Also note that as compared with the results we obtained from principal factors, these results do not differ much.

❑

❑ Technical Note

Finally, we could have estimated our model using the maximum likelihood method by specifying the `ml` option. As with `ipf`, if we do not specify the number of factors, it just so happens that Stata decides to retain more than two factors (it retained three) and, as with `ipf`, it is necessary to re-estimate with the number of factors that we really want. To save paper, we will start by retaining two factors:

```
. factor bg2cost*, ml factors(2)
(obs=527)
Iteration 0:   Log Likelihood =-26.638456
Iteration 1:   Log Likelihood =-6.5089835
Iteration 2:   Log Likelihood =-6.3648616
Iteration 3:   Log Likelihood =-6.3570128
Iteration 4:   Log Likelihood =-6.3565691
Iteration 5:   Log Likelihood =-6.3565452
Iteration 6:   Log Likelihood =-6.3565439
```

(maximum-likelihood factors; 2 factors retained)

Factor	Variance	Difference	Proportion	Cumulative
1	1.02772	0.28110	0.5792	0.5792
2	0.74662	.	0.4208	1.0000

Test: 2 vs. no   factors. chi2(12) = 238.23, Prob > chi2 = 0.0000
Test: 2 vs. more factors. chi2(4) =   12.61, Prob > chi2 = 0.0133

Factor Loadings

Variable	1	2	Uniqueness
bg2cost1	-0.13697	0.42354	0.80185
bg2cost2	0.41413	0.19924	0.78879
bg2cost3	0.62011	0.36904	0.47927
bg2cost4	0.35771	0.09071	0.86382
bg2cost5	-0.37507	0.43574	0.66945
bg2cost6	-0.42929	0.43960	0.62246

In addition to the "standard" output, when you use the `ml` option Stata reports likelihood-ratio tests of the number of factors in the model versus (1) no factors and (2) more factors. The second test is, in reality, a test against a model sufficiently rich to fit the observed correlation matrix perfectly. This test is only approximately chi-squared and we have used the correction recommended by Bartlett (1951). Be aware that there are many variations on this test in use by different statistical packages.

The following comments were made by the analyst looking at these results: "There is, in my opinion, weak evidence of more than two factors. The χ^2 test for more than two factors is really a test of how well you are fitting the correlation matrix. It is not surprising that the model does not fit it perfectly. The significance of 1%, however, suggests to me that there might be a third factor. As for the loadings, they yield a similar interpretation to other factor models we fitted, although there are some noteworthy differences." When we challenged the analyst on this last statement, he added that he would want to rotate the resulting factors before committing himself further.

❑

❑ Technical Note

Going back to the two tests, Stata will sometimes comment, "Note: above tests may not apply; see manual". The approximations used in computing the χ^2 value and degrees of freedom are mathematically justified on the assumption that an *interior* solution to the factor maximum likelihood was found. This is the case in our example above, but that will not always be so.

Another possibility: boundary solutions, called Heywood solutions, often produce uniquenesses of 0 and in that case, at least at a formal level, the test cannot be justified. Nevertheless, we believe that the reported tests are useful even in such circumstances provided they are interpreted cautiously.

This message is also printed when, in principle, there are enough free parameters to completely fit the correlation matrix, another sort of boundary solution. We say "in principle" because the correlation matrix frequently cannot be fit perfectly, so you will see a positive χ^2 with zero degrees of freedom. This warning note is printed because the geometric assumptions underlying the likelihood-ratio test break down.

❑

❑ Technical Note

In maximum likelihood analysis, there is a possibility of more than one local maximum and you may want assurances that the maximum reported is the global maximum. Multiple maxima are especially likely when there is more than one group of variables, the groups are reasonably uncorrelated, and you attempt to fit a model with too few factors.

When you specify the `protect(#)` option, Stata performs # optimizations of the likelihood function, beginning each with random starting values, before continuing with the squared-multiple-correlations initialized solution. Stata then selects the maximum of the maxima and reports it, along with a note informing you if other, local maxima were found. `protect(50)` provides considerable assurance.

If you then wish to explore any of the nonglobal maxima, include the `random` option. This option, which is never specified with `protect()`, uses random starting values and reports the solution to which those random values converge. In the case of multiple maxima, giving the command repeatedly will eventually report all local maxima.

❑

Rotation

Rotation is an attempt to describe the information in several factors by reexpressing them so that loadings on a few initial variables are as large as possible. We have this freedom to reexpress because of the indeterminate nature of the factors. For example, if you find that z_1 and z_2 are two factors, then $z_1 + z_2$ and $z_1 - z_2$ are equally valid solutions. It comes down to which set is more meaningful and interpretable.

❑ Technical Note

Said more technically: We are trying to find a set of q factor variables such that the observed variables can be explained by regressing them on the q factor variables. Usually, q is a small number such as 1 or 2. If $q \geq 2$, there is an inherent indeterminacy in the construction of the factors because any linear combination of the calculated factors serves equally well as a set of regressors. Rotation capitalizes on this indeterminacy to create a set of variables that looks as much like the original variables as possible.

❑

The `rotate` command modifies the results of the last `factor` command to create a set of loadings that are more interpretable than those produced by `factor`.

You may perform a single factor analysis followed by several `rotate` commands, thus experimenting with, say, retaining different numbers of factors and possibly with using different types of rotation. Please remember: If you retain too few factors, the variables for several distinct concepts may be merged, as happens in our example below. If you retain too many factors, several factors may attempt to measure the same concept, causing the factors to get in each other's way and suggest too many distinct concepts after rotation.

▷ Example

Let us rotate the results from our previous analysis, starting with the default principal factor solution reported in the first example of the section *Factor analysis* above. If you look back at the example, you will note that `factor` retained three factors although we made the argument that only two are worth retaining. We commented that you could re-estimate the model specifying the `mineigen()` option and we could also have mentioned the `factors()` option. It is not necessary to re-estimate, because we can tell `rotate` how many factors to retain for the rotation:

```
. rotate, factors(2)
              (varimax rotation)
              Rotated Factor Loadings
    Variable |       1            2     Uniqueness
    ---------+------------------------------------
    bg2cost1 |   -0.09446      0.43223    0.80426
    bg2cost2 |   -0.47327     -0.01425    0.77581
    bg2cost3 |   -0.53161     -0.01239    0.71723
    bg2cost4 |   -0.36294     -0.09851    0.85857
    bg2cost5 |    0.13543      0.50017    0.73149
    bg2cost6 |    0.15820      0.50736    0.71756
```

In this example, the factors are rotated so that the three "negative" items are grouped together, and the three "positive" items are grouped. This is not necessarily a step forward.

We should take note of the uniqueness column. *Uniqueness* is the percentage of variance for the variable that is not explained by the factors. It could be pure measurement error or it could represent something that is measured reliably in that particular variable but not by any of the others. The greater the uniqueness, the more likely that it is more than just measurement error. Values over 0.6 are definitely high; all the variables in this problem are even higher—over 0.71.

If the uniqueness is high, then the variable is not well explained by the factor(s). The quantity "1 − *uniqueness*" is called *communality*.

◁

▷ Example

In this example, we examine 19 variables describing various aspects of health. These variables were collected from a random half of 22,462 visitors to doctors' offices by Tarlov et al. (1989). Factor analysis yields three clear factors. We then examine several rotations of these three factors.

```
. describe
Contains data from sp.dta
  obs:          11,231                     MOS SP Screener Raw Data
  vars:             20                     14 Jul 2000 12:29
  size:        303,237 (70.8% of memory free)
```

variable name	storage type	display format	value label	variable label
patid	float	%9.0g		Case ID
sp1ghp31	byte	%8.0g		Health excellent, very good, good, fair, poor
sp2pf01	byte	%8.0g		How long limit vigorous activity
sp2pf02	byte	%8.0g		How long limit moderate activity
sp2pf03	byte	%8.0g		How long limit walk/climb
sp2pf04	byte	%8.0g		How long limit bend/stoop
sp2pf05	byte	%8.0g		How long limit walk 1 block
sp2pf06	byte	%8.0g		How long limit eat/dress/bath
sp2rkeep	byte	%8.0g		does health keep work-job-hse
sp2rkind	byte	%8.0g		Can't do kind/amount of work
sp2sact0	byte	%8.0g		Last month limit activities
sp2mha01	byte	%8.0g		Last month very nervous
sp2mhp03	byte	%8.0g		Last month calm/peaceful
sp2mhd02	byte	%8.0g		Last month downhearted/blue
sp2mhp01	byte	%8.0g		Last month a happy person
sp2mhc01	byte	%8.0g		Last month down in the dumps
sp2ghp01	byte	%8.0g		somewhat ill

sp2ghp04	byte	%8.0g	Healthy as anybody I know
sp2ghp02	byte	%8.0g	Health is excellent
sp2ghp05	byte	%8.0g	Feel bad lately

Sorted by: patid

We now perform our factorization, requesting that factors with eigenvalues less than or equal to 1 not be retained. Our dataset contains many missing values, a fact you can discover by comparing the number of observations in the dataset (shown by describe as 11,231) with the number of observations used by factor, 8,329. factor uses only complete observations.

```
. factor sp1ghp31-sp2ghp05, mineigen(1)
(obs=8329)
```

(principal factors; 3 factors retained)

Factor	Eigenvalue	Difference	Proportion	Cumulative
1	7.32506	4.88726	0.6873	0.6873
2	2.43779	1.38641	0.2287	0.9160
3	1.05138	0.68662	0.0986	1.0147
4	0.36476	0.07552	0.0342	1.0489
5	0.28924	0.13377	0.0271	1.0760
6	0.15547	0.02951	0.0146	1.0906
7	0.12596	0.10441	0.0118	1.1024
8	0.02155	0.02148	0.0020	1.1045
9	0.00007	0.03729	0.0000	1.1045
10	-0.03722	0.00450	-0.0035	1.1010
11	-0.04172	0.03271	-0.0039	1.0971
12	-0.07443	0.01751	-0.0070	1.0901
13	-0.09194	0.02319	-0.0086	1.0814
14	-0.11513	0.01561	-0.0108	1.0706
15	-0.13074	0.00624	-0.0123	1.0584
16	-0.13698	0.01258	-0.0129	1.0455
17	-0.14956	0.01608	-0.0140	1.0315
18	-0.16564	0.00431	-0.0155	1.0159
19	-0.16995	.	-0.0159	1.0000

Variable	Factor Loadings 1	2	3	Uniqueness
sp1ghp31	-0.65429	-0.05861	0.34895	0.44670
sp2pf01	0.61518	0.32407	-0.00419	0.51652
sp2pf02	0.69049	0.38099	0.22926	0.32551
sp2pf03	0.67373	0.38284	0.16968	0.37074
sp2pf04	0.65131	0.36714	0.23888	0.38394
sp2pf05	0.62350	0.33091	0.27403	0.42665
sp2pf06	0.43672	0.18049	0.22468	0.72622
sp2rkeep	0.68695	0.18325	0.08939	0.48653
sp2rkind	0.72533	0.24854	0.08135	0.40550
sp2sact0	0.65514	-0.07027	0.04680	0.56366
sp2mha01	0.53206	-0.48094	0.12855	0.46909
sp2mhp03	-0.48434	0.57765	-0.12693	0.41562
sp2mhd02	0.52591	-0.60933	0.17036	0.32311
sp2mhp01	-0.50216	0.60714	-0.12672	0.36316
sp2mhc01	0.49556	-0.52768	0.15652	0.45148
sp2ghp01	0.67159	0.02165	-0.36978	0.41176
sp2ghp04	-0.68815	-0.02208	0.42539	0.34500
sp2ghp02	-0.74789	-0.02575	0.44989	0.23759
sp2ghp05	0.61725	-0.27478	-0.16278	0.51700

The first factor is a general health factor. (To understand that claim, compare the factor loadings with the description of the variables as shown by describe above. Also note, just as with the

Physician-Cost data, the sense of some of the coded responses is reversed.) The second factor loads most highly on the five "mental health" items (with names sp2mha01—sp2mhc01). The third factor loads most highly on "general health perception" items—their names have the letters ghp in them. The other items describe "physical health". These designations are based primarily on the wording of the questions, which is summarized in the variable labels.

```
. rotate
              (varimax rotation)
            Rotated Factor Loadings
    Variable |    1          2          3      Uniqueness
```

Variable	1	2	3	Uniqueness
sp1ghp31	−0.28993	0.16325	0.66527	0.44670
sp2pf01	0.58577	−0.02818	−0.37358	0.51652
sp2pf02	0.78374	−0.08700	−0.22950	0.32551
sp2pf03	0.74408	−0.05968	−0.26841	0.37074
sp2pf04	0.75493	−0.08240	−0.19839	0.38394
sp2pf05	0.73367	−0.10930	−0.15206	0.42665
sp2pf06	0.50123	−0.12857	−0.07757	0.72622
sp2rkeep	0.60010	−0.20666	−0.33263	0.48653
sp2rkind	0.65823	−0.16896	−0.36426	0.40550
sp2sact0	0.41481	−0.38759	−0.33770	0.56366
sp2mha01	0.14263	−0.69104	−0.18174	0.46909
sp2mhp03	−0.05581	0.74727	0.15118	0.41562
sp2mhd02	0.08692	−0.80633	−0.13845	0.32311
sp2mhp01	−0.05079	0.78009	0.16035	0.36316
sp2mhc01	0.10614	−0.72029	−0.13578	0.45148
sp2ghp01	0.27007	−0.19585	−0.69061	0.41176
sp2ghp04	−0.25352	0.18694	0.74551	0.34500
sp2ghp02	−0.28271	0.20542	0.80018	0.23759
sp2ghp05	0.17002	−0.47554	−0.47744	0.51700

With rotation, the structure of the data becomes much clearer. The first rotated factor is physical health, the second is mental health, and the third is general health perception. The *a priori* designation of the items is confirmed.

Do not place much emphasis on physical health being the first factor. After rotation, the ordering of the factors is no longer meaningful. Moreover, the importance of any factor must be gauged against the number of variables that purportedly measure it. Here, we included nine variables that measured physical health, five that measured mental health, and five that measured general health perception. Had we started with only one mental health item, it would have had a high uniqueness, but we would not want to conclude that it was therefore largely noise.

Let us now consider retaining only two factors:

(Continued on next page)

```
. rotate, factors(2)
```
                (varimax rotation)
              Rotated Factor Loadings

Variable	1	2	Uniqueness
sp1ghp31	-0.42847	-0.49794	0.44670
sp2pf01	0.21545	0.66110	0.51652
sp2pf02	0.22980	0.75440	0.32551
sp2pf03	0.21649	0.74404	0.37074
sp2pf04	0.21135	0.71717	0.38394
sp2pf05	0.21665	0.67180	0.42665
sp2pf06	0.18749	0.43376	0.72622
sp2rkeep	0.36505	0.61010	0.48653
sp2rkind	0.34708	0.68368	0.40550
sp2sact0	0.51888	0.40610	0.56366
sp2mha01	0.71674	0.02577	0.46909
sp2mhp03	-0.74991	0.07686	0.41562
sp2mhd02	0.80180	-0.07061	0.32311
sp2mhp01	-0.78323	0.08559	0.36316
sp2mhc01	0.72314	-0.03320	0.45148
sp2ghp01	0.46663	0.48348	0.41176
sp2ghp04	-0.47821	-0.49534	0.34500
sp2ghp02	-0.51850	-0.53960	0.23759
sp2ghp05	0.63420	0.23300	0.51700

This rotation does not seem nearly as satisfying. The second factor looks like physical health and general health perception, but some contrast with mental health is included. The first factor is mostly a combination of mental health and general health perception, but has some physical health in it.

◁

▷ Example

The literature suggests that physical health and mental health are not orthogonal to each other. In addition, general health perception may be largely a combination of the two. For these reasons, a promax rotation with two factors is worth trying:

```
. rotate, factors(2) promax
```
                (promax rotation)
              Rotated Factor Loadings

Variable	1	2	Uniqueness
sp1ghp31	-0.24522	-0.51453	0.44670
sp2pf01	-0.03863	0.71076	0.51652
sp2pf02	-0.06063	0.81234	0.32551
sp2pf03	-0.07026	0.80198	0.37074
sp2pf04	-0.06496	0.77280	0.38394
sp2pf05	-0.04162	0.72245	0.42665
sp2pf06	0.02219	0.46274	0.72622
sp2rkeep	0.13564	0.64293	0.48653
sp2rkind	0.08812	0.72532	0.40550
sp2sact0	0.37461	0.40637	0.56366
sp2mha01	0.72848	-0.02771	0.46909
sp2mhp03	-0.80312	0.14325	0.41562
sp2mhd02	0.85413	-0.14044	0.32311
sp2mhp01	-0.84091	0.15547	0.36316
sp2mhc01	0.75831	-0.09311	0.45148
sp2ghp01	0.29025	0.49563	0.41176
sp2ghp04	-0.29752	-0.50777	0.34500
sp2ghp02	-0.32159	-0.55333	0.23759
sp2ghp05	0.56171	0.20683	0.51700

The first factor is defined predominantly by mental health and the second by physical health. General health perception loads on both, but more on physical health than mental health. We think promax rotation was a success here.

◁

Scoring

The `score` command creates a set of new variables that are estimates of the first k factors produced by `factor` or `rotate`, or the first k principal components.

For factor models, two types of scoring are available: regression and Bartlett scoring.

The number of variables may be less than the number of factors created or rotated. If so, the first such factors will be used. If the number of variables is greater than the number of factors created or rotated, the unused factors will be filled with missing values.

▷ Example

We have already demonstrated the use of `score` after principal-component extraction in the section titled *Principal components analysis* above, so let us now turn to factor models. Using our automobile data, we wish to develop an index of roominess based on a car's headroom, rear-seat leg room, and trunk space. We begin by extracting the factors of the three variables:

```
. factor headroom rear_seat trunk
(obs=74)
```

	(principal factors; 1 factor retained)			
Factor	Eigenvalue	Difference	Proportion	Cumulative
1	1.71426	1.79327	1.1799	1.1799
2	-0.07901	0.10329	-0.0544	1.1255
3	-0.18231	.	-0.1255	1.0000

	Factor Loadings	
Variable	1	Uniqueness
headroom	0.72800	0.47002
rear_seat	0.71439	0.48965
trunk	0.82093	0.32607

All the factor loadings are positive, so we have indeed obtained a "roominess" factor. The `score` command will now create the one retained factor, which we will call `f1`:

```
. score f1
```

	(based on unrotated factors)
	Scoring Coefficients
Variable	1
headroom	0.28323
rear_seat	0.26820
trunk	0.45964

If `factor` had retained more than one factor, typing `score f1` would still have added only the first factor to our data. Typing `score f1 f2`, however, would have added the first two factors to our data. `f1` is now our "roominess" index, so we might compare the roominess of domestic and foreign cars:

```
. table foreign, c(mean f1 sd f1) row
```

Foreign	mean(f1)	sd(f1)
Domestic	.2022442	.9031404
Foreign	-.4780318	.6106609
Total	4.51e-09	.8804116

We find that domestic cars are, on average, roomier than foreign cars, at least in our data.

◁

❑ Technical Note

Wait! Are not factors supposed to be normalized to have mean 0 and standard deviation 1? In our example above, the mean is $4.5 \cdot 10^{-9}$ and the standard deviation is .88. Why is that?

Let's take the mean first: The mean is supposed to be zero and $4.5 \cdot 10^{-9}$ is awfully close to zero and, in fact, is zero to the accuracy of a `float` variable. If we had typed `score double f1`, so that `f1` was stored as a `double`, we would have found the mean is $-9.5 \cdot 10^{-17}$, which is also zero to the accuracy of a `double`. The deviation from zero is due to numerical roundoff.

The explanation for the standard deviation of .88, on the other hand, is not numerical roundoff. At a theoretical level, the factor is supposed to have standard deviation 1, but the estimation routines almost never yield that result unless an exact solution to the factor model is found. This happens for the same reason that when you regress y on x, you do not get the same equation as if you regress x on y, unless x and y are perfectly collinear.

By the way, if we had two factors, one would expect the correlation between the two factors to be zero since that is how they are theoretically defined. The matrix algebra, however, does not usually work out for that to be so. It is somewhat analogous to the fact that if you regress y on x and the regression assumption about the errors being uncorrelated with the dependent variable is satisfied, then it automatically cannot be satisfied if you regress x on y.

The covariance matrix of the estimated factors is

$$E(\widehat{f}\widehat{f}') = \mathrm{I} - (\mathrm{I} + \Gamma)^{-1}$$

where

$$\Gamma = \Lambda'\Psi^{-1}\Lambda$$

The columns of Λ are orthogonal to each other, but the inclusion of Ψ in the middle of the equation destroys that relationship unless all the elements of Ψ are equal.

❑

▷ Example

Let's pretend that we work for the K. E. Watt Company, a fictional industry group that generates statistics on automobiles. Our "roominess" index has mean 0 and standard deviation .88, but indexes we present to the public generally have mean 100 and standard deviation 10. First, we wish to rescale our index:

```
. gen roomidx = (f1/.88041161)*10 + 100

. table foreign, c(mean roomidx sd roomidx freq) row format(%9.2f)
```

Foreign	mean(roomidx)	sd(roomidx)	Freq.
Domestic	102.30	10.26	52
Foreign	94.57	6.94	22
Total	100.00	10.00	74

Now when we release our results, we can write, "The K. E. Watt index of roominess shows that domestic cars are, on average, roomier, with an index of 102 versus only 95 for foreign cars".

Now let's find the "roomiest" car in our data:

```
. sort roomidx

. list make roomidx in 1
                    make    roomidx
     74.    Merc. Marquis   116.7469
```

We can also write, "K. E. Watt finds that the Mercury Marquis is the roomiest automobile among those surveyed, with a roominess index of 117 versus an average of 100".

◁

❏ Technical Note

`score` provides two methods of scoring, the default regression scoring, which we have used above, and the optional Bartlett method. An artificial example will best illustrate the use and meaning of the methods. We begin by creating a known-to-be-correct factor model in which the true loadings are 0.4, 0.6, and 0.8. We make the sample size n sufficiently large so that statistical fluctuation due to sample size is not important.

```
. set obs 10000
obs was 0, now 10000

. gen f = invnorm(uniform())

. gen x1 = .4*f + sqrt(.84)*invnorm(uniform())

. gen x2 = .6*f + sqrt(.64)*invnorm(uniform())

. gen x3 = .8*f + sqrt(.36)*invnorm(uniform())

. summ x1 x2 x3
```

Variable	Obs	Mean	Std. Dev.	Min	Max
x1	10000	-.0016167	.9944344	-3.749768	3.89626
x2	10000	-.0060847	.9996945	-3.391357	4.160651
x3	10000	.0024834	.9983335	-3.206443	3.674309

Having concocted our data, the iterated principal factor method reproduces the true loadings most faithfully:

```
. factor x1 x2 x3, ipf factors(1)
(obs=10000)
```

	(iterated principal factors; 1 factor retained)			
Factor	Eigenvalue	Difference	Proportion	Cumulative
1	1.17863	1.17845	1.0000	1.0000
2	0.00018	0.00041	0.0002	1.0002
3	-0.00023	.	-0.0002	1.0000

```
                Factor Loadings
      Variable |        1      Uniqueness
    -----------+--------------------------
            x1 |    0.39535      0.84369
            x2 |    0.57682      0.66727
            x3 |    0.83042      0.31040
```

Let us now compare regression and Bartlett scoring:

```
. score f1
               (based on unrotated factors)
                 Scoring Coefficients
      Variable |        1
    -----------+----------
            x1 |    0.11995
            x2 |    0.22134
            x3 |    0.68499
. score f1b, bartlett
               (based on unrotated factors)
                 Scoring Coefficients
      Variable |        1
    -----------+----------
            x1 |    0.50329
            x2 |    0.52925
            x3 |    0.59698
```

Comparing the two scoring vectors, we see that Bartlett scoring yields larger coefficients and it weights x3 less relative to x1. The regression method is biased insofar as $E(\mathtt{f1})$ is not $\mathtt{f}$, something we can reveal by regressing f1 on f:

```
. regress f1 f
      Source |       SS       df       MS              Number of obs =   10000
    ---------+------------------------------           F( 1,  9998) =25132.99
       Model | 5321.5801        1   5321.5801          Prob > F     =  0.0000
    Residual | 2116.9448     9998  .211736827          R-squared    =  0.7154
    ---------+------------------------------           Adj R-squared =  0.7154
       Total | 7438.52489    9999  .743926882          Root MSE     =  .46015

    ---------+--------------------------------------------------------------
          f1 |     Coef.   Std. Err.      t    P>|t|    [95% Conf. Interval]
    ---------+--------------------------------------------------------------
           f |   .729048   .0045987   158.53   0.000    .7200336    .7380623
       _cons |   .0004368  .0046015     0.09   0.924   -.008583     .0094567
    ---------+--------------------------------------------------------------
```

Note the coefficient on f of .73 < 1. The Bartlett method, on the other hand, is unbiased:

```
. regress f1b f
      Source |       SS       df       MS              Number of obs =   10000
    ---------+------------------------------           F( 1,  9998) =18986.25
       Model | 9898.47671       1   9898.47671         Prob > F     =  0.0000
    Residual | 5212.45427    9998  .521349697          R-squared    =  0.6551
    ---------+------------------------------           Adj R-squared =  0.6550
       Total | 15110.931     9999  1.51124422          Root MSE     =  .72205

    ---------+--------------------------------------------------------------
         f1b |     Coef.   Std. Err.      t    P>|t|    [95% Conf. Interval]
    ---------+--------------------------------------------------------------
           f |  .9943058   .0072161   137.79   0.000    .9801609    1.008451
       _cons |  .0005958   .0072205     0.08   0.934   -.0135578    .0147493
    ---------+--------------------------------------------------------------
```

This difference is not as important as it might seem since the bias in the regression method is only a matter of scaling. We tested for deviations from regression assumptions in both of the above regression models and found nothing (no nonlinearity or heteroskedasticity). This is to be expected since the data have a joint normal distribution and both f1 and f1b are linear combinations of the data.

The regression method is attempting to estimate $f1 = E(f|\text{data})$, not to compute f1 so that $E(f1b|f) = f$. However, the two methods do not produce identical estimators. When the factors are not well determined, the differences can be notable. Here the factor is well determined, so the difference is minimal. The regression estimator, rescaled, is slightly better:

```
. correlate f1 f1b f, means
(obs=10000)
    Variable |      Mean    Std. Dev.          Min          Max
-------------+--------------------------------------------------
          f1 |   2.77e-11     .862512    -3.084572     3.351701
         f1b |   2.16e-10    1.229327    -4.667728     4.665413
           f |  -.0005992    1.000659    -3.918931     3.641588

             |       f1         f1b          f
-------------+---------------------------------
          f1 |   1.0000
         f1b |   0.9431      1.0000
           f |   0.8458      0.8094     1.0000
```

Notice that neither estimator follows the assumption that the scaled factor has unit variance. The regression estimator has a variance less than 1, and the Bartlett estimator has a variance greater than 1.

❑

Saved Results

factor saves in r():

Scalars

r(N)	number of observations	r(chi2_1)	χ^2 test against more factors
r(k_f)	number of retained factors	r(df_1)	degrees of freedom for r(chi2_1)
r(chi2_0)	χ^2 test against no factors	r(lambda#)	#th eigenvalue
r(df_0)	degrees of freedom for r(chi2_0)		

Methods and Formulas

The following is the statistical factor model. Suppose there are p variables and q factors. Let Ψ represent the $p \times p$ diagonal matrix of uniquenesses, and Λ represent the $p \times q$ factor loading matrix. Let f be a $1 \times q$ matrix of factors. Then the standardized (mean 0, variance 1) vector of observed variables x $(1 \times p)$ is given by the system of regression equations:

$$x = f\Lambda' + e,$$

where e is a $1 \times p$ vector of uncorrelated errors with covariance equal to the uniqueness matrix Ψ.

Under the factor model, the correlation matrix of x, called Σ, is decomposed by factor analysis as

$$\Sigma = \Lambda\Lambda' + \Psi$$

Stata does this by an eigenvector calculation. An estimate is found for Ψ, and then the columns of Λ are computed as the eigenvectors, scaled by the square root of the appropriate eigenvalue.

See Lawley and Maxwell (1971), Harman (1976), and Clarke (1970).

Rotation

Varimax rotation (Kaiser 1958) retains the original factor assumption that the factors are orthogonal to each other and have unit variance. Promax rotation (Hendrickson and White 1964) allows the factors to be correlated with each other, but they still have unit variance. Because of the correlation, promax loadings can exceed 1.

Varimax attempts to find an orthogonal rotation matrix $\mathbf{M}$ such that

$$\Lambda = \Lambda_0 \mathbf{M}$$

achieves a maximum of

$$\sum_{r=1}^{k} \sum_{i=1}^{p} (\Lambda_{ir}^2 - d_r)^2$$

where

$$d_r = \sum_{i=1}^{p} \Lambda_{ir}^2 / p$$

This expression has multiple maxima because any exchange of columns of Λ yields an equally good maximum. However, it is known that there is a unique maximum (subject to exchange) for the two-factor problem and, in testing our routines, we did not observe any alternative maxima in our tests for more than two factors.

You should note that there is some disagreement in the literature on what a varimax rotation is. Horst (1965), for example, suggests that the loadings be scaled so that their sum of squares adds to 1 for each variable. This can lead to a different solution if some variables have to be scaled much more than others. Some computer packages (such as SAS) have adopted the Horst scaling as the only option; Stata allows you to select it explicitly with the `horst` option. If you do not select this option, you do not obtain Horst scaling.

This disagreement among software implementations on the varimax solution also leads to disagreements on the promax solution, since the promax rotation is a function of varimax rotation. Let Λ be the varimax loading matrix. Then the promax transform U has columns that minimize

$$\text{trace}(\mathbf{Q} - \Lambda \mathbf{U})'(\mathbf{Q} - \Lambda \mathbf{U})$$

where the elements of Q are formed by taking the corresponding elements of Λ to the promax index power (which Stata defaults to 3), with the sign of Λ. U is then scaled to be consistent with the assumption that the factors have unit variances. The transformed loadings are $\Lambda \mathbf{U}$.

Scoring

The formula for regression scoring (Thomson 1951) in the orthogonal case is

$$\widehat{f} = \Lambda' \Sigma^{-1} x$$

where Λ is the varimax rotated or unrotated loading matrix. For the oblique case, it is

$$\widehat{f} = \Phi \Lambda' \Sigma^{-1} x$$

where $\Phi = (\mathbf{U}'\mathbf{U})^{-1}$ using the scaled U matrix from the promax rotation step.

The formula for Bartlett scoring (Bartlett 1937, 1938) is

$$\Gamma^{-1}\Lambda'\Psi^{-1}x$$

where

$$\Gamma = \Lambda'\Psi^{-1}\Lambda$$

See Harman (1976) and Lawley and Maxwell (1971).

References

Bartlett, M. S. 1937. The statistical conception of mental factors. *British Journal of Psychology* 28: 97–104.

——. 1938. Methods of estimating mental factors. *Nature, London* 141: 609–610.

——. 1951. The effect of standardization on a χ^2 approximation in factor analysis. *Biometrika* 38: 337–344.

Clarke, M. R. B. 1970. A rapidly convergent method for maximum-likelihood factor analysis. *British Journal of Mathematical and Statistical Psychology* 23: 43–52.

Hamilton, L. C. 1992. *Regression with Graphics*, 249–288. Pacific Grove, CA: Brooks/Cole Publishing Company.

——. 1998. *Statistics with Stata 5*, Chapter 12. Pacific Grove, CA: Brooks/Cole Publishing Company.

Harman, H. H. 1976. *Modern Factor Analysis*. 3d ed. Chicago: University of Chicago Press.

Hendrickson, A. E. and P. O. White. 1964. Promax: A quick method for rotation to oblique simple structure. *British Journal of Statistical Psychology* 17: 65–70.

Horst, P. 1965. *Factor Analysis of Data Matrices*. New York: Holt, Rinehart, and Winston.

Hotelling, H. 1933. Analysis of a complex of statistical variables into principal components. *Journal of Educational Psychology* 24: 417–441, 498–520.

Jackson, J. E. 1991. *A User's Guide to Principal Components*. New York: John Wiley & Sons.

Kaiser, H. F. 1958. The varimax criterion for analytic rotation in factor analysis. *Psychometrika* 23: 187–200.

Lawley, D. N. and A. E. Maxwell. 1971. *Factor Analysis as a Statistical Method*. London: Butterworth & Company.

Pearson, K. 1901. On lines and planes of closest fit to systems of points in space. *Philosophical Magazine*, Series 6, 2: 559–572.

Rabe-Hesketh, S. and B. Everitt. 2000. *A Handbook of Statistical Analysis using Stata*. 2d ed. Boca Raton, FL: Chapman & Hall/CRC.

Rencher, A. C. 1998. *Multivariate Statistical Inference and Applications*. New York: John Wiley & Sons.

Spearman, C. 1904. General intelligence objectively determined and measured. *American Journal of Psychology* 15: 201–293.

Tarlov, A. R., J. E. Ware, Jr., S. Greenfield, E. C. Nelson, E. Perrin, and M. Zubkoff. 1989. The medical outcomes study. *Journal of the American Medical Association* 262: 925–930.

Thomson, G. H. 1951. *The Factorial Analysis of Human Ability*. London: University of London Press.

Weesie, J. 1997. smv7: Inference on principal components. *Stata Technical Bulletin* 37: 22–23. Reprinted in *Stata Technical Bulletin Reprints*, vol. 7, pp. 229–231.

Also See

Complementary:	[R] **impute**, [P] **matrix get**
Related:	[R] **alpha**, [R] **canon**, [R] **corr2data**
Background:	*Stata Graphics Manual*, [R] **maximize**

Title

fillin — Rectangularize dataset

Syntax

fillin *varlist*

Description

fillin adds observations with missing data so that all interactions of *varlist* exist, thus making a complete rectangularization of *varlist*. fillin also adds the variable _fillin to the dataset. _fillin is 1 for created observations and 0 for previously existing observations.

Remarks

▷ Example

You have data on something by sex, race, and age group. You suspect that some of the combinations of sex, race, and age do not exist, but if so, you want them to exist with whatever remaining variables there are in the dataset, set to missing. That is, rather than having a missing observation for black females ages 20–24, you want to create an observation that contains missing values:

```
. list
. list, label
            sex      race  age_group        x1       x2
   1.    female     white      20-24     20393     14.5
   2.      male     white      25-29     32750     12.7
   3.    female     black      30-34     39399     14.2
. fillin sex race age_group
. list
            sex      race  age_group        x1       x2   _fillin
   1.    female     white      20-24     20393     14.5         0
   2.    female     white      25-29         .        .         1
   3.    female     white      30-34         .        .         1
   4.    female     black      20-24         .        .         1
   5.    female     black      25-29         .        .         1
   6.    female     black      30-34     39399     14.2         0
   7.      male     white      20-24         .        .         1
   8.      male     white      25-29     32750     12.7         0
   9.      male     white      30-34         .        .         1
  10.      male     black      20-24         .        .         1
  11.      male     black      25-29         .        .         1
  12.      male     black      30-34         .        .         1
```

◁

527

Methods and Formulas

fillin is implemented as an ado-file.

Also See

Complementary: [R] **save**

Related: [R] **cross**, [R] **expand**, [R] **joinby**

Title

---

for — Repeat Stata command

Syntax

Basic syntax

    for *listtype list* : *stata_cmd_containing_X*

Full syntax

    for [*id* in] *listtype list* [\ [*id* in] *listtype list* [\ ...]] [, dryrun noheader

        pause nostop] : *stata_cmd* [\ *stata_cmd* [\ ...]]

where *listtype* and *list* are

if *listtype* is	then	*list* is a
varlist		*varlist*
newlist		*new_varlist*
numlist		*numlist*
anylist		*list of words*

If *ids* are not specified, then

Elements of the	1st	list are used to substitute for	X	in *stata_cmd*	
Elements of the	2nd	list are used to substitute for	Y	in *stata_cmd*	
...	3rd	...	Z	...	
...	4th	...	A	...	
...	5th	...	B	...	
...	6th	...	C	...	
...	7th	...	D	...	
...	8th	...	E	...	
Elements of the	9th	list are used to substitute for	F	in *stata_cmd*	

Description

    for repeats *stata_cmd*. At each repetition, the members of *list* are substituted for the *ids* in *stata_cmd*. More generally, at each repetition, the members of the first *list* are substituted for all occurrences of the first *id* in the *stata_cmds*, members of the second *list* are substituted for all occurrences of the second *id* in the *stata_cmds*, and so forth.

Options

dryrun specifies that *stata_cmd* is not to be executed; for is merely to display the commands that would be run had dryrun not been specified.

noheader suppresses the display of the command before each repetition.

pause pauses output after each execution of *stata_cmd*. This may be useful, for example, when for is combined with the graph command.

nostop does not stop the repetitions if one of them results in an error.

Remarks

▷ Example

Let's do some simple examples which demonstrate the use of the four possible *listtype*s: varlist, newlist, numlist, and anylist. First, for all variables that begin with the letter m, let's replace their values with their values divided by ten.

```
. for var m* : replace X = X/10
-> replace miles = miles/10
(100 real changes made)
-> replace minutes = minutes/10
(100 real changes made)
-> replace marks = marks/10
(100 real changes made)
-> replace myvar = myvar/10
(100 real changes made)
```

A word of caution about using the wildcard character (*): the specification might contain more variables than you intend. For example, if the dataset above had included a string variable called maiden containing maiden names, then m* would have included this variable and for would have attempted to divide the names by ten.

Next, we will generate ten new variables named u1, u2, ..., u10 filled with uniform random numbers.

```
. for new u1-u10 : gen X = uniform()
-> gen u1 = uniform()
-> gen u2 = uniform()
 (output omitted )
-> gen u9 = uniform()
-> gen u10 = uniform()
```

Now, let's count the number of times the values in the variable freq equal 1, 2, 3, 4, or 5.

```
. for num 1/5: count if freq==X
-> count if freq==1
   14
-> count if freq==2
   12
-> count if freq==3
   18
```

```
->  count if freq==4
   36
->  count if freq==5
   20
```

Finally, we place a missing value ('.') in the variable z whenever the variable y is missing or equal to −1.

```
. for any . -1 : replace z = . if y==X
->  replace z = . if y==.
(16 real changes made, 16 to missing)
->  replace z = . if y==-1
(15 real changes made, 15 to missing)
```

If we specify the **noheader** option, the line that indicates which command is being executed would be omitted for each iteration:

```
. for any . -1 , noheader : replace z = . if y==X
(16 real changes made, 16 to missing)
(15 real changes made, 15 to missing)
```

Note that **noheader** is specified as an option to **for**, not as an option to **replace**. Typing

```
for any . -1 : replace z = . if y==X, noheader
```

would be an error. Second, note that **noheader** suppressed the printing of the headers, not the output from **replace**. If we want to suppress all the output, we need to specify **quietly** in front of the entire compound command (see [P] **quietly**); if we specify **quietly**, we do not need to specify **noheader**.

◁

In the examples above, elements from the list are substituted one at a time for the capital X and the command executed. X is the default *id*—the character marking where substitutions are to be made. Other *id*s can be specified by including *id* **in**.

▷ Example

What if we wished to append several similarly named Stata data files to our dataset? We could use **for** to make the task easier.

```
. for num 1/4 , dryrun : append using "my dir\fileX"
->  append using `"my dir\file1"´
->  append using `"my dir\file2"´
->  append using `"my dir\file3"´
->  append using `"my dir\file4"´
```

specifies that **file1**, **file2**, **file3**, and **file4** from the **my dir** directory are to be appended. Notice the use of the **dryrun** option. This indicates that we wish to preview what commands would be executed but not actually execute them. This is especially helpful if you wish to verify that you have specified your **for** command correctly.

We can accomplish the same thing with

```
. for FILENO in num 1/4 , dryrun : append using "my dir\fileFILENO"
  (output omitted)
```

or

```
. for fno in num 1/4 , dryrun : append using "my dir\filefno"
(output omitted)
```

Be careful when specifying ids because all occurrences of *id* are substituted. The command

```
. for f in num 1/4 , dryrun : append using "my dir\filef"
-> append using `"my dir\1ile1"´
-> append using `"my dir\2ile2"´
-> append using `"my dir\3ile3"´
-> append using `"my dir\4ile4"´
```

ends up with filenames like 1ile1 instead of file1.

Some users prefer special characters for the *id*s.

```
. for @ in num 1/4 , dryrun : append using "my dir\file@"
(output omitted)
```

The choice of *id* is yours.

Note that if you refer to filenames containing backslash (\), then you must enclose the filename in double quotes; otherwise, for will think that the backslash is a separator for the for command.

◁

Multiple *list*s are processed concurrently, in parallel. The default ids are X, Y, Z, A, B, C, D, E, and F when you do not specify otherwise.

▷ Example

Let's generate four new variables—x2, x3, x4, and x5—that correspond to the 2nd, 3rd, 4th, and 5th powers of the variable myvar.

```
. for new x2-x5 \ num 2/5 : gen X = myvar^Y
-> gen x2 = myvar^2
-> gen x3 = myvar^3
-> gen x4 = myvar^4
-> gen x5 = myvar^5
```

Or, instead, we could have typed

```
. for VAR in new x2-x5 \ POWER in num 2/5 : gen VAR = myvar^POWER
(output omitted)
```

or even

```
. for num 2/5 : gen xX = myvar^X
(output omitted)
```

to produce the same result.

◁

Multiple commands are allowed with the for command. The backslash (\) is used to separate the commands.

▷ Example

Let's say that we want to perform several regressions and obtain predicted values after each one. With each new regression we add another of the variables we created in our last example. We can perform both the `regress` and the `predict` command in the same `for` command.

```
. for NUM in num 2/5 : quietly reg z m* x2-xNUM \ quietly predict predNUM
-> quietly reg z m* x2-x2
-> quietly predict pred2
-> quietly reg z m* x2-x3
-> quietly predict pred3
-> quietly reg z m* x2-x4
-> quietly predict pred4
-> quietly reg z m* x2-x5
-> quietly predict pred5
```

In fact, if we had not previously generated the x variables we could have included that step in the same `for` command.

```
. for num 2/5 : qui gen xX = myvar^X \ qui reg z m* x2-xX \ qui predict predX
```

◁

❏ Technical Note

If you set version to 5.0 or earlier (see [P] **version**), you will execute an older `for` command which has a different syntax. This ensures that old do-files, ado-files, and programs continue to work. ❏

Methods and Formulas

`for` is implemented as an ado-file.

Acknowledgment

We thank Patrick Royston of the MRC Clinical Trials Unit, London for his contributions to this command.

References

Cox, N. J. 1998a. ip26: Bivariate results for each pair of variables in a list. *Stata Technical Bulletin* 45: 17–19. Reprinted in *Stata Technical Bulletin Reprints*, vol. 8, pp. 78–81.

——. 1998b. ip27: Results for all possible combinations of arguments. *Stata Technical Bulletin* 45: 20–21. Reprinted in *Stata Technical Bulletin Reprints*, vol. 8, pp. 81–83.

Royston, P. 1995. ip8: An enhanced for command. *Stata Technical Bulletin* 26: 12. Reprinted in *Stata Technical Bulletin Reprints*, vol. 5, p. 65.

——. 1996. ip8.1: An even more enhanced for command. *Stata Technical Bulletin* 30: 5–6. Reprinted in *Stata Technical Bulletin Reprints*, vol. 5, pp. 65–66.

Weesie, J. 1997. ip19: Using expressions in Stata commands. *Stata Technical Bulletin* 39: 20–22. Reprinted in *Stata Technical Bulletin Reprints*, vol. 7, pp. 83–85.

——. 1999. gr36: An extension of for, useful for graphics commands. *Stata Technical Bulletin* 49: 8–10. Reprinted in *Stata Technical Bulletin Reprints*, vol. 9, pp. 92–95.

Also See

Complementary:	[P] **quietly**
Related:	[R] **by**, [P] **foreach**, [P] **forvalues**, [P] **while**
Background:	[U] **14.4 varlists**

Title

---
format — Specify variable display format

Syntax

format *varlist* %*fmt*

or

format %*fmt* *varlist*

set dp { comma | period }

Description

format allows you to specify the display format for variables. The internal precision of the variables is unaffected.

set dp lets you globally set the symbol Stata uses to represent the decimal symbol. The default is period, meaning one and a half is displayed as 1.5; comma specifies that it be displayed as 1,5.

Remarks

See [U] **15.5 Formats: controlling how data are displayed** for an explanation of %*fmt*. As a brief review, Stata's three numeric formats are denoted by a leading percent sign % followed by the string *w.d* (or *w,d* if you want European format), where *w* and *d* stand for two integers. The first integer, *w*, specifies the width of the format. The second integer, *d*, specifies the number of digits that are to follow the decimal point. Logic requires that *d* be less than *w*. Finally, a character denoting the format type (e, f, or g) is appended. For example, %9.2f specifies the f format that is nine characters wide and has two digits following the decimal point. In the case of f and g, a c may additionally be suffixed to indicate comma formats. Two more "numeric" formats, %d and %t, are used to display elapsed dates and various time-series formats; see [U] **27 Commands for dealing with dates** and [U] **15.5.4 Time-series formats**. String formats are denoted by %*w*s, where *w* indicates the width of the format.

▷ Example

We have Census data by region and state on median age and population in 1980.

```
. describe
Contains data from census.dta
  obs:            50                          1980 Census data by state
 vars:             4                          6 Jul 2000 17:06
 size:         1,400 (99.8% of memory free)

              storage  display     value
variable name   type   format      label      variable label

state          str14   %14s                   State
region         int     %8.0g       cenreg     Census region
pop            long    %11.0g                 Population
medage         float   %9.0g                  Median age

Sorted by:
     Note:  dataset has changed since last saved
```

535

```
. list in 1/8
              state     region          pop    medage
   1.        Alabama     South      3893888      29.3
   2.         Alaska      West       401851      26.1
   3.        Arizona      West      2718215      29.2
   4.       Arkansas     South      2286435      30.6
   5.     California      West     23667902      29.9
   6.       Colorado      West      2889964      28.6
   7.    Connecticut        NE      3107576        32
   8.       Delaware     South       594338      29.8
```

The **state** variable has a display format of **%14s**. To left-align the state data, we type

```
. format state %-14s
. list in 1/8
          state         region          pop    medage
   1. Alabama            South      3893888      29.3
   2. Alaska              West       401851      26.1
   3. Arizona             West      2718215      29.2
   4. Arkansas           South      2286435      30.6
   5. California          West     23667902      29.9
   6. Colorado            West      2889964      28.6
   7. Connecticut           NE      3107576        32
   8. Delaware           South       594338      29.8
```

Although it seems like **region** is a string variable, it is really a numeric variable with an attached value label. You do the same thing to left-align a numeric variable as you do a string variable: insert a negative sign.

```
. format region %-8.0g
. list in 1/8
          state     region          pop    medage
   1. Alabama     South          3893888      29.3
   2. Alaska      West            401851      26.1
   3. Arizona     West           2718215      29.2
   4. Arkansas    South          2286435      30.6
   5. California  West          23667902      29.9
   6. Colorado    West           2889964      28.6
   7. Connecticut NE             3107576        32
   8. Delaware    South           594338      29.8
```

The **pop** variable would probably be easier to read if we inserted commas. You specify the comma format by appending a 'c':

```
. format pop %11.0gc
. list in 1/8
          state     region          pop    medage
   1. Alabama     South        3,893,888      29.3
   2. Alaska      West           401,851      26.1
   3. Arizona     West         2,718,215      29.2
   4. Arkansas    South        2,286,435      30.6
   5. California  West         23667902       29.9
   6. Colorado    West         2,889,964      28.6
   7. Connecticut NE           3,107,576        32
   8. Delaware    South          594,338      29.8
```

Look at the value of **pop** for observation 5. There are no commas. This number was too large for Stata to insert commas and also respect the current width of 10. Let us try again:

```
. format pop %12.0gc
```

```
. list in 1/8
        state       region          pop    medage
  1. Alabama        South      3,893,888      29.3
  2. Alaska         West         401,851      26.1
  3. Arizona        West       2,718,215      29.2
  4. Arkansas       South      2,286,435      30.6
  5. California     West      23,667,902      29.9
  6. Colorado       West       2,889,964      28.6
  7. Connecticut    NE         3,107,576        32
  8. Delaware       South        594,338      29.8
```

Finally, **medage** would look better if the decimal points were vertically aligned.

```
. format medage %8.1f
. list in 1/8
        state       region          pop    medage
  1. Alabama        South      3,893,888      29.3
  2. Alaska         West         401,851      26.1
  3. Arizona        West       2,718,215      29.2
  4. Arkansas       South      2,286,435      30.6
  5. California     West      23,667,902      29.9
  6. Colorado       West       2,889,964      28.6
  7. Connecticut    NE         3,107,576      32.0
  8. Delaware       South        594,338      29.8
```

Display formats are permanently attached to variables by the **format** command. If you **save** the data, the next time you **use** it, **state** will still be formatted as **%-14s**, **region** will still be formatted as **%-8.0g**, etc.

◁

European formats

Do you prefer that one and one half be written as 1,5 and that one thousand one and a half be written as 1.001,5? Stata will present numbers in that format if, when you set the format, you specify ',' rather than '.' in the following format:

```
. format pop %12,0gc
. format medage %9,2f
. list in 1/8
        state       region          pop    medage
  1. Alabama        South      3.893.888     29,30
  2. Alaska         West         401.851     26,10
  3. Arizona        West       2.718.215     29,20
  4. Arkansas       South      2.286.435     30,60
  5. California     West      23.667.902     29,90
  6. Colorado       West       2.889.964     28,60
  7. Connecticut    NE         3.107.576     32,00
  8. Delaware       South        594.338     29,80
```

Alternatively, you can leave the formats just as they were and instead type **set dp comma**. That tells Stata to interpret all formats as if you had typed the comma instead of the period:

```
. format pop %12.0gc              (put the formats back as they were)
. format medage %9.2f
. set dp comma                    (tell Stata to use European format)
. list in 1/8
```
(same output appears as above)

`set dp comma` affects all of Stata's output, so if you run a regression, display summary statistics, or make a table, commas will be used instead of periods in the output:

```
. tabulate region [fw=pop]
```

Census region	Freq.	Percent	Cum.
NE	49135283	21,75	21,75
N Cntrl	58865670	26,06	47,81
South	74734029	33,08	80,89
West	43172490	19,11	100,00
Total	225907472	100,00	

You can return to using period by typing

```
. set dp period
```

Understand the difference: setting a variable's display format to be in European format will affect how the variable's values are displayed by `list` and in a few other places. Setting `dp` to `comma` will affect every bit of Stata.

Also understand that `set dp comma` affects only how Stata displays output, not how it gets input. When you need to type one and a half, you must type `1.5` regardless of context.

❏ Technical Note

`set dp comma` makes drastic changes inside Stata, and we mention this because some older, user-written programs may not be up to dealing with those changes. If you are using an older user-written program, you might `set dp comma` and then find that the program does not work and instead presents some sort of syntax error.

If, using any program, you do get an unanticipated error, try setting `dp` back to `period`.

Even with `set dp comma`, you might still see some output with the decimal symbol shown as period rather than comma. There are two places in Stata where Stata ignores `set dp comma` because the features are generally used to produce what will be treated as input, and `set dp comma` does not affect how Stata inputs numbers. First,

```
local x = sqrt(2)
```

stores the string "1.414213562373095" in x and not "1,414213562373095", so if some program were to display `x´ as a string in the output, the period would show. Most programs, however, would use `x´ in subsequent calculations or, at the least, when the time came to display what was in `x´, would display it as a number. They would code

```
display ... `x´ ...
```

and not

```
display ... "`x´" ...
```

so the output would be

```
... 1,4142136 ...
```

The other place where Stata ignores `set dp comma` is the **string()** function. If you type

```
. gen str8 res = string(numvar)
```

new variable `res` will contain the string representation of numeric variable `numvar`, with the decimal symbol being period regardless of whether you have previously `set dp comma`. Of course, if you explicitly ask that `string()` use European format,

    . gen str8 res = string(numvar,"%9,0g")

then `string()` honors your request; `string()` merely ignores the global `set dp comma`.

❑

Other effects of display formats, European and non-European

❑ Technical Note

You have data on the age of employees, and you type `summarize age` to obtain the mean and standard deviation. By default, Stata uses its default g format to provide as much precision as possible:

    . summarize age

Variable	Obs	Mean	Std. Dev.	Min	Max
age	204	29.64706	8.914091	18	66

If you attach a `%9.2f` format to the variable and specify the `format` option, Stata uses that specification to format the results:

    . format age %9.2f
    . summarize age, format

Variable	Obs	Mean	Std. Dev.	Min	Max
age	204	29.65	8.91	18.00	66.00

❑

❑ Technical Note

Stata uses the display formats to align column headings as well as to format data. This ensures that the column headings appear above the data they represent. For instance, when you `list` a small portion of your data, you see something like

    . list in 1/5

	empno	sex	age	salary
1.	3000	Male	24	10643
2.	3001	Male	25	23421
3.	3002	Male	32	29661
4.	3003	Male	30	22592
5.	3004	Female	22	14919

The variable names appear directly above the columns.

You look at the data and think that `age` is an integer and needs at most two digits to be displayed correctly. You decide to `format age %2.0f` and then `list` the first five observations again:

    . format age %2.0f
    . list in 1/5

	empno	sex	age	salary
1.	3000	Male	24	10643
2.	3001	Male	25	23421
3.	3002	Male	32	29661
4.	3003	Male	30	22592
5.	3004	Female	22	14919

The variable name `salary` no longer appears right-aligned above the salary figures because `age` has been given a format that is only two characters wide, but there are three letters in the word "age". Stata uses the display format `%2.0f` to format both the data and the column heading, although Stata never takes your formats too literally. If something needs to be displayed and it will not fit in the *%fmt*, Stata temporarily increases the width of the format so that it can produce the display. As a result, the column heading is no longer aligned with the data.

Thus, the width of your formats should be at least as long as the variable name, which in this case is 3:

```
. format age %3.0f
. list in 1/5

          empno    sex   age     salary
    1.     3000    Male   24      10643
    2.     3001    Male   25      23421
    3.     3002    Male   32      29661
    4.     3003    Male   30      22592
    5.     3004  Female   22      14919
```

Let us now apply that rule to the `sex` variable. The word "sex" has three characters in it, so being generous, you decide to `format sex %4s`:

```
. format sex %4s
. list in 1/5

          empno  sex   age     salary
    1.     3000  Male   24      10643
    2.     3001  Male   25      23421
    3.     3002  Male   32      29661
    4.     3003  Male   30      22592
    5.     3004  Female  22      14919
```

Everything appears fine until the fifth observation. When Stata needs to display the word "Female", there is a problem. The word "Female" is six characters long, but the format you specified is only four characters wide. Stata tries to do what you request, but it has one overriding rule: Never misrepresent the data. Six characters will not fit in a four-character-wide field, so Stata temporarily increases the width of the field to six. This results in the misalignment of subsequent variables.

Thus, for string formats the width should also be at least as wide as the longest string. This rule can be generalized: The width of your format should be at least as long as the widest entry that will be displayed with it. We formatted `age %3.0f`. If ages exceeded 999, we would want to make the format at least `%4.0f`.

```
. format sex %6s
. list in 1/5

          empno    sex   age     salary
    1.     3000    Male   24      10643
    2.     3001    Male   25      23421
    3.     3002    Male   32      29661
    4.     3003    Male   30      22592
    5.     3004  Female   22      14919
```

This information is buried in a technical note because the Stata default formats never have these problems. The default format for `byte`s and `int`s is `%8.0g`; for `float`s, `%9.0g`; and for `long`s and `double`s, `%10.0g`. For str*w*, the default format is `%ws` or `%9s`, whichever is wider. The narrowest default format is `%8.0g`, and variable names always contain 8 or fewer characters. When you make a format narrower than 8, however, problems can arise.

❑

❏ Technical Note

The syntax of the `format` command allows a *varlist* and not just a *varname*. Thus, you can attach the %9.2f format to the variables `myvar`, `thisvar`, and `thatvar` by typing

```
. format myvar thisvar thatvar %9.2f
```

❏

Also See

Related: [P] **display**

Background: [U] **15.5 Formats: controlling how data are displayed**,

[U] **15.5.4 Time-series formats**,

[U] **15.6 Dataset, variable, and value labels**,

[U] **27 Commands for dealing with dates**

Title

> **fracpoly** — Fractional polynomial regression

Syntax

> **fracpoly** *regression_cmd yvar xvar*$_1$ $\left[\# \left[\#\ldots\right]\right]$ $\left[xvar_2 \left[\# \left[\#\ldots\right]\right]\right]$ $\left[\ldots\right]$ $\left[xvarlist\right]$
>
> $\left[weight\right]$ $\left[\text{if } exp\right]$ $\left[\text{in } range\right]$ $\left[, \underline{\text{adjust}}(adj\_list) \underline{\text{compare}} \underline{\text{degree}}(\#) \text{ log}\right.$
>
> $\left.\underline{\text{nocon}}\text{stant } \underline{\text{noscal}}\text{ing } \underline{\text{pow}}\text{ers}(numlist) \text{ } regression\_cmd\_options \right]$
>
> **fracpoly** $\left[, \underline{\text{com}}\text{pare}\right]$
>
> **fracplot** $\left[varname\right]$ $\left[, graph\_options\right]$
>
> **fracpred** *newvarname* $\left[varname\right]$ $\left[, \underline{\text{d}}\text{resid } \underline{\text{for}}(varname) \text{ } \underline{\text{stdp}}\right]$
>
> **fracgen** *varname* $\#$ $\left[\#\ldots\right]$ $\left[\text{if } exp\right]$ $\left[\text{in } range\right]$ $\left[, \underline{\text{adjust}}(\text{no} | \text{mean} | \#)\right.$
>
> $\left.\underline{\text{noscal}}\text{ing } \underline{\text{replace}}\right]$

where *regression_cmd* may be **clogit**, **cox**, **glm**, **logistic**, **logit**, **poisson**, **probit**, or **regress**

and where *adj_list* is a comma-separated list with elements *varlist*:{**mean** | # | **no**} except that the first element may optionally be of the form {**mean** | # | **no**} to specify the default for all variables.

Note that **fracplot** and **fracpred**, **dresid** are not allowed after **fracpoly** with **clogit** or **probit**.

fracpoly shares the features of all estimation commands; see [U] **23 Estimation and post-estimation commands**. All weight types supported by *regression_cmd* are allowed; see [U] **14.1.6 weight**.

Description

fracpoly fits fractional polynomials in *xvar*$_1$ to *yvar*. After execution, **fracpoly** leaves variables in the dataset named I*xvar*__1, I*xvar*__2, ..., where *xvar* represents the first four letters of the name of *xvar*$_1$. The new variables contain the best-fitting fractional polynomial powers of *xvar*$_1$.

Covariates other than *xvar*$_1$, which are optional, are specified in *xvar*$_2$, ..., and *xvarlist*. They may be modeled linearly and/or with specified fractional polynomial transformations. Fractional polynomial powers are specified by typing numbers following the variable's name. A variable name typed without numbers following it is entered linearly.

fracplot plots the data and fit, with 95% confidence limits, from the most recently fitted fractional polynomial model. The data and fit are plotted against *varname*, which may be *xvar*$_1$ or another of the covariates (*xvar*$_2$, ..., or a variable from *xvarlist*). If *varname* is not specified, *xvar*$_1$ is assumed.

fracpred creates *newvarname* containing the fitted index or deviance residuals for the whole model, or the fitted index or its standard error for *varname*, which may be *xvar*$_1$ or another covariate.

fracgen creates new variables named *varname*_1, *varname*_2, ..., containing fractional polynomial powers of *varname* using the power(s) (# $\left[\#\ldots\right]$) specified.

Options for use with fracpoly

adjust(*adj_list*) defines the adjustments for the covariates $xvar_1$, $xvar_2$, ..., *xvarlist*. The default is adjust(mean). A typical item in *adj_list* is *varlist*:{mean | # | no}. Items are separated by commas. The first item is special in that *varlist*: is optional, and if omitted, the default is (re)set to the specified value (mean or # or no). For example, adjust(no, age:mean) sets the default to no and adjustment for age to mean.

compare reports significance tests between the best fractional polynomial models of increasing degree.

degree(#) determines the degree of fractional polynomial to be fitted. Default is degree(2); i.e., a model with two power terms.

log displays deviances and (for regress) residual standard deviations for each fractional polynomial model fitted.

noconstant suppresses the regression constant if this is permitted by *regression_cmd*.

noscaling suppresses scaling of $xvar_1$ and its powers.

powers(*numlist*) is the set of fractional polynomial powers from which models are to be chosen. The default is powers(-2,-1,-.5,0,.5,1,2,3) (0 means log).

regression_cmd_options are options appropriate to the regression command in use. For example, for cox, *regression_cmd_options* includes dead(*failvar*), etc. In the case of cox, fracpoly requires that you specify the dead() option to identify the failure/censoring variable.

Options for use with fracplot

graph_options are for use with fracplot and are any of the options allowed by graph, twoway; see [G] **graph options**.

Options for use with fracpred

dresid is for use with fracpred; it specifies that deviance residuals be calculated.

for(*varname*) is for use with fracpred; it specifies (partial) prediction for variable *varname*. The fitted values are adjusted to the value specified by the adjust() option in fracpoly.

stdp is for use with fracpred; it specifies calculation of the standard errors of the fitted values *varname*, adjusted for all the other predictors at the values specified by adjust().

Options for use with fracgen

adjust(no | mean | #) specifies whether *varname* is to be adjusted; the default is adjust(no).

noscaling suppresses scaling of *varname*.

replace specifies that variables named *varname_1*, named *varname_2*, ..., may already exist and, if so, that they may be replaced.

Remarks

Remarks are presented under the headings

> *Introduction*
> *fracpoly*
> *Adjustment*
> *Output with the compare option*
> *fracplot*
> *fracgen*
> *Models with several continuous covariates*
> *Examples*

Introduction

Regression models based on fractional polynomial (FP) functions of a continuous covariate are described by Royston and Altman (1994a). Detailed examples using an earlier and rather more complex version of the present set of commands are presented by Royston and Altman (1994b).

The purpose of FPs is to increase the flexibility afforded by the family of conventional polynomial models. Although polynomials are popular in data analysis, linear and quadratic functions are severely limited in their range of curve shapes, whereas cubic and higher order curves often produce undesirable artifacts, such as "edge effects" and "waves".

A polynomial of degree m may be written

$$\beta_0 + \beta_1 x + \beta_2 x^2 + \cdots + \beta_m x^m$$

whereas a fractional polynomial (FP) of degree m has m integer and/or fractional powers $p_1 < \cdots < p_m$,

$$\beta_0 + \beta_1 x^{(p_1)} + \beta_2 x^{(p_2)} + \cdots + \beta_m x^{(p_m)}$$

where for a power p

$$x^{(p)} = \begin{cases} x^p & \text{if } p \neq 0 \\ \log x & \text{if } p = 0 \end{cases}$$

Note that x must be positive. An FP of first degree ($m = 1$) involves a single power or log transformation of x.

This family of FP functions may be extended in a mathematically natural way to include "repeated powers". An FP of degree m with exactly m repeated powers of p is defined as

$$\beta_0 + \beta_1 x^{(p)} + \beta_2 x^{(p)} \log x + \cdots + \beta_m x^{(p)} (\log x)^{m-1}$$

For example, an FP of second degree ($m = 2$) with repeated powers of 0.5 is

$$\beta_0 + \beta_1 x^{0.5} + \beta_2 x^{0.5} \log x$$

A general FP may include some unique and some repeated powers. For example, one with powers $(-1, 1, 3, 3)$ is

$$\beta_0 + \beta_1 x^{-1} + \beta_2 x + \beta_3 x^3 + \beta_4 x^3 \log x$$

The permitted powers are restricted to the set $\{-2, -1, -0.5, 0, 0.5, 1, 2, 3\}$. While such a limitation is not intrinsic to the approach, the experience of using FPs in data analysis indicates that it is not often worthwhile to include extra powers in the set.

Consider now the use of FPs in regression modeling. If the values of the powers $p_1, \ldots, p_m$ were known, the FP would resemble a conventional multiple linear regression model with coefficients $\beta_0, \beta_1, \ldots, \beta_m$. However, the powers are not (usually) known and must be estimated, together with the coefficients, from the data. Estimation involves a systematic search for the best power or combination of powers from the permitted set. For each possible combination, a linear regression model as just described is fit and the corresponding deviance (defined as minus twice the log likelihood) is noted. The model with the lowest deviance is deemed to have the best fit, and the corresponding powers and regression coefficients constitute the final FP model.

fracpoly

fracpoly finds and reports a multiple regression model comprising the best-fitting powers of $xvar_1$ together with other covariates specified by $xvar_2$, ..., $xvarlist$. The model that is fit depends on the type of *regression_cmd* used.

The regression output for the best-fitting model may be reproduced by typing *regression_cmd* without variables or options. predict, test, etc. may be used after fracpoly; the results will depend on *regression_cmd*.

Note that the standard errors of the fitted values (as estimated following use of fracpoly by using predict or fracpred with the stdp option) are somewhat too low, since no allowance has been made for estimation of the powers.

If $xvar_1$ has any negative or zero values, fracpoly subtracts the minimum of *xvar* from *xvar* and then adds the rounding (or counting) interval. The interval is defined as the smallest positive difference between the ordered values of *xvar*. After this change of origin, the minimum value of $xvar_1$ is positive, so fractional polynomials (which require $xvar_1 > 0$) can be used. Unless the noscaling option is used, fracpoly scales the resulting variable by a power of 10 calculated from the data. The scaling is designed to improve numerical stability when fitting fractional polynomial models.

After execution, fracpoly leaves in the dataset variables named $Ixvar\_\_1$, $Ixvar\_\_2$, ..., which are the best-fitting fractional polynomial powers of $xvar_1$ (calculated, if necessary, following a change in origin and scale as just described, and if adjustment is specified, with a constant added or subtracted to the values following fractional polynomial transformation). Additional variables, whose names follow the same convention, are left in the dataset if $xvar_2$ has been specified.

Adjustment

As discussed by Garrett (1995, 1998), covariate adjustment is a sensible, indeed often essential, step when reporting and interpreting the results of multiple regression models. For this and other reasons, adjustment has been introduced as the default option in fracpoly. As written, the familiar straight line regression function $E(y|x) = \beta_0 + \beta_1 x$ is 'adjusted' to 0 in that $\beta_0 = E(y|0)$. This is fine if $x = 0$ is a sensible base point. However, the sample values of x may not even encompass 0 (usually the case when FP models are contemplated). Then β_0 is a meaningless intercept, and the standard error of its estimate $\widehat{\beta}_0$ will be large. For an FP model $E(y|x) = \beta_0 + \beta_1 x^{(p)}$, the point $x^{(p)} = 0$ may even correspond to $x = \infty$ (consider $p < 0$). The scheme adopted by fracpoly is to adjust to the mean of x. For example, for the FP $E(y|x) = \beta_0 + \beta_1 x^{(p)} + \beta_1 x^{(q)}$, fracpoly actually fits the model

$$E(y|x) = \beta_0 + \beta_1 \left(x^{(p)} - \overline{x}^{(p)} \right) + \beta_2 \left(x^{(q)} - \overline{x}^{(q)} \right)$$

where $\overline{x}$ is the sample mean of the x values, and $E(y|\overline{x}) = \beta_0$, giving β_0 a respectable interpretation as the predicted value of y at the mean of x. This approach has the advantage that plots of the fitted values and 95% confidence intervals for $E(y|x)$ as a function of x, even within a multiple regression model, are always sensible (provided, of course, that the other predictors are suitably adjusted—otherwise, the confidence limits can be alarmingly wide).

Sometimes adjustment to the mean is not appropriate, an example being a binary covariate where often you will want to adjust to the lower value, usually 0 (i.e., not adjust). You should then use the adjust() option to override the default. An example is adjust(x1:mean,x2-x5:no,x6:1).

Output with the compare option

If the compare option is used, fracpoly displays a table showing the best FP model for each degree $\leq m$. A p-value is given for comparing each pair of models whose degrees differ by 1. (The corresponding difference in model degrees of freedom is 2, as one extra power and one extra coefficient are estimated.) As with conventional polynomial regression, the preferred model is normally taken to be the one which is a significantly better fit than that of next lower degree, but not a significantly worse fit than that of next higher degree. The table also presents the *gain* for each FP model. The gain is defined as the deviance of a straight line model minus the deviance of the FP model in question (Royston and Altman 1994a). In general, the larger the gain, the greater the nonlinearity of the relation between *yvar* and *xvar*$_1$ (conditional on the other covariates, if any), and the greater the benefit of choosing an FP model as opposed to a straight line. As with p-values, however, gain depends directly on sample size and is *not* therefore an absolute measure of nonlinearity or of model fit.

fracplot

fracplot actually produces a component-plus-residual plot. For normal-error models with constant weights and a single covariate, this amounts to a plot of the observations with the fitted line inscribed. For other normal-error models, weighted residuals are calculated and added to the fitted values.

For models with additional covariates, the line is the partial linear predictor for the variable in question (*xvar*$_1$ or a covariate), and includes the intercept β_0.

For generalized linear and Cox models, the fitted values are plotted on the scale of the 'index' (linear predictor). Deviance residuals are added to the (partial) linear predictor to give component-plus-residual values. These are plotted as small circles.

fracgen

The basic syntax of fracgen is

fracgen *varname* # [# ...]

Each power (represented by # in the syntax diagram) should be separated by a space. fracgen creates new variable(s) called *varname*_1, *varname*_2, etc. Each variable is labeled according to its power, preliminary linear transformation and adjustment, if applied.

Positive or negative powers of *varname* are defined in the usual way. A power of zero is interpreted as log.

Models with several continuous covariates

fracpoly estimates powers for FP models in just one continuous covariate ($xvar_1$), though other covariates of any kind ($xvar_2$, ..., $xvarlist$) may be included as linear or predefined fractional polynomial terms. An algorithm was suggested by Royston and Altman (1994a) for the joint estimation of FP models in several continuous covariates. It was later refined by Sauerbrei and Royston (1999) and is implemented in mfracpol (see also Royston and Ambler (1998)).

Examples

▷ Example

Consider the serum immunoglobulin-G (IgG) dataset from Isaacs et al. (1983), which consists of 298 independent observations in young children. The dependent variable sqrtigg is the square root of the IgG concentration and the independent variable age is the age of each child. (Preliminary Box–Cox analysis shows that a square root transformation removes the skewness in IgG.) The aim is to find a model which accurately predicts the mean of sqrtigg given age. We use fracpoly to find the best FP model of degree 2 (the default option) and graph the resulting fit:

```
. fracpoly regress sqrtigg age
........
-> gen double Iage__1 = age^-2-.1299 if e(sample)
-> gen double Iage__2 = age^2-7.695 if e(sample)
```

Source	SS	df	MS		Number of obs =	298
					F(2, 295) =	64.49
Model	22.2846976	2	11.1423488		Prob > F =	0.0000
Residual	50.9676492	295	.172771692		R-squared =	0.3042
					Adj R-squared =	0.2995
Total	73.2523469	297	.246640898		Root MSE =	.41566

sqrtigg	Coef.	Std. Err.	t	P>|t|	[95% Conf. Interval]	
Iage__1	-.1562156	.027416	-5.70	0.000	-.2101713	-.10226
Iage__2	.0148405	.0027767	5.34	0.000	.0093757	.0203052
_cons	2.283145	.0305739	74.68	0.000	2.222974	2.343315

Deviance: 319.448. Best powers of age among 44 models fit: -2 2.

. fracplot age

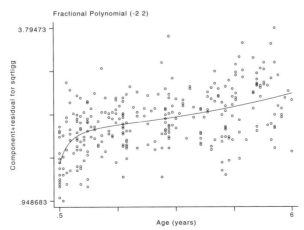

The fitted curve has an asymmetric S-shape. This model has powers $(-2, 2)$ and deviance 319.45. As many as 44 models have been quietly fit in the search for the best powers. Now let us look at models of degree ≤ 4:

```
. fracpoly regress sqrtigg age, degree(4) compare
.................................................................................
> .................................................................................
> ........
-> gen double Iage__1 = ln(age)-1.02 if e(sample)
-> gen double Iage__2 = age^3-21.35 if e(sample)
-> gen double Iage__3 = age^3*ln(age)-21.78 if e(sample)
-> gen double Iage__4 = age^3*ln(age)^2-22.22 if e(sample)
```

Source	SS	df	MS		
Model	22.5754541	4	5.64386353	Number of obs =	298
Residual	50.6768927	293	.172958678	F(4, 293) =	32.63
				Prob > F =	0.0000
				R-squared =	0.3082
				Adj R-squared =	0.2987
Total	73.2523469	297	.246640898	Root MSE =	.41588

sqrtigg	Coef.	Std. Err.	t	P>|t|	[95% Conf. Interval]	
Iage__1	.8761824	.1898721	4.61	0.000	.5024963	1.249868
Iage__2	-.1922029	.0684934	-2.81	0.005	-.3270044	-.0574015
Iage__3	.2043794	.074947	2.73	0.007	.0568767	.3518821
Iage__4	-.0560067	.0212969	-2.63	0.009	-.097921	-.0140924
_cons	2.238735	.0482705	46.38	0.000	2.143734	2.333736

Deviance: 317.744. Best powers of age among 494 models fit: 0 3 3 3.

Fractional polynomial model comparisons:

age	df	Deviance	Res. SD	Gain	P(term)	Powers
Not in model	0	427.539	.49663	—	—	
Linear	1	337.561	.42776	0.000	0.000	1
m = 1	2	327.436	.420554	10.125	0.002	0
m = 2	4	319.448	.415658	18.113	0.020	-2 2
m = 3	6	319.275	.416243	18.286	0.919	-2 1 1
m = 4	8	317.744	.415883	19.818	0.476	0 3 3 3

There is little to be gained by increasing the degree above 2, since the p-values indicate no significant improvement in fit.

Let us compare the curve shape from the $m = 2$ model with that from a conventional quartic polynomial, whose fit turns out to be significantly better than a cubic (not shown). We use the ability of `fracpoly` both to generate the required powers of `age`, namely $(1, 2, 3, 4)$ for the quartic and $(-2, 2)$ for the second degree FP, and to fit the model. We fit both models and graph the resulting curves:

```
. fracpoly regress sqrtigg age 1 2 3 4
-> gen double Iage__1 = age-2.774 if e(sample)
-> gen double Iage__2 = age^2-7.695 if e(sample)
-> gen double Iage__3 = age^3-21.35 if e(sample)
-> gen double Iage__4 = age^4-59.22 if e(sample)
```

Source	SS	df	MS		
Model	22.5835458	4	5.64588646	Number of obs =	298
Residual	50.668801	293	.172931061	F(4, 293) =	32.65
				Prob > F =	0.0000
				R-squared =	0.3083
				Adj R-squared =	0.2989
Total	73.2523469	297	.246640898	Root MSE =	.41585

sqrtigg	Coef.	Std. Err.	t	P>|t|	[95% Conf. Interval]	
Iage__1	2.047831	.4595962	4.46	0.000	1.143302	2.952359
Iage__2	-1.058902	.2822803	-3.75	0.000	-1.614456	-.5033479
Iage__3	.2284917	.0667591	3.42	0.001	.0971037	.3598798
Iage__4	-.0168534	.0053321	-3.16	0.002	-.0273475	-.0063594
_cons	2.240012	.0480157	46.65	0.000	2.145512	2.334511

Deviance: 317.696.

```
. predict fit1
(option xb assumed; fitted values)

. fracpoly regress sqrtigg age -2 2
-> gen double Iage__1 = age^-2-.1299 if e(sample)
-> gen double Iage__2 = age^2-7.695 if e(sample)
```

Source	SS	df	MS			
Model	22.2846976	2	11.1423488			
Residual	50.9676492	295	.172771692			
Total	73.2523469	297	.246640898			

Number of obs =   298
F(2, 295) =   64.49
Prob > F   = 0.0000
R-squared   = 0.3042
Adj R-squared = 0.2995
Root MSE   = .41566

sqrtigg	Coef.	Std. Err.	t	P>|t|	[95% Conf. Interval]	
Iage__1	-.1562156	.027416	-5.70	0.000	-.2101713	-.10226
Iage__2	.0148405	.0027767	5.34	0.000	.0093757	.0203052
_cons	2.283145	.0305739	74.68	0.000	2.222974	2.343315

Deviance: 319.448.

```
. predict fit2
(option xb assumed; fitted values)

. graph sqrtigg fit1 fit2 age, gap(5) xla yla c(.ss) s(oii)
                          l1(Square root of IgG) b2(Age, years)
```

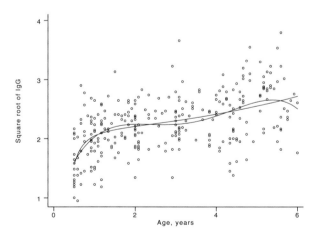

The quartic curve has an unsatisfactory "wavy" appearance, which is implausible in the light of the known behavior of IgG which increases throughout early life. The FP curve increases monotonically and is therefore biologically the more plausible curve. The two models have approximately the same deviance.

◁

▷ Example

Data from Smith et al. (1992) contain times to complete healing of leg ulcers in a randomized controlled clinical trial of two treatments in 192 elderly patients. A number of covariates were available, of which an important one is `mthson`, the number of months since the recorded onset of the ulcer. Since the response variable is time to an event of interest and some (in fact, about one half) of the times are censored, it is appropriate to use Cox regression to analyze the data. We consider FPs in `mthson` adjusting for 4 other covariates: `age`; `ulcarea`, the area of tissue initially affected by the ulcer; `deepppg`, a binary variable indicating presence or absence of deep vein involvement; and `treat`, a binary variable indicating treatment type. We fit FPs of degree 1 and 2:

```
. fracpoly cox ttevent mthson age ulcarea deepppg treat, dead(cens) compare
-> gen double Iage__1 = age-73.45 if e(sample)
-> gen double Iulca__1 = ulcarea-1326 if e(sample)
-> gen double Itrea__1 = treat-1 if e(sample)
........
-> gen double Imths__1 = X^.5-.493 if e(sample)
-> gen double Imths__2 = X^.5*ln(X)+.6973 if e(sample)
   (where: X = (mthson+1)/100)
Iteration 0:   log likelihood = -422.65089
Iteration 1:   log likelihood = -390.49313
Iteration 2:   log likelihood = -383.44258
Iteration 3:   log likelihood = -374.28707
Iteration 4:   log likelihood = -369.31417
Iteration 5:   log likelihood = -368.38104
Iteration 6:   log likelihood = -368.35448
Iteration 7:   log likelihood = -368.35446
Refining estimates:
Iteration 0:   log likelihood = -368.35446

Cox regression -- Breslow method for ties
Entry time 0                              Number of obs   =       192
                                          LR chi2(6)      =    108.59
                                          Prob > chi2     =    0.0000
Log likelihood = -368.35446               Pseudo R2       =    0.1285
```

ttevent censored	Coef.	Std. Err.	z	P>|z|	[95% Conf. Interval]	
Imths__1	-2.81425	.6996385	-4.02	0.000	-4.185516	-1.442984
Imths__2	1.541451	.4703143	3.28	0.001	.6196521	2.46325
Iage__1	-.0261111	.0087983	-2.97	0.003	-.0433556	-.0088667
Iulca__1	-.0017491	.000359	-4.87	0.000	-.0024527	-.0010455
deepppg	-.5850499	.2163173	-2.70	0.007	-1.009024	-.1610758
Itrea__1	-.1624663	.2171048	-0.75	0.454	-.5879838	.2630513

Deviance: 736.709. Best powers of mthson among 44 models fit: .5 .5.
Fractional polynomial model comparisons:

mthson	df	Deviance	Gain	P(term)	Powers
Not in model	0	754.345	—	—	
Linear	1	751.680	0.000	0.103	1
m = 1	2	738.969	12.712	0.000	-.5
m = 2	4	736.709	14.971	0.323	.5 .5

The best-fit FP of degree 2 has powers $(0.5, 0.5)$ and deviance 736.71. However, this model does not fit significantly better than the FP of degree 1, which has power -0.5 and deviance 738.97. The latter model has gain 12.71, showing it to be a significantly better fit than a straight line ($p < 0.001$). We prefer the model with $m = 1$, for which the partial linear predictor is shown below.

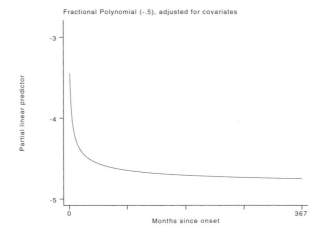
Fractional Polynomial (-.5), adjusted for covariates

The "hazard" for healing is much higher for patients whose ulcer is of recent onset than for those who have had an ulcer for many months.

Notice that `fracpoly` has automatically adjusted the predictors to their mean values, but since in Cox regression there is no constant term, we cannot see the effects of adjustment in the table of regression estimates. The effects would be present if we were to graph the baseline hazard or survival function, since these functions are defined with all predictors set equal to 0.

◁

(*Continued on next page*)

Saved Results

In addition to what *regression_cmd* saves, `fracpoly` saves

Scalars

e(fp_N)	number of nonmissing observations
e(fp_dev)	deviance for FP model of degree m
e(fp_df)	FP model degrees of freedom
e(fp_d0)	deviance for model without *xvar*$_1$
e(fp_s0)	residual SD for model without *xvar*$_1$
e(fp_dlin)	deviance for model linear in *xvar*$_1$
e(fp_slin)	residual SD for model linear in *xvar*$_1$
e(fp_d1), e(fp_d2), ...	deviances for FP models of degree 1,2,...,m
e(fp_s1), e(fp_s2), ...	residual SDs for FP models of degree 1,2,...,m

Macros

e(fp_cmd)	fracpoly
e(fp_depv)	*yvar*
e(fp_rhs)	*xvar*$_1$
e(fp_base)	variables in *xvar*$_2$, ..., *xvarlist* after adjustment and FP transformation
e(fp_xp)	I*xvar*__1, I*xvar*__2 etc.
e(fp_fvl)	variables in model finally estimated
e(fp_wgt)	weight type or ""
e(fp_wexp)	weight expression if `e(fp_wgt)´ ~= ""
e(fp_pwrs)	powers for FP model of degree m
e(fp_x1), e(fp_x2), ...	*xvar*$_1$ and variables in model
e(fp_k1), e(fp_k2), ...	powers for FP models of degree 1,2,...,m

Note that residual SDs are only stored when *regression_cmd* is `regress`.

Methods and Formulas

`fracpoly`, `fracplot`, `fracpred` and `fracgen` are implemented as ado-files.

The general definition of an FP, accommodating possible "repeated powers", may be written in terms of functions $H_1(x), \ldots, H_m(x)$ as follows:

$$\beta_0 + \sum_{j=1}^{m} \beta_j H_j(x)$$

where $H_1(x) = x^{(p_1)}$ and for $j = 2, \ldots, m$,

$$H_j(x) = \begin{cases} x^{(p_j)} & \text{if } p_j \neq p_{j-1} \\ H_{j-1}(x) \log x & \text{if } p_j = p_{j-1} \end{cases}$$

For example, an FP of degree 3 with powers $(1, 3, 3)$ has $H_1(x) = x$, $H_2(x) = x^3$, and $H_3(x) = x^3 \log x$ and equals $\beta_0 + \beta_1 x + \beta_2 x^3 + \beta_3 x^3 \log x$.

An FP model of degree m is taken to have $2m + 1$ degrees of freedom (df): one for β_0 and one for each β_j and its associated power. Since the powers in an FP are chosen from a finite set rather than from the entire real line, the df defined in this way are approximate.

The deviance D of a model is defined as -2 times its maximized log likelihood. For normal-errors models, we use the formula

$$D = n\left(1 - \bar{l} + \log \frac{2\pi\mathrm{RSS}}{n}\right)$$

where n is the sample size, $\bar{l}$ is the mean of the log normalized weights ($\bar{l} = 0$ if the weights are all equal), and RSS is the residual sum of squares as estimated by `regress`.

The gain, G, for an FP model is defined as the deviance for a straight line (i.e., for the model $\beta_0 + \beta x$) minus the deviance for the FP model. The covariates in *xvar*$_2$, ..., *xvarlist*, if any, are assumed to have been fit in each model. The larger the gain, the greater the nonlinearity in the relationship between the outcome variable and x.

The fits of pairs of nested FP regression models with degrees k and $k - 1$ for $k = 2, \ldots, m$ are compared by the `compare` option of `fracpoly`. The p-values reported by `compare` are calculated differently for normal and nonnormal regressions. Let D_k and D_{k-1} be the deviances of the models with degrees k and $k - 1$ respectively. For normal-errors models such as `regress`, a variance ratio F is calculated as

$$F = \frac{n_2}{n_1}\left\{\exp\left(\frac{D_{k-1} - D_k}{n}\right) - 1\right\}$$

where n_1 is the numerator df (here, 2), n_2 is the denominator df (equal to $rdf - 2k$, where rdf is the residual df for the regression model involving only the covariates in *xvar*$_2$, if any, but not x). The p-value is obtained by referring F to an F distribution on $(2, rdf)$ df.

For nonnormal models (`cox`, `glm`, `logistic`, `logit` or `poisson`), the p value is obtained by referring $D_{k-1} - D_k$ to a χ^2 distribution on 2 df. These p values for comparing models are approximate and are typically somewhat conservative (Royston and Altman 1994a).

The component-plus-residual values graphed by `fracplot` are calculated as follows: Let the data consist of triplets $(y_i, x_i, \mathbf{z}_i)$, $i = 1, \ldots, n$, where $\mathbf{z}_i$ is the vector of covariates for the ith observation, after applying possible fractional polynomial transformation and adjustment as described earlier. Let $\widehat{\eta}_i = \widehat{\beta}_0 + \{\mathbf{H}(x_i) - \mathbf{H}(x_0)\}'\widehat{\boldsymbol{\beta}} + \mathbf{z}_i'\widehat{\boldsymbol{\gamma}}$ be the linear predictor from the FP model, as given by the `fracpred` command, or equivalently by the `predict` command with the `xb` option, following use of `fracpoly`. Here, $\mathbf{H}(x_i) = \{H_1(x_i), \ldots, H_m(x_i)\}'$ is the vector of FP functions described above, $\mathbf{H}(x_0) = \{H_1(x_0), \ldots, H_m(x_0)\}'$ is the vector of adjustments to x_0 (often x_0 is chosen to be the mean of the x_i), $\widehat{\boldsymbol{\beta}}$ is the estimated parameter vector, and $\widehat{\boldsymbol{\gamma}}$ is the estimated parameter vector for the covariates. The values $\widehat{\eta}_i^* = \widehat{\beta}_0 + \{\mathbf{H}(x_i) - \mathbf{H}(x_0)\}'\widehat{\boldsymbol{\beta}}$ represent the behavior of the FP model for x at fixed values $\mathbf{z} = \mathbf{0}$ of the (adjusted) covariates. The ith component-plus-residual is defined as $\widehat{\eta}_i^* + d_i$, where d_i is the deviance residual for the ith observation. For normal-errors models $d_i = \sqrt{w_i}(y_i - \widehat{\eta}_i)$ where w_i is the case weight (or 1, if *weight* is not specified). For logistic, Cox, and generalized linear regression models, see [R] **logistic**, [R] **st stcox**, and [R] **glm** respectively for the formula for d_i. The formula for `poisson` models is as for `glm` with `family(poisson)`. For `cox`, d_i is the partial martingale residual (see [R] **st stcox**).

`fracplot` plots the values of d_i and the curve represented by $\widehat{\eta}_i^*$ against x_i. The confidence interval for $\widehat{\eta}_i^*$ is obtained from the variance–covariance matrix of the entire model and takes into account the uncertainty in estimating β_0, $\boldsymbol{\beta}$, and $\boldsymbol{\gamma}$ (but not in estimating the FP powers for x).

`fracpred` with the `for(`*varname*`)` option calculates the predicted index at $x_i = x_0$ and $\mathbf{z}_i = \mathbf{0}$, that is $\widehat{\eta}_i = \widehat{\beta}_0 + \{\mathbf{H}(x_i) - \mathbf{H}(x_0)\}'\widehat{\boldsymbol{\beta}}$. The standard error is calculated from the variance–covariance matrix of $(\widehat{\beta}_0, \widehat{\boldsymbol{\beta}})$, again ignoring estimation of the powers.

Acknowledgment

`fracpoly`, `fracplot`, `fracpred`, and `fracgen` were written by Patrick Royston of the MRC Clinical Trials Unit, London.

References

Becketti, S. 1995. sg26.2: Calculating and graphing fractional polynomials. *Stata Technical Bulletin* 24: 14–16. Reprinted in *Stata Technical Bulletin Reprints*, vol. 4, pp. 129–132.

Garrett, J. M. 1995. sg33: Calculation of adjusted means and adjusted proportions. *Stata Technical Bulletin* 24: 22–25. Reprinted in *Stata Technical Bulletin Reprints*, vol. 4, pp. 161–165.

——. 1998. sg33.1: Enhancements for calculation of adjusted means and adjusted proportions. *Stata Technical Bulletin* 43: 16–24. Reprinted in *Stata Technical Bulletin Reprints*, vol. 8, pp. 111–123.

Isaacs, D., D. G. Altman, C. E. Tidmarsh, H. B. Valman, and A. D. B. Webster. 1983. Serum immunoglobulin concentrations in preschool children measured by laser nephelometry: reference ranges for IgG, IgA, IgM. *Journal of Clinical Pathology* 36: 1193–1196.

Royston, P. 1995. sg26.3: Fractional polynomial utilities. *Stata Technical Bulletin* 25: 9–13. Reprinted in *Stata Technical Bulletin Reprints*, vol. 5, pp. 82–87.

Royston, P. and D. G. Altman. 1994a. Regression using fractional polynomials of continuous covariates: parsimonious parametric modelling (with discussion). *Applied Statistics* 43: 429–467.

——. 1994b. sg26: Using fractional polynomials to model curved regression relationships. *Stata Technical Bulletin* 21: 11–23. Reprinted in *Stata Technical Bulletin Reprints*, vol. 4, pp. 110–128.

Royston, P. and G. Ambler. 1998. sg81: Multivariable fractional polynomials. *Stata Technical Bulletin* 43: 24–32. Reprinted in *Stata Technical Bulletin Reprints*, vol. 8, pp. 123–132.

——. 1999a. sg81.1: Multivariable fractional polynomials: update. *Stata Technical Bulletin* 49: 17–23. Reprinted in *Stata Technical Bulletin Reprints*, vol. 9, pp. 161–168.

——. 1999b. sg81.2: Multivariable fractional polynomials: update. *Stata Technical Bulletin* 50: 25. Reprinted in *Stata Technical Bulletin Reprints*, vol. 9, p. 168.

——. 1999c. sg112: Nonlinear regression models involving power or exponential functions of covariates. *Stata Technical Bulletin* 49: 25–30. Reprinted in *Stata Technical Bulletin Reprints*, vol. 9, pp. 173–179.

——. 1999d. sg112.1: Nonlinear regression models involving power or exponential functions of covariates: update. *Stata Technical Bulletin* 50: 26. Reprinted in *Stata Technical Bulletin Reprints*, vol. 9, p. 180.

Sauerbrei, W. and P. Royston. 1999. Building multivariable prognostic and diagnostic models: transformation of the predictors by using fractional polynomials. *Journal of the Royal Statistical Society*, Series A 162.

Smith, J. M., C. J. Dore, A. Charlett, and J. D. Lewis. 1992. A randomized trial of Biofilm dressing for venous leg ulcers. *Phlebology* 7: 108–113.

Also See

Complementary:	[R] **adjust**, [R] **lincom**, [R] **lrtest**, [R] **predict**, [R] **test**, [R] **testnl**, [R] **vce**, [R] **xi**
Background:	[U] **16.5 Accessing coefficients and standard errors**, [U] **23 Estimation and post-estimation commands**

Title

functions — Quick reference for functions

Description

This entry provides a quick reference for functions allowed by Stata. Matrix functions are not documented here; see [U] **17.8 Matrix functions**. See [U] **16.3 Functions** for additional details about the functions documented here.

Remarks

Function	Description
Mathematical functions	
abs(x)	absolute value
acos(x)	arc-cosine returning radians
asin(x)	arc-sine returning radians
atan(x)	arc-tangent returning radians
comb(n,k)	combinatorial function
cos(x)	cosine of radians
digamma(x)	digamma function $\Gamma'(x)/\Gamma(x)$; for $x > 0$, where $\Gamma(x)$ is the gamma function; digamma function is sometimes called the psi function
exp(x)	exponential
ln(x)	natural logarithm
lnfact(x)	natural log factorial
lngamma(x)	$\ln \Gamma(x)$
log(x)	natural logarithm
log10(x)	log base 10 of x
mod(x,y)	modulus of x with respect to y
sin(x)	sine of radians
sqrt(x)	square root
tan(x)	tangent of radians
trigamma(x)	trigamma function; derivative of digamma function
Statistical functions	
Binomial(n,k,π)	probability of observing k or more successes in n trials when the probability of a success on a single trial is π
binorm(h,k,ρ)	joint cumulative distribution $\Phi(h, k, \rho)$ of bivariate normal with correlation ρ; cumulative over $(-\infty, h] \times (-\infty, k]$

Function	Description
chi2(df,x)	cumulative χ^2 with df degrees of freedom
chi2tail(df,x)	upper-tail cumulative χ^2 with df degrees of freedom
F(df_1,df_2,f)	cumulative F distribution with df_1 numerator and df_2 denominator degrees of freedom.
Ftail(df_1,df_2,F)	upper-tail cumulative F distribution with df_1 numerator and df_2 denominator degrees of freedom
gammap(a,x)	incomplete gamma function $P(a, x)$
ibeta(a,b,x)	incomplete beta function $I_x(a, b)$
invbinomial(n,k,p)	inverse binomial; for $p \leq 0.5$, returns π (π = probability of success on a single trial) such that the probability of observing k or more successes in n trials is p; for $p > 0.5$, returns π such that the probability of observing k or fewer successes in n trials is $1 - p$
invchi2(df,p)	inverse of chi2(); if chi2(df,x)$= p$, then invchi2(df,p)$= x$
invchi2tail(df,p)	inverse of chi2tail(); if chi2tail(df,x)$= p$, then invchi2tail(df,p)$= x$
invF(df_1,df_2,p)	inverse cumulative F distribution; if F(df_1,df_2,f)$= p$, then invF(df_1,df_2,p)$= f$
invFtail(df_1,df_2,p)	inverse upper-tail cumulative F distribution; if Ftail(df_1,df_2,f) $= p$, then invFtail(df_1,df_2, p) $= f$
invgammap(a,p)	inverse incomplete gamma function; if gammap(a,x) $= p$, then invgammap(a,p) $= x$
invnchi2(df,λ,p)	inverse cumulative noncentral χ^2 distribution; if nchi2(df,λ,x) $= p$, then invnchi2(df,λ,p) $= x$ (df must be an integer; $1 \leq df \leq 200$; $0 \leq \lambda \leq 1000$)
invnorm(p)	inverse cumulative normal; if norm(z) $= p$, then invnorm(p) $= z$
invttail(df,p)	inverse of ttail(); if ttail(df,t) $= p$, then invttail($df,$p) $= t$
nchi2(df,λ,x)	cumulative noncentral χ^2 distribution with df degrees of freedom (df must be an integer; $1 \leq df \leq 200$) and noncentrality parameter λ ($0 \leq \lambda \leq 1000$)

Function	Description
$\texttt{normden}(z)$ or $\texttt{normden}(z,\sigma)$	standard normal density; $\texttt{normden}(z,\sigma) = \texttt{normden}(z)/\sigma$ if $\sigma \geq 0$ & $\sigma \neq .$ (*missing*); otherwise, it is $.$ (*missing*)
$\texttt{norm}(z)$	cumulative standard normal
$\texttt{npnchi2}(df,x,p)$	noncentrality parameter λ for noncentral χ^2; if $\texttt{nchi2}(df,\lambda,x) = p$, then $\texttt{npnchi2}(df,x,p) = \lambda$ (df must be an integer; $1 \leq df \leq 200$; $0 \leq \lambda \leq 1000$)
$\texttt{ttail}(df,t)$	upper-tail cumulative Student's t distribution with df degrees of freedom; returns probability $T > t$
$\texttt{uniform}()$	uniform pseudo-random number function; returns uniformly distributed pseudo-random numbers on the interval $[0,1)$; it takes no arguments but the parentheses must be included; it can be seeded with the **set seed** command; see [R] **generate**

Date functions

Function	Description
$\texttt{date}(s_1,s_2)$ or $\texttt{date}(s_1,s_2,n)$	returns the elapsed date corresponding to s_1. s_1 contains the date, recorded as a string, in virtually any format. Months can be spelled out, abbreviated (to three characters), or indicated as numbers; years can include or exclude the century; blanks and punctuation are allowed.
	s_2 is any permutation of m, d, and [##]y with their order defining the order that month, day, and year occur in s_1. ##, if specified, indicates the default century for 2-digit years in s_1; if ## is not specified and s_1 has a 2-digit year, missing values are produced.
	n is a numeric argument that specifies an alternative way to deal with two-digit years. n specifies the largest year that is to be returned when a two-digit year is encountered.
$\texttt{d}(l)$	convenience function to make typing dates in expressions easier; e.g., typing $\texttt{d(2jan1960)}$ is equivalent to typing 1.
$\texttt{mdy}(m,d,y)$	returns the elapsed date corresponding to the numeric arguments of month, day, and year.
$\texttt{day}(e)$	returns the numeric day of the month corresponding to e, the elapsed date.
$\texttt{month}(e)$	returns the numeric month corresponding to e, the elapsed date.
$\texttt{year}(e)$	returns the numeric year corresponding to e, the elapsed date.
$\texttt{dow}(e)$	returns the numeric day of the week corresponding to e, the elapsed date. Sunday $= 0$, Monday $= 1$, ..., Saturday $= 6$.
$\texttt{doy}(e)$	returns the numeric day of the year corresponding to e, the elapsed date.

Function	Description
week(e)	returns the numeric week of the year corresponding to e, the elapsed date.
quarter(e)	returns the numeric quarter of the year corresponding to e, the elapsed date.
halfyear(e)	returns the numeric half of the year corresponding to e, the elapsed date.

String functions

Function	Description
abbrev(s,n)	returns the name s, abbreviated to n characters. s may contain a name, a time-series operated name, or any string. If any of the characters of s are '.', and $n < 8$ or $n = .$, then the value of n defaults to a value of 8. Otherwise, if $n < 5$ or if $n = .$, then n defaults to a value of 5. abbrev() is typically used with variable names and variable names with time-series operators (the period case).
index(s_1,s_2)	returns the position in s_1 in which s_2 is first found or zero if s_1 does not contain s_2. index("this","is") is 3 and index("this","it") is 0.
length(s)	returns the actual length of the string. length("ab") evaluates to 2.
lower(s)	returns the lowercased variant of s. lower("THIS") evaluates to "this".
ltrim(s)	returns s with any leading blanks removed. Thus, ltrim(" this") evaluates to "this".
match(s_1,s_2)	evaluates to 1 if s_1 matches the pattern s_2; otherwise, it returns 0. match("17.4","1??4") returns 1.
real(s)	converts s into a numeric argument. real("5.2")+1 evaluates to 6.2.
reverse(s)	returns reversed s. reverse("hello") evaluates to "olleh".
rtrim(s)	returns s with any trailing blanks removed. Thus, rtrim("this ") evaluates to "this".
string(n, %fmt)	converts n into a string with %fmt display format. string(14610, "%dM-D-CY") evaluates to "January-01-2000".
subinstr(s_1,s_2,s_3,n)	returns s_1 where the first n occurrences in s_1 of s_2 have been replaced with s_3. subinstr("this is this","is","X",1) evaluates to "thX is this". If n is '.', all occurrences are replaced.

Function	Description
subinword(s_1,s_2,s_3,n)	returns s_1 where the first n occurrences in s_1 of s_2 as a word have been replaced with s_3. A word is defined as a space-separated token; a token at the beginning or end of s also counts as being space-separated. subinword("this is this","is","X",1) evaluates to "this X this".
substr(s,n_1,n_2)	returns the substring of s starting at the n_1th column for a length of n_2. substr("abcdef",2,3) evaluates to "bcd". If $n_1 < 0$, the starting position is interpreted as distance from the end of the string. Thus, substr("abcdef",-2,1) evaluates to "e". If n_2 ==., the remaining portion of the string is returned. substr("abcdef",4,.) evaluates to "def".
trim(s)	returns s with any leading and trailing blanks removed. It is identical to ltrim(rtrim(s)). Thus, trim(" this ") evaluates to "this".
upper(s)	returns the uppercased variant of s. upper("this") evaluates to "THIS".

Special functions

Function	Description
autocode(x,n,*xmin*,*xmax*)	partitions the interval from *xmin* to *xmax* into n equal-length intervals and returns the upper bound of the interval that contains x. This function is an automated version of recode() (see below). See [U] **28 Commands for dealing with categorical variables** for an example.
_caller()	returns version of the program or session that invoked the currently running program; see [P] **version**. For use by programmers.
cond(x,a,b)	returns a if x evaluates to *true* (not 0) and b if x evaluates to *false* (0). generate maxinc=cond(inc1>inc2,inc1,inc2) creates the variable maxinc as the maximum of inc1 and inc2 (assuming inc1 and inc2 are not *missing*).
e(*name*)	contains the value of saved result e(*name*). See [U] **21.8 Accessing results calculated by other programs**. Also see [U] **17.8.1 Matrix functions returning matrices**.
e(sample)	evaluates to 1 if the observation was part of the estimation sample; otherwise, 0. See [U] **23.4 Specifying the estimation subsample**.

Function	Description
float(x)	returns the value of x rounded to float. Although you may store your numeric variables as byte, int, long, float, or double, Stata converts all numbers to double before performing any calculations. As a consequence, difficulties can arise when numbers that have no finite binary representation are compared. See [U] **16.10 Precision and problems therein** for more information.
group(x)	creates a categorical variable that divides the dataset into x as nearly equal-sized subsamples as possible, numbering the first group 1, the second 2, and so on.
inlist$(z,a,b,\dots)$	evaluates to 1 if z is a member of the remaining arguments; otherwise, returns 0. The number of arguments is between 2 and 255. All must be reals or all must be strings.
inrange(z,a,b)	evaluates to 1 if it is known that $a \le z \le b$; otherwise, returns 0. The following ordered rules apply: $z = .$ returns 0. $a = .$ and $b = .$ returns 1. $a = .$ returns 1 if $z \le b$; otherwise it returns 0. $b = .$ returns 1 if $a \le z$; otherwise it returns 0. Otherwise, 1 is returned if $a \le z \le b$ In the above, if the arguments are strings, '.' is interpreted as "".
int(x)	returns the integer obtained by truncating x. Thus, int(5.2) is 5 as is int(5.8); int(-5.2) is -5 as is int(-5.8). One way to obtain the closest integer to x is int$(x+\text{sign}(x)/2)$, which simplifies to int$(x+0.5)$ for $x \ge 0$. Use of the round() function, however, is preferred.
matrix(exp)	restricts name interpretation to scalars and matrices; see scalar() function below.
max$(x_1,x_2,\dots,x_n)$	returns the maximum of $x_1, x_2, \dots, x_n$. Missing values are ignored. If all arguments are *missing*, *missing* is returned. For example, max(3+2,1) evaluates to 5.
min$(x_1,x_2,\dots,x_n)$	returns the minimum of $x_1, x_2, \dots, x_n$. Missing values are ignored. If all arguments are *missing*, *missing* is returned.
missing(x)	returns 0 if $x \ne .$ (or $\ne$ "" for a string); otherwise, returns 1
recode$(x,x_1,x_2,\dots,x_n)$	returns *missing* if x is *missing*; x_1 if $x \le x_1$; otherwise x_2 if $x \le x_2$, $\dots$; otherwise x_n if x is greater than $x_1, x_2, \dots, x_{n-1}$. Also see [R] **recode** for another style of recode function.

Function	Description
r(*name*)	contains the value of saved result r(*name*). See [U] **21.8 Accessing results calculated by other programs**; also see [U] **17.8.1 Matrix functions returning matrices**.
reldif(*x, y*)	"relative" difference $\lvert x - y\rvert/(\lvert y\rvert + 1)$.
replay()	function for programmers; see [P] **estimates**.
return(*name*)	contains the value of to-be-saved result return(*name*). See [U] **21.10 Saving results**.
round(x,y)	returns x rounded to units of y. For $y = 1$, this amounts to the closest integer to x; round(5.2,1) is 5 as is round(4.8,1); round(-5.2,1) is -5 as is round(-4.8,1). The rounding definition is generalized for $y \neq 1$. With $y = .01$, for instance, x is rounded to two decimal places; round(sqrt(2),.01) is 1.41. y may also be larger than 1; round(28,5) is 30, which is 28 rounded to the closest multiple of 5. For $y = 0$, the function is defined as returning x unmodified.
s(*name*)	contains the value of saved result s(*name*). See [U] **21.8 Accessing results calculated by other programs**.
scalar(*exp*)	restricts name interpretation to scalars and matrices.
sign(x)	returns *missing* if x is *missing*, -1 if $x < 0$, 0 if $x = 0$, and 1 if $x > 0$.
sum(x)	returns the running sum of x, treating missing values as zero. For example, following the command generate y=sum(x), the ith observation on y contains the sum of the first through ith observations on x. Also see [R] **egen** for an alternative sum function that produces a constant equal to the overall sum.

Time-series functions

Inputting time variables

format	integer conversion	string conversion
%td	mdy(*month, day, year*)	date(*string*, "md[##]y" or "dm[##]Y" ..., [*topyear*])
%tw	yw(*year, week*)	weekly(*string*, "w[##]y" or "[##]yw", [*topyear*])
%tm	ym(*year, month*)	monthly(*string*, "m[##]y" or "[##]ym", [*topyear*])
%tq	yq(*year, quarter*)	quarterly(*string*, "q[##]y" or "[##]yq", [*topyear*])
%th	yh(*year, halfyear*)	halfyearly(*string*, "h[##]y" or "[##]yh", [*topyear*])
%ty	*year*	yearly(*string*, "[##]y", [*topyear*])

Specifying particular dates (date literals)

Stata provides one-letter functions for typing weekly, monthly, quarterly, half-yearly, and yearly dates:

format	function	argument	examples
%td	d()	type day, month, year	d(15feb1998), d(15-5-2002)
%tw	w()	type year, week	w(1998w7), w(2002-25)
%tm	m()	type year, month	m(1998m2), m(2002-5)
%tq	q()	type year, quarter	q(1998q1), q(2002-2)
%th	h()	type year, half	h(1998h1), h(2002-1)
%ty	y()	type year	y(1998), y(2002)

Translating between time units

Stata provides functions to translate any time unit to and from %td daily units:

Input	Output %td daily	%tw weekly	%tm monthly	%tq quarterly	%th half-yearly	%ty yearly
%td		wofd(d)	mofd(d)	qofd(d)	hofd(d)	yofd(d)
%tw	dofw(w)		mofd(dofw(w))	qofd(dofw(w))	hofd(dofw(w))	yofd(dofw(w))
%tm	dofm(m)	wofd(dofm(m))		qofd(dofm(m))	hofd(dofm(m))	yofd(dofm(m))
%tq	dofq(q)	wofd(dofq(q))	mofd(dofq(q))		hofd(dofq(q))	yofd(dofq(q))
%th	dofh(h)	wofd(dofh(h))	mofd(dofh(h))	qofd(dofh(h))		yofd(dofh(h))
%ty	dofy(y)	wofd(dofy(y))	mofd(dofy(y))	qofd(dofy(y))	hofd(dofy(y))	

Selecting periods of time

Stata also has two time-series functions that may be used to select periods of time: tin(d_1, d_2) returns *true* if $d_1 \le t \le d_2$ where t is the time variable previously tsset (see [R] **tsset**); and twithin(), which is the same as tin() except the range is $d_1 < t < d_2$.

See [U] **16.3.4 Time-series functions** for additional details about time-series functions.

Also See

Related:　　　[R] **egen**

Background:　　[U] **16.3 Functions**,
　　　　　　　　　　[U] **17.8 Matrix functions**

Title

> **generate** — Create or change contents of variable

Syntax

> generate [*type*] *newvar*[*:lblname*] =*exp* [if *exp*] [in *range*]
>
> replace *oldvar* =*exp* [if *exp*] [in *range*] [, no̲promote]
>
> se̲t se̲ed #
>
> se̲t ty̲pe { byte | int | long | float | double | str# }

by ... : may be used with generate and replace; see [R] **by**.

Description

generate creates a new variable. The values of the variable are specified by =*exp*. See [R] **egen** for extensions to generate.

replace changes the contents of an existing variable. Since replace alters data, the command may not be abbreviated.

set seed # specifies the initial value of the random number seed used by the uniform() function. # should be specified as a positive integer.

set type specifies the default type assigned to new variables (such as by generate) when the storage type is not explicitly specified. Caution should be exercised when using this command.

Options

no̲promote prevents replace from promoting the variable type to accommodate the change. For instance, consider a variable stored as an integer type (byte, int, or long) and assume you replace some values with nonintegers. By default, replace will change the variable type to a floating point (float or double) and thus correctly store the changed values. Similarly, replace will promote byte and int variables to longer integers (int and long) if the replacement value is an integer but too large in absolute value for the current storage type. replace will promote strings to longer strings. no̲promote prevents replace from doing this; instead, the replacement values are truncated to fit into the current storage type.

(Compatibility with previous releases note: Automatic variable promotion was added in Stata 4.0. If you set version to 3.1 or less, Stata will return to its old behavior and thus old programs and ado-files will work; see [P] **version**.)

Remarks

generate and replace

generate and replace are used to create new variables and to modify the contents of existing variables, respectively. Although the commands do the same thing, they have different names so that you do not accidentally replace values in your data. The details of expressions are covered in [U] **16 Functions and expressions**.

Also see [R] **edit**.

▷ Example

You have a dataset containing the variable age2, which you have previously defined as age^2 (i.e., age^2). You have changed some of the age data and now want to correct age2 to reflect the new values:

```
. generate age2=age^2
age2 already defined
r(110);
```

When you attempt to re-generate age2, Stata refuses, telling you that age2 is already defined. You could drop age2 and then re-generate it, or you could use the replace command:

```
. replace age2=age^2
(204 real changes made)
```

When you use replace, you are informed of the number of actual changes made to the dataset.

◁

You can explicitly specify the storage type of the new variable being created by putting the *type*, such as byte, int, long, float, double, or str8, in front of the variable name. Not specifying a type is equivalent to specifying float. (More correctly, it is equivalent to specifying the default type set by the set type command; see below.)

You may also specify a value label to be associated with the new variable by including ':*lblname*' after the variable name. This is seldom done since you can always associate the value label later by using the label define command; see [U] **15.6.3 Value labels**.

▷ Example

Among the variables in your dataset is name, which contains the first and last name of each person. You wish to create a new variable called lastname, which you will then use to sort the data. name is a string variable, and you type

```
. generate lastname=substr(name,index(name," ")+1,.)
type mismatch
r(109);
```

Since you did not explicitly specify the storage type, Stata attempted to create a float variable called lastname equal to your string expression. Stata realized it could not do that, so it complained and did nothing. You meant to type

```
. generate str12 lastname=substr(name,index(name," ")+1,.)
```

◁

▷ Example

You wish to create a new variable `age2` that is the variable `age` squared. You realize that since `age` is an integer, `age2` will also be an integer and `age2` will certainly be less than 32,766. You therefore decide to store `age2` as an `int` to conserve memory:

```
. generate int age2=age^2
(9 missing values generated)
```

Preceding `age2` with `int` told Stata that the variable was to be stored as an `int`. After creating the new variable, Stata informed us that 9 missing values were generated. Whenever `generate` produces missing values, it informs you.

◁

See [U] **16 Functions and expressions** and [U] **28 Commands for dealing with categorical variables** for more information and examples. Also see [R] **recode** for a convenient way to recode categorical variables.

❏ Technical Note

If you specify the `if` modifier and/or in *range*, the *=exp* is evaluated only for those observations meeting the specified condition and/or in the specified range. The other observations of the new variable are set to missing:

```
. generate int age2=age^2 if age>30
(112 missing values generated)
```

❏

▷ Example

`replace` can be used to change just a single value as well as to make sweeping changes to your data. For instance, say you enter data on the first five odd and even positive integers and then discover that you made a mistake:

```
. list
           odd       even
1.          1          2
2.          3          4
3.         -8          6
4.          7          8
5.          9         10
```

Notice that the third observation is wrong; the value of `odd` should be 5, not −8. We can use `replace` to repair the mistake:

```
. replace odd=5 in 3
(1 real change made)
```

We could also have repaired the mistake by typing `replace odd=5 if odd==-8`.

◁

set seed

set seed # reinitializes the seed for the pseudo-random number generator uniform() and should be specified as a positive integer. If a negative number is specified, it will be made positive. The seed determines the sequence of pseudo-random numbers produced by uniform(). When Stata comes up, it initializes the seed to 123456789, an easy-to-remember nonrandom number that in no way affects the pseudo-randomness of the numbers produced by uniform(). Since Stata initializes the seed to a constant, however, Stata produces the same sequence of random numbers (measured from the start of the session) unless you reinitialize the seed. The seed you select affects only the sequence, not the pseudo-randomness. Without loss of pseudo-randomness, the seed may be set to small numbers; e.g., set seed 2. See [U] **16.3.2 Statistical functions** for details and formulas.

set type

When you create a new variable and do not specify the storage type for the variable, say by typing generate y=x+2, the new variable is made a float. That is, it is made a float if you have not issued the set type command. If earlier in your session you typed set type double, then the new variable would be made a double.

We recommend that set type float and set type double be the only possibilities you consider. Many of Stata's features are implemented as ado-files, and some ado-files do not explicitly specify the storage types of their working variables. While this is especially true of ado-files written by others, this is even true of some of our ado-files. It is understood that such sloppiness on our part is inexcusable, but in the meantime you should not set type int since some ado-files may then produce incorrect results. set type double, on the other hand, is quite safe.

Methods and Formulas

You can do anything with replace that you can do with generate. The only difference between the commands is that replace requires that the variable already exist, whereas generate requires that the variable be new. In fact, inside Stata, generate and replace are the same code! Since Stata is an interactive system, however, we force a distinction between replacing existing values and generating new ones so that you do not accidentally replace valuable data while thinking that you are creating another new piece of information.

References

Gleason, J. R. 1997. dm50: Defining variables and recording their definitions. *Stata Technical Bulletin* 40: 9–10. Reprinted in *Stata Technical Bulletin Reprints*, vol. 7, pp. 48–49.

——. 1999. dm50.1: Update to defv. *Stata Technical Bulletin* 51: 2. Reprinted in *Stata Technical Bulletin Reprints*, vol. 9, pp. 14–15.

Weesie, J. 1997. dm43: Automatic recording of definitions. *Stata Technical Bulletin* 35: 6–7. Reprinted in *Stata Technical Bulletin Reprints*, vol. 6, pp. 18–20.

Also See

Complementary:	[R] **compress**, [R] **rename**
Related:	[R] **drawnorm**, [R] **edit**, [R] **egen**, [R] **encode**, [R] **label**, [R] **recode**
Background:	[U] **15 Data**,
	[U] **16 Functions and expressions**

Title

> **glm** — Generalized linear models

Syntax

> glm *depvar* [*indepvars*] [*weight*] [if *exp*] [in *range*] [, *max_options var_options*
>
> *output_options spec_options*]

max_options are given by

> <u>iterate</u>(#) <u>ltol</u>erance(#) mu(*varname*) <u>nolog</u> search fisher(#) irls

var_options are given by

> oim opg <u>vf</u>actor(#) robust <u>cl</u>uster(*varname*) <u>unbi</u>ased nwest(*wtname*[#])
>
> jknife jknife1 bstrap brep(#) <u>scale</u>(x2 | dev | #) disp(#)
>
> <u>sc</u>ore(*newvar*) t(*varname*)

output_options are given by

> <u>ef</u>orm <u>level</u>(#) <u>trace</u> <u>noheader</u> nodisplay nodots

spec_options are given by

> <u>f</u>amily(*familyname*) <u>link</u>(*linkname*) <u>noconst</u>ant [<u>ln</u>]<u>off</u>set(*varname*)

where *familyname* is a user-written program or one of

> <u>gaus</u>sian | <u>ig</u>aussian | <u>b</u>inomial [*varname*$_N$ | #$_N$] | <u>p</u>oisson | <u>nb</u>inomial [#$_k$] |
>
> <u>gam</u>ma

and *linkname* is a user-written program or one of

> <u>i</u>dentity | log | <u>l</u>ogit | <u>p</u>robit | <u>c</u>loglog | <u>o</u>power # | <u>power</u> # | <u>nb</u>inomial |
>
> <u>logl</u>og | logc

by ... : may be used with glm; see [R] **by**.
fweights, aweights, iweights, and pweights are allowed; see [U] **14.1.6 weight**.
glm shares the features of all estimation commands; see [U] **23 Estimation and post-estimation commands**.
glm may be used with sw to perform stepwise estimation; see [R] **sw**.

Syntax for predict

predict [*type*] *newvarname* [if *exp*] [in *range*] [, *statistic* <u>nooff</u>set <u>stan</u>dardized

<u>stu</u>dentized <u>mod</u>ified <u>adj</u>usted]

where *statistic* is one of

<u>mu</u> | xb | <u>e</u>ta | stdp | <u>a</u>nscombe | <u>c</u>ooksd | <u>d</u>eviance | <u>h</u>at | <u>l</u>ikelihood |

<u>pe</u>arson | <u>r</u>esponse | <u>s</u>core | <u>w</u>orking

These statistics are available both in and out of sample; type predict ... if e(sample) ... if wanted only for the estimation sample.

Description

glm fits generalized linear models. It can estimate models using either IRLS (maximum quasi-likelihood) or Newton–Raphson (maximum likelihood) optimization, which is the default. Previous versions of glm used only IRLS. Users of the previous versions should note this change in default behavior.

See [R] **logistic** and [R] **regress** for lists of related estimation commands.

Options

iterate(*#*) specifies the maximum number of iterations allowed in estimating the model; iterate(50) is the default. You should rarely need to specify iterate().

ltolerance(*#*) specifies the convergence criterion for the change in deviance between iterations; ltol(1e-6) is the default.

mu(*varname*) specifies *varname* as the initial estimate for the mean of *depvar*. This can be useful with models that produce convergence difficulties, such as family(binomial) models with power or odds-power links.

nolog suppresses the iteration log.

search specifies that the command should search for good starting values. This option is only useful for Newton–Raphson optimization (and not when irls is specified).

fisher(*#*) specifies the number of Newton–Raphson steps that should use the Fisher scoring Hessian or expected information matrix (EIM) before switching to the observed information matrix (OIM). This option is only useful for Newton–Raphson optimization (and not when using irls).

irls requests iterated, reweighted least squares (IRLS) optimization of the deviance instead of Newton–Raphson optimization of the log-likelihood. If the irls option is not specified, then the optimization is carried out using Stata's ml commands, in which case all options of ml maximize are also available.

oim specifies that the variance matrix should be calculated using the observed information matrix (OIM) rather than the usual expected information matrix (EIM) if the irls option is specified. The option is ignored if irls is not specified.

opg specifies that the variance matrix be calculated using the Berndt, Hall, Hall, and Hausman (1974), or "B-H-cubed", variance estimator. Another name for this estimator is the outer product of the gradient (OPG) estimator. This estimator only uses the gradient to estimate the variance and avoids the calculation of second derivatives. Note that this option refers only to how the variance is estimated, and does not imply that the B-H-cubed technique is used in the actual optimization. We use the name OPG to avoid this confusion. This option is not allowed when cluster() is specified.

vfactor(#) specifies a scalar by which to multiply the resulting variance matrix. This option allows users to match output with other packages which may apply degrees of freedom or other small sample corrections to estimates of variance.

robust specifies that the Huber/White/sandwich estimator of variance is to be used in place of the traditional calculation; see [U] **23.11 Obtaining robust variance estimates**. robust combined with cluster() allows observations which are not independent within cluster (although they must be independent between clusters).

If you specify pweights, robust is implied; see [U] **23.13 Weighted estimation**.

cluster(*varname*) specifies that the observations are independent across groups (clusters), but not necessarily within groups. *varname* specifies to which group each observation belongs; e.g., cluster(personid) in data with repeated observations on individuals. cluster() affects the estimated standard errors and variance–covariance matrix of the estimators (VCE), but not the estimated coefficients; see [U] **23.11 Obtaining robust variance estimates**. Specifying cluster() implies robust if no other variance estimate is specified.

unbiased specifies that the unbiased sandwich estimate of variances be used. The robust option is implied when unbiased is used.

nwest(*wtname*[*#*]) specifies that a heteroskedasticity and autocorrelation consistent (HAC) variance estimate be used. Newey–West refers to the general form for combining weighted matrices to form the variance estimate. There are three weight kernels built into glm. *wtname* is a user-written program or one of

$$\underline{\text{nw}}\text{est} \; [\#] \; | \; \underline{\text{ga}}\text{llant} \; [\#] \; | \; \underline{\text{an}}\text{derson} \; [\#]$$

If # is not specified, $N - 2$ is assumed.

jknife specifies that the jackknife estimate of variance be used. If cluster() is not specified, then the leave-out strategy is to leave out each observation in model estimation. Otherwise, the strategy is to leave out each group defined by the cluster variable in model estimation.

jknife1 specifies that the one-step jackknife estimate of variance be used.

bstrap specifies that the bootstrap estimate of variance be used.

brep(#) specifies the number of bootstrap samples to consider in forming the bootstrap estimate of variance. The default if brep(199).

scale(x2|dev|#) overrides the default scale parameter. This option is only allowed with Hessian (information matrix) variance estimates.

By default, scale(1) is assumed for the discrete distributions (binomial, Poisson, and negative binomial), and scale(x2) is assumed for the continuous distributions (Gaussian, gamma, and inverse Gaussian).

scale(x2) specifies the scale parameter be set to the Pearson chi-squared (or generalized chi-squared) statistic divided by the residual degrees of freedom, which was recommended by McCullagh and Nelder (1989) as a good general choice for continuous distributions.

scale(dev) sets the scale parameter to the deviance divided by the residual degrees of freedom. This provides an alternative to scale(x2) for continuous distributions and overdispersed or underdispersed discrete distributions.

scale(#) sets the scale parameter to #. For example, using scale(1) in family(gamma) models results in exponential-errors regression. Additional use of link(log) rather than the default link(power -1) for family(gamma) essentially reproduces Stata's ereg command (see [R] **weibull**) if all the observations are uncensored.

disp(#) multiplies the variance of *depvar* by # and divides the deviance by #. The resulting distributions are members of the quasi-likelihood family.

score(*newvar*) creates a new variable, *newvar*, containing each observation's contribution to the score; see [U] **23.12 Obtaining scores**. Note that scores may also be obtained post-estimation using the predict command.

t(*varname*) specifies the variable name corresponding to t; see [R] **xt**. glm does not need to know t() in all cases. When t() is required, it is also assumed that the observations are spaced equally over time. This option is required if nwest is specified.

eform displays the exponentiated coefficients and corresponding standard errors and confidence intervals. For family(binomial) link(logit) (i.e., logistic regression), exponentiation results in odds ratios; for family(poisson) link(log) (i.e., Poisson regression), exponentiated coefficients are rate ratios.

level(#) specifies the confidence level, in percent, for confidence intervals. The default is level(95) or as set by set level; see [U] **23.5 Specifying the width of confidence intervals**.

trace requested that the estimated coefficient vector be printed at each iteration.

noheader suppresses the header information from the output. The coefficient table is still printed.

nodisplay suppresses the output. The iteration log is still printed.

nodots specifies that a dot should not be printed for each fitted model when calculating jackknife or bootstrap estimates. By default, a single dot character is printed for each estimation that is performed. If an iteration does not converge or has collinearity in the variables, a single red 'x' is printed.

family(*familyname*) specifies the distribution of *depvar*; family(gaussian) is the default.

link(*linkname*) specifies the link function; the default is the canonical link for the family() specified.

noconstant specifies that the linear predictor has no intercept term, thus forcing it through the origin on the scale defined by the link function.

[ln]offset(*varname*) specifies an offset to be added to the linear predictor. offset() specifies the values directly: $g\{E(y)\} = \mathbf{x}\boldsymbol{\beta} + varname$. lnoffset() specifies the exponentiated values: $g\{E(y)\} = \mathbf{x}\boldsymbol{\beta} + \ln(varname)$. lnoffset() is most useful with Poisson-like data where *varname* records the person-years of exposure to some hazard and y (*depvar* in the syntax diagram) records the observed number of "deaths".

Options for predict

mu, the default, specifies that predict is to calculate $g^{-1}(\mathbf{x}\widehat{\boldsymbol{\beta}})$, the inverse link of the linear prediction.

xb calculates the linear prediction $\eta = \mathbf{x}\widehat{\boldsymbol{\beta}}$.

eta is a synonym for xb.

`stdp` calculates the standard error of the linear prediction.

`anscombe` calculates the Anscombe (1972) residuals. The aim here is to produce residuals that closely follow a normal distribution.

`cooksd` calculates Cook's distance, which measures the aggregate change in the estimated coefficients when each observation is left out of the estimation.

`deviance` calculates the deviance residuals. Deviance residuals are recommended by McCullagh and Nelder (1989) and by others as having the best properties for examining the goodness of fit of a GLM. They are approximately normally distributed if the model is correct. They may be plotted against the fitted values or against a covariate to inspect the model's fit. Also see the `pearson` option below.

`hat` calculates the diagonals of the "hat" matrix as an analog to simple linear regression.

`likelihood` calculates a weighted average of standardized deviance and standardized Pearson (described below) residuals.

`pearson` calculates the Pearson residuals. Be aware that Pearson residuals often have markedly skewed distributions for non-normal family distributions. Also see the `deviance` option above.

`response` calculates the differences between the observed and fitted outcomes.

`score` calculates the scores used in calculating the sandwich estimate of variance. See the `score()` entry in the *Options* section above.

`working` calculates the working residuals, which are response residuals weighted according to the derivative of the link function.

`nooffset` is relevant only if you specified `offset(`*varname*`)` for `glm`. It modifies the calculations made by `predict` so that they ignore the offset variable; the linear prediction is treated as $\mathbf{x}_j\mathbf{b}$ rather than $\mathbf{x}_j\mathbf{b} + \text{offset}_j$.

`standardized` requests that the residual be multiplied by the factor $(1-h)^{-1/2}$, where h is the diagonal of the hat matrix. This is done to take the correlation between *depvar* and its predicted value into account.

`studentized` requests that the residual be multiplied by one over the square root of the estimated scale parameter.

`modified` requests that the denominator of the residual be modified to be a reasonable estimate of the variance of *depvar*. The base residual is multiplied by the factor $(k/w)^{-1/2}$, where k is either one or the user-specified dispersion parameter, and w is the specified weight (or one if left unspecified).

`adjusted` adjusts the deviance residual to speed up the convergence to the limiting normal distribution. The adjustment deals with adding to the deviance residual a higher-order term which depends on the variance function family. This option is only allowed when `deviance` is specified.

Remarks

Remarks are presented under the headings

> *General use*
> *Variance estimators*
> *User-defined functions*

General use

glm fits generalized linear models of y with covariates $\mathbf{x}$:

$$g\{E(y)\} = \mathbf{x}\boldsymbol{\beta}, \quad y \sim F$$

In the above, $g(\ )$ is called the link function and F the distributional family. Substituting various definitions for $g(\ )$ and F results in a surprising array of models. For instance, if y is distributed as Gaussian (normal) and $g(\ )$ is the identity function, we have

$$E(y) = \mathbf{x}\boldsymbol{\beta}, \quad y \sim \text{Normal}$$

or linear regression. If $g(\ )$ is the logit function and y is distributed as Bernoulli, we have

$$\text{logit}\{E(y)\} = \mathbf{x}\boldsymbol{\beta}, \quad y \sim \text{Bernoulli}$$

or logistic regression. If $g(\ )$ is the natural log function and y is distributed as Poisson, we have

$$\ln\{E(y)\} = \mathbf{x}\boldsymbol{\beta}, \quad y \sim \text{Poisson}$$

or Poisson regression, also known as the log-linear model. Other combinations are possible.

Although glm can be used to estimate linear regression (and, in fact, does so by default), this should be viewed as an instructional feature; regress produces such estimates more quickly, and numerous post-estimation commands are available to explore the adequacy of the fit; see [R] regress and [R] regression diagnostics.

In any case, you specify the link function using the link() option and the distributional family using family(). The allowed link functions are

Link function	glm option
identity	link(identity)
log	link(log)
logit	link(logit)
probit	link(probit)
complementary log-log	link(cloglog)
odds power	link(opower #)
power	link(power #)
negative binomial	link(nbinomial)
log-log	link(loglog)
log-compliment	link(logc)

Define $\mu = E(y)$ and $\eta = g(\mu)$, meaning that $g(\cdot)$ maps $E(y)$ to $\eta = \mathbf{x}\boldsymbol{\beta} + \text{offset}$.

Link function identity is defined as $\eta = g(\mu) = \mu$.

Link function log is defined as $\eta = \ln(\mu)$.

Link function logit is defined as $\eta = \ln\{\mu/(1-\mu)\}$, the natural log of the odds.

Link function probit is defined as $\eta = \Phi^{-1}(\mu)$, where $\Phi^{-1}(\ )$ is the inverse Gaussian cumulative.

Link function cloglog is defined as $\eta = \ln\{-\ln(1-\mu)\}$.

Link function opower is defined as $\eta = \left[\{\mu/(1-\mu)\}^n - 1\right]/n$, the power of the odds. The function is generalized so that link(opower 0) is equivalent to link(logit), the natural log of the odds.

Link function **power** is defined as $\eta = \mu^n$. Specifying **link(power 1)** is equivalent to specifying **link(identity)**. The power function is generalized so that $\mu^0 \equiv \ln(\mu)$. Thus, **link(power 0)** is equivalent to **link(log)**. Negative powers are, of course, allowed.

Link function **nbinomial** is defined as $\eta = \ln\{\mu/(\mu+k)\}$, where $k = 1$ if **family(nbinomial)** is specified and $k = \#_k$ if **family(nbinomial $\#_k$)** is specified.

Link function **loglog** is defined as $\eta = -\ln\{-\ln(\mu)\}$.

Link function **logc** is defined as $\eta = \ln(1 - \mu)$.

The allowed distributional families are

Family	glm option
Gaussian (normal)	family(gaussian)
inverse Gaussian	family(igaussian)
Bernoulli/binomial	family(binomial)
Poisson	family(poisson)
negative binomial	family(nbinomial)
gamma	family(gamma)

family(normal) is allowed as a synonym for **family(gaussian)**.

The binomial distribution can be specified as (1) **family(binomial)**, (2) **family(binomial $\#_N$)**, or (3) **family(binomial $varname_N$)**. In case 2, $\#_N$ is the value of the binomial denominator N, the number of trials. Specifying **family(binomial 1)** is the same as specifying **family(binomial)**; both mean that y has the Bernoulli distribution with values 0 and 1 only. In case 3, $varname_N$ is the variable containing the binomial denominator, allowing the number of trials to vary across observations.

The negative binomial distribution can be specified as (1) **family(nbinomial)** or (2) **family(nbinomial $\#_k$)**. Omitting $\#_k$ is equivalent to specifying **family(nbinomial 1)**. The value $\#_k$ enters the variance and deviance functions; typical values range between .01 and 2; see the technical note below.

You do not have to specify both **family()** and **link()**; the default **link()** is the canonical link for the specified **family()** (except for **nbinomial**):

Family	Default link
family(gaussian)	link(identity)
family(igaussian)	link(power -2)
family(binomial)	link(logit)
family(poisson)	link(log)
family(nbinomial)	link(log)
family(gamma)	link(power -1)

If you do specify both **family()** and **link()**, note that not all combinations make sense. You may choose from the following combinations:

	identity	log	logit	probit	cloglog	power	opower	nbinomial	loglog	logc
Gaussian	x	x				x				
inverse Gaussian	x	x				x				
binomial	x	x	x	x	x	x	x		x	x
Poisson	x	x				x				
negative binomial	x	x				x		x		
gamma	x	x				x				

❏ Technical Note

Some `family()` and `link()` combinations result in models already estimated by Stata. These are:

family()	link()	Options	Other Stata command
gaussian	identity	*nothing* │ irls │ irls oim	regress
gaussian	identity	t(*var*) nwest(nwest #) vfactor(#$_v$)	newey, t(*var*) lag(#) (see note 1)
binomial	cloglog	*nothing* │ irls oim	cloglog (see note 2)
binomial	probit	*nothing* │ irls oim	probit (see note 2)
binomial	logit	*nothing* │ irls │ irls oim	logit or logistic (see note 3)
poisson	log	*nothing* │ irls │ irls oim	poisson (see note 3)
nbinomial	log	*nothing* │ irls oim	nbreg (see note 4)
gamma	log	scale(1)	ereg (see note 5)

Notes:

1. The variance factor $\#_v$ should be set to $n/(n-k)$, where n is the number of observations and k the number of regressors. If not specified, the estimated standard errors will, as a result, differ by this factor.

2. In these cases, since the link is not the canonical link for the binomial family, one must specify the oim option if using irls to get equivalent standard errors. If irls is used without oim, then the regression coefficients will be the same but the standard errors only asymptotically equivalent. If no options are specified (*nothing*), glm will optimize using Newton–Raphson, making it equivalent to the other Stata command.

   See [R] **cloglog** and [R] **probit** for more details about these commands.

3. In these cases, since the canonical link is being used, the standard errors will be equivalent whether the EIM or the OIM estimator of variance is used.

4. Family negative binomial, log-link models—also known as negative binomial regression—are used for data with an overdispersed Poisson distribution. Although glm can be used to estimate such models, use of Stata's maximum-likelihood nbreg command is probably better. In the GLM approach, one specifies family(nbinomial $\#_k$) and then searches for a $\#_k$ that results in the deviance-based dispersion being 1. nbreg, on the other hand, finds the maximum likelihood estimate of $\#_k$ and reports a confidence interval for it; see [R] **nbreg** and Rogers (1993). Of course, glm allows links other than log, and for those links, including the canonical nbinomial link, you will need to use glm. Since the default link for family(nbinomial) is a noncanonical link, standard errors will be only asymptotically equivalent if glm, irls without the oim option is used.

5. glm can be used to estimate exponential regressions, but this requires specifying scale(1). However, censoring is not available with this method. Censored exponential regression may be modeled using glm with family(poisson). The log of the original response is entered into a Poisson model as an offset, while the new response is the censor variable. The result of such modeling is identical to the log relative hazard parameterization of ereg. See [R] **weibull** for details about the ereg command.

In general, where there is overlap between a capability of glm and that of some other Stata command, we recommend using the other Stata command. Our recommendation is not due to some inferiority of the GLM approach. Rather, it is that those other, more specialized commands, by being specialized, provide options and ancillary commands missing in the broader glm framework. Nevertheless, glm does produce the same answers where it should.

Special note. In cases where equivalence is expected, for some datasets one may still see very slight differences in the results, most often only in the latter digits of the standard errors. When comparing glm output to an "equivalent" Stata command, these tiny discrepancies arise for many reasons:

(1) glm uses a general methodology for starting values, while the equivalent Stata command may be more specialized in its treatment of starting values.

(2) When using a canonical link, glm, irls should be equivalent to the maximum likelihood method of the equivalent Stata command, yet the convergence criterion is different (one is in terms of deviance, the other in terms of log-likelihood). These discrepancies are easily resolved by adjusting one convergence criterion to correspond to the other.

(3) In cases where both glm and the equivalent Stata command are using Newton–Raphson, small differences may still occur if the Stata command has a different default convergence criterion than glm. Again, adjusting the convergence criterion will resolve the difference. See [R] **ml** and [R] **maximize** for more details.   ❑

▷ Example

In [R] **logistic**, we estimate a model based on data from a study of risk factors associated with low birth weight (Hosmer and Lemeshow 1989, appendix 1). We can reestimate the model using glm:

```
. xi: glm low age lwt i.race smoke ptl ht ui, f(bin) l(logit)
i.race           _Irace_1-3        (naturally coded; _Irace_1 omitted)

Iteration 0:   log likelihood =  -101.0213
Iteration 1:   log likelihood = -100.72519
Iteration 2:   log likelihood =   -100.724
Iteration 3:   log likelihood =   -100.724

Generalized linear models                    No. of obs      =        189
Optimization      : ML: Newton-Raphson       Residual df     =        180
                                             Scale param     =          1
Deviance          =   201.4479911            (1/df) Deviance =   1.119156
Pearson           =   182.0233425            (1/df) Pearson  =   1.011241

Variance function: V(u) = u*(1-u)            [Bernoulli]
Link function    : g(u) = ln(u/(1-u))        [Logit]
Standard errors  : OIM

Log likelihood    = -100.7239956             AIC             =     1.1611
BIC               =   154.272268
```

low	Coef.	Std. Err.	z	P>|z|	[95% Conf. Interval]	
age	-.0271003	.0364504	-0.74	0.457	-.0985418	.0443412
lwt	-.0151508	.0069259	-2.19	0.029	-.0287253	-.0015763
_Irace_2	1.262647	.5264101	2.40	0.016	.2309024	2.294392
_Irace_3	.8620792	.4391532	1.96	0.050	.0013548	1.722804
smoke	.9233448	.4008266	2.30	0.021	.137739	1.708951
ptl	.5418366	.346249	1.56	0.118	-.136799	1.220472
ht	1.832518	.6916292	2.65	0.008	.4769494	3.188086
ui	.7585135	.4593768	1.65	0.099	-.1418484	1.658875
_cons	.4612239	1.20459	0.38	0.702	-1.899729	2.822176

glm, by default, presents coefficient estimates, whereas logistic presents the exponentiated coefficients—the odds ratios. glm's eform option reports exponentiated coefficients and glm, like Stata's other estimation commands, replays results.

```
. glm, eform
Generalized linear models                      No. of obs      =        189
Optimization        : ML: Newton-Raphson        Residual df     =        180
                                                Scale param     =          1
Deviance          =   201.4479911               (1/df) Deviance =   1.119156
Pearson           =   182.0233425               (1/df) Pearson  =   1.011241

Variance function: V(u) = u*(1-u)               [Bernoulli]
Link function    : g(u) = ln(u/(1-u))           [Logit]
Standard errors  : OIM

Log likelihood    = -100.7239956                AIC             =     1.1611
BIC               =   154.272268
```

low	Odds Ratio	Std. Err.	z	P>|z|	[95% Conf. Interval]	
age	.9732636	.0354759	-0.74	0.457	.9061578	1.045339
lwt	.9849634	.0068217	-2.19	0.029	.9716834	.9984249
_Irace_2	3.534767	1.860737	2.40	0.016	1.259736	9.918406
_Irace_3	2.368079	1.039949	1.96	0.050	1.001356	5.600207
smoke	2.517698	1.00916	2.30	0.021	1.147676	5.523162
ptl	1.719161	.5952579	1.56	0.118	.8721455	3.388787
ht	6.249602	4.322408	2.65	0.008	1.611152	24.24199
ui	2.1351	.9808153	1.65	0.099	.8677528	5.2534

These results are the same as reported in [R] **logistic**.

Included in the output header are values for the Akaike (1973) information criterion (AIC) and the Bayesian information criterion (BIC) (Raftery 1996). Both are measures of model fit adjusted for the number of parameters that can be compared across models. In both cases, a smaller value generally indicates a better model fit. AIC is based on the log-likelihood, and thus is only available when Newton–Raphson optimization is employed. BIC is based on the deviance, and thus is always available.

◁

▷ Example

We use data from an early insecticide experiment, given in Pregibon (1980). The variables are ldose, the log dose of insecticide; n, the number of flour beetles subjected to each dose; and r, the number killed.

```
. list
        ldose          n          r
  1.   1.6907         59          6
  2.   1.7242         60         13
  3.   1.7552         62         18
  4.   1.7842         56         28
  5.   1.8113         63         52
  6.   1.8369         59         53
  7.    1.861         62         61
  8.   1.8839         60         60
```

The aim of the analysis is to estimate a dose–response relationship between p, the proportion killed, and X, the log dose.

As a first attempt, we will formulate the model as a linear logistic regression of p on ldose; that is, take the logit of p and represent the dose–response curve as a straight line in X:

$$\ln\{p/(1-p)\} = \beta_0 + \beta_1 X$$

Since the data are grouped, we cannot use Stata's `logistic` command to estimate the model. Stata does, however, already have a command for estimating a logistic regression on data organized in this way, so we could type

```
. blogit r n ldose
  (output omitted )
```

Instead, we will estimate the model using `glm`:

```
. glm r ldose, family(binomial n) link(logit)
Iteration 0:   log likelihood = -18.824848
Iteration 1:   log likelihood = -18.715271
Iteration 2:   log likelihood = -18.715123
Iteration 3:   log likelihood = -18.715123
```

Generalized linear models			No. of obs	=	8
Optimization	: ML: Newton-Raphson		Residual df	=	6
			Scale param	=	1
Deviance	=	11.23220702	(1/df) Deviance =		1.872035
Pearson	=	10.0267936	(1/df) Pearson =		1.671132
Variance function: V(u) = u*(1-u/n)			[Binomial]		
Link function : g(u) = ln(u/(n-u))			[Logit]		
Standard errors : OIM					
Log likelihood	=	-18.71512262	AIC	=	5.178781
BIC	=	7.073323933			

r	Coef.	Std. Err.	z	P>|z|	[95% Conf. Interval]
ldose	34.27034	2.912141	11.77	0.000	28.56265 39.97803
_cons	-60.71747	5.180713	-11.72	0.000	-70.87149 -50.56346

The only difference between `blogit` and `glm` in this case is how they went about obtaining the answer, although this difference is hidden from us. `blogit` secretly expands the data to contain 481 observations (the sum of n) so that it can run Stata's standard, individual-level logistic command. `glm`, on the other hand, uses the information on the binomial denominator directly. We specified `family(binomial n)`, meaning that variable n contains the denominator. Parameter estimates and standard errors from the two approaches do not differ.

An alternative model, which gives asymmetric sigmoid curves for p, involves the complementary log-log or cloglog function:

$$\ln\big\{-\ln(1-p)\big\} = \beta_0 + \beta_1 X$$

We estimate this model using `glm`:

```
. glm r ldose, family(binomial n) link(cloglog)
Iteration 0:   log likelihood = -14.883594
Iteration 1:   log likelihood = -14.822264
Iteration 2:   log likelihood = -14.822228
Iteration 3:   log likelihood = -14.822228
```

Generalized linear models			No. of obs	=	8
Optimization	: ML: Newton-Raphson		Residual df	=	6
			Scale param	=	1
Deviance	=	3.446418004	(1/df) Deviance =		.574403
Pearson	=	3.294675153	(1/df) Pearson =		.5491125
Variance function: V(u) = u*(1-u/n)			[Binomial]		
Link function : g(u) = ln(-ln(1-u/n))			[Complementary log-log]		
Standard errors : OIM					
Log likelihood	=	-14.82222811	AIC	=	4.205557
BIC	=	-.7124650789			
```
```

r	Coef.	Std. Err.	z	P>|z|	[95% Conf. Interval]	
ldose	22.04118	1.793089	12.29	0.000	18.52679	25.55557
_cons	-39.57232	3.229047	-12.26	0.000	-45.90114	-33.24351

The complementary log-log model is preferred; note that the deviance for the logistic model, 11.23, is much higher than the cloglog model is 3.45. This also is evident by comparing log-likelihoods, or equivalently, AIC values.

This example also shows the advantage of the glm command—one can vary assumptions easily. Note the minor difference in what we typed to obtain the logistic and cloglog models:

```
. glm r ldose, family(binomial n) link(logit)

. glm r ldose, family(binomial n) link(cloglog)
```

Were this not a manual and were we performing this work for ourselves, we would have typed the commands in a more abbreviated form:

```
. glm r ldose, f(b n) l(l)

. glm r ldose, f(b n) l(cl)
```

◁

▷ Example

After glm estimation, predict may be used to obtain various predictions based on the model. We mentioned in the previous example that the complementary log-log link seemed to fit the data better than the logit link. Below, we go back and obtain the fitted values and deviance residuals:

```
. quietly glm r ldose, f(binomial n) l(logit)

. predict mu_logit
(option mu assumed; predicted mean r)

. predict dr_logit, deviance

. quietly glm r ldose, f(binomial n) l(cloglog)

. predict mu_cl
(option mu assumed; predicted mean r)

. predict dr_cl, d

. format mu_logit dr_logit mu_cl dr_cl %9.5f

. list r mu_logit dr_logit mu_cl dr_cl
```

	r	mu_logit	dr_logit	mu_cl	dr_cl
1.	6	3.45746	1.28368	5.58945	0.18057
2.	13	9.84167	1.05969	11.28067	0.55773
3.	18	22.45139	-1.19611	20.95422	-0.80330
4.	28	33.89761	-1.59412	30.36942	-0.63439
5.	52	50.09584	0.60614	47.77644	1.28883
6.	53	53.29092	-0.12716	54.14273	-0.52366
7.	61	59.22216	1.25107	61.11331	-0.11878
8.	60	58.74297	1.59398	59.94723	0.32495

Note that in 6 out of the 8 cases, $|dr\_logit| > |dr\_cl|$. The above represents just the tip of the iceberg as far as available options for predict. See Hardin and Hilbe (2001) for a more in-depth examination.

◁

❏ Technical Note

Stata's xi command prefix may be used with glm. Let us pretend that in the above example, we had ldose, the log dose of insecticide; n, the number of flour beetles subjected to each dose; and r, the number killed—all as before—except now we have results for three different kinds of beetles. Our hypothetical data include beetle, which contains the values 1, 2, and 3.

```
. list

        beetle       ldose         n          r
 1.          1      1.6907        59          6
 2.          1      1.7242        60         13
 3.          1      1.7552        62         18
 4.          1      1.7842        56         28
 5.          1      1.8113        63         52
    (output omitted)
23.          3       1.861        64         23
24.          3      1.8839        58         22
```

Let us assume that, at first, we wish merely to add a shift factor for type of beetle. We could type

```
. xi: glm r i.beetle ldose, f(bin n) l(cloglog)
i.beetle          _Ibeetle_1-3        (naturally coded; _Ibeetle_1 omitted)

Iteration 0:   log likelihood = -79.012269
Iteration 1:   log likelihood =  -76.94951
Iteration 2:   log likelihood = -76.945645
Iteration 3:   log likelihood = -76.945645

Generalized linear models                No. of obs      =        24
Optimization      : ML: Newton-Raphson   Residual df     =        20
                                         Scale param     =         1
Deviance          =   73.76505595        (1/df) Deviance =  3.688253
Pearson           =    71.8901173        (1/df) Pearson  =  3.594506

Variance function: V(u) = u*(1-u/n)      [Binomial]
Link function     : g(u) = ln(-ln(1-u/n)) [Complementary log-log]
Standard errors   : OIM

Log likelihood    = -76.94564525         AIC             =   6.74547
BIC               =  61.05284063
```

r	Coef.	Std. Err.	z	P>|z|	[95% Conf. Interval]	
_Ibeetle_2	-.0910396	.1076132	-0.85	0.398	-.3019576	.1198783
_Ibeetle_3	-1.836058	.1307125	-14.05	0.000	-2.09225	-1.579867
ldose	19.41558	.9954265	19.50	0.000	17.46458	21.36658
_cons	-34.84602	1.79333	-19.43	0.000	-38.36089	-31.33116

We find strong evidence that the insecticide works differently on the third kind of beetle. We now check whether the curve is merely shifted or also differently sloped:

(Continued on next page)

```
. xi: glm r i.beetle*ldose, f(bin n) l(cloglog)
i.beetle          _Ibeetle_1-3        (naturally coded; _Ibeetle_1 omitted)
i.beetle*ldose    _IbeeXldose_#       (coded as above)
Iteration 0:     log likelihood = -67.270188
Iteration 1:     log likelihood = -65.149316
Iteration 2:     log likelihood = -65.147978
Iteration 3:     log likelihood = -65.147978
```

```
Generalized linear models                      No. of obs     =        24
Optimization        : ML: Newton-Raphson       Residual df    =        18
                                               Scale param    =         1
Deviance        =  50.16972096               (1/df) Deviance =  2.787207
Pearson         =  49.28422567               (1/df) Pearson  =  2.738013
Variance function: V(u) = u*(1-u/n)          [Binomial]
Link function    : g(u) = ln(-ln(1-u/n))     [Complementary log-log]
Standard errors  : OIM
Log likelihood   = -65.14797775               AIC            =  5.928998
BIC              =  31.10139798
```

r	Coef.	Std. Err.	z	P>|z|	[95% Conf. Interval]	
_Ibeetle_2	-.79933	4.470882	-0.18	0.858	-9.562098	7.963438
_Ibeetle_3	17.78741	4.586429	3.88	0.000	8.798172	26.77664
ldose	22.04118	1.793089	12.29	0.000	18.52679	25.55557
_IbeeXldos~2	.3838708	2.478477	0.15	0.877	-4.473855	5.241596
_IbeeXldos~3	-10.726	2.526412	-4.25	0.000	-15.67768	-5.774321
_cons	-39.57232	3.229047	-12.26	0.000	-45.90114	-33.24351

We find that the (complementary log-log) dose–response curve for the third kind of beetle has roughly half the slope of that for the first kind.

The results here are unimportant because the data are fictional. What is important is that xi can be combined with glm just as it can with any other Stata estimation command; see [R] **xi**. Also see [U] **28 Commands for dealing with categorical variables**; what is said there concerning linear regression is applicable to any GLM model.

❏

❏ Technical Note

After glm estimation you may perform any of the post-estimation commands you would perform after any other kind of estimation in Stata; see [U] **23 Estimation and post-estimation commands**. If, continuing with the previous example, you wanted to test the joint significance of all the interaction terms, you could type

```
. testparm _I*
 ( 1)  [r]_Ibeetle_2 = 0.0
 ( 2)  [r]_Ibeetle_3 = 0.0
 ( 3)  [r]_IbeeXldose_2 = 0.0
 ( 4)  [r]_IbeeXldose_3 = 0.0
          chi2(  4) =  249.69
        Prob > chi2 =    0.0000
```

If you wanted to print the variance–covariance matrix of the estimators, you would type correlate, _coef (to see it as a correlation matrix) or correlate, _coef cov (to see the covariances themselves).

If you use the linktest post-estimation command, do not forget to specify the family() and link() options on the linktest command; see [R] **linktest**.

❏

Variance estimators

glm offers a multitude of variance options (see *var_options* in the syntax diagram), and gives different flavors of standard errors when used in various combinations. We highlight some of them here, but for a full explanation see Hardin and Hilbe (2001).

▷ Example

Continuing with our flour beetle data, we rerun the most recently displayed model, this time requesting estimation via iterated reweighted least squares (IRLS).

```
. xi: glm r i.beetle*ldose, f(bin n) l(cloglog) ltol(1e-15) irls
i.beetle          _Ibeetle_1-3          (naturally coded; _Ibeetle_1 omitted)
i.beetle*ldose    _IbeeXldose_#         (coded as above)

Iteration 1 : deviance =    54.4141
Iteration 2 : deviance =    50.1942
Iteration 3 : deviance =    50.1697
  (output omitted )
Iteration 26 : deviance =    50.1697
Iteration 27 : deviance =    50.1697
Iteration 28 : deviance =    50.1697
```

Generalized linear models   No. of obs   =   24
Optimization   : MQL Fisher scoring   Residual df   =   18
                (IRLS EIM)   Scale param   =   1
Deviance   =   50.16972096   (1/df) Deviance =   2.787207
Pearson   =   49.28422567   (1/df) Pearson   =   2.738013

Variance Function: $V(u) = u*(1-u/n)$ [Binomial]
Link Function   : $g(u) = \ln(-\ln(1-u/n))$ [Complementary log-log]
Standard Errors   : EIM

BIC   =   31.10139798

r	Coef.	EIM Std. Err.	z	P>|z|	[95% Conf. Interval]	
_Ibeetle_2	-.79933	4.586649	-0.17	0.862	-9.788997	8.190337
_Ibeetle_3	17.78741	4.624834	3.85	0.000	8.7229	26.85192
ldose	22.04118	1.799356	12.25	0.000	18.5145	25.56785
_IbeeXldos~2	.3838708	2.544068	0.15	0.880	-4.602411	5.370152
_IbeeXldos~3	-10.726	2.548176	-4.21	0.000	-15.72033	-5.731665
_cons	-39.57232	3.240274	-12.21	0.000	-45.92314	-33.2215

Note our use of the ltol() option which, although unrelated to our discussion on variance estimation, was used so that the regression coefficients would match precisely those of the previous Newton–Raphson (NR) fit.

Since IRLS uses the expected information matrix (EIM) for optimization, the variance estimate is also based on EIM. If we want optimization via IRLS, yet the variance estimate based on OIM, we specify glm, irls oim:

(*Continued on next page*)

```
. xi: glm r i.beetle*ldose, f(b n) l(cl) ltol(1e-15) irls oim noheader nolog
i.beetle          _Ibeetle_1-3      (naturally coded; _Ibeetle_1 omitted)
i.beetle*ldose    _IbeeXldose_#     (coded as above)
```

r	Coef.	OIM Std. Err.	z	P>|z|	[95% Conf. Interval]	
_Ibeetle_2	-.79933	4.470882	-0.18	0.858	-9.562098	7.963438
_Ibeetle_3	17.78741	4.586429	3.88	0.000	8.798172	26.77664
ldose	22.04118	1.793089	12.29	0.000	18.52679	25.55557
_IbeeXldos~2	.3838708	2.478477	0.15	0.877	-4.473855	5.241596
_IbeeXldos~3	-10.726	2.526412	-4.25	0.000	-15.67768	-5.774321
_cons	-39.57232	3.229047	-12.26	0.000	-45.90114	-33.24351

which, except for the convergence path, is identical to NR. Since the cloglog link is not the canonical link for the binomial family, EIM and OIM produce different results. Both estimators, however, are asymptotically equivalent.

Going back to NR, we can also specify `robust` to get the Huber/White/Sandwich estimator of variance:

```
. xi: glm r i.beetle*ldose, f(b n) l(cl) robust noheader nolog
i.beetle          _Ibeetle_1-3      (naturally coded; _Ibeetle_1 omitted)
i.beetle*ldose    _IbeeXldose_#     (coded as above)
```

r	Coef.	Robust Std. Err.	z	P>|z|	[95% Conf. Interval]	
_Ibeetle_2	-.79933	5.733049	-0.14	0.889	-12.0359	10.43724
_Ibeetle_3	17.78741	5.158477	3.45	0.001	7.676977	27.89784
ldose	22.04118	.8998551	24.49	0.000	20.27749	23.80486
_IbeeXldos~2	.3838708	3.174427	0.12	0.904	-5.837892	6.605633
_IbeeXldos~3	-10.726	2.800606	-3.83	0.000	-16.21508	-5.236912
_cons	-39.57232	1.621306	-24.41	0.000	-42.75003	-36.39462

The Sandwich estimator gets its name due to the form of the calculation—it is the multiplication of three matrices, with the outer two matrices (the "bread") set to the OIM variance matrix. When `irls` is used along with `robust`, the EIM variance matrix is instead used as the bread, and the resulting variance is labeled "Semi-Robust" or "Semi-Huber".

```
. xi: glm r i.beetle*ldose, f(b n) l(cl) irls ltol(1e-15) robust noheader nolog
i.beetle          _Ibeetle_1-3      (naturally coded; _Ibeetle_1 omitted)
i.beetle*ldose    _IbeeXldose_#     (coded as above)
```

r	Coef.	Semi-Robust Std. Err.	z	P>|z|	[95% Conf. Interval]	
_Ibeetle_2	-.79933	6.288963	-0.13	0.899	-13.12547	11.52681
_Ibeetle_3	17.78741	5.255307	3.38	0.001	7.487194	28.08762
ldose	22.04118	.9061566	24.32	0.000	20.26514	23.81721
_IbeeXldos~2	.3838708	3.489723	0.11	0.912	-6.455861	7.223603
_IbeeXldos~3	-10.726	2.855897	-3.76	0.000	-16.32345	-5.128542
_cons	-39.57232	1.632544	-24.24	0.000	-42.77205	-36.3726

The outer product of the gradient (OPG) estimate of variance is one which avoids the calculation of second derivatives. It is equivalent to the "middle" part of the Sandwich estimate of variance, and can be specified by using `glm, opg`, regardless of whether NR or IRLS optimization is used.

```
. xi: glm r i.beetle*ldose, f(b n) l(cl) opg noheader nolog
i.beetle          _Ibeetle_1-3        (naturally coded; _Ibeetle_1 omitted)
i.beetle*ldose    _IbeeXldose_#       (coded as above)
```

r	Coef.	OPG Std. Err.	z	P>|z|	[95% Conf. Interval]	
_Ibeetle_2	-.79933	6.664045	-0.12	0.905	-13.86062	12.26196
_Ibeetle_3	17.78741	6.838505	2.60	0.009	4.384183	31.19063
ldose	22.04118	3.572983	6.17	0.000	15.03826	29.0441
_IbeeXldos~2	.3838708	3.700192	0.10	0.917	-6.868372	7.636114
_IbeeXldos~3	-10.726	3.796448	-2.83	0.005	-18.1669	-3.285097
_cons	-39.57232	6.433101	-6.15	0.000	-52.18097	-26.96368

The OPG estimate of variance is a component of the BHHH (Berndt, Hall, Hall, and Hausman 1974) optimization technique; however, this method of optimization is not available with glm, so only the variance estimation is affected when opg is specified.

◁

▷ Example

The Newey–West (1987) estimator of variance is a sandwich estimator with the "middle" of the sandwich modified to take into account possible autocorrelation between the observations. These estimators are a generalization of those given by the Stata command newey in the case of linear regression. See [R] newey for more details.

For example, consider the dataset given in [R] newey, which has time-series measurements on usr and idle. We want to estimate a linear regression with Newey–West standard errors.

```
. list
         usr      idle      time
 1.       0       100         1
 2.       0       100         2
 3.       0        97         3
 4.       1        98         4
 5.       2        94         5
 (output omitted)
29.       1        98        29
30.       1        98        30
```

By examining the *Methods and Formulas* section of [R] newey, we see that they multiply the variance estimate by a correction factor of $n/(n-k)$, where k is the number of regressors. glm, nwest() does not make this correction, so to get the same standard errors we must use the vfactor() option within glm to manually make the correction.

(Continued on next page)

```
. display 30/28
1.0714286

. glm usr idle, nwest(nwest 3) t(time) vfactor(1.0714286)

Iteration 0:    log likelihood = -71.743396

Generalized linear models                    No. of obs      =         30
Optimization      : ML: Newton-Raphson       Residual df     =         28
                                             Scale param     =   7.493297
Deviance          =    209.8123165           (1/df) Deviance =   7.493297
Pearson           =    209.8123165           (1/df) Pearson  =   7.493297

Variance function: V(u) = 1                  [Gaussian]
Link function    : g(u) = u                  [Identity]
Standard errors  : Weighted Sandwich (Newey-West)
                   Bartlett (Truncation lag 3) weights

Log likelihood    = -71.74339627             AIC             =   4.916226
BIC               =  203.0099217
```

usr	Coef.	Newey-West Std. Err.	z	P>|z|	[95% Conf. Interval]	
idle	-.2281501	.0690928	-3.30	0.001	-.3635694	-.0927307
_cons	23.13483	6.327033	3.66	0.000	10.73407	35.53558

This reproduces the results given in [R] **newey**. We may now generalize this to models other than simple linear regression, and to different kernel weights.

```
. glm usr idle, fam(gamma) link(log) nwest(gallant 3) t(time)

Iteration 0:    log likelihood =   -61.76593
Iteration 1:    log likelihood = -60.963233
Iteration 2:    log likelihood =  -60.95097
Iteration 3:    log likelihood = -60.950965

Generalized linear models                    No. of obs      =         30
Optimization      : ML: Newton-Raphson       Residual df     =         28
                                             Scale param     =    .431296
Deviance          =    9.908506707           (1/df) Deviance =   .3538752
Pearson           =    12.07628677           (1/df) Pearson  =    .431296

Variance function: V(u) = u^2                [Gamma]
Link function    : g(u) = ln(u)              [Log]
Standard errors  : Weighted Sandwich (Gallant)
                   Parzen (Truncation lag 3) weights

Log likelihood    = -60.95096484             AIC             =   4.196731
BIC               =  3.106111944
```

usr	Coef.	Newey-West Std. Err.	z	P>|z|	[95% Conf. Interval]	
idle	-.0796609	.0184647	-4.31	0.000	-.115851	-.0434708
_cons	7.771011	1.510198	5.15	0.000	4.811078	10.73094

glm also offers variance estimators based on the bootstrap (resampling your data with replacement) and the jackknife (re-estimating the model with each observation left out in succession). Also included is the one step jackknife estimate, which, instead of performing full re-estimation when each observation is left out, calculates a one-step NR estimate with the full data regression coefficients as starting values.

```
. glm usr idle, fam(gamma) link(log) bstrap brep(100) nodots
Iteration 0:    log likelihood =  -61.76593
Iteration 1:    log likelihood = -60.963233
Iteration 2:    log likelihood =  -60.95097
Iteration 3:    log likelihood = -60.950965
```

```
Generalized linear models                    No. of obs       =        30
Optimization        : ML: Newton-Raphson     Residual df      =        28
                                             Scale param      = .5980872
Deviance            =   9.908506707          (1/df) Deviance = .3538752
Pearson             =   12.07628677          (1/df) Pearson  =  .431296

Variance function: V(u) = u^2                [Gamma]
Link function    : g(u) = ln(u)              [Log]
Standard errors  : Bootstrap

Log likelihood     =  -60.95096484           AIC              = 4.196731
BIC                =   3.106111944
```

usr	Coef.	Bootstrap Std. Err.	z	P>|z|	[95% Conf. Interval]	
idle	-.0796609	.0165792	-4.80	0.000	-.1121555	-.0471663
_cons	7.771011	1.382203	5.62	0.000	5.061943	10.48008

◁

See Hardin and Hilbe (2001) for a full discussion of the variance options that go with glm, and, in particular, for how the different variance estimators are modified when cluster() is specified. Finally, not all variance options are supported with all types of weights. See help glm for a current table of the variance options that are supported with the different weights.

User-defined functions

glm may be called with a user-written link function, variance (family) function, Newey–West kernel weight function, or any combination of the three.

Syntax of link functions

```
program define progname
        version 7
        args todo eta mu return
        if `todo´ == -1 {
                /* Set global macros for output */
                global SGLM_lt " title for link function "
                global SGLM_lf " subtitle showing link definition "
                exit
        }
        if `todo´ == 0 {
                /* set  η=g(μ) */
                /* Intermediate calculations go here */
                generate double eta = ...
                exit
        }
        if `todo´ == 1 {
                /* set  μ=g⁻¹(η) */
                /* Intermediate calculations go here */
                generate double mu = ...
                exit
        }
```

```
                    if `todo' == 2 {
                            /* set return = ∂μ/∂η */
                            /* Intermediate calculations go here */
                            generate double return = ...
                            exit
                    }
                    if `todo' == 3 {
                            /* set return = ∂²μ/∂η² */
                            /* Intermediate calculations go here */
                            generate double return = ...
                            exit
                    }
                    display as error "Unknown call to glm link function"
                    exit 198
          end
```

Syntax of variance functions

```
program define progname
          version 7
          args todo eta mu return
          if `todo' == -1 {
                    /* Set global macros for output */
                    /* Also check that depvar is in proper range */
                    /* Note: For this call, eta contains indicator for whether each obs. is in est. sample */
                    global SGLM_vt " title for variance function "
                    global SGLM_vf " subtitle showing function definition "
                    global SGLM_mu " program to call to enforce boundary conditions on μ "
                    exit
          }
          if `todo' == 0 {
                    /* set η to initial value. */
                    /* Intermediate calculations go here */
                    generate double eta = ...
                    exit
          }
          if `todo' == 1 {
                    /* set return = V(μ) */
                    /* Intermediate calculations go here */
                    generate double return = ...
                    exit
          }
          if `todo' == 2 {
                    /* set return = ∂V(μ)/∂μ */
                    /* Intermediate calculations go here */
                    generate double return = ...
                    exit
          }
          if `todo' == 3 {
                    /* set return = squared deviance (per observation) */
                    /* Intermediate calculations go here */
                    generate double return = ...
                    exit
          }
          if `todo' == 4 {
                    /* set return = Anscombe residual */
                    /* Intermediate calculations go here */
                    generate double return = ...
                    exit
          }
```

```
            if `todo´ == 5 {
                    /* set return = log-likelihood */
                    /* Intermediate calculations go here */
                    generate double return = ...
                    exit
            }
            if `todo´ == 6 {
                    /* set return = adjustment for deviance residuals */
                    /* Intermediate calculations go here */
                    generate double return = ...
                    exit
            }
            display as error "Unknown call to glm variance function"
            exit 198
        end
```

Syntax of Newey–West kernel weight functions

```
program define progname, rclass
        version 7
        args G j
        /* G is the maximum lag */
        /* j is the current lag */
        /* Intermediate calculations go here */
        return scalar wt = computed weight
        return local setype "Newey-West"
        return local sewtype " name of kernel "
    end
```

Global macros available for user-written programs

Global macro	Description
SGLM_V	program name of variance (family) evaluator
SGLM_L	program name of link evaluator
SGLM_y	dependent variable name
SGLM_m	binomial denominator
SGLM_a	negative binomial k
SGLM_p	power if power() or opower() used, or an argument from a user-specified link function
SGLM_s1	indicator; set to one if scale equal to one
SGLM_ph	value of scale parameter

▷ Example

Suppose we wish to perform Poisson regression with a log link function. Although this is already possible with standard glm, we will write our own version for illustrative purposes.

Since we want a log link, $\eta = g(\mu) = \ln(\mu)$, and for a Poisson family the variance function is $V(\mu) = \mu$.

The Poisson density is given by

$$f(y_i) = \frac{e^{-\exp(\mu_i)} e^{\mu_i y_i}}{y_i!}$$

which results in a log-likelihood of

$$L = \sum_{i=1}^{n} \{-e^{\mu_i} + \mu_i y_i - \ln(y_i!)\}$$

The squared-deviance of the ith observation for the Poisson family is given by

$$d_i^2 = \begin{cases} 2\widehat{\mu}_i & \text{if } y_i = 0 \\ 2\{y_i \ln(y_i/\widehat{\mu}_i) - (y_i - \widehat{\mu}_i)\} & \text{otherwise} \end{cases}$$

We now have enough information to write our own Poisson-log `glm` module. We create the file `mylog.ado`, which contains

```
program define mylog
        version 7
        args todo eta mu return
        if `todo´ == -1 {
                global SGLM_lt "My Log"          /* Titles for output */
                global SGLM_lf "ln(u)"
                exit
        }
        if `todo´ == 0  {
                gen double `eta´ = ln(`mu´)      /*  η = ln(μ) */
                exit
        }
        if `todo´ == 1  {
                gen double `mu´ = exp(`eta´)     /*  μ = exp(η) */
                exit
        }
        if `todo´ == 2 {
                gen double `return´ = `mu´       /*  ∂μ/∂η = exp(η) = μ */
                exit
        }
        if `todo´ == 3 {
                gen double `return´ = `mu´       /*  ∂²μ/∂η² = exp(η) = μ */
                exit
        }
        di as error "Unknown call to glm link function"
        exit 198
end
```

and we create the file `mypois.ado`, which contains

```
program define mypois
        version 7
        args todo eta mu return
        if `todo´ == -1 {
                local y       "$SGLM_y"
                local touse "`eta´"              /* `eta´  marks estimation sample here */
                capture assert `y´>=0 if `touse´        /*  check range of y */
                if _rc {
                        di as error `"dependent variable `y´ has negative values"´
                        exit 499
                }
                global SGLM_vt "My Poisson"              /* Titles for Output */
                global SGLM_vf "u"
                global SGLM_mu "glim_mu 0 ."             /* see Note 1 */
                exit
        }
```

```
             if `todo' == 0 {                   /* Initialization of η; see Note 2 */
                     gen double `eta' = ln(`mu')
                     exit
             }
             if `todo' == 1 {
                     gen double `return' = `mu'                /* V(μ) = μ */
                     exit
             }
             if `todo' == 2 {                                  /* ∂ V(μ)/∂μ */
                     gen byte `return' = 1
                     exit
             }
             if `todo' == 3 {                   /* squared deviance, defined above */
                     local y "$SGLM_y"
                     if "`y'" == "" {
                             local y "`e(depvar)'"
                     }
                     gen double `return' = cond(`y'==0, 2*`mu', /*
                             */ 2*(`y'*ln(`y'/`mu')-(`y'-`mu')))
                     exit
             }
             if `todo' == 4 {                   /* Anscombe residual; see Note 3 */
                     local y "$SGLM_y"
                     if "`y'" == "" {
                             local y "`e(depvar)'"
                     }
                     gen double `return' = 1.5*(`y'^(2/3)-`mu'^(2/3)) / `mu'^(1/6)
                     exit
             }
             if `todo' == 5 {                   /* log-likelihood; see Note 4 */
                     local y "$SGLM_y"
                     if "`y'" == "" {
                             local y "`e(depvar)'"
                     }
                     gen double `return' = -`mu'+`y'*ln(`mu')-lngamma(`y'+1)
                     exit
             }
             if `todo' == 6 {                   /* adjustment to residual; see Note 5 */
                     gen double `return' = 1/(6*sqrt(`mu'))
                     exit
             }
             di as error "Unknown call to glm variance function"
             error 198
     end
```

Notes:

1. `glim_mu` is a Stata program that will, at each iteration, bring $\hat{\mu}$ back into its plausible range should it stray out of it. In this case, `glim_mu` is called with the arguments zero and missing, meaning that zero is the lower bound of $\hat{\mu}$ and there exists no upper bound—such is the case for Poisson models.

2. Here the initial value of η is easy, since we intend to fit this model with our user-defined log link. In general, however, the initialization may need to vary according to the link in order to obtain convergence. If this is the case, the global macro `SGLM_L` is used to determine which link is being utilized.

3. The Anscombe formula is given here because we know it. If we were not interested in Anscombe residuals, we could merely set `return'` to missing. Also, the local macro y is set either to `SGLM_y` if in current estimation, or to `e(depvar)` if this function is being accessed by `predict`.

4. If not interested in ML estimation we could leave out this code entirely and just leave an `exit` statement in its place. Similarly, if not interested in deviance or IRLS optimization, we can set `` `return´ `` in the deviance portion of the code (`` `todo´ ``==3) to missing.

5. This defines the term to be added to the predicted residuals if the option `adjusted` is specified. Again, if we are not interested we can set `` `return´ `` to missing.

We can now test our Poisson-log module by running it on the airline data presented in [R] **poisson**.

```
. list airline injuries n XYZowned

       airline    injuries         n    XYZowned
  1.         1          11    0.0950           1
  2.         2           7    0.1920           0
  3.         3           7    0.0750           0
  4.         4          19    0.2078           0
  5.         5           9    0.1382           0
  6.         6           4    0.0540           1
  7.         7           3    0.1292           0
  8.         8           1    0.0503           0
  9.         9           3    0.0629           1

. gen lnN=ln(n)

. glm injuries XYZowned lnN, fam(mypois) link(mylog) scale(1)

Iteration 0:    log likelihood = -22.557572
Iteration 1:    log likelihood = -22.332861
Iteration 2:    log likelihood = -22.332276
Iteration 3:    log likelihood = -22.332276
```

Generalized linear models		No. of obs	=	9
Optimization	: ML: Newton-Raphson	Residual df	=	6
		Scale param	=	1
Deviance	= 12.70432823	(1/df) Deviance	=	2.117388
Pearson	= 12.7695081	(1/df) Pearson	=	2.128251
Variance function: $V(u) = u$		[My Poisson]		
Link function	: $g(u) = \ln(u)$	[My Log]		
Standard errors	: OIM			
Log likelihood	= -22.33227605	AIC	=	5.629395
BIC	= 6.112654495			

injuries	Coef.	Std. Err.	z	P>|z|	[95% Conf. Interval]	
XYZowned	.6840668	.3895877	1.76	0.079	-.0795111	1.447645
lnN	1.424169	.3725155	3.82	0.000	.6940517	2.154286
_cons	4.863891	.7090501	6.86	0.000	3.474178	6.253603

(Standard errors scaled using dispersion equal to square root of 1)

These are precisely the results given in [R] **poisson**, and are those given had we run `glm, family(poisson) link(log)`. The only minor adjustment we needed to make was to specify the option `scale(1)`. Recall that if `scale()` is left unspecified, `glm` will assume `scale(1)` for discrete distributions, and `scale(x2)` for continuous ones. By default, `glm` will assume that any user-defined family is continuous, since it has no way of checking this. Thus, we needed to specify `scale(1)` since our model is discrete.

Since we were careful in defining the squared deviance, we could have estimated this model using IRLS. Since log is the canonical link for the Poisson family, we would not only get the same regression coefficients, but the same standard errors as well.

◁

▷ Example

Suppose now that we wish to use our log link (`mylog.ado`) with `glm`'s binomial family. This requires some modification since our current function is not equipped to deal with the binomial denominator, which the user is allowed to specify. This denominator is accessible to our link function through the global macro SGLM_m. We now make the modifications and store them in `mylog2.ado`.

```
program define mylog2                                    /* <-- changed */
        version 7
        args todo eta mu return
        if `todo´ == -1 {
                global SGLM_lt "My Log, Version 2"       /* <-- changed */
                if "$SGLM_m" == "1" {                    /* <-- changed */
                        global SGLM_lf "ln(u)"           /* <-- changed */
                }                                        /* <-- changed */
                else     global SGLM_lf "ln(u/$SGLM_m)"  /* <-- changed */
                exit
        }
        if `todo´ == 0  {
                gen double `eta´ = ln(`mu´/$SGLM_m)      /* <-- changed */
                exit
        }
        if `todo´ == 1  {
                gen double `mu´ = $SGLM_m*exp(`eta´)     /* <-- changed */
                exit
        }
        if `todo´ == 2 {
                gen double `return´ = `mu´
                exit
        }
        if `todo´ == 3 {
                gen double `return´ = `mu´
                exit
        }
        noi di "{error: Unknown call to glm link function}"
        exit 198
end
```

We can now run our new log link with `glm`'s binomial family. Using the flour beetle data from earlier, we have

(Continued on next page)

```
. glm r ldose, fam(bin n) link(mylog2) irls
Iteration 1 : deviance =  85.1110
Iteration 2 : deviance =  52.1471
Iteration 3 : deviance =  51.0186
Iteration 4 : deviance =  51.0072
Iteration 5 : deviance =  51.0072
Iteration 6 : deviance =  51.0072
```

```
Generalized linear models                    No. of obs      =          8
Optimization      : MQL Fisher scoring       Residual df     =          6
                    (IRLS EIM)                Scale param     =          1
Deviance          =   51.00716029            (1/df) Deviance =   8.501193
Pearson           =   42.07549795            (1/df) Pearson  =   7.012583

Variance function: V(u) = u*(1-u/n)          [Binomial]
Link function     : g(u) = ln(u/n)           [My Log, Version 2]
Standard errors   : EIM

BIC               =   46.8482772
```

r	Coef.	EIM Std. Err.	z	P>|z|	[95% Conf. Interval]
ldose	7.175578	.50964	14.08	0.000	6.176702	8.174454
_cons	-13.4936	.9601108	-14.05	0.000	-15.37538	-11.61182

◁

For a more detailed discussion on user-defined functions, and for an example of a user-defined
Newey–West kernel weight, see Hardin and Hilbe (2001).

(*Continued on next page*)

Saved Results

glm saves in e():

Scalars

e(N)	number of observations	e(deviance)	deviance
e(k)	number of parameters	e(deviance_p)	Pearson deviance
e(df)	residual degrees of freedom	e(dispers)	dispersion
e(rc)	return code	e(dispers_p)	Pearson dispersion
e(phi)	scale parameter	e(deviance_s)	scaled deviance
e(disp)	dispersion parameter	e(dispers_s)	scaled dispersion
e(df_m)	model degrees of freedom	e(deviance_ps)	scaled Pearson deviance
e(aic)	model AIC	e(dispers_ps)	scaled Pearson dispersion
e(bic)	model BIC	e(vf)	factor set by vfactor(),
e(ll)	log-likelihood, if NR		1 if not set
e(N_clust)	number of clusters	e(N_brep)	number of bootstrap replications
e(power)	power set by power(), opower()		

Macros

e(cmd)	glm	e(wtype)	weight type
e(depvar)	name of dependent variable	e(wexp)	weight expression
e(varfunc)	name of variance function used	e(offset)	offset
e(link)	name of link function used	e(predict)	program used to implement
e(m)	number of binomial trials		predict
e(a)	neg. binomial k	e(clustvar)	cluster variable
e(oim)	set to oim if OIM used	e(cons)	set if noconstant specified
e(se1)	std. error header, line 1	e(opt)	optimization title, line 1
e(se2)	std. error header, line 2	e(opt2)	optimization title, line 2
e(vart)	variance title	e(linkt)	link title
e(varf)	variance form	e(linkf)	link form

Matrices

e(b)	coefficient vector	e(V)	variance–covariance matrix of
e(ilog)	iteration log (up to 20 iterations)		the estimators

Functions

e(sample)	marks estimation sample

Acknowledgments

glm was written by James Hardin and Joseph Hilbe. The previous version of this routine was written by Patrick Royston of the MRC Clinical Trials Unit, London. The original version of this routine was published in Royston (1994). Royston's work, in turn, was based on a prior implementation by Joseph Hilbe, first published in Hilbe (1993). Roger Newson wrote an early implementation (Newson 1999) of robust variance estimates for GLM. Parts of this entry are excerpts from Hardin and Hilbe (2001).

Methods and Formulas

glm is implemented as an ado-file.

The canonical reference on GLM is McCullagh and Nelder (1989). The term "generalized linear model" is from Nelder and Wedderburn (1972), and many people use the acronym GLIM for GLM models. This usage is due to the classic GLM software tool GLIM by Baker and Nelder (1985). See Rabe-Hesketh and Everitt (2000) for additional examples of GLM using Stata.

This discussion highlights the details of parameter estimation and predicted statistics. For a more detailed treatment, and for information on variance estimation, see Hardin and Hilbe (2001).

glm obtains results by iteratively reweighted least squares (IRLS) as described in McCullagh and Nelder (1989), or by maximum-likelihood using Newton–Raphson. The implementation here, however, allows user-specified weights, which we denote v_j for the jth observation. Let M be the number of "observations" ignoring weights. Define

$$w_j = \begin{cases} 1 & \text{if no weights are specified} \\ v_j & \text{if fweights or iweights are specified} \\ Mv_j/(\sum_k v_k) & \text{if aweights or pweights are specified} \end{cases}$$

The number of observations is then $N = \sum_j w_j$ if fweights are specified and $N = M$ otherwise. Each IRLS step is performed by regress using w_j as the weights.

Let d_j^2 denote the squared deviance residual for the jth observation:

For the Gaussian family, $d_j^2 = (y_j - \widehat{\mu}_j)^2$.

For the Bernoulli family (binomial with denominator 1),

$$d_j^2 = \begin{cases} -2\ln(1 - \widehat{\mu}_j) & \text{if } y_j = 0 \\ -2\ln(\widehat{\mu}_j) & \text{otherwise} \end{cases}$$

For the Binomial family with denominator m_j,

$$d_j^2 = \begin{cases} 2y_j\ln(y_j/\widehat{\mu}_j) + 2(m_j - y_j)\ln\{(m_j - y_j)/(m_j - \widehat{\mu}_j)\} & \text{if } 0 < y_j < m_j \\ 2m_j\ln\{m_j/(m_j - \widehat{\mu}_j)\} & \text{if } y_j = 0 \\ 2y_j\ln(y_j/\widehat{\mu}_j) & \text{if } y_j = m_j \end{cases}$$

For the Poisson family,

$$d_j^2 = \begin{cases} 2\widehat{\mu}_j & \text{if } y_j = 0 \\ 2\{y_j\ln(y_j/\widehat{\mu}_j) - (y_j - \widehat{\mu}_j)\} & \text{otherwise} \end{cases}$$

For the gamma family, $d_j^2 = -2\{\ln(y_j/\widehat{\mu}_j) - (y_j - \widehat{\mu}_j)/\widehat{\mu}_j\}$.

For the inverse Gaussian, $d_j^2 = (y_j - \widehat{\mu}_j)^2/(\widehat{\mu}_j^2 y_j)$.

For the negative binomial,

$$d_j^2 = \begin{cases} 2\ln(1 + k\widehat{\mu}_j)/k & \text{if } y_j = 0 \\ 2y_j\ln(y_j/\widehat{\mu}_j) - 2\{(1 + ky_j)/k\}\ln\{(1 + ky_j)/(1 + k\widehat{\mu}_j)\} & \text{otherwise} \end{cases}$$

Let $\phi = 1$ if the scale parameter is set to one; otherwise, define $\phi = \widehat{\phi}_0(n - k)/n$, where $\widehat{\phi}_0$ is the estimated scale parameter and k is the number of covariates in the model (including intercept).

L_j = the log-likelihood for the jth observation is

For the Gaussian family,

$$L_j = -\frac{1}{2}\left[\left\{\frac{(y_j - \widehat{\mu}_j)^2}{\phi}\right\} + \ln(2\pi\phi)\right]$$

For the Binomial family with denominator m_j (Bernoulli if all $m_j = 1$),

$$L_j = \phi \times \begin{cases} \ln\{\Gamma(m_j + 1)\} - \ln\{\Gamma(y_j + 1)\} + \ln\{\Gamma(m_j - y_j + 1)\} & \text{if } 0 < y_j < m_j \\ \quad +(m_j - y_j)\ln(1 - \widehat{\mu}_j/m_j) + y_j \ln(\widehat{\mu}_j/m_j) & \\ m_j \ln(1 - \widehat{\mu}_j/m_j) & \text{if } y_j = 0 \\ m_j \ln(\widehat{\mu}_j/m_j) & \text{if } y_j = m_j \end{cases}$$

For the Poisson family,

$$L_j = \phi \left[y_j \ln(\widehat{\mu}_j) - \widehat{\mu}_j - \ln\{\Gamma(y_j + 1)\} \right]$$

For the gamma family, $L_j = -y_j/\widehat{\mu}_j + \ln(1/\widehat{\mu}_j)$.

For the inverse Gaussian,

$$L_j = -\frac{1}{2}\left\{ \frac{(y_j - \widehat{\mu}_j)^2}{y_j \widehat{\mu}_j^2} + 3\ln(y_j) + \ln(2\pi) \right\}$$

For the negative binomial (let $m = 1/k$),

$$L_j = \phi \left[\ln\{\Gamma(m + y_j)\} - \ln\{\Gamma(y_j + 1)\} - \ln\{\Gamma(m)\} \right.$$
$$\left. - m\ln(1 + \widehat{\mu}_j/m) + y_j \ln\{\widehat{\mu}_j/(\widehat{\mu}_j + m)\} \right]$$

The deviance residual calculated by `predict` following `glm` is $d_j = \text{sign}(y_j - \widehat{\mu}_j)\sqrt{d_j^2}$. The overall deviance reported by `glm` is $D^2 = \sum_j w_j d_j^2$. The dispersion of the deviance is D^2 divided by residual degrees of freedom.

Define the Pearson residual calculated by `predict` following `glm` as

$$r_j = \frac{y_j - \widehat{\mu}_j}{\sqrt{V(\widehat{\mu}_j)}}$$

where $V(\widehat{\mu}_j)$ is the family-specific variance function.

$$V(\widehat{\mu}_j) = \begin{cases} \widehat{\mu}_j(1 - \widehat{\mu}_j/m_j) & \text{if binomial or Bernoulli } (m_j = 1) \\ \widehat{\mu}_j^2 & \text{if gamma} \\ 1 & \text{if Gaussian} \\ \widehat{\mu}_j^3 & \text{if inverse Gaussian} \\ \widehat{\mu}_j + k\widehat{\mu}_j^2 & \text{if negative binomial} \\ \widehat{\mu}_j & \text{if Poisson} \end{cases}$$

The Pearson deviance reported by `glm` is $\sum_j w_j r_j^2$. The corresponding Pearson dispersion is the Pearson deviance divided by the residual degrees of freedom. `glm` also calculates the scaled versions of all these quantities by dividing by the estimated scale parameter.

The response residuals are given by $r_i^R = y_i - \mu_i$. The working residuals are

$$r_i^W = (y_i - \widehat{\mu}_i)\left(\frac{\partial \eta}{\partial \mu}\right)_i$$

and the score residuals are

$$r_i^S = \frac{y_i - \widehat{\mu}_i}{V(\widehat{\mu}_i)} \left(\frac{\partial \eta}{\partial \mu}\right)_i^{-1}$$

Define $\widehat{W} = V(\widehat{\mu})$ and X to be the covariate matrix. h_i, then, is the ith diagonal of the hat matrix given by

$$\widehat{H} = \widehat{W}^{1/2} X (X^T \widehat{W} X)^{-1} X^T \widehat{W}^{1/2}$$

As a result, the likelihood residuals are given by

$$r_i^L = \text{sign}(y_i - \widehat{\mu}_i) \left\{ h_i (r_i')^2 + (1 - h_i)(d_i')^2 \right\}^{1/2}$$

where r_i' and d_i' are the standardized pearson and standardized deviance residuals, respectively. Anscombe residuals are given by

$$r_i^A = \frac{A(y_i) - A(\widehat{\mu}_i)}{A'(\widehat{\mu}_i)\{V(\widehat{\mu}_i)\}^{1/2}}$$

where

$$A(\cdot) = \int \frac{d\mu}{V^{1/3}(\mu)}$$

Deviance residuals may be adjusted (`predict, adjusted`) to make the following correction:

$$d_i^a = d_i + \frac{1}{6}\rho_3(\theta)$$

where $\rho_3(\theta)$ is a family-specific correction. See Hardin and Hilbe (2001) for the exact forms of $\rho_3(\theta)$ for each family.

References

Akaike, H. 1973. Information theory and an extension of the maximum likelihood principle. In *Second international symposium on information theory*, ed. B. N. Petrov and F. Csaki, 267–281. Budapest: Akademiai Kiado.

Anscombe, F. J. 1972. Contribution to the discussion of H. Hotelling's paper. *Journal of the Royal Statistical Society*, Series B 15(1): 229–230.

Baker, R. J. and J. A. Nelder. 1985. *The Generalized Linear Interactive Modelling System, release 3.77*. Oxford: Numerical Algorithms Group.

Berndt, E. K., B. H. Hall, R. E. Hall, and J. A. Hausman. 1974. Estimation and inference in nonlinear structural models. *Annals of Economic and Social Measurement* 3/4: 653–665.

Hardin, J. W. and J. Hilbe. 2001. *Generalized Linear Models and Extensions*. College Station, TX: Stata Press.

Hilbe, J. 1993. sg16: Generalized linear models. *Stata Technical Bulletin* 11: 20–28. Reprinted in *Stata Technical Bulletin Reprints*, vol. 2, pp. 149–159.

——. 2000. sg126: Two-parameter log-gamma and log-inverse Gaussian models. *Stata Technical Bulletin* 53: 31–32. Reprinted in *Stata Technical Bulletin Reprints*, vol. 9, pp. 273–275.

Hosmer, D. W., Jr., and S. Lemeshow. 1989. *Applied Logistic Regression*. New York: John Wiley & Sons. (*Second edition forthcoming in 2001.*)

McCullagh, P. and J. A. Nelder. 1989. *Generalized Linear Models*. 2d ed. London: Chapman & Hall.

Nelder, J. A. and R. W. M. Wedderburn. 1972. Generalized linear models. *Journal of the Royal Statistical Society, Series A*, 135: 370–384.

Newey, W. K. and K. D. West. 1987. A simple, positive semi-definite, heteroskedasticity and autocorrelation consistent covariance matrix. *Econometrica* 55: 703–708.

Newson, R. 1999. sg114: rglm—Robust variance estimates for generalized linear models. *Stata Technical Bulletin* 50: 27–33. Reprinted in *Stata Technical Bulletin Reprints*, vol. 9, pp. 181–190.

Pregibon, D. 1980. Goodness of link tests for generalized linear models. *Applied Statistics* 29: 15–24.

Rabe-Hesketh, S. and B. Everitt. 2000. *A Handbook of Statistical Analysis using Stata*. 2d ed. Boca Raton, FL: Chapman & Hall/CRC.

Rabe-Hesketh, S., A. Pickles, and C. Taylor. 2000. sg129: Generalized linear latent and mixed models. *Stata Technical Bulletin* 53: 47–57. Reprinted in *Stata Technical Bulletin Reprints*, vol. 9, pp. 293–307.

Raftery, A. 1996. Bayesian model selection in social research. In *Sociological Methodology*, vol. 25, ed. P. V. Marsden, 111–163. Oxford: Basil Blackwell.

Rogers, W. H. 1993. sg16.4: Comparison of nbreg and glm for negative binomial. *Stata Technical Bulletin* 16: 7. Reprinted in *Stata Technical Bulletin Reprints*, vol. 3, pp. 82–84.

Royston, P. 1994. sg22: Generalized linear models: revision of glm. *Stata Technical Bulletin* 18: 6–11. Reprinted in *Stata Technical Bulletin Reprints*, vol. 3, pp. 112–121.

Also See

Complementary:	[R] **adjust**, [R] **lincom**, [R] **linktest**, [R] **mfx**, [R] **predict**, [R] **sw**, [R] **test**, [R] **testnl**, [R] **vce**, [R] **xi**
Related:	[R] **cloglog**, [R] **logistic**, [R] **nbreg**, [R] **poisson**, [R] **regress**, [R] **regression diagnostics**, [R] **st streg**, [R] **weibull**, [R] **xtgee**
Background:	[U] **16.5 Accessing coefficients and standard errors**, [U] **23 Estimation and post-estimation commands**, [U] **23.11 Obtaining robust variance estimates**, [U] **23.12 Obtaining scores**

Title

> **glogit** — Logit and probit on grouped data

Syntax

> **blogit** *pos_var pop_var* $\begin{bmatrix} rhsvars \end{bmatrix}$ $\begin{bmatrix} \text{if } exp \end{bmatrix}$ $\begin{bmatrix} \text{in } range \end{bmatrix}$ $\begin{bmatrix} , logit\_options \end{bmatrix}$

> **bprobit** *pos_var pop_var* $\begin{bmatrix} rhsvars \end{bmatrix}$ $\begin{bmatrix} \text{if } exp \end{bmatrix}$ $\begin{bmatrix} \text{in } range \end{bmatrix}$ $\begin{bmatrix} , probit\_options \end{bmatrix}$

> **glogit** *pos_var pop_var* $\begin{bmatrix} rhsvars \end{bmatrix}$ $\begin{bmatrix} \text{if } exp \end{bmatrix}$ $\begin{bmatrix} \text{in } range \end{bmatrix}$ $\begin{bmatrix} , \underline{\text{level}}(\#) \text{ or} \end{bmatrix}$

> **gprobit** *pos_var pop_var* $\begin{bmatrix} rhsvars \end{bmatrix}$ $\begin{bmatrix} \text{if } exp \end{bmatrix}$ $\begin{bmatrix} \text{in } range \end{bmatrix}$ $\begin{bmatrix} , \underline{\text{level}}(\#) \end{bmatrix}$

by ... : may be used with these commands; see [R] **by**.

These commands share the features of all estimation commands; see [U] **23 Estimation and post-estimation commands**.

Syntax for predict

> **predict** $\begin{bmatrix} type \end{bmatrix}$ *newvarname* $\begin{bmatrix} \text{if } exp \end{bmatrix}$ $\begin{bmatrix} \text{in } range \end{bmatrix}$ $\begin{bmatrix} , \{ \text{ n } | \text{ p } | \text{ xb } | \text{ stdp } \} \end{bmatrix}$

These statistics are available both in and out of sample; type predict ... if e(sample) ... if wanted only for the estimation sample.

Description

blogit and **bprobit** produce maximum-likelihood logit and probit estimates on grouped ("blocked") data; **glogit** and **gprobit** produce weighted least squares estimates. In the syntax diagrams above, *pos_var* and *pop_var* refer to variables containing the total number of positive responses and the total population.

The **score** option should be used with caution as only the scores for the "failure" observations will be created. If you need the scores, you should transform the data so that you can use **probit** or **logit**.

See [R] **logistic** for a list of related estimation commands.

Options

logit_options refers to the options allowed by the **logit** command; see [R] **logit**. Most importantly, these include **level()** and **or**; see below.

probit_options refers to the options allowed by the **probit** command; see [R] **probit**. Most importantly, this includes **level()**.

level(#) specifies the confidence level, in percent, for confidence intervals. The default is **level(95)** or as set by **set level**; see [U] **23.5 Specifying the width of confidence intervals**.

or reports the estimated coefficients transformed to odds ratios, i.e., e^b rather than b. Standard errors and confidence intervals are similarly transformed. This option affects how results are displayed and not how they are estimated. **or** may be specified at estimation or when replaying previously estimated results.

Options for predict

n, which is the default, calculates the expected count; that is, the estimated probability times *pop_var*.

p calculates the predicted probability.

xb calculates the linear prediction.

stdp calculates the standard error of the linear prediction.

Remarks

Maximum likelihood estimates

blogit produces the same results as logit and logistic, bprobit as probit, but the "blocked" commands accept data in slightly different "shape". Consider the following two datasets:

```
. use xmpl1, clear
. list
        agecat    exposed    died      pop
   1.      0         0         0        115
   2.      0         0         1          5
   3.      0         1         0         98
   4.      0         1         1          8
   5.      1         0         0         69
   6.      1         0         1         16
   7.      1         1         0         76
   8.      1         1         1         22

. use xmpl2, clear
. list
        agecat    exposed    deaths     pop
   1.      0         0         5        120
   2.      0         1         8        106
   3.      1         0        16         85
   4.      1         1        22         98
```

These two datasets contain the same information; observations 1 and 2 of xmpl correspond to observation 1 of xmpl2; observations 3 and 4 of xmpl1 correspond to observation 2 of xmpl2; and so on.

The first observation of xmpl1 says that, for agecat==0 and exposed==0, 115 subjects did not die (died==0). The second observation says that, for the same agecat and exposed groups, 5 subjects did die (died==1). In xmpl2, the first observation says that there were 5 deaths out of a population of 120 in agecat==0 and exposed==0. These are two different ways of saying the same thing. Both of these datasets are transcriptions from the following table, reprinted in Rothman and Greenland (1998, 255), for age-specific deaths from all causes for tolbutamide and placebo treatment groups (University Group Diabetes Program 1970):

	Age through 54		Age 55 and above	
	Tolbutamide	Placebo	Tolbutamide	Placebo
Dead	8	5	22	16
Surviving	98	115	76	79

The data in xmpl1 are said to be "fully relational", which is computer jargon meaning that each observation corresponds to one cell of the table. Stata typically prefers data in this format. The second form of storing these data in xmpl2 is said to be "folded", which is computer jargon for something less than fully relational.

blogit and bprobit deal with "folded" data and produce the same results that logit and probit would had the data been stored in its "fully relational" representation.

▷ Example

For the tolbutamide data, the fully relational representation would have been preferred. You could then use logistic, logit, and any of the epidemiological table commands; see [R] **logistic**, [R] **logit**, and [R] **epitab**. Nevertheless, there are occasions when the folded representation seems more natural. With blogit and bprobit, you avoid the tedium of having to unfold the data:

```
. use xmpl2, clear

. blogit deaths pop agecat exposed, or
```

Logit estimates

		Number of obs	=	409
		LR chi2(2)	=	22.47
		Prob > chi2	=	0.0000
Log likelihood = −142.6212		Pseudo R2	=	0.0730

_outcome	Odds Ratio	Std. Err.	z	P>|z|	[95% Conf. Interval]
agecat	4.216299	1.431519	4.24	0.000	2.167361	8.202223
exposed	1.404674	.4374454	1.09	0.275	.7629451	2.586175

Had we not specified the or option, results would have been presented as coefficients instead of as odds ratios. The estimated odds ratio of death for tolbutamide exposure is 1.40, although the 95% confidence interval includes 1. (By comparison, these data, in fully relational form, analyzed using the cs command (see [R] **epitab**) produce a Mantel–Haenszel weighted odds ratio of 1.40 with a 95% confidence interval of 0.76 to 2.58.)

We can see the underlying coefficients by replaying the estimation results and not specifying the or option:

```
. blogit
```

Logit estimates

		Number of obs	=	409
		LR chi2(2)	=	22.47
		Prob > chi2	=	0.0000
Log likelihood = −142.6212		Pseudo R2	=	0.0730

_outcome	Coef.	Std. Err.	z	P>|z|	[95% Conf. Interval]
agecat	1.438958	.3395203	4.24	0.000	.7735101	2.104405
exposed	.3398053	.3114213	1.09	0.275	−.2705692	.9501798
_cons	−2.968471	.33234	−8.93	0.000	−3.619846	−2.317097

◁

(*Continued on next page*)

▷ Example

bprobit works like blogit, substituting the probit for the logit-likelihood function.

. bprobit deaths pop agecat exposed

```
Probit estimates                          Number of obs   =       409
                                          LR chi2(2)      =     22.58
                                          Prob > chi2     =    0.0000
Log likelihood = -142.56478               Pseudo R2       =    0.0734
```

_outcome	Coef.	Std. Err.	z	P>|z|	[95% Conf. Interval]	
agecat	.7542049	.170969	4.41	0.000	.4191118	1.089298
exposed	.1906236	.1666057	1.14	0.253	-.1359176	.5171649
_cons	-1.673973	.1619592	-10.34	0.000	-1.991407	-1.356539

◁

Weighted least squares estimates

▷ Example

You have state data for the United States on the number of marriages (marriage), the total population aged 18 years or more (pop18p), and the median age (medage). The dataset excludes Nevada, and so has 49 observations. You create a new variable called medage2 equal to age squared by typing generate medage2=medage^2 and now wish to estimate a logit equation for the marriage rate:

. glogit marriage pop18p medage medage2

Weighted least squares logit estimates for grouped data

Source	SS	df	MS		Number of obs =	49
					F(2, 46) =	12.05
Model	.743083752	2	.371541876		Prob > F =	0.0001
Residual	1.4185293	46	.030837593		R-squared =	0.3438
					Adj R-squared =	0.3152
Total	2.16161305	48	.045033605		Root MSE =	.17561

Logit	Coef.	Std. Err.	t	P>|t|	[95% Conf. Interval]	
medage	-.7581404	.2964699	-2.56	0.014	-1.354903	-.1613775
medage2	.0113728	.0048501	2.34	0.023	.00161	.0211356
_cons	8.243371	4.525708	1.82	0.075	-.8664068	17.35315

◁

▷ Example

You could just as easily have estimated a grouped-probit model by typing gprobit rather than glogit:

. gprobit marriage pop18p medage medage2

Weighted least squares probit estimates for grouped data

Source	SS	df	MS		
Model	.111811933	2	.055905966	Number of obs =	49
Residual	.208841125	46	.004540024	F(2, 46) =	12.31
				Prob > F =	0.0001
				R-squared =	0.3487
Total	.320653058	48	.006680272	Adj R-squared =	0.3204
				Root MSE =	.06738

Probit	Coef.	Std. Err.	t	P>|t|	[95% Conf. Interval]	
medage	-.3075055	.1156941	-2.66	0.011	-.5403857	-.0746254
medage2	.0046296	.0018912	2.45	0.018	.0008228	.0084364
_cons	2.854722	1.767525	1.62	0.113	-.7031222	6.412565

◁

Saved Results

blogit and bprobit save in e():

Scalars

e(N)	number of observations	e(ll)	log likelihood
e(df_m)	model degrees of freedom	e(ll_0)	log likelihood, constant-only model
e(r2_p)	pseudo R-squared	e(chi2)	χ^2

Macros

e(cmd)	blogit or bprobit	e(offset)	offset
e(depvar)	name of dependent variable	e(predict)	program used to implement predict
e(chi2type)	Wald or LR; type of model χ^2 test		

Matrices

e(b)	coefficient vector	e(V)	variance–covariance matrix of the estimators

Functions

e(sample)	marks estimation sample

glogit and gprobit save in e():

Scalars

e(N)	number of observations	e(r2)	R-squared
e(mss)	model sum of squares	e(r2_a)	adjusted R-squared
e(df_m)	model degrees of freedom	e(F)	F statistic
e(rss)	residual sum of squares	e(rmse)	root mean square error
e(df_r)	residual degrees of freedom		

Macros

e(cmd)	glogit or gprobit	e(predict)	program used to implement predict
e(depvar)	name of dependent variable		

Matrices

e(b)	coefficient vector	e(V)	variance–covariance matrix of the estimators

Functions

e(sample)	marks estimation sample

Methods and Formulas

blogit, bprobit, glogit, and gprobit are implemented as ado-files.

Maximum likelihood estimates

The results reported by blogit and bprobit are obtained by maximizing a weighted logit or probit-likelihood function. Let $F(\ )$ denote the normal or logistic-likelihood function. The likelihood of observing each observation in the data is then

$$F(\beta x)^s \left\{ 1 - F(\beta x) \right\}^{t-s}$$

where s is the number of successes and t is the population. The term above is counted as contributing $s + (t - s) = t$ degrees of freedom. All of this follows directly from the definition of logit and probit.

Weighted least squares estimates

The logit function is defined as the log of the odds ratio. If there is one explanatory variable, the model can be written

$$\log\left(\frac{p_j}{1 - p_j} \right) = \beta_0 + \beta_1 x_j + \epsilon_j$$

where p_j represents successes divided by population for the jth observation. (If there is more than one explanatory variable, simply interpret β_1 as a row vector and x_j as a column vector.) The large sample expectation of ϵ_j is zero and its variance is

$$\sigma_j^2 = \frac{1}{n_j p_j (1 - p_j)}$$

where n_j represents the population for observation j. We can thus apply weighted least squares to the observations with weights proportional to $n_j p_j (1 - p_j)$.

As a practical matter, the left-hand-side logit is calculated as the $\log(s_j / f_j)$, where s_j represents the number of successes and f_j represents the number of failures. The weight is calculated as $(s_j f_j)/(s_j + f_j)$.

For gprobit, write $F(\ )$ for the cumulative normal distribution, and define z_j implicitly by $F(z_j) = p_j$, where p_j is the fraction of successes for observation j. The probit model for one explanatory variable can be written

$$F^{-1}(p_j) = \beta_0 + \beta_1 x_j + \epsilon_j$$

(If there is more than one explanatory variable, simply interpret β_1 as a row vector and x_j as a column vector.)

The expectation of ϵ_j is zero and its variance is given by

$$\sigma_j^2 = \frac{p_j(1 - p_j)}{n f^2 \left\{ F^{-1}(p_j) \right\}}$$

where $f\{\ \}$ represents the normal density (Amemiya 1981, 1498). We can thus apply weighted least squares to the observations with weights proportional to $1/\sigma_j^2$.

References

Amemiya, T. 1981. Qualitative response models: A survey. *Journal of Economic Literature* 19: 1483–1536.

Hosmer, D. W., Jr., and S. Lemeshow. 1989. *Applied Logistic Regression*. New York: John Wiley & Sons. (*Second edition forthcoming in 2001.*)

Judge, G. G., W. E. Griffiths, R. C. Hill, H. Lütkepohl, and T.-C. Lee. 1985. *The Theory and Practice of Econometrics*. 2d ed. New York: John Wiley & Sons.

Rothman, K. J. and S. Greenland. 1998. *Modern Epidemiology*. 2d ed. Philadelphia: Lippincott–Raven.

University Group Diabetes Program. 1970. A study of the effects of hypoglycemic agents on vascular complications in patients with adult onset diabetes. *Diabetes* 19, supplement 2: 747–830.

Also See

Complementary:	[R] **adjust**, [R] **lincom**, [R] **lrtest**, [R] **mfx**, [R] **predict**, [R] **test**, [R] **testnl**, [R] **vce**, [R] **xi**
Related:	[R] **clogit**, [R] **cloglog**, [R] **logistic**, [R] **logit**, [R] **mlogit**, [R] **ologit**, [R] **probit**, [R] **scobit**
Background:	[U] **16.5 Accessing coefficients and standard errors**, [U] **23 Estimation and post-estimation commands**, [U] **23.11 Obtaining robust variance estimates**, [R] **maximize**

Title

grmeanby — Graph means and medians by categorical variables

Syntax

> **grmeanby** *varlist* [*weight*] [**if** *exp*] [**in** *range*] , s̲u̲mmarize(*varname*) [m̲e̲di̲an
>
> *graph_options*]

a̲w̲e̲i̲g̲h̲t̲s̲ and f̲w̲e̲i̲g̲h̲t̲s̲ are allowed; see [U] **14.1.6 weight**.

Description

grmeanby graphs the (optionally weighted) means or medians of *varname* according to the values of the variables in *varlist*. The variables in *varlist* may be string or numerical and, if numerical, may be labeled.

Options

s̲u̲mmarize(*varname*) is not optional; it specifies the name of the variable whose mean or median is to be graphed.

m̲e̲di̲an is optional; it specifies the graph is to be of medians, not means.

graph_options are any of the options allowed with **graph, twoway**; see [G] **graph options**.

Remarks

The idea of graphing means of categorical variables was shown in Chambers and Hastie (1992, 3). Since this was shown in the context of an S function for making such graphs, it doubtless has roots going back further than that. **grmeanby** is, in any case, another implementation of what we will assume is their idea.

▷ Example

Using a variation of our auto dataset, we graph the mean of **mpg** by **foreign**, **rep77**, **rep78**, and **make**:

(Continued on next page)

605

. grmeanby foreign rep77 rep78 make, sum(mpg) ylab

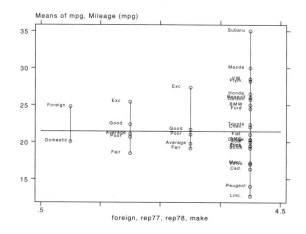

Had we wanted a graph of medians rather than means, we could have typed

. grmeanby foreign rep77 rep78 make, sum(mpg) ylab median

◁

▷ Example

Using a 29,650-observation subsample of men with labor force experience (and other restrictions) from the 1991 Current Population Survey (CPS), we graph the mean of wage:

. grmeanby race hhrel imputed marstat reltohd ftpt, sum(wage) ylab

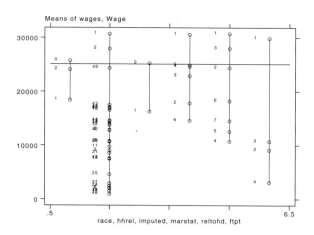

◁

Methods and Formulas

grmeanby is implemented as an ado-file.

References

Chambers, J. M. and T. J. Hastie. 1992. *Statistical Models in S*. Pacific Grove, CA: Wadsworth and Brooks/Cole.

Gould, W. W. 1993. gr12: Graphs of means and medians by categorical variables. *Stata Technical Bulletin* 12: 13. Reprinted in *Stata Technical Bulletin Reprints*, vol. 2, pp. 44–45.

Also See

Background: *Stata Graphics Manual*

Title

> **gsort** — Ascending and descending sort

Syntax

> gsort [+|-] *varname* [[+|-] *varname* ...] [, <u>g</u>enerate(*newvar*) <u>m</u>first]

Description

> **gsort** arranges observations to be in ascending or descending order of the specified variables and so differs from **sort** in that **sort** produces ascending-order arrangements only; see [R] **sort**.
>
> Each *varname* can be numeric or string.
>
> The observations are placed in ascending order of *varname* if + or nothing is typed in front of the name and in descending order if − is typed.

Options

> generate(*newvar*) creates *newvar* containing 1, 2, 3, ..., for each group denoted by the ordered data. This is useful when using the ordering in a subsequent **by**; see [U] **14.5 by varlist: construct** and examples below.
>
> mfirst specifies that missing values are to be placed first in descending order rather than last. With mfirst, descending sorts are in some sense more logically arranged but are, in fact, less useful. They are more logical because Stata treats missing values as $+\infty$; therefore, in an arrangement from high to low values, the missing values ought to be first. Missing-values-first orderings are less useful in programming situations because one can no longer be certain that the largest real value is the first observation. They are less useful in interactive situations because, if one lists the data, one must first wade through the missing, noninformative observations.

Remarks

> **gsort** is almost a plug-compatible replacement for **sort**, the only difference being that you cannot specify a general *varlist* with **gsort**. For instance, **sort alpha-gamma** means to sort the data in ascending order of **alpha**, within equal values of **alpha**, sort on the next variable in the dataset (presumably **beta**), within equal values of **alpha** and **beta**, etc. **gsort alpha-gamma** would be interpreted as **gsort alpha -gamma**, meaning sort the data in ascending order of **alpha** and, within equal values of **alpha**, descending order of **gamma**.

▷ Example

> The difference in *varlist* interpretation aside, **gsort** can be used in place of **sort**. To list the ten smallest incomes in the data,
>
> ```
> . gsort income
> . list name income in 1/10
> ```

or, if you prefer,

```
. gsort +income
. list name income in 1/10
```

To list the 10 largest incomes in the data,

```
. gsort -income
. list name income in 1/10
```

gsort can also be used with string variables. To list all the names in reverse alphabetical order,

```
. gsort -name
. list name
```
◁

▷ Example

gsort can be used with multiple variables. Given a dataset on hospital patients with multiple observations per patient,

```
. gsort id time
. list id time bp
```

lists each patient's blood pressures in the order the measurements were taken.

```
. gsort id -time
. list id time bp
```

lists each patient's blood pressures in reverse-time order.
◁

❏ Technical Note

Say one wished to attach to each patient's records the lowest and highest blood pressures observed during the hospital stay (let's ignore the easier way to achieve this result, egen's min() and max() functions):

```
. egen lo_bp = min(bp), by(id)
. egen hi_bp = max(bp), by(id)
```

(see [R] **egen**). Here is how you could do it using **gsort**:

```
. gsort id bp
. by id: gen lo_bp = bp[1]
. gsort id -bp
. by id: gen hi_bp = bp[1]
```

This works even in the presence of missing values of bp because such missing values are placed last within arrangements regardless of the direction of the sort.
❏

❑ Technical Note

Assume we have a dataset containing x for which we wish to obtain the forward and reverse cumulatives. The forward cumulative is defined as $F(X)$ = the fraction of observations such that $x \leq X$. Again, let's ignore the easier way to obtain the forward cumulative, which would be to use Stata's cumul command

```
. cumul x, gen(cum)
```

(see [R] **cumul**). Eschewing cumul, we could type

```
. sort x
. by x: gen cum = _N if _n==1
. replace cum = sum(cum)
. replace cum = cum/cum[_N]
```

That is, we first place the data in ascending order of x; we used sort but could have used gsort. Next, for each observed value of x, we generated cum containing the number of observations that take on that value (you can think of this as the discrete density). We summed the density, obtaining the distribution, and finally normalized it to sum to 1.

The reverse cumulative $G(X)$ is defined as the fraction of data such that $x \geq X$. To obtain it, one might try simply reversing the sort:

```
. gsort -x
. by x: gen rcum = _N if _n==1
. replace rcum = sum(rcum)
. replace rcum = rcum/rcum[_N]
```

This would work except for one detail: Stata will complain that the data are not sorted in the second line. Stata complains because it does not understand descending sorts (gsort is an ado-file). To remedy this problem, gsort's generate() option will create a new grouping variable that is in ascending order (thus satisfying Stata's narrow definition) and that is, in terms of the groups it defines, identical to that of the true sort variables:

```
. gsort -x, gen(revx)
. by revx: gen rcum = _N if _n==1
. replace rcum = sum(rcum)
. replace rcum = rcum/rcum[_N]
```

❑

Methods and Formulas

gsort is implemented as an ado-file.

Also See

Related: [R] **sort**